# The Mill Iron Site

ʌ ʌ ʌ

# The Mill Iron Site

*Edited by George C. Frison*

University of New Mexico Press
Albuquerque

© 1996 by the University of New Mexico Press
All rights reserved.
*First Edition*

Library of Congress Cataloging in Publication Data
The Mill Iron site / edited by George C. Frison—1st ed.
    p.   cm.
Includes bibliographical references and index.
ISBN 0-8263-1676-X (cl)
    1. Mill Iron Site (Mont.)
    2. Goshen Culture.
    3. Paleo-Indians—Montana
    4. Montana—Antiquities
    I. Frison, George C.
E78.M9M56 1996
978.6'36—dc20                                95-49369
                                                         CIP

*This book is dedicated to
the many professional as well as avocational archaeologists and interested lay persons
whose volunteer efforts contributed significantly to the completion of the Mill Iron site project.*

# Contents

# *Preface*

GERALD R. CLARK
Cheyenne, Wyoming

BURTON D. WILLIAMS
Billings, Montana

This volume reports the results of investigations conducted at the Mill Iron site, a Paleoindian property named after a nearby southeastern Montana community. The site was discovered on public land by Bureau of Land Management (BLM) archaeologists helping the agency meet its responsibility to consider significant prehistoric resources when planning a Federal project. Subsequent work at Mill Iron, led by Dr. George Frison, was a cooperative effort between the University of Wyoming (UW) and the BLM; it is an excellent example of productive archaeological research conducted within the framework of the modern Federal preservation system that was initiated with the National Historic Preservation Act of 1966 (NHPA). In this instance, the academic community and the Federal agency generated the funding and brought together the talent needed to produce important new archaeological information and to share that information with those who helped pay the bill—the interested public, the taxpayer, and the consumer.

Since the early 1970s, Federal land-managing entities such as the BLM, Forest Service, and other agencies that sponsor, assist, permit, or license activities that affect important historic and prehistoric sites have been responding to the NHPA and other laws protecting these kinds of resources. The agencies continue to participate in a national system with legal underpinnings that require historic preservation to be done in the public interest and authorize the use of public funds toward that end. With this tax-supported cultural resource work have come the inevitable bureaucratic structure and governmental control of funding, functions, and end products, which have profoundly influenced archaeology in the West.

On the Northwestern Plains, two decades of archaeological work conducted under the modern Federal preservation system have generated thousands of acres of inventory and many site excavations. However, most professional archaeologists recognize that the quality of contributions to method and theory and to the substantive body of archaeological information from preservation work has been highly variable. Some would argue that a major goal of the system, stemming the loss of archaeological sites and information, has been met to some unknown degree. Others observe a lackluster performance record by major players in the preservation system and identify inefficiencies or outright failures. The Federal agencies have been accused of hiring unqualified preservation personnel, lacking commitment to the preservation system, perpetuating mediocre science through their contracting systems, and failing to provide the kind of direction that might result in better resource management and better archaeology. Private consulting archaeologists have been charged with letting the profit motive reduce their commitment to scientific research. The academic community has been reproached for its failure to take the lead in defining research directions and influencing Federal agencies for productive change. There has also been legitimate debate over whether the preservation system has served the public as intended by the legislation that established it.

Many of the foregoing problems are real; some of them are not as bad as they were in the mid-1980s when the Mill Iron site field work was completed, while others have shown little improvement. In some areas, bureaucracy surrounding the Federal preservation system has actually increased to the detriment of proactive management of important archaeological properties and productive archaeological investigation. Cooperative efforts between Federal land-managing agencies and academia, such as that which produced this volume, are more difficult to initiate today than they were a decade ago.

We believe it is time for everyone involved in the preservation system, including those in academia and the interested public, to reexamine goals, priorities, procedures, and performance within the system. Such a review should seek to understand how the preservation system can be modified to facilitate on-the-ground management of important sites, produce useful archaeological information, and share that information in a meaningful way with the interested public. A review must also examine the direct and indirect costs of the system and assess the public benefits derived from total expenditures; the proportion of total expenditures devoted to bureaucratic process must be carefully scrutinized. A close look at the Mill Iron site investigation and others like it should be included in any system review. Cooperative efforts like these demonstrate that land managers who are willing to assume their role as stewards of important archaeological resources and academic department willing to work within the Federal system can generate cost-effective research while meeting preservation goals.

BLM discovered the Mill Iron site when considering how repair of a stock reservoir by the agency might affect significant archaeological properties. While the reservoir project posed no threat to the site, agency managers committed staff and funding to evaluate its significance with a view toward proactive site management, if warranted. Through a cooperative agreement, the BLM and UW pooled their fiscal resources, expertise, facilities, and equipment and enlisted the help of volunteers to complete a testing program. In this way, the agency obtained detailed information about the site, which was needed to make management decisions, and UW was able to apply the archaeological data that was recovered to its ongoing program of Paleoindian research.

Test excavation conducted under the cooperative agreement in 1984 revealed that the Mill Iron site contained significant Paleoindian deposits. While the BLM acquired useful management information, UW got only enough data from the testing to ask unresolved questions about site formation processes, paleoenvironments, culture history, and culture process. Consequently, support for continued investigation was sought, and the BLM responded with some labor, a field camp, and limited funding for travel and supplies. UW acquired additional funding through a research grant from the National Geographic So-

ciety. Frison and BLM Archaeologist Gerald Clark developed a data recovery plan addressing research and site management goals. The BLM met Federal regulatory requirements associated with additional research, including consultation with the Advisory Council on Historic Preservation.

UW and BLM continued investigations at Mill Iron with an emphasis on public involvement. Students pursuing thesis topics and volunteers, many of them highly qualified professionals, were welcomed to the project. Most persevering of the volunteers was Marshall Lambert, director of the local Carter County (Montana) Museum. When the excavations were complete, Mr. Lambert built a prominent display in the county museum to explain to visitors what the Mill Iron studies had revealed about local and regional prehistory. The BLM donated replicas of Mill Iron artifacts for display in the Carter County Museum and the Montana State Historical Museum to enhance public education and appreciation of the site and to strengthen public support for agency cultural resource management.

This volume represents the final report of the joint UW-BLM Mill Iron site investigations. When the site collections and field notes are permanently housed in the Smithsonian Institution, the BLM will have completed a significant part of its role as steward of this important Paleoindian site. The agency's primary goal of ensuring preservation of important information about prehistory was accomplished, in part, through the cooperative agreement with UW. However, because most of the Mill Iron site remains intact, the BLM must continue to preserve and protect these important cultural deposits to fulfill its role as steward of significant public values.

# Acknowledgments

George C. Frison
University of Wyoming

The Mill Iron site 24CT30 was discovered in 1979 by Jerry Clark and Tom Schley, both employees of the Bureau of Land Management in Montana. A total of 16 years have elapsed between then and the final publication of this volume. During this period, many individuals, organizations, and agencies have contributed toward its final completion.

The Bureau of Land Management (BLM) in the Miles City, Montana District initiated the investigation at the Mill Iron site. Support was provided by this office, the Montana State BLM office, and the Washington D.C. office. I am especially indebted to Jerry Clark and B. J. Earle from the Miles City BLM office and Burton Williams from the Montana State BLM office. Without their continuous and unwavering support, the project would have stalled somewhere along the way. I regard it an honor to have been asked by these three to become the principal investigator of the Mill Iron site, for other Paleoindian specialists were equally qualified to do the work.

The logistics of performing the ground work to begin a project such as Mill Iron are many. In 1982, BLM personnel who performed the inventory of the site area and assisted with the initial mapping of the site include Dave Fraley, B. J. Earle, Mary Bloom, Susan Bupp, Gary Eaton, Bill Freese, Robin Freese, Ray Baker, Diane Rice, Jerry Clark, and Bob Darrow. BLM staff who supported the project in meaningful ways include the following: B. J. Ferber, Ladd Coates, Leonard Farnsworth, Dave Swogger, and Arlene Gunderson who facilitated funding and agreements with adjacent landowners for site access. BLM managers without whose support the project could not have occurred are Alan Pierson, Bob Bennett, Ray Brubaker, Mat Millenbach, and Bruce Whitemarsh. In the Washington Office, John Douglas and Richard Brook helped to obtain funds for the initial site testing.

Funding for site testing and excavation in 1984 and 1985 was provided by the BLM. In 1986, the National Geographic Society funded the excavation and added a supplemental amount to begin the investigation of the bison bonebed in 1987. In 1988, the final site excavations and the subsequent analysis were supported by the National Science Foundation.

Testing of the site under my direction began in 1984. BLM staff who worked there from 1984 through 1986 include Dave Fraley, Mary Bloom, B. J. Earle, Burt Williams, Bonnie Hogan, Ray Baker, Jim Kenderic, Kurt Kunugi, Dale Hanson, Marth Griffith, Bob Bump, Cas Seago, Don Meier, Bill Volk, and Jerry Clark. During this same period, student volunteers from the University of Wyoming included Dale Wedel, Howard Haspel, Dave McKee, Karen Miller, Elizabeth Cartwright, Glen Miller, Kyle Baber, Jennifer Woodcock, and Russell Nelson. Other volunteers were Marshall Lambert, William Woodcock, Sr., Mark Miller, Bill Latady, George Zeimens, Alan Korell, Danny Walker, Marcel Kornfeld, Mike Shean, Ruthann Knudson, Carl Spath, and Rusty Greaves. Besides the geologists whose works appear in this volume, mention must be made of William Eckerle and Jill Onken who participated in the geologic investigations

The salaried crew in 1988 included Eric Ingbar, Dave Rapson, Lawrence Todd, Lee Kreutzer, Kaoru Akoshima, Mike Stafford, Rusty Greaves, John Potter, Galen Burgett, John Lund, and Mary Lou Larson.

Help and support were always provided by Marshall Lambert, curator of the local museum in Ekalaka, Montana. Marshall always seemed to have on hand the badly needed item that would have required a long trip to another town to obtain. William Woodcock, Sr. provided us with aerial photographs of the site and the area. Elston Loken of Ekalaka aided us on several occasions with his backhoe. The Boggs family of Baker, Montana, and the Wollesen family of Mill Iron, Montana, were always tolerant of the constant string of vehicles and the dust clouds raised while driving through their private land in order to gain access to the site. Paleoindian specialists who visited the site and provided meaningful advice and comments included Dennis Stanford, Ruthann Knudson, and C. Vance Haynes, Jr. Will Hubbell took over the position of district manager for the Miles City BLM after the Mill Iron site project began, and his continual support was deeply appreciated. Social life for the crew centered around the Wagon Wheel Cafe and the Old Stand Bar in Ekalaka, Montana. I thank both for making life more pleasant under sometimes less than ideal conditions.

I thank Dave Meltzer of Southern Methodist University for his careful, critical, and time-consuming review of the Mill Iron site manuscript and for pointing out numerous omissions, redundancies, inconsistencies, and faulty syntheses. His efforts were significant towards a final version that was considered acceptable for publication.

A special kind of recognition goes to June Frison, spouse of the principal investigator. With the Mill Iron project, as in all other previous archaeological projects I have undertaken, she has been my sharpest critic but constant and staunchest supporter. Both are important ingredients for success in archaeology.

Inevitably, I have omitted someone or some entity that deserves mention. For this, I ask that you accept my sincere apology.

# CHAPTER ONE

# Introduction

GEORGE C. FRISON
University of Wyoming

The following pages document the discovery, investigation, analysis, and interpretation of the data recovered at the Mill Iron Paleoindian site 24CT30 in southeast Montana. This site has proven instrumental in better defining and understanding the Goshen Paleoindian cultural complex proposed in 1967 (see Irwin-Williams et al. 1973). Before presenting the study of the Mill Iron site, a short review of the events relevant to the Goshen complex (now Goshen-Plainview complex) that occurred before the discovery of the Mill Iron site needs to be presented.

The concept of a Goshen cultural complex came about as a result of archaeological investigations in Goshen County in southeast Wyoming during the late 1950s and early 1960s. Long-term investigations at the stratified Paleoindian Hell Gap site (Figure 1.1) 48GO305 by Harvard University and the University of Wyoming were destined to prove significant in establishing the hitherto poorly known chronology of High Plains Paleoindian cultural complexes. Investigations were about to terminate at the Hell Gap site in mid-August of 1966, when a productive cultural level was encountered underneath, and separated by a sterile level from an overlying Folsom level.

The cultural level in question was rich in debitage and tools but sparse in diagnostic projectile points. A complete projectile point did eventually appear in situ (Figure 1.2a), which at first was thought to be a somewhat aberrant Folsom specimen. However, upon closer examination of the morphology and the manufacture technology of the specimen, the Folsom identification was abandoned, and since it was unequivocally recovered in a cultural level beneath a Folsom level, it was next labeled Clovis. After a still more careful examination, the investigators decided it was neither Folsom nor Clovis, but it bore a close resemblance to the projectile points from the Plainview site in Texas (see Sellards et al. 1947; Wormington 1957:107–108). Plainview, however, was believed to be post-Folsom in age, and since there was no doubt that the cultural level in question at the Hell Gap site underlay a Folsom level, the investigators then decided to give it a different name—Goshen, after the

county in Wyoming where the Hell Gap site is located. Other broken and incomplete Goshen projectile points (Figure 1.2 b–e) along with a large tool assemblage were recovered.

Two of the principal investigators at the Hell Gap site, Henry T. Irwin and Cynthia Irwin-Williams, are no longer alive to provide the badly needed details of the Hell Gap site investigations and to apply their expertise in Paleoindian studies toward the analysis. The published results of the investigations are few: a dissertation at Harvard University (Irwin 1967) and two short summary journal articles (Irwin 1971; Irwin-Williams et al. 1973). Consequently, the following statements on the Hell Gap site are the writer's interpretations of the notes and site records recovered over the last five years from a number of universities throughout the United States to which parts of the Hell Gap site materials had been dispersed.

The Hell Gap site was sealed at the end of the 1966 field season, and for reasons unknown the investigators never returned. Henry Irwin utilized the Hell Gap site materials as a major part of his doctoral dissertaion at Harvard University (1967), in which he proposed a Clovis cultural complex that was composed of an older Blackwater phase (named after the Blackwater Draw site in eastern New Mexico) followed by a Goshen phase. He apparently reasoned that Goshen portrayed a phase of Clovis in which fluting of projectile points changed to a basal thinning and pressure flaking that replaced the percussion flaking so well demonstrated in the Blackwater Clovis phase.

Following Clovis, Irwin proposed the Itama culture (supposedly a Blackfoot term meaning "good hunting") that included a number of phases and subphases. The only one to concern us here is what he designated the Lindenmeier phase with an older Folsom subphase and a later Midland subphase. It is not clear what relationship, if any, Irwin believed to have existed between Goshen and Folsom. No direct mention of Itama is made in the Irwin-Williams et al. summary that includes only a very brief discussion of a succession of cultural complexes as they believed they were represented at the Hell Gap site (1973). Goshen as a

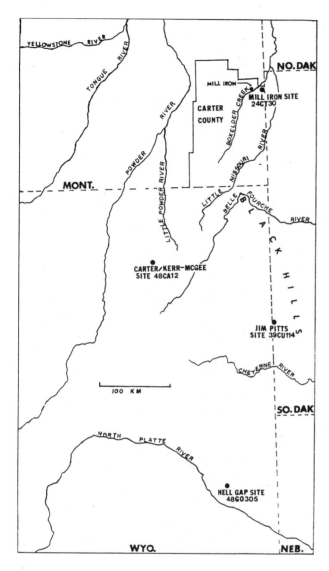

**Figure 1.1.** Locations of known archaelogical sites on the High Plains with Goshen-Plainview components.

**Figure 1.2.** Projectile points from the Hell Gap site labeled as Plainview and later as Goshen (a–e).

cultural complex was largely forgotten for well over a decade, as little appeared to support or add to the Goshen concept as it was described from the Hell Gap site. However, this changed in the early 1980s with the discovery and subsequent investigation of the Mill Iron site 24CT30 in Carter County, located in southeast Montana.

## The Mill Iron Site 24CT30

Interest in the Goshen cultural complex was immediately revived as the result of the discovery and investigation of the Mill Iron site 24CT30 in southeast Montana (Figure 1.1). The site was found during the summer of 1979 as the result of an archaeological survey of a small, isolated block of Bureau of Land Management (BLM) property a short distance from the common meeting point of Montana, North Dakota, and South Dakota. Reservoir construction on this piece of land required archaeological monitoring because of the discovery of late-Paleoindian projectile points on the surface of an area destined to supply fill material for the dam (Figure 1.3). The earthmoving equipment was a day late in getting to the location, so the two BLM archaeologists assigned to monitor the area used the time to investigate the talus slope of a nearby butte, which yielded two Paleoindian projectile points of an entirely different type from the ones from the fill dirt area. The talus of the butte yielded a number of chipped stone items and bison bone over the next two years. Ironically, geological study of the nearby area used as a source of fill material that produced the late-Paleoindian projectile points found earlier proved to be a landform of post-Paleoindian age, and the artifacts that led to the discovery of the Mill Iron site, through unknown causes, were out of place.

The name Mill Iron is derived from the isolated crossroads located about 12 km to the west of the site named Mill Iron in Carter County, Montana (Figure 1.1) that boasts a post office, cafe, a community church, and a country school. The Mill Iron site (Figure 1.3) is located in the Humbolt Hills area, which

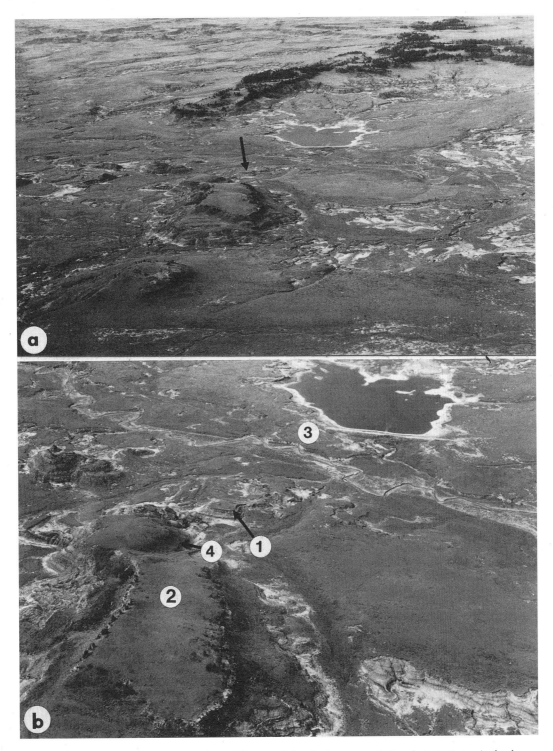

**Figure 1.3.** The Mill Iron site location with part of the timber-covered Humbolt Hills in the background (a). Closer view of the Mill Iron site (b1), the butte to the north (b2), the location of borrow material for the reservoir dam (b3), and the landform remnant that was at one time connected to the Mill Iron site butte (b4).

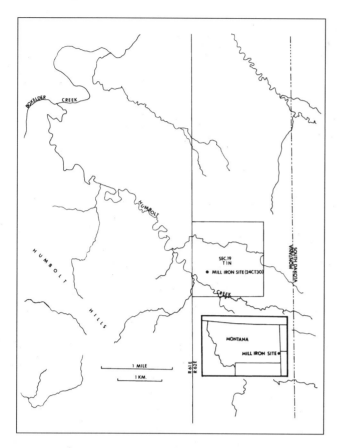

**Figure 1.4.** Map location of the Mill Iron site and vicinity.

is the northernmost extension of the South Dakota–Wyoming Black Hills. The Humbolt Hills are of low relief and capped with relatively soft sedimentary deposits. They are visible from a long distance and present a pleasant contrast to the broad expanse of dreary badland country between the Powder River to the west and the Little Missouri River to the east. These hills are also part of the Custer National Forest and are scattered with patches of juniper and limited quantities of commercial pine timber. The area is good livestock country with adequate grass cover and sufficient water during most years, although livestock operators must plan carefully and store feed for the unpredictable drought years and hard winters that repeatedly occur. Sagebrush is present over most of the area, but it does not tend to crowd out the grasses. Greasewood prevails in low-lying areas of high salinity. Large numbers of deer and pronghorn roam the area with coyotes, bob cats, and foxes as the main predators. One rapidly becomes aware of the large numbers of prairie rattlesnakes, which present no real threat but are continual reminders of the need for a measure of precaution while walking through the area.

The Mill Iron site location can be found on the Humbolt Hills U.S.G.S. Quadrangle, 7.5 minute series, 1:24,000 scale topographic map (Figure 1.4). Humbolt Creek, a meandering ephemeral stream that flows northwesterly into Box Elder Creek, is located just to the west of the Mill Iron site. The

drainage is about 9.5 km long, and the maximum width is about 5.5 km. Box Elder Creek, the major stream draining the area, originates in the low-lying hills of southeast Montana between the Little Powder and the Little Missouri rivers (Figure 1.1). It flows slowly in a northeasterly direction, crosses the extreme northwest corner of South Dakota, and then empties into the Little Missouri River in the southwest corner of North Dakota. Humbolt Creek is dry most of the year, and its flood plain is devoid of brush other than sagebrush. In contrast, Box Elder Creek is a continually flowing stream and is well named for the large number of trees of that species along with cottonwood, chokecherry, buffalo berry, willow, wild rose, and tall wild rye grass that grow on its flood plain.

The Paleoindian cultural level at the Mill Iron site is exposed around parts of the perimeter and over a meter below the surface of a steep-sided, nearly round, flat-topped butte about 20 m in height and 35 m in diameter at the top (Figure 1.5). The surface of the butte slopes gradually towards Humbolt Creek on the west at an angle of about 4 degrees. A narrow extension of the butte about 15 m wide extends westward for a distance of about 40 meters, although it narrows to about 5 m in width where it connects to the main butte. An isolated remnant of the same landform about 22 m long and 12 m wide is located about 20 m south of the western extension of the main butte extension (Figure 1.6). The area of the butte is continually being reduced by erosion: the only inhibiting factor at present is a solid cover of buffalo grass with its extensive root system.

A larger butte about 425 km long and 175 m wide rises about 25 m above the top and to the north of the butte on which the Mill Iron site is located (Figure 1.3). A few scattered pines cling to the side of the larger butte (Figure 1.7): the extent of the exposure of their root systems is testimony to the extreme amounts of erosion occurring in the area during the recent past. The geologic study of the site indicates that the smaller butte on which the Mill Iron site is located was connected to the larger butte in the not too distant past, further testifying to the rates of erosion in the area. A small remnant of a landform is still present on the west side of the larger butte (Figure 1.3b) that was part of the land surface that at one time was a continuous land surface between the two buttes. Other than these and a small land surface a short distance to the west of the site, there is very little of this landform remaining in the Humbolt Creek drainage.

The projectile points (Figure 1.8) and tools recovered from the steep talus slope of the butte were shown at professional meetings for two years following their discovery and were generally regarded as being similar to the Plainview site specimens. There is no doubt that they closely resemble the projectile points from the Plainview site in Texas (see Sellards et al. 1947). However, I suggested that they might also represent Goshen, the nearly forgotten cultural complex suggested earlier at the Hell Gap site. This ultimately led to an invitation by BLM archaeologists to visit the site in 1983. A first-hand look at the site indicated it was probably one with good integrity and I expressed an immediate interest in pursuing test excavations. The Montana BLM agreed to support limited test excavations in 1984 with field help and food and travel expenses, along with some help in the field by BLM archaeologists. The remain-

**Figure 1.5.** Looking south (a) and west (b) at the Mill Iron site. (Arrows point to low-grade coal deposits in the Fort Union Formation.)

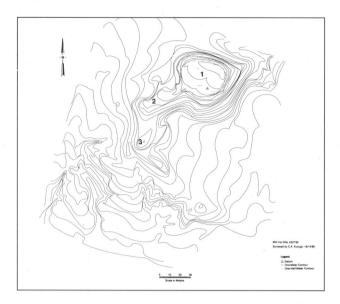

**Figure 1.6.** Topographic map of the Mill Iron site area. The main butte (1), the western extension (2), and the isolated remnant (3).

**Figure 1.7.** Live pine trees with the exposed root systems on the side of the large butte to the north of the Mill Iron site.

**Figure 1.8.** The surface finds on the talus of the Mill Iron site butte. The proximal end and the central, wedge-shaped piece of one (d) were found in situ. Another (e) was broken transversely across the center and the two pieces were found at different times.

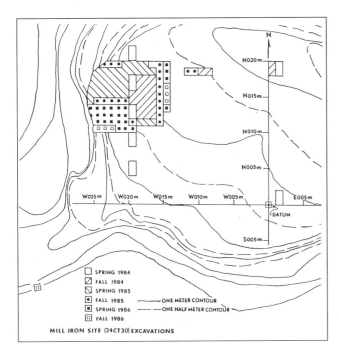

**Figure 1.10.** Test excavations at the Mill Iron site in the spring of 1984 (1, 2) and the block excavations in the fall of 1984. Surveying rod rests on the bottom of the cultural level 1.7 m below the surface.

**Figure 1.9.** Mill Iron site excavations through 1986.

der of the field crew consisted of volunteer help by University of Wyoming and University of New Mexico students and other part-time volunteers, including members of the Wyoming and Montana archaeological societies. The BLM archaeologists had excavated a small test trench in the camp area shortly after the discovery of the site (see Figure 1.19) and gathered soil samples for analysis. The results were inconclusive and they were aware that better field and laboratory facilities and a wider range of specialist consultants were needed for further work.

The first investigations in the spring of 1984 consisted of several 1 x 2 m trenches (Figure 1.9) and produced evidence of a single cultural level over a meter and a half below the surface on the west and north sides of the butte. Several flakes, a broken flake tool, and several bison bone and teeth fragments were recovered in situ but nothing that indicated any unequivocal connection of this level with the surface artifacts recovered earlier. Further testing in the fall of 1984 of a larger block area (Figure 1.10) was more productive and yielded diagnostic projectile points of the same type recovered earlier on the surface along with a few tools, a small amount of debitage, a complete bison mandible, and a few small, broken pieces of long bone. Although encouraging, more data were needed to arrive at any conclusions as to the true nature of the site. In consultation with the BLM archaeologists, we decided that a short period of excavation in both spring and fall to allow analysis of results between times would be preferred over a single, long-term field season.

The BLM once again provided expense money for limited excavation in both spring and fall of 1985, and the same group of volunteers again offered its services. Enough charcoal was recovered from what was believed to have been a surface hearth

of cultural origin to provide an accelerator radiocarbon date of 11,340 ± 120 years B.P. (Beta 16179), a date earlier than expected if the site were of conventional Plainview age. This radiocarbon date strengthened the possibility that the site could be a Goshen manifestation and that the evidence of Goshen found earlier at the Hell Gap site should be reevaluated and given more serious consideration.

Since there were other legitimate needs for the small amount of BLM money available for archaeological site testing, a proposal for further limited site excavation was made to the National Geographic Society and was approved for the 1986 field season. Once again, the site work was done in both the spring and fall and, for the third year, volunteers along with several paid consultants performed the field work. At the end of the 1986 excavations (Figure 1.9), we believed that further work was unlikely to produce other than redundant data and that it was best to leave the remainder of the site for future research since we had recovered what seemed to be a reasonable body of information. Parts of a projectile point and a flake tool were recovered in situ in the buried cultural level that refit to pieces recovered earlier on the talus slope of the butte, leaving no doubt that the surface and site materials were parts of the same cultural assemblage. Pollen, along with limited geologic and soils, studies were completed. A small but informative collection of bison bone was recovered with enough tooth material of proper animal age to allow a seasonality determination.

Bone fragments were recovered throughout the cultural level. This was apparently the result of exposure of the bone for a long enough period, or periods, of time to allow advanced weathering of exposed bone surfaces (Figure 1.11) (see Behrensmeyer 1978). As bone particles loosened, they were moved down the 4 degree slope and over the surface of the then exposed cultural level. However, the bottom surfaces of long bones were intact

**Figure 1.11.** Two pieces of the same bison femur from the camp area that refit.

**Table 1.1.** Accelerator Mass Spectrometer Dates from the Mill Iron Site.

| No. | Lab No. | Date |
| --- | --- | --- |
| | *Camp/Processing Area* | |
| 1 | Beta 13026 | 11,340 ± 120 yrs. B.P. |
| 2 | Beta 16178 | 11,010 ± 140 yrs. B.P. |
| 3 | Beta 16179 | 11,320 ± 130 yrs. B.P. |
| 4 | Beta 20110 | 10,760 ± 130 yrs. B.P. |
| 5 | Beta 20111 | 11,360 ± 130 yrs. B.P. |
| | *Bison Bone Bed* | |
| 6 | NZA 623 | 10,990 ± 170 yrs. B.P. |
| 7 | NZA 624 | 11,560 ± 920 yrs. B.P. |
| 8 | NZA 625 | 11,570 ± 170 yrs. B.P. |
| 9 | AA 3669 | 10,770 ± 85 yrs. B.P. |

There was a legitimate concern of contamination of radiocarbon samples for dating, since the site deposits overlie the widespread Fort Union Formation that contains extensive coal deposits (see Figure 1.5). In one location, a dark level well below the Goshen level soon proved to be channel deposits with a high content of low-grade coal particles and not charcoal (Figures 1.12 and 1.13). However, there does not appear to be any reason to suspect contamination of the charcoal samples used for the radiocarbon dates. All things considered, we believed at this time that the site excavations should be closed and a final report prepared, since no further evidence of cultural significance had been indicated in tests trenches or in profiles exposed on the steep talus slope of the butte. We were aware that the cultural level extended into the western extension of the butte because a distal bison tibia and several long bone fragments along with two chert flakes were recovered there in a profile of a steep bank at about the same depth and in a similar soil horizon as the confirmed Goshen level to the east. After spring runoff and heavy rains, an occasional flake and bone and tooth enamel fragments could be found eroding out at about the same level around the western extension of the butte, but no level as distinct as that at the main butte could be confirmed. However, there was no evidence exposed at this time that we thought could justify opening up new areas on either the main butte or its western extension. Even so, there was the strong belief that somewhere in the area there had been some sort of bison kill to account for the bone in the excavated area of the site.

The snow melted early in the spring of 1987, and I visited the site to see if the spring runoff might have exposed anything of significance. One of the test units on the western extension of the butte (Figure 1.9) from 1986 was placed on the leeward side; consequently, a large snowdrift had formed over it during the preceding winter. As it melted, the runoff water opened a narrow channel where the soft material filling the trench met the original trench wall. In doing so, it also exposed the base of a Goshen projectile point, the point of which rested on a bison rib, which, along with several other ribs and long bones, later proved to be at the eastern edge of a bison bonebed. The test trench had missed the projectile point by about 2 cm, and how

and unweathered indicating they had not been moved from their original position. In one case, for example, the dorsal surface of a bison radius was completely eroded away to within 15 mm of the ventral surface which still remained in pristine condition. Many burned bone fragments were recovered in the camp area and the exposed surfaces of many bones in the bonebed discovered in 1987 were similarly burned. The burning was a post-depositional occurrence and although the cause is undetermined it could have been either the result of deliberate burning for reuse of the site by the human group or accidental grass fires.

The tool assemblage, although small, was adequate for limited site activity interpretations. Enough charcoal was recovered for four more accelerator dates (Table 1.1). Two of these dates bracketed the first date and two others averaged just under 11,000 years B.P. Whichever of these two groups of dates Paleoindian archaeologists consider acceptable, they present several possible interpretations: (1) Goshen was contemporaneous with early Folsom; (2) it was the same age as Clovis; (3) it was a cultural group present on the High Plains between the two. Something to consider concerning radiocarbon dates from the Mill Iron site is that if pine logs of considerable age were there, they could have been used for fuel, and the older dates could reflect charcoal from trees that had been dead for some time.

long it might have been before the bonebed was discovered without this serendipitous event is pure conjecture. Considering the isolated nature of the site, the need to contact landowners to gain access to the area, and the extremely deteriorated nature of the bone that caused it to disintegrate rapidly upon exposure, it is conceivable that the entire bonebed could have eroded away without being noticed.

The National Geographic Society generously supplemented the 1986 grant for limited work in the bison bonebed during 1987. Three more projectile points were found that were of the same type as the ones from the campsite area. However, the exceptionally fragile nature of the bone and its compaction and distortion from the weight of the overburden left no doubt that in order properly to excavate and analyze it would require a substantial amount of funding. A proposal was presented to the National Science Foundation, which was approved, to do the field work during the summer of 1988 and complete the analysis over the following academic year.

The bonebed was not believed to have been the actual kill location but appeared instead to be a pile of stacked single bones and articulated carcass parts about 4.5 m in diameter. Mandibles were present and often in pairs, but skulls had apparently been removed with only a few maxillae parts and upper teeth present. The weight of more than 2 m of overburden combined with the soil chemicals allowed the bones to be compressed into a thin level with varying amounts of deformation. Leaching of material from the bonebed hardened the underlying sandy soil to a depth of several centimeters. We learned later that the south part of the bonebed had been undercut by stream action allowing it to collapse (Figure 1.14). The channel later filled and covered the collapsed section of the bonebed. More recent colluvial material then covered both the channel deposits and the bones, so there was no evidence of the bonebed exposed in profile on the steep talus of the butte. This left little

**Figure 1.12.** Northeast corner of the camp area excavation at the Mill Iron site. Top of cultural level (1), dark level containing low-grade coal particles (b).

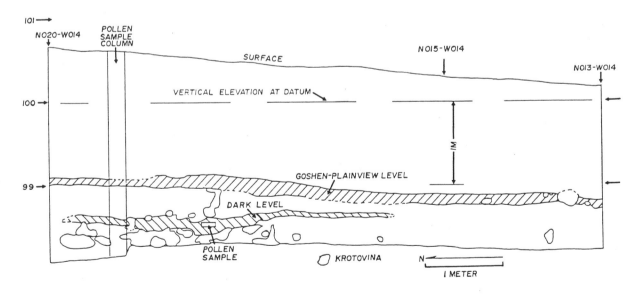

**Figure 1.13.** Profile of part of the north-south trench in the camp area, demonstrating the location of the cultural level and the dark level below.

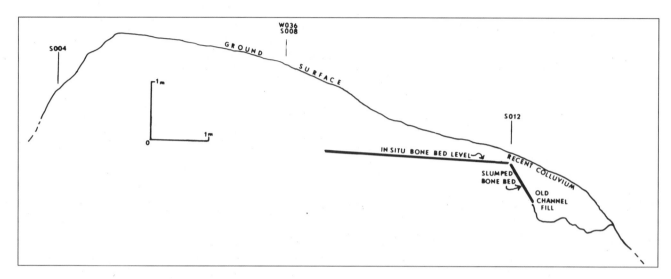

**Figure 1.14.** Schematic diagram of the geologic activities that affected the Mill Iron site bison bonebed.

**Figure 1.15.** Exposure of the top of the Mill Iron site bison bonebed in 1987.

Figure 1.16. Bonebed excavations in progress in 1988.

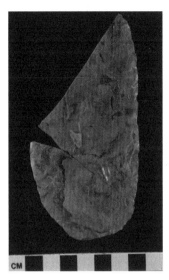

**Figure 1.17.** Two refitted pieces of a large biface from the bonebed.

doubt that the geology of the bonebed area of the site at least was much more complicated than we had been led to believe earlier.

The 1987 tests in the bison bonebed indicated also that the bone was deteriorated to the extent that special treatment would be needed for proper recovery. The bones (Figure 1.15) were badly leached, very fragile, and saturated with salts that would not allow any of the hardening agents commonly used in the field in other Paleoindian bison bonebeds to penetrate and strengthen them enough for casting and removal. Finally, a compound known by the trade name of Acrysol solved this problem and stabilized the bones enough to allow them to be cast and removed.

There were unexpected geologic problems also in the main butte deposits. In the spring 1984 testing, a 1 x 2 m unit was excavated at the southeast side of the main butte (Figure 1.9). The later-to-be-confirmed Goshen level was exposed in profile directly south of this test on the steep talus of the butte. However, the sediments in the test unit were different from those exposed on the talus: the former had a high clay content, while the latter were sandy. What were first thought to be inclusions of charcoal in some of the former ultimately proved to be particles of low-grade coal. Bone fragments and chert flakes were also encountered in a level in the spring 1984 test unit that appeared at the time to be a few centimeters too high in the profile to be the Goshen level. At the time, however, there was no thought that the level in question was not Goshen, and the answer to its elevated position in the trench profile would be explained by further geologic investigation. A test had been made, also in spring 1984, at the northeast part of the main butte (Figure 1.9), where the Goshen level was found at about the same depth as at the southeast and west sides of the butte. This was another indication that the geology of the site was badly in need of more study.

The 1988 site investigations were designed to produce the best possible documentation and recovery of the bison bonebed (Figure 1.16) along with continuation of the soils, geology, and pollen studies. Charcoal for five more accelerator dates was taken from the bison bonebed (Table 1.1). One proved to be a sample contaminated with dead carbon (probably coal), but the others fell into two groups of just over 11,000 years B.P. and just under 11,000 years B.P. as was the case with the campsite area (Table 1.1).

The projectile points from the bonebed are of the same type as those from the campsite. However, we were not able to extend the bonebed level to a direct connection with the campsite cultural level. Before the bonebed excavations in 1988, access to the top of the butte for heavy equipment was at the extreme end of the western extension of the butte, where the slope was not as steep as in all other parts of the butte. The bonebed excavations forced a new road to be constructed on the west side of the main butte (see Figure 3.5) which connected to that part of the site area excavated earlier. In this manner, no part of the cultural level was affected and a profile was cut along the road from the bonebed to the camp area. The profile demonstrated no direct connection between the two site areas due to geologic activity that may have been part of the same event that undercut the south part of the bonebed.

We were unable to refit any broken tools or flakes in the bonebed to their counterparts in the campsite. There is, however, one tool-sharpening flake of material from the camp area so distinctive in color and texture from a large broken biface (Figures 1.17, 4.6) from the bonebed that there is a very high probability that it was detached from the latter at some stage in the resharpening process while it was present in the camp area.

As mentioned earlier, we do not believe that the bonebed is the actual location where the bison were killed. However, there undoubtedly was a geomorphic feature nearby that was used either

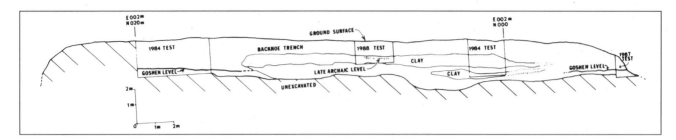

**Figure 1.18.** Schematic diagram of the relationship between the Goshen level and the Late Archaic level at the Mill Iron site.

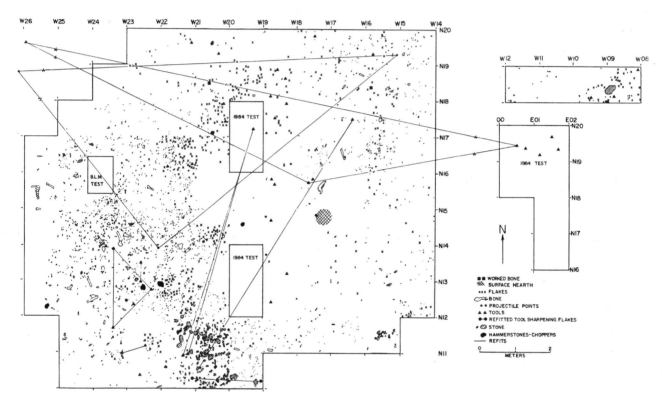

**Figure 1.19.** Map of the main block (camp-processing area) at the Mill Iron site.

in its original form or with some modification as a trap and for which the evidence has been eliminated by erosion since the time of the site activities. From the general character of the area and from studies of other Paleoindian bison kills in the region, an arroyo trap would be the most likely candidate used in the bison procurement strategy. Bison traps utilizing dry arroyos were widespread on the High Plains from Paleoindian to Late Prehistoric times (see Frison 1984, 1991:155-237) and present-day analogs are continually formed and lost through geologic activity.

After the bonebed excavations were completed in late June of 1988, a test unit was placed between the 1984 northeast and southeast tests on the main butte to determine whether or not this part of the butte should be considered for future investigations. A continuation of the supposed Goshen level found in

profile in the 1984 test was encountered. However, exposing part of the level revealed artifacts of Late Plains Archaic age rather than Paleoindian. This brought about the necessity for a return to the site in the late summer of 1988 to reopen trench E-1 and attempt to resolve this stratigraphic problem. The results of this revealed that the Goshen level was indeed missing for a distance of at least 17 m (Figure 1.18) and that the Late Plains Archaic level was contained in a different sedimentary unit from the one containing the Goshen level. This was further evidence of the complexity of the site geology and is discussed in greater detail in Chapter 3, although the problem is not yet solved to the satisfaction of all concerned. Limited pollen and soils studies had been done earlier, but these were expanded in an attempt to obtain a better grasp on the paleoecology.

The Mill Iron site work was officially ended in August of 1988. A large part of the site was excavated (Figure 3.5), although most of the potential site area remains intact for further investigations. The analyses of the materials were completed in 1992. Distribution maps of the camp-processing area (Figure 1.19) and the bonebed (Figure 7.3) were compiled from the field notes. The following pages present the individual results of all of the multi-disciplinary Mill Iron site investigations.

Before pursuing the Mill Iron site further, there is one more reference needed to the Hell Gap site investigations. Irwin (1967:90) states "We would feel that the projectile points of the Goshen level at Hell Gap, the Plainview site, Texas and Domebo in Oklahoma are the same." Later the following qualifiers are stated:

The material culture from the earliest Paleo-Indian occupation at Hell Gap, from Locality 1, has been termed the Goshen Complex. It displays numerous similarities in projectile point typology and has other parallels with the Plainview Complex, first identified at the type site in Texas (Wormington 1957:107–108). Given the range of styles represented at the [Plainview] type locality, a tendency to confuse generalized concave-based lanceolate points with the Plainview type has unfortunately developed, resulting in some confusion concerning both the diagnostic features and chronologic range of Plainview. Rather than add to this confusion, it is preferred to label the Hell Gap material by a different term [Goshen] [Irwin-Williams et al. 1973:46].

This was a strong caveat and, considering the limited amount of data extracted from the lowest Hell Gap site (Goshen) level, one that could probably be justified at that time. On the other hand, documents pertaining to the Hell Gap site indicate that Henry Irwin was revising his dissertation (1967) for publication. This effort unfortunately never came to pass, but he did say in his unfinished efforts at revision that that he was jettisoning the term Goshen and replacing it with Plainview (extracted from Hell Gap site notes and records given to me in 1991 that were stored in a warehouse at Washington State University, Pullman, Washington and in Irwin 1971). Based on what is now known from the Mill Iron site, I am not convinced that this is a good idea at this time. Although there is a remarkable similarity between the Plainview site and Mill Iron site projectile point assemblages, the Goshen projectile point assemblage from Hell Gap is very small. The Hell Gap site Goshen level tool assemblage is large but has only been superficially analyzed and described, and the analysis of the debitage is totally lacking. Consequently, we may discover significant differences between Plainview and Goshen based on extant but unanalyzed data. Until this and the chronological placement of the Plainview cultural complex as it is presently known from the Southern Plains is better understood, the use of Plainview to completely replace Goshen as it is presently known should await further developments and/or the acquisition of new data.

In addition, replacing Goshen with Plainview requires that qualifiers be added, so that the reader will know whether northern Plainview (Goshen) or southern Plainview is the referent. The compromise proposed here is that Goshen as we know it at present be mamed Goshen-Plainview. This acknowledges the close similarity of the projectile point assemblages from both sites and their respective geographic area, and it allows for future analysis of the Hell Gap material. It provides the reader an easy means of geographic separation that is needed because of the presently unresolved differences in the chronologic placement of the two. It is freely admitted, however, that future research may not support this proposed separation. Should this occur, it can easily be changed.

## References Cited

Behrensmeyer, Anna K.
1978    Taphonomic and Ecologic Information from Bone Weathering. *Paleobiology* 4:150–162.

Frison, George C.
1984    The Carter/Kerr-McGee Paleoindian Site: Cultural Resource Management and Archaeological Research. *American Antiquity* 49(2): 288–314.
1991    *Prehistoric Hunters of the High Plains, 2d ed.* Academic Press, Orlando.

Irwin, Henry T.
1967    *The Itama: Late Pleistocene Inhabitants of the Plains of the United States and Canada and the American Southwest.* Unpublished Ph.D. dissertation, Harvard University, Cambridge.
1971    Developments in Early Man Studies in Western North America, 1960–1970. *Arctic Anthropology* 8(2):42-67.

Irwin-Williams, Cynthia, Henry Irwin, George Agogino, and C. Vance Haynes, Jr.
1973    Hell Gap: Paleo-Indian Occupation on the High Plains. *Plains Anthropologist* 18:40–53.

Sellards, E. H., Glen L. Evans, and Grayson E. Meade
1947    Fossil Bison and Associated Artifacts from Plainview, Texas, with Description of Artifacts by Alex D. Krieger. *Bulletin Geological Society of America* 58:927–954.

Wormington, H. M.
1957    *Ancient Man in North America.* Denver Museum of Natural History, Popular Series No. 4.

# CHAPTER TWO

# Spatial Analysis of the Northwestern Block Excavation

Eric E. Ingbar
Carson City, Nevada

Mary Lou Larson
University of Wyoming

Analysis of the spatial distribution of material within archaeological sites furnishes valuable information about site formation, on-site activities including stone tool production, taphonomy, and areal use within the site. The analysis of the spatial distribution in camp areas associated with bonebeds is done rarely, primarily because of the absence of such contiguous areas in most excavations. Although the direct association of the northwest excavation block and the bonebed area of the Mill Iron site is not assumed, this analysis provides information about Paleoindian use of a camp location. If at some time, further analyses associate the two areas, this spatial analysis will provide even more information about Paleoindian existence.

This chapter focuses on the distribution of chipped stone debitage and its attributes in the northwestern excavation area at the Mill Iron site. Our analysis considers the excavation block of approximately 100 square meters (Figure 2.1 [N10-N22/W25-W14]). This area, termed the "northwestern block," has relatively poor bone preservation compared with the bonebed excavation area. Bone in the northwestern block was most often found as small, severely weathered pieces. Such weathering means that the value of spatial analysis of bone is limited in this part of the site (see Chapter 7 concerning spatial relationships within the bonebed). Attribute data, for which we are indebted to Julie Francis and Mary Lou Larson (Chapter 6), are used to examine the natural and behavioral formation of the site. The questions addressed by this analysis include whether the artifact distributions are the result of natural processes, and if not, can the spatial patterns in chipped stone distribution be related to behavioral explanations?

The approximately 100 square meters excavated in the block area comprises a larger excavation than many sites ever receive, but it is quite small relative to the known sizes of ethnographic hunter-gatherer sites (Yellen 1977; O'Connell 1987). The northwestern block area most likely incorporates a small portion of the space used during the tenure of occupation, so generalizations from this small area are best considered tentative.

## Formational Spatial Analyses

Our first concern in this spatial analysis is how the archaeological deposit formed. Here, the issue is whether artifacts have been redeposited or moved across the site surface by natural processes prior to, or during, burial.

Over 3,700 items were point provenienced during excavation of the northwestern block area. In addition to three-dimensional coordinates, long-axis orientation (or strike), dip direction, and dip degrees were taken for almost all items larger than 2 cm maximum length and for most items greater than 1 cm maximum length. The three-dimensional coordinates of mapped items were used to create a contour map of mean elevations across the main block area (Figure 2.1). This map illustrates the approximate elevation and topography of the paleosurface. The paleosurface followed roughly the same surface as the modern surface—that is, a fairly smooth, approximately 3 degree slope to the southwest.

Vertical dispersion of artifacts can indicate the amount of disturbance before and after burial (Hofman 1992; Larson 1990). Backplots, in which the artifacts within a 1 m strip are projected onto a vertical plane, show relatively little dispersion of artifacts within the northwestern block area (Figures 2.2, 2.3). Items follow a narrow elevation band, with very few items sitting much above or below the 5–10 cm zone of maximum occurrence. Examined together, the two backplots show artifacts following a single surface dipping 3–5 degrees to the southwest, in concordance with the paleotopographic reconstruction (Figure 2.1).

If artifacts were *systematically* displaced by post-depositional processes, then they should reveal an orderly pattern of displacement. For instance, low-energy fluvial activity, such as slope-wash, characteristically moves artifacts on slopes so that their long axes align with the slope (Schiffer 1987). Although one cannot exclude the influence of other geomorphic processes at the Mill Iron site, it is probably reasonable to suggest that low-

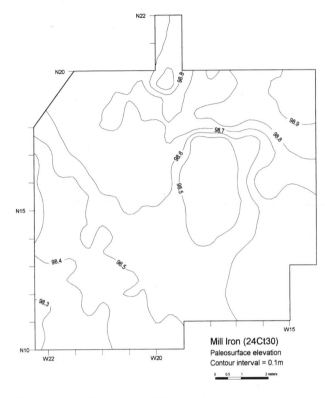

Figure 2.1. Paleotopographic reconstruction, northwestern block area.

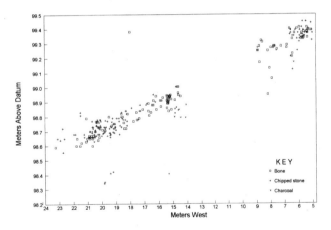

Figure 2.2. Backplot of 1 m wide E-W projection onto N19 grid line.

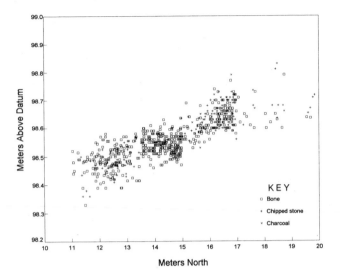

Figure 2.3. Backplot of 1 m wide N-S projection onto W22 grid line.

energy slope processes acted upon the paleosurface. Since the predominant slope is to the southwest, slope processes should have resulted in preferential alignment along a southwest-northeast axis. However, long-axis orientations recorded for 189 artifacts do not show any preferential alignment, either by inspection (Figure 2.4) or statistically (circular coefficient of variation equals 50.9; Davis 1986; Thomas et al. 1986). The

observed pattern may be explained in several ways: (1) the artifacts have not moved at all and hence they lie in their original presumably random orientations; (2) other processes changed artifact orientations following alignment to the slope; (3) slope processes were never sufficiently strong to align artifacts, although other more dominant processes may have affected artifact locations.

An implication of the first possibility is that artifacts should maintain their original dip (or plunge), and that the direction of this plunge should—in general—follow the southwest sloping paleosurface. Table 2.1 shows that amongst the 149 artifacts having complete imbrication data, neither expectation is met. Even objects roughly aligned with the slope, dipping to the southwest, west, or south, have very wide variation in the degree of dip (or plunge). This great variation in dip suggests post-depositional disturbance is the greatest factor determining artifact imbrication. Binding of artifacts by roots, soil expansion and contraction, and frost movement can all alter clast imbrication within a sediment (Johnson and Hansen 1974; Johnson et al. 1974; Schiffer 1987).

Another source of pertinent information on formation processes in the northwestern block is the condition of larger long bones found there. The few long bones found in the northwestern block area (see Appendix 1 and Figure 1.11) were mostly oriented to the southwest. Larger bone pieces showed differential weathering in which the tops of bones were in extremely poor condition, but the undersides were fairly well preserved. This suggests that the larger bones were embedded fairly rapidly in a few centimeters of sediment, leaving their tops exposed to weather. After the upper surfaces of the bones had weathered, but before they disintegrated, additional sediment buried them completely. Thus, although relatively little, some movement has occurred within the deposit as a whole.

The presence of thermal alteration within the chipped stone assemblage from the northwest block provides further evi-

**Table 2.1.** Summary Statistics for Degree of Dip (plunge) by Direction of Dip (strike), Northwestern Block Area.

| Dip direction | n | % | Mean | Stddev. | Minimum | Maximum |
|---|---|---|---|---|---|---|
| N | 8 | 5.4 | 14.9 | 9.1 | 1 | 29 |
| NE | 22 | 14.8 | 28.8 | 21.8 | 1 | 74 |
| E | 8 | 5.4 | 16.9 | 23.3 | 4 | 78 |
| SE | 24 | 16.1 | 15.3 | 15.8 | 0 | 58 |
| S | 13 | 8.7 | 21.2 | 17.6 | 2 | 59 |
| SW | 30 | 20.1 | 17.5 | 14.5 | 2 | 53 |
| W | 21 | 14.1 | 24.7 | 20.0 | 2 | 79 |
| NW | 23 | 15.4 | 17.7 | 11.0 | 4 | 44 |
| Total | 149 | 100.0 | | | | |

dence about formation processes. Thermal alteration within the assemblage varies from destruction of burned items, which leaves angular cuboid fragments, to partial discoloration, crazing, and potlid fracturing. The site's occupants could have intentionally altered the material. However, since thermally altered artifacts are common in the Mill Iron northwest block area (Figure 2.5) and are positively associated with overall artifact frequency (Figure 2.6), the pattern of thermal alteration suggests incidental burning (perhaps by wildfire). However, the timing of the burn episode in relationship to site occupation is unknown.

The archaeological deposits in the northwestern block area formed through fairly rapid shallow burial of the original occupation surface, followed by the formation of a stable surface that persisted long enough for exposed long bone surfaces to weather to a dry state. After this, the second surface was buried and subjected to a variety of minor post-burial processes, which dispersed items above and below the former surface and also tilted them at random angles. Despite this final action, the artifacts are relatively close to their original horizontal locations. Thus, distributional analyses seem feasible and likely will not simply reflect the effects of natural processes.

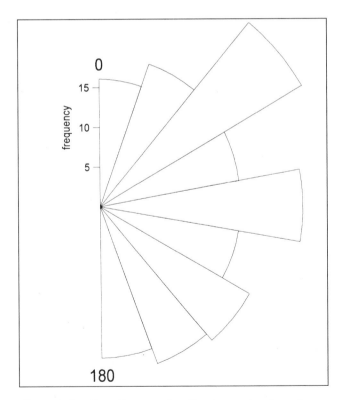

**Figure 2.4.** Rose diagram of artifact long axis orientation, northwest block area (n=157).

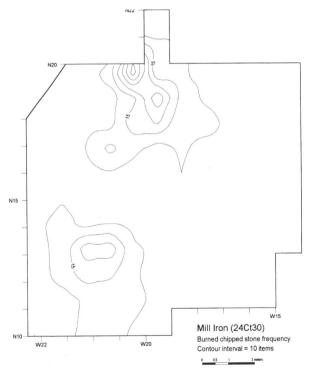

**Figure 2.5.** Density per square meter of thermally altered debitage, northwestern block area.

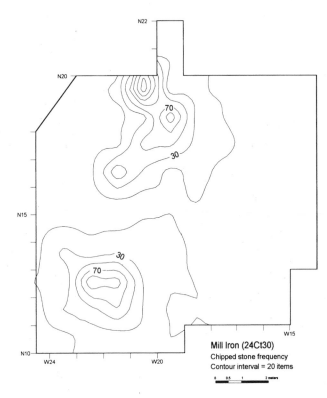

**Figure 2.6.** Density per square meter of debitage throughout northwestern block area.

## Mill Iron Analytical Nodules and Technology

The remainder of this chapter focuses on chipped stone debitage in the northwestern block. Since the study of debitage distributions is of interest only in tandem with the results of the assemblage level analysis, this analysis combines data collected by Francis and Larson (Chapter 6) to understand the spatial distribution of chipped stone. Simply presenting the overall density of chipped stone (Figure 2.6) illustrates the presence of two high-density areas yet conveys no information about possible differences and similarities between them.

Attributes of the chipped stone assemblage that pertain to lithic production (see Chapter 6) were selected as analytical units for our study. Concomitant with this approach is the subdivision of Francis and Larson's raw material groups. For this purpose, minimum analytical nodules (Larson 1990; Larson and Ingbar 1992) based upon similarities in raw material source, artifact color, texture, inclusions, and cortex provide useful subdivisions of the assemblage. Although minimum analytical nodules can be likened to individual cores, they are not intended to be approximations of single blocks of stone, but instead serve as analytical constructs (Larson and Ingbar 1992). Once the material was sorted into analytical nodules, the debitage was tallied into three simple flake types: angular debris or shatter, core reduction flakes, and facial regularization flakes.

Angular debris consists of blocky material fragments, lacking distinctive interior (ventral) surfaces, distinct platforms, or other attributes characteristic of individually removed flakes.

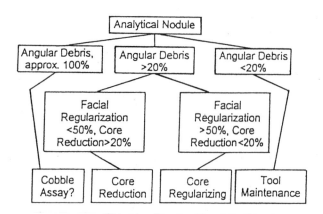

**Figure 2.7.** Key used to characterize technological modes within the Mill Iron debitage assemblage.

Angular debris often results from assaying and initial reduction of material blocks. In low-quality raw materials, it may occur at almost any time, as breakage occurs along pre-existing fractures or planes of weakness. It is most common in initial reduction of blocky raw materials (Crabtree 1972).

Core reduction flakes have simple unprepared platforms, with few scars, irregular or chunky cross-sections and simple dorsal flake scar patterns. Core shaping flakes result from the removal of flakes from large, relatively unshaped, blocks of material. These flakes shape the piece by removing mass. Alternatively, the flakes may be a desired product themselves, in which case shaping of the core is incidental. As such, they are usually considered early in most reduction schemes (Crabtree 1972). Depending upon the lithic production strategy in use, they may also be removed quite late in the use of a core, especially in technologies that rely heavily on simple flake tools (Parry and Kelly 1988).

Facial regularization flakes have relatively complex platforms with potentially many platform scars, generally thin cross-sections with even longitudinal curvature and thinning, and often have complex dorsal flake scar patterns. The archetypal facial regularization flake is a late biface thinning flake, but the type is more broadly defined than just bifacial thinning. Facial regularization flakes shape the surface of a tool (rather than just its edge) and so represent both tool maintenance and tool production. Usually, facial regularization flakes are considered to be later products of stone tool production, since regularizing the surface of a core (whether a block core or a biface) requires some prior control over the shape of the core platform(s).

## Mill Iron Stone Tool Production Activities

Three technological modes are apparent within the Mill Iron debitage: *core reduction, core regularizing,* and *tool maintenance.* These technological modes summarize the dominant stone tool production actions made evident by a nodule's debitage. Core shaping and core regularizing can be considered manufacturing modes: an object is more in progress towards a useful con-

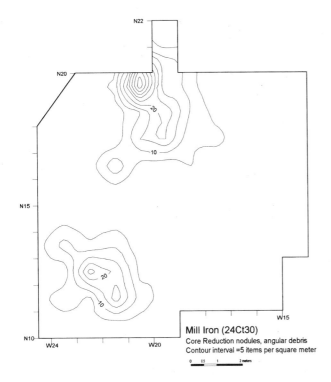

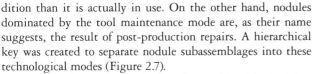

**Figure 2.8.** Density per square meter of angular debris from core reduction nodules, northwestern block area.

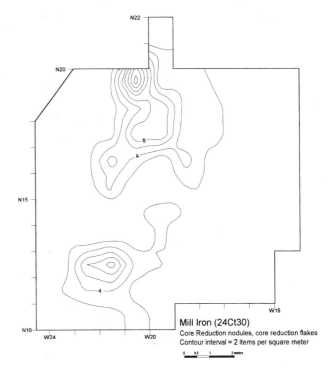

**Figure 2.9.** Density per square meter of core reduction flakes from core reduction nodules, northwestern block area.

dition than it is actually in use. On the other hand, nodules dominated by the tool maintenance mode are, as their name suggests, the result of post-production repairs. A hierarchical key was created to separate nodule subassemblages into these technological modes (Figure 2.7).

Angular debris provides the first key within this classification scheme. Within the Mill Iron assemblage, three different breakpoints occur. The percentage of angular debris provides an initial test within the technological categorization scheme. Nodules with more than 20% shatter are classified as either core shaping or core regularizing nodules. These two manufacturing modes are distinguished from each other by the percentages of facial regularization and core reduction flakes present (Figure 2.7). Nodules having less than 20% angular debris are categorized as tool maintenance assemblages. Tool maintenance nodules contain more than 75% facial regularization flakes and low percentages of core reduction flakes. Debitage within this category consists mostly of retouch flakes produced through maintenance of facially regularized tool edges.

As discussed above, thermal alteration is common in the Mill Iron debitage assemblage. Apparently, it was accidental either during the site's use or following it. Much of the angular debris produced by burning could not be identified as to material type and is not included further in our analysis. Amongst identifiable flake types, nodules, and technological modes, burning is relatively common. However, because we cannot be certain when the burning occurred, a consideration of burning is not included in the following discussion.

## Spatial Distributions of Analytical Nodules

As discussed above, patterns within the distribution of debitage are sought as a means to understanding the activity structure and use-history of the northwest block area. Toward this end, the distribution of analytical nodules is considered in two ways. First, the distribution of flake types contributing to each technological category is examined. Next, the distributions are summarized to permit a more synthetic view of lithic reduction actions within the northwestern block.

### Core Reduction Nodules

The nodules placed in the core reduction class have two distinct spatial peaks: one in the northern part of the block, the other in the southern (Figures 2.8–2.10). Core reduction flakes and angular debris within this technological category are present in both concentrations. Facial regularization flakes are, by definition (Figure 2.7), more sparse than the other two flake types; those present occur most frequently in the northern concentration (Figure 2.10).

Two raw materials comprise most of the nodules within core reduction nodules (Table 2.2). Tongue River silicified siltstone, an abundant low-quality local material, is one contributor to the northern concentration and virtually the sole constituent of the southern concentration (Figure 2.11). Refitting has shown that most of the Tongue River silicified siltstone present in the block area is from the reduction of two to three large blocks of this material (Figures 2.12, 2.13, 4.10, 4.11; see

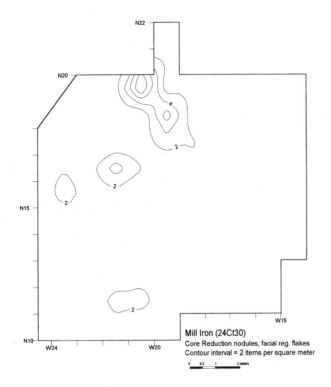

**Figure 2.10.** Density per square meter of facial regularization flakes from core reduction nodules, northwestern block area.

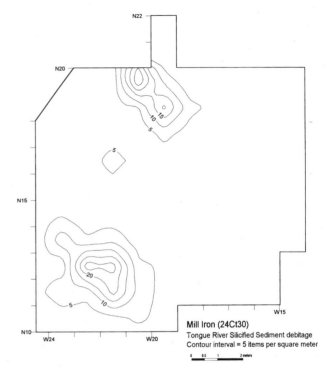

**Figure 2.11.** Density per square meter of Tongue River silicified siltstone debitage, northwestern block area.

**Table 2.2.** Debitage Raw Material Sources Cross-Tabulated by Technological Modes. (See Chapter 6 for raw material type descriptions.)

| | Core Re-duction | Core Regu-larization | Tool Main-tenance |
|---|---|---|---|
| Tongue River Silicified Sediment | XXXX | | |
| Dark Brown Silicified Wood | XXXX | | |
| Gray Porcellanite | | XXXX | |
| Light Brown Silicified Wood | | XXXX | |
| Cobble Chert | | XXXX | |
| Red Porcellanite | | | XXX |
| Red-purple Chert | | | XXX |
| Dendritic Cherts | | | XXX |
| Translucent Red Chert | | | XXX |
| White Chert | | | XXX |
| Pink Chert | | | XXX |
| Other | | | XXX |

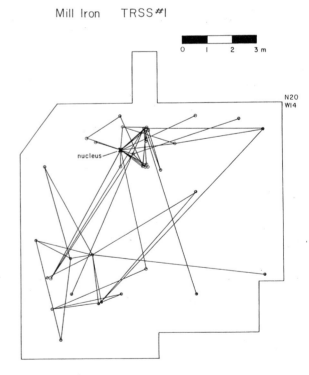

**Figure 2.12.** Location of pieces from refitted core #1 of Tongue River silicified siltstone (TRSS).

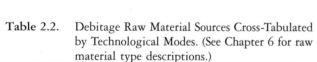

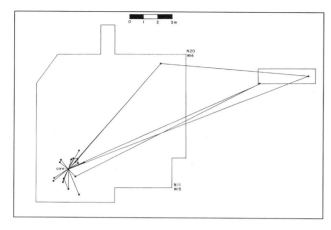

**Figure 2.13.**   Location of pieces from refitted core #2 of Tongue River silicified siltstone (TRSS).

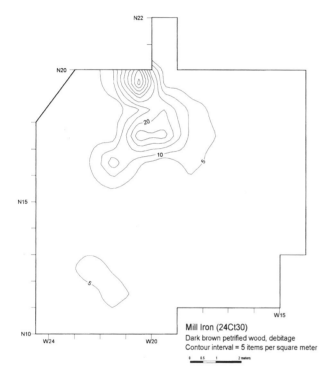

**Figure 2.14.**   Density per square meter of dark brown silicified wood debitage, northwestern block area.

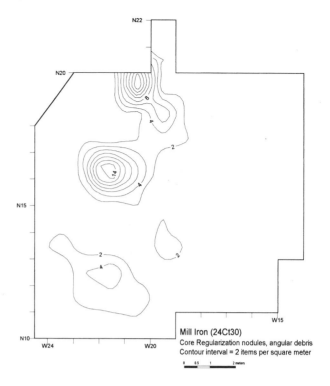

**Figure 2.15.**   Density per square meter of angular debris from core regularization nodules, northwestern block area.

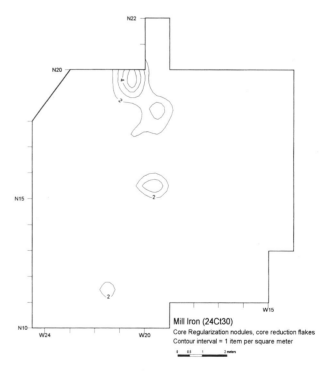

**Figure 2.16.**   Density per square meter of core reduction flakes from core regularization nodules, northwestern block area.

also Figures 2.11, 4.16). Dark brown silicified wood is the other raw material in this technological category. A few tools were produced of this material (Chapters 4 and 5). Almost all of the dark brown silicified wood debitage is confined to the northern concentration (Figure 2.14), where it composes the aggregation of facial regularization flakes, as well as some of the angular debris and core reduction flakes of core reduction nodules. Core reduction nodules occur in the northern and southern portions of the northwest excavation area. Tongue River silici-

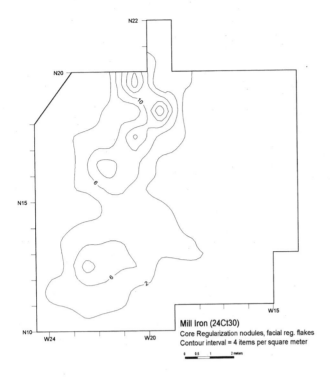

**Figure 2.17.** Density per square meter of facial regularization flakes from core regularization nodules, northwestern block area.

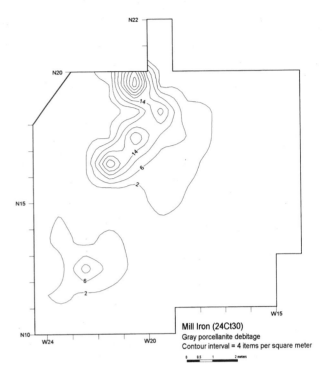

**Figure 2.18.** Density per square meter of gray porcellanite debitage, northwestern block area.

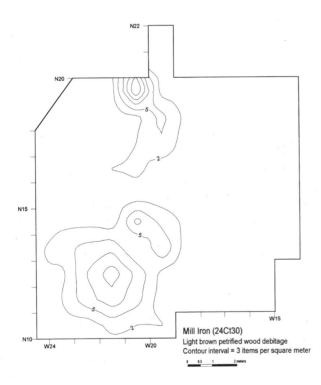

**Figure 2.19.** Density per square meter of light brown silicified wood debitage, northwestern block area.

fied siltstone reduction was limited to initial assay and subsequent early core reduction in both the north and the south, and dark brown silicified wood was reduced somewhat further than Tongue River silicified siltstone primarily in the northern area where some facial regularization flakes were produced.

## Core Regularization Nodules

Most debitage from analytical nodules characterized as core regularization occurs in the northern half of the northwestern block area. Angular debris has two distinct concentrations (Figure 2.15) both in the northern half of the block area. Core reduction flakes are concentrated in a single peak in the northern edge of the excavation area (Figure 2.16), and facial regularization debitage is fairly widespread (Figure 2.17), with two very dense areas in the northern part of the excavation area and a single diffuse aggregation in the southwest corner of the block area.

The two major raw material constituents of the core regularization nodules are gray porcellanite and light brown silicified wood. Gray porcellanite is most frequent in the northern part of the block (Figure 2.18), and light brown silicified wood is about equally frequent in both the northern and southern high-density areas (Figure 2.19). The peak in angular debris centered upon N16.5, W22 (Figure 2.15) is comprised almost entirely of gray porcellanite. Too, the concentration of facial regularization flakes at N18.5, W20 (Figure 2.17) is mostly gray porcellanite debitage.

Overall, the distribution of debitage from core regularization nodules, which represent the later manufacture of stone

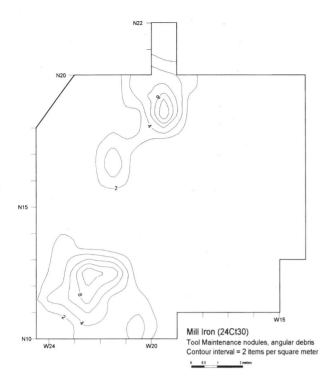

**Figure 2.20.** Density per square meter of angular debris from tool maintenance nodules, northwestern block area.

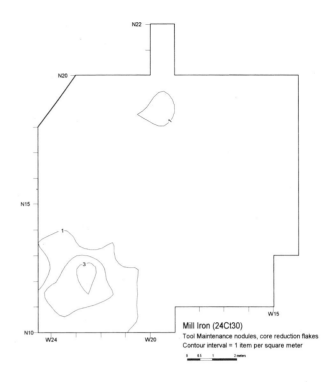

**Figure 2.21.** Density per square meter of core reduction flakes from tool maintenance nodules, northwestern block area.

tools, suggests some spatial differentiation. Most core regularization debris is in the northern part of the excavated area where the two most common material types (gray porcellanite and light brown silicified wood) form a single concentration at approximately N19.5, W21. Two other concentrations are composed of gray porcellanite primarily, as discussed above. In fact, gray porcellanite seems only to occur in discrete concentrations. In contrast to gray porcellanite, light brown silicified wood flakes are more dispersed.

**Tool Maintenance Nodules**

Nodules classed as predominantly maintenance debitage were mostly located in the southern portion of the block area (Figures 2.20, 2.21, and 2.22). The few shatter flakes from these nodules are localized in northern and southern high-density peaks (Figure 2.20). The infrequent core reduction flakes from nodules categorized as tool maintenance follow this distribution too (Figure 2.21). Facial regularization flakes are very dense in the south where the peak density is centered upon N12.5, W21.5 (Figure 2.22). However, low densities of facial regularization flakes occur all over the block area. Debitage from tool maintenance nodules is, thus, the most widespread and also the most densely concentrated of all debitage in the northwestern block area.

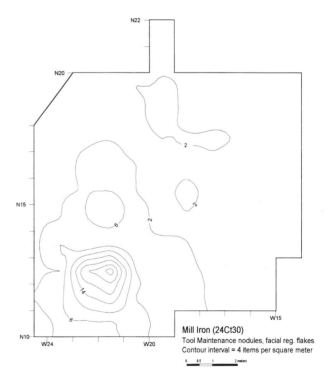

**Figure 2.22.** Density per square meter of facial regularization flakes from tool maintenance nodules, northwestern block area.

## Discussion

A northern aggregation and a southern aggregation are evident from our distributional analysis. The northern aggregation can be further divided into two or three peaks for some technological modes (e.g. Figure 2.17). Several possibilities for interpreting these data exist. First, since each of the two main aggregations is distinct from the other, and they are scattered over just a few square meters, it is quite tempting to interpret these as "activity locations," perhaps primary stone tool manufacture areas. Second, the two aggregations are combinations of quite distinct technological modes and composites of flakes from many raw material sources. Therefore, the pattern could also result from the dumping of lithic debris from some activity area. Third, the aggregations are combinations of episodes of flintknapping, followed by episodes of discard. There is some evidence to support each of these interpretations. The distribution of refitted items suggests activity loci, the distribution of reduction classes suggests dumps in which all debris from various kinds of reduction is piled together, and the distribution of nodules within each technological mode suggests a complex mixture of both activity and discard.

Some relatively clear patterns do, however, emerge from this analysis. First, the composition of the northern and southern aggregations differs. The southern aggregation is dominated by debitage from tool maintenance, whereas the northern aggregation is predominantly core regularization and core reduction. Both core reduction and core regularization produce large flakes that could have been useful primary butchering tools (Frison 1991:314–325). Finer cutting and filleting may, however, have made use of more easily maintained edges, edges that could be resharpened through the butchery process, or in preparation for another kill-butchering event. If they are dumps of lithic debris, then the material from each kind of tool manufacture and use was dumped more or less separately. If they are primary activity loci, then perhaps this is the edge of a butchery assembly line. Finally, if they are simply fortuitous combinations of different technological modes, then there may not have been any activity differentiation within this part of the site.

## References Cited

Crabtree, D.
  1972  *An Introduction to Flintknapping.* Occasional Papers of the Idaho State Museum, No. 28.

Davis, J. C.
  1986  *Statistics and Data Analysis in Geology.* Wiley, New York.

Frison, G. C.
  1991  *Prehistoric Hunters of the High Plains.* 2d ed. Academic Press, New York.

Hofman, J. L.
  1992  Putting the Pieces Together: An Introduction to Refitting. In *Piecing Together the Past: Applications of Refitting Studies in Archaeology*, edited by J. L. Hofman and J. G. Enloe, pp. 1–20. British Anthropological Reports International Series, No. 578.

Johnson, D. L., and K. L. Hansen
  1974  The Effect of Frost-heaving on Objects in the Soil. *Plains Anthropologist* 19:81–98.

Johnson, D. L., D. R. Muhs, and M. L. Barnhardt
  1974  The Effects of Frost-heaving on Objects in Soils, II: Laboratory Experiments. *Plains Anthropologist* 22:133–147.

Larson, M. L.
  1990  *Early Plains Archaic Technological Organization: The Laddie Creek Example.* Ph.D dissertation, Department of Anthropology, University of California at Santa Barbara, Santa Barbara. University Microfilms, Ann Arbor.

Larson, M. L., and E. E. Ingbar
  1992  Perspectives on Refitting: Critique and a Complementary Approach. In *Piecing Together the Past: Applications of Refitting Studies in Archaeology*, edited by J. L. Hofman and J. G. Enloe, pp. 151–162. British. Anthropological Reports International Series, No. 578.

O'Connell, J. F.
  1987  Alyawara Site Structure and its Archaeological Implications. *American Antiquity* 52:74–108.

Parry, W. J., and R. L. Kelly
  1988  Expedient Core Technology and Sedentism. In The *Organization of Core Technology*, edited by J. K. Johnson and C. A. Morrow, pp. 285–304. Westview Press, Boulder.

Schiffer, M. B.
  1987  *Formation Processes of the Archaeological Record.* University of New Mexico Press, Albuquerque.

Thomas, E. F., D. Halverson, and P. L. Guth
  1986  Interactive Rose Diagrams on a Microcomputer. *Geobyte* 2(4):31–33.

Yellen, J. E.
  1977  *Archaeological Approaches to the Present.* Academic Press, New York.

# CHAPTER THREE

# Geology of the Mill Iron Site

JOHN ALBANESE
Casper, Wyoming

## General Geomorphology and Physiography

Archeological Site 24CT30 is located in the southeastern corner of Montana in Section 19, Township 1 North, Range 62 East. The South Dakota–Montana state boundary lies 1.9 km to the south. The topography in the general vicinity of the site is depicted on the U.S.G.S., 7.5 minute Quadrangle Map, Humbolt Hills, Mont.–S. Dak., 1980. This map indicates that the site datum lies on an approximate elevation of 960 m. From a physiographic and structural geologic viewpoint, the site lies at the juncture of the northernmost extension of the Black Hills and the southwestern margin of the Williston Basin (Dobbins and Erdmann 1955).

Site 24CT30 is situated within the valley drained by Humbolt Creek, a fourth-order (scale 1:24000) meandering ephemeral stream that flows to the northwest (310°). The site is located atop a small isolated butte, the crest of which stands 25 ± m above and 275 m northeast of the channel of Humbolt Creek (Figure 3.1). Humbolt Creek is a tributary of Box Elder Creek, the major perennial drainage within the general area. The juncture of Box Elder Creek and Humbolt Creek lies 4.9 km northwest (318°) of the Mill Iron site. The gradient of Humbolt Creek averages 0.00375 (0.2°), while the meandering channel's sinuosity factor is 1.65. The drainage pattern in the general area is rectangular. The predominant (third-order) stream direction is to the northwest ($n$ = 13, mean 248°, st. dev. 129°). The hydrology of the modern drainage system has been locally effected by the construction of a 7 m high dam at the mouth of a system of tributaries to Humbolt Creek. The dam, built in the late 1930s, lies 410 m southwest of Site 24CT30 (Figure 3.1 and 3.2). The resultant 520 m long reservoir is now shallow and infilled with sediment. It holds a minimal amount of water. The rapid influx of sediment into the reservoir testifies to the easy erodibility of bedrock in the area. In the vicinity of Site 24CT30 the tributaries to Humbolt Creek are incised into bedrock of the Hell Creek Formation of Upper Cretaceous Age (Miller et al. 1977). The Hell Creek is composed of interbedded claystones, lignitic shales, coals, and lenses of sandstone. The valley of Humbolt Creek is bordered on the southwest by the Humbolt Hills, a complex of elongate, parallel, flat-topped ridges that trend 310° ± 13° ($n$ = 6). The crest of the Humbolt Hills lies 110 m above and 2.35 km southwest of Humbolt Creek's channel. The crestal portion of the Humbolt Hills is underlain by the basal strata of the Fort Union Formation of Paleocene age, which overlies the Hell Creek Formation (Figures 3.1 and 3.2). The valley is bordered on the northeast by a complex aggregation of elongate ridges that generally parallel the trend of Humbolt Creek. The edge of this ridge system lies 180–300 m northeast of the Humbolt Creek channel (Figure 3.1). The valley floor and slopes plus adjoining ridges are characterized by the presence of abundant, scattered and isolated buttes (erosional remnants) that rise 2–30 m above the surrounding ground surface. The highest are capped by resistant sandstones. Small, local, randomly distributed areas are currently being affected by severe slopewash erosion. In some of these areas, the thin veneer of Quaternary colluvium which overlies bedrock has been completely removed.

Six paired, planar, step-like, Quaternary geomorphic surfaces lie above the flood plain of Humbolt Creek (Figure 3.2). These surfaces, labeled S1 through S6 in ascending order, are the remnants of portions of former valley slopes and/or terrace treads that were formerly at grade to Humbolt Creek (Figure 3.2, 3.3, and 3.4). All individual surfaces decrease in slope angle in a downslope direction. The inclination of an individual surface, e.g. S5, can change from 8.1° at valley edge to 0.48° at valley center. Individual surfaces vary in inclination. Therefore, the height of the riser (step) that separates individual surfaces varies laterally. The most extreme case is the difference in height of the riser that separates surfaces S6 and S5, which depending on locale, varies between 2 m and 9 m. Elevations of the various geomorphic surfaces are shown on Figure 3.3. The crest of the 21 ± m high isolated butte on which the Mill Iron site (24CT30) lies is a remnant of the S6 surface. The surface slope of this 90 m long butte changes from 6° to 3.7° in a westerly

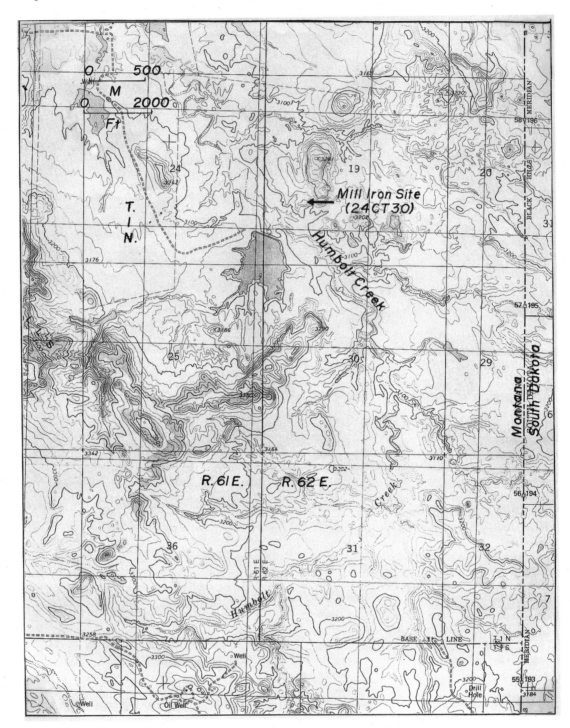

**Figure 3.1.** Topographic map of Mill Iron site (24CT30) and vicinity, contour interval = 6.1 m; reproduced from U.S.G.S., 7.5 minute Quadrangle Map, Humbolt Hills, Montana–South Dakota, 1980.

direction. This surface was formerly connected to the bedrock hill that lies 75 ± m to the northeast of the site (Figures 3.4 and 3.5).

The thickness and type of sediment that lies beneath a given geomorphic surface varies widely within the study area. In general the upslope (valley margin) portion of a surface is underlain by <1–2 m of eolian and/or slopewash colluvium, while surfaces present near the valley center are generally underlain by alluvium. The S6 and S5 surfaces are concentrated along the margins of the Humbolt Creek valley, whereas surfaces S4 through S1 are mainly located in the central portion of the valley. These latter surfaces are typically covered by thin veneer (<50 cm) of eolian and/or slopewash sediment that overlies a thick (>4m) section of braided stream deposits.

Over most of the study area, the S6 surface is underlain by <1 m of Quaternary sediment. However, in the immediate vicinity of Site 24CT30, the S6 surface is underlain by a 5.1 ± m thick prism of Quaternary sediment mainly composed of slopewash colluvium plus basal fluvial deposits. This sediment was deposited within an ancient swale that drained to the west. This "isopach thick" thins rapidly to the northwest and southwest (Figure 3.6). The lower two-thirds of the sediment within the isopach thick is late Pleistocene in age (>10,000 B.P.). During this period, small ephemeral streams drained down valley slopes, covered by a thin veneer of slopewash sediment, into ancestral Humbolt Creek. A preserved remnant of deposits laid down by one of these streams is found 19 m above the valley floor at stadia station 102, which lies 245 m southeast of 24CT30 (Figures 3.3 and 3.4). Here 90 cm of horizontal, thin-bedded, laminated sands and 2.5–5 cm thick interbeds of gravel overlie bedrock. These fluvial sediments are unconformably overlain by 30 ± cm of eolian and slopewash sediment.

Remnants of surface S5 are found only on the margins of the main valley, where they are underlain by 1.5 m or less of sandy slopewash sediment, which is commonly overlain by <30 cm of massive eolian sand. No fluvial sediments were observed beneath the S5 surface. That portion of S5 surface that was originally located near the central portion of the Humbolt Creek valley was removed during later episodes of erosion and downcutting.

Surface S4 is present along valley margins and the central portion of the main valley. The Quaternary sediments that are present beneath the S4 surface on the valley margins are thin (<1 m) eolian and/or slopewash deposits that rest on bedrock. In the central portions of the basin, these same type deposits unconformably overlie thick (4±m) ephemeral stream deposits of Quaternary age. An example of this lateral change in sediment type is present southwest of the Mill Iron site datum. The remnant of an S4 surface lies 60 m southwest of the datum. It is underlain by 50 ± cm of sandy slopewash sediment, which overlies bedrock. A 10 m long, 185 ± cm deep backhoe trench (No. 1) is located 80 m to the southwest of the S4 remnant. The trench lies adjacent to a southwest draining tributary to Humbolt Creek and was excavated into the S4 and S3 surfaces (Figures 3.3 and 3.7). The backhoe trench exposed 56 cm of eolian and slope wash sediment that unconformably overlies 214+ cm of alluvium. With one exception, this same pattern of eolian slopewash sediments unconformably overlying fluvial

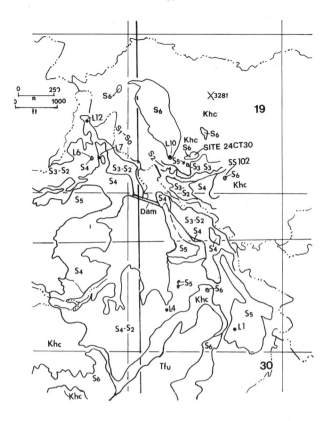

**Figure 3.2.** Topographic and geologic map of the Mill Iron site (24CT30) area, contour interval = 6.1 m. Geologic formation data taken from Miller et al., 1977. Legend as follows: S1–S6 = geomorphic surfaces; Khc = Hell Creek Formation; Tfu = Fort Union Formation; SS102 = statia station; L6 = Locality number.

sediments is present in all exposures of the S4, S3, S2 and S1 surfaces within the study area that lie *south* of Backhoe Trench 1 and within 100 m of the Humbolt Creek channel. The one exception to the pattern noted above exists at the locale of Backhoe Trench 2, which lies 84 m southeast of Backhoe Trench 1. Here the S4 surface is underlain by 306 cm of interbedded Quaternary slopewash sediments. The beds are 20-132 cm thick and overlie 28+ cm of coarse gravels (Figure 3.7).

Three additional backhoe trenches were dug to the southwest and within 110 m of Backhoe Trench 2 (Figure 3.3). Their lengths varied from 7 m to 18 m and they ranged from 1.75 m to 2.5 m in depth. These trenches penetrated surfaces S1 through S3. The same succession of sediment was present beneath all three surfaces, e.g. <1 m of eolian slopewash sediment overlying a thin-bedded fluvial sequence. The thickness of trench exposures varied from 1.5+ m to 1.9+ m (Figure 3.7). The fluvial successions exposed in these trenches as well as in Backhoe Trench 1 are similar. They mainly consist of a complex interfingering of discrete, 3–12 cm thick, horizontal, laminated, very-fine- to fine-grained, well-sorted, sand lenses. Lenses are usually 50–200 cm long; some are composed of clay. Ripple marks are ubiquitous features within sand lenses. Examples of

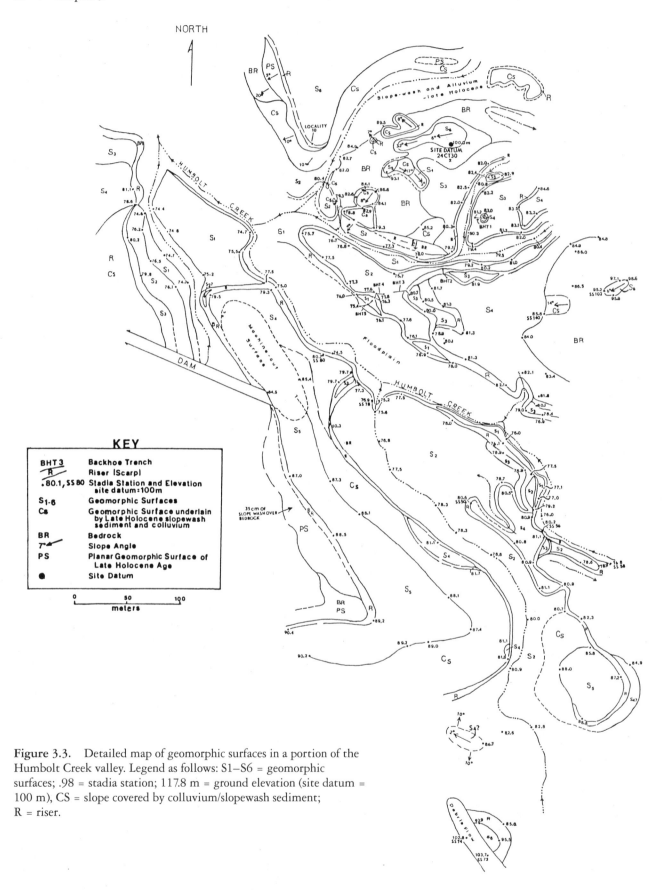

**Figure 3.3.** Detailed map of geomorphic surfaces in a portion of the Humbolt Creek valley. Legend as follows: S1–S6 = geomorphic surfaces; .98 = stadia station; 117.8 m = ground elevation (site datum = 100 m), CS = slope covered by colluvium/slopewash sediment; R = riser.

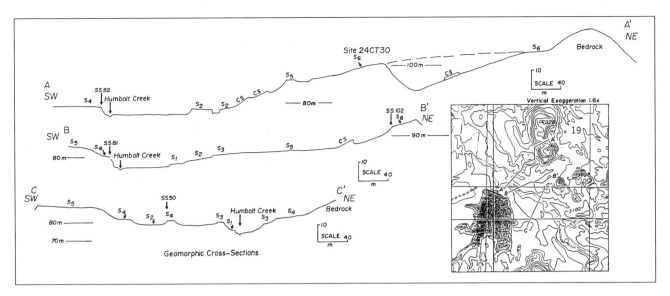

**Figure 3.4.** Geomorphic cross-sections, Humbolt Creek valley. Legend as follows: A–A' = line of cross-section; S1–S6 = geomorphic surfaces; CS = slope covered by colluvium/slopewash sediment; ss82 = stadia station.

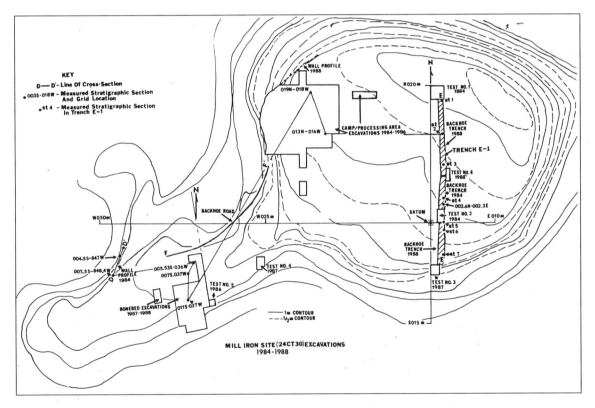

**Figure 3.5.** Topographic map of Mill Iron site (24CT30), contour interval = 1 m (solid line). Legend as follows: E–E' line of cross section; st4 = station in Trench E-1; 19N–18W = site grid location of stratigraphic section.

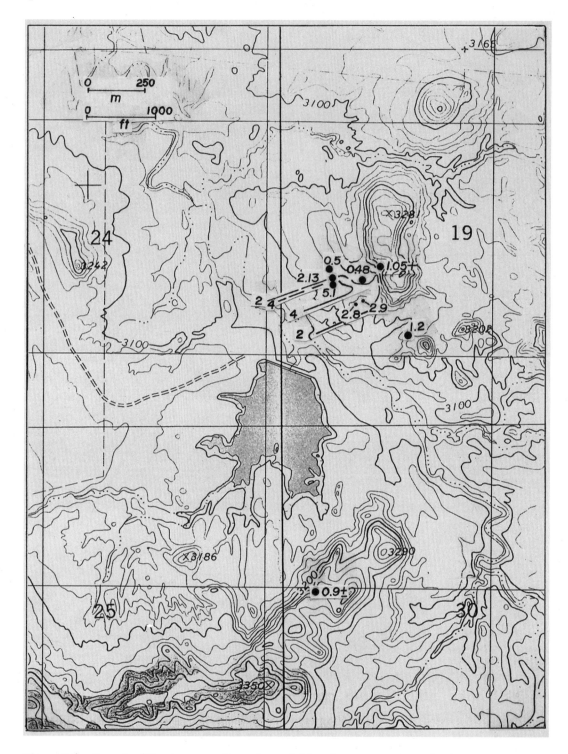

**Figure 3.6.** Isopach of Quarternary sediment beneath S6 surface, contour interval = 2m.

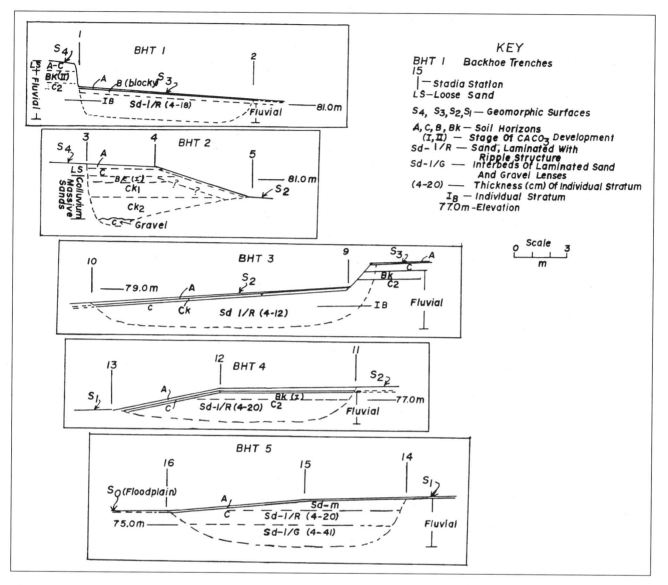

**Figure 3.7.** Geologic cross-sections of Backhoe Trenches 1 through 5.

minor, soft sediment deformation, e.g. convoluted bedding planes, are also present. In Backhoe Trench 5, which was excavated into surface S1, the basal 112 cm of fluvial sediment consists of 3–4 cm thick, 70–250 cm long gravel lenses, which are complexly interbedded with 15–33 cm thick lenses composed of laminated or massive sand. The gravels contain 0.5–2 cm long clasts of rounded to sub-angular concretion fragments (siltstone) and "red clinker" (burned coal beds) imbedded in a coarse sand. Exposures that display thick (3.8–4.4 m) intervals of fluvial sediment beneath the S4, S3 and S2 surfaces are also present in meander scarps that lie southwest of the flood plain of Humbolt Creek. These scarps are intermittently present between stadia stations 82 and 58, a distance of 530 m (Figure 3.3) and display similar sedimentary features, e.g. thin laminated horizontal sand lenses, thin gravel lenses, planar cross-beds, ripple

marks and 2–3 m wide channels filled with sand or gravel. The base of the fluvial sequence can be observed at Locality 12, a meander scarp situated in the most northwestern and downstream portion of the study area (Figure 3.2). Here approximately 3.2 m of fluvial sediment, very similar to that described above, overlies bedrock. The fluvial unit is overlain by 60 ± cm of slopewash sediment, the top of which is the S3 surface.

Surfaces S1–S4 are present in the highly dissected area that lies south of the reservoir (Figure 3.2). Their eroded remnants form a complex mosaic of small pedestals, and elongate "islands" that lie between first- and second-order ephemeral streams. These surfaces are underlain by 1–2 m thick deposits of eolian and slopewash sediment. The thick fluvial sediments that are present along the Humbolt Creek are absent in this area. The dividing line between thick fluvial and adjacent slopewash

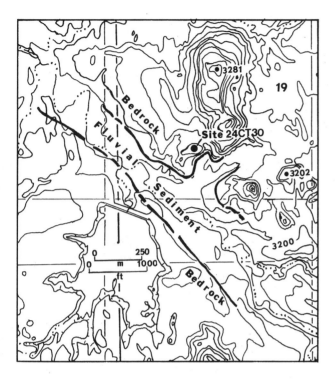

**Figure 3.8.** Map of distribution of Quaternary Alluvial sequence that underlies geomorphic surface S1 through S4.

colluvial facies as displayed beneath the S4–S1 surfaces is sharp and abrupt. It can be mapped with precision in the area adjacent to the reservoir dam where the ground surface has been machine scraped. The fluvial sedimentary unit beneath the S4–S1 surfaces is 215–245 m wide and straddles the modern channel of Humbolt Creek. It also extends northeasterly along the southwest-draining ephemeral streams that lie south of Site 24CT30 (Figure 3.8). Along the main channel, braided stream sediments accumulated within a broad, deep channel depression. This old sediment-filled channel is three times as wide as the modern flood plain of Humbolt Creek.

The S4–S1 geomorphic surfaces that are located near the modern channel of Humbolt Creek are strath (erosional) surfaces and not depositional surfaces as most alluvial terrace treads are commonly thought to be. In Backhoe Trench 1, the fluvial sequence below both the S4 and S3 surfaces was exposed to a depth of 1.5 m. The same individual horizontal beds were observed to continue under both surfaces. The same situation was also observed in Backhoe Trench 3 within the fluvial sediments that lie beneath the S3 and S2 surfaces. At the surface, in the vicinity of stadia stations 78 through 80, located on the southwest bank of Humbolt Creek (Figure 3.3), the same Quaternary fluvial beds can be observed extending beneath surfaces S4 through S2. The geomorphic surfaces formed long after the fluvial sediments were deposited and are not related to the depositional processes.

Surfaces S6 through S4 are underlain by calcareous soils that in general have an A-C-Bkb-Ckb-Cb2 or an A-Bw-Bkb-Ckb-Cb profile. They differ mainly in degree of calcium carbonate

development in the Bk horizon. The soil development beneath the S6 surface at the Mill Iron site contains the thickest (135 cm) and most mature Bk horizon (mostly Stage II calcium carbonate development). At Locality 1 (Figure 3.2), the Quaternary sediment beneath the S5 surface is 127 cm thick and consists mainly of slopewash sediment. An A-C-Akb-Bkb-Ckb soil profile was noted. The Bk horizon is 40 cm thick and displays Stage II calcium carbonate development.

In the vicinity of the previously discussed backhoe trenches, A-C horizons are usually superimposed on the thin eolian slopewash surface veneer, while the Bk horizon is usually superimposed on the underlying fluvial sequence. This situation implies that the top of the Bk horizon coincides with an unconformity surface. A Bk horizon superimposed on the top of the fluvial unit is present beneath the S4 surface at Backhoe Trench 1 and the S3 surface in Backhoe Trench 3. The respective thicknesses of the Bk horizons are 61 cm and 46 cm, and both display Stages I and II development. In Backhoe Trench 1, the soil horizons A-Bw-C are present beneath the T3 surface. The fluvial sediments lie within the C horizon. In Backhoe Trench 3, the S2 surface is underlain by A-C horizons, while in Backhoe Trench 4, the horizons beneath the T2 surface are A-C-Ckb-Cb2. The Ckb horizon is 46 cm thick and lies at the top of the fluvial sequence. At Localities 6 and 7, situated on the opposite side of the valley from Site 24CT30 (see Figure 3.2), the soil development present beneath the S4 surface is similar to that beneath the S4 surface in Backhoe Trench 1. However, at Localities 6 and 7, the soil is developed on 70–90 cm of eolian sand that rests on bedrock rather than fluvial sediment. The Bk horizon at Locality 7 is 65 cm thick, whereas at nearby (45 m) Locality 6, it is 43 cm thick. At both locales, the Bk displays Stages I and II calcium carbonate development and extends 10± cm into bedrock.

A similar S4 soil development is also present in the southeastern portion of the study area on the southwest side of Humbolt Creek. Here in the vicinity of stadia stations 50 and 56 (Figure 3.3), the S4 surface is underlain by 25–50 cm of eolian sand, which unconformably overlies a fluvial sequence similar to that present in the aforementioned backhoe trenches. Entisols with A-C development are superimposed on the eolian sequence, and a truncated Bk horizon is present at the top of the thick (4 + m) alluvial sequence. In the vicinity of stadia station 50, a 33+ cm thick A horizon (eolian) overlies a Bk horizon that varies in exposure thickness from 46+ cm to 110+ cm and in calcium carbonate development from Stage I to Stage II. At stadia station 56, a 48 cm thick A horizon overlies a 60 ± cm thick Bk horizon (Stage II).

In general, the stage of calcium carbonate development of the Bk horizon beneath a given surface increases with age. The Bk horizon beneath the S6 surface is thicker and better developed than the Bk horizon present beneath the S4 surface. However, there is always a caveat or exception to the rule, and in Backhoe Trench 2, the Bk horizon beneath the S4 surface is thin (32 cm) and weakly developed (Stage I). It lies 86 cm beneath the surface and displays Stage I calcium carbonate development. The soil horizons displayed in the trench are A-C-Bkb-Ckb-Cb2 (see Figure 3.8). As mentioned before, the sedimentary section exposed in Backhoe Trench 2 is unusual in that it is mainly composed of slopewash sediment rather than alluvium, which coupled with the weak Bk development makes the setting anomalous. This situation probably resulted from the incision of a gulch or arroyo into the main braided stream section that was later filled with slopewash sediment. The presence of a 30+ cm thick gravel at the base of the trench may be a reflection of the erosional event that created the topographic depression.

Reider (this volume) presents a much more detailed and technical discussion concerning soils than outlined above. He considers soil development to be polygenetic with a Typic Haploboroll forming in late Pleistocene time, under relatively moist conditions, which was later transformed under aridic conditions into a calcareous highly alkaline soil (Aridic Haploboroll or similar soil). The transformation is postulated to have occurred gradually throughout the Altithermal period. Weak soils (Entisols) have developed in post-Altithermal time.

Data concerning the ages of the soils and Quaternary sediment that are associated with geomorphic surfaces S6 through S1 are sparse. Six radiocarbon dates have been secured from the Goshen-Plainview cultural horizon at Site 24CT30, where it lies at an average depth of 170 cm below the S6 surface. Individual dates range between 11,360 B.P. and 10,760 B.P. A late Plains Archaic cultural horizon is also present at Site 24CT30. It lies approximately 75 cm beneath the S6 surface and yielded Pelican Lake style projectile points, ca. 3,000–1,900 B.P. (Frison 1991:29). The horizon was not radiocarbon dated. At Locality 10, situated 160 m west of 24CT30, a radiocarbon date of 1,836 ± 55 B.P. (AZ 3667) was secured from charcoal contained within a cultural level that lies 30 cm beneath the S6 surface. The cultural horizon lies at the base of an eolian sand deposit that unconformably overlies the main Bk horizon. A radiocarbon date of 1370 ± 60 (Beta 26900) was secured from a sandstone slab lined fire hearth that is located 60 ± m southwest (225°) of Locality 1 (Figure 3.2). The 41 cm thick hearth lies 43 cm beneath the top of the S5 surface. It is enclosed within a 130± cm thick section of a clayey, silty, fine-grained sand (50±%) that contains 2.5–7.5 cm thick, 1–3 m long pebble lenses. The hearth lies at the base of an Entisol that unconformably overlies a Bk horizon correlative with the one present at Locality 1. A remnant of the S5 surface, underlain by 150± cm of sandy slope sediment, is located 20± m southwest of the butte on which Site 24CT30 is located (Figure 3.3). A fragment of a Goshen-Plainview projectile point and associated stone artifacts were found on top of the S5 surface at this locale (oral communication from George Frison 1993). The artifacts could very well have washed out of the Goshen-Plainview horizon that outcrops on the rim of the higher and nearby butte.

Late Plains Archaic projectile points of Pelican Lake style also occurred in a buried cultural horizon present at Site 24CT40 (Earl et al. 1982). The previously mentioned Localities 6 and 7, lie within Site 24CT40. The cultural horizon is well displayed at Locality 7, where it lies 51 cm below the S4 surface and 25 cm below the top of the Bk horizon.

From all of the above, one can conclude that the S6, S5 and S4 surfaces existed prior to 2,000 years and that the main episode of pedogenesis that resulted in the creation of the Bk horizon, occurred between 2,000 and 11,000 years. It is obvi-

ous that much of the sediment that now underlies surface S6 was deposited long after the surface was formed. The Pleistocene sediment that *may* have underlain much of the original geomorphic surface was lost to erosional forces quite some time ago. Except for the late Pleistocene sediments in the vicinity of Site 24CT30, all of the sediment now present beneath the S6 surface is Holocene in age.

The S4 surface was intact at the time of the Late Plains Archaic (Pelican Lake) occupation ca. 3,000–1,900 B.P. It has since been incised, and in places it forms the surface of isolated "pedestals," e.g. at Localities 6 and 7 and in the area south of the previously mentioned reservoir. The lower and younger S3, S2 and S1 surfaces formed in Late Holocene time, perhaps as recently as the past 1,200 years (this possibility will be discussed in the concluding section of this paper). The creation of the S3, S2 and S1 surfaces was accompanied by a 5.2–6.7 m lowering of the valley floor of Humbolt Creek.

Geomorphic surfaces of Late Holocene age are present along the slopes of the butte on which Site 24CT30 is situated. These features are eroded remnants of Late Holocene slopewash deposits that formerly mantled the slopes of the butte. The slopewash deposits rest on bedrock and are 0.7–1.5 m thick. They consist of thin-bedded, sandy deposits with abundant, thin, pebble lenses. These deposits have been subjected to recent erosion. They have been completely removed over much of the area. Where preserved, they form 1–1.6 m high pedestals or broader features of similar vertical relief, the surfaces of which slope 5–14° (labeled CS on Figure 3.3). One prominent example of this type of landform is located 240 m southeast of Site 24CT30 at stadia station 140 (Figure 3.3), where an isolated, slope remnant rises 5± m above the general land surface. The surface of the remnant slopes 14° to the west and is underlain by 70 cm of slopewash sediment that rests on bedrock and displays an A-C soil development.

In the vicinity of Site 24CT30, minor 7–20 m wide, low-angle, planar, erosional surfaces are currently forming on hill slopes. These step-like features differ from the slopewash/colluvium slope remnants in that they are cut into bedrock and are bordered in an upslope position by steep scarps that vary from 1.2–4.6 m in height. One such feature lies just west of Site 24CT30 at Locality 10. A 140 m long, 10–20 m wide, west sloping (5°) planar surface is incised into bedrock. It lies adjacent to the edge of the S6 surface and is bordered on the east by a near-vertical scarp that varies from 1.2–2.4 m in height (Figure 3.3). A similar but smaller feature is located 80 m north of the site and adjacent to the edge of the S6 surface. This southerly inclined planar surface is 8± m wide and incised into bedrock. It is bordered on the north by a 4.6 m high scarp, the top of which marks the edge of the S6 surface. The planar surface is incised into the hill slope and stands 2.1 m above the first-order, valley floor (Figure 3.3).

## Quaternary Stratigraphy and Sedimentation

The locale of Site 24CT30 contains the thickest accumulation of Quaternary sediment that was observed beneath the S6 geomorphic surface. At the site, 2.6 m of Quaternary sediment overlies bedrock, while at Locality 10, situated 160 m west of the site datum, 5.1 ± m of Quaternary sediment is present. The thickness of Quaternary sediment decreases markedly to the northwest of Locality 10.

At a point located 20 m northwest of Locality 10, 2 m of Quaternary sediment is present; 80 m further to the northwest, 0.9 m of equivalent sediment is present; 62 m farther to the northwest, 0.5 m of Quaternary sediment overlies bedrock. The thickness of Quaternary sediment beneath the S6 surface also decreases to the southwest of Site 24CT30. At Locality 102, located 260 m to the southwest of the site, 1.2m of Quaternary sediment overlies bedrock (Figure 3.6).

The Quaternary sediment present at and in the vicinity of Site 24CT30 was deposited within an asymmetric, second-order (Scale 1:24000), paleo-swale that in late Pleistocene time drained southwesterly (250°) into ancestral Humbolt Creek. The gradient of the swale was approximately 0.07 (4°), an inclination similar to the gradient (0.063) of the modern first-order ephemeral stream that borders the main site area on the northwest. The paleo-swale originated on the bedrock hill that lies immediately northeast of the site area (Figure 3.2). The Goshen-Plainview cultural horizon at Site 24CT30 was preserved because it lies within a sediment-filled, topographic depression that was not seriously affected by post-depositional episodes of erosion. If the original Goshen-Plainview occupation had been on a higher physiographic surface (drainage divide) that lay away from the paleo-swale, no evidence would remain as the features or artifacts that may have lain there would have been removed by erosion. This is attested to by the fact that outside the general site area, only a thin (<1 m) layer of Late Holocene sediment underlies the S6 surface. The Mill Iron site, like the majority of buried Paleoindian sites present within the Northwestern Plains, is a "geologic freak," which because of a unique set of circumstances and events escaped destruction by subsequent episodes of erosion (Albanese 1977).

The 2.6± m thick Quaternary sedimentary sequence at the site displays complex and rapid lateral changes. No single sedimentary unit or marker bed can be traced across the 90 m long top of the butte on which the site is situated. At this locale, slopewash and colluvial sedimentation have been dominant throughout the Quaternary. However, two episodes of ephemeral stream deposition can be identified. Thin, local eolian sand deposits of Late Holocene age are also present. All of the noneolian Quaternary sediment at the site is derived from the outcrops of Hell Creek Formation exposed on the high hill located to the northeast of the site. As mentioned in the previous discussion on geomorphology of the area, a continuous planar slope (S6) formerly connected the hill and site area. Because they all derive from the same nearby source, all Quaternary noneolian sedimentary facies at the site contain the same type sand grains and pebbles. A ubiquitous ingredient in all sediment is a soft, opaque, spherical grain composed of dolomite that commonly ranges between 0.03 mm and 0.6 mm in diameter, though grains as wide as 1 mm are present. These medium- to coarse-size grains do not react with cold, dilute HCl. They resemble oolites, but lack concentric rings. Sixty-centimeter thick ledges composed entirely of these "spheres" and interstitial silt outcrop on the hill located northeast of the site. Commonly, two to five individual spheres are attached to

each other. The percentage of these "spheroids" within a given Quaternary sediment sample can vary from 1% to 40%. These "spheroids" are interpreted to be oolites that originally formed in the lacustrine environment and whose mineral composition was changed from calcite to dolomite as a result of diagenesis. A second ubiquitous clast common to all sedimentary facies is a rounded quartz sand grain that ranges between 0.1 mm and 0.2 mm in length. This is the most common sand grain size in all stratigraphic units. These grains can constitute up to 80% of a given sediment sample in either slopewash or ephemeral stream sediment. The presence of both medium- to coarse-size spherical (oolite) grains and fine-size sand grains within a given sample results in a striking bimodal appearance. Other common ingredients in all noneolian sediment types are rounded, medium- to coarse size (0.3–0.8 mm) fragments of siltstone, coal and sandstone, which individually can constitute up to an estimated 3% of a given sample. Quartz grains of medium- and coarse-grain size are also present within Quaternary sediments. The percentages of these larger grains are greatest in the western half of the site in both the colluvium and fluvial facies. This situation is probably a reflection of different outcrop source areas for the eastern and western portions of the site. All sedimentary facies contain widely varying percentages of clay and silt. Sand predominates in most sediment, but a transition from clayey, silty sand to sandy, silty clay is not uncommon in the western one-third of the site area.

Pebbles, most commonly composed of sandstone or siltstone, are ubiquitous within colluvium and fluvial facies. Most pebbles range between 0.5 cm and 2.5 cm in length and within colluvium occur as isolated, randomly distributed clasts or in lenses. The lenses range 2–10 cm in thickness and 1–4 m in length. Pebble lenses within colluvium are most common in the northwestern portion of the site in the vicinity of 10–20N, 5–25W. Most slopewash and colluvial deposits and some (but not all) of the fluvial sediments are poorly sorted, which is not surprising considering that the source of most of the sediment probably lies less than 300 m from the site area. Locally, particularly in the east half of the butte, the highest sedimentary unit consists of bimodal, fair- to well-sorted massive sands that generally lack pebbles and are interpreted to be eolian deposits.

Isolated, miniature debris flows within colluvium are common occurrences in the west half of the site area. They are particularly prominent in the vicinity of the Goshen-Plainview bonebed (0–12S, 35–40W). The "flows" commonly consist of 20±% pebbles (1.5–3 cm long) that are randomly distributed within a sand matrix that can vary in grain size from fine to granule. Individual debris flows range 0.2–2 m in length and 2.5–25 cm in thickness. Individual, sandstone slabs that occur with the broad "flat" side parallel to bedding are also a common feature in the western half of the site, particularly at the base of the colluvial sequence. These sandstone slabs are 0.6–1.25 cm thick and 10–25 cm long. The slabs appear to have "slid out" on to an existing ground surface. They are commonly present at the same general stratigraphic level as the debris flows.

Figure 3.9 is a schematic, stratigraphic cross-section drawn through Site 24CT30. It extends from the western to eastern

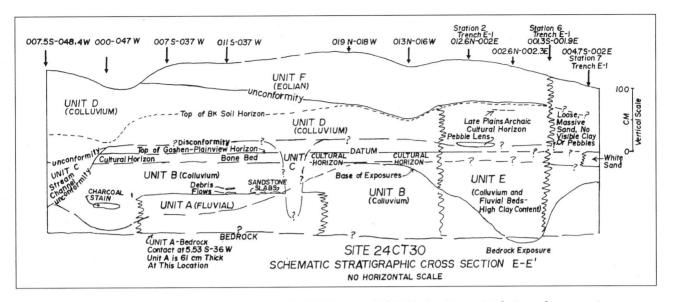

**Figure 3.9.** Schematic stratigraphic cross-section E–E', Mill Iron site (24CT30). See Figure 3.5 for line of cross-section.

portions of the site. The top of the Goshen-Plainview archeological horizon is the horizontal datum on which the cross-section is constructed, a choice necessitated by the lack of a site-wide, lithologic marker. The cultural horizon is a "time marker" that allows correlation across different sedimentary facies. Based on *gross* lithology, and sedimentary structure, six Quaternary sedimentary units can be differentiated within the site area. As indicated on Figure 3.11, no single unit can be identified throughout the entire site area. A brief description of each unit is presented below.

## Unit A

Unit A is the oldest Quaternary stratum in the site area. It can be identified in the western portion of the site in the vicinity of the Goshen-Plainview bison bonebed (4–11S, 35–41W) and along the southwestern portion of the scarp that defines the northwestern margin of the butte on which the site is located (Figure 3.5). Unit A is 65± cm thick and rests on bedrock. The top of the unit lies 43–64 cm below the Goshen-Plainview cultural horizon. The unit is approximately 25± m wide and is a braided stream deposit. The edge of the shallow stream channel within which Unit A was deposited was not observed and it is not known whether the sediments laterally merge into another Quaternary unit or are confined to a channel that is incised into bedrock. Stratification within the unit is horizontal and discontinuous. Two types of sedimentary deposits predominate: channel fills and laminated sand lenses. The two types of deposits interfinger laterally over distances of 0.5–2 m. Channel fills are usually 10–30 cm thick and <1 m long. The channel depressions may be filled with coarse to fine, laminated sand, but more commonly they display a basal gravel (clasts 0.5–5 cm long) that grades upward into medium- to coarse-grained sand. The laminated sand lenses are the most common type of sedimentary structure and consist of well-sorted sand.

They range from 0.5–3 m in length and 20–40 cm in thickness. They commonly display low-angle, planar cross-beds. Laminae are generally horizontal, discontinuous and 1–3 mm thick. The grain size within individual laminae can vary from very-fine to coarse. Black laminae, which consist of coal grains, are a common occurrence.

## Units B and C

Unit B is a sand deposit that accumulated via slopewash and colluvial processes. It varies between 0.6 m and 1.35 m in thickness and with the exception of the eastern third of the site can be identified over most of the area. The Goshen-Plainview cultural horizon lies 8-25 cm below the top of Unit B. The cultural horizon is not marked by the presence of a pedogenic or lithologic contact. The sediment within which the artifacts lie has the same appearance as that which occurs above and below the cultural horizon. The ancient surface was buried by sediment not too long after it was occupied by the Goshen-Plainview peoples.

Unit B overlies Unit A and in most exposures is a massive sand that ordinarily contains 10% or less of randomly distributed and randomly oriented pebbles. Pebbles vary in length (0.5–3 cm), are angular, and are mainly composed of sandstone. However, pebble-size, siltstone concretion fragments are also common. At most locales, the quartz sand grains are predominantly very-fine- to fine-grained (0.1–0.2 mm), though in some trench exposures, medium- to very-coarse-size quartz sand grains were observed. Clay and silt are ubiquitous constituents. Their combined percentage of total sediment commonly exceeds 60% (see Reider this volume for mechanical, grain size analyses of sediments). Sorting is usually poor to very-poor, though as with all generalizations there are exceptions. In the western third of the site, in the vicinity of the Goshen-Plainview bison bonebed (4–11S, 35–40W), the basal

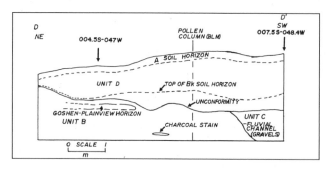

**Figure 3.10.** Geologic cross-section D–D', Mill Iron site (24CT30). See Figure 3.5 for location.

40± cm of Unit B is commonly a laminated (discontinuous laminae, 1–3 mm thick) fine- to medium-grained, well-sorted sand. Random isolate pebble content within the laminated sand varies from an estimated 0% to 8%. The laminated sedimentary structure is suggestive of fluvial deposition. However, the presence of randomly distributed pebbles argues for a slopewash origin. The dividing line between the two processes is not always clear-cut.

Miniature debris flows are a common feature throughout Unit B. They consist of 1.5–3 cm long clasts randomly distributed within a matrix of very poorly sorted, fine-grain to granule-size sand plus varying amounts of silt and clay. The flows are 2.5–25 cm thick and 0.2–2 m long. Debris flows are particularly common at the base of Unit B in the vicinity of 8S-36W where some of the flows rest directly on Unit A. Isolated sandstone slabs that are 0.6–1.25 cm wide and 10–25 cm long also rest on the top of Unit A in the same area. The broad flat sides of the slabs lie parallel to the contact that separates Units A and B. The presence of debris flows and alignments of isolate sandstone slabs just above the Unit A–Unit B contact marks the onset of Quaternary slopewash and colluvial deposition in the area. This event probably reflects the change to a more arid climate and resultant slope instability.

In the western third of the site, the top of Unit B is an unconformity surface. This surface is especially well displayed on the northwest-facing scarp present in the vicinity of OS–47W (Figures 3.5 and 3.10). Here, the erosional event that created the unconformity surface also resulted in the removal of portions of the Goshen-Plainview cultural horizon, which lies 15± m below the unconformity surface. Erosion also resulted in the creation of an ephemeral stream channel, which was subsequently filled with 80+ cm of fluvial deposits that consist of sand and gravel lenses and constitute Unit C. The gravel lenses within Unit C are 7–13 cm thick and 1± m long. The contained pebbles are 0.5-4 cm long. The aforementioned, ephemeral stream paleo-channel that contains Unit C also appears to be present in the vicinity of 11S–38W. Here, a portion of the Goshen-Plainview bison bonebed was removed as a result of lateral undercutting by an ephemeral stream channel. A portion of the bonebed slumped into the channel and was subsequently coveredby 10-50+ cm of interbedded coarse-sand and gravel lenses. The gravel lenses are 1.25–3 cm thick and 30–60 cm

long. At one exposure, the gravel lenses slope 0-5° to the southeast (170°). If the fluvial deposits (Unit C) in the vicinity of OS–11W and 11S–38W correlate, the bison bonebed at 11S–38W was undercut by a stream that drained to the southeast (120°±). This stream did not exist at the time of the Goshen-Plainview occupation. The evidence is clear at OS–47W that the stream channel formed after the time of occupation. Only edges of the channel that contains Unit C were observed within Site 24CT30. The width of the channel has not been determined.

The unconformity at the top of Unit B is not as evident in the eastern two-thirds of the site area, where it appears to coincide with the horizontal contact between Unit B and overlying Unit D. This contact is marked by an abrupt upward increase in the abundance of pebbles.

## Unit D

Unit D is another massive, slopewash colluvium sand deposit. It varies from 60 cm to 130 cm in thickness and overlies Units B and C. It differs from Unit B in that it contains a higher percentage of pebbles (>25%). Nevertheless, the pebbles are similar in size (0.5–7 cm), shape (angular), and composition (sandstone with secondary amounts of siltstone concretion fragments) to those present in Unit B. The pebbles in Unit D occur as randomly distributed clasts and as pebble lenses that vary in inclination from horizontal to 25°. The pebble lenses vary in thickness (2.5–16 cm) and length (1–6 m). They are most abundant in the northwestern portion of the site (10–20N, 5–25W) where four pebble lenses are commonly present within a vertical interval of 60–70 cm. The vertical interval between individual lenses varies between 5 cm and 30 cm. In these areas it is obvious that Unit D is a cumulic deposit that resulted from a series of descrete episodes of slopewash deposition. In places, e.g. 19N, 10–14W, the pebble lenses accumulated within topographic depressions that were 120± cm deep and 3–4 m wide. Small isolated sandstone slabs are another common feature within Unit D, particularly in the northern portion of the site. The "slabs" are 3–10 cm long and are ordinarily tilted 30–40° from the horizontal.

The sand matrix in Unit D is very similar to that present in Unit B. Grain size is predominantly very-fine- to fine-grained (0.1–0.2 mm), but secondary sand fractions that vary from medium to very coarse in size are also present.

## Unit E

In Trench E-1, located in the eastern third of the site (Figure 3.5), Units B and D are present only in the northernmost portion of the trench (Figure 3.11). Their combined lateral equivalent is a 46± m long, 205± cm thick sequence of lenticular beds of slopewash and fluvial origin, herein labeled Unit E. This sediment pile is characterized by a high percentage of clay. Individual beds within the sequence range in thickness (7–20 m) and in length (60–200 cm). They are massive and range in composition from sandy, silty clay to highly clayey, silty sand. Clay content in individual beds is estimated to vary from 40% to 70%. Sand grains are usually very fine to fine in size. Dispersed, angular pebbles (0.5–6 cm long), composed of ferrugi-

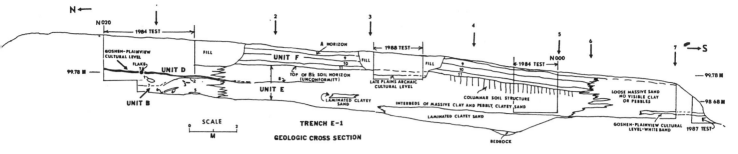

**Figure 3.11.** Geologic cross-section drawn through Backhoe Trench E-1. See Figure 3.5 for location. Legend as follows: 1 = white calcium carbonate concretion, measures 76 × 28 cm, base inclined 10° to south, 2 cm thick halo of light brown iron oxide on upper surface, contains 10±% scattered, fine-size sand grains; 2 = zone (9± cm thick) of dispersed 1–3 cm long pebbles and Stage II calcium carbonate development; 3 = tabular sandstone slabs coated with calcium carbonate, north slab measures 22 × 5 × 2.5 cm and is tilted 36° to south, horizontal south slab measures 13 X 2.5 cm; 4 = zone of dispersed, isolated pebbles (3–5 cm long) within clayey, medium to coarse-grained sand; 5 = horizontal, calcium carbonate concretion, 51 × 15 cm, sandy in upper 4 cm; 6 = calcium carbonate concretion, 18 × 18 cm, Stage III development, tilted 10° north; 7 = isolated chert flake (debitage); 8 = zone of dispersed pebbles 6± cm thick, pebbles are 0.5–2 cm long, tabular and iron stained, pebble orientation varies from horizontal to vertical; 9 = sand, massive, brown, very fine-to fine-grained, silty, moderately well sorted, contains 10±% medium-grain-size "oolites" and 2±% coarse-grain-size "oolites"; 10 = sand, massive, light gray, medium-grain-size (part "oolite" grains), 40±% very-fine to silt-size fraction, changes laterally to very-fine- to fine-grained, very well sorted sand; 11 = sand, massive, light brown, fine- to medium-grained, well sorted, contains two isolated pebbles, 0.5 and 1 cm long, changes laterally to well sorted, very-fine- to fine-grained, silty sand, no pebbles.

nous siltstone concretion fragments can comprise up to 20±% of a given sand lens. Dispersed pebbles can also occur as horizontal alignments within a given layer. In the central portion of Trench E-1 (Figure 3.11) the basal 75± cm of Unit E is an aggregation of thin, discontinuous, interfingering lenses composed of fine- to medium-grained, silty, clayey sand that may contain 10–40% spheroidal "oolitic"-like grains of medium size. This aggregation is 7.3 m long. Individual lenses within the sequence vary in thickness (1.5–2 cm) and length (20–65 cm). They display discontinuous 1-2 mm thick laminae. Some laminae are black and consist of very-fine- to fine-grained coal grains. A few horizontal, 20± cm long, 2.5 cm thick zones of dispersed, 0.5–1 cm long pebbles are present, but pebbles are a minor constituent in this basal unit.

The laminated zone interfingers laterally with colluvium. The basal, laminated portion of Unit E is interpreted to be a braided ephemeral stream deposit. It rests on bedrock and therefore by stratigraphic position could be the stratigraphic equivalent of Unit A. However, the two different units differ markedly in sedimentary structure and lithologic composition. It is obvious that the sediments that comprise each unit were derived from different sources. The same thing can be said for all of Unit E, the high clay content of which indicates a sediment source different from that of the rest of the Quaternary sediment within the site area.

The separate sources may not have differed greatly in distance from the site area but were located in areas with different bedrock lithology. In Trench E-1, Unit E—over a 2 m horizontal interval—interfingers to the north into a sequence of massive, slightly silty, fine- to medium-grained sandy colluvium with low clay content. The colluvium contains dispersed,

0.5–7 cm long, tabular sandstone fragments, the larger of which have an apparent tilt of 18–35° to the south. Isolated, 2.5 cm thick, sandstone slabs, that range in length between 13 cm and 22 cm are also present within the colluvium in the lower half of the trench. Their apparent inclinations vary from horizontal to 36° (south). Unit E, at its southern margin, fades out into a massive, very-fine- to coarse-grained, poorly sorted loose sand that contains "spheroidal" grains of medium size, very few pebbles and minimal clay. The horizontal transition distance between the two types of sediment is 3 m. The massive sand with minimal clay content contains a distinctive, 23 cm thick white zone (not a pedogenic E horizon) that lies 104 cm beneath the ground surface. This "white" band can be traced to the southeast, where it correlates with the top of the Goshen-Plainview bison bone level. Thus, by projection, a portion of the upper-half of Unit E lies at the same stratigraphic position as the upper part of Unit B.

A Late Plains Archaic cultural horizon, that contains Pelican Lake–style projectile points, was encountered in Trench E-1. The cultural horizon lies 15 ± cm beneath the top of Unit E (Figure 3.11). It is enclosed within slopewash sediment that consists of massive fine- to medium-grained, clayey (40% estimated) sand that contains 5% ± scattered, 0.5 cm long pebbles composed of ferruginous siltstone. The cultural horizon occurs at the top of a 135 cm thick soil sequence that is developed on Unit E and consists of A-Bkb-Ckb-Cb horizons. The top of the Bk horizon (scattered calcium carbonate filaments-Stage I) occurs at the level of the cultural horizon. Stage II calcium carbonate development is present 7 cm below the top of the cultural horizon.

A radiocarbon date was not secured from the Pelican Lake

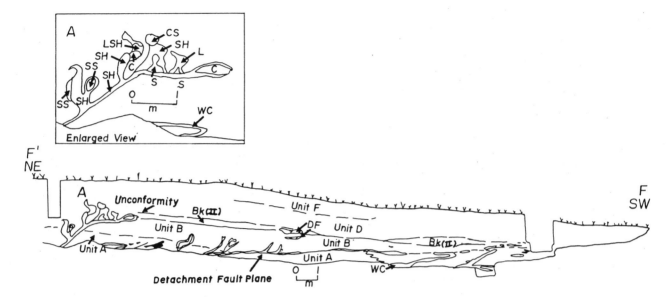

**Figure 3.12.** Geologic cross-section F–F¹ (Backhoe Road), see Figure 3.5 for location. Legend as follows: L = lignite; LSH = lignitic shale; CS = white clayey sand; S = sand; C = calcium carbonate; SS = sandstone; SH = gray shale; WC = white clay; DF = debris flow; SSF = sandstone fragmnent; Bk = calcareous soil horizon, Stage III development.

level. However, the ages of Pelican Lake sites in other portions of the Northwestern Plains range approximately 3,000–1,900 radiocarbon years B.P. (Frison 1991:29). The Goshen-Plainview cultural horizon was not encountered within Unit E. The sediments of Unit E interfinger with those of Units B and D (Figures 3.9 and 3.11) and should therefore be of the same approximate age. The erosional surface that truncates Unit B in the westernmost portion of the site area is not obvious within Unit E, where it may lie parallel to horizontal bedding planes. One possible candidate for the erosional surface is the base of a 6± cm thick, 3.2 m long pebble lens that lies 65–70 cm below the top of Unit E in the northern third of Trench E-1 (Figure 3.11). As indicated on Figure 3.11, the sediment of Unit E interfingers laterally with that of Units B and D. By projection, the stratum that would be the time equivalent of the Goshen-Plainview cultural horizon lies 75–80 cm below the top of Unit E. This situation suggests that a hiatus of 8,000± years is present within the 60± cm thick interval that separates the Pelican Lake cultural horizon and the projected position of the Goshen-Plainview horizon.

## Unit F

Unit F is the youngest stratigraphic unit at the site. A distinguishing feature of Unit F is its essential lack of pebbles. The contact between it and underlying Units D and E is sharp and distinctive. The top of E is an unconformity surface. Unit F is composed of a massive, silty, bimodal sand that consists of very-fine- to fine-grained quartz grains with a secondary component of medium-size, spheroidal "oolitic"-like crystalline grains (previously discussed) which constitute 10–40% of the total sand. Unit F is most readily identified in the northern

half of the site area (5–20N, 0–25W) where it varies in thickness (60–80 cm). In the same area, soil development within Unit F usually consists of a non-calcareous A-C-Ab-Cb sequence, though in a few places an A-C-Ckb, Akb-Cb2 development is present. Outside the northern half of the site area, only a single surface soil with A-C horizons is developed within Unit F. In these areas, the surface soil is usually, but not always, superimposed on a massive "non-pebbly" sand similar to that described above. This pebble-free sand, which is correlated within Unit F, is 25–61 cm in thickness. The A horizon that is superimposed on it is 10–15 cm in thickness. Unit F is interpreted to be an eolian sheet-sand deposit, which in the northern portion of the site accumulated in two main depositional events, each of which was followed by a period of non-deposition and quiescence during which pedogenesis occurred.

The general lack of pebbles in Unit F suggests that when it was deposited, sediment was no longer being delivered to the site area from the bedrock source located to the northeast. The S6 geomorphic surface, which was much more extensive prior to the formation of Unit F was breached by erosion, and the modern isolated butte was formed. A 10 m deep topographic depression developed between the butte and the bedrock hill located to the northeast, after which sediment could only be furnished to the butte top via eolian transport.

Within the site area, Unit F formed after the Pelican Lake cultural occupation ca. 3,000–1,900 years B.P. At previously discussed Locality 10, located 160 m to the west of the site datum, Unit F is 30 cm thick. Here a 7.6 m long cultural horizon, that contains artifacts, fire-cracked rock and charcoal, lies 23–26 cm beneath the surface. This horizon yielded a radiocarbon date of 1,835 ± 55 (AZ 3667). Thus, it would appear that the sediment within Unit F has accumulated during the past 2000 years.

## Soft-Sediment Deformation

Natural and excavated exposures of Quaternary sediment located in the northwestern portion of the site revealed examples of soft-sediment deformation. These features are prominently displayed within Units A and B that are exposed along the scarp that forms the northwest boundary of the butte on which the site lies. Here along the "backhoe road" (Figure 3.5) that is 25 m long, a machine-cut scarp exposure displays examples of faulting. A main, low-angle (10°) detachment fault is present near the base of the exposure. Secondary, imbricate ("sled runner"), reverse faults project upward from the main glide plane (detachment fault). The inclinations of these secondary faults vary between 12° and 60°, but most range between 45° and 60° (Figure 3.12). All fault planes are inclined to the northeast, and movement was to the southwest. Thin intrusive sediment veins and pods of sediment (principally clay) have been injected along fault planes and fractures. The faults formed as a result of the downslope (southwest) movement of the Quaternary sediment of Units A and B, along a major glide plane. The glide plane (main detachment fault) cuts upward across Unit A and then along the contact between Units A and B. This latter portion of the glide plane is marked by a 7 cm thick, white clay lens. The detachment fault plane probably originated within bedrock as some of the injected sediment present along fault planes is of bedrock type, e.g. lignitic shale. "Flame" structures (folds) are present within Unit A and protrude 45–70 cm upward into Unit B. They are the result of sediment squeezing. Unit A also contains examples of inclined intrusive sediment lenses plus miniature fault blocks (horsts and grabens), bounded by small, normal faults with offsets of only a few millimeters.

The above described deformation features formed during the initial stages of the gravitational downslope movement of the prism of Quaternary sediment that underlies Site 24CT30. Fortunately, the downhill movement of sediment was arrested before the threshold of stability was exceeded and a landslide occurred. The creation of the soft-sediment deformation and glide features occurred prior to the initiation of significant pedogenic calcium carbonate deposition, as Stage II calcium carbonate development is superimposed upon the deformation features. Examples of past landslide activity that involved transport of bedrock material were noted within 48 km of the Mill Iron site. One prominent example is present approximately 32 km northwest of Site 24CT30. Here, one of several lobes of bedrock debris is located within a short distance of an abandoned ranch building—a situation that suggests a quite recent age for the landslide event. Other examples are located "closer to home." One is a modern landslide located south of the reservoir near Locality 4 (Figure 3.3). Here large blocks (7± m wide) of surficial sediment with grass still attached have slid down a 20 m high scarp that is inclined 24° to the northwest. A 200± m long, narrow (20 m) debris flow of relatively recent vintage is present in the vicinity of stadia station 74 (Figure 3.3). The flow consists of 1—2 m long sandstone blocks, tilted at angles up to 60° plus sand matrix. Soil development is nil.

## Locality 10

Locality 10 has been mentioned previously in this report. It lies 160 m west of the 24CT30 site datum. It is the locale of a deep backhoe trench and the thickest Quaternary sediment accumulation in the general site area. In descending order, the sedimentary sequence is as follows:

**Unit 4**  30 cm of massive, fine-grained sand that is capped by an A horizon. A cultural horizon lies at the base of the unit. It yielded a radiocarbon date of 1,835 ± 55 B.P. (AZ 36670).

**Unit 3**  76 cm of massive, very-fine- to fine-grained sand that contains 25±% of randomly scattered 0.5–1 cm long pebbles.

**Unit 2**  183 cm of massive, fine- to medium-grained, well-sorted, bimodal sand that contains 2–15% of medium-size "oolite" grains. Unit also contains a few (2–3%) 0.5–1 cm long, randomly distributed pebbles. A 25 cm thick, very-fine-grained, silty, clayey sand zone lies 64 cm from top of unit.

A Bk soil horizon with columnar structure and Stage II calcium carbonate development at its top, is superimposed on all of Unit 3 plus the upper 112 cm of Unit 2. The bottom 28 cm of Unit 2 exhibits a Ck soil horizon.

**Unit 1**  135 cm of fluvial sediment that is characterized by the presence of thin (1–4 cm) interfingering, laminated (1–2 mm) sand lenses that are 40–65 cm in length. Two types of sand predominate; one is very-fine-grained to fine-grained and very well sorted. The other is bimodal, fine- to medium-grained, well sorted with 20–30% coarse-size "oolitic"-like grains.

An auger hole was "drilled" into the floor of the backhoe trench by Vance Haynes and students. It encountered approximately 90 cm of Quaternary sediment above bedrock. This 90 cm interval is probably the basal portion of Unit 1.

Unit 1 is a fluvial deposit that is similar in appearance to the braided stream sediments that underlie geomorphic surfaces S4 through S1 in the central portion of the Humbolt Creek valley. Unit 1 probably represents the deposits of the stream that occupied the bottom of the paleo-swale at the Mill Iron site.

Units 2 and 3 at Locality 10 are approximately the same thickness as Units B and D at Site 24CT30. The units at both locales probably correlate. Unit 4 is of eolian origin and correlates with Unit F at the site.

## Conclusions

The physiographic and geomorphic setting now visible within the Humbolt Creek valley has evolved since the late Pleistocene. During the late Pleistocene, the S6 surface was extant and the channel of Humbolt Creek was essentially in the same horizontal position as at present. The S5–S1 geomorphic surfaces have formed in the past 11,000 years with a resultant 18± m lowering of the valley floor.

The S6 surface at the time it was occupied by the Goshen-Plainview peoples, 11,000 years ago constituted the valley slopes and probably much of the valley floor. Tributary stream channels flowed down slopes and drained into Humbolt Creek. The present S6 remnant is too small to serve as drainage area for a secondary stream capable of transporting significant amounts of alluvium, such as existed at Site 24CT30 during the late Pleistocene (Figure 3.7).

At Site 24CT30 only 50–60 cm of sediment separates the Goshen-Plainview and Pelican Lake horizons. This is a small net accumulation of sediment over an 8,000 year period. A marked hiatus is probably present. One can speculate that the hiatus and lack of significant sedimentation is a reflection of a period of non-deposition and marked erosion, e.g. the Altithermal. However, there is no hard evidence that such an erosional event occurred. One can be certain that the net accumulation of sediment on valley slopes has been minimal during the past 2,000 years—only 30 cm of eolian sand has accumulated during the past 1,800 years at Locality 10, located 160 m west of Site 24CT30. At the site, the equivalent stratum (Unit F) varies between 60 cm and 80 cm in thickness. At Locality 7, only 56 cm of eolian sand overlies the Pelican Lake horizon (ca. 3,000–1,900 B.P.). The dominant mode of documented sedimentation during the past 2,000 years has been the accumulation of thin deposits of slopewash and eolian sediment. Thin veneers of eolian sand are widespread. Eolian deposition has probably occurred throughout the Holocene. The eolian sands that are cemented by pedogenic calcium carbonate probably accumulated prior to the Late Holocene. The high bedrock hill that lies northeast of the site, which served as source for much of the colluvium slopewash sediment at the site, contains scattered eolian deposits at its summit. These eolian deposits overlie thin accumulations of slopewash sediment or bedrock and appear to be of different ages. They are 20–60 cm thick and contain Bk horizons, some of which display Stage II calcium carbonate development. The hill top also displays scattered, cobble- to small-boulder-size, fragments of gray quartzite and gray silificied (petrified) wood. These clasts are highly wind polished, randomly distributed, and rest on bedrock. They are lag deposits that resulted from erosion and the therefore inevitable lowering of the land surface during a portion of the Pleistocene. The silicified wood may be derived from the Fort Union Formation, the base of which at one time lay 30–60 m above the present hill crest.

The backhoe trenches that were dug into the S4 through S1 surfaces all exposed a similar braided stream sequence. The same individual strata are present beneath different terrace strath surfaces, which suggests that the sediment sequence represents one main depositional unit. This alluvial sequence is two to three times as wide as the modern flood plain and formed in a hydrologic regime different from the modern. One can propose that erosion was pronounced on valley slopes and large quantities of sediment were furnished to the valley floor, a situation which resulted in braided stream deposition on a "flat," wide flood plain, a scene quite different from the modern one. The age of the braided stream sequence is not precisely known as no radiocarbon dates or prehistoric artifacts were secured from it. The sequence accumulated during that portion of the 8,000 year period between the Goshen-Plainview and Pelican Lake occupations that occurred prior to the initiation of the calcic pedogenesis and the formation of the "Altithermal" soil. However, the precise time when calcic pedogenesis began is unknown, which still leaves the whole question of age open to conjecture.

The S6 surface at Site 24CT30 was at one time connected to the aforementioned bedrock hill that lies northeast of the site. Narrow remnants of the S6 surface are still present on the west side of the hill (Figures 3.2 and 3.6). The colluvium slopewash sediment that accumulated at the site was derived from the bedrock hill and transported down the T6 slope to the site area. Some time after the Pelican Lake occupation (3,000–1,900 years ago) an erosional cycle began, and slopewash sedimentation ceased at the site. The S6 slope that lies between the site and the hill was partially removed and a 10± m deep topographic depression formed. The resultant topographic "saddle" is 60–90 m wide. (Figures 3.2, 3.4, and 3.6). The slopes of both the topographic depression and the adjoining butte were subsequently covered by a thin veneer (1–2 m) of slopewash sediment. This sediment is currently being removed by erosion. The erosional event that created the butte on which the site lies also resulted in the removal of portions of the S6 and lower surfaces in other parts of the Humbolt Creek valley. The valley floor was lowered 5.2–6.7 m after the time of the Pelican Lake occupation as a consequence of the development of the S3–S1 strath terraces. In the Powder River Basin, 120 km southwest of Mill Iron, the widespread three-tier, Holocene terrace system began to form approximately 1,100 years ago and is still evolving (Albanese 1991). Its initiation was marked by the pronounced entrenchment of stream channels into valley floors. Does that event correlate with the initiation of the post-2,000 years B.P. erosional cycle that created the butte at the Mill Iron site and the S3–S1 strath surfaces? In Wyoming, over 40% of the recorded radiocarbon dates from archaeological sites post-date 2,000 years B.P. (Albanese 1991). If one assumes that the number of radiocarbon dates is an approximation of the number of archaeological sites, the onset of a more arid climate and resultant erosion (as reflected in the initiation of the Holocene terrace system) was accompanied by an influx of prehistoric peoples into the area. The explanation for this seeming contradiction whereby the climate deteriorates and the human population increases may be social rather than ecological.

# References Cited

Albanese, John P.

1977   Paleotopography and Paleoindian Sites in Wyoming and Colorado. In *Paleoindian Lifeways*, edited by Eileen Johnson, pp. 28–47. The Museum Journal XVII, Lubbock, West Texas Museum Association, Texas Tech University.

1991   *The Geoarchaeology of the Eastern Powder River Basin.* Report Submitted to State Historic Preservation Office, Wyoming Archives, Museums and Historical Department, Cheyenne.

Dobbins, C. E., and C. E. Erdmann

1955   Structure Contour Map of the Montana Plains, Oil and Gas Investigations, Map OM 178B. U.S.G. S., Washington, D.C.

Earl, B. J., D. Rice, and R. Freese

1982   *Cultural Resources Inventory of Site 24CT40 (Froggy Butte).* Report Prepared for the Department of the Interior, U.S. Bureau of Land Management, Miles City District Office, Montana.

Frison, George C.

1991   *Prehistoric Hunters of the High Plains.* 2d ed. Academic Press, San Diego.

Miller, M. R., W. M. Bermel, R. N. Bergantino, J. L. Sondereggen, P. M. Norbeck, and F. A. Schmidt

1977   *Compilation of Hydrogeological Data for Southeastern Montana.* Open File Report HY 77-1. Butte, Bureau of Mines and Geology, Montana College of Mineral Science and Technology.

# CHAPTER FOUR

# Flaked-Stone and Worked-Bone Artifacts from the Mill Iron Site

BRUCE A. BRADLEY
Crow Canyon Research Center

GEORGE C. FRISON
University of Wyoming

## Introduction

Although some of this material has already been presented (Bradley and Frison 1988; Frison 1991a:44–46, 1991b: 133–151, 1992: 494–496), this chapter is intended to offer a more detailed description and discussion of the typological and technological attributes of the flaked-stone and worked-bone artifacts from the Mill Iron site. The primary focus will be on manufacture technology and style. Evidence of use wear, breakage, and reflaking will be noted when identified or inferred. However, a use-wear analysis of many tools from the site using a specialized optical instrument is presented in the following chapter. Comparisons with other described artifacts will be made, although these will be primarily with other typologically similar assemblages, specifically the materials from the Plainview site in Texas (Sellards et al. 1947, Knudson 1983). All raw material identifications have been made by George Frison.

Artifacts have been recovered from three areas at the Mill Iron site: 1) the bonebed; 2) the camp area; 3) the modern ground surface (MGS). Refits of fragmentary artifacts between the camp area and the modern ground surface, and the similarity between the artifacts from the camp area and the bonebed, indicate that all of these places are directly related. Therefore, all artifacts are being treated as a single assemblage and aberrant forms are identified.

## Projectile Points

Thirty-one different projectile points and fragments (refits counted as one) are included in this study. Of these, eleven are from the camp area, twelve are from the bonebed, seven from the modern ground surface, and one has conjoining pieces between the modern ground surface and the camp area. Irwin-Williams et al. (1973:46) wrote that "Typical projectile points of the Goshen Complex are lanceolate with parallel to slightly convex or concave sides and concave bases." Although they also

observe that "In overall outline they resemble the Clovis form," at the Mill Iron site, there is a wide range of forms present. This is partly due to their being at different stages in their use cycles, but it is also the case with points believed to be primary forms. To us, there is a greater resemblance in form to Folsom points than there is to Clovis points. Flaking technology is fairly consistent, but flake scar patterns are variable. Characteristically, the points exhibit well controlled and evenly spaced pressure flake scars that include comedial and transmedial terminations. Flake scar orientations are mainly perpendicular to the point axis, except for the basal thinning flakes, which are parallel with it. Material types, general proveniences, condition, dimensions, and weights are given for all of the points in Table 4.1. Dimensions are reported in millimeters as maximums with length (L) taken along the artifact axis (including basal indentation), width (W) perpendicular to length, and thickness (TH), perpendicular to both. The amount of basal indentation (BI) is measured on the artifact axis. The length of the point at the width (LW) is also measured on the axis. Several dimensional ratios are included that help to elucidate proportions including relative elongation (W/L), relative thinness (Th/W), degree of basal indentation (BI/L), and blade shape (LW/L). This information does not include all of the observations we think are of interest, so comments on the individual artifacts are also included. Definitions of some of the terms we use are presented here. In these descriptions we use a number of locational terms that are interchangeable to reduce the redundancy in prose. The terms *proximal, lower,* and *basal* all refer to the approximate half of the projectile point that served as the hafting element. The terms *distal, upper, blade,* and *tip* refer to the approximate half of the projectile that included the pointed end. *Margins* are where two faces come together in an acute angle. *Faces* are the wide surfaces of the points. No attempt was made to define and distinguish between dorsal and ventral faces of the points. *Lateral* refers to the long edges of the points, which are also called *sides.* The term *thinning* is used where it is inferred that the detached flakes removed proportionally more of the face than

**Table 4.1.** Projectile Points.

| Cat. # | Material | Location | Cond. | L | W | Th | BI | LW | W/L | Th/W | BI/L | LW/L |
|---|---|---|---|---|---|---|---|---|---|---|---|---|
| | | | | | | | | (mm) | | | | |
| 266 | Unknown chert | Camp | Comp. | 63.5 | 21.9 | 5.0 | 3.4 | 22.0 | 0.34 | 0.23 | 0.05 | 0.35 |
| 268 | Silicified wood | Camp | Inc. | 66.0 | 25.6 | 4.9 | 2.7 | 28.1 | 0.39 | 0.19 | 0.04 | 0.43 |
| 269 | Silicified wood | Camp | Inc. | 69.3 | 23.1 | 4.7 | 3.8 | 38.9 | 0.33 | 0.20 | 0.05 | 0.56 |
| 274 | Hartville chert? | Camp | Tip frag. | 46.3 | 24.9 | 5.2 | — | — | — | 0.21 | — | — |
| 278/ 279 | Hartville chert | Camp | Comp. | 74.6 | 22.2 | 5.0 | 3.3 | 0.0/ 24.0 | 0.29 | 0.23 | 0.04 | 0.00/ 0.32 |
| 280/ 1508/ 1538 | Hartville chert | MGS (tip), camp (base and midsection | Inc. | 70.8/ 74.5 | 25.4 | 5.6 | 3.1 | 41.1 | 0.34 | 0.22 | 0.04 | 0.00/ 0.55 |
| 284 | Silicified algae | Camp | Base frag. | 33.1 | 25.3 | 5.3 | 6.0 | — | — | 0.21 | — | — |
| 289 | Porcellanite | Camp | Comp. | 47.3 | 18.4 | 4.0 | 0.4 | 5.0 | 0.39 | 0.22 | 0.04 | 0.11 |
| 1577 | Unknown chert | Camp | Base frag. | 16.8 | 18.6 | 3.3 | 0.6 | — | — | 0.18 | — | — |
| 1585 | Hartville chert | Camp | Base frag. | 22.0 | 24.2 | 5.1 | 2.6 | — | — | — | — | — |
| 288 | Silicified wood | Camp | Comp. | 43.5 | 20.7 | 5.1 | 2.3 | 25.4 | 0.47 | 0.24 | 0.05 | 0.58 |
| 271 | Unknown chert | Camp | Base frag. | 24.1 | 24.5 | 5.3 | 4.8 | — | — | 0.22 | — | — |
| 1510 | Porcellanite | Bonebed | Comp. | 62.4 | 24.7 | 6.3 | 0.9 | 30.5 | 0.40 | 0.26 | 0.01 | 0.49 |
| 1582 | Unknown chert | Bonebed | Comp. | 52.4 | 22.2 | 5.2 | 1.8 | 3.0/ 24.0 | 0.42 | 0.23 | 0.03 | 0.06/ 0.46 |
| 1583 | Silicified algae | Bonebed | Comp. | 53.4 | 20.8 | 5.1 | 3.3 | 28.4 | 0.39 | 0.25 | 0.06 | 0.53 |
| 1586 | Hartville chert? | Bonebed | Comp. | 79.5 | 24.2 | 4.4 | 2.6 | 23.2 | 0.30 | 0.18 | 0.03 | 0.29 |
| 1587 | Unknown chert | Bonebed | Comp. | 45.1 | 24.0 | 5.6 | 2.4 | 22.6 | 0.53 | 0.23 | 0.05 | 0.51 |
| 1588 | Hartville chert? | Bonebed | Comp. | 71.4 | 24.0 | 5.5 | 4.0 | 8.1 | 0.34 | 0.23 | 0.05 | 0.11 |
| 1607 | Unknown chert | Bonebed | Comp. | 54.6 | 24.7 | 5.0 | 0.8 | 27.8 | 0.45 | 0.20 | 0.02 | 0.51 |
| 1611/ 1612 | Chert | Bonebed | Tip frag. | 38.1 | 21.9 | 4.4 | — | — | — | — | — | — |
| 1615/ 1616 | Unknown chert | Bonebed | Base frag. | 20.4 | 20.8 | 4.3 | 3.1 | — | — | — | — | — |
| 1617 | Montana agate? | Bonebed | Inc. | 52.9/ 58.9 | 25.5 | 5.2 | 2.0 | 31.2 | 0.43 | 0.20 | 0.03 | 0.00/ 0.53 |
| 1657 | Unknown quartzite | Bonebed | Tip frag. | 17.0 | 19.2 | 4.8 | — | — | — | — | — | — |
| 1655 | Unknown chert | Bonebed | Mid. frag. | 14.1 | 13.5 | 5.1 | — | — | — | — | — | — |
| 270 | Chert | MGS | Base frag. | 14.9 | 22.2 | 4.1 | 3.1 | — | — | — | — | — |
| 272 | Unknown quartzite | MGS | Mid. frag. | 21.2 | 23.9 | 6.3 | — | — | — | 0.26 | — | — |
| 273 | Chert | MGS | Tip frag. | 26.0 | 24.2 | 5.9 | — | — | — | — | — | — |
| 1284 | Hartville chert? | MGS | Tip frag. | 33.0 | 24.1 | 4.8 | — | — | — | — | — | — |
| 1659 | Silicified wood | MGS | Base frag. | 23.0 | 20.3 | 4.2 | 1.1 | — | — | — | — | — |
| 1656 | Unknown chert | MGS | Base frag. | 30.9 | 23.7 | 5.3 | 6.1 | — | — | 0.21 | — | — |
| 1662 | Unknown chert | MGS | Inc. | 58.8 | 21.9 | — | — | — | — | — | — | — |

Italic indicates incomplete measurement and dash indicates dimension not present.

they did of the margin. *Basal thinning* is used where the flake removals were substantial enough to produce a sharp basal margin, regardless of the length of the flake scars. Fluting is not present on any of the points when one defines a *flute* as a flake scar that travels from the basal margin past the point of the hafting element (Sollberger personal communication 1988), in this assemblage identified as the distal point of lateral edge grinding. *Shaping* refers to flakes that did not remove proportionally more of a face than of a margin. *Retouch* is used to describe flakes that were removed after the main shaping and thinning was complete. These flake removals were primarily done to straighten and shape the margins. *Ears* are proximal edge extensions produced at the intersections of the lateral margins and the basal indentations. *Projected ears* are those that extend laterally, or to the side of the lower margins.

Flake scar sequencing is described in terms of spatial relationships between subsequent removals. Selective sequencing is where flakes are detached from locations where there is a particular need at that point in the sequence, regardless of the location of the previous removal. This approach has been called random, but there is little room for true randomness in the production of standardized flaked stone artifacts. Serial flaking is only identified where there is a pattern of three or more flakes removed sequentially adjacent to one another.

Two forms of pressure flaking are identified, primarily based on their terminations, both in location on the points and in relation to one another. *Comedial* is used where flake scars from opposite margins terminate evenly near or at the point axis. (The majority of flake scars on a face must conform to this pattern for this description to be used.) The ultimate expression of this form of pressure flaking is seen on Eden points of the Cody complex (see Bradley and Stanford 1987:405–434). A commonly used synonym is *collateral* (Wormington 1957:107). The second form of pressure flaking is *transmedial.* This is where flake scars from opposite sides interfinger on termination and do not consistently form a distinctive alignment. This is approximately the same as *transverse* (Wormington 1957:107) except that it does not imply either flake scar size or orientation. *Invasive* indicates that a flake scar travels into the body of the point and does not terminate near the edge.

The term *primary form* is used to identify projectile points that we believe were not altered after their initial manufacture. If no interpretation is explicitly included, it is assumed that the projectile point is interpreted as a primary form. Reworking/resharpening is inferred from radical deviations in projectile point forms and flaking technologies or in cases of clear flaking after use breakage. In this assemblage, these activities are more difficult to determine than they have been in some other Paleoindian collections (see for instance Bradley 1974:194–197). These observations on the Mill Iron points are subjective. If they are incorrect, the range in primary forms would be increased.

Number 266 (Figures 4.1a and 1.8a) conforms in shape to the general description of Goshen points. The proximal edges are straight and expand slightly toward the distal portion. The distal edges curve gently to a sharp tip. Two flake scar remnants on one face look as if they were produced by percussion flaking and may represent primary reduction. These scars are in the middle of the point, where there is slightly greater thinning than on either side at the base or tip. Adjacent to these scars, toward the tip, the point has a thickened area where a small pressure flake scar terminates in a shallow step fracture. Pressure flaking on both faces was selective with a wide range of flake scar widths from transmedial with some flaking only slightly invasive. Although most scars are nearly perpendicular to the point axis, some travel at various angles to it. Basal indentation was accomplished with the same types of pressure flaking as seen on the rest of the point. The flakes were produced after the lateral flakes but are not large enough to be considered basal thinning. Margins exhibit fine, abrupt, noninvasive retouch that is selective on the face of the last pressure flaking but nearly continuous on the other (possibly a remnant of platform preparation). Margin grinding extends from the point of maximum width, around the ears, in the basal indentation, and back to the point of maximum width on the other side.

Number 268 (Figures 4.1b and 1.8b) is missing one ear, has a small indented break on the side of the same distal margin,

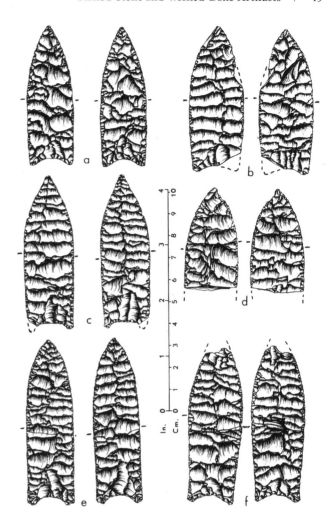

**Figure 4.1.** Mill Iron site projectile points. All were surface finds except for the proximal end and a small wedge-shaped piece of 4.1f that was found in situ in the main block excavation.

and a "squared edge" extending from the tip 13 mm down the opposite side. The indented and squared breaks resulted from flaws in the raw material and probably happened during flaking. The ear was removed with a bend break and probably resulted from use. This piece exhibits no remnants of the primary technology but has well controlled and spaced pressure flake scars on one face. One series of six flake scars was produced in a sequence originating distally and progressing proximally. The flake scars on the other side and same face look serial, but close examination indicates that they are selectively sequenced. The flake scars are nearly comedial in termination and many line up from opposite margins, producing the effect of single continuous flake scars travelling across the entire face. Most of the scars are nearly perpendicular to the point axis.

Pressure flaking on the other face is much less regular and

exhibits selective sequencing. The flakes overlap less regularly at the mid-line and many of the flake scars are not perpendicular to the axis. There is a deep depression near the tip that resulted from a flaw in the raw material, and there is a small area near the center of one face that looks as if it was directly under a cortical surface. Basal indentation was accomplished by the removal of multiple pressure thinning flakes from both faces, after the lateral flaking was completed. Margin retouch is scant, and there are only a few places where selective pressure removed the high spots between flake scars. The lower margins and basal indentation are lightly ground/polished.

Number 269 (Figures 4.1c and 1.8c) is an exquisite example of highly controlled pressure flaking. It has straight proximal margins that expand slightly toward the tip to just over half of the length. At this point, the blade edges curve evenly, straightening just before the tip, which protrudes slightly. This piece has an evenly flat/convex cross-section. One ear is missing, but the other is very slightly projected and squared. The basal concavity is straight with an abrupt turn to the ear. The entire point exhibits highly controlled pressure flaking, and there is no remaining evidence of the primary shaping technology. It undoubtedly began as a tabular piece of the local silicified wood. Pressure flaking is uniformly perpendicular to the point axis, is comedial on one face, and offset transmedial on the other. Final pressure flaking is very well and evenly spaced, but mostly selective in sequence. The look of serial removals is deceptive, and close examination reveals no more than three consecutive serial pressure flake removals. Basal thinning was accomplished by the removal of multiple pressure flakes, on both faces. These truncate the lateral pressure flake scars, indicating that basal thinning was done last. Fine pressure retouch was applied between the flake scars on the distal portion, straightening and sharpening the edges. The basal lateral margins were retouched bifacially and continuously with very fine abrupt flake removals. This evened the margins and prepared them for grinding. A light grinding/polishing of the proximal lateral and basal margins finished this point.

Number 274 (Figure 4.1d) is the distal fragment of a point. The radial/bend break occurred just proximal of the maximum width. The lower edges are nearly straight and then evenly curve to the tip. The cross-section is evenly flat-biconvex. There is no evidence remaining of the primary technology. Controlled, selective, transmedial pressure flake scars are present on both faces. Fine pressure retouch between flake scars is the rule, but one side exhibits very fine, abrupt, unifacial retouch on the proximal half of this piece. Light edge grinding/polishing exists on the lower half of the fragment. A small bit of damage—probably the result of use—is present near the tip.

Number 278/279 (Figures 4.1e and 1.8e) has nearly parallel lower lateral edges that expand slightly toward the tip. At about one-third of the length, the sides begin to contract, then gently curve to a sharp point. Basal ears protrude slightly so that the maximum width of the base is the same as the blade. The ears are squared and the basal indentation is a fairly even arc. In cross-section, the point is nearly plano-convex. Although there is no remnant of the primary technology, this cross-section may indicate that a flake blank was used. The flat face may have been the bulbar surface and the convex side the dorsal surface of a flake. Well spaced, even, selective pressure flaking covers both faces with a comedial pattern on the convex face and transmedial flaking on the flat face. Basal thinning was accomplished by the removal of multiple pressure flakes on both faces. These flakes originated from the interior edge of the basal indentation and were removed after lateral flaking was complete. A very fine bifacial, selective pressure retouch removed the thicker areas between the flake scars, producing sharp and very straight margins. One area of a basal lateral margin also exhibits very fine unifacial steep pressure retouch. The lower lateral margins exhibit light grinding/polishing, but the proximal ears and basal indentation are only very lightly ground. The point was broken through the middle by what appears to be a bend break, probably from use and not manufacture.

Number 280/1508/1538 (Figures 4.1f and 1.8d) consists of three refitted fragments. It has slightly concave to straight proximal lateral edges that expand toward the tip. At just over half of the inferred length, the sides curve toward the tip. The ears protrude slightly; one is squared, and the other comes to a fairly sharp point. The basal concavity is an irregular arc. The cross-section at about one-third of the length is plano-convex but gradually becomes biconvex toward the tip. The point of maximum thickness is very near the surviving distal end. There is no direct evidence of the primary technology or original material form, but the longitudinal section suggests that this point may have been made from a flake with the bulbar/platform end becoming the distal end of the artifact. Well spaced, carefully controlled, selective, transmedial pressure flake scars cover both faces. Some of the flakes near the proximal end terminated in shallow step fractures, and others have relatively deep negative bulbs of applied force. Basal indentation/thinning was done with multiple pressure flake removals, but the resulting scars were substantially obliterated by lateral pressure flaking. This sequence is at variance with many of the other Mill Iron points. Very fine, selective, bifacial retouch was used to finish the point, with one area of abrupt continuous flaking on one distal lateral margin. Light lower lateral edge grinding/polish finished the point. A heavy impact break crushed the tip and caused the point to break across the center in a reflected bend/radial break.

In every respect of flaking and form, this point could be classified as an unfluted Folsom. The final pressure shaping, with minute stepping and deep bulbar scars is very typical of Folsom preform preparation. If channel flakes had been removed from both faces, this piece would be nearly identical to a Folsom point from the Hanson site (Frison and Bradley 1980:50, Figure 31a).

Number 284 (Figure 4.2a)—a projectile point base—has slightly expanding straight sides, very slightly projected, rounded ears, and a deep basal concavity. In cross-section, the piece is slightly plano-convex. There is no indication of the original blank form or primary technology. Pressure flaking is selective, well spaced, comedial on the convex face, and transmedial on the flatter face. Basal pressure flaking is not very invasive but was done after the lateral flaking was completed. Margin retouch is bifacial, very fine, and selective. Light grinding/polishing is present on the lateral and basal margins.

Number 289 (Figure 4.2b) is different in shape from the rest of the points. It is nearly triangular with slightly convex sides and has only the slightest suggestion of a basal indentation. The cross-section is evenly biconvex. There is no evidence of the original blank type or primary technology. Both faces exhibit pressure flaking that is selective and for the most part transmedial. Many of the flake scars expand from the edge inward, and there is a general sense of less care and control than on most of the other points. This is not to say that the point is rough or irregular. The edges are sharp and even. Basal flaking was done, but it is mostly obliterated by lateral flaking. Fine retouch is present, but it occurs on a much smaller proportion of the margins than on most of the other points. We believe that it is very likely that this point resulted from the all-over reworking of a piece of a larger broken point.

Number 1579 (Figure 4.2c) is only a basal fragment of a point. The sides converge very slightly from the proximal toward the distal end, and there is just the slightest suggestion of a basal indentation. There is no evidence of the original blank form or primary technology. There are also very few pressure flake scars intact enough to describe the secondary technology. Substantial bifacial abrupt retouch is present on one lateral edge. Light grinding occurs on the sides and base. Fragmentation was the result of a heavy impact that produced a short "flute" on one face.

Based on the form and flaking of this piece, we believe that it is a reworked projectile point that was broken during use. By itself, it could very easily be mistaken for a basal fragment of a Scottsbluff point or stemmed Cody knife.

Number 1585 (Figure 4.2d) is a base fragment. It conforms well to many of the other points with straight edges that expand slightly toward the distal end, rounded ears, and an indented base. It has a slightly plano-convex cross-section, selective pressure flaking, and basal thinning by multiple pressure flakes on both faces. Retouch is mostly unifacial on both edges. A bend/radial break is nearly perpendicular to the axis.

Number 288 (Figure 4.2e) was made on a piece of silicified wood, as seen by the remnant of cortex on one face. The outline conforms to most of the other points, except it is more irregular. Pressure flaking is selective and doesn't exhibit regularity in either spacing or orientation. Basal thinning is present on one face. Thermal spalling is apparent, probably caused by burning. This point may be considered atypical in the sense that it shows less care than the other specimens. It is possible that it is a reworked piece, but we believe that it is more likely that it was expediently made.

Number 271 (Figure 4.2f) is a basal section with an apparent impact break. Lateral edges are nearly parallel and lightly ground, leaving no basal ears. The basal indentation is slightly asymmetrical with a very light grinding. The cross-section is lenticular, and flaking is transmedial on both faces. Basal thinning flakes extend 10 mm on one side but only 4 mm on the opposite side. A very fine bifacial edge retouch is present on both lateral edges. A notch on one lateral edge near the base appears to be excavation damage.

Number 1510 (Figure 4.3a) is another example of an atypical point, both in form and manufacture technology. The outline and flaking are irregular, it is relatively thick, there is little retouch, and the basal indentation is minimal. Both proximal

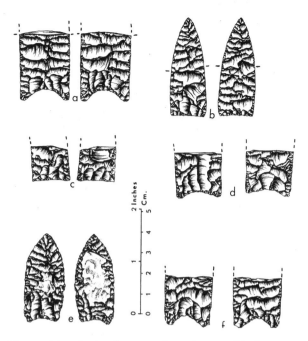

**Figure 4.2.** Projectile points from the main block excavation.

corners have what may be remnants of a break surface. One face has some basal thinning, but it is mostly obliterated by lateral flaking. The proximal lateral margins are heavily ground, and the base is only lightly ground.

We believe it likely that this point is a reworked piece, probably a distal end. If so, the original point would have been quite large. Margin grinding produced a form that might almost be described as stemmed. By itself, this point falls within the range of form and technology of Alberta/Cody points (see Bradley and Frison 1987).

Number 1582 (Figure 4.3b) is typical of Goshen points from the Mill Iron site. The lower lateral margins are nearly straight and expand slightly toward the distal end. The base is indented. Both ears project, one more prominently than the other. The greater projecting ear is squared. Pressure flaking on one face is selective, transmedial, and well spaced. It is offset transmedial (most scars from one side extend past the mid-line) and more irregular on the other face. Multiple basal thinning flakes are present on both faces, and they truncate the lateral pressure flaking. Retouch is selective, fine, and discontinuous. Light grinding is present on the proximal lateral and basal margins. Although not evident, we believe that this piece may be a reworked tip section.

Number 1583 (Figure 4.3c) was made from a piece of raw material that contained flaws in the form of air pockets. In form, it has one straight side and one slightly concave proximal lateral side. The ears are projected, with one pointed and the other rounded. It has a deep basal indentation. Maximum thickness is located near the distal end, possibly due to the location of the material flaws. Pressure flaking is irregular in terms of sequence, spacing, and orientation. Basal thinning is represented by a single flake scar on one face and is nearly obliterated by lateral

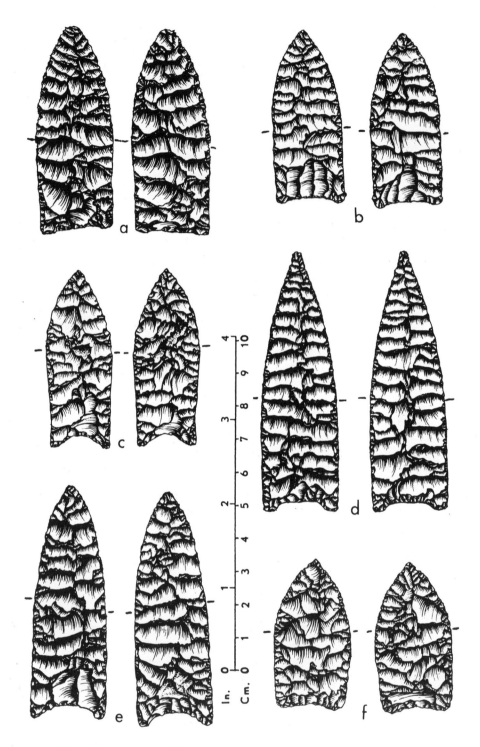

**Figure** 4.3.  Projectile points from the bison bonebed.

flaking everywhere else. Retouch is selective and minimal, and proximal lateral and basal grinding is heavy.

The nature of the raw material might explain why this point is irregular in form and flaking. It is also very possible that this piece was reworked from a larger fragment. Both may be true.

Number 1586 (Figure 4.3d)—unlike several of the previous points—is nearly perfect. Its widest point is just above the base, from where it gradually contracts toward the tip from straight to slightly convex sides. Four millimeters from the distal end, the sides straighten, run nearly parallel, and then abruptly converge to form an extended squared tip. The ears are squared/rounded and not protruded. The basal indentation is straight with abrupt curves into the ears. In cross-section, the artifact is a thin flattened lens shape. Near the center of one face is a small remnant of what might be the bulbar surface of a flake blank. It is also possible that it is part of a percussion flake scar. Pressure flaking is selective, transmedial, and evenly spaced. There are no basal thinning flake scars. Retouch is selective, bifacial, and nearly continuous, producing very straight, sharp edges. Approximately the proximal half of the lateral edges and the base are lightly ground/polished.

This point is an absolutely exquisite piece of flintknapping. It is, however, difficult to see how it could have been used effectively. In order for a point bound to a haft with sinew or some other fiber to be effective as a projectile point, it is necessary for it to be sharp at its widest dimension. Because of the shape of this artifact, the widest area would have been covered with binding (assuming a standard hafting method). This would have greatly reduced its ability to penetrate an animal. Furthermore, although the point was recovered from the bonebed, it is in absolutely perfect condition. Is it possible that this point was intentionally placed in the kill area as some form of offering? We will never know. However, our experience with Paleoindian kill sites indicates that there is usually at least one intact, perfect point. In one case—the Jones-Miller site in eastern Colorado—a ritual area has been postulated in the center of the kill area (Dennis Stanford personal communication).

Number 1588 (Figure 4.3e) is another example of a projectile point that has its greatest width near the base. The lower lateral edges are fairly straight, gradually curving to the tip. The basal indentation is pronounced leaving rounded ears. The cross-section is unevenly plano-convex. An area of the original material exterior surface is present just above the proximal end on one side. The entire point exhibits selective pressure flaking that is for the most part transmedial. Flake scar spacing and orientation is somewhat irregular. Basal thinning flakes were removed from one face. Retouch is scant with several ridges between flake scars removed. Lateral edge grinding extends about half-way up the point. The basal indentation is also ground.

The shape and size of this point is nearly identical to those of Number 1586 (except it lacks a projected tip). One might therefore make the same argument that this piece would not have been very effective as a penetrating implement. Interestingly, these two points were found very close together.

Number 1587 (Figure 4.3f) is in many respects unusual in this assemblage. It is relatively wide and short and has a shallow basal indentation, but no basal thinning. Pressure flake scars form both faces, but the scars are irregularly spaced and oriented. The retouch that is present is less regular than on

many of the other points. One face has a remnant of a percussion flake scar that terminated in a step fracture. This looks very much like the end of a typical Clovis channel flake scar. In fact, alone this point would probably be classified as Clovis. It is possible that it is a reworked Clovis.

Number 1607 (Figure 4.4a) is in some ways an extraordinary point. It has straight and nearly parallel proximal lateral margins that expand slightly just before curving to a sharp tip. The base also appears nearly straight with only a minimal indentation. The cross-section is a flat lens shape. Pressure flake scars are very shallow and difficult to distinguish from one another on one face. They are slightly more distinct on the other face. The proximal lateral margins and base exhibit steep bifacial continuous pressure retouch and heavy grinding/polishing. The overall effect is that the point almost looks stemmed.

We believe that this piece is a mid-section fragment that was reworked on all margins. If so, the original point would have been the largest in the assemblage.

Number 1611/1612 is the distal fragment of a point reconstructed from two pieces. Little can be said concerning the form, but what flaking remains conforms to most of the other points with well spaced pressure flaking and sharp, selective retouch. This fragment resulted from a heavy impact fracture that produced a lateral burin spall on both pieces and a reversed impact "flute."

Number 1615/1616 (Figure 4.5a) is the base of a projectile point reconstructed from two fragments. It is a typical example with slightly projected ears, basal indentation and thinning, and margin retouch and grinding.

Number 1617 (Figure 4.4b) is nearly complete and slightly irregular in shape due to a flaw in the material adjacent to one of the proximal lateral margins. Otherwise, the point has fairly straight proximal lateral margins that expand distally. Just past half of the length, the edges gently curve toward the tip. The ears are not projected but squared. The basal indentation is straight with abrupt curves to the ears. The cross-section is evenly biconvex. Pressure flaking is selective, comedian and transmedial, and irregularly spaced. Retouch is selective and discontinuous. The tip is missing due to impact crushing.

Number 270 is all that remains of this point. It had an indented base and basal thinning.

Number 272 is a medial fragment with a relatively thick, biconvex cross-section. Pressure flaking is selective and irregular. There is little or no retouch or edge grinding. Technologically, it doesn't fit well with the other pieces from the site, and its location on the modern ground surface may indicate that it originated from a different time period.

Number 273 fits well within the range of projectile points recovered from good contexts. It has well controlled and spaced pressure flaking and selective retouch. Edge irregularities probably resulted from use damage. The point was broken with a radial break.

Number 1284 is another typical tip fragment with well controlled and spaced pressure flaking and selective retouch. This too was fractured with a radial break.

Number 1657 is a small tip fragment with a crushing tip impact.

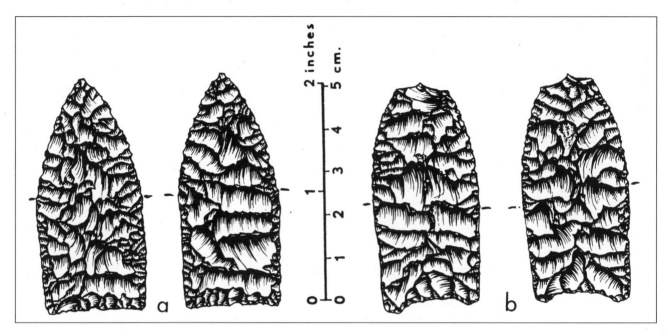

**Figure 4.4.** Projectile points from the bison bonebed.

Number 1655 is a very small medial fragment that resulted from a heavy impact break.

Number 1659 (Figure 4.5b) is a bit unusual in that the basal indentation extends all of the way across the base without producing identifiable ears. It has basal pressure thinning and ground lateral and basal margins.

Number 1656 (Figure 4.5c)—a projectile point base—has very projected ears and a narrow basal indentation. There is no basal thinning. Pressure flaking is well spaced and wide on one face and mostly obliterated by an impact break on the other. The margins show fine continuous retouch. Lateral and basal edge grinding is light. Although similar to other points from the site, this piece looks sufficiently different for us to question its association with the others.

Number 1662 (Figure 4.5d) was originally a large point, possibly the largest from the site assemblage. Both base and tip had been broken and an impact fracture extends at least 26 mm from the distal break down one blade edge. Apparently an attempt was made to rework the remaining part. Both faces were carelessly reflaked, although part of the original fine pressure flaking is still present on both faces. Nearly all of the impact flake scar was removed and the base was reshaped with poorly executed basal thinning flakes on both sides. Only one 11 mm long section of the original blade edge remains that demonstrates the fine edge retouch common to Goshen-Plainview specimens. At this stage of reworking, the effort was apparently abandoned and tool use is evident on the corners formed by the distal transverse break.

## Other Artifacts

The following section will describe the various artifacts that are not considered projectile points. We have divided them into categories based primarily on the locations of modification, although we also use some traditional topological classifications. In these cases, the terms are intended to be descriptive and should not be construed to imply use or function. In many instances, modified flakes have a primary area of modification and other areas with minimal or irregular alterations. Artifacts have been classified with preference given to the main areas of modification. For instance, end retouched artifacts (often called end scrapers) frequently have lightly or irregularly modified edges as well.

We have also tried to place artifact fragments into categories based on their inferred whole forms. This can of course be a tricky business and subject to reassessment. The following table (Table 4.2) is intended to present a complete inventory of

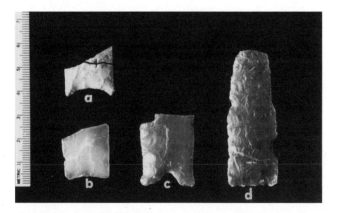

**Figure 4.5.** Projectile point from the bonebed (a), and from the surface of the site (b–d).

the objects we have studied, as well as to present some basic information. Dimensions and weights are given mostly to allow a generalization of artifact sizes and reidentification for pieces that may not be illustrated here. Length (L) is the longest dimension along the flake axis, or if this is not clear, simply the greatest dimension. Width (W) is the maximum dimension perpendicular to length. Thickness (Th) is the maximum dimension perpendicular to the length and width. Right and left sides/margins are determined by the location of the platform and flake axis, with the flake platform toward the observer and the dorsal surface up. Proximal and distal areas are identified based on a division at about half of the length with proximal being at the platform end. Individual descriptions will describe other aspects of the artifacts not included in Table 4.2.

## Bifaces

Number 1589/1606 (Figures 4.6 and 5.3a)—an incomplete biface—consists of two refitting fragments. Technologically, it exhibits well controlled bifacial thinning through the use of diving flakes. There is no evidence of early shaping and thinning, but production of this relatively thin biface probably involved several stages of reduction. Some of the reduction process is seen in the other biface flakes recovered from the site and is discussed later. The major final thinning flakes were struck from a fairly sharp edge and probably from isolated platforms. Although the piece is too fragmentary to see a flaking pattern of sequence, the flake removals were well spaced and platforms constructed on the relatively thick spots between flake scars on the opposite face. Continuous, bifacial, selective pressure retouch is evidenced along the longest remaining edge (on both refitted pieces), but retouch is restricted to between major flake scars on the opposite edge. In fact, one of the two thinning flake scars on this edge was removed after the last pressure flaking in the area. This may indicate that some or most of the retouch in this area is actually platform preparation remnants. Typologically and technologically this biface closely resembles the biface fragments identified as manufacture Stages 4 and 5 at the Hanson site (Frison and Bradley 1980). It also resembles some of the bifaces from the Fenn Clovis cache (Frison 1991a:43, Figure 2.9) but lacks the distinctive percussion overshot thinning flaking.

One tool-sharpening flake from the camp area was almost certainly either removed from this biface or from another biface made from the same piece of raw material. The color and texture of the material is distinctive and totally different from any other stone-flaking material found in either area of the site. It presents a strong argument for a close chronological relationship between the campsite and bonebed areas. A refit could not be made, but the flake could have been from the missing section of the biface or possibly from an earlier resharpening stage.

Number 1618 (Figure 4.7a) is a medium-small biface, distinctively plano-convex in cross-section, and curves slightly from base to tip. Percussion flaking on the flat face is irregular but served to remove most of the cortex from what must have been a naturally flat face. These flakes tended to dive slightly toward the center, but this result is not clearly the product of intent. The opposite face was percussion flaked second, with only a single flake scar near the tip that probably thinned the area. The remaining flake scars curve across the surface. The material is fairly coarse and was probably difficult to percussion thin. Small percussion flakes produced a retouched edge around the distal margins, but it is unclear if this was done to produce a useable edge or if this was platform preparation. This artifact represents early-stage biface manufacture.

Number 101 is a small bifacially flaked artifact, which could be classified as a biface, but its origin may have been the result of use activity and resharpening rather than intentional manufacture. One face exhibits flake scars that originated from a squared edge and ran across the face, removing the opposite side. Flakes were then removed bifacially from the other margin, possibly serving to rejuvenate a wedge-shaped edge. The end adjacent to the squared edge was also abrupt and shows evidence of blows that removed some small flakes. We believe that this piece was possibly originally a fragment of a biface that was used in the same way as the pièce esquillés described below. The main difference is that attrition of this piece did not result in the distinctive shearing seen in the artifacts classified as pièce esquillés.

Number 1607 is a mid-section fragment of a biface that had a pronounced plano-convex cross-section. Diving percussion thinning is evident on the flat face, while non-thinning percussion flaking is evident on the other. This fragment is too small to allow identification of flaking sequences or spacing. Selective, invasive retouch along one edge may indicate that this was once a completed artifact.

Number 1300/1451 (Figure 4.7c) consists of only a basal fragment and a reattached flake. We have identified it as a biface, even though it is not truly bifacial all over. Most of the remaining edges are bifacially flaked with non-invasive shaping flake removals. These were applied to what looks like a flake blank, one face (dorsal) of which retains remnants of cortex, and the other face (ventral) remnants of the bulbar face of a flake. The dorsal face is dominated by a large flake scar that was struck from the proximal end. We believe that it was this flake removal that broke the biface with an end-shock fracture. The ventral face is where the small edge-trimming flake has been refit. This flake was detached just prior to the large flake on the dorsal surface and may have served to isolate a platform for it.

The basic impression of this fragment is that it was broken in an early stage of biface manufacture on a flake blank. The relatively large basal flake resembles early stage fluting/basal thinning, and the reattached flake was probably the result of platform preparation/isolation. This may be the only example of primary projectile point manufacture technology in the Mill Iron assemblage.

## Retouched Flakes

Flakes that exhibit intentional margin flaking are grouped by the location(s) of the main retouch areas in relation to the form of the resulting artifact. If the main flaking is along an edge more or less parallel with the length, it is considered side re-

**Table 4.2.** Flaked Stone Artifacts except Projectile Points.

| Cat. # | Artifact Type | Material | Location | Cond. | L | W | Th |
|---|---|---|---|---|---|---|---|
| | | | | | | (mm) | |
| 1589/ 1606 | Biface | Arikara chert | Bonebed | Frags. (2) | 126.1 | 63.1 | 9.2 |
| 1618 | Biface | Chert | Bonebed | Comp. | 88.2 | 46.5 | 11.4 |
| 101 | Biface | Chert | MGS | Comp. | 45.2 | 31.8 | 10.8 |
| 1607 | Biface | Chert | MGS | Frag. | 25.1 | 49.3 | 17.8 |
| 1300/ 1451 | Biface (and re-attached flake) | Porcellanite | Camp | Frag. | 19.8 | 32.6 | 7.5 |
| 1281 | Single edge retouch | Silicified wood | Camp | Comp. | 65.2 | 32.8 | 8.0 |
| 1595 | Single edge retouch | Silicified wood | MGS | Comp. | 48.2 | 32.6 | 5.2 |
| 97 | Single edge retouch | Unknown chert | Camp | Comp. | 47.8 | 22.8 | 9.2 |
| 275 | Single edge retouch | Hartville chert | Camp | Comp. | 61.6 | 25.1 | 7.1 |
| 276 | Single edge retouch | Chert | Camp | Comp. | 53.8 | 31.3 | 10.0 |
| 282 | Single edge retouch | Chert | MGS | Comp. | 40.7 | 19.2 | 6.0 |
| 1291 | Single edge retouch | Chert | Camp | Comp. | 69.2 | 35.5 | 16.6 |
| 1309 | Single edge retouch | Chert | Camp | Frag. | 23.0 | 25.2 | 11.0 |
| 1580 | Single edge retouch | Porcellanite | Camp | Inc. | 49.6 | 34.0 | 8.0 |
| 1596 | Single edge retouch | Hartville chert | MGS | Inc. | 61.0 | 34.1 | 9.0 |
| 1597 | End Scraper and single edge retouch | Unknown chert | Camp | Inc. | 49.8 | 42.1 | 6.0 |
| 88/ 1286 | Single edge retouch | Silicified wood | Camp | Comp? | 43.2 | 22.3 | 7.1 |
| 1286 | Single edge retouch | Silicified wood | Camp | Inc. | 69.2 | 46.8 | 9.9 |
| 1614 | Single? edge retouch | Hartville chert? | Bonebed | Frag. | 11.01 | 12.8 | 2.8 |
| 1591 | Alternate edge retouch | Silicified wood | Camp | Comp. | 63.0 | 32.2 | 5.9 |
| 1592 | Multiple edge retouch | Porcellanite | Camp | Comp. | 61.1 | 61.2 | 10.2 |
| 1658 | Double edge retouch | Porcellanite | Camp | Comp. | 59.8 | 47.8 | 10.8 |
| 1295/ 1298 | Double edge retouch? | Chert | Camp | Frag. | 31.5 | 27.0 | 4.2 |
| 1297 | Double edge retouch | Chert | Camp | Frag. | 19.0 | 22.4 | 5.0 |
| 1306 | Multiple edge retouch | Chert | Camp | Inc. | 43.4 | 31.0 | 7.8 |
| 1290/ 13A/13B | Double edge retouch | Porcellanite | Camp | Inc. | 62.0 | 30.8 | 8.0 |
| 1292 | Single edge/end retouch | Porcellanite | Camp | Inc. | 50.0 | 59.2 | 8.2 |
| 1310 | Multiple edge retouch | Quartzite | Surface | Frag. | 36.0 | 27.2 | 6.3 |
| 1275 | Double edge retouch | Chert | Camp | Frag. | 37.2 | 19.8 | 6.8 |
| 1293 | End scraper | Chert | Camp | Frag. | 23.3 | 24.0 | 5.1 |
| 1307 | End retouch | Chert | Camp | Frag. | 15.1 | 14.9 | 4.8 |
| 1313 | End scraper | Chert | Camp | Frag. | 16.4 | 17.0 | 5.0 |
| 1315 | End retouch | Chert | Camp | Comp. | 40.8 | 17.8 | 8.7 |
| 1319 | End scraper | Hartville chert | Camp | Comp. | 40.7 | 21.1 | 10.8 |
| 7 | End retouch | Chert | Bonebed | Frag. | 9.2 | 20.9 | 4.0 |
| 285 | End scraper | Chert | Camp | Comp. | 30.2 | 21.9 | 6.0 |
| 84 | End retouch | Chalcedony | MGS | Comp. | 30.0 | 26.6 | 6.8 |
| 1289 | End retouch | Chert | MGS | Comp. | 32.2 | 19.4 | 4.1 |
| 32 | Edge retouch | Chert | Camp | Frag. | 23.0 | 17.9 | 3.9 |
| 43 | End retouch? | Porcellanite | Camp | Frag. | 34.1 | 26.5 | 5.8 |
| 1279 | End retouch | Chert | Camp | Comp. | 42.8 | 20.3 | 9.8 |
| 1294 | Retouched flake | Chert | Camp | Comp. | 33.0 | 18.9 | 4.1 |
| 1316 | Raclette | Chert | Camp | Frag? | 34.3 | 21.4 | 3.1 |
| 1594 | Raclette | Chert | Camp | Comp. | 40.4 | 22.1 | 3.1 |
| 1305 | Graver | Chert | Camp | Comp. | 13.6 | 10.2 | 1.0 |
| 1311 | Graver | Chert | Camp | Comp. | 17.8 | 15.0 | 4.8 |
| 1318 | Burin spall? | Chert | Camp | Comp. | 44.0 | 7.2 | 13.9 |

**Table 4.2** (continued)

| Cat. # | Artifact Type | Material | Location | Cond. | L | W | Th |
|---|---|---|---|---|---|---|---|
| | | | | | | (mm) | |
| 1274 | Edge damaged flake | Chert | Camp | Frag. | 48.8 | 31.9 | 13.8 |
| 1278 | Edge damaged flake | Chert | Camp | Comp. | 28.9 | 32.1 | 5.8 |
| 1280 | Edge damaged flake | Chert | Camp | Comp. | 62.2 | 36.0 | 10.3 |
| 1375 | Edge damaged flake | Chert | Camp | Frag. | *25.1* | *36.2* | 5.0 |
| 1584 | Edge damaged flake | Porcellanite | Bonebed | Comp. | 40.2 | 48.4 | 3.8 |
| 40 | Unmodified flake | Silicified wood? | Camp | Frag. | *25.5* | *30.2* | 9.3 |
| 204 | Unmodified flake | Hartville chert? | Camp | Frag. | *20.2* | *19.4* | 2.2 |
| 277 | Utilized flake | Porcellanite | Camp. | Frag. | *29.3* | *29.8* | *3.0* |
| 1562 | Graver | Chert | Camp | Frag. | *10.7* | 7.9 | 1.8 |
| 1581 | Unmodified flake | Porcellanite | Camp | Comp. | 41.8 | 22.3 | 3.5 |
| 197 | Unmodified flake | Chert | Bonebed | Comp. | 26.3 | 17.2 | 2.1 |
| 1314 | Unmodified flake | Chert | Bonebed | Comp. | 22.0 | 21.4 | 3.0 |
| 1608 | Utilized flake | Chert | Bonebed | Comp. | 33.8 | 20.7 | 2.5 |

Italic indicates incomplete measurement.

touch. If the flaking concentrates more or less perpendicularly to the length, it is considered end retouch. Traditionally these retouch locations would correspond to side scrapers and end scrapers respectively. Several fragments exhibit minimal or irregular retouch that suggests that the main retouch was on the missing portion. We have classified these pieces in categories as if they were complete. Evidence is documented for each such classification.

## Single Side Retouch

Number 1281 (Figure 4.8e) is an angular, tabular piece of silicified wood that has been retouched unifacially along one of the long sides. The retouched edge is slightly convex. The retouch is shallow and produced a sharp edge. Damage to this edge is evident. Although this piece of material is the same stone type as at least two of the projectile points (Numbers 268 and 269), it is a bit smaller than both. The first stage of flaking such a piece into a projectile point would be the production of a beveled platform edge. It is possible that this is what the retouch represents, but we would expect platform beveling to be more abrupt. We believe that this was a cutting tool.

Number 1595 (Figure 4.8k) is very similar to the previous one, in that it is a natural slab of silicified wood with one long side unifacially retouched. In this case the edge is straight, and the retouch is continuous along the entire edge. The edge angle is more obtuse than on Number 1281 (Figure 4.8e), but it is still sharp. This was a cutting or scraping tool.

A short, thick, curved blade-like flake served as the blank for tool Number 97 (Figure 4.8d). It has a relatively large, plane platform that exhibits light reduction and grinding. The flake was struck from the side of a core that had a pronounced ridge, removing an area of cortex. A single flake scar remains on the non-cortical area of the dorsal surface. This flake scar is not parallel with the flake axis but is nearly perpendicular. Although the length is just slightly longer than twice the width, this is

not a blade. Shallow unifacial retouch is present along the sharp edge opposite the abrupt cortical side. The retouch is on a slightly concave edge. Edge damage is also evident. This implement is heavily burned and has a number of potlid fractures.

Number 275 (Figure 4.8h) is a long blade-like flake with a single primary ridge. The main flake scar on the right side is parallel with the flake axis, while the flake scar on the left side runs at about 35 degrees to the axis. This flake scar is wide, slightly curved, and undulates slightly. It resembles biface thinning flake scars. The flake platform is small, only slightly convex, bifacial, and lightly ground. Although this flake could be classified as a blade, we believe that it was produced in an early stage of biface manufacture. This does not preclude the possibility that the biface surface was prepared in such a way as to allow the production of this blade-like flake. Even though no bifacial cores have been recovered from Mill Iron, the later Folsom and earlier Clovis flaked stone assemblages have this type of core (Frison and Bradley 1980:18-22; Bradley 1991:370). One side exhibits unifacial retouch with some being invasive and scalar (terminating in hinge/step fractures). This retouch left a sharp edge. The amount of artifact narrowing resulting from this retouch is minimal. In other instances, flakes have been retouched to the extent that an elongated form is produced. This has sometimes led to the mistaken conclusion that an implement was made on a blade. Edge damage is noted on both the retouched and opposing unretouched edges.

Abrupt unifacial retouch is present on the proximal half of the right side of Number 276 (Figure 4.8g). The flake has a large dihedral platform (point of percussion on a ridge between two surfaces or flake scars), is curved at the distal end, expands from the platform to the distal end, and retains three major flake scars. One of these is parallel with the flake axis, but the other two are nearly perpendicular to it. The distal end of this flake removed a large "knot" from the surface that resulted from internal flaws in the material. This flake was probably produced in an early to intermediate stage of biface production.

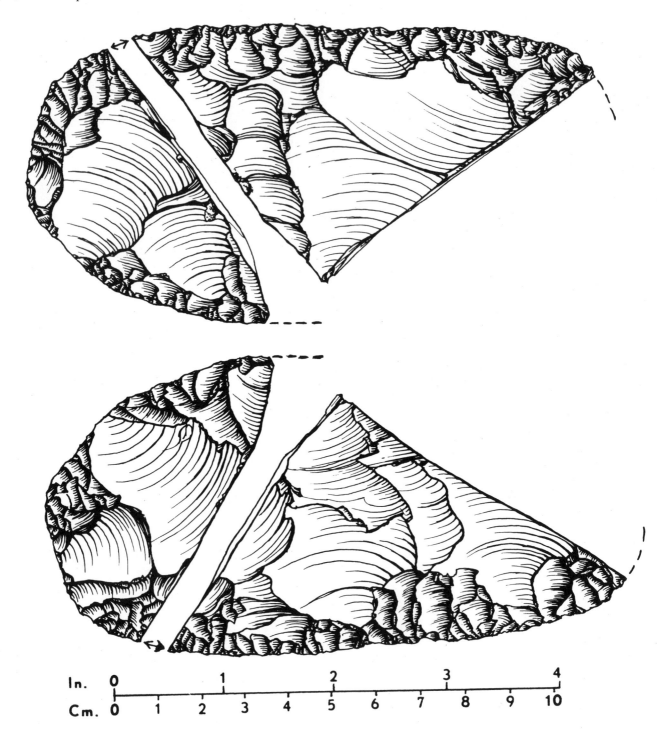

**Figure 4.6.** Refitted biface from the bison bonebed.

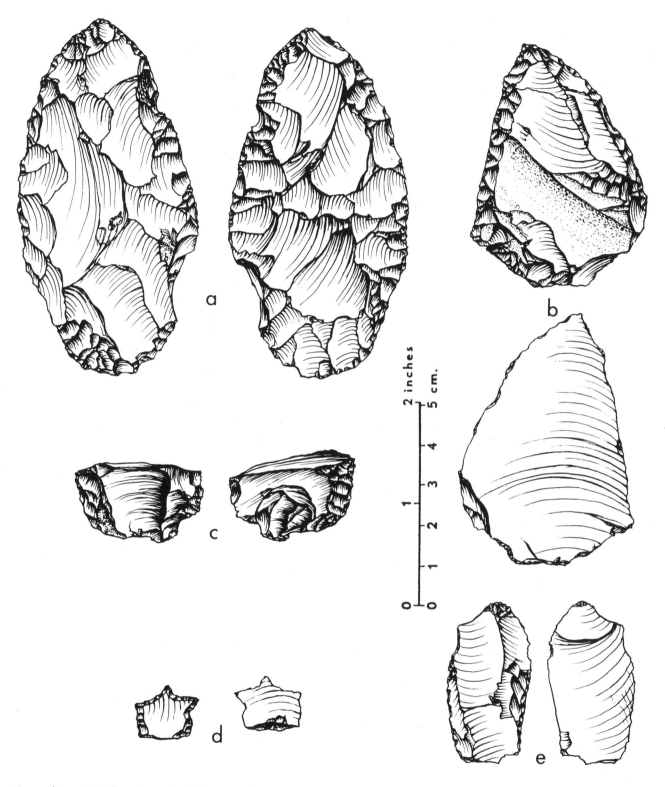

**Figure 4.7.** Tools from the main block excavation.

**Figure 4.8.** Tools from the surface and main block excavation.

It is also possible that it was struck from a discoidal core. The retouch is abrupt and only part of the edge is still sharp. If this retouch was opposite a sharp edge, we would probably consider it as intentional backing. In this case, however, the opposite side is nearly square due to a flaw in the material. This probably served as an implement.

Number 282 (Figures 4.8i and 5.4f) is a medium-small biface flake. It was struck next to a relatively thick, subcortical area and probably contributed substantially to the thinning of the biface. The platform is small, straight, and bifacial. Because of the thick area, the flake is quite curved and slightly twisted. The thin right margin was unifacially retouched along the entire edge, with a focus on the proximal portion. The resulting edge is convex proximally and straightens distally. Although neither acute nor abrupt, the retouch produced an evenly sharp edge.

Number 1291 (Figure 5.3g) is a steeply ridged flake blade that retains cortex on the left side, has a large flake scar on the right that probably originated from the same core platform as the flake blade, and has a flake scar at the distal end that originated from the central ridge before this flake blade was struck. Like Number 97 (Figure 4.8d), this piece was removed from the side of a core, plunged toward the end, and is slightly twisted. The platform is small, plain, and slightly reduced. Unifacial, scalar retouch extends along the entire right margin, producing a nearly straight edge. Although the general edge angle is quite steep, the scalar retouch produced a fairly sharp edge. The heaviest retouch is toward the proximal end, accentuating the distally expanding form. Recent flaking (trowel damage) is present on the left proximal edge and edge damage occurs along most of the rest of the edge (probably old damage).

Number 1309 is a small artifact fragment. It is the proximal segment of another flake blade with a strong ridge, left of which is cortex and right of which is a flake scar and a couple of superimposed spall scars. It has an unprepared, plain, cortical platform. The sharp right margin exhibits small, acute angle retouch.

Number 1580 (Figure 5.5a) is a classic example of an early-stage biface thinning flake. It has a very small bifacial platform and the dorsal flake scars originated from the same edge as the flake. A cortical area is present on the distal right surface. The distal end of the flake is missing, and the break truncates the retouch along the left side. This retouch is unifacial, regular, at a medium angle, and extends only a very short way from the edge. The retouched area is straight.

Number 1596 (Figure 4.8c) is similar to the preceding artifact. This one is an early- or middle-stage biface thinning flake. The platform is wide, bifacial, and slightly lipped. The dorsal flake scars originated from the same biface edge as the flake and converge toward the distal end, which is missing. There is a continuous unifacial retouch along the entire length of the remaining left side. This formed a slightly convex edge, extends a maximum of 7 mm onto the surface, and produced a medium acute angle. Retouch is also present on the proximal right margin. This retouch is scalar and produced an acute, slightly convex edge. The distal break occurred (probably during use) on a material flaw after the left edge retouch was done.

Number 1597 (Figure 5.4d)—the distal portion of a large,

thin, wide biface thinning flake—exhibits a small area of unifacial retouch on its right margin. The dorsal surface is dominated by two flat flake scars: one traveling in the same direction as the flake, and the other originating from the opposite direction. A limited area of small flake scars is present on the very distal end of the flake and originated from a shallow hinge fracture. In our experience, this type of flaking frequently occurs during the flake detachment because of rebounding against the biface from which it is removed. This may be the case here.

Numbers 88 and 1286 are two pieces of a highly layered tabular material. They exhibit small areas of unifacial retouch. Flaking on both is fairly abrupt, restricted to one area, irregular, and shot through with internal fractures. The two pieces conjoin, with the smaller (Number 88) clearly having been flaked after breaking from the larger. It is unclear what was being attempted with these pieces.

Number 1614 is a very small flake fragment that has abrupt unifacial retouch along one edge. The retouch is truncated by breaks at both ends. It isn't possible to determine what type of tool this came from.

## Multiple Side Retouch

Number 1591 (Figures 4.8j and 5.4e) is a piece of silicified wood that exhibits unifacial retouch on two opposing sides. These sides were flaked from opposite faces of the natural piece, creating a bibeveled cross-section. Retouch is continuous along each side, is regular, and at a medium angle. The edges are neither sharp nor dull. One side is slightly concave and the other fairly straight.

Number 1592 (Figure 5.6b) is a relatively large flake of porcellanite. It displays unifacial retouch around most of the edges. The platform of the flake is crushed, and the flake form could indicate that it was struck either from a core or from an early stage of biface manufacture. Overall, the shape of this piece is off-round, with most areas of retouch on convex edges. The heaviest retouch is on the left side, where the flaking is quite steep in the area where a dorsal ridge was fairly pronounced. Except for this area, retouch seems to have been fairly light with the removal of only a small proportion of the original flake. Edge damage is apparent on most retouched areas.

Number 1658 (Figure 4.7b) was produced by abrupt unifacial retouch along two edges of a large, partially cortical porcellanite flake. The platform is wide, thin, and polyhedral (multiple facets that don't originate from the platform margin). Retouch extends along almost all non-platform margins, converging at the distal end. A traditional topological category for this tool is a convergent side scraper. Retouch removed a substantial amount of the right side and may represent one or more resharpenings.

Number 1295/1298 (Figure 5.6g) comprises two pieces of a flake that fit together to form a piece of an implement. The flake platform is intact and is wide, slightly convex, facetted, lightly battered, and ground. Although the pieces that are present exhibit retouch on only one side, artifact Number 1297, which is probably a piece of the same implement, shows retouch on two edges (see below). The conjoined fragment has minor unifacial retouch on the right edge that is sharp and concave. The retouch is truncated by the flake break.

Number 1297 (Figure 5.6f) is a medial fragment of a retouched flake tool that was probably a piece of the same tool as artifact Number 1295/1298 (Figure 5.6g). The distal end is a thermal break, while the proximal is a bend break. The retouch on the right side is sharp and concave and truncated by both breaks. The retouch on the left side is sharp, straight, and is truncated by the distal thermal break but looks as if it was—at least partly—done after the proximal break.

Number 1306 (Figure 5.5b). A biface thinning/shaping flake exhibits a bifacial "nibbled" retouch along all of the non-platform edges. The platform is small, thin, and bifacial. The flake expands from the platform to about half-way to the distal end. The flake was struck at a prominent ridge and removed a deep hinge fracture scar that had originated from the opposite side of a biface. The retouch is very short, quite irregular, and bifacial. Although we believe that most of this is intentional retouch, some of it may have resulted from use. Part of the distal end is missing as the result of a bend fracture.

Number 1290/13A/13B is an elongated biface thinning/shaping flake with retouch along both sides. It has been reconstructed by the conjoining of three flake fragments. Even so, a distal portion and a medial fragment are still missing. The original flake was elongated, expanded from the platform to about half the length and then converged toward the end. The platform is straight, bifacial and heavily ground. Grinding was mostly done to the dorsal edge of the platform, greatly strengthening it. Most of the dorsal surface of the flake is covered by a flake scar that originated from the same biface margin and is parallel with this flake's axis. The right side exhibits a sharp invasive retouch where some of the flakes terminated in hinge fractures. The proximal portion of the left side has the same type of retouch. Although it is difficult to be sure, the retouch does not seem to have removed much of the sides of the original flake.

Number 1292 (Figure 5.6a) was produced by the regular unifacial retouching of the left side and a portion of the distal end of a large, porcellanite, biface thinning flake. The proximal end of the flake is missing due to a radial break that originated on a central dorsal ridge. Dorsal flake scars exhibit multidirectional origins, and there is the suggestion of a sub-cortical remnant in the center of the flake. The flake terminated in a rebounded hinge fracture. This flake was removed from a large biface, and it would have greatly flattened one face. It was probably from an intermediate stage of manufacture. Retouch was applied to sharp flake edges and is very regular and sharp. The left side is straight, and the distal retouch formed a convex edge. This flake was only minimally reduced in size by this retouch.

Number 1310—the distal fragment of a quartzite flake—has minimal, irregular, abrupt retouch along all unbroken edges. The dorsal surface of the fragment exhibits two parallel flake scars that meet in a median ridge, originating from the same direction as the flake, and the ridge is on the flake axis. There is also a small portion of a flake scar on the distal end that originated from a different direction. Although the edges

have been modified by retouch, the original flake sides were probably also parallel to the flake axis. The proximal portion is missing, but thickening at the break indicates that the flake was probably never more than about twice as long as the remaining piece. This piece exhibits a slight curve at the distal end. When intact, this flake could have been classified as a struck blade. The irregularity and abruptness of the retouch might indicate that it may have resulted from use rather than from intentional modification.

Number 1275 (Figure 4.8a) is the proximal portion of a flake that exhibits heavy retouch on the right side and minimal retouch on the left side. The platform is straight, wide, and relatively thick. It was bifacially prepared with facetting, dorsal reduction, light battering, and grinding. The dorsal surface has a flake scar on the left side that originated from the same direction as the flake and formed a straight central ridge on the flake axis. The right side has been heavily retouched, but there are remnants of flake scars that seem to have originated from the right. After retouching, which probably removed a substantial portion of the right side, this piece resembles a struck blade, and it may have been a blade before retouching, but not with parallel dorsal flake scars.

## End Retouch

This category would normally include those implements called end scrapers. There are, however, several pieces that have flake-end retouch that would not be considered end scrapers. Most of the artifacts in this category exhibit some retouch or modification on the lateral sides, but the distal retouch is dominant. We have also chosen to include two proximal fragments in this category that we believe are the remnants of end-retouched tools.

Number 1293 (Figure 5.4a) is the distal end of an end scraper made on a jasper flake. The unifacial retouch is at a medium angle and forms two fairly straight distal edges that meet in a slight projection. The removal of only one or two more small retouch flakes would have produced an evenly convex end. It is possible that this implement was broken while it was being resharpened. The maximum width is located at the sides of the distal retouch. The dorsal flake scars of the original flake look as if they originated at and traveled in the same direction as the flake. The shallow double ridge may indicate that the flake was a struck blade. Side retouch is abrupt and somewhat irregular. A potlid fracture on the ventral surface indicates that this piece was burned.

Number 1307 (Figure 5.4b) is a small single-ridged jasper flake fragment that exhibits medium-angle retouch on its distal end. This piece is quite small with a retouched distal width of only 17.1 mm. The flake contracted toward the distal end.

Only the distal end of Number 1313 (Figure 5.3c) is present. The flake on which it was made has a single central ridge and two dorsal flake scars that run parallel to the flake axis. Retouch is only on the end and produced a convex edge with a medium sharp angle. This small tool does not look as if it was resharpened. It broke through the center with a pronounced bend break. The retouched end is only 17.2 mm wide.

Number 1315 (Figure 5.4c), an end-retouched implement,

was made on a relatively thick flake with a single ridge. The dorsal surface on the left is cortex with a single flake scar running parallel to the flake axis on the right. The flake platform is crushed, probably resulting from collapse during flake removal due to weakness caused by the cortex. The end retouch is at a medium-sharp angle, but the slight curve of the flake at the distal end produced a sharp cutting edge. It is not possible to tell how much this tool may have been reduced in length due to resharpening. There is some edge damage on the sides and some trowel damage in one area as well.

Number 1319 (Figure 5.2g) is a classic example of an exhausted end scraper. It was made on a thick flake that has a plain, ground, and slightly lipped platform. The sides are steeply retouched so that the tool expands from the proximal end to the points where the distal convex retouch meets them. A slight notch on the left side may have been intentionally produced. End retouch is steep, but small hinged flakes left the edge fairly sharp. Edge damage is present on the distal end. This tool is well configured for hafting in a slot or socket.

Number 7 is only a small fragment of the distal end of a tool. It was made on a thin cortical flake. The retouch is medium-sharp, regular, and formed a convex edge. The tool may have broken on a flaw in the material, possibly during manufacture.

Number 285 (Figures 4.8f and 5.2h) is a fairly flat, single-ridged flake with a large, thick, plain platform. The dorsal surface exhibits two main flake scars that seem to run parallel to the flake axis, but the one on the right is oriented from the distal end. Steep and somewhat irregular side retouch formed this piece, so that it expands from the proximal end to meet the distal end retouch. This retouch is medium-sharp and produced a very even, convex end.

Number 84 (Figure 5.2i) is another single-ridged flake. The flake platform is facetted, and both dorsal flake scars run parallel to the flake axis and are oriented from the direction of the platform. The right side has a small area of retouch near the distal end. The left side is retouched unifacially on the bulbar (ventral) surface with several bulb-thinning flake removals. This succeeded in removing only a portion of the bulb of applied force. This retouch was probably accomplished with percussion. The distal retouch is fairly steep, although fine hinge and step fractures left the edge sharp. It is irregularly convex.

Number 1289 is an end scraper that was made on a cortical flake struck from a nodule of jasper. The flake platform is small and plain. The flake cross-section is thin plano-convex. Discontinuous retouch is present on the right edge. The distal end is retouched to a sharp edge angle and is evenly convex.

Number 32 (Figure 5.4g) is the proximal end of what we believe was an end-retouched piece, probably an end scraper. This is the only item in the assemblage that can be described as a true blade. It has a small platform that is facetted, reduced, and lightly ground. The dorsal surface has two ridges that are parallel to both the sides and the flake axis. Medium-sharp retouch extends along most of the right edge. The distal end is missing due to a radial break originating from one of the central ridges. There is some edge damage on the left edge. Although we believe that this piece was most likely part of an end scraper, it may have been something else.

Number 43 (Figure 5.4h) is another proximal flake frag-

ment that we believe may have had distal retouch. The platform is missing, and the dorsal flake scars indicate that the flake probably came from a biface. There is fine sharp retouch along the right edge and abrupt damage along the left. The distal end is missing due to a bend break or perverse fracture. Once again, this fragment may or may not have been part of an end scraper.

Number 1279 (Figure 5.2c) is an unusual piece in that the retouched end is proximal rather than distal. A thick single-ridged, curved flake was selected for this implement. The platform was removed by retouching. The dorsal surface exhibits flake scars: two on the right, approximately perpendicular to the flake axis, and one on the left, also nearly perpendicular. In addition, about two-thirds of the left area is cortex. The proximal end is unifacially retouched, with two straight sections converging to a point. The retouch is invasive and ranges from medium-sharp to abrupt. The remaining edges of the flake exhibit edge damage from light to heavy.

## Raclettes

The term *raclette* is used here to classify flakes that exhibit abrupt, short unifacial flaking on a thin edge. This flaking is extremely short and seen only by careful inspection. It may have resulted either from intentional modification or possibly through use. We have separated these items from other flakes that exhibit edge damage primarily based on the regularity and evenness of the edge flaking. We believe that this regularity indicates intentional modification.

Number 1294 (Figure 5.5f) is a medium-sized biface thinning flake with a small plain platform. It is curved and has dorsal flake scars with varied orientations. Although it is difficult to determine, this flake may have helped remove the bulb of applied force of a larger flake. The distal left edge, distal end, and a small segment of the right edge have abrupt, regular flaking.

Number 1316 is a fragment of a flake of heavily burned chert. Potlid fractures and crazing are present. One edge has regular abrupt flaking, which produced a shallow concavity. There is also the suggestion that additional retouch may have been present before fracturing by burning. It is possible that this is a piece of a larger retouched implement.

Number 1594 (Figure 4.7e) is a classic example of a late-stage biface thinning flake. It has a small, slightly convex platform that was facetted, reduced and ground. Dorsal flake scars are nearly parallel with the flake axis, with those on the proximal two-thirds originating from the same direction as the flake, and with the one on the distal third originating from the opposite direction. The bulb of applied force bounced, nearly causing the flake to terminate in a hinge fracture. Instead, it progressed smoothly past the mid-line of the biface, terminating in a feathered fracture. It also removed the remnant of a bounced, or hinged fracture near the center of the biface. It is the sort of flake that would be considered very successful in final biface manufacture. If it had terminated in the short hinge fracture, it would have been a disaster. Approximately half of the left edge has short, abrupt, even flaking that produced a shallow concavity.

**Figure 4.9.** Percussion flake with a facetted and ground platform from the main block excavation.

## Gravers

*Gravers* are simply small pointed projections flaked into the edge of a flake or other tool. We are using this term simply to conform to a traditional typological category and are not intending to imply any particular use or function.

Number 1305 (Figure 5.2d) is a small sharp projection that was produced by abruptly retouching a very small biface flake fragment along one edge. This was done by making two adjacent concavities. It is not possible to determine whether or not this retouching was done on this small fragment. Even if the flake was complete when the retouching was done, the tool would not have been much larger than it is.

Number 1562 is only a proximal fragment. The platform is crushed, but a tiny graver point similar to Number 1305 (Figure 5.2d) was flaked on the platform end. The lateral sides are parallel, and the piece resembles a microblade. However, this is not an uncommon form for flakes resulting from bifacial retouch.

Number 1311 (Figure 4.7d) is a triple graver. A small core edge-trimming flake served as the blank for its production. The flake was struck from a piece of chert that had not been previously flaked in the same area. The platform is thick, wide, and completely cortical. The dorsal flake surface looks natural, although not cortical. The longitudinal section of the flake is triangular. Three separate projections were produced by unifacial abrupt retouch, with three shallow notches and one straight area. All of the non-platform margins of the flake were retouched.

## Burin Spall

In the case of Number 1318 (Figure 5.6d), a long, narrow flake was struck that removed the edge of a unifacially retouched implement. This implement was probably a side-retouched piece. The burin spall has a plain platform that was probably part of a break through the original tool. It is possible that this flake was struck in an attempt to rejuvenate the retouched edge, but it was not successful because the resulting edge would have been obtuse. Although this piece can be classified as a burin spall, this is not intended to imply that the knappers at Mill Iron were intentionally producing burins.

## Edge Damaged Flakes

Five flakes have been recovered from the Mill Iron site that exhibit edge alteration resulting from flaking. The flaking is, however, inconsistent, irregular, and non-invasive. It is our impression that this damage resulted from use or post-depositional forces, rather than intentional retouch.

Number 1274 (Figure 4.8b) is the distal portion of a blade-like flake. Two parallel flake scars form most of the dorsal surface and produced a fairly straight dorsal ridge. The flake removal ended in a hinge-through that removed a portion of the core base. This flake may have resulted from intentional blade production. There is heavy edge damage along the lateral margins, especially on the right side.

Number 1278 (Figure 5.7b) is a flake that was struck from the edge or side of a core or biface and exhibits minor flaking on its distal edge. The flake platform is plain, and the dorsal surface retains some cortex, adjacent to the platform and a single flake scar remnant. The flake terminated in a shallow hinge fracture. Although it isn't clear what the form of the material was, this flake is typical of products of discoidal cores.

Number 1280 (Figure 5.5e) is an elongated flake that is very curved and expands toward the distal end. The right dorsal side is quite steep and retains cortex. The remaining dorsal surface has flake scar remnants that have many orientations. The platform is wide, plain, and partly missing due to crushing—probably when the flake was struck. Although not a blade, this is the type of flake removal that is commonly produced while preparing a nodular core for blade removals. The naturally concave left side exhibits heavy bifacial edge damage. This artifact was also heavily burned as seen by crazing and potlid fractures.

Number 1375 is the distal end of a flake, possibly from a biface. A concave area on the left edge, and the distal edge, exhibit unifacial edge damage. This flake is also burned.

Number 1584 (Figure 5.5g) is a large, thin bifacial thinning flake of porcellanite that has a single unifacially flaked notch on the right side. The platform is facetted and possibly isolated. Dorsal flake scars have multiple orientations, and the flake terminated in a shallow hinge fracture. The notch was produced by the removal of one or two pieces of the very thin flake edge. We believe that this occurred accidentally, probably after deposition. This is a very common type of break when thin flakes are stepped on.

## Unmodified Flakes

Eight flakes and fragments are included in the assemblage that does not exhibit any obvious modification other than the fact

Figure 4.10. Chopper or anvil stone from the main block excavation.

Figure 4.11. Manufacture flakes refit to the chopper in figure 4.10.

that some are fragmented. This is not to say that they are debitage. Only microscopic examination can determine whether or not they may have been used in some capacity.

Number 40 is the distal end of a flake that has a mostly cortical dorsal surface. The sides of the flake are nearly parallel, and the distal end removed a natural protrusion on the piece of raw material. Although this could have been from initial biface preparation, it is just as likely it was from a core.

Number 204 is a biface flake fragment with a small area of cortex present near the distal end. Little can be said other than that it is quite thin. This looks as if it may have been from the large biface (Numbers 1589 and 1606), but no refit could be found.

Number 277 (Figure 5.8d) is a fragment of the distal end of a thin biface flake that terminated in a rebound hinge fracture.

Number 1581 (Figure 4.9) retains an excellent example of platform preparation of biface flakes. The platform is relatively wide, lipped, convex, facetted, reduced, and ground. The distal end of the dorsal surface is cortical. The flake terminated in a shallow step fracture on a material flaw. This flake resulted from careful individual platform preparation.

Number 197 is a small biface shaping flake that is thin and flat. It has a small, straight, facetted platform. It probably came either from final biface manufacture or from resharpening. It is the same material as Number 1608 and may have come from the same biface.

Number 1314 (Figure 5.8b), a small biface reduction flake, has a wide, facetted, straight platform, is slightly curved, and expands to a shallow hinge termination.

Number 1608 (Figure 5.7d) is a medium-sized biface flake with a crushed platform and a cortex on the proximal dorsal face. It terminates in a feather fracture. Although in size and form similar to a final biface manufacture flake, the cortex may indicate that it came from an early stage. On the other hand, it is also possible to complete a biface without removing all of the cortex. Much depends on the form of the original raw material. This flake looks like it may have come from the same biface as Number 197.

## Other Artifacts

This category is a catch-all in that it includes several pieces that obtained their forms as the result of use rather than through intentional modification. One exception is a chopper (Number 16620) made of a relatively inferior material known as Tongue River Silicified Sediment that changes rapidly in texture from a material that flakes in places with a choncoidal fracture to one that immediately adjacent may separate along fracture planes with all intergrades. The tool in question (Figure 4.10) was deliberately shaped with symmetrical, rounded chopping edges on opposite ends, each with working edge angles of nearly 90 degrees. Both working edges demonstrate

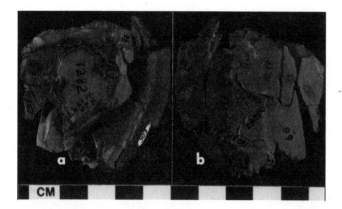

**Figure 4.12.** Pièce esquillé with refitted manufacture and use flakes from the main block excavation.

heavy use. The tool could have been used in the hand as a chopper, or it could have been partially buried and used as an anvil over which large bones could have been broken.

Although this tool appears rather crude, it was deliberately formed according to a preconceived plan because the two working edges and edge angles are almost identical: the tool was designed with a knowledge of what was needed to smash bison bones. There is no doubt that the tool was made on the site, because numerous manufacture flakes were refitted (Figure 4.11; see also Chapter 3 for a map of the refitted flakes). It is significant also, that this material is better for this kind of tool use than the more brittle cherts that tend to break under heavy, continuous chopping use.

A larger chopper (Number 1663) was made from the same material but in this case, only a few large spalls were removed to form a blunt point. This tool was also made on the site, since most of the manufacture flakes were refitted (see Chapter 3 for a flake distribution map). Two tabular pieces of low-grade petrified wood averaging 3.0 and 3.7 cm in thickness, nearly round in outline form, and 10–13 cm in diameter were recov-

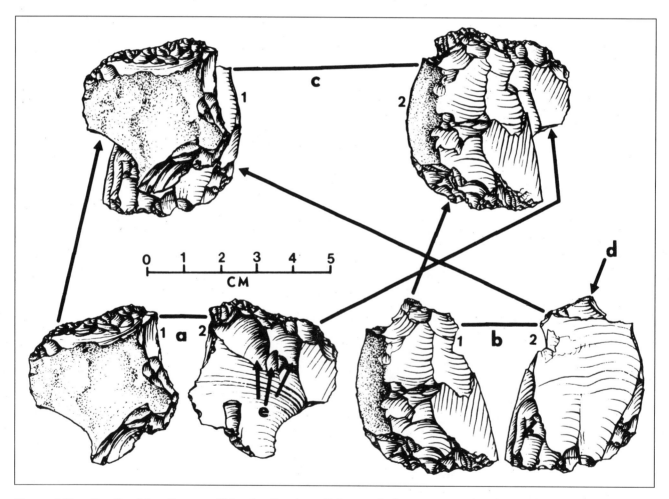

**Figure 4.13.** Details of the pièce esquillé and refitted use flakes made from a large manufacture flake that refits to the chopper in Figure 4.10.

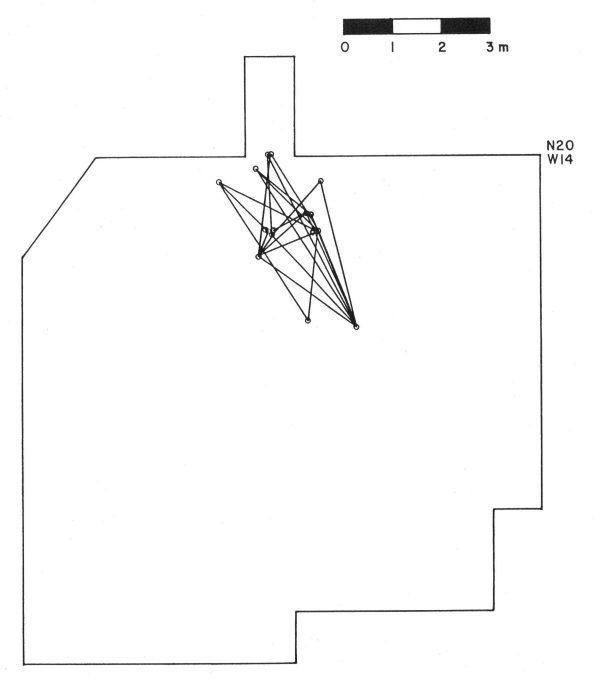

**Figure** 4.14. Distribution of flakes refitted to the pièce esquillé in Figure 4.12.

**Figure 4.15.** Pièce esquillé and refitted use flakes made from a large manufacture flake that refits to the chopper in Figure 4.10.

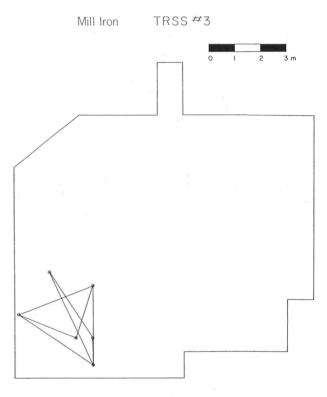

Mill Iron     TRSS #3

0  1  2  3 m

**Figure 4.16.** Distribution of flakes that refit to the pièce esquillé in Figure 4.15.

ered and both demonstrate chopper and/or hammerstone use (Numbers 31 and 1654).

## Pièces Esquillés

Number 1282 (Figure 4.12), a tool with a heavily battered poll 15.9 mm thick, was split through the center as the result of a heavy blow, presumably during use. The two broken pieces were refitted (Figure 4.13), and a number of flakes that were removed presumably first by manufacture and then by subsequent use of the tool were refitted (Figure 4.12).

The poll end was hit with a blow that detached a flake (Figure 4.13b2d) and simultaneously initiated the split from the opposite end so that the two separate striking platforms merged into a single flake scar (Figure 4.13b2). As the tool split, one of the pieces apparently remained stationary, while the other progressed forward and removed flakes from the center outward, as demonstrated on the conjoining faces of the split (Figure 4.13a2e). This would suggest that the tool was wedged tightly when it split and that one piece was forced to move against the other while both were held together under pressure. Subsequent to the split, one piece (Figure 4.13b) was utilized further, although it was then reversed so that the original distal end became the poll end. A number of flakes were recovered in the camp area and were refit (Figures 4.13 and 4.14): most appear to be use rather than manufacture flakes. A broken biface (Figure 4.7c) was once thought to have been part of this tool but further analysis suggests this is probably not the case.

One of the pieces that refits to the large chopper (Figure 4.11) was also used as a pièce esquillé. A sharp point was formed on one end (Figure 4.15a) and repeated blows to the other end removed several flakes, some of which were refit (Figures 4.15b and 4.16). Several flakes were refit to another similar tool of the same material but could not be refit to the chopper. However, there is little doubt that it came from the same body of manufacture flakes.

## Summary

The assemblage of flaked stone artifacts that has been recovered from the Mill Iron site is incomplete because of incomplete site preservation and excavation and because it doesn't represent the total range of activities. It is therefore necessary to infer technological processes from mostly finished, used, and in most cases, discarded artifacts.

### Raw Materials

The stone selected for flaking includes small tabular pieces of silicified wood, small nodules of jasper, porcellanite (which occurs in large cobbles)—all available locally—and Hartville cherts (which are available in large blocks in southeastern Wyoming). Although all types of fine-grained materials were used for the production of projectile points, blade flakes, blades, and end scrapers, these tool forms tended to be made from medium-sized nodules of jasper and chert. (For a more

**Table 4.3.** Size Comparisons of Plainview and Mill Iron Projectile Points.

| Site | Range | Mean | n | Range | Mean | n | Range | Mean | n | Range | Mean | n |
|------|-------|------|---|-------|------|---|-------|------|---|-------|------|---|
| | L (mm) | | | W (mm) | | | Th (mm) | | | BI (mm) | | |
| Mill Iron | 45.1–79.5 | 62.3 | 13 | 18.4–25.6 | 23.2 | 16 | 3.3–5.6 | 4.9 | 17 | 0.4–6.0 | 2.8 | 16 |
| Plainview | 50.5–74.0 | 64.8 | 10 | 20.5–26.0 | 23.3 | 15 | 5.0–7.6 | 5.8 | 14 | 1.6–3.8 | 2.2 | 10 |

**Table 4.4.** Projectile Comparisons of Projectile Points between Mill Iron and Plainview Sites.

| Site | Range | Mean | n | Range | Mean | n | Range | Mean | n | Range | Mean | n |
|------|-------|------|---|-------|------|---|-------|------|---|-------|------|---|
| | W/L (mm) | | | Th/W (mm) | | | LW/L (mm) | | | BI/L (mm) | | |
| Mill Iron | 0.29–0.53 | 0.38 | 13 | 0.18–0.25 | 0.21 | 17 | 0.11–0.56 | 0.41 | 13 | 0.01–0.06 | 0.04 | 13 |
| Plainview | 0.30–0.52 | 0.38 | 10 | 0.19–0.34 | 0.25 | 13 | 0.04–0.68 | 0.42 | 9 | 0.02–0.05 | 0.03 | 7 |

detailed treatment of the raw material sources and forms see Chapter 6, this volume.)

## Primary Technologies

Two basic technological processes seem to be represented in the flaked stone artifacts: bifacial reduction for the production of large bifaces and projectile points, and core reduction for the production of flakes and blade flakes, primarily for the manufacture of end scrapers.

Bifacial flaking incorporated direct percussion and pressure thinning and shaping. The large bifaces were produced mostly with direct percussion with substantial thinning accomplished by the removal of diving flakes. There is no evidence that overshot flaking typical of Clovis (Bradley 1982:203-208; 1991:370) was being done. In form and technique, the large bifaces closely resemble those from the Hanson site (Frison and Bradley 1980:31–42). Platform preparation for percussion biface flaking tended to include facetting, reducing, and grinding. Platform isolation, while present, is not common. Platforms also tend to be straight to only slightly convex. These characteristics more closely resemble Clovis platform preparation than they do Folsom (Bradley 1991:373).

There is little direct evidence that flake blanks were being used to produce projectile points, a common practice at the Plainview site (Knudson 1983). Possible exceptions are a small biface (Figure 4.7c) broken in manufacture by end shock and two projectile points. The number of unmodified flakes recovered was very low, and with the possible exception of the resharpening of a single biface in the bonebed, the manufacture of the small biface, and flaking resulting from tool use, there is little evidence that flaking was taking place at the site.

Only a single small core has been recovered from the site, and this was from the modern ground surface. Its association with the in-place artifacts from the camp and bonebed areas is questionable. Without cores to examine, the remaining core flakes are only suggestive of the technology involved. There is evidence that nodular materials were having cortex removed by the production of elongated flakes. Occasionally this process

seems to have been continued so that flake blades, and possibly even true blades were being made. The main purpose for these products seems to have been for the production of end scrapers. Irwin-Williams et al. (1973:46) note that "This industry (Goshen) contains the highest incidence of true blades of any Paleoindian complex at Hell Gap." Struck blades are sometimes considered to be a Clovis trait in the southern Plains (Hester 1972:92), and they are very rare or absent in Folsom assemblages.

There are also retouched tools made on relatively large flakes that could either have been from flake cores or from the early stages of biface manufacture. A number of implements was also made by retouching unmodified pieces of tabular raw material, and many others were made on biface flakes.

## Secondary Technologies

Projectile point manufacturing sequences are also not well represented in the assemblage. Several points were made from the local, tabular silicified woods, and the sizes and shapes of the raw material would probably have limited the methods that could be employed. One projectile point (Figure 4.1a) retains two flake scar remnants that may have resulted from percussion flaking. Another (Figure 4.3d) has a small remnant of what may be a bulbar surface of a flake blank, and still another (Figure 4.7c) may have resulted from projectile point manufacture failure. All the rest of the projectile points exhibit flaking that was possible using pressure techniques. Pressure flaking included thinning, shaping, and fine margin retouching. Pressure thinning and shaping was primarily selective in sequence, although a series of three flake scars was not uncommon. Sequencing can be generalized as selective. Flake scars are usually close to perpendicular to the points' axes, with comedial and transmedial patterns standard. Flake scar spacing ranges from very uniform to irregular, with some exceptional examples of controlled flaking. Retouch was applied selectively, primarily to remove ridges between flake scars. This produced sharp straight and even edges, especially on distal lateral margins. Abrupt, usually bifacial and continuous, retouch was also done,

**Figure 4.17.** Mammoth rib tool handle or weaponry haft from the main block excavation.

mainly along proximal margins that were then ground/polished, and especially as a process of reworking. Basal thinning is common and usually consisted of several pressure flake removals from each face. These thinning flakes do not extend very far and cannot be considered fluting. Selective bifacial pressure retouch is also present on the large fragmented biface.

Flake tool manufacture seems to have been done primarily with percussion flaking, probably with an antler billet. In only one instance is pressure flaking on a flake tool inferred, and this is a tentative interpretation.

### Finished Forms

There is a fairly wide range of projectile point primary forms in the Mill Iron assemblage. Reworked pieces make an additional contribution to the typological range. The closest well-described analogues are the points from the Plainview site in Texas (Sellards et al. 1947, Knudson 1983). Tables 4.3 and 4.4 present comparative metrical data measurements for the Plainview points taken from Knudson 1973. Even when the broken and reworked pieces are included, the only apparent difference is that the Mill Iron points are, on average, thinner than those from Plainview. In addition to the measurements, outlines also represent nearly the same ranges of variation. The only significant technological difference is that several of the Plainview points retain remnants of original flake blank surfaces, while they are lacking on the Mill Iron points.

Other Goshen points have been found in the northern High Plains, specifically at the Carter Kerr-McGee and Kaufmann Cave sites in northern Wyoming (Frison 1991a:44–46, 52), and in the North Park area of Colorado (Kornfeld et al. 1993) and more recently from the Jim Pitts site in the South Dakota Black Hills (James Donohue, personal communication 1993). Initially, the Goshen points at the Carter Kerr-McGee site were considered to be a Clovis variant (Frison 1984:305), but further study indicates that they have a greater technological similarity to Goshen points. Our opinion is that they are actually

somewhere in between the two and may indicate the process of transition from Clovis to Goshen.

The Mill Iron points can be classified as Goshen (Irwin-Williams et al. 1973:46), but they are basically the same, technologically and typologically as Plainview. Traditionally, the earliest described type takes name precedence and subsequent points are called by this name. Although basically identical in form and manufacture, Goshen and Plainview points are associated with assemblages that have significantly different dates and stratigraphic relationships. Goshen points from the northern High Plains are securely dated at around 11,000 B.P. (see Chapter 1) and have been found in stratigraphic context below Folsom components at more than one site. These include the Hell Gap (Irwin-Williams et al. 1973:46) and Carter Kerr-McGee sites (Frison 1984:288–314).

Recent investigations at the Plainview and Lubbock Lake sites in Texas have yielded dates for Plainview assemblages of around 10,000 B.P. (Eileen Johnson, personal communication). Plainview materials have not been recovered in direct stratigraphic association with Folsom materials at either of these localities. There is a report of Plainview stratigraphically above Folsom at the Lake Theo site in Texas (Johnson et al. 1982:113–137), but we have, at this time, been unable to obtain descriptions of the Plainview materials. If this new information is correct, Plainview materials in the southern High Plains are significantly older than previously thought (Wormington 1957:108). They are still substantially younger than Goshen materials in the northern High Plains, and it is difficult to see how this particular style and technology could survive for this length of time, with the whole Folsom phenomenon happening in between.

At this time, we have to think that there is a lot we don't know about what was happening and that it is probably appropriate to retain both the Goshen and Plainview designations. What is unclear to us is how the non-projectile point technologies compare, primarily because of a lack of information in both areas. Perhaps a detailed study of the Goshen materials

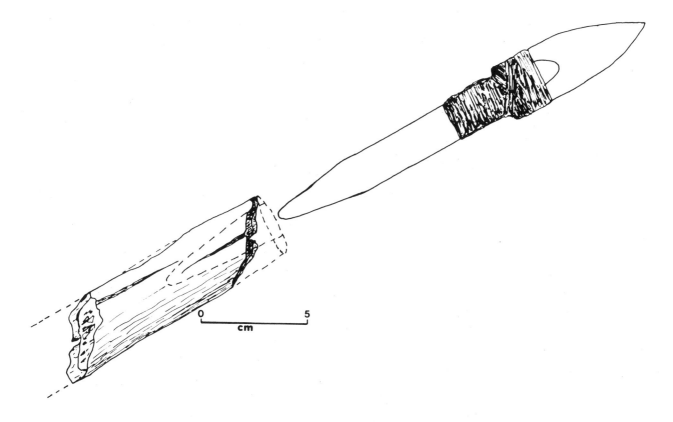

**Figure 4.18.** One suggested possible use for the mammoth rib tool in Figure 4.17.

from the Hell Gap site will allow a better understanding of Goshen, but it will take additional excavated materials to provide comparative information from a Plainview assemblage.

Other Goshen-like point styles have been noted in the western United States, for example Belen in the Middle Rio Grande Valley in New Mexico (Judge 1973:69-72). Unfortunately, sample sizes are small and stratigraphic context and dating are lacking. The Milnesand site assemblage (Sellards 1955:336–344) also resembles Goshen materials, but it generally lacks basal indentation, basal thinning is minimal, flaking is more irregular, and it is proportionally thicker. Although these artifacts lack rounded bases, they otherwise look like Agate Basin points (Frison and Stanford 1982:82–104).

Very few bifaces were recovered from Mill Iron. Those present resemble both Clovis and Folsom forms, but are not particularly diagnostic of either.

The sample of retouched flake tools is fairly small and any of the forms may be found in most Paleoindian assemblages in the High Plains. We see nothing diagnostic in any of the categories. Interestingly, spurred end scrapers are not present.

## Worked Bone

A mammoth rib fragment was recovered in the camp-processing area. The specimen was broken on both ends (Figure 4.17)

and is the only bone from the area that demonstrated extensive rodent chewing. After removal of a heavy coat of caliche, one end exhibited a carefully drilled conical-shaped hole. This was first interpreted as a tool haft, except that conical holes do not function well in holding a tool that is subject to stress from directions other that directly toward the bottom of the cone.

In ethnographic collections from Eskimo groups, pieces of whale ribs are shaped in similar manner on one end to hold conical-shaped foreshafts, and the other end is attached to the end of wooden harpoon shafts. The similarity between the two items led to a suggestion that the Mill Iron specimen might have been used as the end of a main shaft. The conical end of experimental Clovis points mounted on wooden foreshafts and used successfully with an atlatl and dart on African elephants (see Frison 1989) happens to fit the hole in the mammoth rib (Figure 4.18) and this is suggested as a possible use.

This artifact cannot be used as a valid claim for the presence of or the procurement of mammoths at the Mill Iron site. However, there should have been mammoth bone available for some time after their supposed extinction during Clovis times. This could be a tool type with considerable time depth. The only other humanly modified piece of bone recovered at the Mill Iron site is part of an object that was probably egg-shaped and may have been decorative—perhaps a pendant. It was probably about 35 mm in length, 25 mm wide, and 3.1

mm thick. Both faces and the edge were ground to shape, and it was burned to the extent of being nearly calcined to a light color. No evidence of a drilled hole is present on the recovered piece but would probably have been in the part or parts not recovered if it were there. The object strongly suggests a piece made from the blade of a bison scapula and a shallow, incised line may represent part of an applied decorative pattern. It resembles quite closely a bone item recovered from the Folsom level at the Agate Basin site (Frison and Craig 1982; Figure 2.109k).

## Conclusions

The Mill Iron flaked stone artifact assemblage clearly does not represent all of the technological and typological processes and forms that were being employed by Goshen peoples. The forms and processes that are present have a strong affinity to Folsom assemblages but also retain some characteristics more typical of Clovis. The presence of a blade flake technology in Goshen assemblages is more reminiscent of Clovis than Folsom, as is basic bifacial platform preparation. We are unwilling, however, to imply that Goshen represents a transitional stage between Clovis and Folsom. Of particular interest is the lack of projec-tile point fluting. Clovis fluting seems to be an extension of the normal Clovis biface thinning processes, applied to the base near the end of the manufacturing sequence. It probably served well as hafting preparation. Folsom fluting, on the other hand, is so elaborate and inefficient that it has been suggested that its primary function may have been ritual (Bradley 1991:374–379). Whatever the purpose for fluting in Clovis and Folsom assemblages, the lack of it in Goshen is somewhat perplexing. The form and proportions of the finished points, as well as the technology, in no way precluded fluting as an option. Why then is it lacking? If Goshen does intervene between Clovis and Folsom, how is it that fluting is not present? We suppose that it is possible that Clovis is succeeded by two different technological approaches with one (Folsom) continuing and developing a fluted point technology, and the other (Goshen) abandoning it. Perhaps this may help in understanding the Goshen/Plainview and Midland/Folsom questions. Perhaps not.

Goshen points are technologically distinct enough from Clovis to suggest that if they did develop from Clovis, we should expect that intermediate forms and technologies will some day be identified. Perhaps the small sample from the Carter Kerr-McGee site represents such an intermediate stage.

## References Cited

Bradley, Bruce A.
1974    Comments on the Lithic Technology of the Casper Site Materials. In *The Casper Site: A Hell Gap Bison Kill on the High Plains*, edited by George Frison, pp. 191–197. Academic Press, San Diego.
1982    Flaked Stone Technology and Typology. In *The Agate Basin Site: A Record of the Paleoindian Occupation of the Northwestern High Plains*, edited by George Frison and Dennis Stanford, pp. 181–212. Academic Press, New York.
1991    Flaked Stone Technology in the Northern High Plains. *In Prehistoric Hunters of the High Plains. 2d ed.*, pp. 369–395. Academic Press, San Diego.
Bradley, Bruce A., and George C. Frison
1987    Projectile Projectile Points and Specialized Bifaces from the Horner Site. In *The Horner Site: The Type Site of the Cody Cultural Complex*, edited by George C. Frison and Lawrence Todd, pp. 199–232. Academic Press, Orlando.
1988    Typology and Technology of the Mill Iron Site Flaked Stone Tools. Paper presented at the 53rd Annual Meeting of the Society for American Archaeology, Phoenix.
Bradley, Bruce A., and Dennis J. Stanford
1987    The Claypool Study. In *The Horner Site: The Type Site of the Cody Cultural Complex*, edited by George Frison and Lawrence Todd, pp. 405–434. Academic Press, Orlando.
Frison, George C.
1984    The Carter/Kerr-McGee Paleoindian Site: Cultural Resource Management and Archaeological Research. *American Antiquity* 49(2):288–314.
1989    Experimental Use of Clovis Weaponey and Tools on African Elephants. *American Antiquity* 54(4):766–784.
1991a   *Prehistoric Hunters of the High Plains*. 2d ed. Academic Press, San Diego.
1991b   The Goshen Paleoindian Complex: New Data for Paleoindian Research. In *Clovis Origins and Adaptations*, edited by Robson Bonnichsen and Karen Turnmire, pp. 133–151. A Peopling of the Americas Publication, Center for the Study of the First Americans. Oregon State University, Corvallis.
1992    The Goshen Cultural Complex—Where Does it Fit in the Paleoindian Cultural Sequence? *Research & Exploration* 8(4):494–496.
Frison, George C., and Bruce A. Bradley
1980    *Folsom Tools and Technology at the Hanson Site, Wyoming*. University of New Mexico Press, Albuquerque.
Frison George C., and Carolyn Craig
1982    Bone, Antler, and Irory Artifacts and Manufacture Technology in the Agate Basin Site. In *The Agate Basin Site: A Record of the Paleoindian Occupation of the Northwestern High Plains*, edited by George C. Frison and Dennis J. Stanford, pp. 161–173. New York, Academic Press.
Frison, George C., and Dennis J. Stanford (editors)
1982    *The Agate Basin Site: A Record of the Paleoindian Occupation of the Northwestern High Plains*. Academic Press, New York.

Hester, James J.
1972    *Blackwater Locality No. 1: A Stratified Early Man Site in Eastern New Mexico.* Fort Burgwin Research Center, vol. 8:1–238.

Irwin-Williams, Cynthia, Henry Irwin, George Agogino, and C. Vance Haynes, Jr.
1973    Hell Gap: Paleoindian Occupation of the High Plains. *Plains Anthropologist* 18(59):40–53.

Johnson, Eileen, Vance T. Holliday, and Raymond W. Neck
1982    Lake Theo: Late Quaternary Paleoenvironmental Data and New Plainview (Paleoindian) Date. *North American Archaeologist* 3(2):113–137.

Judge, W. James
1973    *Paleo-Indian Occupation of the Central Rio Grande Valley in New Mexico.* University of New Mexico Press, Albuquerque.

Kornfeld, Marcel, Jan Saysette, and James Miller
1993    Goshen-Plainview Complex at Upper Twin Mountain Sites, Colorado: One Avenue for Further Research. Unpublished Manuscript on file at the Department of Anthropology, University of Wyoming, Laramie, Wyoming.

Knudson, Ruthann
1983    *Organizational Variability in Late Paleoindian Assemblages.* Washington State University, Laboratory of Anthropology, Reports of Investigations No. 60.

Sellards, E. H.
1955    Fossil Bison and Associated Artifacts from Milnesand, New Mexico. *American Antiquity* 20(4):336–344.

Sellards, E. H., Glen L. Evans, and Grayson E. Meade
1947    Fossil Bison and Associated Artifacts from Plainview, Texas, with Description of Artifacts by Alex D. Krieger. *Bulletin, Geological Society of America* 58:927–954.

Wormington, H. Marie
1957    *Ancient Man in North America.* Denver Museum of Natural History, Popular Series No. 4.

# CHAPTER FIVE

# Lithic Microwear Studies of the Mill Iron Site Tools

KAORU AKOSHIMA
Sendai University, Japan

GEORGE C. FRISON
University of Wyoming

## Introduction

The introduction of high-power microscopy (magnifications around 300x) and the use of systematic experiments to build a reference framework by Keeley (1977, 1978, 1980) combine to represent a significant landmark in lithic microwear studies. Keeley's method is based on the premise that variability in tool polishes represents tool use on different mediums (e.g. hide, wood, bone, etc.). He also recognizes other categories of microwear, including microchipping and striations. Mill Iron site tools were analyzed in a similar manner using the methods developed by the Tohoku University Experimental stone tool use project developed at its Laboratory of Archaeology and directed by Professor C. Serizawa. Variability in tool use was determined by about 230 experiments using tool types made of different silicious materials, and new experiments are continually added. Generally speaking, it has been confirmed that the influence of raw material differences on tool microwear patterns is minimal. Microwear analysts agree that resultant polish types on different rocks of cryptocrystalline silica are almost identical. The Tohoku University experiments produced polishes that were classified into 11 types (Table 5.1).

Examination of the Mill Iron site tool polishes was made with an Olympus BHM-J microscope and a Zeiss metallurgical microscope at magnifications between 200X and 500X. Microflaking examination was done with a Bausch and Lomb stereoscopic microscope at magnifications of 30X to 60X along with a hand magnifier. Artifact surfaces were cleaned with alcohol to remove finger grease, but pretreatment of the rock surfaces (such as metal coating for electron microscopy) was not deemed necessary.

Conventional microwear analysis (e.g. Keeley 1976; Vaughn 1985) has been oriented toward behavioral reconstruction and largely disregarded surface-modified specimens as unsuitable for analysis. However, we believe this attitude is unsatisfactory from an organizational viewpoint. Surface modification is not just caused by post-depositional disturbances, and as a result relevant pieces of information can often be gleaned from surface alteration phenomena. This is analogous to taphonomic study of faunal remains in that the way in which specimens were modified can give us clues to past organizational data. Analysis of tool surface conditions from this perspective may be classified as "microwear taphonomy," a concept still mostly lacking in present-day tool microwear studies.

Not all Mill Iron stone tool surfaces were altered post-depositional to the site activities. It is most likely that much of the alteration occurred before deposition and thus reflects some organizational characteristics of the past system. There does appear to be a relationship between tool types and tool surface modification—a phenomenon not yet satisfactorily explained. End scrapers and gravers tend generally to be altered, while utilized flakes and retouched flakes demonstrate varying degrees of modification from mint condition to heavily modified. There is a relationship also between raw material types and tool surface condition (Table 5.2). Chert (which includes a variety of non-local materials along with locally occurring Arikara Formation chert, a commonly utilized silicified algae deposit) tends to be more altered than other materials. Silicified wood, which includes high-quality material as well as several low-quality local materials behaves much like chert in this respect. If all surface alteration was post-depositional, all tool types of the same material should exhibit similar degrees of modification, which is not the case.

At the Mill Iron site it appears that characteristics of activity areas were relevant factors in lithic tool surface alteration. In the northern lithic cluster in the main site area (Figure 2.6), heavily patinated pieces are concentrated, which is thought to represent more curated aspects of the technology, while tools with fresh surfaces are found around the more extensive outside activity areas. In the southern lithic cluster area (Figure 2.6), tools with fresh surfaces (end scrapers and scrapers made from "curated blanks," as demonstrated by microwear patterns) aggregate around an area of local material reduction, while heavily surface modified tools tend to scatter more widely in extensive activity areas. This observation suggests that the idea of "microwear taphonomy" needs to be integrated into activity area analysis with a serious consideration of both raw material and tool types.

**Table 5.1.** Polish Types of Siliceous Hard Shale (Tohoku University Classification) (From Akoshima 1993).

| Polish Type | Contrast and Texture | Extension | Other Characteristics | Worked Materials (Less Common Materials) |
|---|---|---|---|---|
| A | Very bright and smooth | Covers wide area rather evenly | "Filled-in" striations, "Comet-shaped" pits; when underdeveloped resembles type B | Non-woody plants (bamboo) |
| B | Bright and smooth, round and "domed" appearance | Well-defined patches develop on high points | Clear striations | Wood, bamboo (bone, non-woody plants) |
| C | Relatively bright but rough | Covers wide area rather evenly with flat patches; patches are ill-defined | With numerous pits of various size/shape, depressions, striation; often surrounds types D1 and D2 | Sawing soaked antler (and bone) |
| D1 | Bright and smooth; very flat and lacks "roundness"; includes "melted snow" type | Flat polish patches are well-defined | Directional undulations often constitute wide striated features | Bone, antler (wood) |
| D2 | Bright but less smooth than D1 | Polish patches are well-defined | Patch surface undulates with numerous parallel, sharp striations | Bone, antler, wood (bamboo) |
| E1 | Dull and relatively rough | Polish patches are small and confined | Numerous tiny pits and very minutely rugged ("rugose"); usually accompanies types E2, F1, F2 | Hide, meat (wood) |
| E2 | Dull and relatively rough, "matte" texture | Patches are less confined and sometimes flat; when developed, patches grow and "roundness" increases | Numerous tiny pits and very minutely rugged ("rugose"); usually accompanies types E1, F1, F2 | Hide, meat |
| F1 | Dull and rough, sometimes "greasy luster" | Patches are not well-defined; polish follows microtopography (on both elevations and depressions) | Coarse "rugged" appearance; type F1 often develops into type D1 on antler/bone | Dry antler, bone, hide, meat, wood |
| F2 | Very dull, weak | Polish follows microtopography | Often accompanies other types | Generic polish, hide, meat (wood, bone) |
| X | Dull, "battered" appearance | Extends widely | Very "rugged"; full of pits, depressions; striations everywhere | Soil (digging, etc.) or any other material in contact with soil |
| Y | Relatively bright but no contrast (even brightness), variable texture | Entire surface is covered | Random striations; various pits | "Patination" polish, polish on naturally worn surface |

**Table 5.2.** Raw Material and Tool Surface Condition.

| Raw Material | Mint | Good | Altered | Heavily modified | Total |
|---|---|---|---|---|---|
| Chert | 1 | 4 | 7 | 14 | 26 |
| Chalcedony | 0 | 4 | 2 | 3 | 9 |
| Silicified Wood | 0 | 6 | 6 | 2 | 14 |
| Porcellanite | 2 | 2 | 1 | 3 | 8 |
| Other | 1 | 0 | 0 | 0 | 0 |
| Total | 4 | 16 | 16 | 22 | 57 |

**Table 5.3.** Tool Type and Number of IUZs (EUs) per Tool.

| Tool Type | No clear IUZs | 1 | 2 | 3 | 4 | 5 | 6 | Total |
|---|---|---|---|---|---|---|---|---|
| Biface | 6 | 4 | 1 | 0 | 0 | 0 | 0 | 11 |
| End scraper | 0 | 1 | 1 | 3 | 2 | 1 | 0 | 8 |
| Scraper/retouched | 8 | 4 | 5 | 3 | 0 | 1 | 1 | 22 |
| Graver | 2 | 0 | 0 | 0 | 0 | 1 | 0 | 3 |
| Utilized flake | 2 | 5 | 2 | 3 | 4 | 0 | 0 | 16 |
| Total | 18 | 14 | 9 | 9 | 6 | 3 | 1 | 60 |

**Table 5.4.** Edge Type and Edge Shape of Mill Iron Site Tools.

| Edge Type | Straight | Convex | Concave | Pointed | Total |
|---|---|---|---|---|---|
| Unprepared | 21 | 8 | 2 | 0 | 31 |
| Microretouch | 5 | 2 | 4 | 0 | 11 |
| Scraper | 12 | 23 | 0 | 0 | 35 |
| Break | 11 | 0 | 2 | 0 | 13 |
| Hinge | 0 | 1 | 0 | 0 | 1 |
| Projection | 0 | 0 | 0 | 7 | 7 |
| Corner | 0 | 0 | 0 | 3 | 3 |
| Notch | 0 | 0 | 3 | 0 | 3 |
| Total | 49 | 34 | 11 | 10 | 104 |

## The Microwear Analyzed Sample from the Mill Iron Site

There are two major clusters of lithic artifacts and debitage in the main Mill Iron site area as is shown in terms of items per square meter (Figure 2.6). However, when only formal tools are plotted, the distribution is somewhat different (Figure 5.1a). The southern cluster is located in the same place as the general cluster, but the northern cluster extends toward the east. The tendency is more evident when the number of re-

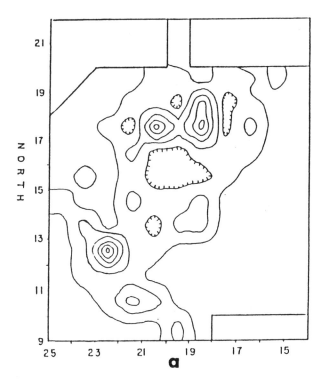
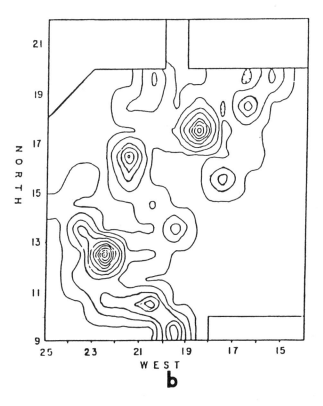

**Figure 5.1.** Tool distribution (a) and distribution of retouched IUZs (or EUs) at the Mill Iron site camp area (b).

Table 5.5. Raw Material and Background Polish Type.

| Raw Material | Background Polish | | | | |
| --- | --- | --- | --- | --- | --- |
| | Fresh | Soil sheen | White patina | Other | Total |
| Chert | 4 | 19 | 0 | 2 | 25 |
| Chalcedony | 2 | 5 | 0 | 2 | 9 |
| Silicified wood | 5 | 9 | 0 | 0 | 14 |
| Porcellanite | 3 | 0 | 5 | 0 | 8 |
| Other | 1 | 0 | 0 | 0 | 1 |
| Total | 15 | 33 | 5 | 4 | 57 |

touched EUs (employable units), which are the morphological working edge units (Knudson 1983), or IUZs (independent use zones) (Vaughn 1985) are used for calculation (Figure 5.1b; see also Table 5.3). There are several "working edge clusters" across a wider area of the site, and only a few of them overlap with debitage clusters. Different types of EUs—projections; corners; notches; straight, convex, or concave edges (Table 5.4)—have different localities of high density. It is difficult to interpret these patterns as such because we lack interpretive frameworks that focus on the organizational characteristics of these aspects of site formation.

A notable feature repeatedly encountered here is what might be called "multiple stage edge/ridge rounding" or "multiple stage surface modification." That is, different degrees of surface/edge abrasion are recognized on single specimens. This phenomenon is considered to reflect complicated use histories, some even prior to the Mill Iron occupational episode, including blank curation and later conversion to formal tools. The phenomenon has not yet been fully recognized in the field of lithic use-wear studies, so the new equivalent term is introduced here. Distinctive multiple-stage abrasion is found on as many as 35% of the total tool assemblage. The ratio varies for different tool classes: 73% for bifaces, 63% for end scrapers, at least 14% for retouched flakes, and 25% for utilized flakes.

The bonebed area yielded only a relatively small number of lithics, the majority of which are whole or fragmentary projectile points. Tools include two conjoined pieces to form a partial biface and several flakes with retouch, some of which is deliberate and some resulting from use. Many smaller flakes were recovered on waterscreens and appear to be the result of projectile points shattering on impact and tool use and resharpening.

Sixty artifacts were analyzed to identify "IUZ" or "independent use zones" (see Vaughn 1985). The proportion of tools that exhibit no single clear IUZ varies among the tool types, which does not necessarily mean that the tools were not used. Rather, it often—if not always—means that the tools were utilized in a way that makes application of the experimental use-wear framework used in the analysis more difficult. Put another way, when a tool was utilized repeatedly and in various complicated tasks as expected in the case of curated tools, the resultant use-wear patterns can be difficult and too complicated to interpret with any acceptable degree of reliability. In addition, more sur-

face alteration phenomena can be expected because of longer tool life.

The sample analyzed accounts for 91% of all the utilized lithic tools recovered in the Mill Iron site excavations as determined by visual examination. Several tools had to be eliminated from the analysis for various reasons beyond the control of the writers (e.g. the raw materials are too coarse, the surface is totally patinated, the edge is coated with some unidentified substance). Projectile points were not analyzed, because we did not believe that the Tohoku University experimental program utilized was designed for this weaponry category.

## Tool Surface Conditions

Tool surface condition is an assessment of the non-cultural modifications of the artifact and is a critical factor to successful microwear analysis. In the case of Mill Iron site artifacts, not all the specimens retain satisfactorily fresh surfaces. Out of the pieces examined (excluding coarse-grained quartzite materials), only 7% retain original, mint-condition surfaces. Twenty-seven percent retain surfaces fresh enough for detailed functional interpretation. Another 27% underwent some degree of surface modification, but still some use-wear traces could be detected. Thirty-eight percent was totally patinated or surface-altered, rendering microwear analysis difficult.

The dominant type of surface alteration is soil sheen (SS) that could easily be identified on 34 specimens. Five specimens were altered by white patination, and four specimens were affected by other miscellaneous types of alteration. Porcellanite is the only material that is covered with white patination, which may be the result of its porous texture (see Table 5.5).

## Functional Interpretation of Tool Classes

In this section, description and interpretation of microwear patterns are provided on a piece-by-piece basis. In this case, the sample is small: only 48 of 60 specimens yielded interpretable IUZs. Illustrations are presented with marginal indications of utilized portions. Some of the illustrations are somewhat schematic to demonstrate portions and motions utilized. The sample used accounts for 91% of all retouched and/or utilized (judged visually) artifacts, except projectile points. Seventy percent of the analyzed artifacts demonstrate use zones with interpretable wear patterns.

Symbols used to demonstrate types of tool use are as follows: D1/D2, bone and/or antler; E1, rawhide; E2, dry hide/leather; B, wood/plant. Post-depositional surface alteration includes BS (bright spots) and SS (soil sheen) (see Table 5.6).

### Bifaces

#### Artifact No. 1308 (Silicified wood, Figure 5.2a)
No retouch or edge resharpening was done after breakage. That is, all flaking scars precede the break. Surface condition is generally good enough to reveal multiple-stage surface modification. Some scar surface is covered with soil sheen, while other areas are fresh, meaning that the soil sheen is not post-depositional. There are weak polish patches along the lateral sides of

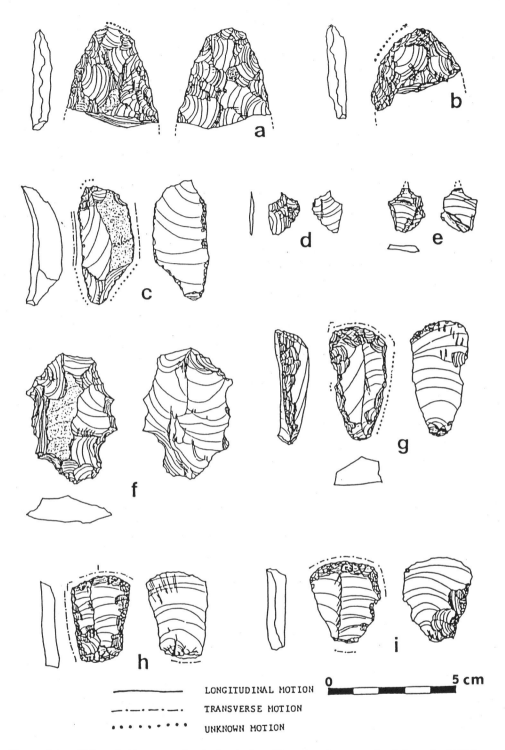

LONGITUDINAL MOTION
TRANSVERSE MOTION
UNKNOWN MOTION

0                    5 cm

**Figure 5.2.** Bifaces (a,b), gravers (c–e), denticulate (f ), and end scrapers (g–i) from the Mill Iron site camp area.

**Table 5.6.** Tool Type and Dominant Polish Type.

| Tool Type | Dominant Polish Type | | | | | | | Other use—polish | Bright spot BS | Soil sheen SS | Total |
|---|---|---|---|---|---|---|---|---|---|---|---|
| | B | D1 | D2 | E1 | E2 | F1 | F2 | | | | |
| Biface | 0 | 2 | 0 | 0 | 1 | 0 | 0 | 1 | 0 | 2 | 6 |
| End Scraper | 0 | 2 | 0 | 2 | 4 | 0 | 0 | 5 | 4 | 8 | 25 |
| Scraper/Retouched flake | 0 | 5 | 1 | 11 | 2 | 3 | 2 | 1 | 6 | 2 | 33 |
| Graver | 0 | 0 | 0 | 0 | 1 | 0 | 0 | 0 | 1 | 2 | 4 |
| Utilized flake | 1 | 8 | 0 | 8 | 3 | 1 | 3 | 3 | 1 | 5 | 33 |
| Total | 1 | 17 | 1 | 21 | 11 | 4 | 5 | 10 | 12 | 19 | 101 |

the biface, but they are sporadic and do not extend to the larger areas of the edges. Rather, it is the pointed end of the biface that retains intense use-wear traces. On both aspects of the pointed edge, combination of flat type polish (D1) and numerous obliquely oriented striations are found. It is not clear whether the biface was put to use mainly on the pointed end, or the end received less edge rejuvenation compared to lateral edges. The latter case is most likely, considering the fact that there are differences in patination of individual retouch scars.

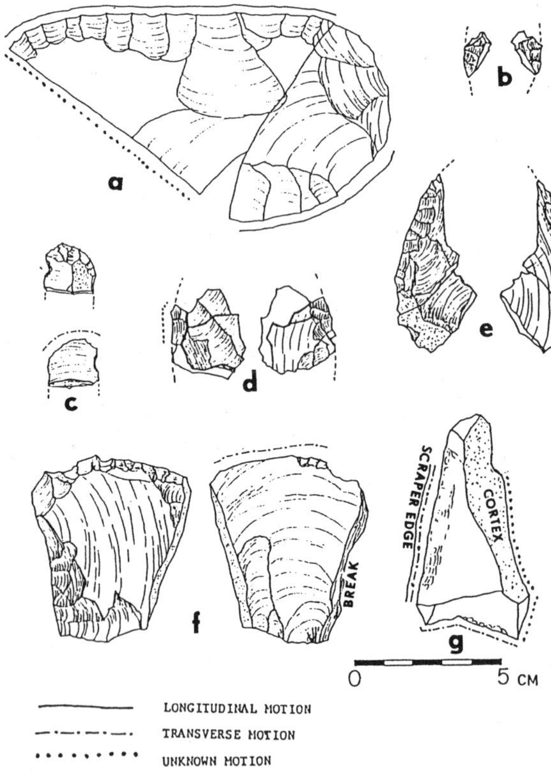

**Figure 5.3.** Biface (a) from the bison bonebed and retouched flakes (b, d–g) and an end scraper (c) from the Mill Iron site camp area.

and that numerous striations are found on ridges in the central interior portions of both aspects of the biface.

### Artifact No. 1288 (Silicified wood, Figure 5.2b)
The intensity of surface modification varies among retouch scars. Various types of polish patches are seen, and striations run in various directions along an edge. The implement was utilized, but the method of use cannot be reconstructed within our experimental framework. It is suspected that the biface retains traces from many use episodes, which were further compounded by some rejuvenation.

### Artifact No. 1589 and 1606 (Arikara chert, Figure 5.3a)
This large biface (128 X 62 X 7 mm) was broken into two pieces that were recovered 2.5 m apart in the bonebed. Its entire surface is covered with strong soil sheen, and use-wear polishes are detectable only when they are very intense. Many parts of flake scar ridges are rounded, but the degree of rounding varies, suggesting that the rounding is not the result of post-depositional effects. In fact, some marginally retouched scars (i.e., those flaked latest) retain fresh ridges. The varied rounding and altered surface seem to represent a history of use trajectory. Therefore, it cannot be assumed that all of the reconstructed activities were conducted at this spot.

A long lateral edge (131 mm) exhibits a clear wear pattern movement parallel to the edge. Striations run dominantly in this direction on both aspects, sometimes extending several millimeters into the interior on scar ridges. The same pattern of parallel striations is also seen along the other lateral edge, although the majority of the edge has been lost because of breakage. The broken edges demonstrate sharp contrast in terms of degree of rounding. One side of the triangle is unusually heavily rounded, and it almost constitutes a narrow "attrition facet" on the aspect shown in the sketch (Figure 5.3a). Patches of E2 type polish, that suggest work on dry hide/leather, are found on the abraded facet. Striations are also extremely numerous there, but they run in multiple directions. Various types of microflaking scatter irregularly. The same broken edge, but on the opposite face, demonstrates less rounding. The other broken but refitted edges are fresh. There, neither face of two pieces demonstrates rounding since there are no clear patterned striations on the refitted broken edges. In sum, the biface had probably been brought to the Mill Iron site after some extended use history. Its lateral sides were used mainly in longitudinal motions, and a broken end was utilized in mixed motions, possibly on hide. It was then broken and discarded without further use.

### Artifact No. 913 (Chert or chalcedony, Figure 5.3b)

All the surface of this small biface fragment is covered with soil sheen. Even broken edges are surface modified. There is no difference in strength of soil sheen between the bifacial edge and three broken sides, indicating that surface patination occurred after it was broken and discarded. No use-wear interpretation is possible on this specimen.

### Artifact No. 381 and 923 and 893 (Silicified wood, Figure 5.3d)

Three refitted flakes are part of a biface shattered by heat. However, the restored portion retains a 13 mm section of an edge of the tool. The edge retains some traces of use that consist of flat and bright polish patches (D1 type) with multiple striations mostly perpendicular to the edge. Moderate edge rounding is also present.

Multiple-stage surface modifications are notable on this specimen that are both pre-depositional and post-depositional. For the former case, some later (younger) flake scars exhibit less surface alteration. For the latter case, the ventral aspect of the tool, which cannot be older than other bifacial flake scars, exhibits much more intense surface modification. Only one face of the tool fragment was altered heavily after it was detached by heat shattering.

### Artifact No. 16 and 17 (Chert, Figure 5.3e)

A large irregular fracture that seems to be one of the latest flaking attempts was probably the cause leading to discard. The flaked lateral edge of the biface exhibits no rounding. Some degree of white patination can be detected under the microscope around the entire periphery of the tool. Sporadic weak patches of indeterminate polish are seen along the bifacial edge and scar ridges on both aspects. The weak polish is not found on the broken edge, so it is probable that these are traces of a previous use episode before the failed thinning attempts. No clear pattern of striations is found. The specimen was not, however, intensively utilized since the polish is only very weak.

## Gravers

### Artifact No. 1279 (Chert, Figure 5.2c)

Whether or not this should be classified as a graver is equivocal since a unilateral retouch forms a sharp corner. Microwear traces are found along the entire periphery of the implement. Multiple-stage rounding is noted on this tool: both lateral edges and dorsal ridges are very heavily rounded, while rounding around the graver projection, including the tip itself, is light and only moderate. Both lateral edges exhibit traces of use including but not limited to transverse motion that produced perpendicular striations. There, microflaking scars distribute bifacially, and polish patches are of various types (E2, F1, BS, and SS). The *least* utilized portion was on and around the graver tip. The tip edge is not only less rounded, but the

polish is also less intense. A probable interpretation of the implement is that it was converted into a graver after a substantial amount of former utilization. Judging from heavy rounding, the tool (or blade blank) had another use life before the Mill Iron site episode of use.

### Artifact No. 1305 (Chert, Figure 5.2d)

The surface is shiny under magnification due to raw material quality plus some soil sheen. All the periphery is very sharp, and no rounding is recognized. Clear striations or polish patches are not found. The graver tip is fresh. The implement was not used.

### Artifact No. 229 (Silicified wood, Figure 5.2e)

This is a double graver, but one of the graver tips is missing. The surface is covered with some soil sheen, and the entire periphery is affected by white patination. No clear striations or strong polish are found even on the graver projection, which should have been detectable if present. The implement was deliberately shaped but apparently not used.

## Denticulate

### Artifact No. 49 (Quartzite, Figure 5.2f)

The denticulate is oval-shaped. Its entire periphery is a continuous serrated working edge. It is unfortunate that the raw material is coarse-grained quartzite, a material not accommodated in our experimental program.

## End Scrapers

### Artifact No. 1319 (Chert, Figure 5.2g)

The surface is shiny even to the eye. All the surface is polished, and it is a good example of heavy soil sheen. However, there are areas where intensity and type of polish is very distinctive and different from the background, making some functional interpretation possible along with additional information from edge rounding and microflaking. It is regrettable that inference of the worked material is impossible due to the intense surface modification.

The ventral side of the end scraper edge shows very heavy edge rounding. The area is also distinctly covered with a strong polish, which is bright but of rough texture. The polish type is not that of BS, which often occurs on surface-modified specimens. Heavy edge rounding is seen along the right lateral edge. This area is also strongly polished. The main polish type is typical BS there. The left lateral edge with a notch exhibits moderate edge rounding. Strong polish is found here also, again including BS type. Heavy rounding is seen on sharp corners of both sides of the scraper edge. The implement was an intensely utilized scraper. The scraper edge and both lateral edges were utilized in scraping tasks.

### Artifact No. 285 (Chert, Figure 5.2h)

The scraper edge was utilized in a scraping motion, probably on dry hide. Polish observed is E2 type overlying soil sheen. Striations run perpendicular to the edge, which is moderately rounded. However, about one-third of the scraper edge toward the left side underwent resharpening since polish there is weaker and rounding is minimal. The ventral aspect of the proximal end also shows signs of the same usage. Lateral edges are relatively fresh, although the left lateral edge exhibits some traces of transverse motions.

Multiple-stage ridge rounding is observed. The dorsal spine ridge and the platform edge of the flake blank are very heavily rounded, while ridges between secondary retouch scars on the scraper edge and on the lateral edges show virtually no rounding. In addition, the surfaces inside the retouch scars are usually fresher than on the ventral face of the tool. On the ventral surface, bright spots—BS—are also found on corners. A most probable interpretation of this phenomenon is that the implement was retained in the system for a considerable duration of time prior to retouch and use as a dry hide scraper.

### Artifact No. 84 (Chert, Figure 5.2i)

Three use zones are identified: the scraper edge, the distal half of the right lateral edge, and the dorsal face of the proximal end. Polishes consist of extended rough matt type—E2—surrounded by F1. Perpendicular striations accompany the polish, and the edges are moderately rounded. This microwear combination is a typical dry hide scraping pattern. The right half of the scraper edge is less rounded and the polish changes to the lighter E1 type, probably reflecting the edge resharpening. The edge is also recessed to a straight line. There is a notch in the middle of the right lateral edge, but neither clear polish (except soil sheen) nor rounding is found around the notch. Possibly this portion of the tool was not utilized. The left lateral edge exhibits some traces of transverse motions. The left lateral edge is retouched but no distinctive polish is present.

### Artifact No. 1293 (Chert, Figure 5.4a)

Two straight end scraper edges converge to form a sharp corner. Use-wear traces are found on both edges and on the corner. Patterned striations running perpendicular to the edge are clear on both edges. Polish is difficult to identify because of the surface alteration by soil sheen which covers the entire specimen. The tool was also burned and potlid fractures are present on both the dorsal and ventral surfaces. However, a narrow band of E1 type use-wear exists along the right scraper edge. Edge rounding is minimal. Other sides including the lateral edges and broken proximal end exhibit no use-wear traces. The functional inference for this implement is scraping wet hide.

### Artifact No. 1307 (Chert, Figure 5.4b)

Multiple-stage ridge rounding is again attested by a stark contrast between the dorsal spine ridge and retouch scar ridges. Rounding of the dorsal ridge is very heavy. Both lateral edges are partially retouched, and there are differences in the degrees of edge rounding there, indicating that all of the retouch or micro-retouch was not applied at one time but was instead the result of sequential episodes. Ridges on the scraper edge are relatively fresh and show little rounding.

As to the function of the tool, the scraper edge and lateral edges exhibit traces of use. The surface is covered with rather strong soil sheen, and use polish is not detectable. However, the scraper edge retains a particular micro-topographic feature that indicates scraping motion. It is a continuous step-like structure of micro-depression and elevation, that is a diffused variation of a "comet-shaped" depression (Keeley 1980). The scraper edge itself is moderately rounded. The left lateral edge was used in transverse motion as is confirmed by striations that are both oblique and perpendicular to the edge. The lateral edge rounding is heavy, but it is abruptly terminated by the end scraper working edge retouch, indicating that the lateral rounding preceded manufacture of the end scraper edge. The tool is broken, and its proximal half is missing. The broken end is sharp and not rounded. No use-wear traces are found there.

To summarize the above observations, the use trajectory of this specimen is reconstructed as follows. 1) The tool was made and used to the extent that ridges were abraded and probably the lateral sides were used at the same time; 2) it was converted into an end scraper and was in fact utilized in scraping; 3) a break occurred; and it was left at the Mill Iron site without further salvage attempts or use on the break. It could also have been broken post-depositionally.

### Artifact No. 1315 (Chert, Figure 5.4c)

This composite tool is an end scraper with a notch on the right lateral side. A second notch at the right corner of the end scraper edge was deepened slightly as the result of damage during excavation. The tool does demonstrate multiple-stage edge rounding. The dorsal spine ridge and both lateral edges are well rounded, but the retouched end scraper edge demonstrates no attrition. The recently damaged part of the right corner shows no wear pattern or surface alteration as would be expected. Surface condition is fresher inside retouch scars relative to the ventral face of the tool. Used portions include the scraper edge, the notches, and the right lateral edge. Perpendicular to oblique striations are found on the edges as well as microflaking scars, but the type of use cannot be determined.

## Atypical End Scraper

### Artifact No. 1597 (Chert, Figure 5.4d)

The entire surface of this tool is heavily affected by soil sheen. However, some portions of edges demonstrate use-wear traces such as rounding and striations, indicating that this composite scraper tool was actually put to use. A part of the ventral aspect of the right lateral edge is covered with well-developed flat polish and accompanying striations that run perpendicular to the edge, which is also rounded. This portion was probably used in transverse motion. The small end scraper edge at the distal end of the flake is rounded with stronger polish bands and striations running perpendicular to the edge, leaving little doubt that this portion was used in scraping. On the proximal broken end, relatively heavy edge rounding is found. The left lateral edge has an area of BS polish on the ventral aspect. In sum, the specimen was intensely used on all of its peripheral edges including the lateral one and the broken edge. A deliberate or accidental burin spall was removed from the broken end, but there is no typical burin use identified suggesting that the removal could have been accidental.

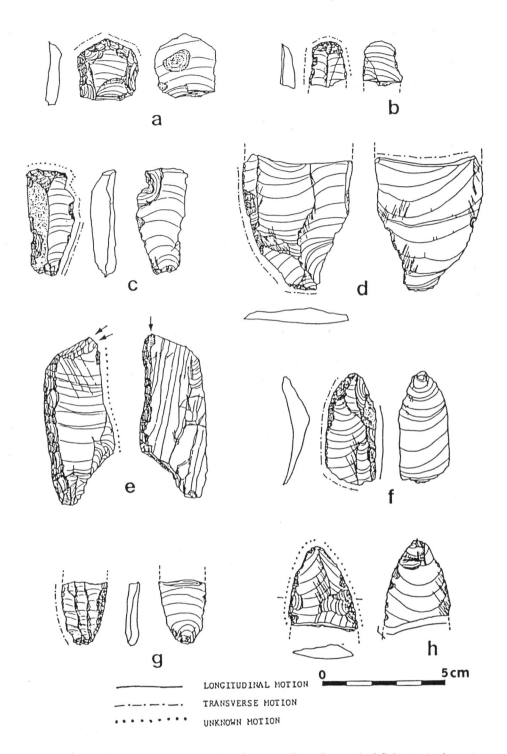

**Figure 5.4.** End scrapers (a–c), atypical end scraper (d), and retouched flakes (e–h) from the Mill Iron site camp area.

### Artifact No. 1313 (Chert, Figure 5.3c)

The scraper edge demonstrates microwear patterns of an actual scraping task. The edge is not rounded, but some striations run perpendicularly to the edge. A very narrow band of strong polish patches of E1 type is located on the very edge. The patches are seen on both projections and concavites of the edge line, suggesting soft worked materials. The pattern is interpreted to be the result of scraping rawhide in a relatively clean condition. Lateral edges are moderately rounded—much more so than the working end scraper edge—and patches of bright spots (BS) are identified. The broken proximal end, however, exhibits no wear traces. It is sharp and neither polish nor striations can be observed there. The implement is another example that demonstrates multiple-stage rounding.

### Retouched Flakes/Scrapers

### Artifact No. 1591 (Silicified wood, Figure 5.4e)

This tool was made from a flat piece of petrified wood formed by separation along annual growth rings and has an alternate beveled edge retouch. Most of the surface of this double side scraper is shiny under magnification due to surface alteration, and the implement is not suitable for microwear analysis. No distinctive use-wear polish can be detected on either scraper edge. Moderate edge rounding is seen along an edge. Possible burin facets on one end were carefully studied, but no clear microwear evidence of this kind of use was found.

### Artifact No. 282 (Chert, Figure 5.4f)

The surface is altered and covered with soil sheen. However, multiple-stage rounding can still be observed. The proximal portion of the dorsally retouched left lateral edge shows no rounding at all, while the continuous distal half of the same edge is moderately rounded. Both lateral edges and the distal right lateral edge were probably used longitudinally, and the left lateral and distal edges were used transversely as demonstrated by striations. Some of the observed polish patches may be natural and post-depositional since they include bright spots, and the surfaces *inside* the retouch scars are similarly altered with soil sheen.

### Artifact No. 32 (Chert, Figure 5.4g)

The entire surface is shiny under magnification due to surface patination. All the edges are also moderately rounded, including the broken distal end. Striations and microflaking are found on a lateral edge, while the opposite edge is backed. Striations are perpendicular and microchipping is continuous unifacially, indicating transverse motion.

### Artifact No. 43 (Porcellanite, Figure 5.4h)

The surface condition of this side scraper/backed knife is exceptionally good, and detailed functional reconstruction was possible. Dorsal ridges are somewhat abraded and polished (E1-F2 type interpreted as "prehension wear"). The right lateral side is the only rounded edge observed on the implement. Striations and microflaking are few at that location, but clear polish patches (E1-F2) are seen, suggesting soft worked materials such as rawhide/meat. The other lateral edge exhibits

oblique striations and polish (D2-F1) suggestive of bone/antler contact. The distal edge on the broken end demonstrates evidence of use after breakage in a longitudinal motion. Polish patches (D1-F1) are seen as narrow bands along the very edge, accompanying striation patterns parallel to the edge. Microflaking scars are of both scalar and stepped varieties. Traces of bone/antler contact are also strongly indicated at the right distal corner where striations run parallel to the edge with polish patches (D1-F1) indicating possible incising motion.

### Artifact No. 1580 (Porcellanite, Figure 5.5a)

The surface of the single side scraper is patinated and not ideal for microwear analysis. However, sporadic patches of weak polish of indeterminate type are visible along both lateral edges. They somewhat resemble the E1 type, as is found on another porcellanite artifact (Figure 5.5d). Slight edge rounding is also seen along both edges on the ventral side. Neither worked materials nor motion can be determined due to surface conditions and coarseness of the raw material.

### Artifact No. 1306 (Chert, Figure 5.5b)

All the peripheral edges except a distal break are covered with continuous micro-retouch. However, the surface is heavily patinated and not suitable for microwear analysis.

### Artifact No. 1304 (Silicified wood, Figure 5.5c)

This tool is part of a broken biface and was used for scraping. The scraper edge was produced with thinly flaked removals using the ventral face as a platform. Partial striations, both perpendicular and oblique, at that location suggest transverse motion employing the corners as well as the edge. The right broken edge also exhibits traces of some use subsequent to the break in the form of dry-hide-type polish and various striations. Both edges are moderately rounded.

### Artifact No. 1609 (Porcellanite, Figure 5.5d)

The lithic material is relatively coarse-grained, but the surface condition of this scraper recovered in the bonebed is exceptionally good. Weak polish appears along the scraper edge and the broken end. The polish is restricted to the very edge only as a narrow band and does not extend to the interior area. The polish is seen on both ventral and dorsal aspects. The polish is of E1 type, which is brighter and smoother, but develops as tiny patches. It is experimentally related mainly to rawhide processing. Slight edge rounding is found along the scraper edge. The implement was probably used in scraping rawhide. Both the scraper edge and a steep broken edge were utilized.

### Artifact No. 50 (Silicified wood, Figure 5.3f)

Multiple-stage surface modification and multiple-stage edge rounding are both observed on this large atypical end scraper. The ventral face is fresh, as opposed to the dorsal aspect, which is heavily affected by soil sheen. Part of the scraper edge retains traces from scraping activity in the form of a band of polish, rounding, and perpendicular striations. The other part of the scraping edge demonstrates evidence of resharpening since the portion toward the left side of the scraping edge exhibits no rounding or clear striations. It is known from the flake scar se-

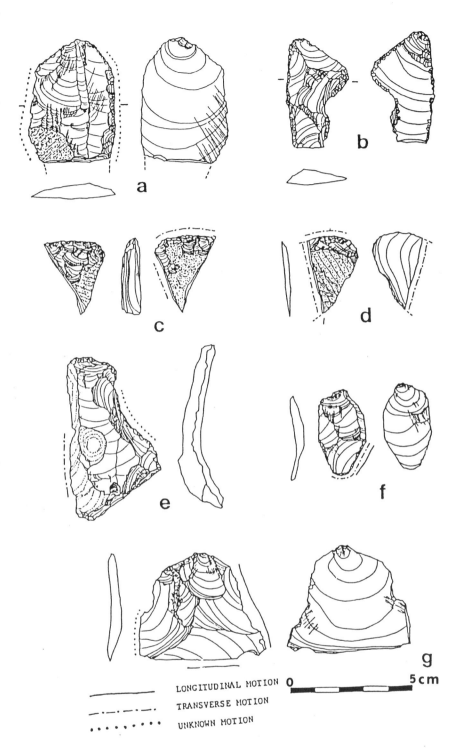

**Figure 5.5.** Retouched flakes (a–e), and a raclette-like tool (f) from the camp area and a retouched flake (g) from the bison bonebed at the Mill Iron site.

quences that retouches on both the end scraper edge and on the left lateral edge were done after the lateral break. It is not known what materials were worked with this tool.

### Artifact No. 1291 (Chert, Figure 5.3g)

This large side scraper (70 mm long) is made of the same pink chert raw material as another end scraper (Figure 5.4c). It is interesting that the same phenomenon of multiple-stage edge rounding is also found on this specimen. The contrast is very sharp between the un-retouched portion and retouched portion of edges. The left lateral edge that constitutes the side scraper edge exhibits virtually no rounding. On the other hand, the distal end, covered with larger microflaking or micro-retouch, and the right lateral edge are both heavily rounded. The notch is actually the result of excavation damage and, as would be expected, demonstrates no rounding or evidence of use. Conditions of dorsal ridges contrast sharply; dorsal spine ridges are heavily rounded as opposed to ridges between retouch scars, which are fresh.

The entire surface is affected by numerous bright-spot polishes and heavy soil sheen and, because of that, use-wear polish is not readily detectible. Microflaking scars are numerous along the entire periphery. Perpendicularly directed striations are found on the distal edge. The implement apparently had a relatively long use-life before it was converted into a side scraper.

### Artifact No. 1292 (Porcellanite, Figure 5.6a)

The surface of this double scraper is fresh and very suitable for microwear observation. The distal scraper edge was produced on a hinge fracture, but no clear microwear was found on the hinge. Possible utilized portions are the other right lateral scraper edge and the left half of the proximal break that was utilized after the bulbar part was gone. Polish is very weak on both edges (E1-F2 type), and striations are not distinctive. The use of the specimen, if any, was not intensive.

### Artifact No. 1592 (Porcellanite, Figure 5.6b)

The surface condition of this double side scraper is satisfactory to identify weak polish patches. Dorsal scar ridges are rounded, but the ventral surface is fresh. Scraper edges are not rounded. Polish patches of indeterminate types scatter along two convergent scraper edges. They are relatively strong at the pointed part at the juncture of the two edges. Microflaking scars are also seen there, but no clear patterned striations are found. Method of use and worked materials are unknown.

### Artifact No. 1301 (Arikara chert, Figure 5.6c)

All four sides are unifacially retouched to form the small, rectangular-shaped scraper. All four edges demonstrate little rounding and are still sharp. Only one lateral side exhibits patterned striations perpendicular to the edge.

### Artifact No. 1318 (Chert, Figure 5.6d)

This is the edge of a tool removed in the form of a burin spall, which appears to have been deliberate in order to rejuvenate a tool. The scraper edge retains use-wear traces in the form of polishes of E1, D1, F1, and F2 types along with partial longitudinal striations and edge rounding on all except the notched

portion, which is unused. The proximal part of the other lateral side also exhibits some use-wear in the form of D1-F1 polish patches and mostly scalar-shaped continuous microflaking. The implement was made of the same pink chert as Figures 5.3g and 5.4c, but the multiple-stage rounding is not identified on this piece.

### Artifact No. 353 (Chert, Figure 5.6e)

This small, thin piece appears to be an edge rejuvenation flake. A portion of a previous scraper edge was detached with this resharpening flake. However, no clear use-wear traces are found on the scraper edge. Surface condition is good.

### Artifact No. 1297 (Chert, Figure 5.6f)

This mid-section of double side scraper of chert was broken as a result of intense heat on one end, and the opposite break edge demonstrates a microwear pattern from transverse motion. Perpendicular striations are dominant on its dorsal intersection, and both scalar and stepped microflaking scars are unifacially continuous from the dorsal face to the break. Striations in several directions indicate the right lateral edge was also put to use. Both edges are moderately rounded and patches of use polish (D1 and E1) are observed. This is probably part of the same tool as Figure 5.6g.

### Artifact No. 1295 and 1298 (Chert, Figure 5.6g)

This tool was burned. Some polish and rounding are observed but are sporadic. No clear IUZ is identified, and it is of the identical material as Figure 5.6f, but the pieces do not refit.

## Utilized Flakes

### Artifact No. 1280 (Chert, Figure 5.5e)

This tool was burned and demonstrates numerous potlid fractures, several of which were recovered and refit. Some polish patches and bands are identified as they differ from the background burned surface. The distal half of the left lateral edge displays a scraping pattern of microflaking in the form of thin and larger sporadic scars on the ventral surface and deep scalar scars plus some continuous stepped scars on the dorsal surface. Striations are perpendicular, and the observed polish band is E2 type. This portion of the tool was probably used in hide scraping. The right lateral edge is concave and covered with micro-retouch. Some patches of B type polish are found here, which is the sole example of "wood/plant variety" identified among the whole Mill Iron site assemblage that has presently been analyzed.

The implement is made of pink chert, the same material as Figure 5.4c (an end scraper) and Figure 5.3g (a side scraper), and the pattern of multiple-stage edge/ridge rounding is again recognized. All the peripheral edges are heavily rounded, but some ridges between retouch scars are relatively fresh.

It is conventionally understood that the category "utilized flakes" represents a typical part of expedient technologies. However, in the case of the Mill Iron site assemblage, it is suspected that some blanks (flakes and blades) were saved and transported, sometimes being retouched later into other classes of tools, and this specimen is one such example. Accordingly, it cannot be assumed *a priori* that the detected tasks such as hide scraping or wood working were in fact carried out at the Mill Iron site simply because this kind of use-wear is found on "utilized flakes."

### Artifact No. 1294 (Silicified wood, Figure 5.5f)

Both faces are covered with soil sheen, but possible use-wear traces are extant on the convex distal end and distal half of the right lateral edge. Scalar microflaking scars occur dorsally on the distal end. Striations are perpendicular as well, suggesting transverse motion here. On the lateral portion, striations of both longitudinal and transverse directions accompany E1 type polish. Microflaking is continuous through two edges. Both edges are moderately rounded, probably from use, because the other lateral edge remains sharp and not rounded.

### Artifact No. 1584 (Porcellanite, Figure 5.5g)

The surface condition of this thin flake recovered in the bonebed is very good and almost ideal for microwear detection. Along the right lateral edge, microflaking scars appear irregularly. They distribute on both ventral and dorsal aspects, indicating cutting morions. Weak polish patches are found on both aspects along the edge, but they are confined to the extreme edge and do not extend to the interior area. The polish is dull, and it is a combination of E1 and F2 type, that is, a combination of tiny smooth, brighter patches and generic weak polish. This polish type experimentally relates mainly to hide and meat working. No edge rounding is recognized there. Along the distal and left lateral edges, the same use-wear pattern is seen. The flake was probably used in cutting rawhide/meat. The main working edge was right lateral, but other edges were also used. However, there is no positive evidence of bone contact on the specimen.

### Artifact No. 127 (Silicified wood, Figure 5.7a)

Surface condition is good. Use-wear traces are found on a nibbled edge and on a broken end. A graver-like projection that terminates with a straight edge rather than a point has use-wear traces on the straight edge. On the ventral side of a lateral edge, there are polished areas extending up to several millimeters into the interior. The polished band is of atypical E2 type, that is, bright but with rough texture and also pitted. Keeley (1980) and Vaughn (1985) would call this "matt texture." The polish is not limited to higher portions of the microtopography. This type of polish resembles those experimentally produced on very gritty hide. There are also small patches of D1 type polish. Edge rounding is seen on both ventral and dorsal aspects of the graver-like edge. Microflaking scars of various shapes distribute irregularly on both aspects. On the ventral side of the graver-like edge, there are bright polish patches of indeterminate type.

Along the broken end, striations run oblique to the edge on the ventral side. They accompany an indeterminate-type polish and irregular microflaking scars, but little edge rounding is observed here. On the dorsal side, there are sporadic polish patches of flat (D1) type polish suggesting work on bone/antler.

The tool was utilized on three edges. Worked materials probably included hide and bone, but it was used under dirty conditions and with various motions.

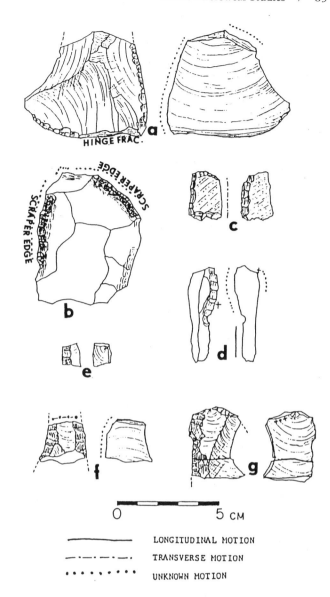

**Figure 5.6.** Retouched flakes (a–c, e–g) and a burin-like, tool-sharpening spall (d) from the Mill Iron site camp area.

### Artifact No. 1278 (Silicified wood, Figure 5.7b)

This piece is marginally nibbled or broken for almost its entire periphery. It has four IUZs. Striations run perpendicular to oblique. The polish includes evident D1 type, indicating probable contact with bone/antler. All edges are moderately rounded.

### Artifact No. 1272 (Silicified wood, Figure 5.7c)

Surface condition is relatively good, but slight soil sheen alteration occurs locally. Along the distal edge where bifacial microflaking scars are seen, there are bands and patches of polish on both aspects. Among them is a distinctive brighter type extending across the ventral surface. This polish type did not occur in our experimental framework, and the worked materi-

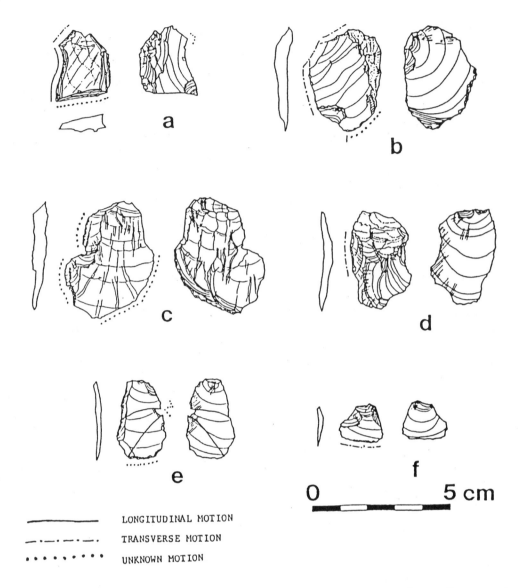

LONGITUDINAL MOTION

TRANSVERSE MOTION

UNKNOWN MOTION

0                    5 cm

**Figure 5.7.** Atypical burin (a), and retouched flakes from the camp site area (b, c, e, f); retouched flake (d) from the bison bonebed at the Mill Iron site.

als are undetermined. However, toward the lateral side of the same edge, probable F1 plus D1 bone/antler type polish clearly appears. Microflaking scars of various types are found almost continuously along the distal edge as well as light edge rounding. The strong undetermined type polish is also found on the other lateral edge at the ventral face together with D1-F1 polish, which is the same combination pattern as on the other edge. The flake was used mainly on the distal and right lateral edges. The left lateral edge was also utilized but with less intensity. Worked materials are not certain, but probably included bone. The motion of use is unknown.

### Artifact No. 1608 (Chert, Figure 5.7d)
A lateral edge is covered with unifacial micro-retouch that is predominantly scalar on the dorsal aspect, but the edge is not rounded. Surface condition is good. Sporadic weak polish with brighter patches appears along the ventral aspect. Flat patches of D1 type are surrounded by wider areas of "greasy" type (F1), which is a typical bone/antler contact pattern. The same combination of polishes is also found on the dorsal fringe of micro-retouch scars. Natural bright spots (BS) make sporadic appearances on various parts of both faces of the tool. The flake was used on the micro-retouched edge. It was used mainly in a scraping motion plus some other complex movements. The worked materials probably include bone.

### Artifact No. 851 and 286 (Porcellanite, Figure 5.7e)
The lithic material is coarse-grained and the surface is somewhat patinated. The flake was broken into two pieces recovered 3.7 m apart. A lateral edge of the original flake shows some microflaking, but neither polish nor striation is found there. After the flake was broken, its central portion received a light retouch, and a notch was produced. The notch was carefully examined, but only faint patches of indeterminate weak polish were found. The notch is not rounded or striated and its use was minimal. However, a broken corner of the proximal portion exhibits polish patches of E1-F2 type, suggesting contacts with a meaty substance. The distal end of the flake has continuous unifacial microflaking of scalar type plus indeterminate weak polish, but it cannot be determined whether or not the use of the distal end was before or after its breakage.

### Artifact No. 260 (Porcellanite, Figure 5.7f)
The lithic raw material is coarse-grained, and the surface is patinated. The specimen is not suitable for polish observation. However, the distal edge exhibits continuous but unifacial microflaking of a scalar type. Perpendicular striations and moderate edge rounding are also found there. This small thin flake of bifacial reduction was used with a whittling/scraping motion on its distal end.

### Artifact No. 38 (Chert, Figure 5.8a)
Four steep edges were put to use probably in scraping. Three of them are edges formed by breaks. All directional indicators display transverse patterns perpendicular to oblique stria, scraping patterns of microflaking, rounding, and polish bevels. The worked materials are not known. The polish includes the

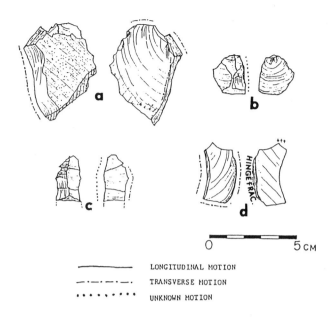

LONGITUDINAL MOTION
TRANSVERSE MOTION
UNKNOWN MOTION

**Figure 5.8.** Retouched flakes from the camp site area at the Mill Iron site.

dry hide type (E2), but the microflaking suggests harder worked materials.

### Artifact No. 1314 (Chert, Figure 5.8b)
It appears that this flake was detached from a biface that was used as a core. It is very thin (3 mm) and the dorsal scar pattern demonstrates radial directions of force that are known to occur on a biface. The right lateral edge has unifacially continuous microflaking scars. The worked material or motion is unknown. The surface is altered by soil sheen. Bright spots are also found, but the edges are not rounded.

### Artifact No. 1277 and 281 and 1276 (Chert, Figure 5.8c)
The blade was broken into three pieces recovered in separate locations. Both lateral edges exhibit some microflaking scars. The worked material is unknown since the surface is heavily altered by soil sheen. What is informative on the specimen is its multiple-stage edge/ridge rounding. Both lateral sides and the dorsal spine ridge are rounded especially the right lateral edge, but the edge on the distal breakage is not rounded indicating that it was not used after breakage and that there is probably more of the tool still present at some location in the site.

### Artifact No. 277 (Porcellanite, Figure 5.8d)
The flake is hinge fractured. Three steep edges exhibit perpendicular striations indicative of transverse use as indicated in the figure. Edges on breaks are moderately rounded. The dominant polish is type E1 for all edges. Polish patches are numerous on the intersection between the hinge-fractured end and the dorsal face. The most likely worked material was fresh hide.

## Conclusions

One hundred and four independent use zones (IUZs) were identified on 42 of the Mill Iron tools examined. More edges exhibit microwear traces, but only those that are interpretable within the Tohoku University experimental framework are considered here. The breakdown of edge types by morphology (straight, convex, concave, pointed) is shown in Table 5.2.

Most numerous are scraper edges (35), two-thirds of which are convex. Twenty-seven of these are unifacially retouched. Next most numerous are unprepared sharp edges (31) with no preparation retouch and recognizable only by microwear analysis. The majority (21) are straight edges and 13 of these are the result either of breaks or deliberate snaps. This is a category usually overlooked in use-wear studies. Eleven cases demonstrate micro-retouched edges that consist of continuous tiny flaking scars that are usually smaller than one or two millimeters in size and can be the result of deliberate retouch or heavy use-wear. Nine of the 11 are micro-retouched unifacially.

Edge angles have conventionally been thought to be indicative of functional diversity (Wilmsen 1970, 1974), but there is another view that this is too simplistic (see Yerkes 1987). Mill Iron site edge angles separate into a trimodal distribution which is classified as follows: 1) sharp, less than 35 degrees; 2) moderate, 35–70 degrees; and 3) thick, steeper than 70 degrees. This includes all edge angles and not just retouched edges.

Thirty-one edges out of 101 exhibit surface modification polishes. Polish variety is suggestive of the worked material, although the correlation is not always exact. Polish usually appears in combinations. The E1 variety in combination with another is the most numerous (E1-F2, E1-E2, E1-SS, etc.) with 21 occurrences, suggesting use on rawhide and/or meat. There are 18 cases of the bone/antler variety (D1 and D2). Eleven edges are interpreted as having been used on dry hide/leather

(E2 variety). Only one case bears polish suggestive of use on wood/plant (B type). Nine cases have indeterminate polishes (F1 and F2 varieties). Ten edges exhibit polishes that did not occur in any of our experimental results.

Motion is inferred mainly by the direction of striations and the disposition and type of microchipping. Transverse motion is dominant in the Mill Iron sample. Forty-eight edges are considered to have been moved largely transversely to the edge in scraping and/or whittling tasks. Only nine cases are considered to have longitudinal motions. Four edges show signs of mixed motions and the direction of movement could not be determined for edges.

There is no clear relationship between striation patterns and degrees of edge rounding, except the tendency that edges that are not rounded do not accompany patterned striations. There is, however, a correlation between rounding and microchipping Bifacially scarred edges tend to be more heavily rounded than unifacially scarred edges. Edges with both scalar and stepped scars tend to be more heavily rounded than edges with dominantly scalar scars.

It is readily noticeable that almost all tool usage suggested by microwear studies of the Mill Iron assemblage indicates a relation to faunal exploitation. This is no surprise considering the nature of the site. However, the main site area cannot be interpreted as the main activity area where the faunal assemblage (the bison) was butchered and/or processed since the faunal remains in the main site area represent only a small portion of the number of animals found in the bonebed. Erosion in the Mill Iron site area has undoubtedly left only a small part of the total site so that originally there were probably more extensive activity areas than the one investigated, assuming that all the animals recovered in the bonebed were butchered and processed at the site. Possibly also, there are activity areas still intact in the unexcavated area of the butte, and some of these could reflect more intense activity than the area investigated.

## References Cited

Akoshima, Kaoru
1993    *Microwear Patterns and Distributional Variability in Terminal Palaeolithic Site Structure.* Unpublished Ph.D. dissertation, Department of Anthropology, University of New Mexico, Albuquerque.

Keeley, Lawrence H.
1976    Microwear on Flint: Some experimental Results. In *Second International Symposium on Flint*, edited by F. Engelen, pp. 49–51. Nederlandse Geologische Vereniging, Maastricht.

1977    The Functions of Paleolithic Flint Tools. *Scientific American* 237(5):108–126.

1978    Preliminary Microwear Analysis of the Meer Assemblage. In *Les Chasses de Meer*, edited by F. Van Noten, pp. 73–86. Dessertationes Archaeologicae Gandenses 18. De Tempel, Brugge.

1980    *Experimental Determination of Stone Tool Uses: A Microwear Analysis.* University of Chicago Press, Chicago.

Knudson, Ruthann
1983    *Organizational Variability in Late Paleo-Indian Assemblages.* Washington State University Laboratory of Anthropology Reports of Investigations No. 60.

Vaughn, P.
1985    *Use-Wear Analysis of Flaked Stone Tools.* University of Arizona Press, Tucson AZ.

Wilmsen, Edwin N.
1970    *Lithic Analysis and Cultural Inference: A Paleo-Indian Case.* University of Arizona Press, Tucson AZ.

1974    Lindenmeier: A Pleistocene Hunting Society. Harper & Row, New York.

Yerkes, Richard W.
1987    *Prehistoric Life on the Mississippi Flood Plains.* University of Chicago Press, Chicago.

# CHAPTER SIX

# Chipped-Stone Raw Material from the Mill Iron Site

JULIE FRANCIS
Wyoming Department of Transportation

MARY LOU LARSON
University of Wyoming

## Introduction

This chapter examines raw materials present in the chipped-stone assemblage from the Mill Iron site (24CT30) in southeast Montana, and, where possible, determines the sources of these materials. Laboratory analysis of the assemblage, combined with an examination of geologic data from the general area, indicate that locally available raw materials are dominant. However, small amounts of dendritic chert and an unknown variety of quartzite are represented. These materials could have been obtained from several different source areas ranging 160-400 km from the site. Results of the analysis also suggest that utilization and production strategies varied considerably between different raw material types.

## Methods

A total of 1,709 tools and debitage from 1985, 1986, 1987, and 1988 excavations were examined. These included material which had been found in situ and had been recovered from 1/4 in and 1/8 in dry screening and waterscreening through 1/16 in mesh. This sample did not include 1986 waterscreen materials or some Tongue River silicified sediment debitage, which had already been refit onto two of the large choppers recovered from the site (Figures 2.12, 2.13, and 4.11). It is estimated that over 90% of all chipped-stone artifacts were examined.

Based on macroscopic visual characteristics, materials were first sorted into raw material types which approximate analytical nodules (Chapter 2), that is items which could have been derived from the same core or tool. These raw material types were then assigned to probable source areas. At the same time, all artifacts were classified into morphological types and size grades (Table 6.1). Primary, secondary, and tertiary flakes indicate core reduction activities, while tool manufacture and maintenance includes bifacial reduction flakes, pressure flakes, and small tool resharpening flakes. The shatter category includes both angular debris and small pieces of flake shatter. Tools

were grouped into fairly common morphological types (utilized, retouched flakes, scraper, biface, graver, projectile point, etc.). Evidence of burning, the particular part of the item present, and striking platform attributes—when observable—were also noted.

## Mill Iron Raw Material Types and Sources

Seventeen different raw material types found in the Mill Iron assemblage are thought to have been obtained from at least six different source areas (Figure 6.1). These include the immediate site area, the Fort Union Formation, two sources in other Tertiary formations, and two non-local sources. Materials available within a few kilometers of the site dominate. The most common of these are three varieties of silicified wood. These can be described as dark and light brown translucent cherts, sometimes resembling Knife River flint. Growth rings are apparent in the material, and cortex is a weathered, yellow limonitic stain. Silicified wood occurs in the immediate site area as lag deposits resting on Cretaceous age surfaces and was observed on the butte where the site is located (Albanese 1988, personal communication). The material is ultimately derived from the Fort Union Formation.

Tongue River silicified sediment (TRSS) also occurs in the immediate site area. This is an indurated quartz siltstone—dull, and light to medium gray or buff in color. It often exhibits orange limonitic staining on weathered surfaces (Christensen 1984:15). In primary context, the material occurs at the contact of the Ludlow Member and the overlying Tongue River Member of the Fort Union Formation (Keyser and Fagan 1987:233). Where erosion has removed the Tongue River Member, TRSS often occurs as a dense surface lag deposit of large angular boulders on older Cretaceous surfaces (Keyser and Fagan 1987:233). Christensen (1984:11) has documented this situation several kilometers north of the Mill Iron site, and large chunks of the material are present in the immediate area of the site.

**Table 6.1.** Lithic Classification System.

*Raw Material Types/Analytical Nodules*
    Silicified wood—dark brown, light brown, opaque (patinated) white
    Tongue River silicified sediment
    Porcellanite—gray, red
    Cobble cherts—opaque red/purple, translucent red, pink/gray (burned), white/gray, green, miscellaneous burned
    Arikaree chert
    Yellow dendritic chert
    Quartzite
    Unknown—yellow, black

*Artifact Types*
    Primary flake—unmodified flake having between 75% and 100% cortex the dorsal surface and no intentional dorsal flake scars. Striking platforms are generally unprepared.
    Secondary flake—unmodified flake having between 1% and 75% cortex on the dorsal surface and one or two dorsal flake scars. Striking platforms are generally unprepared.
    Tertiary flake—unmodified flake having less than 1% cortex on the dorsal surface and three or more dorsal flake scars. Striking platforms are generally unprepared.
    Tool manufacture/maintenance flake—unmodified flake with no cortex, numerous dorsal scars, and prepared platforms. Such flakes are often thin and are highly curved. Platforms are commonly lipped. Includes biface reduction, resharpening, and pressure flakes.
    Shatter—shows no definite flake attributes.
    Utilized flake—edge modification due to use only.
    Retouched flake—working edge has been intentionally shaped to a desired shape.
    Scraper
    Graver
    Burin
    Biface
    Projectile point
    Chopper
    Pièces equillés
    Other—tool is too burned and fragmentary to ascertain form.

*Size Grades*
    1 = greater than 2 in. in longest dimension
    2 = between 1 and 2 in. in longest dimension
    3 = between ½ and 1 in. in longest dimension
    4 = between ¼ and ½ in. in longest dimension
    5 = between ⅛ and ¼ in. in longest dimension
    6 = less than ⅛ in. in longest dimension

*Burning*
    No visible evidence
    Evidence of color change, crazing, potlidding, etc.

*Part or Portion of Item Present*
    Proximal
    Distal
    Complete
    Midsection
    Lateral fragment
    Unknown

*Striking Platform Attributes*
    Absent—broken, crushed, or item has been modified to the extent that the strking platform is no longer apparent.
    Cortical/unprepared
    Non-cortical/unprepared
    Non-cortical/prepared

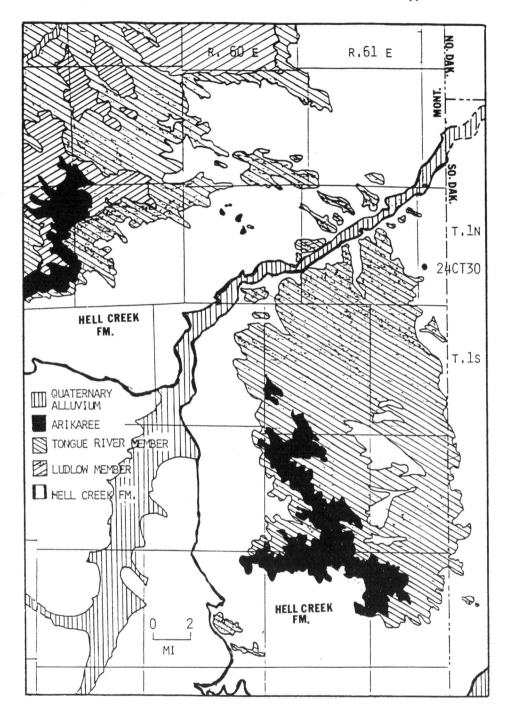

**Figure 6.1.** Geologic map of the Mill Iron area (from Miller et al. 1977).

**Figure 6.2.** Alternating strata of exposed Arikaree chert located approximately 19 kilometers southwest of the Mill Iron site.

Two varieties of porcellanite were also noted. This material is a metamorphosed shale produced by the burning of coal seams in the Fort Union Formation and is most commonly a dull gray or maroon color (Fredlund 1976). Porcellanite is found over much of the Powder River Basin in both Wyoming and Montana, although it did not outcrop on-site (Frison 1988, personal communication). The porcellanite present in the Mill Iron assemblage was likely obtained from primary sources in the Fort Union Formation, which is extensively exposed a little over 1.6 km from the site in the Humbolt Hills and on the west side of Box Elder Creek. Thus, porcellanite is considered a local source in this analysis.

Several varieties of chert present in the Mill Iron assemblage were obtained from gravel deposits. The original nodules were probably no greater than 15 cm in diameter, and the materials can be distinguished by the distinctive weathered limestone cortex. The most common of the cobble cherts is an opaque red or purple chert, which is probably ultimately derived from Permo-Pennsylvanian age formations. An opaque white to yellow to gray chert with no macroscopic inclusions is also fairly common. When burned, this material apparently turns light pink. The specific source for the cobble cherts is unknown. However, given the high frequency of these materials in the assemblage, a local source is quite likely. The materials were most likely obtained from Tertiary age gravels, lag deposits, or possibly from Quaternary deposits along major drainages, such as Box Elder Creek or the Little Missouri River. Thus, sources for the cobble cherts could easily occur within a few kilometers of the site area.

Small amounts of what was identified as Arikaree chert were also noted in the assemblage. This is generally an opaque white to beige to light brown material. Banding and small round white inclusions are common. The Miocene age Arikaree Formation is thought to be the source. This formation is exposed as close as 14 km southwest of the site (Figure 6.1).

Two specific raw material types are thought to have been brought into the site from some distance. The first of these is an opaque yellow Mississippian age chert with small black dendritic inclusions. No cortex was observed on any of these artifacts. Given the large size of the projectile points made from this material, procurement from a primary geologic source is likely. Mississippian age formations are extensively exposed in the Black Hills nearly 160 km south, in the Big Horn Mountains approximately 320 km southwest, and in the Hartville Uplift 400 km south of the Mill Iron site. This high-quality raw material was extensively quarried in all of these areas (Francis 1983; Frison 1982:174; David Eckles 1988, personal communication).

Minuscule quantities of quartzite were also observed in the assemblage. This was a tan to gray to maroon material of medium- to coarse-grain and sugary appearance. The material may have been derived from the Cloverly Formation which is extensively exposed in the Black Hills, Big Horns, and Hartville Uplift. Visually, this material resembles some documented sources from the southern Black Hills (Tratebas 1982). Cloverly quartzites were extensively quarried in all of the above areas. A specific source cannot be suggested.

A small number of cherts were classified as unknown. Most of these were extensively burned, making raw material identifications tenuous. These could simply be cobble cherts.

## Utilization Patterns of Mill Iron Chipped-stone Raw Materials

Figure 6.3 presents percentage breakdowns of the Mill Iron debitage assemblage by raw material type. Frequencies are presented in Table 6.2. Silicified wood occurs most commonly, comprising nearly 32% of the assemblage. This is followed by cobble cherts, Tongue River silicified sediment, and porcellanite. Thus, nearly 73% of the assemblage consists of raw materials known to occur within a few kilometers of the site. If one presumes that the cobble cherts also occur within a few kilometers of the site, nearly 95% of the assemblage can be considered local. Arikaree chert, of which the nearest possible source is about 19 km away and is here considered non-local, constitutes less than 1%, while the non-local dendritic chert and quartzite comprise 3% of the assemblage.

Table 6.3 presents the raw material frequencies of tool types in the Mill Iron tool assemblage. Relative frequencies are presented in Figure 6.4. Of the tools analyzed, utilized and retouched flakes comprise 50% of all tools, while over 20.6% are projectile points. When broken down by raw material type (and excluding unknown raw materials), patterning exists between the proximity of raw materials to the site and the raw material types of some tools. There is a significant but weak association between local raw materials and utilized flakes, retouched flakes and scrapers (Table 6.4 top: $X^2 = 8.814$, df = 1, $p < .01$, phi = .261). The pièces esquillés (Chapter 4) are manufactured on Tongue River silicified siltstone and porcellanite, raw materials available nearby or on the site itself. The two silicified wood choppers are manufactured from material available on-site. Non-local raw materials appear more frequently as

RAW MATERIAL TYPES

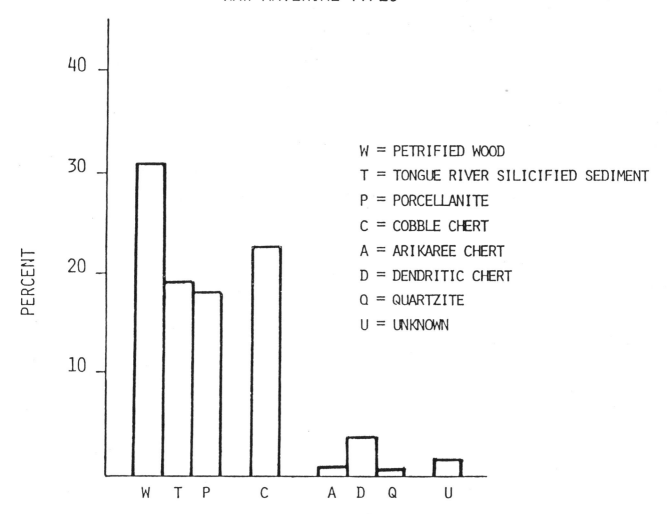

W = PETRIFIED WOOD
T = TONGUE RIVER SILICIFIED SEDIMENT
P = PORCELLANITE
C = COBBLE CHERT
A = ARIKAREE CHERT
D = DENDRITIC CHERT
Q = QUARTZITE
U = UNKNOWN

**Figure 6.3.** Relative frequencies of Mill Iron site chipped stone debitage by raw material type.

**Table 6.2.** Mill Iron Debitage Frequencies.

| Raw Material | Primary | Secondary | Tertiary | Tool Manufacture | Shatter | Nodule Total | Material Total | % Mat | % Total Mat |
|---|---|---|---|---|---|---|---|---|---|
| Gray Porcellanite | 1 | 2 | 53 | 150 | 56 | 262 | | 82.91 | |
| Red Porcellanite | 0 | 0 | 3 | 46 | 5 | 54 | | 17.09 | |
| Subtotal | | | | | | | 316 | | 20.09 |
| LBSW | 0 | 0 | 10 | 96 | 56 | 162 | | 32.46 | |
| DBSW | 14 | 26 | 66 | 69 | 147 | 322 | | 64.53 | |
| OWSW | 0 | 2 | 7 | 3 | 3 | 15 | | 3.01 | |
| Subtotal | | | | | | | 499 | | 31.72 |
| TRSS | 9 | 13 | 47 | 2 | 256 | 327 | 327 | 100.00 | 20.79 |
| CCR/P | 0 | 0 | 32 | 85 | 41 | 158 | | 45.53 | |
| CCTR | 0 | 0 | 4 | 13 | 15 | 32 | | 9.22 | |
| CCP/G | 0 | 2 | 8 | 74 | 24 | 108 | | 31.12 | |
| CCW/G | 0 | 1 | 1 | 5 | 2 | 9 | | 2.59 | |
| CCMB | 0 | 1 | 2 | 11 | 26 | 40 | | 11.53 | |
| Subtotal | | | | | | | 347 | | 22.06 |
| Arikaree | 0 | 1 | 0 | 3 | 1 | 5 | 5 | 100.00 | 0.32 |
| Dendritic | 0 | 0 | 2 | 38 | 6 | 46 | 46 | 100.00 | 2.92 |
| Quartzite | 0 | 0 | 1 | 10 | 0 | 11 | 11 | 100.00 | 0.70 |
| Unknown | 0 | 1 | 1 | 18 | 2 | 22 | 22 | 100.00 | 1.40 |
| Total | 24 | 49 | 237 | 623 | 640 | 1,573 | 1,573 | | 100.00 |

*Key*

| | | | |
|---|---|---|---|
| LBSW | Light brown silicified wood | Arikaree | Arikaree chert |
| DBSW | Dark brown silicified wood | Dendritic | Yellow dendritic chert |
| OWSW | Opaque white silicified wood | Quartzite | Unknown quartzite |
| TRSS | Tongue river silicified sediment | Unknown | Unknown chert |
| CCR/P | Opaque red/purple cobble chert | UYC | Unknown chert |
| CCTR | Translucent red cobble chert | UBC | Unknown black chert |
| CCP/G | Pink/grey cobble chert | | |
| CCMB | Miscellaneous burned cobble chert | | |
| CCG | Green cobble chert | | |

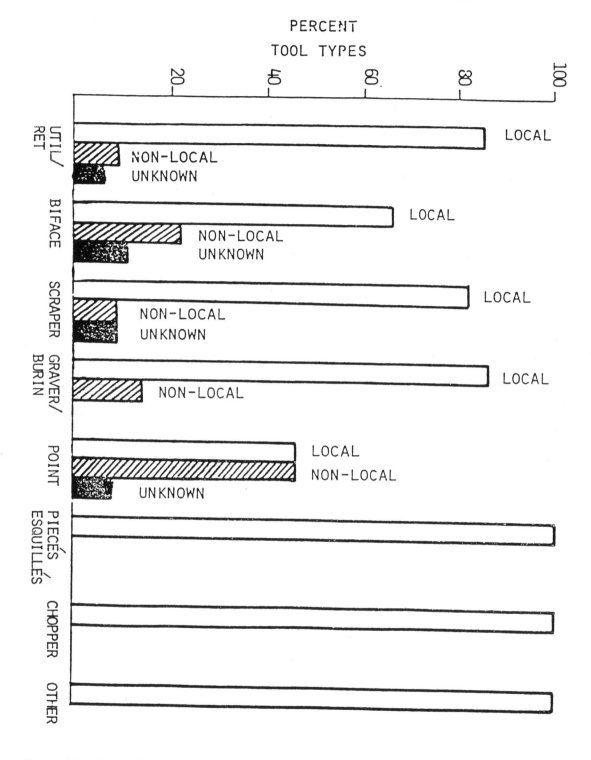

**Figure 6.4.** Relative frequencies of Mill Iron site chipped stone tools by local versus non-local or unknown raw material type.

**Table 6.3.** Mill Iron Tool Type Frequencies.

| Raw Material | UT/RET | Biface | Scaper | Graver/Burin | Point | Piece Esquilles | Chopper | Other | Nodule Total | Material Total | % Material | % Total Mat. |
|---|---|---|---|---|---|---|---|---|---|---|---|---|
| Gray Porcellanite | 13 | 0 | 0 | 0 | 0 | 3 | 0 | 0 | 16 | | 69.57 | |
| Red Porcellanite | 3 | 0 | 2 | 0 | 2 | 0 | 0 | 0 | 7 | | 30.43 | |
| Subtotal | | | | | | | | | | 23 | | 16.91 |
| LBSW | 10 | 0 | 0 | 2 | 4 | 0 | 0 | 2 | 18 | | 38.30 | |
| DBSW | 8 | 6 | 1 | 3 | 6 | 0 | 2 | 2 | 28 | | 59.57 | |
| OWSW | 1 | 0 | 0 | 0 | 0 | 0 | 0 | 0 | 1 | | | |
| Subtotal | | | | | | | | | | 47 | | 34.56 |
| TRSS | 1 | 0 | 0 | 0 | 0 | 0 | 2 | 0 | 3 | 3 | 100.00 | 2.21 |
| CCR/P | 8 | 0 | 5 | 0 | 0 | 0 | 0 | 2 | 15 | | 45.45 | |
| CCP/G | 11 | 0 | 1 | 1 | 0 | 0 | 0 | 0 | 13 | | 39.39 | |
| CCW/G | 3 | 0 | 0 | 0 | 1 | 0 | 0 | 0 | 4 | | 12.12 | |
| CCG | 1 | 0 | 0 | 0 | 0 | 0 | 0 | 0 | 1 | | 3.03 | |
| Subtotal | | | | | | | | | | 33 | | 24.26 |
| Arikaree | 0 | 2 | 0 | 0 | 3 | 0 | 0 | 0 | 5 | 5 | 100.00 | 3.68 |
| Dendritic | 5 | 0 | 1 | 0 | 8 | 0 | 0 | 0 | 14 | 14 | 100.00 | 10.29 |
| Quartzite | 1 | 0 | 0 | 1 | 2 | 0 | 0 | 0 | 4 | 4 | 100.00 | 2.94 |
| UYC | 2 | 1 | 1 | 0 | 2 | 0 | 0 | 0 | 6 | | 85.71 | |
| UBC | 1 | 0 | 0 | 0 | 0 | 0 | 0 | 0 | 1 | | 14.29 | |
| Subtotal | | | | | | | | | | 7 | | 5.15 |
| Column totals | 68 | 9 | 11 | 7 | 28 | 3 | 4 | 6 | 136 | 136 | | 100.00 |

*Key*

| | | | |
|---|---|---|---|
| LBSW | Light brown silicified wood | Arikaree | Arikaree chert |
| DBSW | Dark brown silicified wood | Dendritic | Yellow dendritic chert |
| OWSW | Opaque white silicified wood | Quartzite | Unknown quartzite |
| TRSS | Tongue river silicified sediment | Unknown | Unknown chert |
| CCR/P | Opaque red/purple cobble chert | UYC | Unknown chert |
| CCTR | Translucent red cobble chert | UBC | Unknown black chert |
| CCP/G | Pink/grey cobble chert | | |
| CCMB | Miscellaneous burned cobble chert | *Tool Types* | |
| CCG | Green cobble chert | UT/RET | Utilized flake/retouched flake |

## ARTIFACT TYPES

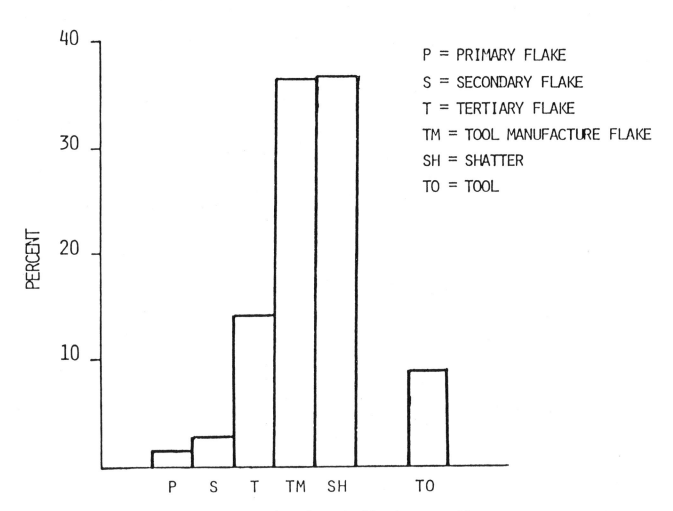

**Figure 6.5.** Relative frequencies of artifact types for Mill Iron site chipped stone assemblage.

projectile points than as other tools when compared to artifacts made on local raw materials (Table 6.4 bottom: $X^2$ = 15.81, df = 1, p < 0.001, phi = 0.350).

Figure 6.5 presents a percentage breakdown by general artifact type for the entire assemblage. Flakes which exhibit any kind of cortex at all (primary and secondary) account for only 4.3% of all artifacts, while the tool manufacture category constitutes 36%. Tools comprise nearly 8% of the Mill Iron assemblage. Thus, on-site reduction of cores of locally available materials is not the principal activity represented by these chipped-stone artifacts. Rather, it is apparent that nearly all raw materials (Tongue River silicified sediment and dark brown silicified wood are the exceptions) were brought into the site as finished or nearly finished tools. This inference is supported by

the size grade distributions (Figure 6.6). Over 47% of all artifacts were 1/4 in the longest dimension. This is an excellent example of how enhanced recovery techniques can provide a more complete picture of lithic reduction activities which occurred at a given locality.

Comparison of the debitage assemblages between Tongue River silicified sediment and the other local raw material types (porcellanite, silicified wood, and cobble cherts) illustrates differing aspects of raw material utilization strategies (Figure 6.7). The Tongue River silicified sediment presents a marked contrast. Tool manufacture flakes are almost non-existent, while almost 80% of Tongue River debitage consists of shatter (primarily angular debris). This is indicative of the specialized use of the Tongue River silicified sediment for the two large chop-

**Table 6.4.** Comparison of Local Versus Non-Local Tool Types from the Mill Iron Site.

| Raw Material | Tool Type | |
| --- | --- | --- |
| | Utilized Flk/ Retouched Flk/ Scrapers | Other Tools & Proj. Points |
| Local | 68 | 38 |
| Non-local | 7 | 16 |

N = 129    X² = 8.814    df = 1, p < .01, Phi = .261

| Raw Material | Projectile Point | All Other Tools |
| --- | --- | --- |
| Local | 13 | 93 |
| Non-local | 11 | 12 |

N = 129    X² = 15.81    df = 1, p < .001, Phi = .350

pers recovered from the excavations. Because of the predominance of shatter or angular debris, the debitage does not appear to be the product of intentional or systematic tool production. Rather it appears to the by-product of use.

For all but TRSS and dark brown silicified wood, debitage is dominated by tool manufacture and shatter flakes, with low frequencies of cortex flakes (Table 6.2). This is probably indicative of nearly finished tools being brought into the site and the occurrence of tool regularizing and resharpening (see Chapter 2). Dark brown silicified wood also has a higher percentage of primary and secondary flakes than the other local raw materials (12.4%) and an even higher percentage than TRSS. See Chapters 2 and 4 for a discussion of the differences between the use of Tongue River silicified siltstone and dark brown silicified wood at the Mill Iron site. An extremely high incidence of burned silicified wood (48% of all this raw material type exhibits evidence of burning) accounts for the high relative frequency of shatter.

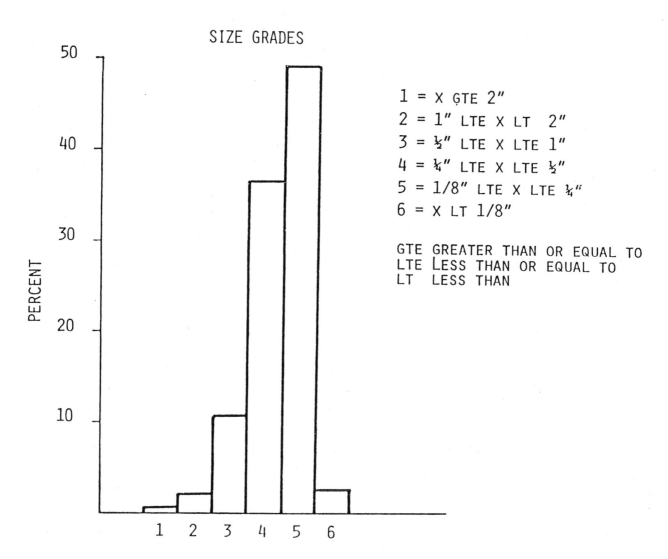

**Figure 6.6.** Relative frequencies of size grades for Mill Iron site chipped stone assemblage.

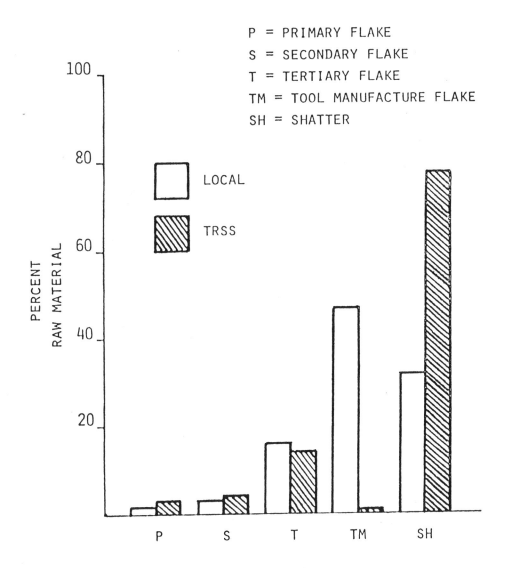

**Figure 6.7.** Comparison of Mill Iron debitage types for Tongue River Silicified Sediment and other local raw materials.

NON-LOCAL DEBITAGE

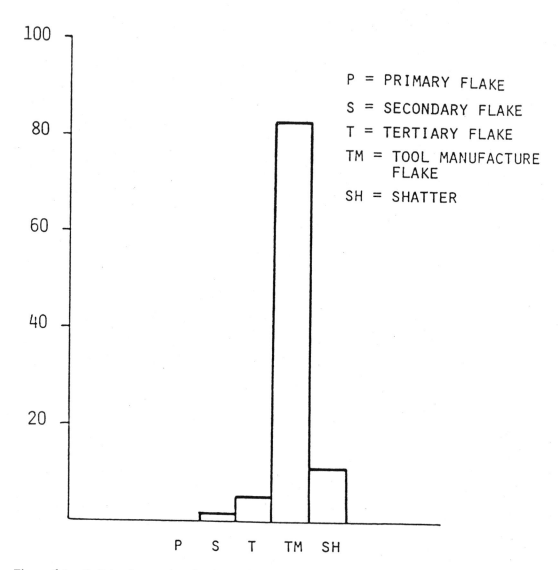

P = PRIMARY FLAKE

S = SECONDARY FLAKE

T = TERTIARY FLAKE

TM = TOOL MANUFACTURE
FLAKE

SH = SHATTER

**Figure 6.8.** Relative frequencies of Mill Iron flake types from non-local debitage.

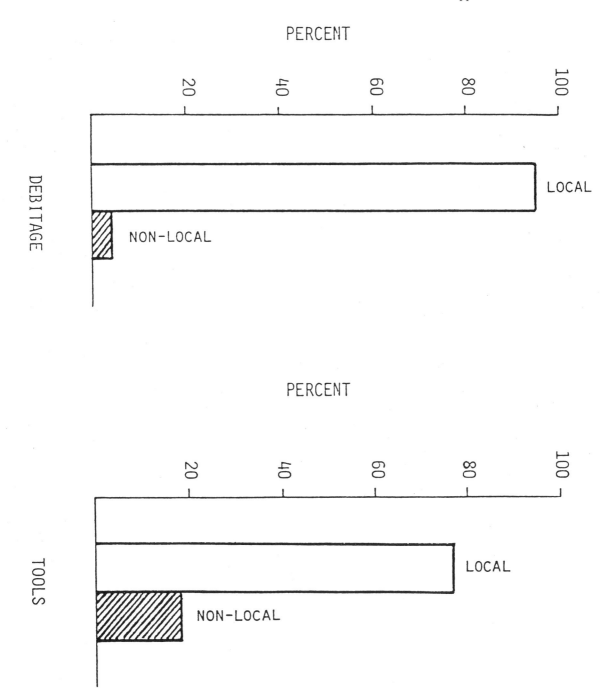

**Figure 6.9.** Relative frequencies of Mill Iron site local and non-local debitage and tools.

Within the non-local debitage (Arikaree chert, dendritic chert, and quartzite; Figure 6.8), tool manufacture flakes comprise over 80% of flakes. Shatter, in this case small fragments of flake shatter, decreases dramatically (11.3%), compared with the local raw materials (41.89%). Primary flakes are non-existent. It is notable that the one secondary flake in this portion of the Mill Iron assemblage is of Arikaree chert, possibly available within the comparatively close distance of 19 km from the site. The lack of primary and secondary flakes of the dendritic chert and quartzite along with the predominance of tool manufacture and maintenance flakes suggest that the non-local materials were brought into the Mill Iron site as finished tools. This inference is reinforced by a comparison of the relative frequencies of local and non-local debitage and tools (Figure 6.9). Local materials make up nearly 95% of all flakes, while non-local materials only amount to just under 4%. When only the tools are examined, the percentage of non-local materials jumps to nearly 17%, an increase of almost 13 percentage points.

## Summary and Conclusions

Raw materials, either available in the immediate site area or within a few kilometers of the locality, dominate the Mill Iron chipped-stone assemblage, with marked contrasts in the utilization strategies for different material types. The Tongue River silicified sediment and dark brown silicified wood suggest expedient utilization of large cobbles available in the immediate site area for use as choppers in the butchering and dismemberment process and the dark brown silicified wood is also used in core reduction. For porcellanite, cobble cherts, and

the remaining silicified wood, procurement and the vast majority of tool manufacture occurred at other localities, and finished or nearly finished tools were brought into the site. With regard to non-local materials, specific sources remain speculative at this time, with either the Black Hills, Hartville Uplift, or Bighorn Mountains as possible sources. Regardless of the specific source utilized, these items were brought to the Mill Iron site as finished tools. The small amount of dendritic chert exhibits a relatively narrow range of variability in terms of visual characteristics. Certainly the artifacts could have been manufactured from material available within one outcrop. Interestingly, 57% of the dendritic chert are projectile points, while 35% are utilized or retouched flakes (see Chapter 5 and 11 for discussion of this phenomenon). The homogeneous nature of these materials, both in terms of the tool type and raw material variability, suggests that the source area may have been part of the regular settlement round for the site occupants. Given the distant sources from which these materials were likely obtained, a fairly large area for the regular settlement round seems likely.

Though specific sources for many of the Mill Iron raw materials remain speculative, additional research at the site should include systematic survey of the surrounding area to locate potential raw material sources. It is particularly important to locate sources of porcellanite and the cobble cherts. Similarly, future research to document the range of variability, both visually and geochemically, of Mississippian age cherts in the Black Hills, Bighorns, and Hartville Uplift, is critical if we wish to examine raw material procurement strategies and settlement rounds with any degree of confidence.

## References Cited

Christensen, Kim C.
  1984  *The Stratigraphy and Petrography of a Light-Colored Siliceous Horizon within the Fort Union Formation (Paleocene), Southeastern Montana.* M.S. thesis, Department of Geological Engineering, Montana College of Mineral Science and Technology, Butte, Montana.
Francis, Julie E.
  1983  *Procurement and Utilization of Chipped Stone Raw Materials: A Case Study from the Bighorn Mountains and Basin of North-Central Wyoming.* Unpublished Ph.D. dissertation, Department of Anthropology, Arizona State University, Tempe, Arizona.
Fredlund, Dale E.
  1976  Fort Union Porcellanite and Fused Glass; Distinctive Materials of Coal Burn Origin on the Northwestern Plains. *Plains Anthropologist* 21(73):207-212.
Frison, George C.
  1982  Raw Stone Flaking Sources. In *The Agate Basin Site:*

*A Record of the Paleoindian Occupation of the Northwestern High Plains*, edited by George C. Frison and Dennis J. Stanford, pp. 173-178. Academic Press, New York.
Keyser, James D. and John L. Fagan
  1987  ESP: Procurement and Processing of Tongue River Silicified Sediment. *Plains Anthropologist* 32(117):233-256.
Miller, M. R., W. M. Bermel, R. N. Bergantino, J. L. Sonderberger, P. M. Norbeck, and F. A. Schmidt
  1977  Compilation of Hydrogeological Data for Southeastern Montana. *Bureau of Mines and Geology Open File Report HY-77-1.* Montana College of Mineral Science and Technology, Butte, Montana.
Tratebas, Alice E.
  1982  Quartzite Quarries in the Black Hills. Paper presented at the 40th Plains Conference, Calgary, Alberta, Canada.

# CHAPTER SEVEN

# Taphonomy of the Mill Iron Site Bison Bonebed

LEE ANN KREUTZER
National Park Service

## Introduction

Identifying the causes of the morphological, quantitative, and spatial variability exhibited by faunal assemblages is the goal of taphonomic research. Much of this work is specifically and explicitly aimed at distinguishing the products of human action from those of non-cultural processes (e.g., Bunn 1981, 1986; Butler 1987, 1990; Fisher 1992; Grayson 1988; Kreutzer 1988; Livingston 1988, 1989; Morey and Klippel 1991; Shipman and Rose 1983; Todd and Frison 1986). This effort ultimately allows archaeologists to explore the ecological contexts in which past cultural systems operated.

The relationships between natural and cultural variables are complex, but one can observe that an abundance of the former generally corresponds to a dearth of the latter. The dynamics of post-occupational, attritional processes are often such that the original "target" assemblage characteristics are obscured or distorted—even destroyed. Therefore, sites with good preservation and high integrity conventionally have been considered to hold greater analytic potential than those subjected to long-term chemical and physical attrition, or biological and geological disturbances.

However, those attritional processes are a product of their environment. While modifying some parts of the record, they also leave behind evidence of the environmental context of the site. In view of this, one might better regard a disturbed, weathered site as a rich source of formational, environmental, and ecological information than as an analytically barren heap of bones.

In this sense, the Mill Iron, Montana bonebed (24CT30) (Figure 7.1) is a treasure. It comprises a variably weathered bison assemblage that has been subject to long-term surface exposure, carnivore ravaging, rodent gnawing and burrowing, subsequent burial and crushing, erosion, and chemical and mechanical deterioration associated with root growth and the presence of soluble salts in the soil. These and other processes have clearly altered the composition of the bonebed since Paleoindian times, also obliterating much of the bone surface that

might have borne direct evidence of human action. The same processes that have blurred that economic record, however, have left evidence of a complex formational history that reveals the local and regional environmental contexts in which Paleoindian subsistence activities occurred.

## The Mill Iron Bison Bonebed

The Mill Iron locality has yielded two Paleoindian sites: a campsite with bison (*Bison bison* cf. *antiquus*) remains, a single mammoth (*Mammuthus* spp.) bone, lanceolate projectile points, and other lithic artifacts (Frison 1988, 1991); and a bison (*B. bison* cf. *antiquus*) bonebed yielding projectile points of the same type as those in the campsite.

Work conducted by the University of Wyoming began at the Paleoindian campsite in 1984, after the discovery of a projectile point at the locality. The nearby, separate bone deposit was exposed during geological testing in 1987, as work at the camp drew to a close. Between 1984 and 1988, excavators recovered bison remains both from the camp context and from the bonebed (Frison 1988, 1991).

The bison bonebed was located approximately 25 m southwest of the Paleoindian camp, on an isolated terrace remnant (Figure 7.2). Although they may be related parts of a single occupation, the camp and bonebed may instead represent temporally distinct events. The presence of the same diagnostic projectile point type in both areas does argue that the occupations were at least culturally affiliated and roughly contemporaneous.

Further, Todd et al. (this volume) observe that tooth wear and molar eruption stages exhibited by mandibles from the camp and the bonebed indicate that animals in both sites died in the spring season. Whether the bison were killed during a single event, in two or more closely spaced events, or in different years (Todd et al., this volume), remains undetermined. There is to date no direct evidence that definitely establishes the functional and precise chronological relationships between the two sites.

**Figure 7.1.** Bison bonebed location (a), and top of part of the bonebed in 1988 (b) at the Mill Iron site.

In this analysis, only specimens recovered from the bonebed assemblage are considered, because the precise nature of the relationship between these two Paleoindian locations remains uncertain, and because, even if temporally related, the two locations are functionally distinct.

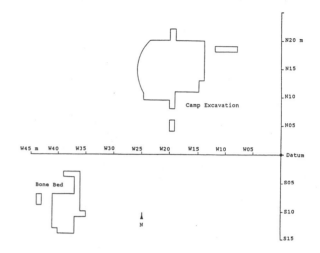

**Figure 7.2.** Bonebed and campsite locations at the Mill Iron site.

## Bonebed Excavation and Description

Excavation of the bonebed began shortly after its discovery in 1987. The datum originally established for the camp excavation was retained, and the grid was extended to the south to incorporate the bonebed. Site datum elevation was arbitrarily established at 100 m, and excavation elevations were measured relative to this arbitrary point: e.g., a bone lying 2.5 below datum would be recorded at an elevation of 97.5 m. An EDM was used to collect three-dimensional provenience data; orientation and inclination were measured with compasses and clinometers.

During the first brief field season, the bonebed surface was partly exposed and mapped. Bones were treated with a solution of white glue and water, and covered for protection until the next field session (Todd and Rapson 1988a). Work continued for a week in October 1987, when more of the deposit was exposed and bone removal began.

Much of the excavation was accomplished with bamboo picks and brushes. Large, fragile bones and some articulated units were jacketed for removal. Exposed specimens that could not be removed at that time were again mapped, treated with white glue and water, and covered for protection over the winter.

Excavation resumed in June 1988, when it was discovered that rabbits had burrowed under the protective cover and scattered some bones in the southeastern portion of the midden. In addition, moisture had dissolved the glue and caused some of the weaker, more vulnerable specimens to exfoliate or crumble. This difficulty was exacerbated by the crystallization of mineral salts on some bone surfaces. Such specimens were cleaned and consolidated with an acrylic solution of Acrysol and water. Excavation and bone removal resumed, continuing until the margins of the concentration were identified and all the exposed specimens were recorded and collected.

Spatial data show that the bones were distributed in a compact, kidney-shaped layer concentrated in an area of roughly 4 x 5 m² (Figure 7.3). They lay on the fine fluvial sands of an

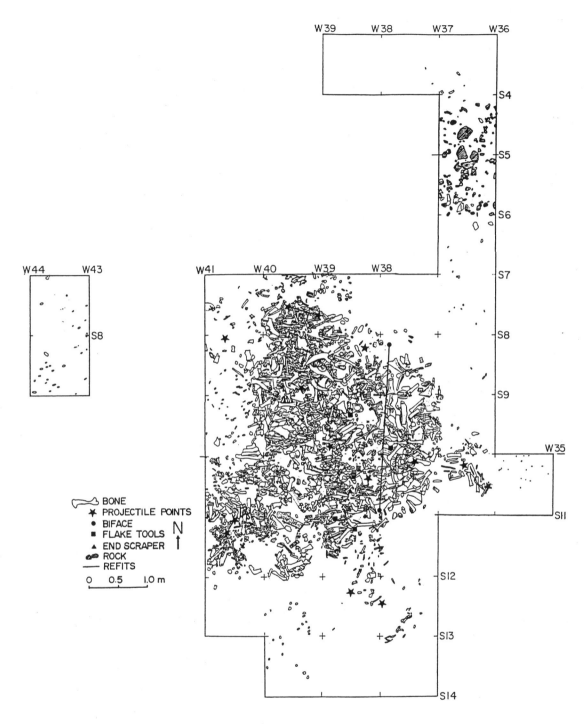

**Figure 7.3.** Plan view of the Mill Iron site bison bonebed.

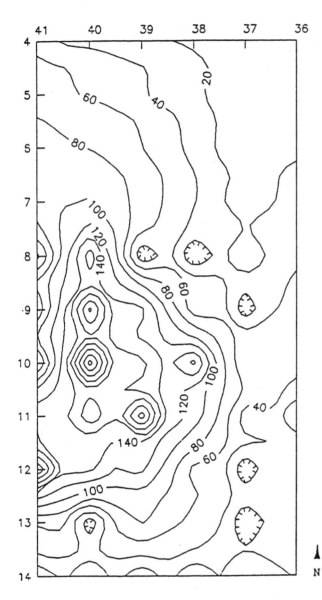

**Figure 7.4.** Bone density contour map of the Mill Iron site bonebed. Contours represent intervals of 20 specimens; tic marks designate 1 m intervals.

areas within the bonebed proper. A cluster of large rocks with a few scattered bone fragments just to the north of the Mill Iron bonebed, however, may be a related feature.

The southeastern portion of the deposit was truncated in prehistoric times by a stream that cut into the bonebed and caused it to slump into the channel (Figure 1.14; Eckerle 1990). Limited scattering is evident to varying degrees along the remaining boundaries, but a test pit 3 m to the west of the main excavation yielded only a few unidentifiable bone fragments.

Mapped and recovered from the bonebed were 3,073 bison bone and tooth specimens and 23 chipped-stone artifacts, including eight projectile points and three bifaces.

## Data Collection

As the specimens were exposed in the field, skeletal part identification and provenience information were entered directly into a computer database. Bone identifications were recorded using the coding system employed in previous University of Wyoming investigations (Table 7.1; see Todd 1983, 1987a:121-23), wherein element, portion, and segment are noted for each specimen. Every specimen, then, has a tripartite code "name" that identifies, as precisely as possible, the particular part of the skeleton it represents. Orientation, dip, and maximum length measurements were also recorded.

In the lab, additional taphonomic data were recorded for each specimen. The coded descriptions of taphonomic attributes are used in conjunction with the skeletal-part field codes. For instance, the location of gnawing on part of an element is described using portion and segment codes. Some analyses, however, incorporate two additional coding systems, previously devised for studies of bone mineral density (Lyman 1982, 1984) and carcass-part food utility (Emerson 1990a).

In all three systems, various skeletal parts are assigned simple alphabetic codes. However, while nominally similar, they are not redundant: the coding systems were independently constructed to address different analytical questions. Because the three systems are in current usage, all are retained here rather than merged into yet a fourth system.

1) General skeletal-part identification follows the system used by Todd (1987a) and others in analyses of several Plains faunal assemblages.
2) Bone mineral density scan site codes largely follow Lyman (1982, 1984), whose system is employed in investigations of density-related issues.
3) Bison-carcass utility codes are those devised by Emerson (1990a) for investigations of body-part food values.

Table 7.2 shows how these coding systems relate to the bison skeleton and to each other. The importance of these relationships will become evident as the various analyses are discussed below.

entrenched, ephemeral stream channel, and were buried by slopewash and debris flow deposits (Eckerle 1990). The midden was a single layer of bones with no intervening geological strata, indicative of one depositional event. Although concentrated within a small area and possibly representing a deliberately placed pile (Frison 1988), the bones had not been sorted and stacked by element, as at the Olsen-Chubbuck (Wheat 1972), Casper (Frison 1974) and Lubbock Lake (Johnson 1987) bison kill/butchery sites.

A density contour map (Figure 7.4) shows that the highest specimen frequencies occur toward the western side of the bonebed, thinning out gradually toward the edges. There is otherwise no clear clustering identifiable as separate activity

**Table 7.1.**   Skeletal Element, Portion, and Segment Codes Used in Mill Iron Analyses.

*A. Skeletal Element*

*Cranium/Teeth*

| | | |
|---|---|---|
| CRN = cranium | MUN = unidentified molar | PMX = maxillary premolar |
| HY = hyoid | PUN = unidentified premolar | IC = incisor |
| MMR = mandibular molar | MR = mandible | TFR = tooth fragment |
| PMR = mandibular premolar | MMX = maxillary molar | TTH = unidentified tooth |

*Axial Skeleton*

| | | |
|---|---|---|
| AT = atlas vertebra | SN = sternal element | SA = sacral vertebra |
| CE = cervical vertebra | RB = rib | SAC = complete sacrum |
| LM = lumbar vertebra | AX = axis vertebra | MN = manubrium |
| CA = caudal vertebra | TH = thoracic vertebra | VT = unidentified vertebra or vertebra fragment |

*Appendicular Skeleton, Forelimb*

| | | |
|---|---|---|
| SC = scapula | MC = metacarpal | CPR = radial carpal |
| HM = humerus | MCF = fifth metacarpal | CPS = fused second and third |
| RD = radius | CP = unidentified carpal | CPF = fourth carpal |
| UL = ulna | CPU = ulnar carpal | |
| RDU = radius-ulna | CPI = intermediate carpal | |

*Appendicular Skeleton, Hind Limb*

| | | |
|---|---|---|
| PV = complete pelvis | LTM = lateral malleolus | TRC = fused central & fourth |
| IM = innominate | MT = metatarsal | TRS = fused 2nd and 3rd |
| FM = femur | TR = unidentifed tarsal | TRF = first |
| PT = patella | CL = calcaneus | |
| TA = tibia | AS = astragalus | |

*Appendicular Skelton, Other*

| | | |
|---|---|---|
| PHF = first phalanx | PH = unidentified phalanx | SE = unidentified sesamoid |
| PHS = second phalanx | SEP = proximal sesamoid | MP = metapodial |
| PHT = third phalanx | SED = distal sesamoid | |

*Fragments*

| | |
|---|---|
| LB = long bone | FB = flat bone |
| CB = cancellous bone | US = unidentifiable fragment |

*B. Portion*

*Long Bones and General Codes*

| | |
|---|---|
| CO = complete | BL = blade of rib or scapula |
| PR = proximal | FK = bone flake, less than half the circumference of a shaft |
| PSH = proximal end and more than half the shaft | US = unspecified |
| PRS = proximal end and less than half the shaft | TR = trochlea |
| DS = distal end | DSE = distal epiphysis |
| DSS = distal end and less than half the shaft | DF = diaphysis |
| DSH = distal end and more than half the shaft | DDS = distal diaphysis |
| DPR = proximal diaphysis | PRE = proximal epiphysis |
| DFD = diaphysis and distal epiphysis | HE = head |
| DFP = diaphysis and proximal epiphysis | CDL = condyle |
| SH = long bone shaft | CP = capitulum |

*Scapula*

| | | |
|---|---|---|
| GN = glenoid portion | GNB = glenoid and blade fragment | GS = glenoid and spine |

*Ulna*

| | |
|---|---|
| ANC = trochlear notch | OLC = olecranonal portion |

**Table 7.1.** (continued)

*Cranium*

| | | |
|---|---|---|
| PAR = parietal | EN = tooth enamel | SR = skull roof |
| FN = frontal | SKO = other combination of | BRC = braincase |
| ZGO = zygomatic | fragment | NSL = nasal |
| LC = lacrimal | JUG = jugal process | PAL = palatine |
| INV = incisive | MX = maxilla | TW = toothrow |
| OCC = occipital | PET = petrous | TMP = temporal |

*Mandible*

| | | |
|---|---|---|
| HRM = horizontal ramus | ANG = hyoid angle | BDR = border |
| DRM = dentary ramus | DAM = DRM + RAM | BOD = hyoid body |
| EN = tooth enamel | RAM = ascending ramus | |
| TW = tooth row | SYM = symphysis | |

*Innominate*

| | | |
|---|---|---|
| IL = ilium | ILD = caudal IL | ACP = AC + PB |
| IS = ischium | ISD = caudal IS | ILC = cranial IL |
| PB = pubis | ACS = AC + IS | ISC = cranial IS |
| AC = acetabulum | ACL = AC + IL | PBS = pubic symphysis |

*Vertebrae*

| | | |
|---|---|---|
| CN = centrum | AEP = anterior epiphysis | AP = articular process |
| CNN = centrum + neural arch | ACN = articular surface and | NAS = neural arch and spine |
| CNS = CN + dorsal spine process | centrum | PEP = posterior epiphysis |
| CNW = atlas: centrum + wings | DNS = dens | DCN = dens and centrum |
| TSP = transverse spinous process | SP = dorsal spinous process | |

*C. Segment*

| | | |
|---|---|---|
| CO = complete | L = left | FR = fragment |
| PR = proximal | R = right | US = unspecified |
| DS = distal | EN = tooth enamel | IN = interior |
| LT = lateral | HB = split rib blade | EX = exterior |
| ME = medial | PL = posterolateral | DT = deltoid tuberosity (HM) |
| CR = cranial (anterior) | PM = posteromedial | SF = supracondaloid fossa (FM) |
| CD = caudal ( posterior) | AM = anteromedial | MO = minor trochanter (FM) |
| DR = dorsal | AL = anterolateral | EG = edge |
| VN = ventral | FO = fore | |
| ACT = acetabular portion | HD = hind | |

## The Mill Iron Bison MNI

In their analysis of the Mill Iron bison teeth and mandibles, Todd et al. (this volume) calculated a Minimum Number of Individuals (MNI) of 29, based on right mandibular second molars recovered from the bonebed proper. The post-cranial and mandibular bone material provided an MNI of 21, based on second cervical vertebrae (Appendix 2). This post-cranial MNI provides the basis for the statistical analyses presented in this chapter.

Regardless of which MNI is used in calculating relative *bone* frequencies, quantitative relationships among those relative abundances remain the same. The decision to proceed with the post-cranial MNI would become statistically inappropriate only if teeth were included in the quantitative analyses.

Teeth are not included because they are structurally and compositionally different from bone (see Currey 1990, Hillson 1986 for discussion), and cannot be expected to respond to attritional processes in the same manner as bones. For instance, teeth are not as vulnerable to scavenging carnivores, they split differently, and their brittleness causes them to fragment more rapidly than bone (Toots 1965; Behrensmeyer 1978; Todd et al., this volume). Therefore, including tooth abundances in the weathering, carnivore ravaging, and other taphonomic analyses undertaken here is neither necessary nor useful.

## Herd Sex Ratio

Modern bison exhibit a high degree of sexual dimorphism, with mature bulls often weighing twice as much as mature cows (McHugh 1972; Wheat 1972). Assuming the same was true of ancient forms of bison, element size differences can be used to determine the ratio of bulls to cows in a zooarcheological assemblage.

**Table 7.2.** Field Identification, Utility, and Scan Site Codes Used in Mill Iron Bonebed Analysis.

| Element | Scan Site Equivalent | Mill Iron Equivalent | Bison Utility Equivalent |
|---|---|---|---|
| *Mandible | DN | MR | MAND |
| Atlas | AT | AT | ATLAS |
| Axis | AX | AX | AXIS |
| Cervical | CE | CE | C3C7 |
| *Sternebra | ST | SN | STER |
| Thoracic | TH | TH | THOR |
| *Lumbar | LU | LM | LUMB |
| *Sacrum | SC | SA | SPEL (sacrum-pelvis) |
| *Rib | RI | RB | RIBS |
| *Scapula | SP | SC | SCAP |
| *Humerus | HU | HM | PHUM, DHUM |
| *Radius | RA | RD | PRUL, DRUL |
| Ulna | UL | UL | PRUL, DRUL |
| *Radial Carpal | SCA | CPR | CARP |
| *Intermediate Carpal | LUN | CPI | CARP |
| *Ulnar Carpal | CUN | CPU | CARP |
| Second/Third Carpal | TM | CPS | CARP |
| Fourth Carpal | UNC | CPF | CARP |
| Metacarpal | MC | MC | PMTC, DMTC |
| *Fifth Metacarpal | FIF | MCF | CARP |
| *First Phalanx | P1 | PHF | 1ST, PPHA |
| *Second Phalanx | P2 | PHS | 2ND, PPHA |
| *Third Phalanx | P3 | PHT | 3RD, PPHA |
| Ilium | IL | IL | SPEL |
| Ischium | IS | IS | SPEL |
| *Pubis | PU | PB | SPEL |
| Acetabulum | AC | AC | SPEL |
| *Femur | FE | FM | PFEM, DFEM |
| *Patella | PA | PT | PATE |
| *Tibia | TI | TA | PTIB, DTIB |
| *Calcaneum | CA | CL | TARS |
| *Naviculo-Cuboid | NC | TRC | TARS |
| Astragalus | AS | AS | TARS |
| Second/Third Tarsals | 2&3 | TRS | TARS |
| *Lateral Malleolus | LATMAL | LTM | TARS |
| *Metatarsal | MR | MT | PMTC, DMTC |

*Asterisks signify coding differences between scan site and Mill Iron element codes.

The procedure involves making a series of measurements for each element of interest, often long bones, using calipers and an osteometric board (e.g., Bedord 1974, 1978; Duffield 1973; Smiley 1978). Standard osteometric conventions, such as those published by von den Driesch (1976), are followed for each element. Next, data collected for two measurements of the same element (e.g., breadth and width of proximal radii) are cross-plotted for visual identification of size-clustering. Multivariate statistical analyses are also useful for this purpose (e.g., Bedord 1978).

**Table 7.3.** Bison Radius Measurements of Fused Distal Epiphyses (after Todd 1987a).

| Specimen | Side | RD4 (mm) | RD9 (mm) | Sex |
|---|---|---|---|---|
| L13-16-131 | R | 90 | 52 | F |
| L13-23-29 | R | — | 42 | F |
| L13-23-42 | R | 88 | 49 | F |
| L13-23-26 | R | 93 | 50 | F |
| L13-24-46 | R | 103 | 54 | M |
| M13-7-106 | L | 97 | 52 | F |

These procedures require that the skeletal parts to be measured are relatively complete, that the particular elements selected are known to be proportional to overall animal size, and that they can be determined to be from mature animals. Obviously, measurements of a broken or deteriorated specimen will under-represent the size of the animal, and metric data from the bones of large, immature males may cluster with those of adult females. To determine whether a fossil is from a mature animal, its stage of epiphyseal fusion is compared to known fusion rates in modern bison (Duffield 1973; Koch 1934).

The generally poor preservation and fragmentary nature of the Mill Iron bones severely limit the number of specimens suitable for such analysis. Specimens are frequently damaged heavily, or missing the diaphyseal portion by which fusion stage may be determined. Consequently, the sample of measurable elements is small. In such instances, the metric data may not group into clearly identifiable clusters.

Despite these difficulties, Todd and Rapson (1988a) identified five radii with complete epiphyseal union at the distal end. Metric data from these specimens (see Todd and Rapson 1988a; Todd 1987a for descriptions of measurement sites) indicate that four belong to small bison, probably cows, and one to a larger animal, probably a bull (Todd and Rapson 1988a). Subsequent excavation, although recovering more radii, added only one that was both mature and complete enough for measurement (L13-16-131); it falls into the cow grouping (Table 7.3). Although the data are limited, it appears that the assemblage may be dominated by cows.

The sex ratio of a zooarchaeological assemblage, however, does not necessarily reflect the sex ratio of the original death assemblage (e.g., Bedord 1978; Speth 1983; Speth and Parry 1980). Given the possibility of selective destruction, as well as the small sample size of measurable elements, identification of the Mill Iron assemblage as a cow-dominated herd should be considered tentative.

## Paleotopography and Bonebed Structure

If a bison trap once existed within Mill Iron's ephemeral stream channel, extensive terrace erosion and weathering have destroyed conclusive evidence of its presence. The absence of such evidence, together with distributional and other characteristics of the bonebed itself, initially led investigators to discount the

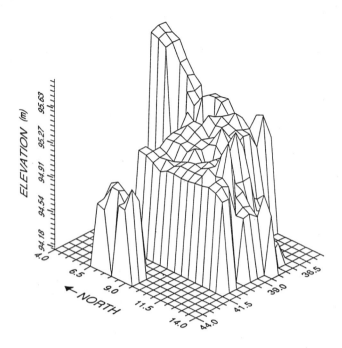

**Figure 7.5.** Surface map depicting topography of ancient surface on which the bones were deposited. Specimen elevations indicate their distance below datum, arbitrarily established at 100 m. (Note vertical exaggeration.)

**Table 7.4.** Mean Elevations (meters) of Specimens Across Mill Iron Bone Bed.

| Units South | Mean Elevation | SD | Minimum Elevation | Maximum Elevation | Number of Specimens* |
|---|---|---|---|---|---|
| S4–S5 | 95.92 | 0.05 | 95.83 | 95.99 | 12 |
| S5–S6 | 95.74 | 0.15 | 95.58 | 95.89 | 3 |
| S6–S7 | 95.44 | 0.08 | 95.36 | 95.53 | 4 |
| S7–S8 | 95.24 | 0.16 | 94.27 | 96.30 | 243 |
| S8–S9 | 95.25 | 0.13 | 94.86 | 96.21 | 516 |
| S9–S10 | 95.27 | 0.08 | 94.69 | 95.55 | 701 |
| S10–S11 | 95.24 | 0.08 | 94.64 | 06.06 | 742 |
| S11–S12 | 95.14 | 0.23 | 94.18 | 96.28 | 575 |
| S12–S13 | 94.80 | 0.37 | 94.00 | 95.76 | 196 |
| S13–S14 | 94.83 | 0.43 | 94.23 | 95.25 | 10 |
| | | | | | 3,002 |

*71 specimens from the assemblage are unprovenienced.

kill-site hypothesis, and to explain it in another manner (Frison 1990, 1991).

The bone midden, for instance, may be the remains of a secondary butchery site, to which economically valuable carcass parts were carried for processing from a nearby kill site (e.g., Landals 1990), as yet undiscovered by archaeologists. The lack of clear physical evidence for a trap, the absence of complete skulls, and the low incidence of articulated units and complete articulated skeletons at Mill Iron meet Wheat's (1971, 1978, 1979) identifying criteria for butchery (as opposed to kill) sites. The absence of complete crania is particularly interesting in this respect, as they are present at other Paleoindian bison kill sites.

Another possibility is that the midden is a dump, where camp and butchery refuse was disposed. Wheat's criteria for butchery sites could as well apply to such a situation. However, the facts that the bonebed appears to be a discrete stack or pile (Frison 1990, 1991) and that it contains a number of projectile points and other tools suggest that it was the site of some organized activity rather than a place into which garbage was flung.

Before these alternatives can reasonably be considered, the possibility that geological processes were instrumental in creating the bonebed must be evaluated. As the accumulation lies on the sands of an entrenched stream channel at the foot of a slope, it could plausibly be a slopewash or alluvial deposit. Hydraulic processes are capable of producing sorted accumulations that can mimic the structure and distribution of a butchery or kill site (Behrensmeyer 1975, 1978; Boaz and

Behrensmeyer 1976; Hanson 1980; Todd 1987b; Todd and Frison 1986; Voorhies 1969). Particle size, stratification, bone orientation and dip, and the morphological characteristics of the bones themselves, however, argue that these geological processes are not responsible for the structure of the Mill Iron bison bonebed (Eckerle 1990).

The bonebed lay on a south- and west-dipping surface. A three-dimensional surface map, plotted for the excavation area from basal bone elevations (Figure 7.5), indicates an ancient slope rising nearly 2 m at the north end of the bone concentration, and a somewhat gentler slope toward the eastern side.

To describe the distribution of the assemblage across the site, specimen numbers were totaled for each east/west transect (Table 7.4). The bone counts show a gradual increase in number from north to south, with the peak occurring within and between transects S9 and S912. Figure 7.6 illustrates this graphically. The histogram shows a numerical distribution skewed toward the south (downslope) side of the site; the curve indicates relative mean elevations for each transect. The figure shows the following.

1) Lower elevations and relatively low numbers of specimens lie at the southern extremity of the bonebed, where geologists have identified a stream channel that cut into the midden and caused it to slump. The bone population consequently declines there.
2) Between transects S11 and S7, where most specimens occur, the slope levels out.
3) At transect S7, the slope begins an ascent to the north, and the bone populations correspondingly drop. As Table 7.4 indicates, there are fewer than 10 specimens on the slope.
4) There is a small numerical peak at the top of the slope (transect S5), representing 12 specimens. The site map shows this clearly as a distinct cluster of large rocks with a few scattered bone fragments among them.

The ancient topography of the site consisted of a slope to the north with a leveled area at the foot, where the bones are concen-

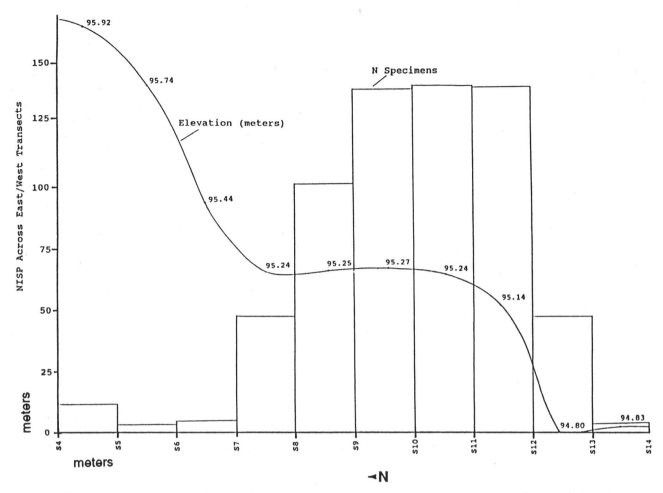

Figure 7.6. Histogram depicts distribution of NISP across east-west transects; curve plots specimen distances below arbitrary datum, tracing the ancient slope. The greatest numbers of specimens occur between transects S6 and S12, where the slope levels.

trated. Significantly, bones are most numerous in the *center* of the flattened area at the foot of the slope (Figure 7.6). Had the material moved downslope, the greatest accumulation would occur at the foot of the slope directly at the grade change (Figure 7.7).

The possibility that the bones are an alluvial deposit is likewise slim. If considered as sedimentary particles, the bone and tooth specimens represent an extremely poorly sorted concentration that is incongruous with the fine sands surrounding it. The "particles" include articulated rib and vertebral units, single units, isolated teeth and tiny fragments. Flume experiments (Behrensmeyer 1988; Boaz and Behrensmeyer 1976; Hanson 1980; Voorhies 1969) have shown that water currents will sort objects according to their size, shape, and density. This being the case, one would not expect to find such a wide size range of specimens in either a channel fill or lag deposit. Nor, given the variables that influence hydraulic sorting, would one expect stone tools to be carried along with bones by stream currents and to be deposited together with them. The presence of lithics among the Mill Iron bones is more parsimoniously explained by structured human activity than as a coincidental convergence of unrelated lithics and bones in a low-energy stream bed.

Experimental studies of fluvial transport demonstrate that bones will become aligned both parallel with and transverse to the direction of current (Toots 1965; Voorhies 1969). Rose diagrams provide a means of assessing whether the long axes of bones are preferentially oriented, and they have been used to

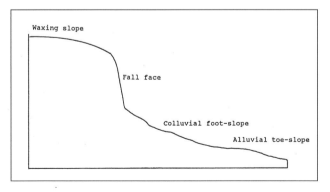

Figure 7.7. Schematic diagram showing deposition of colluvium at foot of a slope (after Small and Clark 1982).

**Table 7.5.** Sums of Specimens Grouped by Orientation (20 degree) Classes.

| Orientation (degrees) | Number of Specimens |
|---|---|
| 1– 20 | 232 |
| 21– 40 | 216 |
| 41– 60 | 193 |
| 61– 80 | 221 |
| 81–100 | 187 |
| 101–120 | 178 |
| 121–140 | 163 |
| 141–160 | 192 |
| 161–180 | 183 |
| | 1,765 |

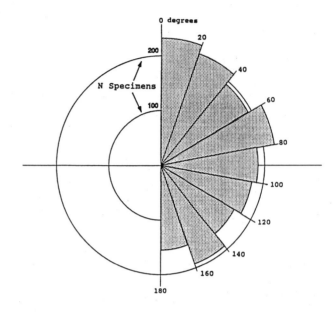

**Figure 7.8.** Rose diagram of specimen orientations, across 20-degree units at Mill Iron bone bed. Pattern shows no preferred orientation.

describe patterning in a number of archaeological sites (e.g., Johnson 1990; Kreutzer 1988; Rapson 1990a; Shipman 1981; Todd and Frison 1986). At Mill Iron, bone orientation is random and fairly evenly distributed across 20 degree orientation classes (Table 7.5, Figure 7.8). Such a distribution is not indicative of a high-energy fluvial environment capable of moving or orienting bison elements.

Nor does dip, the degree of inclination of the bone specimens, suggest that such an environment existed at Mill Iron. Of the 1,654 specimens for which dip was recorded, 1,452 (87.8%) assume a relatively stable position, with inclinations of 30 degrees or less. Inclinations of greater than 30 degrees were recorded for the remaining 202 (12.2%) specimens. Following Rapson (1990a), orientation and dip are illustrated by a cyclographic projection (Figure 7.9). Orientations are shown between 0 and 180 degrees; degrees of dip, from 0 on the right to 90 on the left, are indicated on the horizontal scale. Points along the rim of the hemisphere thus indicate specimens with little or no inclination, whereas items near the center are nearly vertical. Here, the assemblage is primarily (but not exclusively) planar in distribution. The 12.2% of the specimens located nearer the center of the projection do not display preferred orientation; rather, they are randomly distributed across orientation classes. Nevertheless, this percentage of relatively steep dips appears high when compared to other sites, such as Bugas-Holding (Rapson 1990a, 1990b).

Some of this is attributable to the channel cutting that caused slumping (hence, steep inclinations) in the southeastern portion of the site. Some may also be due to reworking of the site by burrowing rodents, and to trampling by people and carnivores. However, many of these measurements are exaggerated by the overall slope of the old depositional surface itself. For example, bones lying on a surface with a 10-degree slope will yield a dip measurement of at least 10 degrees. The surface map (Figure 7.5) clearly illustrates an inclination to the north and a more subtle one to the east. Specimens lying on these slopes therefore show a steeper angle of dip and hence should not be assumed to be indicative of a high-energy depositional environment.

Finally, even though much of the assemblage is moderately to heavily weathered, those elements in fair-to-good condition

are not rounded or abraded, as is common among hydraulically transported bones (Behrensmeyer 1988; Shipman 1981).

Although geological processes have acted upon the bonebed, they do not account for its location, distribution, or composition. Human predation better explains these characteristics, and the kill/butchery hypotheses can now be considered more closely.

The possibility that the Mill Iron bonebed is a kill site cannot at this point be ruled out. The butchery-site criteria outlined by Wheat (1971, 1978, 1979) are only generalizations, not diagnostics, and (as Todd 1983 and 1987b points out) can be duplicated in a variety of other situations. This means that under some circumstances a kill site might look like a butchery locale.

On the other hand, the site's paleotopography is not inconsistent with the possibility that a trap once existed there. The surface map shows a northern slope that might have served as a wall of a trap into which the animals were driven, perhaps over the bank or down the channel (Eckerle 1990). In the absence of the clear, physical remains of a bison trap, the remains of the bison themselves may provide some answers.

## Carcass Utility and Skeletal Part Frequencies

Patterned human activity at a kill or butchery site should result in patterned distribution and frequencies of the abandoned bones (e.g., Frison 1973; Wheat 1967, 1972; White 1956). Zooarchaeologists have long attempted to derive cultural meaning from the patterns they define (e.g., Brain 1969; Daly 1969; Perkins and Daly 1968; White 1952, 1953, 1956). These efforts generally argue that variability reflects human predation, butchery and transport (e.g., Speth 1983, Thomas and

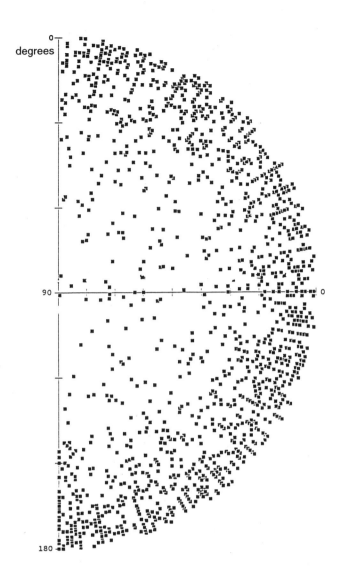

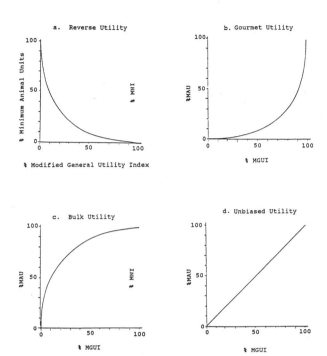

**Figure 7.10.** Family of curves generated by %MAU-MGUI plots (after Binford 1978).

## Carcass Utility Indices

Binford (1978) has argued that element frequencies may be best understood in terms of the relative economic values of different anatomical units. His analyses of modern Nunamiut caribou kills suggest that hunters' selection of carcass parts to be transported elsewhere is prioritized according to the relative food value of those parts (Binford 1978). For instance, lower limb bones with little muscle tissue, marrow, and fat are of relatively low utility, and they are usually discarded on-site; femora, ribs, and thoracic vertebrae are high-utility parts, carried away from the kill to be consumed elsewhere.

Accordingly, Binford (1978: 72–75) developed his well-known Modified General Utility Index (MGUI), listing caribou *(Rangifer tarandus)* and sheep *(Ovis aries)* body parts by the amount of muscle, marrow and grease they provide. These values were then used to develop a series of idealized curves, wherein relative body-part utility values are plotted against corresponding skeletal-part abundances (Binford 1978, Figure 2.18). The resulting curves (Figure 7.10) are purported to model human predatory behavior.

For example, Binford (1978) reports that Nunamiut kill/butchery assemblages are predominantly composed of low-utility elements that are discarded during butchery and left behind, as the more valuable parts are carried away. Plotting the relative abundances of the elements against their MGUI values produces a negative hyperbolic curve (Binford 1978:79–80), commonly called a *reverse utility curve* (Thomas and Mayer 1983) (Figure 7.10a).

**Figure 7.9.** Cyclographic projection showing orientation and dip of Mill Iron bones. Orientations are shown between zero and 180 degrees; degrees of dip, from zero on the right to 90 on the left, are indicated on the horizontal scale. Points along the rim of the hemisphere indicate specimens with little or no inclination, whereas items near the center are nearly vertical (after Rapson 1990a).

Mayer 1983), or that it results from taphonomic processes that differentially transport or destroy bones (e.g., Binford and Todd 1982; Grayson 1988; Klein and Cruz-Uribe 1984; Kreutzer 1988; Lyman 1985). Both of these possibilities must be evaluated in order to explain quantitative patterning of the Mill Iron assemblage.

Conversely, the high-utility assemblage will be recognizable as a *gourmet utility curve* (Figure 7.10.b), identified for sites to which the valuable parts were transported and processed, and at which they were ultimately discarded—a processing, secondary butchery, or consumption site, for example.

## Constraints and Limitations

Binford's utility indices, as well as more recent, simplified indices (e.g., Jones and Metcalfe 1988; Metcalfe and Jones 1988) are constructed exclusively on the basis of food product values. They do not include utility values for other products such as hides, hair, hooves, sinew, horns or antlers. While no one claims that food is the limiting interest in these animals, there are overriding reasons for the "oversight."

First, most of these non-bone industrial materials can be collected from *large mammal* carcasses without destroying or removing skeletal parts from the site. Thus, while other scales of utility may factor in large-prey selection and scheduling, they are not generally recognizable from skeletal abundances.

Second, no method has been devised by which utility values can be validly, reliably, and meaningfully assigned to these non-food products. A kilogram of flesh, fat, or marrow represents a measurable number of kilocalories, grams of protein, and other nutrients essential to human survival. Accordingly, its value can be quantified on ordinal or ratio scales of measurement. An 80 lb hide, on the other hand, represents—what? A season's shelter; a winter's warmth? And is an 80 lb hide twice as valuable as a 40 lb hide? While hides might be counted (i.e., one bison skeleton represents one hide), it seems such data may be useful only at a nominal scale of measurement.

Bone itself may be considered an industrial material, useful for a variety of tools and utensils (see Lowie 1954; McHugh 1972; Wheat 1982). Quantifying bone's industrial value is possible and reasonable, in that bone utility is related to *measurable* properties, such as strength and stiffness (Carter and Hayes 1977; Currey 1984; Evans 1973; Martin and Burr 1989; Schaffler and Burr 1988; Shipman et al. 1985).

Undeniably, selective removal of particular elements for non-food use would affect the resulting skeletal abundances (Frison 1974; Sharp 1989). To date, however, no one has developed a bone industrial-utility index and attempted to use it to explain skeletal abundances in the archaeofaunal record.

These issues are not trivial, for non-food products in some cases may be as important as food value to human predators. Ethnographic reports, for instance, indicate that hunters sometimes selectively killed bison cows rather than bulls, because their hides are thinner and more workable, or killed bulls preferentially to cows, because their hides are tough and made better shields or lodge covers (Ewers 1955, 1958; Roe 1972). At this time, however, archaeologists can neither identify nor control for such contingencies in archaeological assemblages. When skeletal frequencies demonstrate a strong and convincing preference for one sex over the other, researchers generally reason that the phenomenon is linked to food value.

Gifford-Gonzalez (1989, 1991) and Yellen (1991a, 1991b) have discussed at length the weaknesses inherent in food utility models. As generalizations built on limited samples, such indices cannot replicate, predict, or explain all variability that people might generate within a bone assemblage. Hence, utility indices are most useful when treated as idealized models that generate and focus questions, not as diagnostic templates that purport to answer them. Making sense of archaeofaunal assemblages may incorporate curve fitting and pattern recognition but must ultimately depend on other kinds of information as well (Grayson 1989, Lyman 1991).

## Implications for the Mill Iron Assemblage

Aware of these limitations, a number of researchers have cautiously used utility curves to describe and probe the meaning of skeletal frequencies in archaeofaunal assemblages (e.g., Borrero 1990; Brink and Dawe 1989; Emerson 1990a, 1990b; Grayson 1988; Landals 1990; Sharp 1989; Speth 1983; Thomas and Mayer 1983). Such curves are also of interest in the analysis of the Mill Iron bonebed, as each of the possible kill/butchery scenarios holds implications for the skeletal-part constituency of the assemblage.

1) If the bonebed is a kill site from which valuable carcass parts were removed, the assemblage should consist primarily of abandoned, low-utility elements, and a reverse utility curve is expected. A significant, negative rank-ordinal correlation coefficient should exist between skeletal frequencies and utility values.

2) If the bonebed is a secondary butchery site, to which valuable parts were carried for subsequent processing, the assemblage would be expected to consist mostly of high-utility elements and should produce a gourmet or bulk utility curve, with a significant, positive rank-ordinal correlation existing between the two variables.

3) A refuse heap would likely resemble a secondary butchery site in constituency. As a campside dump, it would be an accumulation of high-utility parts that have been stripped of nutrients and tossed aside.

4) Another possibility is that Mill Iron is a place where bison were both killed and butchered, with the muscle stripped away and the bones discarded on-site (e.g., Frison 1970, 1974, 1978, 1991; Frison et al. 1976; Wheat 1972). Such an assemblage would comprise both high- and low-utility body parts, and would be in keeping with other Paleoindian butchery kill assemblages, such as those of the Casper, (Frison 1974), Horner (Todd 1987a, 1987b) and Jones-Miller sites (Stanford 1978). In that case, relative skeletal frequencies should be unrelated to body-part utility, as all elements should be present in approximately the same proportions as they existed in the living animals.

For Mill Iron, arraying skeletal abundances against corresponding utility values may suggest, not identify, a site history from among those described above. The suggested history can then be examined in light of other lines of evidence. Constructing a utility curve is an important initial step in the analysis.

There is legitimate concern, however, as to whether caribou

**Table 7.6.** Bison Carcass Utility (S)MTP values (Emerson 1990a) and Mill Iron Skeletal Abundances.

| Plot Code | Carcass Unit | *Scan Site | (S)MTP Value | Value Rank | MI %MAU | %MAU Rank |
|---|---|---|---|---|---|---|
| 1 | ATLAS | AT1 | 5.0 | 4 | 38.1 | 12.5 |
| 2 | AXIS | AX1 | 6.2 | 6 | 100.0 | 21 |
| 3 | C3C7 | CE1 | 44.2 | 15 | 43.8 | 16 |
| 4 | THOR | TH1 | 86.8 | 20 | 11.4 | 4 |
| 5 | LUMB | LU1 | 83.2 | 19 | 22.9 | 8 |
| 6 | SPEL | IL2 | 56.2 | 16 | 90.4 | 20 |
| 7 | RIBS | RI2 | 100.0 | 21 | 10.9 | 3 |
| 8 | SCAP | SP1 | 21.7 | 11.5 | 88.1 | 19 |
| 9 | PHUM | HU2 | 21.7 | 11.5 | 4.8 | 2 |
| 10 | DHUM | HU5 | 20.5 | 10 | 42.9 | 15 |
| 11 | PRUL | RA2 | 13.5 | 9 | 40.5 | 14 |
| 12 | DRUL | RA5 | 9.8 | 7 | 38.1 | 12.5 |
| 13 | CARP | (Avg'd) | 5.4 | 5 | 24.3 | 9 |
| 14 | PMP | MP1 | 4.9 | 3 | 33.3 | 11 |
| 15 | DMP | MP6 | 2.9 | 2 | 47.6 | 17 |
| 16 | PFEM | FE2 | 62.7 | 17.5 | 11.9 | 5 |
| 17 | DFEM | FE6 | 62.7 | 17.5 | 2.4 | 1 |
| 18 | PTIB | TI2 | 36.3 | 14 | 14.3 | 6 |
| 19 | DTIB | TI5 | 21.9 | 13 | 21 | 7 |
| 20 | TARS | (Avg'd) | 11.6 | 8 | 52.4 | 18 |
| 21 | PHA | (Avg'd) | 1.9 | 1 | 30.3 | 10 |

*MAU percentages are based on the scan sites that best represent Emerson's carcass units.

and sheep provide an appropriate utility model here, as they are anatomically quite different from bison. Emerson (1990a) solves the difficulty by providing a set of utility indices specifically for bison. She first measures the muscle tissue, marrow, and bone grease yielded by the carcasses of four bison: a pregnant, 6-to-7-year-old female killed in spring, a 16½-year-old cow killed in fall, a 1½-year-old male killed in fall, and a 4-year-old bull killed in spring. Appendicular elements such as femora, humeri, radii and tibiae are cut in half, and product values are measured for each half-element. From those measurements, Emerson constructs separate tables of utility values for meat, marrow, grease, and total products (a combination of the three). These are then standardized by setting the highest value to 100% and scaling the other values respectively. Separate indices for each food product are provided for each individual animal, combined female values, combined male values, and total combined values for all four bison, so that the most appropriate model can be selected for a given analysis.

As the Mill Iron assemblage appears to be composed primarily of cows of reproductive age, model (S)MTP (Standardized, Modified for "rider elements", Total Products utility: Emerson 1990a, Table 8.5), for the spring adult female (SAF) was selected for the analysis. The carcass-part utility values shown in Table 7.6 do not constitute Emerson's complete (S)MTP index, but are representative of most of it. These carcass units were selected to correspond to skeletal units used in other parts of this analysis. Omitted are utility values for the skull, sternum, and caudal vertebrae, because other kinds of data (to which the

utility values will be compared later in this analysis) are not available for those elements.

Skeletal abundances, against which utilities are to be plotted, can be tallied in several ways. (For a review of these counting methods and their problems, see Grayson 1979, 1984; Klein and Cruz-Uribe 1984).

Here, Minimum Number of Elements (MNE) for each part is derived following the counting conventions described by Grayson (1988) and Lyman (1991, 1992): a particular element portion or landmark is selected to represent each anatomical unit, and only bone specimens that include that portion or landmark are counted. This ensures that the numerous fragments of a single bone are not tallied as separate elements.

The resulting MNEs are converted to Minimal Animal Units (MAU), by dividing MNE by the number of times that element occurs in a complete skeleton. For instance, there are 11 proximal femora; bison skeletons have two of these, providing an MAU of 5.5 ($^{11}$/$_2$). This step standardizes the element counts, which otherwise would be higher for those elements (ribs and vertebrae) occurring more than twice in the skeleton.

Finally, the MAUs are further standardized by setting the highest MAU to 100% and scaling the other values accordingly. Mill Iron MAUs and their standardized equivalents (hereafter referred to as %MAUs) are presented in Table 7.7; these and other element counts are also provided in Appendix 2.

Arraying the Mill Iron %MAU values against 21 of Emerson's (S)MTP carcass unit values produces the relationship shown in Figure 7.11. A simple visual comparison of this scatterplot to

**Table 7.7.** Bison Carcass (S)MTP Utility Values (Emerson 1990a) and Mill Iron Skeletal Abundances.

| Carcass Unit | (S)MTP | Value Rank | *Scan Site | MI MAU | MI %MAU | %MAU Rank | VD | VD Rank |
|---|---|---|---|---|---|---|---|---|
| ATLAS | 5.0 | 4.0 | AT1 | 8.0 | 38.1 | 11.5 | 0.52 | 17.0 |
| AXIS | 6.2 | 6.0 | AX1 | 21.0 | 100.0 | 21.0 | 0.65 | 20.0 |
| C3C7 | 44.2 | 15.0 | CE1 | 9.2 | 43.8 | 13.0 | 0.37 | 7.0 |
| THOR | 86.8 | 20.0 | TH1 | 2.4 | 11.4 | 5.0 | 0.42 | 11.0 |
| LUMB | 83.2 | 19.0 | LU1 | 9.5 | 45.2 | 14.5 | 0.31 | 3.0 |
| SPEL | 56.2 | 16.0 | AC1 | 10.5 | 50.0 | 17.0 | 0.53 | 18.0 |
| RIBS | 100.0 | 21.0 | RI2 | 2.3 | 10.9 | 4.0 | 0.35 | 5.5 |
| SCAP | 21.7 | 11.5 | SP1 | 18.5 | 88.1 | 20.0 | 0.50 | 15.5 |
| PHUM | 21.7 | 11.5 | HU1 | 0.5 | 2.4 | 2.0 | 0.24 | 1.0 |
| DHUM | 20.5 | 10.0 | HU5 | 7.0 | 33.3 | 8.5 | 0.38 | 8.0 |
| PRUL | 13.5 | 9.0 | RA1 | 8.5 | 40.5 | 12.0 | 0.48 | 13.5 |
| DRUL | 9.8 | 7.0 | RA5 | 8.0 | 38.1 | 11.0 | 0.35 | 5.5 |
| CARP | 5.4 | 5.0 | UNCI | 9.5 | 45.2 | 14.5 | 0.44 | 12.0 |
| PMP | 4.9 | 3.0 | MP1 | 7.0 | 33.3 | 8.5 | 0.56 | 19.0 |
| DMP | 2.9 | 2.0 | MP6 | 10.0 | 47.6 | 16.0 | 0.50 | 15.5 |
| PFEM | 62.7 | 17.5 | FE2 | 2.5 | 11.9 | 7.0 | 0.34 | 4.0 |
| DFEM | 62.7 | 17.5 | FE6 | 0.5 | 2.4 | 2.0 | 0.26 | 2.0 |
| PTIB | 36.3 | 14.0 | TI1 | 0.5 | 2.4 | 2.0 | 0.41 | 9.5 |
| DTIB | 21.9 | 13.0 | TI5 | 4.0 | 19.0 | 6.0 | 0.41 | 9.5 |
| TARS | 11.6 | 8.0 | AS1 | 11.0 | 52.4 | 18.0 | 0.72 | 21.0 |
| PHA | 1.9 | 1.0 | P12 | 7.7 | 36.7 | 10.0 | 0.48 | 13.5 |

*MAU percentages are calculated based on the most abundant element portion that best corresponds to Emerson's carcass units. These element portions are identified by scan site.

Binford's utility curves shows some similarity to a reverse utility curve. A rank-ordinal comparison using Spearman's rho demonstrates a weak, negative relationship exists: higher utility parts *tend* to appear less frequently relative to lower utility parts and Mill Iron %MAUs ($rs = -0.46$, $p = 0.037$).

These results are in keeping with the kill-site hypothesis, suggesting that nutritionally valuable parts are missing because they were carried away for consumption elsewhere. This in itself does not, however, falsify or rule out other explanations.

This is because, once again, matters are more complex than they first appear: the economic properties of fat, marrow and protein content are *not independent* of certain bone structural properties (Brink and Dawe 1989; Klein 1989; Lyman 1985, 1991, 1992; Marshall and Pilgram 1991) that help determine a bone's mechanical strength.

One study of bone fracture mechanics, for instance, reported that a 5% increase in mineral density resulted in a 30% increase in the ability of bone to resist fracture (Wright and Hayes 1977). Such properties should also influence the resistance of bone to mechanical and chemical attrition (e.g., Brain 1976, 1981; Binford and Bertram 1977; Hare 1980; Henderson 1987; Waldron 1987). Recognizing this, Binford (1978) himself cautioned that the complexity of bone decay processes may preclude the use of butchery models in interpreting many archaeological assemblages. Whether the Mill Iron frequencies are better explained by bone mechanical properties than by economic ones must next be determined.

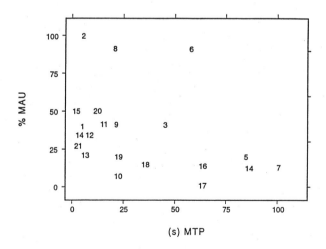

**Figure 7.11.** Scatterplot of Mill Iron %MAU values against Emerson's (S)MTP values. Skeletal parts plotted here are identified in the "Plot Codes" column of Table 7.6.

## Mineral Density Measurement and Bone Mechanical Properties

Numerous investigators have explored the relationships between bone properties and differential survivorship in the archaeological record (e.g., Behrensmeyer 1975; Binford and Bertram 1977; Boaz and Behrensmeyer 1976; Brain 1967, 1969, 1976, 1981; Guthrie 1967; Klein 1989; Lyman 1982, 1984, 1985; Shipman 1977, 1981; Voorhies 1969). Some of the earliest investigations strongly implicated bone mineral density, measured as the ratio of bone mass to its volume, as a determinant of survivorship. As a result of this and more recent research (e.g., Emerson 1990 a/b; Galloway et al. 1991; Kreutzer 1992a, 1992b; Lyman 1982, 1984, 1985, 1991, 1992; Snyder et al. 1991), bone mineral density is currently the best understood of the variables affecting bone survivorship.

Lyman's (1982, 1984) analysis with medical scanning equipment is perhaps the most widely utilized and cited bone density study to date. Using single-photon absorptiometry, he was able to isolate and measure bone mineral in the skeletons of modern artiodactyls: 13 deer (Odocoileus hemionus and O. virginianus), one incomplete pronghorn antelope (Antilocapra americana), and three partial domestic sheep (Ovis aries). Lyman's deer bone data showed significant rank-ordinal correlation between density and skeletal abundances in paleontological, archaeological, and ethnoarchaeological assemblages (Lyman 1982, 1984). The results point to a significant tendency for high-density specimens to survive in greater numbers than do low-density bones. These findings concur with predictions earlier made by Brain (1969), Binford and Bertram (1977), and others.

Patterned skeletal abundances, then, can result from human predation or from differential survivorship mediated by mineral density or other bone material properties (e.g., Kreutzer 1992b). However, correlation between density and skeletal part abundances, or between carcass-part utility values and skeletal abundances, does not necessarily demonstrate causal relationships between those variables. Using Binford's (1978) carcass-part food values, Lyman (1985, 1991, 1992) established that skeletal-part densities are significantly and negatively correlated with MGUI values. That is, high-utility parts are consistently of low mineral density, whereas low-utility parts are of higher density.

Significantly for the faunal analyst, this means that a reverse utility pattern could result from human predation, carnivore gnawing, density-mediated attrition, or from some other variable not yet considered. Bones with more muscle, fat, and marrow are both preferentially consumed and preferentially susceptible to natural destructive processes.

The complex interdependence among these variables demands caution on the part of the analyst attempting to explain quantitative patterning. Correlation between utility and %MAU does not necessarily mean that human predation caused the patterning (Lyman 1985, 1991, 1992; Grayson 1988, 1989). By the same token, neither does correlation between bone density and %MAU necessarily show that post-occupational, density-mediated attrition produced the pattern.

Grayson (1988) has noted that reverse utility patterns produced by human predation should have significant negative %MAU-MGUI correlations, but non-significant MAU-bone density correlations. Conversely, a reverse utility curve caused by destruction will show non-significant %MAU-MGUI relationships, and significant, positive MAU-density correlations. Hence, by examining and comparing both kinds of relationships, one might determine whether human predation or natural attrition better explains the quantitative patterning apparent within a faunal assemblage. Lyman (1991:130) provides a table in which he classifies correlation coefficient sets along with their possible interpretations.

## Bison Bone Density and the Mill Iron Skeletal Abundances

Lyman's (1982, 1984) deer bone density data have been used in numerous analyses since their publication a decade ago (e.g., Brink and Dawe 1989; Fisher 1992; Grayson 1988, 1989; Klein 1989; Kreutzer 1992a; Lyman 1985, 1988; Marshall and Pilgram 1991). Good reason exists to believe, however, that deer bone data do not provide the most appropriate density model for large bovids such as bison. Deer and bison bone densities, while significantly correlated, exhibit taxon-specific differences that can be explained in terms of functional anatomy relating to body size, locomotion, and rutting behavior (Kreutzer 1992a, 1992b).

In order to address questions regarding bison skeletal part survivorship at Mill Iron, this analysis therefore utilizes bone mineral density data collected from 12 modern bison skeletons (Table 7.8; Kreutzer 1992a, 1992b), using technology similar to that employed by Lyman (1982, 1984).

The single-beam photon densitometer with which Lyman measured cervid bone densities is not powerful enough to provide valid measurements for the more robust bison elements. Instead, Kreutzer (1992a, 1992b) employed a dual-energy X-ray densitometer, which is more powerful but which operates on broadly the same principles. Because photon and dual X-ray technology is described in detail elsewhere (Kreutzer 1992a, 1992b), it will not be reviewed here.

For consistency and comparability, the bison scan site placement and coding largely follows Lyman's (Figure 7.12; refer to Table 7.1 for scan site code equivalents), although some scan sites vary due to morphological differences between deer and bison elements. The resulting data (Table 7.9) must be assumed to be representative, on an ordinal level, of the bone mineral densities of extinct forms of bison, such as that at Mill Iron. Archaeological bone specimens have not themselves been scanned because of the difficulty of distinguishing between biogenic mineral density and diagenetic mineral density (Hare 1980; Sillen 1989) in ancient specimens.

## Mill Iron Relative Abundances and Bison Bone Density

The Mill Iron faunal specimens were assigned "scan sites" corresponding to those measured on the modern bison skeletons. For instance, a proximal humerus from the assemblage might

**Table 7.8.** Bison Skeletons Measured by Dual Energy X-Ray Densitometer (from Kreutzer 1992a: 275).

| Museum or collection | Accession Number | Sex | Age (years) | Collection Area |
|---|---|---|---|---|
| Burke Memorial Washington State Museum, University of Washington | 12548 | F | 15 | Woodland Park Zoological Gardens, Seattle, Washington |
| University of Wyoming, Department of Anthropology Comparative Collections | 8529B | M | 8+ | Bison Pete Gardner Herd Wheatland, Wyoming |
| | 8530B | M | 10+ | Bison Pete Herd |
| | 8330B | M | 10+ | Bison Pete Herd |
| | 8222B | F | 17+ | Bison Pete Herd |
| | 8331B | F | 15+ | Bison Pete Herd |
| | 8402B | M | 4.5 | Bud Harris Herd Laramie, Wyoming |
| | W500 | M | 12+ | State of Kansas Herd, Kingman |
| | 8500B | F | 12+ | Downare Herd, Harsell, Colorado |
| | 8506B | F | 12+ | Downare Herd |
| | 8501B | F | 12+ | Downare Herd |
| Private Collection | not accessioned | M | 4+ | Best Butcher, Rose Hill, Kansas |

include scan sites HU1 and HU2. Presence of a scan site was recorded if any portion of it was recognizable on the specimen; a scan site did not have to be complete in order to be recorded. Scan site MNEs and MAUs, tallied according to the same conventions described earlier, are provided for 88 scan sites (Table 7.10), along with their corresponding volume densities.

Spearman's rho shows the MNEs for the 88 scan sites to be significantly correlated with the bison bone volume densities: $r_s = 0.43$, $p < 0.00006$. As an additional test, the Mill Iron %MAUs were compared again to density values, but limiting the comparison to the 21 scan sites corresponding to Emerson's carcass units. The relationship is significant ($r_s = 0.64$, $p < 0.005$) and the correlation higher than for the %MAU-MGUI comparison (−0.46).

Mill Iron skeletal frequencies, then, might be explained either by density-mediated, post-occupational destruction, or by human selection and removal of high-utility parts. This is not surprising, given the relationship between bone density and carcass-part utility. In fact, a comparison of (S)MTP utility values and volume density produces a rank-order correlation coefficient of −0.58 ($p < 0.01$), showing the two to be significantly and negatively related.

The coefficients summarized in Table 7.11 show the following.

1) A weak but significant, negative relationship exists between bison total product utility values and Mill Iron %MAUs, indicating that total product utility does predict skeletal abundances at Mill Iron.
2) A significant, positive correlation exists between bison bone volume density and Mill Iron skeletal part abundances, identified by scan site, suggesting that density-mediated destruction is also a predictor of skeletal abundances at the site.
3) A significant relationship exists between bison carcass utility and bison bone volume density, demonstrating that nutritionally valuable parts tend to be low-density parts.

The results are equivocal: either density or utility could explain the Mill Iron abundances. Grayson (1989), finding similar relationships in an analysis of archaeological marmot bones, has argued that in such cases it is wise to attribute the patterning to density-mediated destruction. He points out that destructive processes are so universal and diverse that nearly every assemblage has been influenced by them.

If such is indeed the case at Mill Iron, it holds implications for the hypotheses regarding site function. The relative skeletal abundances of the recovered assemblage are not representative of those comprised by the assemblage when it was first abandoned by people.

The lack of complete skulls, for instance, may be attributable to density-mediated attrition. Although some of the specimens classified as "flat bone" may be skull fragments, crania are mainly represented by petrosals, teeth, and occipitals— probably the most mineral-dense, nutrient-poor parts of a bison's body. People interested in maximizing their nutritional payload are unlikely to have broken open the skulls and carried these heavy, inedible parts away from a kill locality for processing elsewhere. Those skull parts are present in the assemblage either because people carried complete bison skulls to the site for later processing, or because the animals were killed and butchered there.

People may have broken open the Mill Iron crania for access to the brain cavity or to remove the horns. The relative paucity of skull parts at the Hudson-Meng bonebed has been attributed to such butchery procedures (Agenbroad 1978), and other sites, such as Glenrock (Frison 1970), have yielded bison skulls with holes clearly chopped through the frontals. No such direct evidence exists at Mill Iron, however, nor were any heavy chopping or battering tools recovered from that midden.

Carnivore gnawing, an obvious possibility, does not easily account for skull-part representation in the assemblage. Haynes (1982) has observed, for instance, that wolves are unable to break open bison crania for access to the brain cavity. At modern, scavenged sites, bison skulls tend to remain intact unless disturbed by people.

Exposure and weathering are the mostly likely explanation for Mill Iron's skull-part frequencies. In their re-analysis of Hudson-Meng, Rapson and Todd (1992) report that the upward surfaces of bison crania are heavily weathered, whereas the lower skull portions are well preserved. They suggest that the gradual sedimentation buried and protected the lower portions (including mineral-dense petrosals and occipitals), while the facial bones remained exposed to surface conditions for a lengthier period. Differential weathering and presumed differences in skull-part mineral density thus explain cranial-part frequencies at Hudson-Meng (Rapson and Todd 1992) and likewise at Mill Iron.

Regardless of the agent of destruction, the presence of dense, inedible cranial parts argues that whole skulls were once present in the Mill Iron bonebed. That, coupled with a strong case for density-mediated attrition of the assemblage as a whole, weakens the argument that Mill Iron is strictly a butchery site, *sensu* Wheat (1971, 1978, 1979). The Mill Iron bonebed may, after all, be the remains of a combined kill/butchery site.

The next task, then, is to consider physical evidence of attrition, identify the agents, and determine whether it is sufficient to explain the Mill Iron skeletal abundances.

## Weathering and Disarticulation

Human predation, carnivore gnawing, or any other process that preferentially destroys structurally weak, low-mineral parts could produce relative abundances like those of the Mill Iron assemblage. Further, just as any *one* of the above described processes could create these patterns and curves, so could any combination of them acting together.

Weathering is clearly one of the significant contributors to the differential destruction of the Mill Iron assemblage. Bone specimens were coded according to the six-stage weathering classification developed by Behrensmeyer (1978) and modified by Todd (1983, 1987a) (Table 7.12).

Bone weathering at Mill Iron is highly variable, ranging from slight to severe even within a single element class (Figure 7.13). Even so, the assemblage's weathering profile for specimens identifiable to element (Figure 7.14) shows that most of the assemblage is moderately to severely weathered. The unimodal distribution exhibits no "gaps" or other quantitative irregularities between weathering classes, which is consistent with single-event deposition.

Microenvironmental conditions, including slope, soil conditions, vegetation, exposure to sunlight, and a host of other variables (Behrensmeyer 1978; Gifford 1981; Hare 1980; Lyman and Fox 1989; Miller 1975; Todd 1983) can cause weathering to vary across even a small site. One might expect, then, to find spatially defined weathering trends across a site; however, no such weathering distribution is clearly identifiable at Mill Iron. This may be because the assemblage is concentrated in a relatively small area and has become so disturbed that distributions existing earlier in the site's formational history are no longer discernible.

## Weathering Stages and Element Ratios

Figure 7.15 illustrates the changing relative abundances of identifiable elements in progressively more advanced weathering stages. (Table 7.13 provides NISPs for each weathering stage.) Because these ratios are based on NISP values, those elements that are most abundant in a bison skeleton and those most susceptible to fragmentation into identifiable pieces will naturally dominate the profiles.

Not suprisingly, then, the most abundant elements within

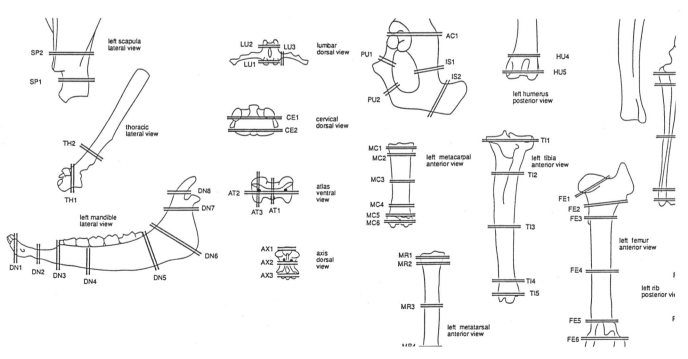

**Figure 7.12.** Locations of scans on bison bones.

**Table 7.9.** Mean Volume Densities (VD), Mean Linear Densities (LD), and Standard Deviations (SD) for Bison and Deer Bones.

| Scan Site | Bison VD LD | N N | SD SD | Deer VD LD | N N | SD SD |
|---|---|---|---|---|---|---|
| 2&3CP | 0.50 | 9 | 0.08 | * | | |
| | 1.11 | 9 | 0.08 | * | | |
| AC1 | 0.53 | 7 | 0.22 | 0.27 | 23 | 0.07 |
| | 1.31 | 7 | 0.55 | 0.93 | 23 | 0.32 |
| AS1 | 0.72 | 12 | 0.07 | 0.47 | 22 | 0.08 |
| | 1.86 | 12 | 0.20 | 0.91 | 22 | 0.16 |
| AS2 | 0.62 | 12 | 0.06 | 0.59 | 22 | 0.08 |
| | 2.23 | 12 | 0.22 | 1.33 | 22 | 0.20 |
| AS3 | 0.60 | 12 | 0.08 | 0.61 | 22 | 0.08 |
| | 2.33 | 12 | 0.20 | 1.19 | 22 | 0.21 |
| AT1 | 0.52 | 11 | 0.07 | 0.13 | 11 | 0.04 |
| | 1.67 | 11 | 0.48 | 0.50 | 11 | 0.20 |
| AT2 | 0.91 | 11 | 0.32 | 0.15 | 11 | 0.05 |
| | 1.58 | 11 | 0.61 | 0.53 | 11 | 0.19 |
| AT3 | 0.34 | 11 | 0.08 | 0.26 | 11 | 0.08 |
| | 1.83 | 11 | 0.56 | 0.80 | 11 | 0.24 |
| AX1 | 0.65 | 11 | 0.22 | 0.16 | 8 | 0.30 |
| | 1.50 | 11 | 0.33 | 0.89 | 8 | 1.11 |
| AX2 | 0.38 | 10 | 0.06 | 0.10 | 8 | 0.02 |
| | 2.09 | 10 | 0.61 | 0.58 | 8 | 0.19 |
| AX3 | 0.97 | 10 | 0.32 | 0.16 | 8 | 0.04 |
| | 1.41 | 10 | 0.35 | 1.00 | 8 | 0.33 |
| CA1 | 0.46 | 10 | 0.04 | 0.41 | 20 | 0.06 |
| | 1.76 | 10 | 0.23 | 0.74 | 20 | 0.08 |
| CA2 | 0.80 | 10 | 0.19 | 0.64 | 20 | 0.09 |
| | 2.01 | 10 | 0.33 | 0.72 | 20 | 0.12 |
| CA3 | 0.49 | 10 | 0.07 | 0.57 | 20 | 0.06 |
| | 2.34 | 10 | 0.28 | 1.49 | 20 | 0.18 |
| CA4 | 0.66 | 10 | 0.09 | 0.33 | 19 | 0.07 |
| | 1.23 | 10 | 0.30 | 0.37 | 19 | 0.09 |
| CE1 | 0.37 | 8 | 0.07 | 0.19 | 6 | 0.04 |
| | 2.02 | 8 | 0.46 | 0.83 | 6 | 0.27 |
| CE2 | 0.62 | 8 | 0.21 | 0.15 | 6 | 0.03 |
| | 1.44 | 8 | 0.38 | 0.69 | 6 | 0.16 |
| CUNEIF | 0.43 | 12 | 0.11 | * | | |
| | 1.33 | 12 | 0.30 | * | | |
| DN1 | 0.53 | 10 | 0.14 | 0.55 | 16 | 0.70 |
| | 0.94 | 10 | 0.07 | 0.43 | 16 | 0.59 |
| DN2 | 0.61 | 10 | 0.05 | 0.57 | 15 | 0.06 |
| | 1.48 | 10 | 0.15 | 0.39 | 15 | 0.06 |
| DN3 | 0.62 | 10 | 0.07 | 0.55 | 15 | 0.08 |
| | 1.54 | 10 | 0.14 | 0.44 | 15 | 0.05 |
| DN4 | 0.53 | 3 | 0.05 | 0.57 | 16 | 0.09 |
| | 1.63 | 3 | 0.08 | 0.66 | 16 | 0.13 |
| DN5 | 0.49 | 10 | 0.05 | 0.36 | 15 | 0.08 |
| | 1.31 | 10 | 0.24 | 0.40 | 15 | 0.07 |
| DN6 | 0.57 | 10 | 0.07 | 0.31 | 16 | 0.10 |
| | 0.97 | 10 | 0.11 | 0.26 | 16 | 0.08 |
| DN7 | 0.79 | 10 | 0.12 | 0.43 | 16 | 0.15 |
| | 1.17 | 10 | 0.15 | 0.33 | 16 | 0.10 |

**Table 7.9.** (continued)

| Scan Site | Bison VD LD | N N | SD SD | Deer VD LD | N N | SD SD |
|---|---|---|---|---|---|---|
| DN8 | 0.79 | 10 | 0.11 | 0.61 | 16 | 0.16 |
| | 0.83 | 10 | 0.14 | 0.25 | 16 | 0.05 |
| FE1 | 0.31 | 12 | 0.03 | 0.41 | 26 | 0.07 |
| | 2.14 | 12 | 0.19 | 1.03 | 26 | 0.19 |
| FE2 | 0.34 | 12 | 0.05 | 0.36 | 25 | 0.08 |
| | 1.57 | 12 | 0.23 | 0.72 | 25 | 0.14 |
| FE3 | 0.34 | 12 | 0.03 | 0.33 | 26 | 0.06 |
| | 1.81 | 12 | 0.29 | 1.05 | 26 | 0.20 |
| FE4 | 0.45 | 12 | 0.04 | 0.57 | 26 | 0.07 |
| | 2.40 | 12 | 0.35 | 1.29 | 26 | 0.16 |
| FE5 | 0.36 | 12 | 0.08 | 0.37 | 26 | 0.06 |
| | 2.30 | 12 | 0.22 | 1.15 | 26 | 0.17 |
| FE6 | 0.26 | 12 | 0.04 | 0.28 | 23 | 0.03 |
| | 2.54 | 12 | 0.28 | 1.78 | 23 | 0.21 |
| FE7 | 0.22 | 12 | 0.03 | * | | |
| | 1.54 | 12 | 0.19 | * | | |
| 5MC | 0.62 | 8 | 0.32 | * | | |
| | 0.67 | 8 | 0.30 | * | | |
| HU1 | 0.24 | 10 | 0.02 | 0.24 | 22 | 0.05 |
| | 2.59 | 10 | 0.36 | 1.32 | 22 | 0.31 |
| HU2 | 0.25 | 10 | 0.04 | 0.25 | 23 | 0.05 |
| | 2.02 | 10 | 0.31 | 0.96 | 23 | 0.17 |
| HU3 | 0.45 | 10 | 0.03 | 0.53 | 23 | 0.06 |
| | 2.79 | 10 | 0.46 | 1.32 | 23 | 0.17 |
| HU4 | 0.48 | 10 | 0.03 | 0.63 | 23 | 0.05 |
| | 2.77 | 10 | 0.42 | 1.43 | 23 | 0.21 |
| HU5 | 0.38 | 10 | 0.07 | 0.39 | 23 | 0.05 |
| | 2.62 | 10 | 0.31 | 1.44 | 23 | 0.21 |
| HYOID | 0.36 | 9 | 0.36 | * | | |
| | 0.43 | 9 | 0.33 | * | | |
| IL1 | 0.22 | 7 | 0.14 | 0.20 | 23 | 0.06 |
| | 1.14 | 7 | 0.41 | 0.44 | 23 | 0.13 |
| IL2 | 0.52 | 7 | 0.13 | 0.49 | 23 | 0.05 |
| | 1.78 | 7 | 0.24 | 1.05 | 23 | 0.35 |
| IS1 | 0.50 | 7 | 0.16 | 0.41 | 23 | 0.06 |
| | 1.19 | 7 | 0.44 | 1.08 | 23 | 0.15 |
| IS2 | 0.19 | 7 | 0.17 | 0.16 | 23 | 0.05 |
| | 0.55 | 7 | 0.28 | 0.44 | 23 | 0.14 |
| LATMAL | 0.56 | 12 | 0.38 | * | | |
| | 1.02 | 12 | 0.12 | * | | |
| LU1 | 0.31 | 10 | 0.08 | 0.29 | 6 | 0.03 |
| | 1.76 | 10 | 0.42 | 1.03 | 6 | 0.18 |
| LU2 | 0.11 | 10 | 0.04 | 0.30 | 6 | 0.03 |
| | 1.17 | 10 | 0.37 | 1.20 | 6 | 0.11 |
| LU3 | 0.39 | 10 | 0.07 | 0.29 | 4 | 0.07 |
| | 0.65 | 10 | 0.19 | 0.19 | 4 | 0.02 |
| LUN | 0.35 | 12 | 0.03 | * | | |
| | 1.39 | 12 | 0.14 | * | | |
| MC1 | 0.59 | 11 | 0.12 | 0.56 | 18 | 0.06 |
| | 2.06 | 11 | 0.27 | 1.21 | 18 | 0.20 |
| MC2 | 0.63 | 11 | 0.06 | 0.69 | 18 | 0.04 |
| | 2.07 | 11 | 0.29 | 1.21 | 18 | 0.17 |
| MC3 | 0.69 | 11 | 0.04 | 0.72 | 18 | 0.05 |
| | 2.12 | 11 | 0.27 | 1.18 | 18 | 0.15 |
| MC4 | 0.60 | 11 | 0.05 | 0.58 | 18 | 0.08 |
| | 1.82 | 11 | 0.19 | 0.78 | 18 | 0.10 |

**Table 7.9.** (continued)

| | | | | | | |
|---|---|---|---|---|---|---|
| MC5 | 0.46 | 11 | 0.05 | 0.49 | 18 | 0.08 |
| | 1.72 | 11 | 0.23 | 0.94 | 18 | 0.15 |
| MC6 | 0.53 | 11 | 0.05 | 0.51 | 18 | 0.04 |
| | 1.91 | 11 | 0.21 | 1.03 | 18 | 0.12 |
| MR1 | 0.52 | 10 | 0.05 | 0.55 | 23 | 0.05 |
| | 2.57 | 10 | 0.26 | 1.62 | 23 | 0.22 |
| MR2 | 0.59 | 10 | 0.03 | 0.65 | 23 | 0.04 |
| | 2.52 | 10 | 0.31 | 1.55 | 23 | 0.21 |
| MR3 | 0.67 | 10 | 0.04 | 0.74 | 22 | 0.06 |
| | 2.43 | 10 | 0.26 | 1.43 | 22 | 0.16 |
| MR4 | 0.51 | 10 | 0.04 | 0.57 | 23 | 0.07 |
| | 1.84 | 10 | 0.18 | 0.89 | 23 | 0.11 |
| MR5 | 0.40 | 10 | 0.03 | 0.46 | 22 | 0.07 |
| | 1.61 | 10 | 0.16 | 0.96 | 22 | 0.16 |
| MR6 | 0.48 | 10 | 0.04 | 0.50 | 7 | 0.04 |
| | 1.88 | 10 | 0.17 | 1.18 | 7 | 0.12 |
| NC1 | 0.48 | 11 | 0.06 | 0.39 | 3 | 0.03 |
| | 1.70 | 11 | 0.15 | 0.89 | 3 | 0.07 |
| NC2 | 0.64 | 11 | 0.21 | 0.33 | 3 | 0.03 |
| | 1.63 | 11 | 0.25 | 0.79 | 3 | 0.11 |
| NC3 | 0.77 | 11 | 0.20 | 0.62 | 3 | 0.11 |
| | 1.64 | 11 | 0.21 | 1.18 | 3 | 0.18 |
| PA | * | | | 0.31 | 2 | 0.01 |
| | * | | | 0.69 | 2 | 0.02 |
| P11 | 0.48 | 21 | 0.08 | 0.36 | 9 | 0.04 |
| | 1.77 | 21 | 0.22 | 0.60 | 9 | 0.09 |
| P12 | 0.46 | 21 | 0.06 | 0.42 | 9 | 0.05 |
| | 1.47 | 21 | 0.19 | 0.54 | 9 | 0.10 |
| P13 | 0.48 | 21 | 0.06 | 0.57 | 9 | 0.10 |
| | 1.75 | 21 | 0.27 | 0.80 | 9 | 0.14 |
| P21 | 0.41 | 19 | 0.14 | 0.28 | 32 | 0.07 |
| | 1.53 | 19 | 0.24 | 0.40 | 32 | 0.10 |
| P22 | * | | | 0.25 | 32 | 0.04 |
| | * | | | 0.28 | 32 | 0.05 |
| P23 | 0.46 | 19 | 0.13 | 0.35 | 29 | 0.14 |
| | 1.44 | 19 | 0.19 | 0.36 | 29 | 0.05 |
| P31 | 0.32 | 19 | 0.09 | 0.25 | 18 | 0.03 |
| | 1.06 | 19 | 0.18 | 0.28 | 18 | 0.04 |
| PU1 | 0.55 | 6 | 0.11 | 0.46 | 8 | 0.04 |
| | 1.21 | 6 | 0.13 | 0.46 | 8 | 0.11 |
| PU2 | 0.39 | 6 | 0.23 | 0.24 | 3 | 0.08 |
| | 0.48 | 6 | 0.12 | 0.20 | 3 | 0.04 |
| RA1 | 0.48 | 12 | 0.05 | 0.42 | 22 | 0.08 |
| | 2.46 | 12 | 0.49 | 1.12 | 22 | 0.21 |
| RA2 | 0.56 | 12 | 0.06 | 0.62 | 23 | 0.06 |
| | 2.42 | 12 | 0.45 | 1.15 | 23 | 0.27 |
| RA3 | 0.62 | 12 | 0.04 | 0.68 | 23 | 0.11 |
| | 2.14 | 12 | 0.32 | 1.18 | 23 | 0.23 |
| RA4 | 0.42 | 12 | 0.06 | 0.38 | 23 | 0.05 |
| | 1.83 | 12 | 0.22 | 0.88 | 23 | 0.12 |
| RA5 | 0.35 | 12 | 0.05 | 0.43 | 22 | 0.08 |
| | 1.90 | 12 | 0.28 | 1.20 | 22 | 0.26 |
| RI1 | 0.27 | 18 | 0.08 | 0.26 | 18 | 0.06 |
| | 0.81 | 18 | 0.21 | 0.29 | 18 | 0.06 |
| RI2 | 0.35 | 18 | 0.09 | 0.25 | 19 | 0.06 |
| | 0.94 | 18 | 0.30 | 0.31 | 19 | 0.05 |

**Table 7.9.** (continued)

| | | | | | | |
|---|---|---|---|---|---|---|
| RI3 | 0.57 | 18 | 0.17 | 0.40 | 19 | 0.10 |
| | 1.04 | 18 | 0.31 | 0.31 | 19 | 0.09 |
| RI4 | 0.55 | 18 | 0.11 | 0.24 | 18 | 0.09 |
| | 0.92 | 17 | 0.21 | 0.27 | 18 | 0.09 |
| RI5 | 0.33 | 18 | 0.08 | 0.14 | 6 | 0.04 |
| | 0.65 | 18 | 0.20 | 0.23 | 6 | 0.06 |
| SC1 | 0.27 | 12 | 0.09 | 0.19 | 11 | 0.05 |
| | 1.53 | 12 | 0.46 | 0.60 | 11 | 0.16 |
| SC2 | 0.26 | 12 | 0.05 | 0.16 | 11 | 0.03 |
| | 1.25 | 12 | 0.20 | 0.53 | 11 | 0.13 |
| SCA | 0.42 | 12 | 0.06 | * | | |
| | 1.64 | 12 | 0.22 | * | | |
| SP1 | 0.50 | 12 | 0.08 | 0.36 | 23 | 0.09 |
| | 1.59 | 12 | 0.31 | 0.75 | 23 | 0.19 |
| SP2 | 0.48 | 12 | 0.12 | 0.49 | 23 | 0.11 |
| | 1.40 | 12 | 0.22 | 0.75 | 23 | 0.18 |
| SP3 | 0.28 | 12 | 0.19 | 0.23 | 23 | 0.05 |
| | 0.84 | 12 | 0.17 | 0.50 | 23 | 0.11 |
| SP4 | 0.43 | 12 | 0.16 | 0.34 | 22 | 0.07 |
| | 0.89 | 12 | 0.09 | 0.40 | 22 | 0.10 |
| SP5 | 0.17 | 12 | 0.10 | 0.28 | 23 | 0.05 |
| | 0.50 | 12 | 0.07 | 0.28 | 23 | 0.05 |
| ST | * | | | 0.22 | 1 | — |
| | * | | | 0.22 | 1 | — |
| TH1 | 0.42 | 9 | 0.15 | 0.24 | 8 | 0.06 |
| | 1.65 | 9 | 0.45 | 0.69 | 8 | 0.20 |
| TH2 | 0.38 | 9 | 0.11 | 0.27 | 8 | 0.05 |
| | 0.75 | 9 | 0.15 | 0.23 | 8 | 0.05 |
| TI1 | 0.41 | 10 | 0.07 | 0.30 | 24 | 0.04 |
| | 2.30 | 10 | 0.29 | 1.56 | 24 | 0.25 |
| TI2 | 0.58 | 10 | 0.09 | 0.32 | 25 | 0.05 |
| | 2.19 | 10 | 0.28 | 1.23 | 25 | 0.18 |
| TI3 | 0.76 | 10 | 0.06 | 0.74 | 25 | 0.06 |
| | 2.34 | 10 | 0.28 | 1.45 | 25 | 0.12 |
| TI4 | 0.44 | 10 | 0.04 | 0.51 | 25 | 0.05 |
| | 2.00 | 10 | 0.22 | 1.02 | 25 | 0.14 |
| TI5 | 0.41 | 10 | 0.03 | 0.50 | 24 | 0.08 |
| | 2.26 | 10 | 0.31 | 1.38 | 24 | 0.27 |
| TM | 0.52 | 11 | 0.07 | * | | |
| | 1.36 | 11 | 0.17 | * | | |
| UL1 | 0.34 | 12 | 0.07 | 0.30 | 23 | 0.06 |
| | 1.13 | 12 | 0.24 | 0.36 | 23 | 0.09 |
| UL2 | 0.69 | 13 | 0.14 | 0.45 | 23 | 0.07 |
| | 1.43 | 13 | 0.29 | 0.59 | 23 | 0.11 |
| UL3 | * | | | 0.44 | 5 | 0.06 |
| | * | | | 0.42 | 5 | 0.11 |
| UNC | 0.44 | 10 | 0.03 | * | | |
| | 1.34 | 10 | 0.14 | * | | |

*Scan site data unavailable.

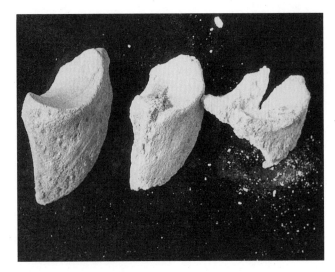

**Figure 7.13.** Variable weathering on bison phalanges from the Mill Iron site bison bonebed.

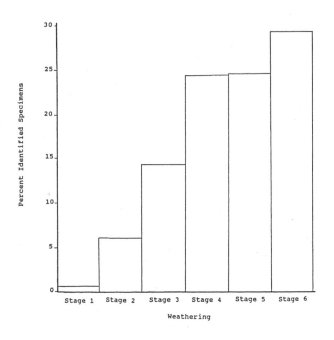

**Figure 7.14.** Histogram illustrates distribution of identified specimens across six weathering stages. Most of the assemblage is moderately to heavily weathered, with nearly 30% of the specimens classified as Stage 6.

each weathering stage tend to be phalanges, ribs, and vertebrae. Of interest here are the changing relative abundances of these elements through the sequence of weathering stages.

**Stage 1:** This class consists of nine identifiable specimens, seven of which are phalanges. One might expect the least-weathered specimens to be the most mineral-dense, but phalanges rank in the mid-range of volume densities. The prevalence of phalanges in this and other lightly weathered stages may be due to two factors. First, they hold little interest for human consumers because they do not bear much edible soft tissue, so are often left intact after limb disarticulation (e.g., Frison 1974). Second, under dry conditions, bison hide and ligaments desiccate and harden into a protective "shelter" (Todd 1983) that shields the skeleton from sun and rain. In particular, Hill (1979) notes that mummification of bovid feet occurs in arid environments. Although hide and tissue might be removed by people and carnivores from most of the other elements, any remaining on the abandoned phalanges would shield them, for a time, from weathering. This might explain the appearance of phalanges in the least-weathered stages. On the other hand, if mummification of the distal limbs did occur, one might expect to find articulated phalanges in the bonebed. In fact, only disarticulated phalanges were found.

**Stage 2:** Phalanges continue to dominate the assemblage, but now are accompanied by carpals, tarsals and long bones.

**Stage 3:** Here, the distribution seems almost evenly spread among element classes, but vertebrae and other axial elements begin to appear for the first time.

**Stage 4:** Ribs, crania, and vertebrae become relatively more abundant, although most other element classes are represented by a few specimens.

**Stage 5:** Ribs, crania, and vertebrae increasingly dominate the relative abundances. The actual numbers of other element fragments drop only slightly (Table 7.13), although relative to the much more abundant axial elements, they virtually disappear from the graph.

**Stage 6:** Ribs, crania, vertebrae and upper forelimb elements comprise most of the elements in this weathering class. Across the weathering stage sequence, axial elements become increasingly more abundant in the advanced weathering stages, and peak in stages 5 or 6. The same is generally true for upper limb bones but not for phalanges, carpals, and tarsals, which tend to peak earlier in the sequence. Yet the axis and atlas, portions of which are highly mineral-dense, are absent in the early weathering stages and abundant in the advanced ones. This is unexpected, given the correlation of mineral density with element survivorship at Mill Iron. It also seems contradictory because assemblage MAUs, based on normed, independent element parts, clearly show that these elements are also most abundant within the assemblage. This apparent contradiction might be explained by the fact that while portions of these elements are very dense, other parts are not, and weathering codes were assigned on the basis of overall specimen condition.

Consider the elements that comprise weathering stages 1 and 2. The most abundant of these are phalanges and carpals, which may have been covered with dried tissue that protected them from deterioration (Figure 7.15). Tarsals may have been similarly protected, but they also happen to be among the densest bones in the bison skeleton. Portions of the mandibles and tibia, also relatively abundant in the early weathering stages, are similarly dense. Aside from these, virtually all of the remaining assemblage falls into weathering stages 4 to 6. Overall, the relative distributions of element NISPs follow predictions based on mineral density. The atlas and axis are the exceptions. For reasons that remain unclear, their representation

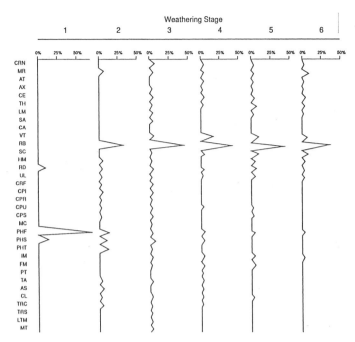

**Figure 7.15.** Relative abundances of elements across weathering stages. Phalanges dominate the least-weathered portion of the assemblage.

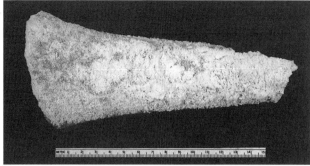

**Figure 7.16.** Salt crystal accumulation on a bison long bone.

across weathering categories appears to be inconsistent with both their mineral density and their abundance within the assemblage.

Most of the assemblage, however, is intensively weathered. Although it is generally reasoned that burial significantly slows bone weathering (see Lyman and Fox 1989), such may not be the case at Mill Iron because of the presence of soluble salts in, and the related alkalinity of, the surrounding matrix.

## Salt Weathering

To date, no analysis has been undertaken to identify the particular salt(s) found at Mill Iron, but gypsum is a likely possibility (C. V. Haynes, personal communication). Further, project geologists report neither grain size nor pH analyses, as their interests lay primarily in geomorphological issues. However, two sediment samples procured from a plaster-jacketed element (from 38.867W, 7.900S, at an arbitrary elevation of 95.378 m) provided pH measurements of 8.6 (Kreutzer 1992b).

Just as saline solutions penetrate rock and cause it to disintegrate (e.g., Cooke and Smalley 1968; Wellman and Wilson 1965), such solutions are capable of weathering other objects in the ground. Field observations at Mill Iron strongly point to salt crystal growth from solution (Yatsu 1988) as a major cause of bone deterioration within the assemblage (Fig. 7.16).

In the lab, the presence or absence of visible salts was noted for each specimen examined. Table 7.14 shows the number of specimens exhibiting salt precipitation in each element class, and provides the percentage of each class that shows visible salts. For instance, five of the 22 astragali, or 22.7%, exhibit

salt crystals. Most of the damage is to appendicular elements; radii appear to be particularly susceptible, with nearly 55% showing visible crystals. These patterns may relate to microstructural properties of the elements.

As noted earlier, salt precipitation on the bone surface occurs after exposure to moisture, including the moisture provided as a result of the application of a consolidant solution. The specimens were cleaned and conserved by several individuals working separately, and were not treated identically. As a result, the apparent pattern of soluble salts across elements may reflect variability in post-recovery treatment as much as it reflects actual diagenetic conditions. Further, the absence of visible surface salts does not necessarily mean that none are present within the bone. It is difficult, then, to quantify the occurrence of salt weathering across the assemblage, and to explain why it appears to cause differential destruction within the assemblage (Figure 7.16).

Nevertheless, its damaging effects on exposed bone are obvious, and salt weathering clearly has contributed to assemblage attrition. As burial may not have significantly slowed this or other bone-weathering processes (see Lyman and Fox 1989), the weathering profile itself cannot be regarded as firm evidence for long-term surface exposure.

## Skeletal Disarticulation

The paucity of articulated skeletal units, however, is in keeping with an assemblage that has been subject to extensive disturbance at or near the ground surface. No complete, articulated bison skeletons were found at Mill Iron, and only 33 articulated skeletal units (not including tooth rows or fused elements) were recorded during excavation. Of these, 28 are vertebral segments, two are forelimb joints, and three are rear limb units including tarsals (Table 7.15).

Todd (1983, 1987a) considered appendicular articulations and conjoined specimens in assessing the degree of post-depositional disturbance at the Horner II bison bonebed. No attempt was made to match and conjoin scattered elements at Mill Iron, because of the generally poor condition of the assemblage. However, articulated specimens were recorded as they were encountered in the field.

**Table 7.10.** Volume Density and Mill Iron Bonebed %MAUs for 88 Scan Sites.

| Scan Site | MNE | MAU | %MAU | VD |
|---|---|---|---|---|
| 2&3CP | 7 | 3.5 | 16.7 | 0.50 |
| AC1 | 21 | 10.5 | 50.0 | 0.53 |
| AS1 | 22 | 11.0 | 52.4 | 0.72 |
| AS2 | 21 | 10.5 | 50.0 | 0.62 |
| AS3 | 22 | 11.0 | 52.4 | 0.60 |
| AT1 | 8 | 8.0 | 38.1 | 0.52 |
| AT2 | 8 | 8.0 | 38.1 | 0.91 |
| AT3 | 12 | 12.0 | 57.1 | 0.34 |
| AX1 | 21 | 21.0 | 100.0 | 0.65 |
| AX2 | 6 | 6.0 | 28.6 | 0.38 |
| AX3 | 3 | 3.0 | 14.3 | 0.97 |
| CA1 | 8 | 4.0 | 19.0 | 0.46 |
| CA2 | 14 | 7.0 | 33.3 | 0.80 |
| CA3 | 13 | 6.5 | 30.9 | 0.49 |
| CA4 | 13 | 6.5 | 30.9 | 0.66 |
| CE1 | 46 | 9.2 | 43.8 | 0.37 |
| CE2 | 26 | 5.2 | 24.8 | 0.62 |
| CUN | 12 | 6.0 | 28.6 | 0.43 |
| DN1 | 13 | 6.5 | 30.9 | 0.53 |
| DN2 | 24 | 12.0 | 57.1 | 0.61 |
| DN3 | 26 | 13.0 | 61.9 | 0.62 |
| DN4 | 36 | 18.0 | 85.7 | 0.53 |
| DN5 | 25 | 12.5 | 59.5 | 0.49 |
| DN6 | 21 | 10.5 | 50.0 | 0.57 |
| DN7 | 21 | 10.5 | 50.0 | 0.79 |
| DN8 | 17 | 8.5 | 40.5 | 0.79 |
| FE1 | 11 | 5.5 | 26.2 | 0.31 |
| FE2 | 5 | 2.5 | 11.9 | 0.34 |
| FE3 | 4 | 2.0 | 9.5 | 0.34 |
| FE4 | 5 | 2.5 | 11.9 | 0.45 |
| FE5 | 7 | 3.5 | 16.7 | 0.36 |
| FE6 | 1 | 0.5 | 2.4 | 0.26 |
| HU1 | 1 | 0.5 | 2.4 | 0.24 |
| HU2 | 2 | 1.0 | 4.8 | 0.25 |
| HU3 | 11 | 5.5 | 26.2 | 0.45 |
| HU4 | 19 | 9.5 | 45.2 | 0.48 |
| HU5 | 18 | 9.0 | 42.9 | 0.38 |
| IL1 | 15 | 7.5 | 35.7 | 0.22 |
| IL2 | 38 | 19.0 | 90.5 | 0.52 |
| IS1 | 15 | 7.5 | 35.7 | 0.50 |
| IS2 | 5 | 2.5 | 11.9 | 0.19 |
| LATMAL | 6 | 3.0 | 14.3 | 0.56 |
| LU1 | 24 | 4.8 | 22.9 | 0.31 |
| LU2 | 14 | 2.8 | 13.3 | 0.11 |
| LU3 | 4 | 0.8 | 3.8 | 0.39 |
| LUNAR | 10 | 5.0 | 23.8 | 0.35 |
| MP1 | 14 | 7.0 | 33.3 | 0.56 |
| MP2 | 15 | 7.5 | 35.7 | 0.61 |
| MP3 | 14 | 7.0 | 33.3 | 0.68 |
| MP4 | 15 | 7.5 | 35.7 | 0.55 |
| MP5 | 14 | 7.0 | 33.3 | 0.43 |
| MP6 | 20 | 10.0 | 47.6 | 0.50 |

**Table 7.10.** (continued)

| | | | | |
|---|---|---|---|---|
| NC1 | 12 | 6.0 | 28.6 | 0.48 |
| NC2 | 9 | 4.5 | 21.4 | 0.64 |
| NC3 | 10 | 5.0 | 23.8 | 0.77 |
| P11 | 59 | 7.4 | 35.2 | 0.48 |
| P12 | 64 | 8 | 38.1 | 0.46 |
| P13 | 57 | 7.1 | 33.8 | 0.48 |
| P21 | 46 | 5.7 | 27.1 | 0.41 |
| P23 | 50 | 6.25 | 29.8 | 0.46 |
| P31 | 30 | 3.7 | 17.8 | 0.32 |
| PU1 | 10 | 5.0 | 23.8 | 0.55 |
| RA1 | 17 | 8.5 | 40.5 | 0.48 |
| RA2 | 17 | 8.5 | 40.5 | 0.56 |
| RA3 | 13 | 6.5 | 30.9 | 0.62 |
| RA4 | 15 | 7.5 | 35.7 | 0.42 |
| RA5 | 16 | 8.0 | 38.1 | 0.35 |
| RI1 | 50 | 1.8 | 8.6 | 0.27 |
| RI2 | 65 | 2.3 | 10.9 | 0.35 |
| RI3 | 125 | 4.5 | 21.4 | 0.57 |
| SC1 | 10 | 10.0 | 47.6 | 0.27 |
| SC2 | 3 | 3.0 | 14.3 | 0.26 |
| SCA | 10 | 5.0 | 23.8 | 0.42 |
| SP1 | 37 | 18.5 | 88.1 | 0.50 |
| SP2 | 33 | 16.5 | 78.6 | 0.48 |
| SP3 | 18 | 9.0 | 42.8 | 0.28 |
| SP4 | 23 | 11.5 | 54.8 | 0.43 |
| SP5 | 5 | 2.5 | 11.9 | 0.17 |
| TH1 | 33 | 2.4 | 11.4 | 0.42 |
| TH2 | 25 | 1.8 | 8.6 | 0.38 |
| TI1 | 1 | 0.5 | 2.4 | 0.41 |
| TI2 | 6 | 3.0 | 14.3 | 0.58 |
| TI3 | 7 | 3.5 | 16.7 | 0.76 |
| TI4 | 6 | 3.5 | 16.7 | 0.44 |
| TI5 | 9 | 4.5 | 21.4 | 0.41 |
| UNC | 12 | 6 | 28.6 | 0.44 |
| UL1 | 3 | 1.5 | 7.1 | 0.34 |
| UL2 | 15 | 7.5 | 35.7 | 0.69 |

**Table 7.11.** Correlation Coefficients for Mill Iron %MAUs, (S)MTP, and VD.

| Correlation | N | $r_s$ | P |
|---|---|---|---|
| (S)MTP.SAF — MI %MAU | 21 | −0.47 | > .004 |
| MI %MAU — VD, all scan sites | 88 | +0.44 | > .001 |
| MI %MAU — VD, scan sites corresponding to utility units | 21 | +0.64 | > .005 |
| (S)MTP.SAF — VD | 21 | −0.58 | >.001 |

**Table 7.12.** Weathering Stage Classification, from Behrensmeyer (1978) and Todd (1983, 1987a).

| | |
|---|---|
| 1 | Unweathered, dry |
| 2 | Limited surface weathering; some longitudinal cracking |
| 3 | Light surface flaking, deeper cracking |
| 4 | Patches of fibrous bone, moderate flaking and cracking |
| 5 | Deep cracking, extensive flaking |
| 6 | Bone falling apart |

To compare the Horner articulation data to that of other sites, Todd (1987a:141-143) calculated the maximum number of *potential* articulations for each joint. He did this by tallying MNEs for the articular ends of the bone pairs comprising each joint, and then using the lower of the two MNEs as the number of potential articulations for that joint. Consider the knee joint, for instance: the Horner assemblage included 104 distal femora and 95 proximal tibia (Todd 1987a:146). By Todd's calculations, the maximum number of possible knee articulations was 95. Using this number, he then calculated the percentage of articulations that actually occurred for each joint. In this example, there were 30 distal femur/proximal tibia articulations, so 31.58% of the potential articulations were actually recorded at Horner II (Todd 1987a). These figures could then be compared to standardized data from other sites.

Such comparisons carry with them the same limitations inherent in analyses of skeletal-part relative abundances: many different kinds of processes might account for the patterning, and there is no analytical yardstick by which objective meaning might be ascribed. Disarticulation and scattering of elements might result from intensive carcass processing by human beings, short-term carnivore ravaging, geological and fluvial processes operating over a lengthy period, post-burial rodent burrowing, or trampling. Data comparisons simply indicate in what manner assemblages vary, but do not address why those differences exist.

With these limitations in mind, standardized appendicular articulations for the Mill Iron assemblage are presented in Table 7.16. Discounting the fused element pairs, leg joint articulations are uncommon in the assemblage.

Superimposing these data on the graphs Todd (1987a) provides for Horner, Casper, and Olsen-Chubbuck (Figure 7.17), one can see that Mill Iron has strikingly fewer joint articulations. The only reasonable conclusion to be drawn from this, however, is that undetermined processes causing limb-joint disarticulation operated more intensely or for a lengthier period at Mill Iron than at the other bonebeds. The strongest argument for lengthy surface exposure remains that provided by the geological evidence, discussed earlier. The bone weathering profile, weathering distributions, and disarticulation data do not falsify the hypothesis.

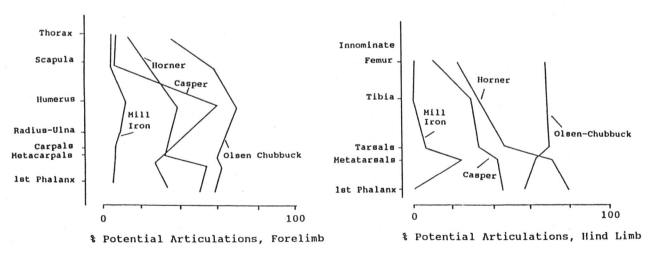

**Figure 7.17.** Comparison of percentages of potential articulations of forelimb and rear limb elements from Casper, Olsen-Chubbuck, Horner, and Mill Iron (After Todd 1987a).

**Table 7.13.** Mill Iron Bison Bone Weathering by Identified Elements.

| Element | Stage 1 | Stage 2 | Stage 3 | Stage 4 | Stage 5 | Stage 6 | Total |
|---|---|---|---|---|---|---|---|
| AS | 0 | 6 | 3 | 9 | 4 | 0 | 22 |
| AT | 0 | 0 | 0 | 7 | 6 | 12 | 25 |
| AX | 0 | 0 | 3 | 4 | 8 | 10 | 25 |
| CA | 0 | 0 | 1 | 0 | 2 | 0 | 3 |
| CE | 0 | 0 | 11 | 19 | 31 | 26 | 87 |
| CL | 0 | 3 | 4 | 5 | 5 | 1 | 18 |
| CPF | 0 | 0 | 3 | 4 | 4 | 2 | 13 |
| CPI | 0 | 3 | 2 | 2 | 0 | 3 | 10 |
| CPR | 0 | 2 | 4 | 2 | 1 | 1 | 10 |
| CPS | 1 | 2 | 2 | 3 | 7 | 4 | 19 |
| CPU | 0 | 1 | 4 | 0 | 6 | 1 | 12 |
| CRN | 0 | 0 | 12 | 12 | 10 | 15 | 49 |
| FM | 0 | 1 | 3 | 9 | 8 | 5 | 26 |
| HM | 0 | 2 | 4 | 2 | 5 | 15 | 28 |
| IM | 0 | 0 | 3 | 18 | 13 | 27 | 61 |
| LM | 0 | 0 | 3 | 2 | 14 | 18 | 37 |
| LTM | 0 | 1 | 2 | 2 | 1 | 0 | 6 |
| MC | 0 | 1 | 2 | 1 | 2 | 2 | 8 |
| MCF | 0 | 0 | 1 | 2 | 0 | 0 | 3 |
| MR | 0 | 5 | 9 | 14 | 10 | 44 | 82 |
| MT | 0 | 0 | 4 | 1 | 3 | 5 | 13 |
| PH | 0 | 1 | 0 | 1 | 1 | 1 | 4 |
| PHF | 6 | 13 | 11 | 16 | 11 | 10 | 67 |
| PHS | 1 | 9 | 16 | 19 | 2 | 2 | 49 |
| PHT | 0 | 10 | 7 | 5 | 5 | 4 | 31 |
| PT | 0 | 0 | 3 | 3 | 1 | 0 | 7 |
| RB | 0 | 32 | 116 | 176 | 145 | 184 | 653 |
| RD | 1 | 3 | 4 | 3 | 6 | 14 | 31 |
| SA | 0 | 0 | 1 | 0 | 6 | 4 | 11 |
| SC | 0 | 0 | 1 | 14 | 12 | 40 | 67 |
| TA | 0 | 3 | 2 | 5 | 3 | 4 | 17 |
| TH | 0 | 0 | 2 | 7 | 29 | 26 | 64 |
| TRC | 0 | 6 | 1 | 4 | 2 | 1 | 14 |
| TRS | 0 | 2 | 2 | 2 | 1 | 0 | 7 |
| UL | 0 | 2 | 6 | 5 | 2 | 11 | 26 |
| VT | 0 | 2 | 13 | 61 | 78 | 40 | 194 |
| Total | 9 | 110 | 265 | 439 | 444 | 532 | 1,799 |

**Table 7.14.** Bone Specimens Exhibiting Visible Salt Crystals on Surface.

| Element | Number with Salts | %MNE with Salts |
|---|---|---|
| AS | 5 | 22.7 |
| AX | 1 | 4.0 |
| CE | 4 | 4.6 |
| CL | 2 | 11.1 |
| CPF | 1 | 7.7 |
| CPI | 2 | 20.0 |
| CPS | 4 | 21.1 |
| CPU | 1 | 8.3 |
| CRN (MX) | 1 | 8.3 |
| FM | 5 | 19.2 |
| HM | 4 | 14.3 |
| IM | 8 | 13.1 |
| LB | 1 | 1.0 |
| LM | 2 | 5.4 |
| MP | 2 | 14.3 |
| MR | 1 | 1.0 |
| MT | 1 | 7.7 |
| PHF | 4 | 6.0 |
| PHS | 16 | 31.3 |
| PHT | 3 | 9.7 |
| RB | 31 | 4.7 |
| RD | 17 | 54.8 |
| SA | 1 | 9.0 |
| SC | 4 | 6.0 |
| TA | 2 | 11.8 |
| TH | 1 | 1.6 |
| TRC | 3 | 21.4 |
| UL | 3 | 11.5 |
| US | 3 | 0.4 |
| VT | 2 | 0.5 |
| Total | 135 | |

**Table 7.15.** Summary of Skeletal Articulations.

| Articulated Unit | Number of Articulation Units |
|---|---|
| Axial: | |
|     Cervicals | 15 |
|     Thoracics | 3 |
|     Lumbar/Sacral | 7 |
|     Unidentified Vertebrae | 3 |
| Forelimb: | |
|     Humerus/radius-ulna | 2 |
| Hind limb: | |
|     Tibia/Tarsals | 1 |
|     Metatarsals/Tarsals | 2 |

**Table 7.16.** Percentage Potential Articulations for Mill Iron Long Bone Elements (after Todd 1987a).

| Element | MNE | Joint | Potential Articulation | Recorded Articulation | % Potential |
|---|---|---|---|---|---|
| DS humerus | 18 | | | | |
| PR ulna | 14 | HM-UL | 14 | 1 | 7.14 |
| PR radius | 17 | HM-RD | 17 | 1 | 5.88 |
| DS tibia | 9 | | | | |
| Astragalus | 22 | TA-AS | 9 | 1 | 11.11 |
| DS metatarsal | 5 | | | | |
| Tarsals | 12 | MT-TR | 5 | 2 | 40.00 |

**Table 7.17.** Gnawing Codes.

| | |
|---|---|
| 0 | None observed |
| 1 | Light to moderate rodent |
| 2 | Extensive rodent |
| 3 | Crenulated |
| 4 | Pitting |
| 5 | Scoring |
| 6 | Chipping |
| 7 | Puncture |
| 8 | Furrowing |

## Carnivore Modification

People were not the only consumers interested in the Mill Iron bison carcasses. Shortly after, or perhaps during human occupation, carnivores began gnawing the remains. In so doing, they destroyed some parts, turned some into unidentifiable scrap, and modified others in a patterned manner. Carnivores, like people, consume carcass parts in a sequential manner that is largely determined by the food value and accessibility of those parts (Binford 1981; Blumenschine 1986a, 1986b, 1988; Brain 1981; Burgett 1990; Haglund 1991; Haynes 1980a, 1980b, 1982; Marean et al. 1992). Carnivores also leave a variety of toothmarks and patterned damage on bone (Binford 1981; Bonnichsen 1979; Haynes 1983; Johnson 1983, 1985; Maguire et al. 1980; Morlan 1980; Wilson 1983). Each specimen from the Mill Iron bonebed was examined for evidence of gnawing, which was coded by type, following Todd (1987a) and Burgett (1990) (Table 7.17). Kinds of gnaw marks observed include crenulation of chewed edges, pitting and punctures, tooth scoring, and furrowing, as defined by Binford (1981:45-49). On many specimens, more than one of these kinds of gnaw marks are found together on the same segment of bone.

However, bone weathering and exfoliation is so severe across the assemblage that many specimens no longer retain cortical surfaces. Where exfoliation or severe surface deterioration obscures more than half of a specimen's surface, surface modification was recorded as indeterminate.

Some long bones were too fragile to handle for examination or had exfoliated cortical surfaces, but nonetheless exhibited extensive damage, usually to the articular ends. In many cases, damage morphology closely resembled that exhibited by other Mill Iron specimens of the same element, where the morphology is clearly associated with toothmarks. In some instances, anomalous marks were observed, but because of the condition of the specimen, the agent that caused them could not be determined.

A secondary classification was created whereby specimens were recorded as ungnawed (no visible toothmarks, weathering stage 4 or less), gnawed (toothmarks visible), and indeterminate (surface exfoliated or otherwise obscured) (Table 7.18). Some deteriorated specimens (weathering stages 5 or 6) exhibited damage morphology typical of carnivore gnawing, as identified on other specimens of the same element within the assemblage. These were counted among the gnawed specimens in the analysis, following the approach taken by Todd (1987a) and Todd and Rapson (1988a, 1988b). Indeterminate specimens constitute a separate class and are not counted among the gnawed or ungnawed specimens.

## Carnivore Modification of Long Bones

Proximal-to-distal structural differences in long bones make portions of these elements differentially vulnerable to destructive processes. This being the case, the percentages of complete long bones present in an assemblage should be indicative of the degree of attrition undergone by the assemblage: the lower the percentages of complete long bones, the greater the amount of destruction. Likewise, the percentage difference between counts of long bone proximal and distal articular ends is thought to be indicative of differential destruction (Richardson 1980). Element classes with approximately equal numbers of proximal and distal articular ends are considered to have been subjected to little attrition. Although taphonomists use such comparisons to assess the intensity of destruction within an assemblage, they generally caution that its *cause* is not necessarily identified. Inferences regarding the agent(s) of differential destruction across long bone classes must be based upon physical evidence, such as tooth scoring. The Mill Iron bison assemblage bears an abundance of such evidence.

Of the 3,073 recorded Mill Iron specimens, 2,789 are bone

(that is, not teeth or tooth fragments). Of the bone specimens, 1,357 (48.66%) are indeterminate. Of the remaining 1,432 specimens, 199 (13.90%) show evidence of carnivore gnawing. The bulk of this modification occurs on the long bone speci-

mens, of which 63% of determinate specimens are gnawed (Table 7.19).

The locations of gnawing on the long bones are indicated in Table 7.20. Each specimen is identified by portion, as indicated by its density scan site locations. For example, L14-21-49 is a humeral distal shaft and articular end, which includes scan sites HU3, HU4 and HU5.

Long bone damage morphologies and distributions have been described in detail by Binford (1981), who considers certain distributions of damage across humeri to be particularly indicative, if not diagnostic, of carnivore ravaging. Here, the predominance of scan sites HU3, HU4, and HU5 indicates that most of the humeral specimens are shafts and distal ends, missing the head and proximal diaphysis. This distribution has been reported in numerous carnivore-ravaged assemblages (Brain 1967, 1969, 1981; Binford 1981; Haynes 1982; Morey and Klippel 1991; Richardson 1980). However, such a pattern may also be produced, as mentioned earlier, by other attritional processes, or by people breaking long bones at mid-shaft for removal of marrow.

Binford (1981) has suggested that plotting the ratios of proximal to distal humeri and proximal to distal tibiae within an assemblage provides a means of assessing the severity of attrition. Those classes with many distal ends and few proximal ends fall into what Binford (1981) has characterized as a "zone of destruction." The Mill Iron data fall into that zone (Figure 7.18).

Binford's "zone of destruction" is arbitrarily defined, providing a convenient standard for comparing and categorizing as-

**Table 7.18.** Summary of Carnivore Gnawing on Mill Iron Assemblage.

| Element | No Visible Gnawing | Visible Gnawing | Indeterminate |
|---|---|---|---|
| CRN | 47 | 0 | 0 |
| HY | 4 | 0 | 0 |
| MR | 46 | 4 | 37 |
| AT | 7 | 1 | 17 |
| AX | 12 | 0 | 13 |
| CE | 31 | 2 | 54 |
| TH | 20 | 2 | 42 |
| LM | 5 | 0 | 32 |
| SA | 1 | 0 | 10 |
| IM | 24 | 1 | 36 |
| CA | 1 | 0 | 2 |
| VT | 83 | 7 | 104 |
| RB | 454 | 35 | 168 |
| SC | 36 | 1 | 30 |
| HM | 4 | 12 | 12 |
| RD | 5 | 8 | 18 |
| UL | 8 | 11 | 7 |
| CPF | 6 | 2 | 4 |
| CPI | 4 | 1 | 5 |
| CPR | 7 | 0 | 4 |
| CPS | 10 | 1 | 8 |
| CPU | 5 | 0 | 7 |
| MC | 3 | 1 | 4 |
| MCF | 3 | 0 | 0 |
| FM | 2 | 17 | 7 |
| PT | 1 | 3 | 2 |
| TA | 6 | 5 | 6 |
| AS | 12 | 2 | 8 |
| CL | 4 | 6 | 9 |
| LTM | 6 | 0 | 0 |
| TRC | 9 | 1 | 4 |
| TRS | 6 | 0 | 1 |
| MT | 5 | 2 | 6 |
| MP | 8 | 1 | 5 |
| SE | 13 | 3 | 6 |
| PHF | 18 | 33 | 16 |
| PHS | 21 | 20 | 10 |
| PHT | 10 | 11 | 10 |
| PH | 2 | 0 | 2 |
| LB | 30 | 3 | 69 |
| US | 205 | 3 | 494 |
| CB | 0 | 0 | 35 |
| FB | 49 | 0 | 53 |
| Subtotal | 1,233 | 199 | 1,357 |
| Total | | | 2,789 |

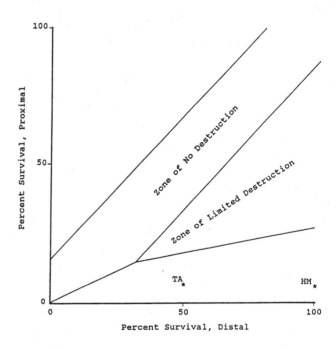

**Figure 7.18.** Ratios of proximal to distal humeri and tibiae of Mill Iron bison, plotted on Binford's (1981) "Zone of Destruction" graph.

**Table 7.19.** Summary of Carnivore Modification of Long Bones from the Mill Iron Assemblage.

| Element | None (1) | Gnawed (2) | Indeterminate (3) | % Gnawed (4)[a] | % Indeterminate (5)[b] |
|---|---|---|---|---|---|
| Humerus | 4 | 12 | 12 | 75.00 | 42.86 |
| Radius | 5 | 8 | 18 | 61.53 | 58.06 |
| Ulna | 8 | 11 | 7 | 57.89 | 26.92 |
| Metacarpal | 3 | 1 | 4 | 25.00 | 50.00 |
| Femur | 2 | 17 | 7 | 89.47 | 26.92 |
| Tibia | 6 | 5 | 6 | 45.45 | 35.29 |
| Metatarsal | 5 | 2 | 6 | 15.38 | 50.00 |
| Long Bone Totals | 33 | 56 | 60 | 62.92 | 40.27 |

[a]Percentage of GNW = 1 or 2 for all specimens *except* those with severely exfoliated or deteriorated surfaces.

Percentage of gnawed specimens = $\dfrac{\text{Col. 2} \times 100}{\text{Col. 1} + \text{Col. 2}}$

[b]Percentage of exfoliated or deteriorated specimens (GNW = 3) for which evidence of gnawing could not be determined.

Percentage of indeterminate specimens = $\dfrac{\text{Col. 3} \times 100}{\text{Col. 1} + \text{Col. 2} + \text{Col. 3}}$

semblage patterns, even though it has no inherent, objective meaning. No independent analytical measuring stick exists by which an assemblage may be judged severely, moderately, or slightly damaged by attritional processes. Likewise, this descriptive device provides no means for identifying the cause of the pattern: comparisons with modern assemblages with known taphonomic histories may only *suggest* agents of destruction. These possibilities can then be considered in light of physical evidence, such as tooth scoring or hammer impact marks.

At Mill Iron, humeri, tibia, and femora exhibit the most intensive differential articular-end survivorship (Table 7.21). Proximal humeri and tibia, and distal femora tend to be missing. Given the abundant toothmarks documented on these elements, carnivore gnawing is a likely cause of this pattern.

### Carnivore Modification of Other Elements

Other elements also exhibit evidence of carnivore gnawing. Because they comprise the bulk of the assemblage and are too numerous to be listed in table format, non-long-bone elements are summarized here.

Of the non-long-bone elements, gnawing is most abundant on ribs. Only one of the 40 clearly carnivore-chewed rib specimens exhibits gnawing on the head and neck. This suggests that the ribs were chewed while they were still attached to the thoracic vertebrae. Haynes (1982) has noted that wolves typically attack the rib blades, leaving the proximal ends still attached to the vertebrae. Frison (1970, 1974) and Zeimens (1982), on the other hand, concluded that the abundances of rib heads at Glenrock, Casper, and Agate Basin, respectively, were the result of a butchery procedure whereby people lifted the animal's rib cage to snap the ribs near the vertebral col-

umn. The paucity of rib heads at Stewart's Cattle Guard, a site to which preferred carcass parts apparently were transported, was similarly interpreted (Jodry and Stanford 1992). People may have removed bison rib-slabs in this manner at Mill Iron, but the gnawing evident on the recovered blade fragments indicates that carnivores are at least partially responsible for the pattern of rib destruction at Mill Iron.

Few vertebrae displayed clear evidence of carnivore gnawing, although they were highly fragmented and most had lost their spines and transverse processes. Such damage might have occurred during butchery, but carnivores are known to destroy spinous processes (Richardson 1980).

Innominates show little evident carnivore damage. The most abundant portions of innominates are ilium fragments, usually associated with mineral-dense acetabular remnants. Corresponding to this is the presence of a number of femoral head fragments with the fovea still visible. These femoral fragments typically exhibit tooth scoring not on the proximal articular surface itself, but in the exposed cancellous bone. This could have occurred if the femur heads were gnawed while still attached to the acetabulum: the proximal-most portions of the heads would be protected in the acetabulum while the rest was removed by gnawing.

Phalanges, as well, appear to have been favored targets. There are 33 gnawed first phalanges, most of them punctured and furrowed on the plantar side. The same pattern is evident on 23 gnawed second phalanges. There are, however, only 10 carnivore-gnawed third phalanges, most of which are missing the distal-most tips and are furrowed on the dorsal surfaces.

Speth (1983) notes that the distal-most limb bones, including phalanges, contain fluid fat and are relatively rich in that substance even in times of nutritional stress. Ungulate lower limb bones in wolf kills often remain ignored and hide-bound

**Table 7.20.** Mill Iron Carnivore Modification, Locations[1] on Limb Bones.

| | | | A. Humerus | | | | |
|---|---|---|---|---|---|---|---|
| Specimen | HU1 | HU2 | HU3 | HU4 | HU5 | GNW[2] | Location |
| L13-24-114 | X | | | | | 1 | Cancellous |
| L14-1-133 | | X | | | | 0 | |
| M13-9-3 | | X | | | | 0 | |
| M14-1-126 | | X | | | | 0 | |
| M14-10-112 | | X | X | X | | 1 | Proximal shaft |
| L14-21-49 | | | X | X | | 1 | Distal shaft |
| M13-4-78 | | | X | X | | 3 | |
| M13-3-53 | | | X | X | X | 3 | |
| L13-25-72 | | | X | X | X | 1 | Shaft, epicondyles |
| L13-23-40 | | | X | X | X | 1 | Shaft, epicondyles |
| L13-25-105 | | | X | X | X | 1 | Shaft, condyles |
| L13-17-13 | | | X | X | X | 1 | Shaft, epicondyles |
| L13-16-7 | | | X | X | X | 0 | |
| M13-5-109 | | | X | X | X | 1 | Trochlea, epicondyles |
| M13-6-139 | | | X | X | X | 3 | |
| M13-13-67 | | | | X | | 3 | |
| L13-24-94 | | | | X | X | 3 | |
| M13-7-108 | | | | X | X | 3 | |
| L13-23-69 | | | | X | X | 2 | Proximal shaft |
| M13-14-65 | | | | X | X | 3 | |
| M13-8-3 | | | | X | X | 1 | Epicondyles |
| M13-6-10 | | | | X | X | 3 | |
| L14-20-7 | | | | X | X | 1 | Trochlea, shaft |
| L14-21-32 | | | | | X | 1 | Capitulum |
| M14-10-46 | | | | | X | 3 | |
| M14-10-85 | | | | | X | 3 | |
| M14-1-125 | | | | | X | 3 | |
| M13-13-3 | | | | | X | 3 | |

| | | | B. Radius-Ulna | | | | |
|---|---|---|---|---|---|---|---|
| Specimen | RA1 | RA2 | RA3 | RA4 | RA5 | GNW | Location |
| M13-14-65 | X | | | | | 3 | |
| M13-5-108 | X | | | | | 3 | |
| M13-6-18 | X | X | | | | 3 | |
| M13-4-71 | X | X | | | | 3 | |
| M13-14-69 | X | X | | | | 3 | |
| M13-13-1 | X | X | | | | 3 | |
| L13-16-27 | X | X | X | | | 3 | |
| L13-23-45 | X | X | X | | | 3 | |
| L13-25-47 | X | X | X | X | | 1 | Proximal shaft |
| L13-17-10 | X | X | X | X | | 1 | Distal shaft |
| L13-16-131 | X | X | X | X | X | 1 | Shaft |
| L13-24-26 | X | X | X | X | X | 1 | Distal shaft |
| L13-24-46 | X | X | X | X | X | 3 | |
| L14-20-8 | X | X | X | X | X | 1 | Proximal, distal shaft |
| L13-23-29 | X | X | X | X | X | 3 | |
| L13-23-42 | X | X | X | X | X | 3 | |
| M13-7-106 | X | X | X | X | X | 3 | |

[1]Approximate, descriptive scan sites have been assigned to some shaft fragments that actually lie between two scan sites.
[2]GNW: 0 = No visible carnivore gnawing on specimens of weathering stage 4 or lower
    1 = Presence or gnawing (scoring, crenulation, punctures, pitting, or furrowing)
    2 = Probable gnawing (morphology typical of carnivore modification) on exfoliated specimens
    3 = Indeterminate (surface exfoliated, burned, or otherwise obscured)

**Table 7.20.** *(continued)*

| | | | *B. Radius-Ulna* | | | | |
|---|---|---|---|---|---|---|---|
| Specimen | RA1 | RA2 | RA3 | RA4 | RA5 | GNW | Location |
| M13-5-31 | | X | | | | 0 | |
| L13-23-46 | | X | | | | 3 | |
| M14-10-112 | | X | X | X | | 1 | Proximal shaft |
| M13-3-103 | | | X | | | 3 | |
| L13-23-97 | | | X | X | | 1 | Shaft ends |
| L13-23-83 | | | X | X | X | 3 | |
| L13-23-68 | | | | X | X | 3 | |
| M13-3-36 | | | | X | X | 1 | Shaft |
| M13-3-62 | | | | | X | 3 | |
| L13-16-64 | | | | | X | 0 | |
| L13-17-30 | | | | | X | 0 | |
| L13-25-48 | | | | | X | 0 | |
| M13-14-71 | | | | | X | 3 | |
| M13-5-137 | | | | | X | 0 | |

| | UL1 | UL2 | UL3 | Shaft | GNW | Location |
|---|---|---|---|---|---|---|
| L13-25-73 | X | X | | | 2 | Olecranon, shaft |
| L13-23-66 | X | X | | | 3 | |
| L14-20-9 | | X | | | 2 | Olecranon |
| L13-23-44 | | X | | | 1 | Proximal |
| M13-14-70 | | X | | | 1 | Olecranon |
| M13-3-52 | | X | | | 2 | Olecranon |
| M13-13-2 | | X | | | 2 | Olecranon |
| L13-16-143 | | X | | | 1 | Olecranon |
| L13-16-28 | | X | | | 1 | Olecranon |
| L13-23-50 | | X | | | 2 | Olecranon |
| L13-23-64 | | X | | | 1 | Proximal |
| M13-6-30 | | X | | | 3 | |
| M13-5-34 | | X | | | 0 | |
| M13-7-158 | | X | | | 1 | Olecranon |
| L14-17-22 | | | | X | Shaft | |
| L13-25-143 | | | | X | 0 | |
| M14-10-54 | | | | X | 3 | |
| L13-16-100 | | | | X | 0 | |
| M14-10-64 | | | | X | 3 | |
| M13-5-105 | | | | X | 3 | |
| L13-24-165 | | | | X | 0 | |
| L13-15-11 | | | | X | 3 | |
| M13-3-123 | | | | X | 3 | |
| M13-6-107 | | | | X | 0 | |
| L13-16-34 | | | | X | 0 | Shaft |
| L13-16-40 | | | | X | 0 | Shaft |

| | | | *C. Femora* | | | | |
|---|---|---|---|---|---|---|---|
| Specimen | FE1 | FE2 | FE3 | FE4 | FE5 | FE6 | GNW Location |
| M14-11-4 | X | | | | | | 1 Cancellous |
| M14-10-45 | X | | | | | | 1 Cancellous |
| M13-8-18 | X | | | | | | 1 Cancellous |
| M13-4-169 | X | | | | | | 2 Lateral |
| L13-23-65 | X | | | | | | 0 |
| L13-23-119 | X | | | | | | 0 |
| L13-17-42 | X | | | | | | 1 Shaft |
| M13-7-104 | X | X | | | | | 2 Trochlea |

**Table 7.20.** *(continued)*

### C. Femora

| Specimen | FE1 | FE2 | FE3 | FE4 | FE5 | FE6 | GNW | Location |
|---|---|---|---|---|---|---|---|---|
| M13-3-48 | X | X | X | X | | | 2 | Trochlea |
| L13-16-5 | X | X | X | X | X | | 2 | Distal, trochlea |
| M13-5-129 | X | X | X | X | X | | 1 | Trochlea, distal shaft |
| L13-23-43 | | X | X | | | | 2 | Trochlea |
| M13-5-182 | | X | | | | | 3 | |
| L13-17-43 | | | X | | | | 1 | Edge |
| L13-25-175 | | | X | X | X | | 1 | Shaft ends |
| M13-17-12 | | | | X | X | | 2 | Shaft ends |
| M13-5-182b | | | | | X | | 3 | |
| M13-3-46 | | | | | X | | 2 | Distal shaft |
| L13-18-5 | | | | | X | | 3 | |
| L13-23-39 | | | | | X | | 3 | |
| M13-14-66 | | | | | | X | 1 | Medium condyle |
| L13-23-143 | | | | | | X | 3 | |
| L13-16-201 | | | | | | X | 3 | |
| M13-7-217 | | | | | | X | 2 | Cranial |
| L13-17-60 | | | | | | X | 2 | Cranial |
| M14-10-176 | | | | | | X | 3 | |

### D. Tibiae

| Specimen | TI1 | TI2 | TI3 | TI4 | TI5 | GNW | Location |
|---|---|---|---|---|---|---|---|
| L13-17-86 | X | | | | | 0 | |
| M13-7-109 | | X | X | X | | 3 | |
| L13-15-80 | | X | X | X | X | 1 | Proximal shaft |
| L13-16-33 | | X | X | X | X | 1 | Anterior crest, shaft |
| L13-25-136 | | X | X | X | X | 1 | Proximal shaft |
| M14-1-21 | | X | X | X | X | 3 | |
| M14-1-27 | | X | X | X | X | 1 | Proximal, distal shaft |
| M13-9-4 | | | X | | | 0 | |
| L13-22-120 | | | X | | | 0 | |
| M13-8-4 | | | X | X | | 3 | |
| M14-11-47 | | | | X | | 0 | |
| L13-24-108 | | | X | X | X | 3 | |
| M14-11-48 | | | | | X | 3 | |
| M13-15-65 | | | | | X | 0 | |
| M13-13-14 | | | | | X | 3 | |
| L13-13-1 | | | | | X | 0 | |
| M13-6-55 | | | | | X | 1 | Edge |

### E. Metapodials

| Specimen | MC1 | MC2 | MC3 | MC4 | MC5 | MC6 | GNW | Location |
|---|---|---|---|---|---|---|---|---|
| M13-6-19 | X | X | X | | | | 3 | |
| M13-15-1 | X | X | X | X | X | | 0 | |
| M13-4-177 | X | X | X | X | X | X | 3 | |
| L13-24-188 | X | X | X | X | X | X | 0 | |
| L13-25-74 | X | X | X | X | X | X | 3 | |
| L13-18-8 | X | X | X | X | X | X | 3 | |
| L13-23-41 | X | X | X | X | X | X | 0 | |
| L13-17-91 | | | | X | X | X | 1 | Shaft |
| | MT1 | MT2 | MT3 | MT4 | MT5 | MT6 | | |
| M14-10-113 | X | | | | | | 0 | |
| L13-7-212 | X | X | | | | | 3 | |

**Table 7.20.** *(continued)*

| | | | | | | | | | |
|---|---|---|---|---|---|---|---|---|---|
| L13-17-16 | X | X | X | | | | | 0 | |
| L13-24-31 | X | X | X | | | | | 0 | |
| L13-24-109 | X | X | X | X | | | | 1 | Distal shaft |
| L13-24-95 | X | X | X | X | X | | | 3 | |
| M13-6-72 | X | X | X | X | X | X | | 3 | |
| M13-8-100 | X | X | X | X | X | X | | 3 | |
| L14-20-23 | | X | X | X | | | | 1 | Proximal shaft |
| M14-10-144 | | | | X | X | | | 3 | |
| M13-14-68 | | | | X | X | X | | 3 | |
| M14-10-140 | | | | | X | | | 0 | |
| L13-24-97 | | | | | | X | | 0 | |

| | MP1 | MP2 | | | | MP6 | | |
|---|---|---|---|---|---|---|---|---|
| M13-7-150 | X | | | | | | 0 | |
| M14-10-147 | | X | | | | | 0 | |
| M14-10-184 | | X | | | | | 0 | |
| M13-14-65 | | | | | | X | 3 | |
| M14-10-10 | | | | | | X | 3 | |
| M13-6-142 | | | | | | X | 3 | |
| M14-10-104 | | | | | | X | 0 | |
| M13-6-9 | | | | | | X | 0 | |
| M14-10-97 | | | | | | X | 0 | |
| M13-3-66 | | | | | | X | 3 | |
| M14-1-144 | | | | | | X | 0 | |
| M13-6-20 | | | | | | X | 3 | |
| M14-10-234 | | | | | | X | 1 | Condyle, cancellous |

**Table 7.21.** Mill Iron Bison Long Bone Fragmentation.

| EL | Number complete (1) | Fragments (2) | Proximal (3) | Distal (4) | Max (5)[a] | Percent complete (6)[b] | Percent difference (7)[c] |
|---|---|---|---|---|---|---|---|
| HU | 0 | 9 | 1 | 18 | 18 | 0 | 89.47 |
| RD | 7 | 15 | 9 | 7 | 16 | 43.75 | 6.67 |
| MC | 5 | 0 | 2 | 1 | 7 | 71.43 | 3.57 |
| FM | 0 | 11 | 11 | 5 | 11 | 0 | 37.50 |
| TA | 0 | 7 | 1 | 9 | 9 | 0 | 80.00 |
| MT | 2 | 4 | 4 | 3 | 8 | 25.00 | 9.09 |

[a]Number of complete elements plus the greater of proximal or distal ends.

[b]Percentage of complete elements = $\dfrac{\text{Col. 1} \times 100}{\text{Col. 5}}$

[c]Percentage difference between proximal and distal end counts (Richardson 1980): $\dfrac{([\text{Col. 1} + \text{Col. 3}] - [\text{Col. 1} + \text{Col. 4}]) \times 100}{(\text{Col. 1} + \text{Col. 3}) + (\text{Col. 1} + \text{Col. 4})}$

**Table 7.22.** Burning Codes.

| | |
|---|---|
| 0 | None |
| 1 | Localized carbonization |
| 2 | Carbonized |

**Table 7.23.** Burned and Unburned MNEs.

| Element | Burned | Unburned |
|---|---|---|
| AS | 2 | 20 |
| AT | 1 | 11 |
| AX | 5 | 16 |
| CE | 6 | 40 |
| CA | 0 | 3 |
| CL | 2 | 12 |
| CPF | 0 | 12 |
| CPI | 2 | 8 |
| CPR | 1 | 9 |
| CPS | 1 | 18 |
| CPU | 0 | 12 |
| CRN | 2 | 14 |
| FM | 3 | 8 |
| HM | 6 | 12 |
| IM | 3 | 35 |
| LM | 3 | 21 |
| MC | 0 | 7 |
| MP | 5 | 1 |
| MR | 3 | 13 |
| MT | 1 | 7 |
| PHF | 2 | 62 |
| PHS | 4 | 46 |
| PHT | 2 | 28 |
| RB | 6 | 59 |
| RD | 1 | 16 |
| SA | 2 | 3 |
| SC | 3 | 34 |
| TA | 2 | 7 |
| TH | 1 | 32 |
| TRC | 1 | 11 |
| TRS | 0 | 7 |
| UL | 1 | 13 |

as carnivores concentrate on more accessible elements with greater bulk payloads (e.g., humeri). In an intensively scavenged assemblage, however, this liquid fat reservoir could be a valuable source of nutrition, even if consumed late in the sequence. This could explain carnivore interest in phalanges at Mill Iron.

Of the moderately well preserved portion of the assemblage as a whole, 13.85% exhibit evidence of carnivore gnawing. Recall also that 63% of the moderately to well preserved long bone specimens possess physical evidence of gnawing. The patterns of long bone destruction, coupled with the abundance of toothmarked specimens, are enough to justify the conclusion that much of the attrition of the Mill Iron bonebed is attributable to carnivores.

## Burning, Cuts, and Other Modification

The depositional environment of the Mill Iron locality argues that most of the bonebed was exposed for years as it was gradually buried by slopewash. Further evidence of lengthy exposure duration is offered by the distribution of burned bone across the site.

## Burned Bone

Coloration has long been considered a criterion for the identification of bone burned at different temperatures (e.g., Baby 1954; Binford 1963; Pfeiffer 1977; Shipman et al. 1984; Ubelaker 1984; Buikstra and Swegle 1989; McCutcheon 1992). For the Mill Iron assemblage, each specimen was examined in the lab for evidence of discoloration due to burning. Initial efforts to distinguish specimens calcined as a result of burning from those calcined as a result of weathering were abandoned when it became apparent that such discrimination could not be reliably made. Specimens with no apparent burn-related discoloration, therefore, were all classified as unburned, even though some burn-calcined specimens may be among them (Table 7.22).

Although approximately 15% of the assemblage is identified as burned, only a few small specimens of charcoal were recovered in the field. There were no ashbeds or evidence of hearths in the excavated area. The absence of such features is typical of Paleoindian sites, but it is likely that any such evidence that once existed at the bonebed would have been weathered, washed, or blown away.

There are several possibilities that can account for the presence of burned bone. First, it may have been burned by people in the course of processing or cooking. If this were the case, one would expect burning to be patterned across element classes. This assumes that people selected and processed particular carcass parts, rather than treating all parts identically, and it predicts that burning should occur preferentially on some elements. It should not occur randomly.

However, non-random burning across element classes could result as well from range fire, no matter what the cause of such fire. The effects of open-flame burning on fresh and weathered bones are poorly understood because little research has been undertaken on that subject. It is likely that fire differentially alters elements, depending on bone morphology, microstructure, or other variables (e.g., Pfeiffer 1977). Such appears to be the case, for instance, among *Lepus* and *Ovis* remains from Danger Cave, thought to have burned long after initial deposition (Grayson 1988).

Consequently, a non-random pattern might occur in a faunal assemblage that has been subject *either* to human processing or range fire, or even some combination of the two. If a non-random pattern of burning is identified, the problem then is to determine its cause by examining other lines of evidence.

This analysis uses chi-square to examine the distribution of

**Table 7.24.** Adjusted Residuals for Burned and Unburned Element and Element-Group MNEs.

| Element | Burned | Unburned |
|---|---|---|
| CRN/MR | 1.03 | −1.03 |
| CE | 1.55 | −1.55 |
| LM/SA | 1.28 | −1.28 |
| TH/RB | −1.09 | 1.09 |
| SC | −0.44 | 0.44 |
| HM[1] | 3.28 | −3.28 |
| RD/UL | −0.71 | 0.71 |
| CARPALS | −1.48 | 1.48 |
| MP[2] | 2.82 | −2.82 |
| PH[2] | −2.65 | 2.65 |
| IM/FM | 0.48 | −0.48 |
| TA | 1.20 | −1.20 |
| TARSALS | −0.29 | 0.29 |

[1]p < .01; [2]p < .001

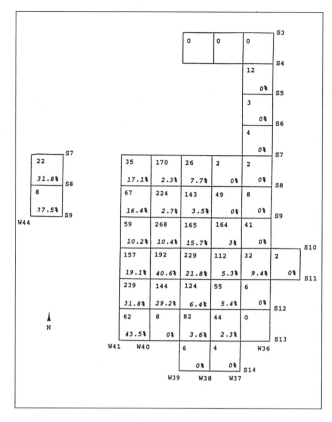

**Figure 7.19.** Distributions of burned and unburned bone across the Mill Iron bonebed. In each meter square unit, the uppermost number designates the number of bone specimens recovered from that unit; the lower number, in italics, designates the percentage identified as burned.

burning across element classes. In doing that, NISP counts are not used because of the high degree of bone fragmentation within the assemblage, which leads to problems of specimen interdependence. Instead, MNE counts are derived for burned elements and unburned elements (Table 7.23).

For purposes of chi-square analysis, some element classes have been pooled to increase their sample size (crania with mandibles, all cervical vertebrae, thoracic vertebrae with ribs, lumbar vertebrae with sacrae; innominates with femora; all phalanges, and radii with ulnae). The result shows that burning is non-random across the assemblage as a whole ($X^2$ = 33.78, p < 0.01).

An analysis of single-cell adjusted residuals (Everitt 1977) identifies the element categories that are responsible for the significant chi-square result (Table 7.24): humeri and metapodials are burned more often than predicted by chance, whereas phalanges are burned less frequently.

In open-flame bone-burning experiments, Buikstra and Swegle (1989) found that green bones (fleshed and de-fleshed) burned white, gray, and blue, whereas dry bones burned brown or tan. If cooking produced burned bone at Mill Iron, that burning would have occurred while the bone was still green. However, burn colors across the assemblage mostly grade from a light pink/tan to dark brown (7.5YR in the Munsell color chart), although a few dark gray specimens also occur.

This color range corresponds to that reported by Mc-Cutcheon (1992) for artiodactyl bone burned experimentally in a muffle oven at low temperatures (184-340°C). Low temperatures such as these are typical of range fires.

Significantly, 31 burned specimens exhibit the most intense carbonization or scorching on *interior* bone: cancellous parts and the insides of long bone shafts and epiphyses. Frequently, *all* of the discoloration or carbonization is on the interior surfaces, which would not have been exposed directly to flame, whereas the exterior surfaces appear unaltered or slightly discolored. Buikstra and Swegle (1989) describe this pattern for experimen-

tally burned dry dog femora: interior bone is darkened, whereas minimal (if any) color change occurs on the surfaces of those elements. The same phenomenon is noted by Spennemann and Colley (1989) in the experimental burning of dry cow bones. Neither this pattern nor the tan/brown coloration is reported for experimentally burned, fresh specimens. Buikstra and Swegle attribute this phenomenon to the loss of combustible organic substance in the cortex of dry or weathered bone, and combustion of organic material remaining in the protected interior bone.

Burning occurred at Mill Iron, then, after weathering had already removed organics from the exposed portions of the bone. Range fire best accounts for the burning pattern described above.

This explanation is further supported by the spatial distribution of burned bone within the site. Figure 7.19 shows the ratios of burned to unburned bone in each 1 x 1 unit. The ratios of burned bone diminish toward the northern and eastern peripheries, which is where slopewash would first begin accumulating in the bonebed.

The vertical distribution of the bone along east/west transects is more informative. A backplot of the S12 transect (Figure 7.20; see Figure 7.3 for transect locations) shows that most

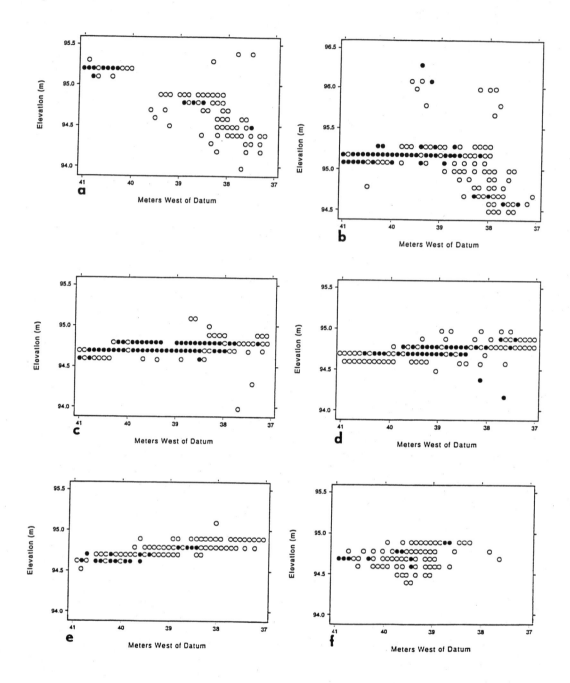

**Figure 7.20.** Vertical distribution of burned and unburned specimens across east-west transects. The filled black circles designate burned specimens; empty circles designate unburned specimens. Elevations are relative to an arbitrary datum elevation of 100 m. The backplot (a) illustrates the vertical distribution along transect S13 to S12. Unburned specimens dominate the slump on the eastern end of the transect, while burned bones are common on the level area above. Unburned bone continues to dominate the slump sediment in transect S12 to S11 (b). Most of the bone west of that area is burned. Those specimens above the 95.5 elevation mark may owe their location to bioturbation. Burned bone is abundant in transect S11 to S10 (c), which is north of the slump area. The backplot for transect S10 to S9 (d) shows the slope rising in elevation toward the east. The number of burned specimens at the higher elevation correspondingly drops, perhaps because they were partly buried by slopewash when the ground fire burned over. As the slope continues to rise in transect S9 to S8 (e), numbers of burned specimens diminish. Burned bone now occurs mostly at the foot of the slope to the west. Transect S8 to S7 yielded few burnt specimens (f).

of the burned bone lies at the relatively level upper elevations and in the westernmost unit, whereas unburned bone is distributed along a steep declination in the eastern units. This slope is actually part of the slump area along the southeastern border of the feature, the site of the old channel cut. The few specimens that are scattered at much higher elevations may owe their position to rodent burrowing or other biogenic disturbances. The same pattern occurs in transect S11 (Figure 7.20b), which was also clipped by the stream. As in the first instance, burned bone lies on the old surface while unburned bone is distributed downslope.

Figure 7.20c shows the distribution of burned and unburned bone along transect S10. Here is seen the beginning of a topographical incline toward the east, with unburned bone concentrated on the upslope, eastern edge and burned bone downslope to the west. The slope steepens along S9 (Figure 7.20d), again with burned bone on the higher, eastern edge of the transect. This pattern recurs in transect S8, whereas S7, itself situated at the foot of the northern slope, is composed mostly of unburned bone (Figures 7.20e, 7.20f).

The sediment itself gives no indication of oxidation resulting from burning. Range fires do not necessarily leave behind visible alteration of the sediment across which they burn (Bellomo 1990); nor do such fires typically burn everything (i.e., all bone specimens) over which they pass, nor objects protected by a thin covering of sediment (Ahler et al. 1990). Because fire is not uniform in intensity, and because it does not move uniformly across open terrain (Connor and Cannon 1990; Pyne 1982; Rowe and Scotter 1973), the effects of a ground fire should be variable across an assemblage.

This analysis provides several converging lines of evidence favoring range fire as the overriding explanation for burned bone at Mill Iron.

1) The brown coloration and carbonization on element interiors argue that burning occurred after the bone was substantially weathered.
2) The clustering of unburned specimens in the cutbank along the southeastern quarter suggests that this cut and subsequent slumping occurred *before* fire burned across the assemblage. Given the irregular movement of range fires across the ground surface, it is possible that these unburned bones were simply missed by the flames and later were undercut and buried. That scenario, however, invokes coincidence to explain the concentration of unburned bone in the slump deposits.
3) The distribution of unburned specimens along the upslope northern and northeastern perimeters of the bonebed indicates that slopewash had already begun covering the edges of the accumulation when the fire burned through: even a thin covering of soil can protect bone from burning (Ahler et al. 1990).

## Rodents, Roots, and Insects

Rodents also were attracted to the bonebed, leaving toothmarks on 126 specimens (4% of the assemblage). Short, paired toothmarks are most abundant on rib fragments (45% of the rodent-gnawed specimens), and ribs exhibit the most extensive damage. In general, rodents focused on thin elements and irregularly shaped bones with chewable edges, and ignored

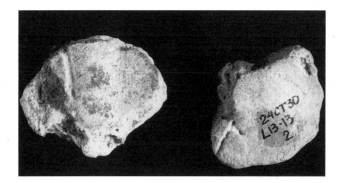

**Figure 7.21.** An example of invertebrate tunneling on Mill Iron bison bone.

large, cylindrical limb bones. However, one long bone shaft exhibits rodent gnawing on an interior layer of cortical bone that had been exposed by exfoliation, showing that rodents continued to chew bone even after it was heavily weathered. In some instances, gnawing may have occurred after the bone was initially buried: on many specimens, interior bone exposed by rodent gnawing is of a different color than surface bone. Such specimens may have been encountered by rodents during tunneling, evidence for which is abundant at the site.

Root etching is seen on just 17 bones, but modern roots were still present on or through 324 specimens when examined in the laboratory. This recent growth had caused or contributed to bone fragmentation.

Small boreholes and larger channels with shallow U-shaped cross-sections occur on 11 specimens (Figure 7.21). These may have been produced by carrion-feeding arthropod invertebrates. Insect damage to bone has long been noted on both modern and paleontological specimens (e.g., Hinton 1945, Kitching 1980, Watson and Abbey 1986).

More recently, Jodry and Stanford (1992:111) described probable beetle boreholes in specimens from the Folsom age bison assemblage at Stewart's Cattle Guard, CO. The features they describe, however, differ in two ways from those occurring on the Mill Iron specimens. First, the channels run *across* rather than into the Mill Iron bone surfaces, and are generally less than 0.5 mm deep. Second, the Mill Iron features are smaller in diameter, 1–6 mm, as opposed to 9–14 mm in the Stewart's Cattle Guard material.

At Mill Iron, the channels, sometimes occurring two to a specimen, are found on the articular surfaces of tarsals, carpals, and a first phalanx, along the surface of a proximal rib blade fragment, and at the distal epiphyseal line of a tibia. Five are straight, terminating in a widened, scooped-out chamber, and four are Y- or L-shaped. Channel lengths range 6–50 mm; "entry" widths range 2–6 mm; none are dendritic or otherwise resemble root etching. The boreholes occur in mid-shaft of two severely weathered first phalanges and in a rib blade fragment.

A variety of invertebrates, including dermestid beetles, are attracted to decaying remains (Nuorteva 1977) and are capable of causing such damage by tunneling into bone or between articulated elements. Susanne Miller (personal communication)

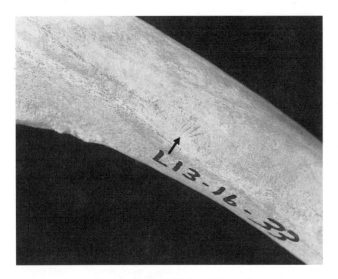

**Figure 7.22.** Cut marks on Mill Iron bison rib.

has observed dermestid beetle tunneling on modern surface bone recovered from Smith Creek Cave, NV, and similar damage to buried archaeological and paleontological material recovered along with insect casings from the cave's deposits. She also provides descriptions and metric data for damage occurring on immature artiodactyl remains during bone cleaning in dermestid colonies at the Idaho Museum of Natural History. On Miller's comparative skeletons, insect burrowing occurs on proximal and distal long bones, and burrow widths range 3.4–4.8 mm. These widths fall within the range observed on the Mill Iron specimens. Miller (personal communication) further reports finding dermestid damage on the foam stripping used on the box containing the beetle colony, and the foam samples she provides show both linear and bifurcated tunnels.

The dermestid damage described by Miller closely resembles the channeling that occurs on the Mill Iron specimens. Some of the tinier boreholes, however, being much smaller and of a different nature than the horizontal tunneling, may be the product of a different organism.

## Cuts and Breaks

Most of the specimens are dry-fractured or crushed by the weight of overlying sediment. Broken edges of long bones and ribs are usually heavily weathered and modified by dry breakage. This, coupled with cortical exfoliation, makes identification of green breakage difficult. Only 37 specimens exhibit possible green breakage; 10 (27%) are long bone shafts, and the remainder are rib blades with oblique breaks.

Because of the condition of the bone, shallow surface markings such as cuts appear rarely within the Mill Iron assemblage. However, cuts (linear marks with V-shaped cross-sections) are evident on eight specimens, V-shaped notches (possible chop marks) on six, and anomalous gouges on two.

Notches occur on three humeri, on the medial and lateral sides of distal end, and on the trochlea. These correspond to disarticulation marks (Hd-1, Hd-2) observed by Binford

(1981:123) on Nunamiut-butchered caribou. The mark on the medial surface is 2 mm wide and approximately as deep, and the specimen exhibits a short, longitudinal cut at mid-shaft. Notching also appears along the ridge of the cranial articular surface of a burned axis, at the base of a scapular glenoid fossa and on a ventral rib below the head.

Beveled, V-shaped gouges are seen on the dorsomedial edge of one intermediate carpal, and a similar mark is seen in the center of the ventral surface of a fused second and third carpal. There are no corresponding marks on the opposite sides of these elements, so they do not appear to be rodent or carnivore toothmarks. They may be butchery-related. Frison (1970) finds cut marks, but not gouges, on bison carpals from the Glenrock assemblage.

Cuts are most abundant on proximal ribs. A series of parallel, transverse marks are spread over approximately 4 cm, along the caudal border of one proximal rib blade (Figure 7.22). These marks are distal to the tubercle, which, along with the rib head, is missing. On some ribs, sets of parallel or subparallel cuts occur along the ventral or dorsal ridges of the proximal blade. These are comparable to filleting marks described by Binford (1981) on the Nunamiut caribou, and marks observed by Grayson (1988) on mountain sheep bones from Last Supper Cave.

Two crossing, perpendicular cuts occur on the dorsal side of a first phalanx; four subparallel cuts, oblique to the long axis of the shaft are found on the lateral, caudal side of a tibia, at about mid-shaft.

In the absence of true diagnostics for butchery-related cuts and other human modification (Lyman 1987), it is difficult to identify positively the agent that produced a particular mark. Consequently, some analysts (e.g., Grayson 1989) also look for the patterned occurrence of cuts across elements. Just 16 Mill Iron specimens exhibit possible butchery-related modification, making such patterning difficult to identify. However, modification does tend to group on distal humeri and proximal ribs in locations where disarticulation and filleting marks have been described ethnographically (e.g., Binford 1982).

The numerous lithic artifacts found among the bones show that people did utilize the bison carcasses at Mill Iron. Direct physical evidence of butchery or marrow processing, however, is both rare and equivocal.

## Summary and Conclusions

Analytic interest in the Mill Iron bison bonebed extends well beyond the period of its occupation and use by human beings. Its taphonomic history records its original environmental context and the effects of changing conditions with the passage of time.

Topographic and geological evidence shows that the Mill Iron bonebed is not an alluvial deposit, although it was affected by later stream cutting that washed away part of the feature. Instead, it is the death site of at least 29 bison, perhaps mostly cows, killed in a single episode approximately 10,700 years ago (Haynes et al. 1992). The deaths appear to be the result of human predation, given the presence of projectile points and other lithic tools among the bones, but the possibility that the midden is a scavenged natural-death assemblage cannot be excluded.

Exactly how the animals were trapped is unclear: the fact that the midden occurs in an ancient stream channel comprises the only geomorphic evidence of a possible impoundment or drive lane. Whether it actually served as such, or whether some other form of corral once existed at the site, remains unresolved. In this regard, the Mill Iron midden is similar to a number of other Paleoindian period bonebeds, including Horner (Todd 1987a) and Jones-Miller (Stanford 1978).

The lack of clear evidence for a trap, together with the absence of complete skulls, the lack of complete articulated bison skeletons, and the low incidence of articulated units cause the bonebed to resemble others thought to be secondary butchery features. Several lines of evidence, however, suggest that this resemblance is superficial, created in large part by taphonomic processes. For instance, statistical comparisons of skeletal-part frequencies with bison carcass utility values show that low-value parts occur with significantly greater frequency than do high-value parts. This is the opposite of what is expected at a secondary butchery or processing site, such as Stewart's Cattle Guard, where high-value parts comprise the bulk of the assemblage.

Further, the presence of petrous skull parts and maxillary molars indicate that whole skulls did once exist at the site. How the crania became fragmented and what became of the other fragments remains unclear, but breakage and processing by people is one possibility; weathering is a second.

Severe carnivore ravaging may account for the paucity of articulated units at Mill Iron. Those units that do remain are mostly vertebral segments, typical of carnivore-scavenged sites. Even if human hunters left some carcasses intact at the site, it is likely that wolves, coyotes, and other carnivores would disarticulate them.

Given this evidence, the Mill Iron assemblage better fits a kill/butchery model than that of a secondary butchery feature. Statistical comparisons of skeletal-part frequencies with carcass utility values in fact suggest that valuable parts may have been *removed* from the original assemblage, rather than selected to comprise it.

The relative abundance of less-valuable parts compared to that of choice parts, however, is better attributed to density-mediated differential survivorship than to human transport. Carnivore ravaging, extensive weathering, and natural burning, in addition to possible human processing activity, are attritional processes that would preferentially remove weaker parts, leaving behind the mineral-dense elements that comprise the bulk of this assemblage. Regardless of whether the relative skeletal abundances are due primarily to natural or cultural processes, or to some combination of the two, the patterning does not support the original interpretation of the feature as a secondary butchery site. Rather, it appears to be a site where the animals were both killed and butchered.

The attritional processes that contributed to the quantitative patterning of the assemblage also modified bone surfaces, often exfoliating cortical bone that may have borne cuts or impact marks. As a result, direct evidence of specific butchering activities is severely limited. The presence of stone tools, fewer than 20 cut and chop marks, and destruction of skulls is the best evidence of human activity at the feature.

The depositional context of the site argues that the bones were left exposed on the surface for a long time before they were completely buried by slopewash. This hypothesis is not contradicted by the weathering profile, weathering stage distributions, joint articulations, degree of carnivore ravaging, nor any other portion of the analysis. During this period, the assemblage was disturbed by carnivores and rodents, utilized by insects, weathered, and at one point was partially eroded by a stream and subsequently burned over by a range fire. After burial, the assemblage was subjected to impregnation by mineral salts, additional rodent disturbance and modification, and crushing by the accumulating weight of the slopewash deposits. Root etching may have been obliterated by subsequent weathering, but the lack of soil development (Eckerle 1990) suggests that vegetation was sparse.

Morphological and distributional characteristics of the bison bonebed record a complex taphonomic history at Mill Iron. While this, undeniably, exists at the expense of direct evidence of ancient human activity, the information it provides is equally valuable to our understanding of the site.

## References Cited

Agenbroad, L. D.
1978    *The Hudson-Meng Site: An Alberta Bison Kill in the Nebraska High Plains.* University Press of America, Washington, D.C.

Ahler, S. A., P. R. Picha, R. D. Sayler, and R. D. Seabloom
1990    Effects of Prairie Fire on Selected Artifact Classes. Paper presented at the 55th Annual Meeting of the Society for American Archaeology, Las Vegas.

Baby, R. S.
1954    *Hopewell Cremation Practices.* Ohio Historic Society Papers in Archaeology 1.

Bedford, J. N.
1974    Morphological Variation in Bison Metacarpals and Metatarsals. In *The Casper Site*, edited by G. C. Frison, pp. 199–240. Academic Press, New York.
1978    A Technique for Sex Determination of Mature Bison Metapodials. In *Bison Procurement and Utilization: A Symposium*, edited by L. B. Davis and M. Wilson, pp. 40–43. Plains Anthropologist Memoir 14.

Behrensmeyer, A. K.
1975    The Taphonomy and Paleoecology of Plio-Pleistocene Vertebrate Assemblages East of Lake Rudolf, Kenya. *Bulletin of the Museum of Comparative Zoology* 146(10):473–578.
1978    Taphonomic and Ecologic Information from Bone Weathering. *Paleobiology* 4(2):150–162.

1988 Vertebrate Preservation in Fluvial Channels. *Palaeogeography, Palaeoclimatology, Palaeoecology* 63:183–199.

Bellomo, R. V.
1990 Identifying Traces of Natural and Humanly Controlled Fire in the Archaeological Record: The Role of Actualistic Studies. Paper presented at the 55th Annual Meeting of the Society for American Archaeology, Las Vegas.

Binford, L. R.
1963 An Analysis of Cremations from Three Michigan Sites. *Wisconsin Archaeologist* 44:98–110.
1978 Nunamiut Ethnoarchaeology. Academic Press, New York.
1981 *Bones: Ancient Men and Modern Myths*. Academic Press, New York.

Binford, L. R., and J. B. Bertram
1977 Bone Frequencies—and Attritional Processes. In *For Theory Building in Archaeology*, edited by L. R. Binford, pp. 77–153. Academic Press, New York.

Binford, L. R., and L. C. Todd
1982 On Arguments for the "Butchering" of Giant Geladas. *Current Anthropology* 23(1):108–110.

Blumenschine, R. J.
1986a *Early Hominid Scavenging Opportunities: Implications of Carcass Availability in the Serengeti and Ngorongoro Ecosystems*. British Archaeological Reports International Series No. 283, Oxford.
1986b Carcass Consumption and the Archaeological Distinction of Scavenging and Hunting. *Journal of Human Evolution* (15):639–659.
1988 An Experimental Model of the Timing of Hominid and Carnivore Influence on Archaeological Bone Assemblages. *Journal of Archaeological Science* 15:483–502.

Boaz, N. T., and A. K. Behrensmeyer
1976 Hominid Taphonomy: Transport of Human Skeletal Parts in an Artificial Fluviatile Environment. *American Journal of Physical Anthropology* 45:53–60.

Bonnichsen, R.
1979 *Pleistocene Bone Technology in the Beringian Refugium*. Archaeological Survey of Canada Paper No. 89. Mercury Series, National Museum of Man, Ottawa.

Borrero, L. A.
1990 Fuego-Patagonian Bone Assemblages and the Problem of Communal Guanaco Hunting. In *Hunters of the Recent Past*, edited by B. Davis and B. O. K. Reeves, pp. 373-399.

Brain, C. K.
1967 Hottentot Food Remains and their Bearing on the Interpretation of Fossil Bone Assemblages. *Namib Desert Research Station Scientific Paper* 32:1–11.
1969 The Contributions of the Namib Desert Hottentots to an Understanding of Australopithecine Bone Accumulations. *Namib Desert Research Station Scientific Paper* 39:13–22.
1976 Some Principles in the Interpretation of Bone Accumulations Associated with Man. *In Human Origins*, edited by G. L. Isaac and E. McCown, pp. 97–116. W. A. Benjamin, Menlo Park, California.
1981 *The Hunters or the Hunted? An Introduction to African Cave Taphonomy*. University of Chicago Press, Chicago.

Brink, J. E., and B. Dawe
1989 *Final Report of the 1985 and 1986 Field Season at Head-Smashed-In Buffalo Jump, Alberta*. Archaeological Survey of Alberta No. 16. Alberta Culture and Multiculturalism Historical Resources Division, Edmonton.

Buikstra, J. E., and M. Swegle
1989 Bone Modification Due to Burning: Experimental Evidence. *In Bone Modification*, edited by R. Bonnichsen and H. Sorg, pp. 247–258. Center for the Study of the First Americans, Orono, Maine.

Bunn, H. T.
1981 Archaeological Evidence for Meat-Eating by Plio-Pleistocene Hominids from Koobi Fora and Olduvai Gorge. *Nature* 291:574–577.
1986 Patterns of Skeletal Representation and Hominid Subsistence Activities at Olduvai Gorge, Tanzania, and Koobi Fora, Kenya. *Journal of Human Evolution* 15:673–690.

Burgett, G. R.
1990 *The Bones of the Beast: Resolving Questions of Faunal Assemblage Formation Processes Through Actualistic Research*. Ph.D. dissertation, University of New Mexico, Albuquerque. University Microfilms, Ann Arbor.

Butler, V. L.
1987 Distinguishing Natural from Cultural Salmonid Deposits in the Pacific Northwest of North America. In *Natural Formation Processes and the Archaeological Record*, edited by T. Nash and M. D. Petraglia, pp. 131–149. British Archaeological Reports International Series No. 352, Oxford.
1990 *Distinguishing Natural from Cultural Salmonid Deposits in Pacific Northwest North America*. Ph.D. dissertation, University of Washington, Seattle. University Microfilms, Ann Arbor.

Carter, D. R., and W. C. Hayes
1977 Compact Bone Fatigue Damage—I. Residual Strength and Stiffness. *Journal of Biomechanics* 10:325–337.

Connor, M. A., and K. P. Cannon
1990 Forest Fires as a Site Formation Process in the Rocky Mountains of Northwestern Wyoming. Paper presented at the 55th Annual Meeting of the Society for American Archaeology, Las Vegas.

Cooke, R. U., and I. J. Smalley
1968 Salt Weathering in Deserts. *Nature* 220:1226–1227.

Currey, J.
1984 *The Mechanical Adaptations of Bones*. Princeton University Press, Princeton.
1990 Biomechanics of Mineralized Skeletons. In *Skeletal Biomineralization: Patterns, Processes and Evolutionary*

*Trends,* vol. 1 edited by J. G. Carter, pp. 11-25. Van Nostrand Reinhold, New York.

Daly, P.

1969    Approaches to Faunal Analysis in Archaeology. *American Antiquity* 34:146–153.

Duffield, L. F.

1973    Aging and Sexing the Post-Cranial Skeleton of Bison. *Plains Anthropologist* 18:132–39.

Eckerle, W.

1990    Geoarchaeology of the Mill Iron Archaeological Site: Postglacial Environments on the Great Plains of Southeastern Montana. Unpublished Report to Department of Anthropology, University of Wyoming, Laramie.

Emerson, A. M.

1990a   *Archaeological Implications of Variability in the Economic Anatomy of* Bison bison. Ph.D. dissertation, Washington State University, University Microfilms, Ann Arbor.

1990b   Bison Body Part Utility: Applications and Considerations of Carcass Use or Bone Destruction. Paper presented at the 48th Annual Conference of the Plains Anthropological Society, Oklahoma City.

Evans, F. G.

1973    *Mechanical Properties of Bone.* Charles C. Thomas, Springfield.

Everitt, B. S.

1977    *The Analysis of Contingency Tables.* Wiley, New York.

Ewers, J. C.

1955    *The Horse in Blackfoot Indian Culture.* Bureau of American Ethnology Bulletin No. 159. Smithsonian Institution, Washington, D.C.

1958    *The Blackfeet.* University of Oklahoma Press, Norman.

Fisher, J. W., Jr.

1992    Observations on the Late Pleistocene Bone Assemblage from the Lamb Spring Site, Colorado. In *Ice Age Hunters of the Rockies,* edited by D. J. Stanford and J. S. Day, pp. 51–82. Denver Museum of Natural History and University Press of Colorado, Niwot, CO.

Frison, G. C.

1970    *The Glenrock Buffalo Jump, 48CO304: Late Prehistoric Period Buffalo Procurement and Butchering on the Northwestern Plains.* Plains Anthropologist Memoir 7, Pt. 2.

1973    *The Wardell Buffalo Trap, 48SU301: Communal Procurement in the Upper Green River Basin, Wyoming.* Anthropological Papers of the Museum of Anthropology, University of Michigan No. 48.

1974    *The Casper Site: A Hell Gap Bison Kill on the High Plains.* Academic Press, New York.

1978    Animal Population Studies and Cultural Inference. In *Bison Procurement and Utilization: A Symposium,* edited by L. B. Davis and M. Wilson, pp. 44–52. Plains Anthropologist Memoir 14.

1988    Paleoindian Subsistence and Settlement During Post-Clovis Times on the Northwestern Plains, the Adjacent Mountain Ranges, and Intermontane Basins. In *Americans Before Columbus: Ice-Age Origins,* edited by R. C. Carlisle, pp. 83–106. Ethnology Monographs No. 12., Pittsburgh.

1990    Clovis, Goshen, and Folsom: Lifeways and Cultural Relationships. In *Megafauna and Man: Discovery of America's Heartland,* edited by L. D. Agenbroad, J. I. Mead, and L. W. Nelson, pp. 100–108. The Mammoth Site of Hot Springs, South Dakota, Inc. and Northern Arizona University, Hot Springs, S.D.

1991    *Prehistoric Hunters of the High Plains,* 2d ed. Academic Press, New York.

Frison, G. C., M. Wilson, and D. J. Wilson

1976    Fossil Bison and Artifacts from an Early Altithermal Period Arroyo Trap in Wyoming. *American Antiquity* 41(1):28–57.

Galloway, A., P. Willey, and L. Snyder

1991    Bone Density Determinants of Carnivore Scavenging and Bone Survival. Paper Presented at the 43rd Meeting of the American Academy of Forensic Sciences, Anaheim.

Gifford, D. P.

1981    Taphonomy and Paleoecology: A Critical Review of Archaeology's Sister Disciplines. *Advances in Archaeological Method and Theory* 4: 365–438.

Gifford-Gonzalez, D.

1989    Ethnographic Analogues for Interpreting Modified Bones: Some Cases from East Africa. In *Bone Modification,* edited by R. Bonnichsen and M. Sorg, pp. 179–246. Center for the Study of the First Americans, University of Maine, Orono.

1991    Gaps in Zooarchaeological Analyses of Butchery. Paper presented at the 1991 Visiting Scholar's Conference, "Bones to Behavior," Southern Illinois University, Carbondale.

Grayson, D. K.

1979    On the Quantification of Vertebrate Archaeofaunas. *Advances in Archaeological Method and Theory* 2:199–237.

1984    *Quantitative Zooarchaeology: Topics in the Analysis of Archaeological Faunas.* Academic Press, New York.

1988    *Danger Cave, Last Supper Cave, and Hanging Rock Shelter: The Faunas.* Anthropological Papers of the American Museum of Natural History 66.

1989    Bone Transport, Bone Destruction, and Reverse Utility Curves. *Journal of Archaeological Science* 16:643–652.

Guthrie, R. D.

1967    Differential Preservation and Recovery of Pleistocene Large Mammal Remains in Alaska. *Journal of Paleontology* 41:243–246.

Haglund, W. D.

1991    *Applications of Taphonomic Models to Forensic Investigations.* Ph.D. dissertation, University of Washington, Seattle. University Microfilms, Ann Arbor.

Hanson, C. B.

1980    Fluvial Taphonomic Processes: Models and Experiments. In *Fossils in the Making: Vertebrate Taphonomy and Paleoecology*, edited by A. K. Behrensmeyer and A. P. Hill, pp. 156–181. University of Chicago Press, Chicago and London.

Hare, P. E.
1980    Organic Geochemistry of Bone and its Relation to the Survival of Bone in the Natural Environment. In *Fossils in the Making: Vertebrate Taphonomy and Paleocology*, edited by A. K. Behrensmeyer and A. P. Hill, pp. 208–222. University of Chicago Press, Chicago and London.

Haynes, C. V., Jr., R. P. Beukens, A. J. T. Jull, and O. K. Davis
1992    New Radiocarbon Dates for some Old Folsom Sites: Accelerator Technology. In *Ice Age Hunters of the Rockies*, edited by D. J. Stanford and J. S. Day, pp. 83–100. Denver Museum of Natural History and University Press of Colorado, Niwot, CO.

Haynes, G.
1980a   Evidence of Carnivore Gnawing on Pleistocene and Recent Mammalian Bones. *Paleobiology* 6(3):341–351.
1980b   Prey Bones and Predators: Potential Ecologic Information from Analysis of Bone Sites. *Ossa International Journal of Skeletal Research* 7:75–97.
1982    Utilization and Skeletal Disturbances of North American Prey Carcasses. *Arctic* 35(2):266–281.
1983    A Guide for Differentiating Mammalian Carnivore Taxa Responsible for Gnaw Damage to Herbivore Limb Bones. *Paleobiology* 9(2):164–172.

Henderson, J.
1987    Factors Determining the State of Preservation of Human Remains. In *Death, Decay and Reconstruction: Approaches to Archaeology and Forensic Science*, edited by A. Boddington, A. N. Garland and R. C. Janaway, pp. 43–54. Manchester University Press, Manchester.

Hill, A.
1979    Disarticulation and Scattering of Mammal Skeletons. *Paleobiology* 5(3):261–274.

Hillson, S.
1986    *Teeth*. Cambridge University Press, Cambridge.

Hinton, H. E.
1945    *Monograph of the Beetles Associated with Stored Products*, vol. 1. British Museum, London.

Jodry, M. A., and D. J. Stanford
1992    Stewart's Cattle Guard Site: An Analysis of Bison Remains in a Folsom Kill-Butchery Campsite. In *Ice Age Hunters of the Rockies*, edited by D. J. Stanford and J. S. Day, pp. 101–168. Denver Museum of Natural History and University Press of Colorado, Niwot, CO.

Johnson, E.
1983    A Framework for Interpretation in Bone Technology. In *Carnivores, Human Scavengers & Predators: A Question of Bone Technology*, edited by G. M. LeMoine and A. J. MacEachern, pp. 55–94. Proceedings of the 15th Annual CHACMOOL Conference, The Archaeological Association of the University of Calgary, Alberta.
1985    Current Developments in Bone Technology. *Advances in Archaeological Method and Theory* 8: 157–235.
1987    Cultural Activities and Interactions. In *Lubbock Lake: Late Quaternary Studies on the Southern High Plains*, edited by E. Johnson, pp. 120–158. Texas A & M University Press, College Station.
1990    The Clovis-Age Bonebed at Lubbock Lake Revisited. Paper presented at the 48th Plains Anthropological Conference, Oklahoma City.

Jones, K. T., and D. Metcalfe
1988    Bare Bones Archaeology: Bone Marrow Indices and Efficiency. *Journal of Archaeological Science* 15: 415–423.

Kitching, J. M.
1980    On some Fossil Arthropoda from the Limeworks, Makapansgat, Potgietersrus. *Palaeontologia Africana* 26:63–68.

Klein, R. G.
1989    Why does Skeletal Part Representation Differ Between Smaller and Larger Bovids at Klasies River Mouth and other Archeological sites? *Journal of Archaeological Science* 16:363–381.

Klein, R. G., and K. Cruz-Uribe
1984    *The Analysis of Animal Bones from Archeological Sites*. University of Chicago Press, Chicago and London.

Koch, W.
1934    The Age Order of Epiphyseal Union in the Skeleton of the European Bison (*Bos Bonansus L.*) *Anatomical Record* 61:371–376.

Kreutzer, L. A.
1988    Megafaunal Butchering at Lubbock Lake, Texas: A Taphonomic Re-Analysis. *Quaternary Research* 30:221–231.
1992a   Bison and Deer Bone Mineral Densities: Comparisons and Implications for the Interpretation of Archaeological Faunas. *Journal of Archaeological Science* 19:271–294.
1992b   *Taphonomy of the Mill Iron, Montana (24CT30) Bison Bonebed*. Ph.D. dissertation, University of Washington, Seattle. University Microfilms, Ann Arbor.

Landals, A.
1990    The Maple Leaf Site: Implications of the Analysis of Small-Scale Bison Kills. In *Hunters of the Recent Past*, edited by L. B. Davis and B. O. K. Reeves, pp. 122–151. Unwin Hyman, London.

Livingston, S. D.
1988    *The Avian and Mammalian Faunas from Lovelock Cave and the Humboldt Lakebed Site*. Ph.D. dissertation, University of Washington, Seattle. University Microfilms, Ann Arbor.
1989    The Taphonomic Interpretation of Avian Skeletal Part Frequencies. *Journal of Archaeological Science* 16:537–547.

Lowie, R. H.
1954    *Indians of the Plains*. University of Nebraska Press, Lincoln and London.

Lyman, R. L.
1982    *The Taphonomy of Vertebrate Archaeofaunas: Bone Density and Differential Survival of Fossil Classes*. Ph.D. dissertation, University of Washington, Seattle. University Microfilms, Ann Arbor.
1984    Bone Density and Differential Survivorship of Fossil Classes. *Journal of Anthropological Archaeology* 3:259–299.
1985    Bone Frequencies: Differential Transport, In Situ Destruction, and the MGUI. *Journal of Archaeological Science* 12:221–236.
1987    Archaeofaunas and Butchery Studies: A Taphonomic Perspective. *Advances in Archaeological Method and Theory* 10:249–337.
1988    Was There a Last Supper at Last Supper Cave? In *Danger Cave, Last Supper Cave, and Hanging Rock Shelter: the Faunas*, edited by D. K. Grayson, pp. 81–104. American Museum of Natural History Anthropological Papers 66(1).
1991    Taphonomic Problems with Archaeological Analyses of Animal Carcass Utilization and Transport. In *Beamers, Bobwhites, and Blue-Points: Tributes to the Career of Paul W. Parmalee*, edited by J. R. Purdue, W. E. Klippel, and B. W. Styles, pp. 125–138. Illinois State Museum Scientific Papers 23, Springfield.
1992    Anatomical Considerations of Utility Curves in Zooarchaeology. *Journal of Archaeological Science* 19:7–22.

Lyman, R. L., and L. Fox.
1989    A Critical Evaluation of Bone Weathering as an Indication of Bone Assemblage Formation. *Journal of Archaeological Science* 16:293–317.

Maguire, J. M., D. Pemberton, and M. H. Collett
1980    The Makapansgat Limeworks Grey Breccia: Hominids, Hyaenas, Hystricids or Hillwash? *Palaeontologia Africana* 23:75–98.

Marean, C. W., L. M. Spencer, R. J. Blumenschine, and S. D. Capaldo
1992    Captive Hyaena Bone Choice and Destruction, The Schlepp Effect and Olduvai Archaeofaunas. *Journal of Archaeological Science* 19:101–121.

Marshall, F., and T. Pilgram
1991    Meat Versus Within-Bone Nutrients: Another Look at the Meaning of Body Part Representation in Archaeological Sites. *Journal of Archaeological Science* 18:149–163.

Martin, R. B., and D. B. Burr
1989    *Structure, Function, and Adaptation of Compact Bone*. Raven Press, New York.

McCutcheon, P. T.
1992    Burned Archaeological Bone. In *Deciphering a Shell Midden*, edited by J. K. Stein, pp. 347–370. Academic Press, New York.

McHugh, T.
1972    *The Time of the Buffalo*. University of Nebraska Press, Lincoln and London.

Metcalfe, D., and K. T. Jones
1988    A Reconsideration of Animal Body-Part Utility Indices. *American Antiquity* 53(3):486–504.

Miller, G. J.
1975    A Study of Cuts, Grooves, and Other Marks on Recent and Fossil Bone, II. Weathering Cracks, Fractures, Splinters, and Other Similar Natural Phenomena. In *Lithic Technology: Making and Using Stone Tools*, edited by E. Swanson, pp. 211–226. Aldine, Chicago.

Morlan, R. E.
1980    *Taphonomy and Archaeology in the Upper Pleistocene of the Northern Yukon Territory: A Glimpse of the Peopling of the New World*. Archaeological Survey of Canada 94, Mercury Series. National Museum of Man, Ottawa.

Morey, D. F., and W. E. Klippel
1991    Canid Scavenging and Deer Bone Survivorship at an Archaic Period Site in Tennessee. *Archaeozoologia* IV:11–28.

Nuorteva, P.
1977    Sarcosaprophagous Insects as Forensic Indicators. In *Forensic Medicine: A Study in Trauma and Environmental Hazards*, edited by C. G. Tedeschi, W. G. Eckert, and L. G. Tedeschi, pp. 1072–1095. W. B. Saunders & Co., Philadelphia.

Perkins, D., and P. Daly
1968    A Hunter's Village in Neolithic Turkey. *Scientific American* 219(5):97–106.

Pfeiffer, S.
1977    *The Skeletal Biology of Archaic Populations of the Great Lakes Region*. Archaeological Survey of Canada 64, Mercury Series. National Museum of Canada, Ottawa.

Pyne, S. J.
1982    *Fire in America: A Cultural History of Wildland and Rural Fires*. Princeton University Press, Princeton, New Jersey.

Rapson, D. J.
1990a   *Pattern and Process in Intra-Site Spatial Analysis: Site Structural and Faunal Research at the Bugas-Holding Site*. Ph.D. dissertation, University of New Mexico, Albuquerque. University Microfilms, Ann Arbor.
1990b   Decomposing Faunal Assemblages: Applying Attribute-Based Spatial Techniques to the Evaluation of Formational Context at the Bugas-Holding Site. Paper presented at the 48th Plains Anthropological Conference, Oklahoma City.

Rapson, D. J., and L. C. Todd
1992    1992 Excavations at the Hudson-Meng Bison Bonebed: Analytic Approaches for Evaluating Bonebed Formation. Paper presented at the 1992 Annual Meeting of the Plains Anthropological Society, Lincoln, NE.

Richardson, P. R. K.
1980    Carnivore Damage on Antelope Bones and its Archaeological Implications. *Palaeontologia Africana* 23:109–125.

Roe, F. G.
1972    *The North American Buffalo: A Critical Study of the Species in its Wild State,* 2d ed. University of Toronto Press, Toronto.

Rowe, J. S., and G. W. Scotter
1973    Fire in the Boreal Forest. *Quaternary Research* 3:444–464.

Schaffler, M. B., and D. B. Burr
1988    Stiffness of Compact Bone: Effects of Porosity and Density. *Journal of Biomechanics* 21(1):13–16.

Sharp, N. D.
1989    Redefining Fremont Subsistence. *Utah Archaeology* 1989:19–31.

Shipman, P.
1977    *Paleoecology, Taphonomic History and Population Dynamics of the Vertebrate Assemblage from the Middle Miocene of Fort Ternan, Kenya.* Ph.D. thesis, New York University. University Microfilms, Ann Arbor.

1981    *Life History of a Fossil: An Introduction to Taphonomy and Paleoecology.* Harvard University Press, Cambridge.

Shipman, P., G. Foster, and M. Schoeninger
1984    Burnt Bones and Teeth: An Experimental Study of Color, Morphology, Crystal Structure and Shrinkage. *Journal of Archaeological Science* 11:307–325.

Shipman P., and J. Rose
1983    Evidence of Butchery and Hominid Activities at Torralba and Ambrona: An Evaluation Using Microscopic Techniques. *Journal of Archaeological Science* 10:465–474.

Shipman, P., A. Walker, and D. Bichell
1985    *The Human Skeleton.* Harvard University Press, Cambridge.

Sillen, A.
1989    Diagenesis of the Inorganic Phase of Cortical Bone. In *The Chemistry of Prehistoric Human Bone,* edited by T. D. Price, pp. 211–229. Cambridge University Press, Cambridge.

Skinner, M. F., and O. C. Kaisen
1947    *The Fossil Bison of Alaska and Preliminary Revision of the Genus.* Bulletin of the American Museum of Natural History 89(3).

Small, R. J., and M. J. Clark
1982    *Slopes and Weathering.* Cambridge University Press, New York.

Smiley, F. E.
1978    Changes in the Cursorial Ability of Wyoming Holocene Bison. In *Wyoming Contributions to Anthropology,* vol. 1, edited by F. E. Smiley and J. L. Hofman, pp. 105–126. University of Wyoming Publications 42.

Snyder, L., A. Galloway, and P. Willey
1991    Bone Density Measures and Survival of Human and Nonhuman Skeletal Remains in Archaeological Contexts. Paper presented at the 56th Annual Meeting of the Society for American Archaeology, New Orleans.

Spennemann, D. H. R., and S. M. Colley
1989    Fire in a Pit: The Effects of Burning on Faunal Remains. *Archaeozoologia* III/1(2):65–70.

Speth, J. D.
1983    *Bison Kills and Bone Counts: Decision Making by Ancient Hunters.* University of Chicago Press, Chicago and London.

Speth, J. D., and W. J. Parry
1980    *Late Prehistoric Bison Procurement in South-Eastern New Mexico: The 1978 Season at the Garnsey Site (LA-18399).* University of Michigan Museum of Anthropology Technical Report 8. Ann Arbor.

Stanford, D. J.
1978    The Jones-Miller Site: An Example of Hell Gap Bison Procurement Strategy. In *Bison Procurement and Utilization: A Symposium,* edited by L. B. Davis and M. Wilson, pp. 90–97. Plains Anthropologist Memoir 14.

Thomas, D. H., and D. Mayer
1983    Behavioral Faunal Analysis of Selected Horizons. In *The Archaeology of Monitor Valley: 2. Gatecliff Shelter,* edited by D. H. Thomas, pp. 353–391. Anthropological Papers of the American Museum of Natural History 59.

Todd, L. C.
1983    *The Horner Site: Taphonomy of an Early Holocene Bison Bonebed.* Ph.D. dissertation, University of New Mexico, Albuquerque. University Microfilms, Ann Arbor.

1987a   Taphonomy of the Horner II Bonebed. In *The Horner Site: The Type Site of the Cody Cultural Complex,* edited by G. C. Frison and L. C. Todd, pp. 107–198. Academic Press, New York.

1987b   Analysis of Kill-Butchery Bonebeds and Interpretation of Paleoindian Hunting. In *The Evolution of Human Hunting,* edited by M. H. Nitecki and D. V. Nitecki, pp. 225–266. Plenum Press, New York and London.

Todd, L. C., and G. C. Frison.
1986    Taphonomic Study of the Colby Site Mammoth Bones. In *The Colby Mammoth Site: Taphonomy and Archaeology of a Clovis Kill in Northern Wyoming,* edited by G. C. Frison and L. C. Todd, pp. 27-90. University of New Mexico Press, Albuquerque.

Todd, L. C., and D. J. Rapson
1988a   Bonebed Analysis and Paleoindian Studies: The Mill Iron Site. Paper presented at the 53rd Annual Meeting of the Society for American Archaeology, Phoenix.

1988b   Long Bone Fragmentation and Interpretation of Faunal Assemblages: Approaches to Comparative Analysis. *Journal of Archaeological Science* 15:307–325.

Todd, L. C., D. J. Rapson, and J. L. Hofman
1992    Dentition Studies of Mill Iron and Other Early Paleoindian Bison Bonebed Sites. Unpublished manuscript.

Toots, H.
1965 Orientation and Distribution of Fossils as Environmental Indicators. In *Sedimentation of Late Cretaceous and Tertiary Outcrops, Rock Springs Uplift: Wyoming Geological Association Guidebook*, 19th Field Conference, edited by R. H. DeVoto and R. K. Bitter, pp. 219–229.

Ubelaker, D. H.
1984 *Human Skeletal Remains: Excavation, Analysis, and Interpretation*. Manuals in Archaeology 2. Taraxacum, Washington, D. C.

von den Driesch, A.
1976 *A Guide to the Measurement of Animal Bones from Archaeological Sites*. Peabody Museum Bulletin 1. Peabody Museum of Archaeology and Ethnology.

Voorhies, M. R.
1969 *Taphonomy and Population Dynamics of an Early Pliocene Vertebrate Fauna, Knox County, Nebraska*. University of Wyoming, Laramie.

Waldron, T.
1987 The Relative Survival of the Human Skeleton: Implications for Palaeopathology. In *Death, Decay and Reconstruction: Approaches to Archaeology and Forensic Science*, edited by A. Boddington, A. N. Garland, and R. C. Janaway, pp. 55–64. Manchester University Press, Manchester.

Watson, J. A. L., and H. M. Abbey
1986 The Effects of Termites (Isoptera) on Bone: Some Archeological Implications. *Sociobiology* 11(3):245–254.

Wellman, H. W., and A. T. Wilson
1965 Salt Weathering, a Neglected Geological Erosive Agent in Coastal and Arid Environments. *Nature* 205(4976):1097–1098.

Wheat, J. B.
1967 A Paleo-Indian Bison Kill. *Scientific American* 216:44–52.
1971 Lifeway of Early Man in North America. *Arctic Anthropology* 8(2):22–31.
1972 *The Olsen-Chubbuck Site: A Paleo-Indian Bison Kill*. Society for American Archaeology Memoir 26.
1978 Olsen-Chubbuck and Jurgens sites: Four Aspects of Paleo-Indian Economy. In *Bison Procurement and Utilization: A Symposium*, edited by L. B. Davis and

M. Wilson, pp. 84–89. Plains Anthropologist Memoir 14.
1979 *The Jurgens Site*. Plains Anthropologist Memoir 15.
1982 Bone Technology at Jurgens, Olsen-Chubbuck and Little Box Elder. *Canadian Journal of Anthropology* 2(2):169–177.

White, T. E.
1952 Observations on the Butchering Technique of Some Aboriginal Peoples, No. 1. *American Antiquity* 17:337–338.
1953 A Method of Calculating the Dietary Percentages of Various Food Animals Utilized by Aboriginal Peoples. *American Antiquity* 18:396–398.
1956 The Study of Osteological Materials in the Plains. *American Antiquity* 21:401–404.

Wilson, M. C.
1983 Canid Scavengers and Butchering Patterns: Evidence From a 3600-year-old Bison Bonebed in Alberta. In *Carnivores, Human Scavengers & Predators: A Question of Bone Technology*, edited by G. M. LeMoine and A. MacEachern pp. 95–140. Proceedings of the 15th Annual CHACMOOL Conference, The Archaeological Association of the University of Calgary, Calgary, Alberta.

Wright, T. M., and W. C. Hayes
1977 Fracture Mechanics Parameters for Compact Bone—Effects of Density and Specimen Thickness. *Journal of Biomechanics* 10:419–430.

Yatsu, E.
1988 *The Nature of Weathering: An Introduction*. Sozosha, Tokyo.

Yellen, J. E.
1991a Small Mammals: !Kung San Utilization and the Production of Faunal Assemblages. *Journal of Anthropological Archaeology* 10:1–26.
1991b Small Mammals: Post-Discard Patterning of !Kung San Faunal Remains. *Journal of Anthropological Archaeology* 10:152–192.

Zeimens, G. M.
1982 Analysis of Postcranial Bison Remains. In *The Agate Basin Site: A Record of the Paleoindian Occupation of the Northwestern High Plains*, edited by G. C. Frison and D. J. Stanford, pp. 213–239. Academic Press, New York.

# CHAPTER EIGHT

# Dentition Studies of the Mill Iron and Other Early Paleoindian Bison Bonebed Sites

LAWRENCE C. TODD
Colorado State University

DAVID J. RAPSON
University of Wyoming

JACK L. HOFMAN
University of Kansas

## Introduction

For over twenty years, analysis of molar eruption and wear has been a prominent feature in the interpretation of bison bonebeds from western North America (e.g., Frison and Reher 1970; Reher 1974; Reher and Frison 1980; Frison 1982a; Todd et al. 1990; Clark and Wilson 1981). Such studies have demonstrated the utility of dental analysis in the determination of season of death and estimation of herd composition, and as the basis for interpretations about predation and processing of bison by Paleoindians (Frison 1982b, 1991a; Klein and Cruz-Uribe 1984; McCartney 1990; Todd 1991). This study of the Mill Iron site lower molars has several purposes. The first is documentation of the collection in order to provide information on the dental age groups represented, the season of death, and the number of animals in the collections. Second, we discuss spatial attributes of the teeth and mandibles and present several interpretations about the Mill Iron site's formational history. Finally, we review comparable data from tooth eruption and wear studies of several other bison bonebeds associated with Goshen or Folsom artifacts to examine some regional and temporal patterns.

The data base from the Mill Iron site incorporates all lower molars from both the bonebed (Table 8.1) and other areas of the site (Table 8.2). Complete tooth rows and isolated molars are included in this study. As documented by Kreutzer (this volume), the Mill Iron site has a complex formational history. Of particular relevance to analysis of the dentitions are the processes of crystal growth due to soil salts. Although tooth enamel is a very dense, durable material, other portions of the tooth, and particularly tooth structure, are not equally durable. Many of the Mill Iron teeth have had much of the dentine de-

stroyed, presumably by processes related to mineral crystal formation. As exposed during excavations, bison "teeth" in the Mill Iron assemblage are frequently little more than fragile, often fragmentary, enamel husks. Especially in some of the younger dental age groups, this condition presents difficulties in assessing the degree of wear. During the process of dentine deterioration, enamel tended to split and separate along the crests of the tooth cusps. This separation can mimic light wear in cases where only a thin band of dentine is exposed.

## Documentation of the Mill Iron Lower Molars

Archaeological descriptions of bison teeth generally follow the cusp and wear surface terminology of Frison et al. (1976; see also Frison 1982a, 1991b). Following Wilson (e.g., Clark and Wilson 1981), we use the term "ectostylid" rather than "exostylid" and refer to the mesial infundibula (Hilson 1986) as the "prefossetid" and to the distal infundibula as the "postfossetid." We also use a modified version of a system for documenting tooth wear patterns developed by Payne (1973, 1987), which classifies wear based on the pattern of exposed dentine on the occlusal surfaces. This system is used together with narrative description and measurement of teeth comparable to those used on other studies of bison dentition (e.g., Frison et al. 1976; Reher 1974; Reher and Frison 1980; Clark and Wilson 1981). Documentation of eruption and wear patterns begins with drawings of occlusal surfaces similar to Grant's (1982) tooth wear stage illustrations (Figure 8.1). In addition to allowing efficient documentation of degree of wear, we have found that when used in conjunction with narrative descriptions these drawings provide a convenient method for inter-assemblage comparisons (Todd et al. 1990).

**Table 8.1.** Bison Lower Teeth from the Mill Iron Bonebed.

| Number | Teeth | PR | SD | GRP | AGE | M1S | M1M | M1E | M1MS | M1DS | M1L | M1EC | M2S | M2M | M2E | M2MS | M2DS | M2L | M2EC | M3S | M3M | M3E | M3MS | M3DS | M3L | M3EC |
|---|---|---|---|---|---|---|---|---|---|---|---|---|---|---|---|---|---|---|---|---|---|---|---|---|---|---|
| L13-15-49 | $P_2$–$P_4$ | | R | | | MIS | — | — | — | — | — | — | MIS | — | — | — | — | — | — | MIS | — | — | — | — | — | — |
| L13-23-169 | $P_3$–$M_2$ | | L | | | I | — | — | — | — | — | — | I | — | — | — | — | — | — | MIS | — | — | — | — | — | — |
| M13-13-75 | $M_2$ | | R | | | MIS | — | — | — | — | — | — | I | — | — | — | — | — | — | MIS | — | — | — | — | — | — |
| M13-14-81 | $M_2$–$M_3$? | | N | | | MIS | — | — | — | — | — | — | I | — | — | — | — | — | — | MIS | — | — | — | — | — | — |
| M13-15-9 | $M_2$ | | R | | | MIS | — | — | — | — | — | — | 9e | — | — | — | — | — | 18.2 | MIS | — | — | — | — | — | — |
| M13-17-5a | $M_1$ | | R | | | I | — | — | — | — | — | 0.0 | MIS | — | — | — | — | — | — | MIS | — | — | — | — | — | — |
| M13-3-131 | $M_2$–$M_3$ | | L | | | MIS | — | — | — | — | — | — | I | — | — | — | — | — | — | I | — | — | — | — | — | — |
| M13-3-69 | $dP_4$–$M_2$ | | L | | | I | — | — | — | — | — | — | I | — | — | — | — | — | — | MIS | — | — | — | — | — | — |
| M13-6-66 | $P_4$–$M_3$ | | L | | | I | — | — | — | — | — | — | I | — | — | — | — | — | — | I | — | — | — | — | — | — |
| M13-7-105 | $M_3$ | | R | | | MIS | — | — | — | — | — | — | MIS | — | — | — | — | — | — | I | — | — | — | — | — | 13.8 |
| M14-10-65 | $P_4$–$M_1$ | | L | | | I | — | — | — | — | — | — | MIS | — | — | — | — | — | — | MIS | — | — | — | — | — | — |
| M13-3-113 | $dP_3$–$M_3$ | | L | 2 | 1.2 | 8D | 53.8 | 55.7 | 13.3 | 12.8 | 34.7 | 10.8 | M | — | — | — | — | 40.5 | 20.8 | Z | — | — | — | — | — | — |
| M13-3-37 | $dP_3$–$M_2$ | | R | 2 | 1.1 | 9C | 54.8 | — | — | — | — | 9.0 | M | — | — | — | — | — | 20.2 | MIS | — | — | — | — | — | — |
| L13-16-135 | $P_2$,$P_3$,$dP_4$, $M_1$–$M_3$ | | R | 3 | 2.1 | 10a | 44.5 | — | 14.1 | 13.7 | 33.1 | 0.0 | 7e | 64.4 | — | 15.6 | 13.9 | 41.2 | 13.7 | M | — | — | — | — | — | — |
| L13-25-200 | $P_2$,$dP_3$–$M_3$ | | L | 3 | 2.2 | 9e | — | — | — | — | — | — | 8a | — | — | — | — | — | — | M | — | — | — | — | — | — |
| L13-25-50 | $P_3$,$dP_4$–$M_3$ | | L | 3 | 2.2 | 9e | 45.9 | — | — | — | — | 3.2 | 8b | 64.7 | — | — | — | — | 13.4 | M | — | — | — | — | — | — |
| M13-14 | $M_1$ | | R | 3 | 2.1 | 9e | — | 48.0 | — | 13.8 | — | 2.4 | MIS | — | — | — | — | — | — | MIS | — | — | — | — | — | — |
| M13-6-80 | $dP_4$–$M_3$ | A24 | L | 3 | 2.0 | 9e | 49.9 | 55.0 | 14.6 | 14.6 | 35.9 | 5.2 | 3d | 69.8 | 72.0 | — | — | — | 15.6 | M | — | — | — | — | — | — |
| M13-6-87 | $P_4$–$M_3$ | A24 | L | 3 | 2.1 | 9e | 49.6 | — | — | — | — | 5.0 | I | 70.8 | — | — | — | — | — | M | — | — | — | — | — | — |
| M14-5-104 | $M_1$–$M_2$ | | R | 3 | 2.1 | I | — | — | — | — | — | — | — | — | — | — | — | — | — | MIS | — | — | — | — | — | — |
| L13-15-66 | $P_2$–$M_3$ | | L | 4 | 2.9 | 11a | 41.8 | 40.7 | 14.0 | 13.7 | 31.7 | 0.0 | 9e | 59.4 | — | 14.3 | 14.4 | 37.2 | 6.8 | 3e | 65.6 | — | — | — | — | — |
| L13-17-92 | $P_2$–$M_3$ | | R | 4 | 3.1 | 11a | 42.9 | — | — | — | — | 0.0 | 9e | 59.2 | — | — | — | — | 8.7 | 4c | 65.1 | — | — | — | — | 17.4 |
| L13-18-11 | $M_1$–$M_3$ | | L | 4 | 3.1 | 11a | — | — | — | — | — | 0.0 | 9d | 62.8 | — | — | — | — | — | I | 67.9 | — | — | — | — | — |
| M13-13-77 | $M_1$ | | R | 4 | 3.1 | 11a | 39.8 | — | — | — | — | 0.0 | MIS | — | — | — | — | — | — | MIS | — | — | — | — | — | — |
| M13-15-8 | $M_2$–$M_3$ | | R | 4 | 3.0 | MIS | — | — | — | — | — | — | 9c | 60.8 | 63.5 | 13.7 | 14.0 | 37.8 | — | U | — | — | — | — | — | — |
| M13-4-59 | $P_4$–$M_3$ | | L | 4 | 3.0 | 11a | — | — | — | — | — | 0.0 | 9d | 54.1 | — | — | — | — | 9.3 | 3c | 63.9 | — | — | 14.7 | — | — |
| M13-4-62 | $M_2$–$M_3$ | | R | 4 | 3.0 | 11a | — | — | — | — | — | — | 9e | — | — | — | — | — | 10.6 | 3c | — | — | — | — | — | 12.2 |
| M13-6-43 | $P_3$–$M_3$ | | R | 4 | 3.1 | 9e | 40.8 | — | — | — | — | 1.7 | 9e | 56.3 | — | — | — | — | 9.8 | I | 63.5 | — | — | — | — | 15.5 |
| M13-6-74 | $P_3$–$M_3$ | | L | 4 | 3.2 | 10a | 38.5 | — | — | — | — | 0.0 | 9e | 57.4 | — | — | — | — | 7.5 | I | — | — | — | — | — | — |
| M14-11-24 | –$M_3$ | | R | 4 | 3.0 | MIS | — | — | — | — | — | — | 9c | 61.6 | 64.6 | — | 17.1 | 42.6 | 12.7 | 3c | 67.4 | 68.5 | 14.7 | — | — | 23.5 |
| M13-17-5 | $M_3$ | | R | 5 | 4.1 | MIS | — | — | — | — | — | — | MIS | — | — | — | — | — | — | 6a | 64.3 | — | — | — | — | 13.4 |
| M13-5-61 | $M_3$ | | L | 5 | 4.1 | MIS | — | — | — | — | — | — | MIS | — | — | — | — | — | 10.6 | 6b | 62.2 | — | — | — | — | — |
| M14-10-65a | $M_1$–M3 | | R | 5 | 4.1 | 10a | 35.1 | 39.6 | 13.2 | 13.1 | 27.3 | 0.0 | 9e | — | — | 14.1 | 14.8 | 34.9 | — | I | — | — | — | — | — | — |
| M14-10-7 | $M_2$–$M_3$ | | L | 5 | 4.1 | MIS | — | — | — | — | — | — | 9e | 51.7 | 51.4 | — | 14.8 | — | 5.8 | 9g | — | 58.1 | 13.6 | 13.0 | — | 11.8 |
| L13-15-112 | $P_2$–$M_3$ | | L | 6 | 5.1 | 11a | 33.1 | 34.6 | 15.3 | 15.2 | 30.4 | 0.0 | 9e | — | 15.9 | 14.9 | 37.0 | 0.9 | 10e | — | 14.8 | 13.9 | — | 11.6 | | |
| L13-17-108 | $P_3$–$M_3$ | | R | 6 | 5.1 | 11a | 32.2 | — | — | — | — | 0.0 | 9e | — | — | — | — | — | 2.6 | 9g | 65.2 | — | — | — | — | 10.1 |
| L13-25-102 | $P_3$–$M_3$ | | R | 6 | 5.0 | 11a | 31.8 | — | — | — | — | 0.0 | I | 52.2 | — | — | — | — | 0.0 | I | — | — | — | — | — | — |
| M13-14-88 | $M_2$ | | R | 6 | 5.1 | MIS | — | — | — | — | — | — | 9e | 51.9 | 47.6 | 14.4 | 15.0 | 36.1 | 0.2 | ,IS | — | — | — | — | — | — |
| M13-14-90 | $M_1$ | | R | 6 | 5.1 | 11a | 28.1 | — | 15.7 | 15.0 | 29.3 | 0.0 | MIS | — | — | — | — | — | — | MIS | — | — | — | — | — | — |
| M13-5-59 | $P_2$–$M_3$ | A22 | R | 6 | 5.1 | I | — | — | — | — | — | 0.0 | 9e | 51.9 | — | — | — | — | 1.3 | 11a | 59.9 | — | — | — | — | 14.2 |
| M13-5-60 | $P_2$–$M_3$ | A22 | L | 6 | 5.1 | 11a | 32.2 | — | — | — | — | 0.0 | 9e | 50.0 | — | — | — | — | 3.1 | 11b | 60.7 | — | — | — | — | 13.3 |
| M13-8-23 | $P_4$–$M_3$ | | R | 6 | 5.1 | I | — | — | — | — | — | — | I | — | — | — | — | 0.0 | — | 11e | 58.4 | 61.6 | — | — | — | 8.0 |
| M14-10-83 | $P_3$–$M_3$ | | R | 6 | 5.1 | 11a | 29.9 | — | 14.6 | 14.7 | 28.3 | 0.0 | 9e | — | 15.2 | 15.4 | 35.5 | 3.7 | 10e | — | — | 14.5 | 14.7 | — | — |
| M14-11-1 | $M_3$ | | L | 6 | 5.1 | MIS | — | — | — | — | — | — | MIS | — | — | — | — | — | — | 11c | 57.2 | 58.9 | 14.6 | 14.7 | — | 12.7 |
| M14-11-23 | $P_4$–$M_2$ | | L | 6 | 5.1 | 11a | 28.4 | 29.8 | 15.6 | 15.1 | 28.7 | 0.0 | 9e | 46.8 | — | 15.3 | 15.3 | 35.7 | 2.4 | MIS | — | — | — | — | — | — |
| L13-16-41 | $P_2$–$M_3$ | A21 | R | 7 | 6.1 | 11a | 23.7 | — | — | — | — | 0.0 | 10a | 41.8 | — | — | — | — | 0.0 | 11b | 55.8 | — | — | — | — | 5.3 |
| L13-16-42 | $P_2$–$M_3$ | A21 | L | 7 | 6.1 | 11a | 25.6 | 25.9 | — | 16.0 | 28.5 | 0.0 | 10a | 42.3 | — | 16.3 | 16.5 | 35.4 | 0.0 | 11b | — | — | 16.0 | 15.4 | — | — |
| M13-3-60 | $M_2$ | | R | 7 | 6.1 | MIS | — | — | — | — | — | — | I | 39.4 | — | — | — | — | 0.0 | MIS | — | — | — | — | — | — |
| M13-6-67 | $P_2$–$M_3$ | | L | 7 | 6.1 | 11a | 26.2 | — | 15.6 | 15.7 | — | 0.0 | 10a | 45.9 | — | — | 15.8 | — | 0.0 | 11c | 57.4 | — | — | — | — | 9.6 |
| M14-1-127 | $M_1$–$M_3$ | A48 | L | 7 | 6.1 | I | — | — | — | — | — | — | I | — | — | — | — | — | — | I | — | — | — | — | — | — |
| M14-1-128 | $P_2$–$M_3$ | A48 | R | 7 | 6.1 | I | — | — | — | — | — | — | I | — | — | — | — | — | — | I | — | — | — | — | — | — |
| M13-13-76 | $M_3$ | | L | 8 | 7.1 | MIS | — | — | — | — | — | — | MIS | — | — | — | — | — | — | 12a | 50.2 | 51.4 | 16.7 | 15.0 | — | 0.0 |
| M13-4-166 | $P_3$–$M_3$ | C16 | L | 8 | 7.1 | 15b | 17.3 | — | 15.4 | 15.9 | 25.7 | 0.0 | 11a | — | — | 16.1 | 15.5 | 35.4 | 0.0 | 11c | — | — | 15.7 | — | — | 6.2 |
| M13-4-167 | $P_4$–$M_3$ | C16 | R | 8 | 7.1 | 15b | — | — | — | — | — | — | 11a | — | — | — | — | — | — | 11C | — | — | — | — | — | — |
| M13-9-3 | $M_2$–$M_3$ | | R | 8 | 7.1 | MIS | — | — | — | — | — | — | 10A | 32.8 | 34.7 | 17.5 | 16.3 | 32.6 | 0.0 | 12a | 47.9 | — | 16.3 | 15.0 | — | 0.0 |
| M14-1-136 | $P_2$–$M_3$ | A49 | R | 8 | 7.1 | 11a | — | — | — | — | — | — | 10a | — | — | — | — | — | — | 12a | — | — | — | — | — | — |
| M14-1-137 | $P_2$–$M_3$ | A49 | L | 8 | 7.1 | 11a | 18.4 | 18.0 | 16.6 | 16.6 | 27.4 | 0.0 | 10a | 32.8 | 31.0 | 18.1 | 16.6 | 32.3 | 0.0 | 12a | — | — | 16.6 | 15.4 | — | — |
| L13-25-176 | $M_2$–$M_3$ | | L | 9 | 8.1 | MIS | — | — | — | — | — | — | 11a | 27.4 | 27.8 | — | 17.6 | — | 0.0 | 12a | 38.3 | 38.5 | 15.5 | 15.9 | — | 0.0 |
| M13-17-9 | $M_3$ | | R | 9 | 8.1 | MIS | — | — | — | — | — | — | MIS | — | — | — | — | — | 0.0 | 12a | 41.9 | — | — | — | — | 0.0 |
| M13-3-100 | $M_2$–$M_3$ | A09 | L | 9 | 8.1 | MIS | — | — | — | — | — | — | I | — | — | — | — | — | 0.0 | 12a | 38.8 | — | — | — | — | — |
| M13-3-99 | $M_1$–$M_3$ | A09 | R | 9 | 8.1 | I | — | — | — | — | — | 0.0 | I | — | — | — | — | — | 0.0 | 12a | 38.7 | — | — | — | — | 0.0 |
| L13-17-118 | $P_2$–$M_3$ | | R | 10 | 9.1 | 15b | 11.1 | — | — | — | — | 0.0 | 11a | 25.7 | — | — | — | — | 0.0 | 12a | 34.4 | — | — | — | — | 0.0 |
| L13-23-37 | $P_2$–$M_3$ | A02 | R | 10 | 9.1 | 16a | 12.1 | — | — | — | — | 0.0 | 11a | 25.3 | — | — | — | — | 0.0 | 12a | 32.7 | — | — | — | — | 0.0 |
| L13-23-38 | $P_2$–$M_3$ | A02 | L | 10 | 9.1 | 15a | 9.5 | — | — | — | — | 0.0 | 11a | 21.2 | — | — | — | — | 0.0 | 12a | 32.2 | — | — | — | — | 0.0 |
| L13-25-86 | $M_1$–$M_3$ | | L | 10 | 9.1 | 16a | 9.6 | 11.1 | 18.8 | 19.0 | — | 0.0 | 11a | 26.5 | — | 18.6 | 17.4 | 32.6 | 0.0 | 12a | — | — | 16.8 | 15.6 | — | 0.0 |
| L13-25-196 | $P_4$–$M_3$ | | R | 13 | 12.1 | 16a | — | 8.3 | — | — | — | 0.0 | 17c | — | 8.7 | — | 20.6 | — | 0.0 | 13a | — | — | — | — | 17.5 | 0.0 |
| L14-21-43 | $P_2$–$M_3$ | | L | 13 | 12.1 | 16a | 4.8 | 8.1 | 17.8 | — | — | 0.0 | 17c | 9.0 | 7.8 | — | 20.9 | 30.0 | 0.0 | 13a | 12.7 | 16.8 | 28.8 | 17.0 | — | 0.0 |
| M13-6-27 | $P_4$–$M_3$ | | R | 14 | 13.1 | 19a | 0.2 | — | — | — | — | 0.0 | 19a | 2.3 | — | — | — | — | — | MIS | — | — | — | — | — | — |

NUMBER, identification number; TEETH, teeth present; PR, pair identification; SD, side; GRP, dental age group; AGE, estimated age in years; $M_1$S, $M_1$ wear stage; $M_1$M, $M_1$ metaconid height; $M_1$E, $M_1$ entoconid height; $M_1$MS $M_1$ occlusal width, mesial; $M_1$DS, $M_1$ occlusal width, distal; $M_1$L, $M_1$ occlusal length; $M_1$EC, $M_1$ ectostylid distance to wear; $M_2$S, $M_2$ wear stage; $M_1$M, $M_2$ metaconid height; $M_2$E, $M_2$ entoconid height; $M_2$MS, $M_2$ occlusal width, mesial; $M_2$DS, $M_2$ occlusal width, distal; $M_2$L, $M_2$ occlusal length; $M_2$EC, $M_2$ ectostylid distance to wear; $M_3$S, $M_3$ wear stage; $M_3$M, $M_3$ metaconid height; $M_3$E, $M_3$ entoconid height; $M_3$MS, $M_3$ occlusal width, mesial; $M_3$DS, $M_3$ occlusal width, distal; $M_3$L, $M_3$ occlusal length; $M_3$EC, $M_3$ ectostylid distance to wear.

Eruption stages for unworn teeth are coded (Table 8.3), and several dimensions are measured for each molar. Although there is a clear relationship between tooth eruption/wear patterns and an animal's chronological age, this relationship is not one-to-one (Gifford-Gonzalez 1991). Therefore, we use the term "dental age groups" (Hilson 1986:182) to describe the series of dentitions with similar eruption and wear patterns.

The dental age groups are equated with corresponding approximate chronological ages based on comparisons with eruption and wear schedules for modern bison teeth (Reher and Frison 1980). The dental age groups can also be compared to dental age groups described from other Plains bison bonebeds (Tables 8.4 and 8.5) to provide a relative scale for examining season of death. In addition to the narrative descriptions, we have reexamined several of the assemblages listed in Tables 8.4 and 8.5 and completed occlusal surface drawings to aid in their comparison. For example, the younger dental age groups from the Mill Iron site are shown together with examples from the Hawken site to illustrate the similarities and differences in wear patterns.

Molar measurements (Figure 8.2) include: metaconid height (cemento-enamel junction to crown), entoconid height, mesial (anterior) width at the occlusal surface, distal (posterior) width at occlusal surface, length of occlusal surfaces, and distance from crown of ectostylid to exposed dentine of occlusal surface. Metric data on all Mill Iron molars are included in Tables 8.1 and 8.2.

Combining eruption and wear stage data with metric attributes, such as dental crown height (metaconid height), yields a series of distinct dental age groups. As illustrated in Figure 8.1, occlusal surface illustrations are on the left, the dental age group is in the central column, and a series of schematic 'Payne-like' (Payne 1973, 1987) representations of the wear pattern and the corresponding wear stage designation for lower molars are in the right-hand column. The wear stage codes used here (Figures 8.3 and 8.4) differ somewhat from Payne's (1987) system. We have included codes for wear to the ectostylid (e.g., Figure 8.4:10a) and also for documentation of the small ovals of enamel that are common at the mesial and

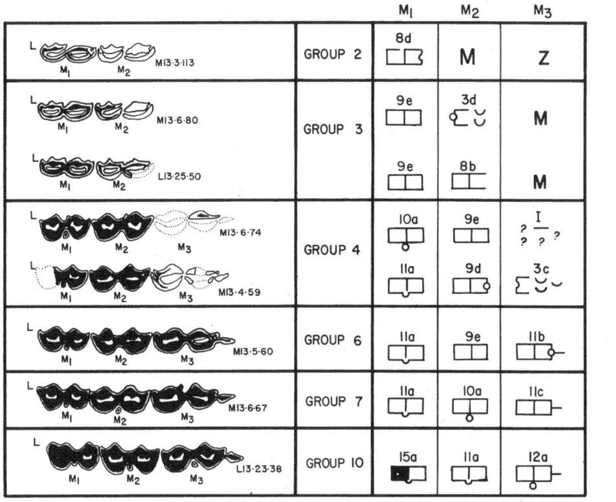

**Figure 8.1.** Examples of occlusal surface illustrations and eruption and wear codes.

distal margins of bison molars during early stages of wear (e.g., Figure 8.3:4b, 4c). In assigning wear codes to specific wear patterns, we have followed the system outlined by Payne in which:

> numbers are based on the sequence of steps by which wear progresses. Starting with an unworn tooth as 0, one is added each time another cusp comes into wear, or the exposed dentine of one cusp joins up with the dentine of another . . . A similar approach is used for stages in the gradual erasure of the infundibula, each of which first breaks down into two smaller infundibula which are then eliminated one after the other . . . The letter suffixes are used to distinguish variants with the same numerical score [Payne 1987:609–612].

Measurement of the relative state of "eruption" of unworn teeth, such as the distance of a tooth crown below the alveolus as illustrated for a sample of 78 known-age-at-death (age group 2) bison in Figure 8.5, can also aid in identification of the range of variation in archaeological samples.

**Table 8.2.** Bison Lower Teeth from Mill Iron Camp-Processing Area.

| Number | Teeth | SD | GRP | AGE | M1S | M1M | M1E | M1MS | M1DS | M1L | M1EC | M2S | M2M | M2E | M2MS | M2DS | M2L | M2EC | M3S | M3M | M3E | M3MS | M3DS | M3L | M3EC |
|---|---|---|---|---|---|---|---|---|---|---|---|---|---|---|---|---|---|---|---|---|---|---|---|---|---|
| N12/W19 | M₁ | L | — | — | 11a | — | — | — | — | — | 0.0 | MIS | — | — | — | — | — | — | MIS | — | — | — | — | — | — |
| N15/W23 | P₃–M₃ | R | — | — | I | — | — | — | — | — | — | I | — | — | — | — | — | — | I | — | — | — | — | — | — |
| N13/W13 | M₁ | L | 4 | 3.1 | 10a | 39.8 | — | 15.7 | 15.1 | — | 0.0 | MIS | — | — | — | — | — | — | MIS | — | — | — | — | — | — |
| NO #D | M₃ | L | 4 | 3.1 | MIS | — | — | — | — | — | — | MIS | — | — | — | — | — | — | I | 62.7 | — | — | — | — | 10.9 |
| STEPA 16 | M₃ | L | 4 | 3.1 | MIS | — | — | — | — | — | — | MIS | — | — | — | — | — | — | I | 65.7 | — | 14.8 | — | — | 17.4 |
| STEPC 15 | M₂–M₃ | L | 4 | 3.1 | I | — | — | — | — | — | — | 9e | 57.8 | 62.1 | — | — | — | 11.5 | MIS | — | — | — | — | — | — |
| N13/W22 | M₂ | R | 4 | 3.1 | MIS | — | — | — | — | — | — | 9e | 60.9 | — | — | — | — | 12.2 | MIS | — | — | — | — | — | — |
| STEPC 14 | M₂–M₃ | R | 4 | 3.1 | MIS | — | — | — | — | — | — | 9d | — | — | — | — | — | 12.0 | 3c | — | — | — | — | — | 17.2 |
| BLOCK 2 | P₂–3, dP₄, M₁–M₃ | L | 5 | 4.0 | 11a | 35.5 | — | — | — | — | 0.0 | 9d | 55.7 | — | — | — | — | 8.9 | I | — | — | — | — | — | — |
| 24CT30-2 | M₃ | R | 6 | 5.1 | MIS | — | — | — | — | — | — | MIS | — | — | — | — | — | — | I | 57.9 | — | — | — | — | — |
| BANK 1 | P₃–M₃ | R | 6 | 5.1 | I | — | — | — | — | — | — | I | — | — | — | — | — | — | 11c | 57.7 | — | — | — | — | 7.6 |
| NO #C | M₃ | R | 6 | 5.1 | MIS | — | — | — | — | — | — | MIS | — | — | — | — | — | — | 11c | 57.8 | — | — | — | — | 10.0 |
| NO #E | M₁ | R | 6 | 5.1 | 11a | 31.0 | — | — | — | — | 0.0 | MIS | — | — | — | — | — | — | MIS | — | — | — | — | — | — |

NUMBER, identification number; TEETH, teeth present; PR, pair identification; SD, side; GRP, dental age group; AGE, estimated age in years; M1S, M1 wear stage; M1M, M1 metaconid height; M1E, M1 entoconid height; M1MS M1 occlusal width, mesial; M1DS, M1 occlusal width, distal; M1L, M1 occlusal length; M1EC, M1 ectostylid distance to wear; M2S, M2 wear stage; M1M, M2 metaconid height; M2E, M2 entoconid height; M2MS, M2 occlusal width, mesial; M2DS, M2 occlusal width, distal; M2L, M2 occlusal length; M2EC, M2 ectostylid distance to wear; M3S, M3 wear stage; M3M, M3 metaconid height; M3E, M3 entoconid height; M3MS, M3 occlusal width, mesial; M3DS, M3 occlusal width, distal; M3L, M3 occlusal length; M3EC, M3 ectosylid distance to wear.

**Table 8.3.** Dental Eruption Codes Used in Description of the Mill Iron Lower Dentitions (for Wear Codes see Figures 3 and 4).

| Code | Description |
|------|-------------|
| Z | Dental crypt is not open at the alveolar surface; tooth forming within jaw. |
| C | Dental crypt open at the alveolar surface; tooth is not visible. |
| O | Dental crypt open and the tooth is visible below the alveolar surface of the jaw. Measurement of the distance from the lingual alveolar surface to the upper surface of the metaconid used as an indication of the relative state of "eruption"; for the "O" stage these are recorded as negative numbers. |
| M | Metaconid and often the protoconid erupted through the alveolar bone; entoconid and hypoconid still below the alveolar bone. Measurement of the distance from the lingual alveolar surface to the upper surface of the metaconid used as an indication of the relative state of "eruption"; for the "M and E" stages these are recorded as positive numbers. |
| E | Metaconid and entoconid above the alveolar bone, but the tooth is not yeat to the level of the other teeth. Measurement of the distance from the lingual alveolar surface to the upper surface of the metaconid used as an indication of the relative state of "eruption"; for the "M and E" stages these are recorded as positive numbers. |
| U | At the level of the other teeth but unworn. |
| I | Eruption/wear stage indeterminate; damaged specimen. |

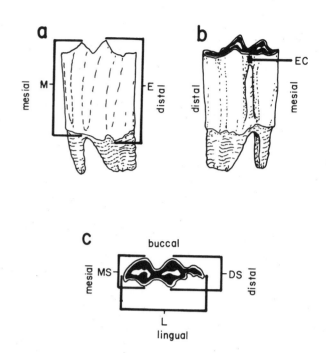

**Figure 8.2.** Locations of measurements taken on Mill Iron lower molars; a) lingual view: M = metaconid height, E = entoconid height; b) buccal view: EC = ectostylid to wear; c) occlusal view: MS = mesial width of occlusal surface, DS = distal width of occlusal surface, L = occlusal surface length. (All measurements in mm.)

For the Mill Iron sample, dental age groups 2–5 are determined by patterns of molar eruption and wear. Groups 6–13 are based on crown heights with the $M_1$ metaconids emphasized for younger groups (6 and 7) and $M_2$–$M_3$ metaconids given greater attention for the older dental age groups. $M_1$ metaconids are not used exclusively since, as noted below, there is a tendency for the rate of $M_1$ attrition to decrease as animals grow older. Exclusive reliance on the $M_1$ in assigning dental groups to older animals can lead to an underestimation of dental age.

The techniques used here for determining dental age groups and season of bison mortality differ in several key respects from the tooth crown height approaches used by other researchers (e.g., Klein and Cruz-Uribe 1983, 1984; Klein et al. 1981; Gifford-Gonzalez 1991). In particular, dental age groups for the younger animals in bison assemblages are assigned primarily on the basis of *both* molar eruption and wear patterns. Crown heights are used as the primary criterion only after all molars are in full wear.

## Dental Age Groups, Seasonality, Molar Attrition, and MNI

A total of 81 mandibles or partial tooth rows have been recorded from the Mill Iron site. Sixty-eight specimens are

from the bonebed (Table 8.1), and 13 are from other areas of the site (Table 8.2). Minimum number of individuals (minimal distinction MNI) estimates, based on counts of lower molars (Figure 8.6), indicate that at least 29 animals (i.e., there are 29 right $M_2$s) are represented in the bonebed area and as many as five additional animals (based on 5 right $M_3$s) are represented in collections from the camp/processing area. As discussed below, when the teeth are partitioned by dental age group, the MNI estimates for the site increase slightly.

Most of the lower molars have been assigned to dental age groups based on attributions of eruption and attrition. For younger animals, a combination of eruption and wear can be used to segregate the teeth into a series of distinct groups. Comparison with modern specimens, with published eruption and wear schedules (Reher and Frison 1980), in combination with descriptions of eruption and wear patterns from other bison assemblages (Table 8.4 and 8.5) allows age-at-death estimates to be assigned to the younger dental age groups from Mill Iron.

Once all molars are fully erupted and in wear (dental age groups 6 and above), the metaconid method (Frison 1991b) is used. Metaconid heights (Figure 8.2) from catastrophic mass mortality sites tend to fall into discrete clusters, assumed to represent individual age cohorts. Incremental attrition of $M_1$ metaconids (Figure 8.7) has been widely used in bison mortality studies and, together with wear class codes (Figures 8.3 and 8.4) and attrition of the other molars (Figure 8.8), provides the

LEFT

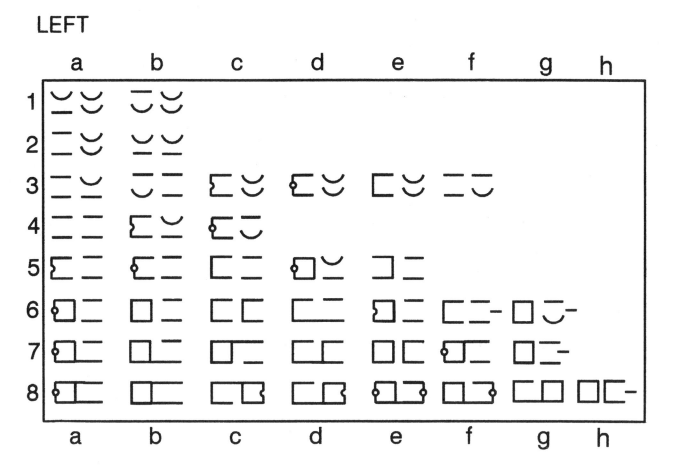

**Figure 8.3.**   Wear codes for bison lower molars in light to moderate wear (following Payne 1987).

LEFT

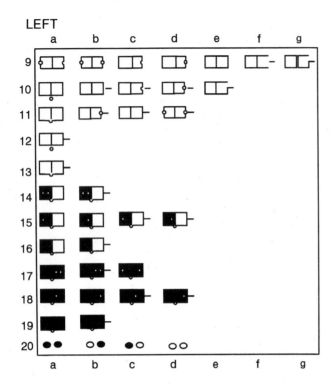

**Figure 8.4.** Wear codes for bison lower molars in advanced wear (following Payne 1987).

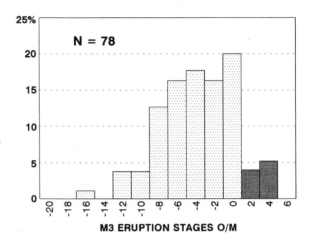

**Figure 8.5.** Distance of $M_3$ metaconid from alveolus for dental age group 2 modern comparative bison.

basis for separating the worn Mill Iron teeth into dental age groups. Given the fragmentary nature of many of the teeth, metaconid measurements were not always possible. Although, as noted by Gifford-Gonzalez (1991:54), measurements other than crown heights may be less susceptible to damage, and hence allow inclusion of a larger number of specimens into the analysis, metaconid heights are used here to allow broader comparisons with other Plains bison assemblages.

Teeth with damaged or fragmentary metaconids can often be assigned to dental age groups based on alternate patterns of sequential attrition. For instance, in bison, height of the second cusp (entoconid: Figure 8.2), is highly correlated with the metaconid height (Figure 8.9) for all molars and can be used to estimate dental age when the metaconid is unmeasurable.

In addition to metaconid heights, other metric attributes show distinct patterns of incremental attrition. For example, as a molar wears, the distance between the ectostylid crown and the exposed dentine of the occlusal surface decreases until the ectostylid eventually comes into wear. Although the timing of ectostylid wear can be individually variable and should not be relied on exclusively, it does provide a good indication of relative dental age. Measurement of ectostylid to wear distance on a series of modern, comparative specimens (University of Wyoming), illustrates this pattern (Figure 8.10). Group 2 ectostylids are never worn. In group 3, the $M_1$ ectostylid is in wear on less than 40% of the older individuals, with most being 4–5

mm from wear; ectostylids on $M_2$ and $M_3$ are never worn. Even when the ectostylid is in wear, it maintains a distinct oval separating it from the rest of the tooth by a band of enamel (Figure 8.4; wear code 10a). The first molar ectostylids on group 4 are usually (over 85%) in wear and often form a continuous dentine surface with the rest of the occlusal surface (Figure 8.4: wear code 11a). When the group 4 $M_1$ ectostylids are unworn, their crowns are always less than 5 mm from the occlusal surface.

Average distances from the ectostylid crown to the occlusal surface by dental age group for the Mill Iron lower molars are illustrated in Figure 8.11. This pattern of attrition is comparable to that observed on the modern bison and adds an additional criterion for assigning damaged specimens from the Mill Iron site to dental age groups.

A final consideration in the estimation of a bison's age at death based on dental ages, is an apparent variation in the rate of molar attrition as a bison's age increases. In a discussion of the Ayers-Frazier bison trap, Clark and Wilson note that:

[a] graph of metaconid height versus age, using mean values calculated for successive age groups, shows that $M_1$ attrition *generally slows down in the sample with increasing age*. This was also noted in the Garnsey (New Mexico) sample (Wilson 1980), but to a lesser extent [Clark and Wilson 1981:63; emphasis added].

This tendency for $M_1$ attrition to slow with increasing age is also indicated in the Mill Iron sample. As described for the Hawken site mandibles (Frison et al. 1976:39–40), where identification of older dental age groups relied more heavily on the $M_3$ metaconid heights rather than the $M_1$ metaconid heights, here we use $M_1$ metaconid heights primarily for the younger age groups, and then rely more heavily on $M_2$ and $M_3$ metaconid heights for dental age groups 8 and older.

**Table 8.4.** Summary of Mandibular Eruption and Wear for Selected Bison Assemblages with Dental Age Estimates of Less than N+.5 Years.

| Garnsey (Wilson 1980) | Scottsbluff (Todd et al. 1990) | Lipscomb (Todd et al. 1990) | Wardell (Reher 1973) |
|---|---|---|---|
| *0.0–0.1 years.* Fetal and neonatal individuals with no dental wear or very slight wear on crests of dP$_3$ and dP$_4$. M$_1$ is still below the level of the alveolus as a bud. | No Group 1 specimens. | No Group 1 specimens. | *0.4 years.* All deciduous incisors and premolars in place. dP$_2$ and dP$_3$ slightly to moderately worn; dP$_4$ slightly worn; both cusps of m$_1$ erupted from jaw, but still below the level of the other teeth and unworn. |
| *1.0 years.* dP$_4$ in full wear except for anterior ectostylid. M$_1$ erupted to level of dP$_4$ and in wear on facets I–VI; facets VII–VIII very lightly worn; ectostylid not in wear and still well below crown. M$_2$ erupted in bud. | *1.1–1.2 years.* All deciduous premolars are in wear. Facets I–VIII are in wear on the M$_1$s (facets VII–VIII in light wear) and the ectostylids are 8 to 14 mm from wear. The M$_2$s are unerupted or just beginning to erupt with the metaconid and protoconid visible in the open crypt behind the first molar with the metaconids at or slightly below the alveolus. | *1.2–1.4 years.* The M$_1$s are fully erupted with full wear on facets I–VIII. the M$_2$s are either partially erupted with only the first cusp above the jaw to erupted nearly to level of the M$_1$s but always unworn. Based on Reher and Frison's (1980:64–70) erupted schedules of bison molars, which indicates that the M$_2$ begins erupting at 1.1 to 1.2 years and starts in wear before 1.5 years, a dental age of 1.2–1.4 years is indicated. | *1.4 years.* dP$_2$ and dP$_3$ well worn; dP$_4$ moderately to well worn, roots beginning to show on all dP's as they are pushed out; M$_1$ only moderately worn; M$_2$ erupted to about the level of other teeth and unworn or with slight wear on the first cusp; M$_3$ still being formed in the jaw, first cusp sometimes visible where jaw is opening behind M$_2$. |
| *2.0 years.* dP$_4$ heavily worn and may be starting to cup in preselenid; both ectostylids in wear. M$_1$ strongly to moderately bilophodont; enamel base remains below level of alveolus. M$_1$ ectostylid unworn or lightly worn on tip to a circle. M$_1$ in full wear through facet VIII. M$_2$ erupted close to level of M$_1$, all facets showing wear but only lightly on VII–VIII. M$_2$ ectostylid unworn and not far above alveolus. M$_3$ unerupted and in bud. | *2.1–2.2 years.* The deciduous premolars are heavily worn. M$_1$s are in full wear with the ectostylids at 4–5 mm from wear. Facets I–VI on the M$_2$s are in full wear and facets VI–VIII in light wear. The M3s are visible in the crypt behind the M$_2$ and the metaconids are 5–7 mm above the alveolus. | *2.2–2.5 years.* The M$_1$s are in full wear with the ectostylids on two specimens having dentine surface connected to the rest of the tooth, and in wear but with the dentine still encircled with enamel on another. Ectostylids on the remaining three first molars are about 3 mm from wear. The M2s vary from full wear on facets I–VI with light wear on facets V–VI on one specimen, to wear on facets I–VIII on other specimens. The M$_3$ first two cusps are always erupted, but the hypoconulid is never above the jaw. Third molars are unworn. | *2.4 years.* dP$_2$ and dP$_3$ extremely worn, with most of the roots showing, P$_2$ and P$_3$ sometimes visible underneath; dP$_4$ also extremely worn, but with less of the roots showing; M$_1$ and M$_2$ moderately to well worn; first cusp of M$_3$ erupted second cusp always visible but often not entirely free of jaw, third cusp never visible, no wear or only slight wear on first cusp. |

**Table 8.4.**   *(continued)*

| Garnsey (Wilson 1980) | Scottsbluff (Todd et al. 1990) | Lipscomb (Todd et al. 1990) | Wardell (Reher 1973) |
|---|---|---|---|
| *3.0 years.* One specimen, damaged. $M_3$ in full wear on facets I–II, light on III–VI, and unworn on VII–IX'. $M_3$ strongly bilophodont; ectostylid not yet visible at alveolus. | *3.1–3.3 years.* The first molar is in full wear. On two $M_1$s the ectostylid is worn, but still separated by a ring of enamel; on the others the enamel is worn through. $M_2$ is in full wear with the ectostylid not yet in wear. The first two cusps of the M3s are erupted to the level of the second molar. Facets I–II are in wear on all specimens, I–III in wear on one, and facets IV–VIII in light wear on one specimen. The hypoconulid is below the level of the alveolus in one specimen, but slighly above the alveoli of the others. | *3.2–3.5.* $M_1$ and $M_2$ are in full wear with the ectostylids on all $M_1$s in wear but still separated from the rest of the occlusal surface by a ring of enamel. The ectostylids on the second molars are 9–10 mm from wear. The hypoconulids of the $M_3$s are erupted but unworn. Facets I–IV are in wear on all $M_3$s. On one specimen facets V–VI are in light wear while facets VII–IX' are unworn. On the right mandible with the same specimen number, facets VII is also in wear. Facets V–VIII are in wear on one mandible. | *3.4 years.* $P_4$ usually partly erupted and unworn; $M_1$ and $M_2$ in regular use; third cusp of $M_3$ erupted above jaw line but never worn, moderate wear on first cusp, slight wear on second cusp. |
| *4.0 years.* One specimen, lacking $M_1$. $M_2$–$M_3$ strongly bilophodont; both have enamel bases still well below level of alveolus. $M_2$ ectostylid worn to a small circle. $M_3$ ectostylid just visible above level of alveolus. Anterior face of $M_3$ hypoconulid (facet IX) in wear, but IX' not yet worn. | *4.1–4.2 years.* The $M_1$s are in full wear; ectostylids are worn, but still separated by a ring of enamel. The second molars are in full wear and the ectostylids are not yet in wear. The $M_3$s are fully erupted and all have wear on facets I–VIII. The hypoconulid (facets IX and IX') is in wear but not connected to the rest of the occlusal surface in two of the specimens. | No group 5 specimens. | *4.4 years.* Third cusp of $M_3$ erupted to about full height, slightly worn with dentine exposed but still bordered by continuous enamel, first cusp well worn, second cusp moderately to well worn. |

**Table 8.5.** Summary of Mandibular Eruption and Wear for Selected Bison Assemblages with Dental Age Estimates of N+.5 Years or Greater.

| Glenrock (Frison and Reher 1970) | Casper (Reher 1974; see also Horner II ([Todd 1987b] and Ayers-Frazier [Clark and Wilson 1981] for other N+.6) | Hawken (Frison et al. 1976) | Agate Basin (Agate Basin Component) (Frison 1982a) |
|---|---|---|---|
| *0.5 years.* All deciduous incisors and premolars in place, $dP_2$ and $dP_3$ moderately to well worn, $dP_4$ moderately worn; $M_1$ erupted but usually not to the level of the other teeth, $M_1$ is unworn or slightly worn on the highest cusp; partially formed $M_2$ can sometimes be seen in the opening behind $M_1$. | *0.6 years.* $dP_{2-4}$ in place and in wear on all cusps; $M_1$ erupted to level of other teeth, usually moderate wear on first cusp, slight wear on anterior side of second cusp; $M_1$ of some specimens has only slight wear on first cusp; tip of first cusp of $M_2$ can be seen in the jaw behind $M_1$, occasionally this protrudes 1–2 mm above the jaw. | *0.7 years.* All deciduous premolars in wear. $M_1$ erupted with wear on facets I–VI; wear on facets V and VI light. $M_2$ not yet erupted although visible in opening behind $M_1$. $M_3$ in bud, totally enclosed behind $M_2$. | *0.8–0.9 years.* All deciduous premolars in wear. Wear on facets I–VIII on $M_1$. $M_2$ unerupted but visible in the opening behind $M_1$ just below the level of the alveolus. $M_3$ is in the early bud stage and totally enclosed behind $M_2$. |
| *1.5 years.* $dP_2$, $dP_3$, and $dP_4$ well worn and have roots showing as they are being pushed out; $M_1$ moderately worn; $M_2$ usually unworn and not full erupted or shows only slight wear; $M_3$ still being formed in the jaw and can be seen through the opening behind $M_2$. | *1.6 years.* No specimens of this age were recovered at the Casper site. We can infer that animals of this age would have had the second molar erupted to the level of the other teeth with slight wear on the second cusp. | *1.7 years.* All deciduous premolars still in place. $M_1$ fully erupted and in wear. $M_2$ erupted; specimens vary as to wear. Some have very light wear on facets I and II. On other facets I and II show more wear with light wear on III and IV. $M_3$ not erupted but visible in opening behind $M_2$. | *1.6–1.8 years.* All deciduous premolars in place. $M_1$ is now fully erupted and has been reduced in length by several millimeters through wear. $M_2$ is erupted and there is considerable variance in wear. On one specimen there is light wear only on facets I and II; on another the wear is extended to facets V and VI. $M_3$ is not erupted but visible in the opening behind $M_2$, still below the level of the aveolus. The $P_4$ has not yet pushed above the level of the alveolus. |
| *2.5 years.* $dP_2$ and $dP_3$ extremely worn, sometimes sitting on partially erupted permanent tooth and just barely rooted in the jaw. $P_2$ and $P_3$ accordingly are usually partially erupted or close to eruption; $dP_4$ extremely worn, but not pushed out as far as other deciduous premolars; $M_1$ and $M_2$ moderately to well worn; 1st and 2nd cusps of $M_3$ erupted, but never the 3rd cusp. | *2.6 years.* $dP_2$ and $dP_3$ still in place or $P_2$ and $P_3$ erupted to varying extents. It should be stressed that the premolars in bison can vary almost two years in their eruption and are not useful indicators of age. $dP_4$ is usually still in place and well worn; $M_1$ and $M_2$ are in regular wear, cusps on both are quite pointed; first two cusps only of $M_3$ are erupted above jaw line, but not to level of other teeth and show no wear. | *2.7 years.* $dP_2$ and $dP_3$ lost. $P_2$ and $P_3$ in place with little or no wear. $dP_4$ still in place but being pushed up by $P_4$ which is usually visible above the alveolus. $M_1$ and $M_2$ in full wear. Ectostylid on $M_1$ just beginning to wear. $M_3$ erupted but with either no wear or light wear on facets I–II. Hypoconulids still below level of jaw but may be visible. | *2.6–2.9 years.* $P_2$ and $P_3$ are usually in place and show little wear. Either $dP_2$ or $dP_3$ or both may still be in place but are soon to be lost. The $dP_4$ is still in wear but $P_4$ is pushing it upward and it is visible well above the alveolus. $M_1$ and $M_2$ are in full wear and the exostylid on $M_1$ is either beginning or is actually in wear. $M_3$ is erupted and varies from no wear on any facets to wear on facets I and II and even light wear on facets III and IV. The hypoconulid is still below the level of the alveolus but is visible. |

**Table 8.5.** *(continued)*

| Glenrock (Frison and Reher 1970) | Casper (Reher 1974; see also Horner II ([Todd 1987b] and Ayers-Frazier [Clark and Wilson 1981] for other N+.6) | Hawken (Frison et al. 1976) | Agate Basin (Agate Basin Component) (Frison 1982a) |
|---|---|---|---|
| | *3.6 years.* $P_2$ and $P_3$ usually erupted to level of other teeth and showing slight wear; $dP_4$ still in place but being pushed out by $P_4$ and the roots are exposed, fossettes in $dP_4$ usually obliterated; $M_1$ and $M_2$ in regular wear; all cusps of $M_3$ above jaw line but tooth is not yet completely erupted, first cusp of $M_3$ moderately worn, second cusp unworn or with slight wear, third cusp is never worn. | *3.7 years.* All premolars erupted and $P_4$ just coming into wear. $M_1$ and $M_2$ in full wear and facets I–VIII on $M_3$ usually in wear; wear may be very light or absent on VII and VIII. On two specimens wear is evident on facet VII and none on VIII. Hypoconulid erupted above alveolus but not yet in wear. | *3.6–3.9 years.* $P_2$ and $P_3$ are in wear; $dP_4$ may rarely be in place but is usually gone. Light wear is present on $P_4$. Wear on $M_3$ varies. Usually it is present on facet I to VIII, with none on the hypoconulid. Wear may be light on facet VII with none on facet VIII on the one extreme and light wear may be present on the hypoconulid on the other extreme. Exostylid on $M_2$ is not yet in wear. |
| *3.5 years.* $P_2$ and $P_3$ moderately worn; $P_4$ partially erupted and unworn or fully erupted and only slightly worn; $M_1$ and $M_2$ in regular use; 3rd cusp of $M_3$ erupted but always unworn. | | | |
| *4.5 years.* $P_2$, $P_3$, and $P_4$ moderately to well worn; $M_1$ and $M_2$ in regular use; 3rd cusp of $M_3$ slightly worn, usually just through enamel exposing dentine in small area; posterior style between 2nd and 3rd cusps always unworn. | *4.6 years.* $P_2$–$P_4$ fully erupted and in moderate to regular wear; first two cusps of $M_3$ in regular wear, third cusp worn on anterior side; earlier-in-the-fall wear on the third cusp is surrounded by continuous enamel, but at the Casper site a thin band of wear may continue across to join wear pattern on second cusp. | *4.7 years.* All premolars in place and in wear. Exostylid on $M_2$ usually in wear. Hypoconulid of $M_3$ in wear but often the cusp still appears isolated from remainder of tooth. These are essentially mature animals. Although there is some bimodality in crown height measurements, the first five age groups are discrete eruption groups, with no intermediate specimens. | *4.6–4.9 years.* All permanent premolars and molars are in place and in full wear. Hypoconulid on $M_3$ is in wear but on some specimens the enamel is separated from the remainder of the tooth. On others, however, wear has advanced so that the enamel on the hypoconulid joins the enamel on the remainder of the tooth on both lingual and buccal aspects. Exostylid on $M_2$ is usually just ready to come into wear. |

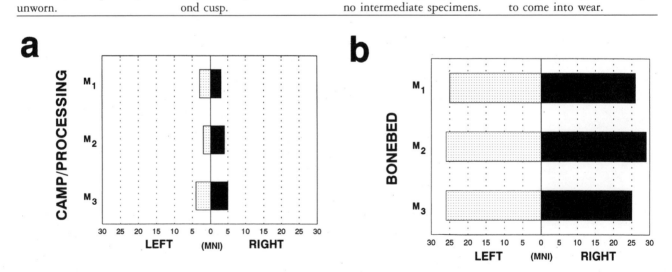

**Figure 8.6.** Frequency of lower molars by side from Mill Iron (a) camp/processing area, and (b) bonebed.

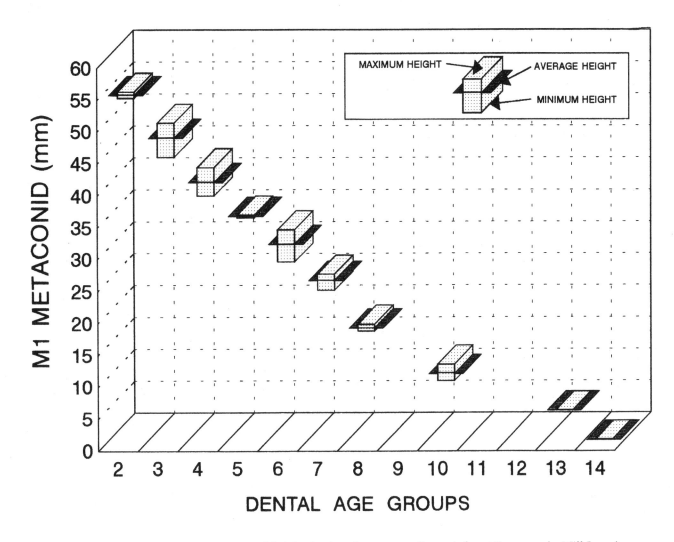

**Figure 8.7.** Range and Average M₁ metaconid heights by dental age groups for teeth from all areas at the Mill Iron site.

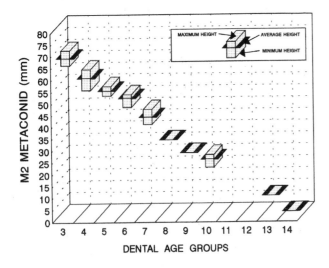

**Figure 8.8.**  Range and Average M₂ metaconid heights by dental age groups for teeth from all areas at the Mill Iron site.

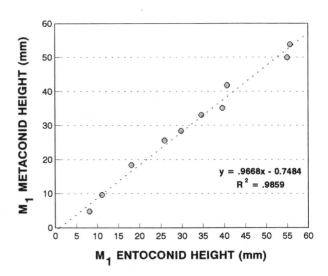

**Figure 8.9.**  Relationship between Mill Iron site $M_1$ metaconid and entoconid heights.

## Dental Age Group Descriptions

In the following descriptions, all lower teeth from the site are described as a single sample. No distinction is made between teeth from the bonebed and those from other areas of the site since in all cases, the patterns of eruption and wear of specimens from the camp/processing area fit well within the range of variation for dental age groups defined by the larger bonebed sample. All but 13 of the 81 molars or tooth rows from the Mill Iron site have been assigned to dental age groups.

**Group 1 (full-term fetus or neonate)** There are no group 1 specimens represented in the Mill Iron sample. Based on the older dental age groups, group 1 specimens are expected to be either newborn calves or full-term fetuses. Given the potential for differential bone preservation noted by Kreutzer (this volume), and the deteriorated, fractured condition of many of the teeth from even the more mature animals, the under-representation of group 1 specimens is not unusual. Although teeth are generally among the most durable portions of a skeleton, the molars, including the M1s, are not fully formed in newborns and would be less likely to be preserved than the teeth from older individuals. Examination of several full-term fetuses and newborns in the University of Wyoming comparative collections, which correspond in dental age to the Mill Iron group 1, indicates that only 20–30 mm of the M1 crowns have formed at birth, and the roots of the premolars are not completely formed. Even in dental age group 2, M1 roots are not complete and M2 enamel is still forming. Skinner and Kaisen (1947:Plate 12, 1A and 3A) provide good illustrations of the stages of molar crown and root formation in bison mandibles of comparable age to the Mill Iron group 1 and 2 specimens.

**Group 2 (1.1–1.2 years)** The two group 2 lower dentitions are both from the bonebed and may represent the left and right tooth rows of a single individual. These two specimens represent the youngest animal recovered. The MNI for group 2 is 1 (Table 8.6). The M1s are in full wear (Figure 8.12) and are coded as wear classes 8d or 9c (Figures 8.3 and 8.4). The ectostylids are at 9–11 mm below the occlusal surfaces (Figure 8.11) and the roots are almost fully formed but still open at their lower margins. The M2s are erupting, with the metaconids approximately 12 mm above the alveolus; the enamel is fully formed and approximately 5 mm of the root has developed. The mesial margin of the M2s is about 13 mm below the occlusal surface at the distal margin of the M1s. The M3s are not visible at the distal margins of the M2s, but the crowns are developing in the jaw with at least 25 mm of enamel having been formed.

As illustrated in Figure 8.12, the group 2 specimens from Mill Iron exhibit more advanced wear than group 1 specimens (0.7 yr) from the Hawken site. Group 1 specimens from Hawken represent individuals that died several months before the spring calving season, while group 2 from Mill Iron are individuals that are slightly older, but having died during or near the calving period. Thus, there is only a several months', rather than a year's, difference in age between the group 1 from Hawken and group 2 from Mill Iron. In comparison with other bison assemblages (Tables 8.4 and 8.5), the Mill Iron group 2 specimens exhibit very slightly more advanced wear than the Garnsey group 2 sample (1.0 yr) and are most similar to that of the Scottsbluff group 2 assemblage (1.1–1.2 yr). Mill Iron group 2 is inferred to be a spring to early-summer mortality.

**Group 3 (2.0–2.2 years)** This group contains seven dentitions, including one mandible pair. All group 3 specimens are

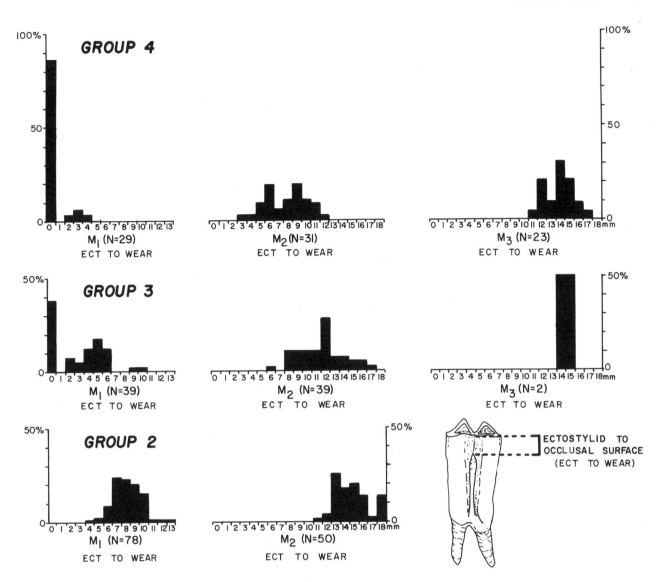

**Figure 8.10.** Ectostylid to wear measurements of modern, comparative bison mandibles, University of Wyoming, Department of Anthropology collection (N+.5–.7 dental age groups combined.)

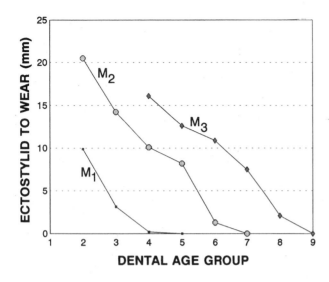

**Figure 8.11.** Average distance from crown on ectostylid to occlusal surface (approximate distance of ectostylid from coming into wear).

**HAWKEN**

**MILL IRON**

**Figure 8.12.** Comparison of Hawken group 1 (0.7 year) with Mill Iron group 2 (1.1–1.2 year) lower dentitions.

from the bonebed and the MNI is 4, based on the count of right M1s (Table 8.6). M1s are in full wear (Figure 8.13) with the ectostylids just beginning to wear (L13-16-135; wear code 10a) or only 3-5 mm below the occlusal surfaces (Table 8.1); the roots are either fully formed and closed or nearly closed at the lower margin. M2s are erupted to the level of M1 with wear varying from only facets I–IV to wear across facets I–VIII, ectostylids well below the occlusal surfaces, and the roots fully formed but still open. M3s are beginning to erupt with the metaconids at about 10 mm above the alveolus but with the mesial margin still 9–10 mm below the level of the distal margin of the M2 occlusal surface. The hypoconulids are below the alveolus with the crypt often closed. The M3 enamel is not fully formed.

The Mill Iron group 3 specimens represent a more extreme wear than all but the most extensively worn group 2 specimens at Hawken (Figure 8.13). The Mill Iron dental age is similar to, or slightly greater than, that described for Garnsey (Table 8.4) or comparable to Scottsbluff (Table 8.4). Mill Iron group 3 is interpreted to be a late-spring to early-summer mortality.

**Group 4 (3.0–3.2 years)** The 16 dentitions in this group include 10 from the bonebed and six from other areas of the site (Tables 8.1 and 8.2). A MNI of 5 for the bonebed is based on the frequency of right M2s and M3s (Table 8.6). The MNI of 3 from other areas is derived from the left M3s (Table 8.7). When all teeth from the site are combined into a single group 4 sample, an MNI of 7 is obtained, based on the number of left M3s and right M2s (Table 8.8).

Premolars 2–3 (P2–3) are erupted and exhibit very light wear. The M1s are in full wear with ectostylids in wear (wear

codes 10a or 11a) in all but one specimen (M13-6-43; wear code 9e) and usually fully connected to the rest of the occlusal surface (Figure 8.14). The M1 roots are fully formed and completely closed. The M2s are in full wear (code 9e) except for an occasional enamel oval (M13-4-59 and L13-18-11; wear code 9d) or incomplete closure (M14-11-24; wear code 9c) at the distal margin of the occlusal surface. The M2 ectostylids are about 7-10 mm below the occlusal surface (Tables 8.1 and 8.2), and the roots are fully formed but still open. The M3s are erupted to the level of M2 with wear varying from facets I-II to facets I-VI. Facets I and II are always partially connected, and occasionally fully connected at their mesial margins. The hypoconulids are above the alveolus, but always unworn.

Most of the Mill Iron group 4 specimens exhibit greater wear than group 3 from the Hawken site (Figure 8.14). Mill Iron group 4 corresponds most closely to the descriptions of the Garnsey and Scottsbluff samples (Table 8.4) and suggests mortality near or slightly after a spring calving period.

**Group 5 (4.0–4.2 years)** Five specimens representing this group have been identified in the Mill Iron collection. Four are from the bonebed (Table 8.1) and one is from the camp/processing area (Table 8.2). The group 5 bonebed MNI is 2 based on right M2s (Table 8.6). The MNI for the entire collection (Table 8.8) is also 2, based on the numbers of left M2s, left M3s, and right M3s. Wear on M3 (Figure 8.14; M13-17-5 and M13-5-61) has progressed across facets I-VIII with either light polish or no wear on the hypoconulid (facet IX and IX').

# HAWKEN

H2912

H2896

H2872

H2900

H2846

# MILL IRON

MI3·6·80

LI3·16·135

LI3·25·50

LI3·25·200

**Figure 8.13.** Comparison of Hawken group 2 (1.7 year) with Mill Iron group 3 (2.0–2.2 years) lower dentitions.

**Table 8.7.** Frequency of Lower Molars by Dental Age Group, Side, NISP, and MNI for Mill Iron Camp-Processing Area.

| Dental Age Group | | Side L | R | NISP | MNI | Maximum MNI |
|---|---|---|---|---|---|---|
| Group 4 (3.1 yr): | $M_1$ | 1 | 0 | 1 | 1 | |
| | $M_2$ | 1 | 2 | 3 | 2 | 3 |
| | $M_3$ | 3 | 1 | 4 | 3 | |
| Group 5 (4.1 yr): | $M_1$ | 1 | 0 | 1 | 1 | |
| | $M_2$ | 1 | 0 | 1 | 1 | 1 |
| | $M_3$ | 1 | 0 | 1 | 1 | |
| Group 6 (5.1 yr): | $M_1$ | 0 | 2 | 2 | 2 | |
| | $M_2$ | 0 | 1 | 1 | 1 | 3 |
| | $M_3$ | 0 | 3 | 3 | 3 | |
| Total Camp-Processing MNI | | | | | | 7 |

**Table 8.6.** Frequency of Lower Molars by Dental Age Group, Side, NISP, and MNI for Mill Iron Bone Bed.

| Dental Age Group | | Side L | R | NISP | MNI | Maximum MNI |
|---|---|---|---|---|---|---|
| Group 2 (1.1 yr): | $M_1$ | 1 | 1 | 2 | 1 | |
| | $M_2$ | 1 | 1 | 2 | 1 | 1 |
| | $M_3$ | 1 | 0 | 1 | 1 | |
| Group 3 (2.1 yr): | $M_1$ | 3 | 4 | 7 | 4 | |
| | $M_2$ | 3 | 3 | 6 | 3 | 4 |
| | $M_3$ | 3 | 2 | 5 | 3 | |
| Group 4 (3.1 yr): | $M_1$ | 4 | 3 | 7 | 4 | |
| | $M_2$ | 4 | 5 | 9 | 5 | 5 |
| | $M_3$ | 4 | 5 | 9 | 5 | |
| Group 5 (4.1 yr): | $M_1$ | 0 | 1 | 1 | 1 | |
| | $M_2$ | 1 | 1 | 2 | 2 | 2 |
| | $M_3$ | 1 | 2 | 2 | 2 | |
| Group 6 (5.1 yr): | $M_1$ | 3 | 6 | 9 | 6 | |
| | $M_2$ | 3 | 6 | 9 | 6 | 6 |
| | $M_3$ | 3 | 5 | 8 | 5 | |
| Group 7 (6.1 yr): | $M_1$ | 3 | 2 | 5 | 3 | |
| | $M_2$ | 3 | 3 | 6 | 3 | 3 |
| | $M_3$ | 3 | 2 | 5 | 3 | |
| Group 8 (7.1 yr): | $M_1$ | 2 | 3 | 5 | 3 | |
| | $M_2$ | 2 | 3 | 5 | 3 | 3 |
| | $M_3$ | 3 | 3 | 6 | 3 | |
| Group 9 (8.1 yr): | $M_1$ | 2 | 1 | 3 | 2 | |
| | $M_2$ | 2 | 1 | 3 | 2 | 3 |
| | $M_3$ | 3 | 1 | 4 | 3 | |
| Group 10 (9.1 yr): | $M_1$ | 2 | 2 | 4 | 2 | |
| | $M_2$ | 2 | 2 | 4 | 2 | 2 |
| | $M_3$ | 2 | 2 | 4 | 2 | |
| Group 13 (12.1 yr): | $M_1$ | 1 | 1 | 2 | 1 | |
| | $M_2$ | 1 | 1 | 2 | 1 | 1 |
| | $M_3$ | 1 | 1 | 2 | 1 | |
| Group 14 (13.1 yr): | $M_1$ | 0 | 1 | 1 | 1 | |
| | $M_2$ | 0 | 1 | 1 | 1 | 1 |
| | $M_3$ | 0 | 1 | 1 | 1 | |
| Total Bone Bed MNI | | | | | | 31 |

## HAWKEN

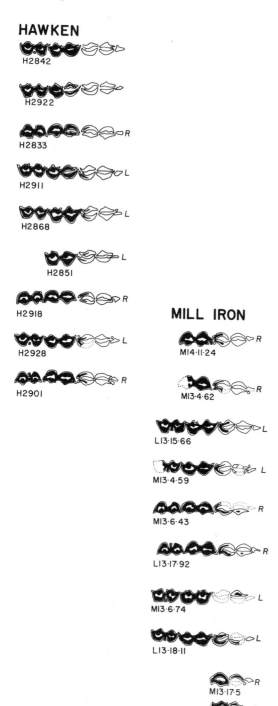

**Figure 8.14.** Comparison of Hawken group 3 (0.7 year) with Mill Iron groups 4 (2.9–3.2 year) and 5 (4.1 years: M13-17-5 and M13-5-61) lower dentitions.

**Table 8.8.** Frequency of Lower Molars by Dental Age Group, Side, NISP, and MNI for Mill Iron Site, all Areas.

| Dental Age Group | | Side L | Side R | NISP | MNI | Maximum MNI |
|---|---|---|---|---|---|---|
| Group 2 (1.1 yr): | $M_1$ | 1 | 1 | 2 | 1 | |
| | $M_2$ | 1 | 1 | 2 | 1 | 1 |
| | $M_3$ | 1 | 0 | 1 | 1 | |
| Group 3 (2.1 yr): | $M_1$ | 3 | 4 | 7 | 4 | |
| | $M_2$ | 3 | 3 | 6 | 3 | 4 |
| | $M_3$ | 3 | 2 | 5 | 3 | |
| Group 4 (3.1 yr): | $M_1$ | 5 | 3 | 8 | 5 | |
| | $M_2$ | 5 | 7 | 12 | 7 | 7 |
| | $M_3$ | 7 | 6 | 13 | 7 | |
| Group 5 (4.1 yr): | $M_1$ | 1 | 1 | 2 | 2 | |
| | $M_2$ | 2 | 1 | 3 | 2 | 2 |
| | $M_3$ | 2 | 2 | 4 | 2 | |
| Group 6 (5.1 yr): | $M_1$ | 3 | 8 | 11 | 8 | |
| | $M_2$ | 3 | 7 | 10 | 7 | 8 |
| | $M_3$ | 3 | 8 | 11 | 8 | |
| Group 7 (6.1 yr): | $M_1$ | 3 | 2 | 5 | 3 | |
| | $M_2$ | 3 | 3 | 6 | 3 | 3 |
| | $M_3$ | 3 | 2 | 5 | 3 | |
| Group 8 (7.1 yr): | $M_1$ | 2 | 3 | 5 | 3 | |
| | $M_2$ | 2 | 3 | 5 | 3 | 3 |
| | $M_3$ | 3 | 3 | 6 | 3 | |
| Group 9 (8.1 yr): | $M_1$ | 2 | 1 | 3 | 2 | |
| | $M_2$ | 2 | 1 | 3 | 2 | 3 |
| | $M_3$ | 3 | 1 | 4 | 3 | |
| Group 10 (9.1 yr): | $M_1$ | 2 | 2 | 4 | 2 | |
| | $M_2$ | 2 | 2 | 4 | 2 | 2 |
| | $M_3$ | 2 | 2 | 4 | 2 | |
| Group 13 (12.1 yr): | $M_1$ | 1 | 1 | 2 | 1 | |
| | $M_2$ | 1 | 1 | 2 | 1 | 1 |
| | $M_3$ | 1 | 1 | 2 | 1 | |
| Group 14 (13.1 yr): | $M_1$ | 0 | 1 | 1 | 1 | |
| | $M_2$ | 0 | 1 | 1 | 1 | 1 |
| | $M_3$ | 0 | 1 | 1 | 1 | |
| Total MNI | | | | | | 35 |

**Group 6 (4.9–5.2 years)** This group contains 15 specimens: 11 from the bonebed, including one mandible pair, and the rest from the camp/processing area (Tables 8.1 and 8.2). The MNI for the bonebed is 6, based on right $M_1$s (Table 8.6). Three animals are represented in other areas of the site by right $M_3$s (Table 8.7). The combined MNI of 8 for the entire site is derived from the numbers of right $M_1$s and $M_3$s (Table 8.8).

All premolars are in place with the $P_4$ in moderate wear either at the level of or slightly below the $M_1$. The $M_1$s are in full wear and the ectostylids are connected to the remainder of the tooth (wear class 11a). The $M_1$ cemento-enamel junction is near, but still below, the alveolus. $M_2$s are in full wear (Figure 8.15; wear code 9e), except for the ectostylids, which are still about 1–4 mm from wear. Third molars vary in wear. On some, facets I–IV are in wear and connected, although still separate from facets VI–IX, which are also in wear (L13-17-108; wear code 10e), while other specimens have all facets connected by wear (M13-5-60; wear code 11b). On 3 $M_3$s, (L13-17-108, L13-15-112, and M14-10-83) the hypoconulid is connected only to the hypoconid, but still separated from the entoconid. Several $M_3$s have a separate enamel cusp between the hypoconid and hypoconulid (Figure 8.15:L13-15-112, M14-11-1, and M14-10-83), which is lightly worn on two specimens and unworn on the third.

In comparison with other assemblages (Tables 8.4 and 8.5), this group exhibits slightly more advanced wear than the most advanced group 5 specimens from the Agate Basin site (4.9 years).

**Group 7 (6.0–6.2 years)** For group 7 and older age groups, all specimens are from the bonebed. The total of six group 7 specimens includes two mandible pairs. The MNI of 3 is based on the frequency of left molars and right $M_2$s. $M_2$s are in full wear (code 10A) with the ectostylid lightly worn, but not connected to the rest of the tooth (Figure 8.16). $M_3$ is in full wear with the hypoconulid connected (codes 11b and 11c), but occasionally with a small oval of enamel remaining at the distal margin (code 11b). $M_3$ ectostylids are unworn and 5–10 mm below the occlusal surface (Figure 8.11).

**Group 8 (7.0–7.2 years)** There are also six specimens and two mandible pairs in group 8. The MNI of 3 is derived from the number of right molars and left M3s (Table 8.6). M1s are in full wear and in one mandible pair (M13-4-166 and M13-4-167) the prefossetid is reduced in size (Figure 8.16). Ectostylids are connected to the M1s and M2s. M3s are usually in full wear (wear code 12a) with the ectostylids in wear, but not connected to the main occlusal surface. On one specimen (M13-4-166) the M3 ectostylid is still 6 mm from wear.

**Group 9 (8.0–8.2 years)** The four group 9 specimens (including one mandible pair) are distinguished primarily by the M2 and M3 metaconid heights (Table 8.1), since all M1s are either damaged or missing. The MNI of 3 is obtained from the left M3. All teeth are in full wear. M3 ectostylids are in wear, but never connected to the rest of the tooth (wear code 12a).

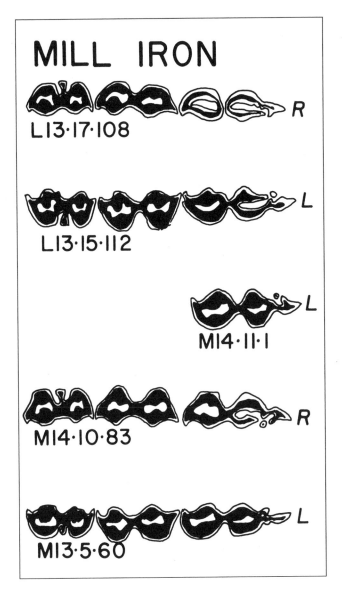

**Figure 8.15.** Mill Iron dental age group 6 (5.1 years) lower molars.

**Group 10 (9.0–9.2 years)** This group contains one mandible pair and two additional tooth rows (Table 8.1). There are two of each of the molars (Table 8.6) for an MNI of 2 for the group. $M_1$ prefossetids are either completely worn away (L13-23-37 and L13-25-86; wear code 16a) or reduced to only a single small oval at either the mesial (wear code 15a) or distal (wear code 15b) ends of the fossetid (Figure 8.16). $M_3$ ectostylids are still not connected to the primary occlusal surface.

**Groups 11–12 (10.0–11.2 years)** No specimens are assigned to this age range. Based on the differences in M2 (Figure 8.8)

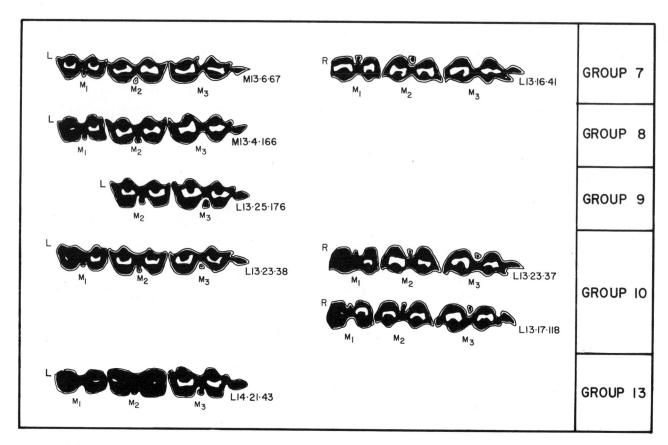

**Figure 8.16.** Examples of Mill Iron dental age groups 7–13.

## Season of Mortality and Molar Attrition Rates

In a preliminary study of the first season's mandibles from the bonebed (Todd and Rapson 1987), we incorrectly attributed a late-fall to early-winter season of death to the Mill Iron site bison. However, as described above, all the younger age group specimens where both eruption and wear patterns can be used indicate a season of death during the late spring or early summer. This corresponds to mortality at, or very near, the calving season. Although no newborn calves or full-term fetal remains have been recovered, the relatively fragile, incompletely formed molars of the younger animals may not have survived the complex formational history indicated by taphonomic analysis of the bonebed (Kreutzer, this volume).

Within the bonebed, many of the teeth are part of complete or nearly complete tooth rows, while in other areas isolated teeth are more common. This difference is evident in the average numbers of teeth per tooth row (Table 8.9). Results of a two-tailed $t$-test refute the null hypothesis that there is no statistically significant difference between the two samples (Table 8.9). The greater scattering of mandibular teeth outside of the bonebed is probably related to differences in bone preservation across the site area. Although differential preservation is evident within the bonebed (Kreutzer, this volume), there seems to be an even greater preservational difference between the bonebed and other areas of the site.

and M3 metaconid heights (Figure 8.17) between the dental age group 10 specimens and the next clustering of metaconid heights, we estimate that at least two dental age groups are not represented in the Mill Iron sample.

**Group 13 (12.0–12.1 years)** The two specimens (Table 8.1) in this group (one left and one right) yield a MNI of 1 (Table 8.6). M1 is heavily worn with the prefossetids obliterated, the postfossetids greatly reduced, and the base of the ectostylids almost completely worn away (Figure 8.16). Fossetids on the M2 are reduced to small ovals at the mesial and distal margins of the tooth (wear code 17c) and only a small remnant of the base of the ectostylid remains. M3 is in full wear with the ectostylids connected to the rest of the tooth (wear code 13a).

**Group 14 (13.0–13.1 years)** The molars from the single fragmentary mandible assigned to this group (Table 8.1) are heavily worn. All fossetids on both the M1 and M2 are nearly worn away (wear code 19a), and the enamel on both metaconids is almost completely gone (Figure 8.17). This mandible represents an individual near the end of its potential life-span. Within one to perhaps two more years the M1 and M2 would be worn down to the roots and grazing would become difficult. The M3 ectostylid is connected to the main occlusal surface (wear code 13a).

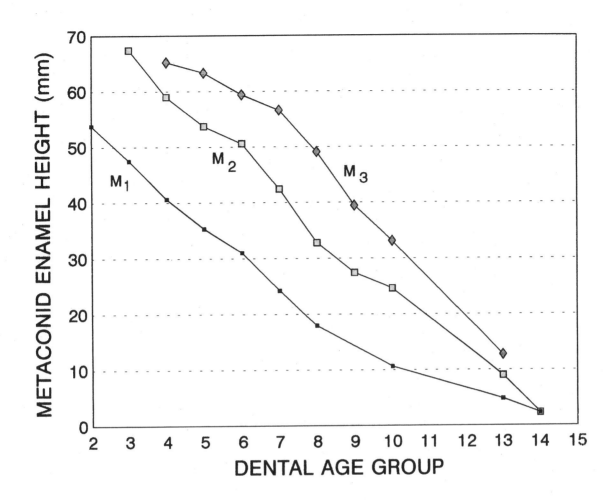

**Figure 8.17.** Average metaconid height of lower molars by dental age group.

Study of rates of attrition of molars from Plains bison bonebeds has the potential to contribute to the development of more refined interpretations of Pleistocene/Holocene paleoecology (e.g., Fawcett 1987; Frison 1982a; Guthrie 1990:179–185). For example, at Mill Iron, the average attrition rates range from 4.5 (M1s) to 5.9 (M2s) mm/year (Table 8.10). Rates of attrition for all teeth in the 5- to 8-year-old animals (dental age groups 6–9) seem especially high (Table 8.11). Following the line of reasoning developed by Fawcett (1987), this pattern may provide evidence of a period of less than optimal grazing conditions, followed by several years of somewhat improved range conditions before the animals died. In addition, the average rate of attrition of the Mill Iron molars is higher than that reported from Late Prehistoric sites. In this sense, the Mill Iron sample is yet another example of a pattern previously noted by Frison (1982a:251):

whatever the underlying causes for the differences in bison

tooth wear from site to site and between time periods, the results indicate a shorter life span for the late-Pleistocene-early-Holocene bison than for the bison of the Late Prehistoric Period.

## Minimum Number of Animals

As discussed in the age group descriptions, the development of MNI estimates for bison at the Mill Iron site has been undertaken in two ways. First, frequencies of molars from the bonebed and camp/processing areas were examined to provide a minimum distinction MNI using all available teeth differentiated by side. Second, only those molars assigned to dental age groups (Tables 8.6–8.8) were tabulated. For both approaches, we report the bonebed area and the camp/processing area separately, as well as combining the two data sets to provide an estimate of the total number of animals at the site (Figure 8.18).

**Table 8.9.** Two-Sample *T*-Test of Total Number of Teeth (Molars and Premolars) in Tooth Rows for the Mill Iron Bonebed and Camp-Processing Samples.

| Sample | Mean | SD | N | *T*-Statistic | df | p |
|---|---|---|---|---|---|---|
| Bonebed | 3.54 | 1.85 | 68 | 2.464 | 79 | 0.05 |
| Other areas | 2.15 | 1.79 | 13 | | | |

Based on the frequency of right $M_2$s, the bonebed minimum distinction MNI is 29 (Figure 8.6). For the camp/processing area, the minimal distinction MNI of 5 is based on right $M_3$s (Figure 8.6). Tables 8.6 through 8.8 give molar frequencies partitioned by dental age group.

When dental age group divisions are taken into account, the remains of at least 31 animals are represented in the bonebed (Table 8.6). In the camp/processing area, a MNI based on dental age groups of seven bison, all from about 3–5 years of age, is indicated (Table 8.7). Comparison of the dental age structure between the bonebed and the camp/processing area shows that most of the animals at the site are prime-age individuals—there are few very young or very old animals (Figure 8.19). As noted above, it is likely that this restricted pattern of dental age group representation is not necessarily an accurate reflection of the death assemblage, or of the depositional assemblage, since molars of the younger animals may not have survived. Especially with the dispersed bone from the camp/processing area, the scattered, fragmentary nature of tooth rows suggests that by the time of archaeological excavation, any incompletely formed molars may have deteriorated into non-identifiable tooth enamel fragments.

**Table 8.11.** Average Annual Attrition Rates for Mill Iron Lower Molars, all Areas of the Site.

| Dental Age Span | Average Attrition (mm/yr) | | |
|---|---|---|---|
| | $M_1$ | $M_2$ | $M_3$ |
| 1.1–2.1 years | 6.3 | | |
| 2.1–3.1 years | 6.9 | 8.4 | |
| 3.1–4.1 years | 5.3 | 5.3 | 1.9 |
| 4.1–5.1 years | 4.3 | 3.1 | 3.9 |
| 5.1–6.1 years | 5.8 | 8.2 | 2.8 |
| 6.1–7.1 years | 7.3 | 9.6 | 7.5 |
| 7.1–8.1 years | — | 5.4 | 9.7 |
| 8.1–9.1 years | — | 2.8 | 6.3 |
| 9.1–12.1 years | 1.8 | 5.2 | 6.8 |
| 12.1–13.1 years | 4.6 | 6.7 | |

If all teeth from the site are combined and counted by dental age group (Table 8.8), an MNI of 35 is indicated. Although a larger number of animals would be indicated if the two areas (bonebed and camp/processing) were treated as separate samples (see Grayson 1984), at present we feel that a conservative estimate derived from the combined sample is more appropriate.

### Other Goshen and Folsom Sites

Recently, collections of bison molars from several Folsom sites of approximately the same age as the Mill Iron site have been studied using the same techniques (Todd et al. 1990, 1992; Todd and Hofman 1992). Results of several of these studies are summarized here as the basis for a more general discussion of interpretations of the Mill Iron collections.

**Table 8.10** Average Metaconid Heights (mm) of Bison Molars from the Mill Iron Site, all Areas.

| Dental Age Group | $M_1$ | | | $M_1$ | | | $M_1$ | | |
|---|---|---|---|---|---|---|---|---|---|
| | Mean | STD | N | Mean | STD | N | Mean | STD | N |
| 2 | 53.8 | 0.71 | 2 | | | | | | |
| 3 | 47.5 | 2.69 | 4 | 67.4 | 3.35 | 4 | | | |
| 4 | 40.6 | 1.58 | 6 | 59.0 | 2.66 | 10 | 65.2 | 1.83 | 8 |
| 5 | 35.3 | 0.28 | 2 | 53.7 | 2.82 | 2 | 63.3 | 1.48 | 2 |
| 6 | 31.0 | 1.99 | 8 | 50.6 | 2.28 | 5 | 59.4 | 2.65 | 8 |
| 7 | 25.2 | 1.31 | 3 | 42.4 | 2.68 | 4 | 56.6 | 1.13 | 2 |
| 8 | 17.9 | 0.78 | 2 | 32.8 | — | 2 | 49.1 | 1.63 | 2 |
| 9 | — | — | — | 27.4 | — | 1 | 39.4 | 1.66 | 4 |
| 10 | 10.6 | 1.25 | 4 | 24.6 | 2.35 | 4 | 33.1 | 1.15 | 3 |
| 13 | 4.8 | — | 1 | 9.0 | — | 1 | 12.7 | — | 1 |
| 14 | 0.2 | — | 1 | 2.3 | — | 1 | — | — | 0 |
| Average Yearly Attrition | 4.5 | | | 5.9 | | | 5.3 | | |

Mean = average metaconid height
STD = standard deviation
N = number of measurable specimens

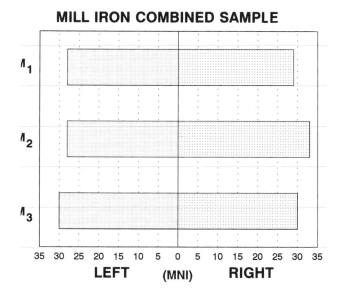

**MILL IRON COMBINED SAMPLE**

Figure 8.18. Frequency of Lower Molars by side from Mill Iron (a) Camp/Processing Area, and (b) bonebed.

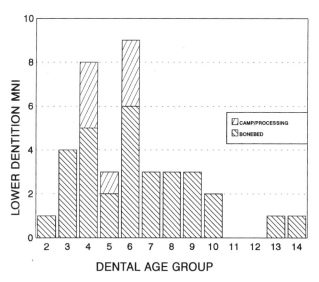

Figure 8.19. Age structure of Mill Iron site bison by dental age groups.

Ongoing excavations at the Upper Twin Mountain Goshen bonebed have produced a series of bison lower molars. These teeth are described here to allow comparison with the Mill Iron collection. The younger dental age groups from the Folsom type site are also described, since the Folsom and Mill Iron collections may be roughly contemporaneous (Haynes et al. 1992). Descriptions of the small sample of lower teeth from the Folsom bonebed at the Lake Theo site in Texas (Harrison and Smith 1975) are also included. Finally, the molars from the younger animals at the Lipscomb Folsom bonebed are described in Table 8.4 and illustrated by Todd et al. (1990).

### Upper Twin Mountain (5GA1513)

The Upper Twin Mountain site near Kremling, Colorado, has been under investigation by the University of Wyoming for the last several years. The site consists of a small bison bonebed and associated Goshen points. Although there is, as yet, no chronometric date for the site, projectile-point typology suggests a comparable age to Mill Iron. The assemblage of lower molars from the Upper Twin Mountain site (5GA1513), which includes specimens from excavations through the 1992 field season, as well as several loose teeth recovered from the surface, is described here. This discussion focuses on the basic description of the mandibular dentition (Table 8.12), on preliminary estimates of season of death, and on developing a MNI estimate for the site (Table 8.13). Since field work at the site is continuing, the preliminary nature of this summary must be emphasized. Additional field work may provide a larger sample of lower teeth and some of the present interpretations may have to be reevaluated.

A total of 62 lower molars is listed in Table 8.12. There are 13 each (Figure 8.20) of right first ($M_1$s) and second molars ($M_2$s), which indicates at least 13 animals are represented. A more refined estimate of the MNI is developed by partitioning the teeth into eruption and wear groups. Such partitioning (Table 8.13) provides a maximum distinction MNI estimate of 15 animals for the bonebed.

### Dental Age Group Descriptions

The following description of the 5GA1513 lower teeth gives a preliminary overview of the assemblage. There are no calves (group 1) in the Upper Twin Mountain sample.

**Group 2** The two specimens in this group represent at least two individuals (Table 8.13), based on marked differences in wear patterns (Figure 8.21) and metric attributes (Table 8.12). Both dentitions exhibit considerably less wear than group 2 specimens from the Hawken site (Frison et al. 1976), which have been assigned a dental age of 1.7 years (Figure 8.21). Reher and Frison's (1980:64–70) bison molar eruption schedules indicate that the $M_2$ begins erupting at 1.1–1.2 years and starts to wear at about 1.5 years. The younger animal from Upper Twin Mountain (5GA1513-164) is represented by a partial right tooth row ($dP_4$–$M_2$) with the $M_1$ in full wear. The $M_2$ metaconid is above the alveolus, but still 10 mm below the level of the $M_1$ and unworn. This indicates a dental age for 5GA1513-164 that is slightly younger than the group 2 specimens at the Wardell (Reher 1973; 1.4 years) and Glenrock (Frison and Reher 1970; 1.5 years) sites, which have $M_2$s erupted to about the level of the other teeth, but generally unworn or with only slight wear. The Upper Twin Mountain specimen is comparable with the older specimens from Scottsbluff (Todd et al. 1990; 1.1–1.2 years) or the younger animals represented at Lipscomb (Todd et al. 1990; 1.2–1.4 years). Based on these comparisons with eruption schedules and archaeological samples, 5GA1513-164 is assigned a dental age of 1.2 years.

The second specimen in this group (5GA1513-456), consists

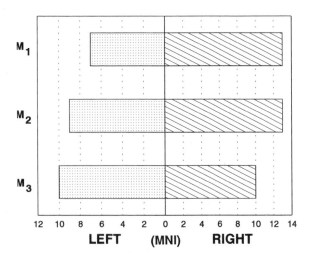

**Figure 8.20.** Frequency of Upper Twin Mountain lower molars by side.

of a series of three loose molars (left $M_1$–$M_3$) and premolars ($Dp_4$ and $P_4$). Although the relative eruption of $M_2$ cannot be determined, it has light wear on facets I–II (Figure 8.21), and therefore was probably at or very near the level of $M_1$. The light wear on facets I–II is comparable with the 1.4–1.5 yr dental age descriptions from Wardell (Reher 1973) and Glenrock (Frison and Reher 1970) and slightly less advanced than the dental age 1.6 specimens from Horner II (Todd 1987b) or Ayers-Frazier (Clark and Wilson 1981:62). 5GA1513-456 is therefore assigned a dental age of about 1.5 years.

**Group 3** Group 3 is represented by a pair of mandibles (5GA1513-284 and 5GA1513-455; Table 8.12) indicating an MNI of 1. $M_1$ is in full wear with the ectostylid in light wear but not connected to the rest of the tooth. $M_2$ is nearly in full wear, with only the distal margins of the hypoconid and entoconid not fully connected (Figure 8.22). Facets I–II of $M_3$ are in light wear (Figure 8.22), and although the rami are fragmented it appears that the hypoconulids are still below the alveolus. This pattern of eruption and wear is comparable with that described for the Hawken site bison (Frison et al. 1976; dental age of 2.7) where the $M_3$ is erupted with either no wear, or light wear, on facets I–II. The Upper Twin Mountain specimens are also comparable with the younger group 3 specimens from the Agate Basin component in Area 2 of the Agate Basin site (Frison 1982a; dental ages 2.6–2.9 years). $M_3$ wear is more advanced than that described for the 2.6 year group at the Casper site (Reher 1974). Based on these comparisons, the group 3 mandible pair from Upper Twin Mountain is assigned a dental age of 2.7 years (Table 8.13).

**Group 4** There is a total of four partial tooth rows in group 4 (Table 8.12), and a MNI of 3 is based on three right tooth rows (Table 8.13). M1s are in full wear with the ectostylids in wear and connected to the occlusal surface on both specimens with complete first molars (5GA1513-163 and 5GA1513-477). M2s are in full wear and their ectostylids are 7–10 mm from wear (Table 8.12). All third molars are worn on facets I–IV with variable light wear on facets V–VIII (Figure 8.22). This wear is similar to the group 4 descriptions from the Wardell site (Reher 1973; dental age 3.4 years) and Casper (Reher 1974:117–118), but slightly less than at Hawken (Frison et al. 1976; dental age 3.7 year) or at Agate Basin (Frison 1982a:244). The dental age

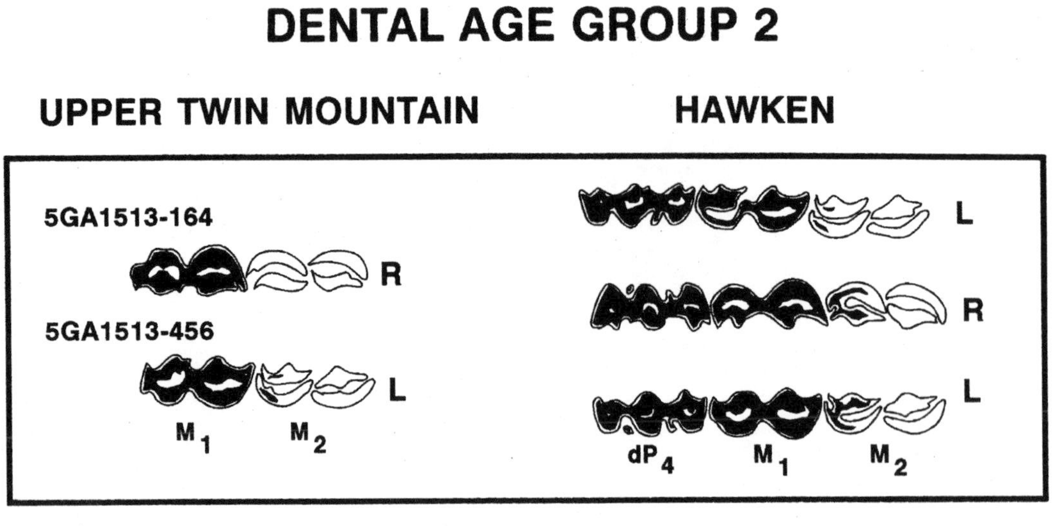

## DENTAL AGE GROUP 2

### UPPER TWIN MOUNTAIN                    HAWKEN

**Figure 8.21.** Comparison of Upper Twin Mountain group 2 with several group 2 specimens from the Hawken site.

8.12. Bison Lower Dentitions from 5GA1513.

| Number | SD | Teeth | PR | GP | M1M | M1E | M1T | M2M | M2E | M2T | M3M | M3E | M3T |
|---|---|---|---|---|---|---|---|---|---|---|---|---|---|
| 5GA15-13-164 | R | dP$_4$–M$_2$ | | 2 | 47.5 | 48.0 | 11.2 | 67.8 | — | 18.6 | — | — | — |
| 5GA1513-456 | L | dP$_4$–M$_3$ | | 2 | 45.7 | 48.8 | 9.8 | 68.9 | — | 22.0 | — | — | — |
| 5GA1513-284 | L | P$_2$–M$_3$ | 1 | 3 | 37.9 | 42.9 | — | 57.9 | — | — | 68.4 | — | 19.9 |
| 5GA1513-455 | R | P$_2$–M$_3$ | 1 | 3 | 38.3 | 42.9 | 0.0 | — | — | 12.9 | — | — | 17.9 |
| 5GA1513-163 | R | P$_4$–M$_3$ | | 4 | 37.6 | — | 0.0 | 60.8 | — | 7.5 | 64.3 | — | 19.1 |
| 5GA1513-34 | R | P$_3$–M$_3$ | | 4 | — | — | — | 58.2 | — | 10.0 | 70.6 | 72.3 | 17.4 |
| 5GA1513-51 | L | M$_2$–M$_3$ | | 4 | — | — | — | — | — | — | — | — | — |
| 5GA1513-477 | R | P$_3$–M$_3$ | | 4 | — | 44.7 | 0.0 | 59.5 | — | — | 69.1 | — | — |
| 5GA1513-170 | R | P$_2$–M$_3$ | | 5 | 39.8 | 40.9 | 0.0 | 58.2 | — | — | — | — | — |
| 5GA1513-457 | R | M$_3$ | | 5 | — | — | — | — | — | — | — | — | 18.5 |
| 5GA1513-458 | L | M$_3$ | | 5 | — | — | — | — | — | — | — | — | 3.8 |
| 5GA1513-53a | R | M$_1$ | | 5 | 36.2 | 36.3 | 0.0 | — | — | — | — | — | — |
| 5GA1513-53B | R | M$_2$ | | 5 | — | — | — | 52.3 | 54.3 | 0.0 | — | — | — |
| 5GA1513-54 | L | M$_2$–M$_3$ | | 5 | — | — | — | 55.8 | — | 5.6 | 64.1 | — | — |
| 5GA1513-32 | L | P$_2$–M$_3$ | | 7 | 24.8 | 30.0 | 0.0 | 40.4 | — | 0.0 | 52.4 | — | 7.8 |
| 5GA1513-485 | L | P$_2$–M$_2$ | 4 | 7 | — | — | 0.0 | — | — | 0.0 | — | — | — |
| 5GA1513-484 | R | P$_3$–M$_2$ | 4 | 7 | 27.4 | — | 0.0 | 42.0 | — | 0.0 | — | — | — |
| 5GA1513-459 | L | M$_3$ | | 7 | — | — | — | — | — | — | — | 53.1 | 0.0 |
| 5GA1513-460 | R | M$_2$ | | 7 | — | — | 0.0 | 39.3 | 42.3 | 0.0 | — | — | — |
| 5GA1513-461 | R | M$_1$ | | 7 | 24.3 | 24.7 | 0.0 | — | — | — | — | — | — |
| 5GA1513-486 | R | P$_1$–M$_3$ | | 8 | 16.2 | 17.8 | 0.0 | 33.5 | 34.6 | 0.0 | (39.6) | — | — |
| 5GA1513-144 | R | P$_4$–M$_3$ | | 8 | — | — | — | 29.8 | 29.5 | 0.0 | 42.7 | 42.6 | 0.0 |
| 5GA1513-33 | L | M$_1$–M$_3$ | 3 | 8 | — | — | — | 30.4 | 32.1 | 0.0 | 42.7 | — | 0.0 |
| 5GA1513-588 | R | P$_4$–M$_3$ | 3 | 8 | — | — | — | — | — | 0.0 | 40.7 | — | 0.0 |
| 5GA1513-268 | R | P$_3$–M$_3$ | 2 | 9 | 13.4 | — | 0.0 | 25.5 | — | 0.0 | 35.8 | — | 0.0 |
| 5GA1513-269 | L | P$_2$–M$_3$ | 2 | 9 | — | — | 0.0 | 25.2 | — | 0.0 | — | — | 0.0 |
| 5GA1513-476 | L | P$_3$–M$_3$ | | 11 | (9.6) | — | 0.0 | (14.0) | — | 0.0 | — | — | 0.0 |

Number, catalog number; SD, side; Teeth, teeth present; PR, mandible pair designation; GP, eruption and wear group; M1M, M$_1$ metaconid height: M1E, M$_1$ entoconid height; M1T, M$_1$ distance of ecostylid from wear; M2M, M$_2$ metaconid height; M2E, M$_2$ entoconid height; M2T, M$_2$ distance of ectostylid from wear; M3M, M$_3$ metaconid height; M3E, M$_3$ entoconid height; M3T, M$_3$ distance of ectostylid from wear. Measurements in parentheses indicate estimates for damaged specimens.

# DENTAL AGE GROUPS 3-4

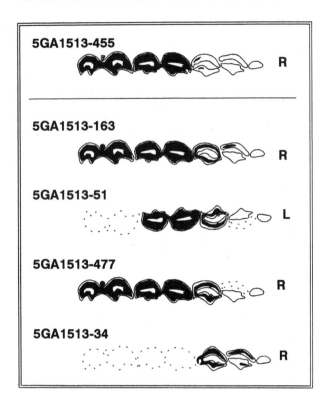

**Figure 8.22.** Upper Twin Mountain Dental Age groups 5 (5GA1513-455) and 4 (5GA1513-163, 5GA1513-51, 5GA1513-477, and 5GA1513-34).

# DENTAL AGE GROUPS 5, 7, 8

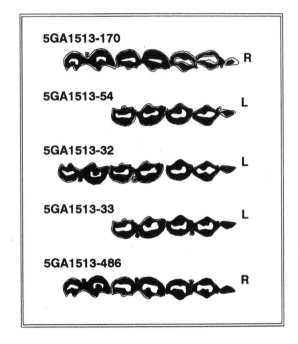

**Figure 8.23.** Upper Twin Mountain Dental Age groups 5 (5GA1513-170 and 5GA1513-54), 7 (5GA1513-32), and 8 (5GA1513-33 and 5GA1513-486).

estimate for group 4 at Upper Twin Mountain is 3.4–3.6 years (Table 8.13).

**Group 5** The five partial tooth rows in this group (Table 8.12;5GA1513-53a and 5GA1513-53b seem to be from the same individual so are counted only once in the NISP) represent a MNI of 2 based on two left M2s, two left M3s, and two right M3s. The M3s are in full wear, including the hypoconulids (facets I–IX'), which are not fully connected to the rest of the occlusal surface or are connected only by a very thin band of dentine (Figure 8.23). Based on comparisons with the Casper (Reher 1974) and Hawken (Frison et al. 1976) group 5 descriptions, hypoconulids begin to be connected to the remainder of the occlusal surface at 4.6–4.7 years, although at 4.7 (Hawken), it is still often isolated by a ring of enamel (Frison et al. 1976). At 4.5 years (Glenrock; Frison and Reher 1970), the hypoconulid is only lightly worn and is not connected. Based on these comparisons, the dental age of group 5 at Upper Twin Mountain is estimated to be 4.6–4.7 years.

**Group 6** Based on a gap in metaconid heights, no dental age group 6 specimens are represented at Upper Twin Mountain (Figure 8.24).

**Group 7** All teeth are in full wear. Therefore, this group is distinguished by metaconid heights (Figure 8.24). A MNI of 2 for this group is based on two each of each left molar and on two right M2s and M3s (Table 8.12). Based on the dental ages of groups 2–5, these mandibles indicate animals about 6.4–6.7 years old at time of death (Figure 8.23). Two of the mandibles in this group (5GA1513-484 and 5GA1513-485) are broken behind the M2s, perhaps as a result of human butchering/processing.

**Group 8** This group contains a mandible pair and two additional right partial tooth rows for a MNI of 3. Based on the dental ages of groups 2–5, these mandibles indicate animals about 7.4–7.7 years of age (Figure 8.23).

**Group 9** This group contains a single mandible pair for a MNI of 1. Based on metaconid heights (Figure 8.24), this individual may have been about 8.4–8.7 years old.

**Group 11** The oldest dental age group at Upper Twin Mountain is evidenced by a single fragmentary mandible (5GA1513-476). Although the teeth are damaged, approximate metaconid heights of $M_1$ and $M_2$ suggest that this individual is at least 2 years older than the group 9 specimens. The group 11 $M_2$ estimated metaconid height is over 11 mm less than the average group 9 $M_2$ metaconid height (Table 8.12).

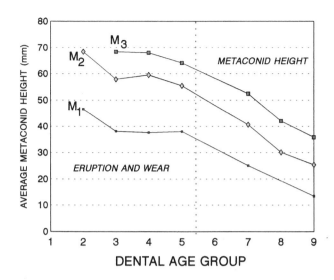

**Figure 8.24.** Average annual metaconid attrition for Upper Twin Mountain lower molars. Dental age groups 1–5 determined by combination of eruption and wear patterns; groups 6–9 based on metaconid heights only.

**Table 8.13.** Summary of Upper Twin Mountain (5GA1513) Lower Dentitions

| Group | NISP | MNI | Dental Ages |
|---|---|---|---|
| 1 | 0 | 0 | — |
| 2 | 2 | 2 | 1.2–1.5 yr |
| 3 | 2 | 1 | 2.7 yr |
| 4 | 4 | 3 | 3.4–3.6 yr |
| 5 | 5 | 2 | 4.6–4.7 yr |
| 6 | 0 | 0 | (5.4–5.7 yr) |
| 7 | 6 | 2 | (6.4–6.7 yr) |
| 8 | 4 | 3 | (7.4–7.7 yr) |
| 9 | 2 | 1 | (8.4–8.7 yr) |
| 10 | 0 | 0 | (9.4–9.7 yr) |
| 11 | 1 | 1 | (10.4–10.7 yr) |
| Total | 26 | 15 | |

NISP = number of identified specimens (number of partial tooth rows or loose teeth).
MNI = minimum number of individuals based on most frequent molar by side (Table 8.12).

## Season of Death and Herd Composition

Dental age estimates for the 5GA1513 bonebed suggest mortality during the fall or early winter. With the exception of the youngest group 2 specimen (5GA1513-456), the range of dental ages is between N + .5 and N + .7 years. This corresponds to a period of about 6 to 8 months after a presumed spring calving season. The number of mortality events is difficult to assess given the small number of animals. The group 2 mandibles, particularly 5GA1513-164, are from animals that may have died slightly earlier in the year than the other age classes, suggesting the possibility of multiple kill events. However, given the relatively tight age structure represented by the other dentitions, the young group 2 specimen is most probably the result of a slightly out-of-season birth.

Based on tooth eruption and wear groups, at least 15 bison are represented (Table 8.13). No very young animals and only a single old animal have been identified in the sample. Only three animals are under 3 years of age, while nine are prime adults from 3.4–9 years old. Due to the fragmentary condition of the mandibles, no attempt has been made to estimate the sex of the animals represented, although one distal humerus, proximal radius articulation is clearly from a large bull. Based on measurements of the proximal radius (RD4 = 105.1 mm; RD9 = 58.4 mm; see Todd [1987a] for measurement descriptions) specimen (5GA1513-26) falls within the size range of large bulls from other Paleoindian bonebeds (Todd 1987b). Although the other forelimb bones are highly fragmentary and not measurable, most appear to be smaller and could be from cows.

Although the sample size is small, several trends in dental attrition rates are indicated (Table 8.14). First, the difference between the average $M_1$ metaconid heights between the youngest animals (group 2) and the oldest individual with measurable molars (group 9) is 33.2 mm, yielding an annual average attrition rate of 4.7 mm/year. Average attrition of the $M_2$ (6.1 mm) and $M_3$ (5.4 mm) is slightly higher. These are very similar to the attrition rates from Mill Iron (Table 8.10). The Upper Twin Mountain and Mill Iron molars exhibit relatively high rates of attrition in comparison with those documented at later sites (see Fawcett 1987). The trend identified by Frison (1991b), for greater annual attrition during the late Pleistocene and early Holocene in relation to the late Holocene is supported by these two additional samples.

However, Figures 8.24 and 8.25 both indicate that the high rate of attrition between groups 2 and 3 is followed by a period of below average attrition through group 5. Although this pattern may be due to sample size, the low rates of attrition for groups 3–5 could indicate several years of favorable grazing conditions prior to the mortality. Following Fawcett's (1987) discussion of wear rates, the increased attrition between groups 2 and 3 might be indicative of a severe deterioration in range conditions in the year immediately preceding the animals' deaths. As noted above, continued study of these differences in attrition rates may, with further research, provide valuable additional information of early Holocene bison ecology.

## Folsom, Lake Theo, and Lipscomb

Although Frison (1978, 1991b) presents a preliminary discussion of the mandibles from the Folsom type site collections in the Denver Museum of Natural History (DMNH), the DMNH collections represent only a small portion of the material recovered from the site with most of the assemblage being at the American Museum of Natural History (AMNH). As part of a general reinvestigation of Folsom age bison assem-

**Table 8.14.** Average Metaconid Height for Upper Twin Mountain (5GA1513) Lower Molars (number of measurable specimens in parentheses).

| Dental Age Group | Average Metaconid Height (mm) | | |
|---|---|---|---|
| | $M_1$ | $M_2$ | $M_3$ |
| 2 | 46.6 | 68.4 | (0) |
| | (2) | (2) | |
| 3 | 38.1 | 57.9 | 68.4 |
| | (2) | (1) | (1) |
| 4 | 37.6 | 59.5 | 68.0 |
| | (1) | (3) | (3) |
| 5 | 38.0 | 55.4 | 64.1 |
| | (2) | (3) | (1) |
| 6 | (0) | (0) | (0) |
| 7 | 25.1 | 40.6 | 52.4 |
| | (3) | (3) | (1) |
| 8 | (0) | 30.1 | 42.0 |
| | | (2) | (3) |
| 9 | 13.4 | 25.4 | 35.8 |
| | (1) | (2) | (1) |
| Average Attrition | 4.7 | 6.1 | 5.4 |

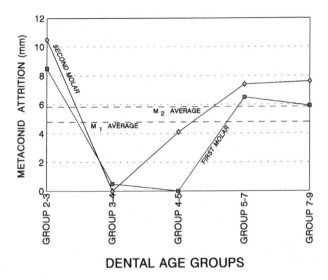

**Figure 8.25.** Differences between Upper Twin Mountain Dental age groups based on average molar attrition relative to combined average attrition (groups 2 to 9) for $M_1$ and $M_2$.

blages, including the Folsom, Lake Theo, and Lipscomb collections reported here (Todd and Hofman 1992), we have recorded all of the bison mandibles from both the DMNH and AMNH. The following discussion of the Folsom site mandibles is based on the combined DMNH and AMNH assemblage.

**Folsom** Only the younger age groups are described here. Crown heights are not available for many of the Folsom site molars since most of the mandibles are complete and the cemento-enamel junction is below the alveolus.

**Group 1:** Although no group 1 individuals are in Denver, the AMNH collection contains four calf mandibles with the $M_1$s unworn and slightly (2-5 mm) below the level of the $dP_4$s (eruption code E), and one isolated first molar with light wear on facets I–II (Figure 8.26; wear code 2a). The $dP_4$s are in full wear, although neither preectostylid or postectostylid is in wear. Based on the count of left $M_1$s, the MNI for dental age group 1 is 3. Reher and Frison (1980:65) note that for bison, the $M_1$ starts "erupting around 0.1 to 0.2 years; [and] continues erupting through late summer, by October to November (ca. 1.5 years) the facets I–II are beginning to wear as [the] molar is almost fully erupted." This suggests a dental age of about 0.4–0.5 years for the Folsom site group 1 cohort.

**Group 2:** The seven dental age group 2 specimens yield a MNI of 4, based on the number of left tooth rows. The $dP_4$s are in full wear with the postectostylid usually in wear and connected to the crown (Figure 8.27). The preectostylid is either unworn or lightly worn, but still separated from the crown by a distinct enamel ring. $M_1$s are in full wear (wear codes 9d and 9e) with the ectostylids more than 5 mm below the occlusal surface. The $M_2$s are either unworn, or with light wear on facet I or facets

I–II. The $M_3$s are forming in the jaw, but have not yet begun to erupt. The $M_2$ eruption schedules are similar to that for $M_1$. The wear on group 2 $M_2$s is slightly less than that described for the 1.6 year dental age group at Ayers-Frazier (Clark and Wilson 1981:61). The Folsom site dental age group 2 cohort is interpreted to represent animals at about 1.5 years of age.

**Group 3:** The six specimens in this group have the $M_3$ erupting (still 5–8 mm below the distal margin of $M_2$) and unworn, or with light wear (wear code 1a or 3c) on facets I or I–II. The MNI is 3 based on right $M_3$s. In comparison with other assemblages (Tables 8.4 and 8.5), this group is interpreted to represent 2.4–2.5-year-old animals.

The three youngest dental age groups at the Folsom site represent a series of tightly clustered annual cohorts. This supports an interpretation of the site as either a single catastrophic mortality or as a series of smaller, closely spaced deaths in the early fall. The tightly clustered cohorts also indicate a short calving period similar to that of modern bison.

**Lake Theo** Excavations were undertaken at the Lake Theo site in 1974 (Harrison and Smith 1975) and again in 1977 (Harrison and Killen 1978) by the Panhandle-Plains Historical Museum (P-PHM) of Canyon Texas, and all collections from the site are currently at the P-PHM. The 1974 excavations exposed the densest concentration of bone found at the site (Harrison and Smith 1975:Figure 5) and focused on the Folsom level. Only the lower teeth from the 1974 excavations are discussed here.

A total of 22 mandibles or mandible fragments, plus 10 loose molars or molar fragments has been documented during our inventory of the Lake Theo site collections (Todd and Hofman 1992). A minimal distinction MNI for mandibles of 10 is derived from the left $M_2$s. Only seven of the tooth rows can be assigned to dental age groups.

**Group 2:** The five group 2 mandibles exhibit a pattern of eruption and wear comparable with, or very slightly more advanced than, the group 2 dentitions from the Lipscomb site (Todd et al. 1990:Figure 2). The $M_1$s are in full wear with ovals of dentine present at both the mesial and distal occlusal surfaces. The $M_2$s are unworn and either erupted to the level of the $M_1$ or still slightly below the level of $M_1$. The crown of the $M_3$ is formed in the jaw but not visible behind $M_2$. Reher and Frison (1980:65) state that the $M_2$ "begins erupting around 1.1 to 1.2 years." By about 1.5 years, $M_2$ is fully erupted and beginning to wear on the mesial facets. The dental age at death of the Lake Theo group 2 mandibles is therefore estimated at 1.4 to 1.5 years.

**Group 3:** The two mandibles in this group are probably from a single individual. Both $M_1$ ectostylids are in wear, but are separated from the rest of the occlusal surface by an enamel ring. The $M_2$s are in full wear with enamel ovals remaining only at the distal margins of the occlusal surfaces. The $M_3$s are erupted to the level of the other molars and the mesial facets (I–II) are in light wear. The hypoconulid is below the level of the alveolus. Wear is similar or slightly more advanced than that reported for the Lipscomb site group 3 dentitions (Todd et al. 1990:Figure 3). Reher and Frison (1980:65) describe the $M_3$ as beginning to erupt:

> . . . by 2.1 to 2.2 years; by fall (2.5 years) the first two sets of cusps (metaconid, protoconid, hypoconid, entoconid) are well erupted, [and] light wear may occasionally occur on facets I–II, often the second set of cusps is not fully erupted and the third cusp (hypoconulid) is not erupted at all.

The dental ages of the group 3 specimens at Lake Theo are estimated to be 2.5 to 2.6 years.

Although there are only four individuals represented by group 2 and 3 dentitions, all indicate fairly tightly clustered dental ages from N + .4 to N + .6 years. This indicates a fall mortality for the Lake Theo bison and supports Harrison and Smith's (1975:81) initial assessment of the seasonality of the site. The sample is not large enough to address the question of number of events: the bonebed could be the result of a single event, of several closely spaced events, or a series of events over a number of years, each occurring at nearly the same season.

**Lipscomb** The 55 animals from the Lipscomb bison quarry are interpreted as having died during a single event, or several closely spaced events, during the late summer to early fall (Todd et al. 1990, 1992). As with the Folsom sample, most of the teeth from Lipscomb are in relatively complete mandibles and metaconid heights are not available for most specimens. Therefore, estimates of dental attrition and dental age groups for the older animals have yet to be attempted. The estimated ages for Lipscomb bison are in the N + .2 to N + .5 range and are thus inferred to represent deaths slightly later in the year (in reference to calving season) than those of the Mill Iron sample. Preservational conditions at Lipscomb, as at Mill Iron, appear to have reduced the number of dental age group 1 (calves) in this assemblage, in addition to the less rigorous collection techniques employed here (Todd et al. 1992).

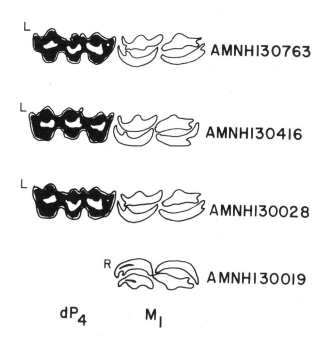

**Figure 8.26.** Dental age group 1 specimens from the Folsom type site (specimen AMNH-130043 not illustrated).

## Summary and Conclusions

Analysis of the Mill Iron lower molars indicates that the mortality event(s) took place during the spring, either at, or near, the calving season. There are no indications that the bonebed and the camp/processing areas are different seasonal episodes. The patterns of eruption and wear in both areas indicate spring mortality. On the other hand, based on the dentitions, there is no compelling evidence to demonstrate that the two areas are the result of closely interrelated sets of events or activities. Although the bonebed seems to be a single mass death, whether the other animals from the site died during that specific event, during a series of several closely spaced events, or even during a series of same-season events separated by relatively long time periods (perhaps years or decades), cannot be determined.

At least 35 bison are represented at the Mill Iron site. Since only a portion of the deposit has been excavated and a portion of the bonebed of unknown size has apparently been removed by subsequent erosion, this estimate is probably a very low approximation of the actual number of animals once present. The differences in age structure and bone frequency/condition between the two areas may be, at least in part, the result of differences in formational histories. Kreutzer (this volume) notes that the bonebed area has undergone a wide range of post-mortem modifications that make direct interpretations of human actions difficult. The portions of the site designated as the camp/processing area may have been modified to an even greater degree. Therefore, we are hesitant to infer differences in human activities across the site based on differences in bison bones.

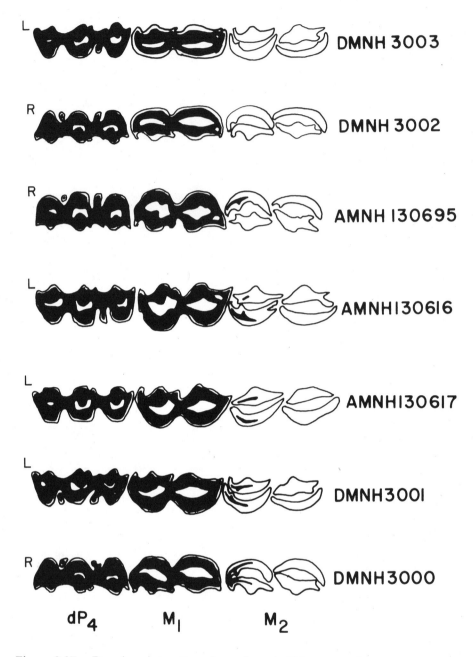

**Figure 8.27.** Dental age group 2 specimens from the Folsom type site.

**Table 8.15.** Season estimates for Goshen/Folsom/Plainview sites.

| Site | Seasonality Evidence | N[a] | Season | Dental Ages | Reference |
|------|------|------|--------|-------------|-----------|
| Mill Iron | Bison dentition | 81 | Spring to early summer | N+.0 to N+.1 | This chapter |
| Lipscomb | Bison dentition | 18 | Late summer to early fall | N+.2 to N+.5 | Todd et al. 1990 |
| Lake Theo | Bison dentition | 7 | Early fall | N+.4 to N+.5 | Todd and Hofman 1992 |
| Folsom | Bison dentition | 33 | Early fall | N+.4 to N+.5 | Todd and Hofman 1992 |
| Hanson | Bison dentition | 1 | Late fall to early winter | | Frison 1991b:160 |
| Sheaman | Bison dentition | 2 | Late spring to early summer | N+.1 to .25 | Frison 1982a:260 |
| Agate Basin Folsom Level | Bison dentition | 3[b] | Late winter to early spring | ca. N+.9 | Frison 1982a |
| Upper Twin Mountain | Bison dentition | 26 | Fall to early winter | N+.4 to N+.7 | This chapter |
| Indian Creek: Downstream Occupation 1 | Faunal remains | | Spring to early summer | | Davis and Greiser 1992:266 |
| Upstream Locus D | Faunal remains | | Spring | | Davis and Greiser 1992:269 Davis et al. 1987 |

[a] = Number of individual speciments (NISP) used to determine seasonality, not MNI.

[b] = Only a single calf mandible, and 2 near-term fetal individuals

Table 8.15 summarizes the seasonality data from several Goshen and Folsom sites. Unlike most later Paleoindian bonebeds, which are often winter deaths (Frison 1982b; Todd 1991; Todd et al. 1990), Mill Iron, Lipscomb, Lake Theo, and Folsom all occurred earlier in the year during the spring, summer, or fall. The Upper Twin Mountain site represents mortality in the late fall or early winter. The Agate Basin Folsom level at N + 0.9, and the Plainview site at N + 0.3 (Fawcett 1987:402) also represent early-spring to summer mortalities for bison associated with Folsom/Goshen/Plainview assemblages. In addition, the FA6-II Plainview locality at Lubbock Lake (Johnson 1987:126; Johnson and Holliday 1981) may be a small winter kill as is the Clovis bison kill at Murray Springs (Wilson et al. 1994). As with any discussion based on a few sites, the apparent patterning of warm-season deaths during Goshen/Folsom/Plainview times may be an artifact of small sample size, rather than an accurate reflection of prehistoric hunting patterns.

However, the current data, based on the dentition studies presented here, strongly suggest a difference in the predominant seasonality of the multi-animal bison bonebed sites associated with earlier versus later Paleoindian artifacts in western North America. At present, rather than focusing on what this apparent difference might mean in terms of understanding changes in Paleoindian land use and subsistence activities, we would like to highlight one of the predominant similarities that seems to characterize all Paleoindian bonebed sites. Regardless of season of mortality, none of the Paleoindian site exhibits processing features or other evidence of preparation of large quantities of food products for long-term storage.

## References Cited

Clark, Gerald R., and Michael Wilson
  1981  The Ayers-Frazier Bison Trap (24PE30): A Late Middle Period Bison Kill on the Lower Yellowstone River. *Archaeology in Montana* 22(1):23–77.
Davis, Leslie B., and Sally T. Greiser
  1992  Indian Creek Paleoindians: Early Occupation of the Elkhorn Mountains' Southeast Flank, West-Central Montana. In *Ice Age Hunters of the Rockies,* edited by D. J. Stanford and J. S. Day, pp. 225–283. University Press of Colorado, Niwot.
Davis, Leslie B., Sally T. Greiser, and T. Weber Greiser
  1987  Spring Cleanup at a Folsom Campsite in the Montana Rockies. *Current Research in the Pleistocene* 2:45–46.
Fawcett, William B.
  1987  *Communal Hunts, Human Aggregations, Social Varia-tion, and Climatic Change: Bison Utilization by Prehistoric Inhabitants of the Great Plains.* Unpublished Ph.D. dissertation, Department of Anthropology, University of Massachusetts, Amherst.
Frison, George C.
  1978  *Prehistoric Hunters of the High Plains.* Academic Press, New York.
  1982a  Bison Dentition Studies. In *The Agate Basin Site: A Record of the Paleoindian Occupation of the Northwestern High Plains,* edited by G. C. Frison and D. J. Stanford, pp. 240–260. Academic Press, New York.
  1982b  Paleo-Indian Winter Subsistence Strategies on the High Plains. In *Plains Indian Studies: A Collection of Essays in Honor of John C. Ewers and Waldo R. Wedel,* edited by D. H. Ubelaker and H. J. Viola, pp. 193–201. Smithsonian Contributions in Anthro-

pology No. 30. Smithsonian Institution, Washington, D.C.

1991a    The Goshen Paleoindian Complex: New Data for Paleoindian Research. In *Clovis Origins and Adaptations,* edited by R. Bonnichsen and K. L. Turnmire, pp. 133–151. Center for the Study of the First Americans. Oregon State University, Corvallis.

1991b    *Prehistoric Hunters of the High Plains,* 2d ed. Academic Press, San Diego.

Frison, George C., and Charles A. Reher

1970    Age Determination of Buffalo by Teeth Eruption and Wear. In The Glenrock Buffalo Jump, 48CO304, edited by G. C. Frison. *Plains Anthropologist Memoir* 7:46–50.

Frison, George C., Michael Wilson, and Diane J. Wilson

1976    Fossil Bison and Artifacts from an Early Altithermal Period Arroyo Trap in Wyoming. *American Antiquity* 41(1):28–57.

Gifford-Gonzalez, Diane

1991    Examining and Refining the Quadratic Crown Height Method of Age Estimation. In *Human Predators and Prey Mortality,* edited by M. C. Stiner, pp. 41–78. Westview Press, Boulder, Colorado.

Grant, A.

1982    The Use of Tooth Wear as a Guide to the Age of Domestic Ungulates. In *Ageing and Sexing Animal Bones from Archaeological Sites,* edited by B. Wilson, C. Grigson, and S. Payne, pp. 91–108. British Archaeological Reports 109, Oxford.

Grayson, D. K.

1984    *Quantitative Zooarchaeology.* Academic Press, New York.

Guthrie, R. Dale

1990    *Frozen Fauna of the Mammoth Steppe: The Story of Blue Babe.* University of Chicago Press, Chicago.

Harrison, Billy R., and H. C. Smith

1975    Excavations at the Lake Theo Site, PPHM-A917, Briscoe County, Texas. *Panhandle-Plains Historical Review* 48:70–106.

Harrison, Billy R., and Kay L. Killen

1978    *Lake Theo: A Stratified, Early Man Bison Butchering and Camp Site, Briscoe County, Texas.* Special Archaeological Report No. 1. Panhandle-Plains Historical Museum, Canyon, Texas.

Haynes, C. Vance, Jr., Roelf P. Beukens, A. J. T. Jull, and Owen K. Davis

1992    New Radiocarbon Dates for Some Old Folsom Sites: Accelerator Technology. In *Ice Age Hunters of the Rockies,* edited by D. J. Stanford and J. S. Day, pp. 83–100. University Press of Colorado, Niwot.

Hilson, Simon

1986    *Teeth.* Cambridge University Press, Cambridge.

Johnson, Eileen

1987    *Lubbock Lake, Quaternary Studies on the Southern High Plains.* Texas A & M University Press, College Station.

Johnson, Eileen and Vance T. Holliday

1981    Late Paleoindian Activity at the Lubbock Lake Site. *Plains Anthropologist* 26:173–193.

Klein, Richard, and K. Cruz-Uribe

1983    The Computation of Ungulate Age (Mortality) Profiles from Dental Crown Heights. *Paleobiology* 9:70–78.

1984    *The Analysis of Animal Bones from Archaeological Sites.* University of Chicago Press, Chicago.

Klein, R. G., C. Wolf, L. G. Freeman, and K. Allwarden

1981    The Use of Dental Crown Heights for Constructing Age Profiles of Red Deer and Similar Species in Archaeological Samples. *Journal of Archaeological Science* 8:1–31.

McCartney, Peter H.

1990    Alternative Hunting Strategies in Plains Paleoindian Adaptations. In *Hunters of the Recent Past,* edited by Leslie B. Davis and Brian O. K. Reeves, pp. 111–121. Unwin Hyman, London.

Payne, Sebastian

1973    Kill-off Patterns in Sheep and Goats: The Mandibles from Asvan Kale. *Anatolian Studies* 23:281–303.

1987    Reference Codes for Wear States in the Mandibular Cheek Teeth of Sheep and Goats. *Journal of Archaeological Science* 14:609–614.

Reher, Charles A.

1973    The Wardell *Bison bison:* Population dynamics and archaeological interpretation. In *The Wardell Buffalo Trap 48SU301: Communal Procurement in the Upper Green River Basin, Wyoming,* edited by G. C. Frison. Appendix II. University of Michigan, Museum of Anthropology, Anthropological Papers No. 48.

1974    Population Study of the Casper Site Bison. In *The Casper Site: A Hell Gap Bison Kill on the High Plains,* edited by G. C. Frison, pp. 113–124. Academic Press, New York.

Reher, Charles A., and George C. Frison

1980    The Vore Site, 48CK302, A Stratified Buffalo Jump in the Wyoming Black Hills. *Plains Anthropologist Memoir* No. 16.

Skinner, Morris F., and Ove C. Kaisen

1947    The Fossil *Bison* of Alaska and Preliminary Revision of the Genus. *Bulletin of the American Museum of Natural History* 89(3):123–256.

Todd, Lawrence C.

1987a    Bison Bone Measurements. In *The Horner Site: The Type Site of the Cody Cultural Complex,* edited by G. C. Frison and L. C. Todd, pp. 371–403. Academic Press, Orlando.

1987b    Taphonomy of the Horner II Bonebed. In *The Horner Site: The Type Site of the Cody Cultural Complex,* edited by G. C. Frison and L. C. Todd, pp. 107–198. Academic Press, Orlando.

1991    Seasonality Studies and Paleoindian Subsistence Strategies. In *Human Predators and Prey Mortality,* edited by M. C. Stiner, pp. 217–238. Westview Press, Boulder, Colorado.

Todd, Lawrence C., and Jack L. Hofman

1992    Variation in Folsom Age Bison Assemblages: Implications for the Interpretation of Human Action. In *Folsom Archaeology: An Overview of Early Holocene Environments and Human Adaptations,* edited by D. J. Stanford and M. Jodry, in press. Smithsonian Institution Press, Washington, D.C.

Todd, Lawrence C., Jack L. Hofman, and C. B. Schultz
1990    Seasonality of the Scottsbluff and Lipscomb Bison Bonebeds: Implications for Modeling Paleoindian Subsistence. *American Antiquity* 55:813-827.
1992    Faunal Analysis and Paleoindian Studies: A Reexamination of the Lipscomb Bison Bonebed. *Plains Anthropologist* 37(139):137–165.

Todd, Lawrence C., and D. J. Rapson
1987    Bonebed Analysis and Paleoindian Studies: The Mill Iron Site. Paper presented at the 53rd Annual Meeting of the Society for American Archaeology, Phoenix.

Wilson, Michael
1980    Population Dynamics of the Garnsey Site Bison. In *Late Prehistoric Bison Procurement in Southeastern New Mexico: The 1978 Season at the Garnsey Site (LA-18399),* edited by J. D. Speth and W. J. Parry, pp. 88–129. *Museum of Anthropology, University of Michigan Technical Reports* No. 12.

Wilson, Michael, Lawrence C. Todd, and George C. Frison
1994    Bison Dentitions from the Murray Springs Site, Arizona. In *The First Arizonans: Clovis Occupation of the San Pedro Valley, 9000 B.C.,* edited by C. Vance Haynes, Jr. University of Arizona Press, Tucson, in press.

# CHAPTER NINE

# Paleoenvironmental Interpretations for the Mill Iron Site: Stratigraphic Pollen and Phytolith Analysis

LINDA SCOTT CUMMINGS

Golden, Colorado

## Introduction

Patterns of occupation and exploitation of resources during Paleoindian times were affected by paleoenvironmental conditions, as they were at other times. Reconstruction of the paleoenvironment at the Mill Iron site relies on two data bases: pollen and phytoliths. Because pollen grains and phytoliths preserve relatively well in diverse conditions, they may be extracted from their surrounding matrix for analysis.

Pollen and phytolith samples were examined from stratigraphic deposits to identify vegetation in the vicinity of the Mill Iron Site beginning slightly prior to its utilization by the Goshen population and extending until the present with an hiatus of an indeterminate amount of time prior to 3,000 B.P. Pollen and phytolith samples were extracted from single soil samples collected stratigraphically from the profile of the excavation block during the 1986 field season. Radiocarbon ages from the bonebed in this area varied from 10,760 to 11,360 B.P. The pollen record encompassed samples immediately below the bonebed, from the bonebed, and between the bonebed and the present surface. In addition, samples were collected from the present surface to provide information on modern pollen rain. The summer of 1986 was relatively wet, and vegetation was relatively lush. The summer of 1989 experienced a severe drought, and local vegetation was sparse and obviously drought-stressed, so samples of the present ground surface were recollected for pollen analysis and comparison with those from 1986, a relatively wet year.

The pollen record includes pollen distributed from both regional and local vegetation having specific ecologic requirements. Pollen types that are most abundant in the pollen record are usually wind transported. This category of pollen includes most of the tree population in this area, as well as many of the shrubs, grasses, and forbs, such as Cheno-ams (*Atriplex*—saltbush and others), sagebrush *(Artemisia),* and sedges (Cyperaceae). The most aerodynamic pollen types (*Pinus* is a good example) may be transported hundreds, if not thou-

sands of miles on the wind. The majority of the pollen represented in this pollen record is transported by wind and represents plants in the immediate vicinity of the remnant in which the site rests, as well as from the surrounding area for several miles' distance. Fluctuations in pollen frequency noted in samples from the present ground surface reflect primarily density of vegetation in the immediate vicinity of the area sampled. Differences in arboreal pollen, primarily *Pinus* pollen, may be related to wind transport patterns, density of local vegetation, and distance from the nearest stand of pine. Pollen that must rely on insects or animals for transport are recovered more rarely from the stratigraphic pollen record, and usually in small quantities. Some of the plants that rely on insects for pollination are imperfectly or incompletely insect pollinated and disperse a portion of their pollen on the wind. The High-spine Asteraceae are a good example of this mechanism of pollination.

Phytoliths are silica bodies produced by plants when soluble silica in the ground water is absorbed by the roots and carried up to the plant via the vascular system. Evaporation and metabolism of this water result in precipitation of the silica in and around the cellular walls. The general term phytoliths, while strictly applied to opal phytoliths, also may be used to refer to calcium oxylate crystals produced by a variety of plants, including *Opuntia* (prickly pear cactus). Opal phytoliths, which are distinct and decay-resistant plant remains, are deposited in the soil as the plant or plant parts die and break down. They are, however, subject to mechanical breakage, erosion, and deterioration in high pH soils. Phytoliths are usually introduced directly into the soils in which the plants decay. Transportation of phytoliths occurs primarily by animal consumption, man's gathering of plants, or by erosion or transportation of the soil by wind, water, or ice.

Types of grass short-cell phytoliths recovered from this site generally may be lumped into the groups Festucoid, Chloridoid, and Panicoid. Exceptions occur primarily for the bilobate and polylobate forms, which may represent members of the Panicoid group or a few Festucoid grasses, such as *Stipa* and *Dan-*

*thonia.* Elongate phytoliths are of no aid in interpreting either paleoenvironmental conditions or the subsistence record since they are produced by all grasses and because at present there is no recognized key to their identification. Elongate phytoliths are easily broken in the soil, and because each fragment is counted as an individual phytolith, soil movement that serves to break the phytoliths would also increase the relative frequency of this type. For these reasons, elongate phytoliths were not included in the phytolith count. Phytoliths tabulated to represent "total phytoliths" include the grass short-cells (Festucoid, Panicoid bilobate and polylobate, and Chloridoid). Frequencies for all other phytoliths and other bodies recovered are calculated by dividing the number of each type recovered by the "total phytoliths."

The Festucoid class of phytoliths is ascribed primarily to the subfamily Pooideae, which grows most abundantly in cool, moist climates. However, Brown (1984) notes that Festucoid phytoliths are produced in small quantity by nearly all grasses. Therefore, while they are typical phytoliths produced by the subfamily Pooideae, they are not exclusive to this subfamily. Some Festucoid grasses, notably *Stipa* and *Danthonia,* produce bilobate and occasionally polylobate phytoliths, which are not separated from other bilobates in this record.

Chloridoid phytoliths are found primarily in the subfamily Chloridoideae, warm-season grasses that grow in arid to semi-arid areas and require less available soil moisture. Twiss (1987:181) also notes that some members of the subfamily Chloridoideae produce both bilobate and polylobate (Panicoid) and Festucoid phytoliths. Chloridoid grasses are most abundant in the American Southwest (Gould and Shaw 1983:120).

Panicoid phytoliths, which include bilobates and polylobates in this study, occur in warm-season or tall grasses that frequently thrive in humid conditions. "According to Gould and Shaw (1983, p. 110) more than 97% of the native US grass species (1,026 or 1,053) are divided equally among three subfamilies Pooideae, Chloridoideae, and Panicoideae" (Twiss 1987:181). While some of the bilobate and polylobate forms recovered in this study may represent Festucoid (*Stipa* or *Danthonia*) or Chloridoid grasses, the majority were well-lobed, which is typical of Panicoid forms. Therefore, in this study, the bilobate and polylobate forms are lumped under the designation Panicoid.

Buliform phytoliths are produced by grasses in response to wet conditions (Irwin Rovner, personal communication, January 1991) and are to be expected in wet habitats of flood plains and other places. Phytoliths referred to as "pillows" are the same as those reported by Rovner (1971). While these phytoliths are described, no taxonomic significance has been assigned. They most probably represent grasses and are inferred here to represent wetter conditions.

Other phytoliths recovered in this study include trichomes and towers, both produced by a variety of grasses. Other forms noted include calcium oxalate crystals produced by *Opuntia* (prickly pear cactus).

Diatoms and sponge spicules were also noted. Diatoms indicate wet conditions. Sponge spicules may represent fresh water sponges that live in rivers and streams. Their presence in these samples probably indicates wind transport of riverine deposits. Their recovery in upland soils is noted to accompany loess deposits derived from flood plains in Illinois (Jones and Beavers 1963).

Pollen and phytolith analyses also included identification of starch granules to general categories. Several roots have been examined for starches to build a key for identifying archaeological starches. Examination of *Balsamorhiza* roots for starch granules did not yield identifiable granules. Tracheids were abundant and the root was very fibrous. *Typha* (cattail) roots contained a very small starch granule with hila that exhibited a cross under crossed polar illumination. In addition, numerous raphids were observed. Roots from *Lomatium* (biscuit root), a member of the Apiaceae, yielded both small solid starches and a larger starch granule, with hila, that exhibited a cross under crossed polar illumination. The larger starch granules, with hila, appeared to be combinations of three of the smaller solid starch granules. Shooting star (*Dodecatheon*) root starch granules were ovate to D-shaped without a central hilum. They exhibited no pattern under crossed polar illumination. The single *Calochortus* (sego lily) specimen examined for starch granules did not yield any. The specimen was small, and the failure to recover starch granules may simply reflect poor growing conditions during that season. Bitterroot (*Lewisia*) exhibited gum-drop shaped starch granules. These starch granules occurred singly, paired, or attached in groups of three. Poaceae seeds exhibited a variety of starch granules, some with hila and some without. These starch granules were highly variable in size and may be referred to as "solid" or "with hila". The hila varied from single points to more complex linear hila. Starch granules were both round and angular in shape. Only Poaceae-type and Apiaceae-type starches were observed in sediments from the Mill Iron site.

## Methods

A chemical extraction technique based on flotation was used for the removal of pollen from the large volume of sand, silt, and clay with which they were mixed. This particular process was developed for extraction of pollen from soils where preservation has been less than ideal and pollen density is low.

Hydrochloric acid (10%) was used to remove calcium carbonates present in the soil, after which the samples were screened through 150 micron mesh. Zinc bromide (density 2.0) was used for the flotation process. The samples were mixed with zinc bromide while still moist immediately after centrifugation to remove the dilute hydrochloric acid and water. All samples received a short (10-minute) treatment in hot hydrofluoric acid to remove any remaining inorganic particles. The samples were then acetolated for 3 minutes to remove any extraneous organic matter.

A light microscope was used to count the pollen to a total of 100 to 200 pollen grains at a magnification of 500x. Pollen preservation in these samples varied from good to poor. Comparative reference material collected at the Intermountain Herbarium at Utah State University and the University of Colorado Herbarium was used to identify the pollen to the family, genus, and species level, where possible.

Pollen aggregates were recorded during identification of the pollen. Aggregates are clumps of a single type of pollen, and may be interpreted to represent pollen dispersal over short distances, or the actual introduction of portions of the plant represented into an archaeological setting. Aggregates were included in the pollen counts as single grains, as is customary. The presence of aggregates is noted by an "A" next to the pollen frequency on the pollen diagram.

Indeterminate pollen includes pollen grains that are folded, mutilated, and otherwise distorted beyond recognition. These grains are included in the total pollen count, as they are part of the pollen record.

Extraction of phytoliths from these sediments also was based on heavy liquid flotation. First hydrogen peroxide (30%) was used to destroy the organic fraction from 50 ml of sediment. Once this reaction was complete, 50 ml. of sodium pyrophosphate (0.1 molar solution) was added to the mixture to suspend the clays. The sample then was sieved through 150 micron mesh. The sample was allowed to settle for two hours, then the supernatant, which contained clay, was poured off. This settling time allowed the phytoliths to settle to the base of the beaker. The samples were mixed with water, allowed to settle for two hours, and the supernatant discarded several times until it was clear. The last two times the sample was allowed to settle the time was reduced to one hour. This procedure removes most of the clays. Once most of the clays were removed, the silt and sand size fraction was dried. The dried silts and sands then were mixed with zinc bromide (density 2.3) and centrifuged to separate the phytoliths, which will float, from the other silica, which will not.

Phytoliths, in the broader sense, may include opal phytoliths and calcium oxalate crystals. Calcium oxalate crystals were formed by *Opuntia* (prickly pear cactus) and were separated rather than destroyed using this extraction technique since it employs no acids. Any remaining clay was floated with the phytoliths and further removed by mixing with sodium pyrophosphate and distilled water. The samples then were rinsed with distilled water, then alcohols to remove the water. After several alcohol rinses, the samples were mounted in Canada balsam for counting with a light microscope at a magnification of 500x.

## Discussion

The Humbolt Hills, located to the southwest of the Mill Iron site area, provide the greatest topographic relief in this area and support local pine woodlands. The badlands area in which the Mill Iron site is situated lies between the Little Missouri River on the east and Box Elder Creek on the west. Humbolt Creek, an intermittent tributary of Box Elder Creek, flows nearest the site. The Hell Creek Formation underlies the Mill Iron site, and both the Hell Creek and Fort Union Formations are noted in the area. Sandstone and shale are present in both formations. Weathering of these formations contributes Late Cretaceous and Paleocene pollen to the pollen record. Mixing of Late Cretaceous and Paleocene pollen with Holocene pollen is more evident in some stratigraphic columns examined from the Mill Iron site than others. Stratigraphic records exhibiting large quantities of redeposited pollen from the Late Cretaceous and Paleocene are not included in this discussion.

The Mill Iron site is situated near the southern margin of the Pleistocene continental glaciation. Estimated rates of reces-

sion of the ice sheet indicate that it could still have been within 500 km of the site at 11,300 B.P. However, more recent data indicate accelerated recession around 12,000 B.P., suggesting that the ice sheet may have been farther removed from this area by the Goshen occupation. The presence of wooly mammoth (*Mammuthus primigenius*) along the earliest shores of Lake Agassiz, approximately 300 km to the north/northeast, has been interpreted to represent tundra conditions approximately 11,500 B.P. (Harrington and Ashworth 1986 in Eckerle 1990:8). Extrapolation of vegetation noted elsewhere on the northern plains, especially the post-glacial vegetation reported by Wright (1970) for the eastern Dakotas, has been used by others to postulate local vegetation in the vicinity of the Mill Iron site (Eckerle 1990:19). Specific examination of the pollen record from the Mill Iron site does not provide evidence of any of the postulated vegetation systems, which usually include *Picea* (spruce) forests for this area. Patchy vegetation, rather than regional vegetation zonation with diverse community types is also postulated for the early post-glacial (Guthrie 1984).

Modern vegetation in the badlands to the east of Box Elder Creek is supported by silty range (Soil Conservation Service, n.d.). Plants typical in this area include western wheatgrass, thickspike wheatgrass, bluebunch wheatgrass, green needle grass, needle-and-thread grass, big bluestem, little bluestem, side oats grama, American vetch, as well as biscuitroot, buffaloberry, and currant (Eckerle 1990:7). Wheatgrasses and needle grasses produce Festucoid phytoliths, bluestem grasses and some needle grasses produce Panicoid phytoliths, and grama grasses produce Chloridoid phytoliths. Modern vegetation on top of the remnant is dominated by sedges (Cyperaceae) and grasses (Poaceae), although sagebrush (*Artemisia*) is also noted. The west slope of the remnant supports more shrubby plants, including rabbitbrush (*Chrysothamnus*—a High-spine Asteraceae), greasewood (*Sarcobatus*), and sagebrush (*Artemisia*). The south side of the remnant is dominated by saltbush (*Atriplex*—a Cheno-am), although it also supports grasses (Poaceae), greasewood (*Sarcobatus*), rabbitbrush (*Chrysothamnus*—a High-spine Asteraceae), and sagebrush (*Artemisia*). *Artemisia* is an important component of the mixed grassland surrounding the remnant.

Pollen samples were collected from the present ground surface in several areas in the immediate vicinity of the site to evaluate present vegetation and the accompanying pollen rain during both a drought year (1989) and the wetter conditions of 1986. The 100 m wide arroyo to the west of the site was sampled, as was the top of the remnant, the south-facing slope, and two locations farther from the site that exhibited more abundant sagebrush than in the immediate area of the site. Only the samples representing the top of the remnant and south-facing slope were collected both years.

Samples representing the present ground surface during the drought year (1989) were collected from the top of the remnant (1), from the arroyo to the west of the site (2), from the south-facing slope of the remnant (3), a sagebrush/grass area near a stock tank (4), and near the edge of the sagebrush/grass area and nearby pines (5) (Table 9.1). Pollen samples were collected near the stock tank to examine the effect on the pollen record of large-scale disturbance by grazing animals, and from the edge of a sagebrush/grass area near a stand of pines to observe the quantity of *Pinus* pollen much closer to the stand of pines.

The quantity of *Pinus* pollen recovered from these samples is largest in the samples collected from the remnant and its immediate vicinity (Figure 9.1, Table 9.2). The sample collected closest to the pines (5) displayed a slightly smaller amount of *Pinus* pollen, while that from the sagebrush/grass area near the stock tank displayed the least *Pinus* pollen. *Juniperus* pollen was highest in the arroyo, but was present in small quantities in most of the modern samples. Modern pollen recovery assists in understanding distribution of pollen from both local and regional vegetation, as does information concerning pollen transport. *Pinus* pollen is very aerodynamic, travels long distances, and produced in large quantities. Tree pollen in general is released into the atmosphere high off the ground, while grass and herb pollen is released next to the ground. Trajectories for pollen transport are also important in pollen recovery. A "rain shadow"

effect may be observed often near the boundary of forested areas, where tree pollen, such as *Pinus*, does not drop directly to the ground in large quantities, but instead is carried on the wind to be deposited some distance from the forest. When local vegetation is sparse and produces little pollen, such as on the remnant, regional vegetation, such as *Pinus*, will be represented more prominently in the pollen record. This scenario is visible in sample 1, representing the remnant, in the pollen record.

Cheno-am pollen was expected to be highest on the south-facing slope. Sample 3 from the south-facing slope and sample 5 collected near the pines exhibited the highest frequencies of Cheno-am pollen. Recovery of the slightly larger Cheno-am pollen frequency from sample 3 indicates that Cheno-am pollen is, indeed, more abundant in the pollen record from the drier habitat than from areas where moisture loss is less severe. At present, there is not a sufficient quantity of *Atriplex* or other Chenopodiaceae in the modern vegetation to contribute significantly to the pollen record.

**Table 9.1.** Provenience Data for Samples from the Mill Iron Site.

| Sample No. | Depth (cmbpgs) | Stratum | Stratum Description | Pollen Counted | Phytos Counted |
|---|---|---|---|---|---|
| 1 | 0 | | Modern control from top of remnant, 1989 | 200 | |
| 2 | 0 | | Modern control from west of site in drainage, 1989 | 200 | |
| 3 | 0 | | Modern control from south-facing slope, 1989 | 200 | |
| 4 | 0 | | Modern control from *Artemisia*/Poaceae vegetation near stock tank, 1989 | 200 | |
| 5 | 0 | | Modern control from *Artemisia*/Poaceae vegetation near pines, 1989 | 200 | |
| 30 | 0 | | Modern control from east and south of site, 1986 | 200 | 200 |
| 32 | 0 | | Modern control from *Artemisia*/Poaceae vegetation west of site, 1986 | 200 | 200 |
| 1 | 10 | I | | 200 | 201 |
| 2 | 20 | II | | 200 | 200 |
| 3 | 25.5 | I | | 200 | 200 |
| 4 | 29.5 | III | | 200 | 200 |
| 5 | 33 | IV | | 200 | 25 |
| 6 | 36 | V | | 200 | 100 |
| 7 | 40 | VI | | 200 | 203 |
| 8 | 46 | VII | | 200 | 201 |
| 9 | 56 | VIII | | 200 | 200 |
| 10 | 66 | VIII | | 200 | 201 |
| 11 | 76 | XI | Pelican Lake horizon (3,000 B.P.) | 100 | 201 |
| 12 | 86 | XI/XII | | 200 | 200 |
| 13 | 96 | XII | | 100 | 200 |
| 14 | 106 | XII | | 200 | 200 |
| 15 | 116 | XII | | 200 | 200 |
| 16 | 126 | XII | | 200 | 200 |
| 17 | 136 | XII | | 200 | 201 |
| 18 | 146 | XII/XIII | | 200 | 200 |
| 19 | 156 | XIII | Cultural, Goshen-Plainview | 100 | 200 |
| 20 | 166 | XIII | Cultural, Goshen-Plainview | 200 | 420 |
| 21 | 176 | XIII | Cultural, Goshen-Plainview | 200 | 201 |
| 22 | 186 | XIV | | 100 | 200 |
| 28 | | L.4 | N13/W24 Bones (98.36) Cultural, Goshen-Plainview | 200 | 200 |
| 29 | | L.5 | N13/W21 NW Quad, Cultural, Goshen-Plainview | 200 | 100 |
| 31 | | | N19/W7 NW Quad (99.39), Cultural, Goshen-Plainview | 200 | 200 |

*Artemisia* pollen was greatly elevated in samples 4 and 5, and relatively consistent in the samples collected from the immediate vicinity of the site. This indicates that the *Artemisia* pollen reflected in the stratigraphic record is probably a composite of that produced by sagebrush in the general area of the site. Cheno-am/*Artemisia* ratios, used to interpret the prehistoric vegetation communities, are similar for samples 1 and 3 representing the top of the remnant and the south-facing slope respectively. Samples examined from the drainage, near the trees, and the stock tank also close to the trees exhibited a markedly different signature, more like that of Zone C following the Goshen occupation.

Cyperaceae pollen was highest on top of the remnant and on the south-facing slope, the two driest locations sampled. Members of the Cyperaceae are adapted to very different habitats and often mix with grasses. In the modern vegetation, Cyperaceae pollen is abundant in areas with various dry soils, indicating the presence of dry-tolerant members of this family. Poaceae pollen was relatively consistent in the modern samples, being slightly depressed in samples 4 and 5 collected near the stock tank and closest to the pines. This area also contained the largest quantity of *Rhus trilobata* pollen, reflecting the presence of squawberry bushes near the interface of the sagebrush/grass and pine communities. Pollen representing riparian habitats associated with nearby Humbolt Creek were scattered and include *Salix* and *Typha*.

The pollen rain generated by the present vegetation in a wet year is reflected in pollen samples 30 and 32 in the pollen diagram (Figure 9.1, Table 9.2). Sample 30 was collected on top of the remnant near the excavations, while sample 32 was collected below the remnant in a grassy area that also supported various herbs and shrubs. The pollen record reflected is very similar to that of the drought years. *Artemisia* (sagebrush) pollen dominates the record and grasses and sedges (Poaceae and Cyperaceae) are represented as lesser components of the pollen record even though they compose a large portion of the vegetation community. Wind transport accounts for the presence of the arboreal pollen recorded, which includes *Alnus, Betulaceae, Juniperus, Picea, Pinus, Quercus, Salix,* and *Ulmus.* Juniper and pines are the most numerous trees noted on nearby hills. Juniper is the most common tree in wooded draws and dissected areas, although various hardwoods, including oak, are also present. *Pinus* pollen is present through transport from the hills to the south of the site. The presence of *Ulmus* pollen may be the result of long distance transport of that grain, or possibly its redeposition in the soil from an earlier era.

The herbaceous and shrubby plants represented in the pollen record at the surface include Cheno-ams, *Sarcobatus, Artemisia,* Low-spine and High-spine Asteraceae, *Ceanothus,* Cornaceae, Cyperaceae, *Ephedra,* Geraniaceae, Poaceae, Lamiaceae, Liliaceae, Rosaceae, *Cercocarpus,* and Saxifragaceae. Some of these pollen types, such as *Ephedra,* are present through long-distance transport of the pollen, as Mormon tea was not recorded in the vicinity of the site.

Comparisons between the two samples examined from the present ground surface from the 1986 excavations (wet year) and the 1989 excavations (drought year) display more similarity than was expected. This is probably attributable to mixing

**Table 9.2.** Pollen Types Observed in Samples from the Mill Iron Site.

| Scientific Name | Common Name |
|---|---|
| *Arboreal Pollen* | |
| *Abies* | Fir |
| *Acer negundo* | Box elder |
| *Alnus* | Alder |
| Betulaceae | Birch family |
| *Juniperus* | Juniper |
| *Picea* | Spruce |
| *Pinus* | Pine |
| *Populus* | Cottonwood |
| *Quercus* | Oak |
| *Salix* | Willow |
| *Ulmus* | Elm |
| *Non-Arboreal Pollen* | |
| Cheno-ams | Includes amaranth and pigweed family |
| *Sarcobatus* | Greasewood |
| Asteraceae: | Sunflower family |
| *Artemisia* | Sagebrush |
| Low-spine | Includes ragweed, cocklebur, etc. |
| High-spine | Includes aster, rabbitbrush, snakeweed, sunflower, etc. |
| Liguliflorae | Includes dandelion and chicory |
| Cornaceae | Dogwood family |
| Brassicaceae | Mustard family |
| Cyperaceae | Sedge family |
| *Ephedra nevadensis*-type | Mormon tea |
| *Ephedra torreyena*-type | Mormon tea |
| *Eriogonum* | Wild buckwheat |
| *Erodium* | Heron-bill |
| *Euphorbia* | Spurge |
| Geraniaceae | Geranium family |
| Poaceae | Grass family |
| Lamiaceae | Mint family |
| Fabaceae | Legume or pea family |
| *Petalostemon* | Prairie-clover |
| Liliaceae | Lily family |
| Onagraceae | Evening primrose family |
| *Opuntia* | Prickly pear cactus |
| *Phlox* | Phlox |
| *Polygala* | Milkwort |
| Primulaceae | Primrose family |
| Rhamnaceae | Buckthorn family |
| *Ceanothus* | Buckbrush |
| *Rhus* | Sumac |
| Rosaceae | Rose family |
| *Cercocarpus* | Mountain mahogany |
| *Holodiscus* | Spirea, ocean spray |
| Saxifragaceae | Saxifrage family |
| *Saxifraga* | Saxifrage |
| *Shepherdia* | Buffaloberry |
| Solanaceae | Potato/tomato family |
| *Typha angustifolia*-type | Cattail |
| Apiaceae | Parsley/carrot family |
| *Urtica* | Nettle |
| *Spores* | |
| *Selaginella densa* | Little clubmoss |

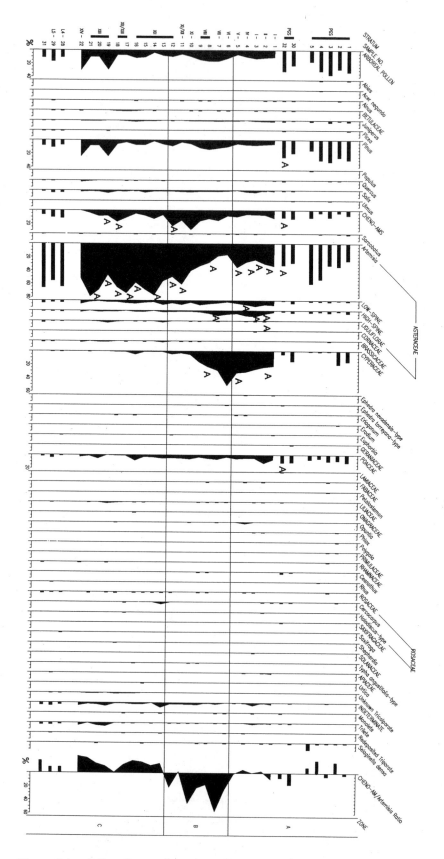

**Figure 9.1.** Pollen diagram from the Mill Iron site 24CT30.

of pollen from several years in the surface sediments. Pollen production is expected to be lower during drought years than wet years. In addition, annual and perennial herbaceous plants are expected to be fewer in number during drought years. More *Pinus* pollen was recovered during the drought year, probably as a result of a severe decrease in local pollen production by grasses and forbs. More *Artemisia* pollen was recovered from the arroyo to the west of the remnant than from the top of the remnant during both the dry and wet years. Considerably more Cyperaceae pollen was recovered from the top of the remnant than from the arroyo both years, although the frequencies were slightly more similar during 1986. Poaceae pollen was reduced in 1989, the drought year, but still present in similar quantities in the remnant and arroyo samples. Most differences in local plant composition between the top of the remnant, the arroyo, and the drier south-facing slope were not immediately evident in the pollen record. The most visible difference appears to be the quantity of Cyperaceae pollen present.

Cyperaceae seems to be a common element of the local plant community on top of the remnant and on the south-facing slope, but not elsewhere. Recovery of Cyperaceae pollen from the top of the remnant and south-facing slope, the two driest habitats sampled, suggests that at present the Cyperaceae pollen represents sedges that thrive in dry conditions and may be used as an indicator of dry conditions. Because the Cyperaceae family is large and includes sedges that are well adapted to different conditions including wet conditions, interpretation of discontinuous populations of Cyperaceae as indicating similar conditions is not possible. However, the large quantity of Cyperaceae pollen recovered from the upper samples of the 1986 excavation block is contiguous with the present population, suggesting that it may represent an increase in sedges well adapted to dry conditions on the top of the remnant. Cyperaceae appears to have displaced *Artemisia* as a major component of the local vegetation on top of the remnant beginning in stratum VIII, climaxing in stratum VI, and continuing to the present. This dramatic change in the vegetation may coincide with erosion and separation of the remnant from the surrounding landforms.

Phytolith frequencies for modern samples collected from the top of the remnant and south-facing slope are dominated by Festucoid forms, indicating a dominance in the local vegetation by wheatgrasses and needle grasses. Grama grasses, which produce Chloridoid phytoliths, are observed in frequencies smaller than those of either Zones B or C. Bilobate forms, probably representing Panicoid (bluestem) grasses and needle grasses are present in low frequencies. The phytolith record represents a grass population dominated by cool-season grasses, with a significant short grass (warm-season) presence.

## Stratigraphic Record

A stratigraphic column of pollen samples was collected at 10 cm intervals from the east wall of the 1986 block excavations in the camp/processing area, with closer intervals sampled when a single strata was not 10 cm thick. The pollen column encompasses three samples from the cultural level (19–21) near the bottom of the record, and a single sample below the cultural level. Radiocarbon ages indicate that the site was occupied ap-

proximately 11,000 B.P. Five radiocarbon ages have been reported to date from the bone concentration within the cultural level. They are 11,340 ± 120, 11,010 ± 140, 11,320 ± 130, 11,360 ± 130, and 10,760 ± 160 B.P. Therefore, it is expected that the pollen record represents a period of time from prior to 11,000 B.P. until the present. Albanese (this volume) notes that only 50–60 cm of sediment accumulated between the Goshen-Plainview and Pelican Lake horizons. A marked hiatus between the accumulation of the Goshen-Plainview deposits and the Pelican Lake horizon, at 3,000 B.P., is noted to occur in the pollen record at approximately sample 12, or the interface between stratum XI and stratum XII. Final correlation of strata with pollen samples and depths was made several years after excavation and pollen sample collection. Therefore, this boundary should be considered approximate.

Several local vegetation types are considered to be indicators of variations in the paleoclimatic conditions at this site. The Cheno-ams were selected since saltbush *(Atriplex)* is noted to grow most abundantly on the south-facing slope of the remnant. This is the driest environmental niche in the vicinity of the site, and therefore an increase in Cheno-am pollen relative to the present values is interpreted to indicate warming and/or drying conditions.

Sedges (Cyperaceae) appear to occupy relatively dry econiches in the vicinity of the site, and their frequencies are very mobile. Association of high frequencies of Cyperaceae pollen with modern samples collected from the top of the remnant as well as from the south-facing slope, the two driest habitats, indicate that these sedges are well adapted to dry and possibly drought conditions. The sedges noted in the lusher vegetation in the arroyo do not appear to be particularly well represented in the pollen record.

The *Artemisia* (sagebrush) frequencies also display considerable variation in the pollen record. Sagebrush have long tap roots and may withstand a significant amount of drying, provided that there has been sufficient winter snowpack to wet the soil thoroughly to a great depth (West 1979). Sagebrush is not as severely affected by summer droughts as many grasses. Sagebrush is also the dominant vegetation observed in many areas that experience summer drought. Sagebrush was a very large component of the late-glacial and post-glacial vegetation (Mehringer 1985) and was associated with an expanding steppe environment described as cold and dry. Large quantities of sagebrush pollen are frequently accompanied by grass and juniper pollen during the late-glacial and post-glacial. Analogue steppe communities are found today at relatively high elevation in northern Wyoming. Baker and Waln correlate the dominance of *Artemisia* pollen in Wyoming with "cold conditions and an open, tundra-like environment" (1985:198).

*Pinus* pollen is also expected to fluctuate with environmental conditions. It may increase with cooler and/or moister conditions, and decrease with warmer and/or drier conditions. *Pinus* pollen may also increase in relation to other pollen as a result of long distance transport when local vegetation becomes sparse.

In addition to noting fluctuations in these three major pollen groups (Cheno-ams, Cyperaceae and *Artemisia*), the Cheno-am and *Artemisia* pollen counts were transformed into ratios that depict changes in the local vegetation and environmental conditions. Ratios are commonly used within pollen analysis in an effort to elucidate trends in the pollen data that may otherwise be obscured by the fluctuating pollen curves. A Cheno-am to *Artemisia* ratio was calculated for this site using raw data. It was hoped that this ratio would shed additional light on the fluctuations of these two major taxa, which fluctuate primarily in opposition to one another throughout the High Plains. Increasing Cheno-am values, when in an area that supports *Atriplex,* are associated with intervals of reduced effective moisture and perhaps increased soil alkalinity and increased temperatures, while increasing *Artemisia* values represent cooler and/or more mesic intervals, particularly when accompanied by increases in the Poaceae or *Pinus* frequency. The ratios are diagrammed about the mean (Figure 9.1), with deviations to the left indicating a cooler and/or moister conditions, while deviations to the right indicate warmer and/or drier conditions.

The lower portion of the pollen record (samples 13–22) is characterized by very high *Artemisia* pollen frequencies, fluctuating *Pinus* values, low quantities of Cyperaceae pollen, and Cheno-am frequencies similar to present. These general conditions persist prior to the occupation at the base of the record until immediately before the Stratum XII/XI interface (sample 12). This time period is designated Zone C on the pollen diagram. The Cheno-am/*Artemisia* ratio records vegetation very different than modern that is usually interpreted to indicate cooler and/or more mesic conditions than present. *Artemisia* is known to thrive in conditions with adequate winter moisture and summer droughts. Large quantities of *Artemisia* pollen recorded in other studies and noted to be typical of the glacial and post-glacial vegetation, and has been interpreted to represent colder climates (Baker and Waln 1985; Mehringer 1985). However, *Artemisia* is not used as an indicator of colder summer temperatures at the Mill Iron site. Other pollen that is observed during this zone either in larger frequencies or more regularly than in other portions of the pollen record include: Liguliflorae, Brassicaceae, Rhamnaceae, and Rosaceae. Rhamnaceae and Rosaceae represent shrubs, which in the modern plant communities near the site occur in the drainages or near the margin of forested areas. In addition, trilete spores representing ferns are more numerous in these earlier deposits.

The pollen record from the earliest zone (Zone C) indicates environmental conditions supported vegetation communities that were different in their frequency composition than those of today. Shrubs appear to have been more abundant in the immediate vicinity of the site than they are today. This probably reflects response to paleoclimatic conditions that were different than modern climatic conditions, as well as the fact that the remnant was not yet separated from surrounding land forms by erosion. High *Pinus* pollen values are recorded below the cultural level and at the top of the cultural sequence. This suggests that a larger population of pines grew in the hills in the vicinity of the site approximately 11,000 B.P. or that local vegetation became sparse at these intervals, allowing an over-representation of pine in the pollen record. There is no other direct evidence to suggest drought, so it seems more likely that the increase in *Pinus* pollen represents an increase in local pine populations. The fact that these frequencies are not regularly observed throughout the cultural samples suggests that the increase in population was slight or that the population of pine fluctuated considerably at this time. A mosaic of pine stands is probable, with shrubs supported near the margins of treed areas.

The phytolith record for the base of the stratigraphic column, including Strata XIV through XII (Figure 9.2), exhibits co-dominance by Festucoid and Chloridoid phytoliths, including samples examined from the bonebed. In fact, Festucoid phytoliths slightly dominate this record only at the base and the top of Zone C. This mixture suggests approximately equal quantities of cool-season and warm-season, drought tolerant grasses, a situation very different from today's grass population, which is dominated by Festucoid grasses. Above the bonebed, Festucoid phytoliths decline, while Chloridoid phytoliths increase, indicating warming and drying conditions at this time. This phytolith record suggests response in the grass community to seasonal climatic fluctuations, specifically the increased amount of solar radiation during the summer months that would have resulted in warmer, drier summers.

A dramatic reversal in Festucoid and Chloridoid phytolith frequencies is observed near the end of this zone. Diatoms are noted to spike in sample 16 from Stratum XII. This large spike of diatoms suggests a relatively short-lived episode of extremely wet conditions or local puddling of water. It is interesting to note that this is followed in samples 13 and 14 from the upper portion of Stratum XII and sample 12 from the Stratum XII/Stratum XI interface with large frequencies of Festucoid phytoliths, suggesting increases in moisture at this time. This is accompanied by slight increases in buliform and pillow-shaped phytoliths, both of which are expected to increase with greater moisture. This short-lived increase in the Festucoid grass population appears to represent a brief period of cooler temperatures and/or more mesic conditions. The approximate nature of the correlation of pollen samples with soil strata makes assignment of a date to this climatic change problematic.

Following this period, the pollen record undergoes marked changes in Zone B. This zone extends from Stratum V–Stratum XI (samples 6 through 11). The lower portion of Zone B correlates with the Late Archaic, approximately 3,000 B.P. (John Albanese, personal communication, February 1993). The early portion of this zone displays evidence of a moderately large Cheno-am population, probably reflecting saltbush (*Atriplex*). In addition, the *Artemisia* pollen frequencies note a general decline compared to earlier deposits. The Cyperaceae frequencies replace *Artemisia* later in this zone as the dominant pollen type, and experience a steady rise in population throughout most of this zone.

The Cheno-am/*Artemisia* ratio records a vastly different vegetation pattern and climatic situation for Zone B from the one observed in Zone C. The declining *Artemisia* pollen frequencies are accompanied first by sharply increasing Cheno-ams, suggesting at least warming of the environment, and possibly drying. The conditions that fostered the dominance of sagebrush on the steppe approximately 11,000 B.P. have changed, and the sagebrush population declines in favor of saltbush and later sedges. Brassicaceae pollen drops out of the pollen record during this zone. The on-site vegetation types record warm and dry conditions particularly throughout the central portion of Zone B. A reduction in shrubs such as *Atriplex,* which produces

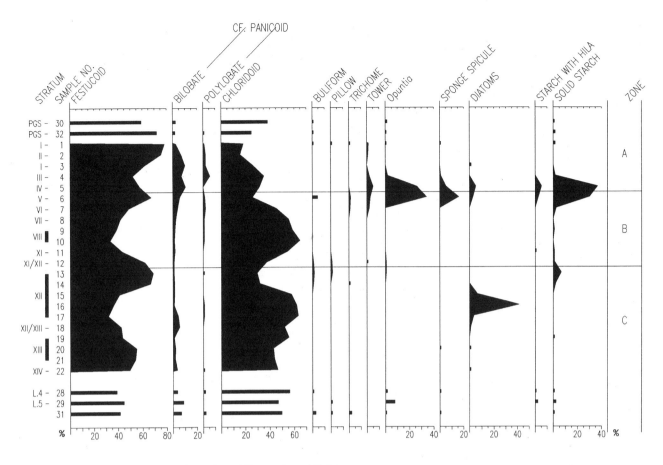

**Figure 9.2.** Phytolith diagram from the Mill Iron site 24CT30.

large quantities of Cheno-am pollen, and *Artemisia,* which also produces large quantities of pollen, is observed. Instead, Cyperaceae (sedges), which do not produce large quantities of pollen, increase in the local vegetation community. The *Pinus* frequencies increase toward the end of this zone, suggesting that local vegetation density declined and introduced less pollen into annual local pollen rain, thus allowing *Pinus* to be overrepresented through long distance transport from nearby hills. The *Salix* pollen frequencies remain stable during this period, indicating that streams through this area are not impacted by any potential drying, and continue to support well-developed riparian communities. This is also evidenced by the presence of *Typha angustifolia*-type pollen recorded in this zone.

The phytolith record exhibits a rapid change from the short-lived increase in Festucoid phytoliths and decline in Chloridoid phytoliths that represent Neoglacial conditions to a dominance of the record by Chloridoid phytoliths and concomitant decline in Festucoid phytoliths, representing the Medithermal. Panicoid phytoliths increase slightly near the end of this interval. Relatively warm and dry conditions during the central portion of Zone B apparently resulted in increases in Chloridoid grasses, such as side oats grama, over Festucoid grasses, such as wheatgrasses and needle grass. Bluestem, a Panicoid grass, and needle grasses probably in-

creased late in this interval. These conditions also caused an increase in the Cyperaceae population on top of the remnant and probably contributed to declining *Artemisia* populations.

Zone A is the uppermost zone denoted for this pollen record. The vegetation and environmental conditions are similar to those of the present, with few exceptions. The *Pinus* pollen frequencies are not as high as at present, suggesting that there has been a recent advance in the pine population, and/or an influence on the pine population through fire control. Cyperaceae pollen continues as a major element of the pollen record until nearly the present. The prairie appears to have supported a mixture of grasses and sedges from the middle of Zone B through the present. The Cheno-am/*Artemisia* ratio fluctuates around the average indicating slightly cooler and/or moister conditions during this zone, becoming slightly warmer and/or drier at present. This zone records more moderate climatic conditions than previous zones.

The upper portion of the phytolith record exhibits increasing Festucoid and Panicoid frequencies, accompanied by declining Chloridoid frequencies. *Opuntia* phytoliths are noted to peak near the interface of Zones A and B at the same time there is an increase in sponge spicules and immediately before a small peak in diatoms. These sponge spicules and diatoms recovered indicate a brief interval of increased moisture. This is noted in the phytolith record by increases in buliform and Festucoid phytoliths in sample 6. The phytolith record suggests that Panicoid grasses, such as bluestem, and needle grasses increased in the recent past, then declined to modern levels. Festucoid grasses, including wheatgrasses and needle grasses, also recently increased to approximately modern levels, whereas Chloridoid grasses, such as side oats grama, have declined from previous levels to modern frequencies.

## Regional Comparisons

Paleoenvironmental trends in the pollen record from the Mill Iron site may be compared with those from several sites in western North Dakota, as well as western Montana, northwestern and southwestern Wyoming, and southeastern Idaho. Major climatic episodes within the past 11,000 years include the Anathermal, a period of warming following the last glaciation, followed by the Hypsithermal or Altithermal, a warm period that is frequently ascribed to 7,000 to 4,000 B.P. The Hypsithermal is followed by the Neoglacial and Medithermal episodes, which are periods of cooler, more mesic conditions and warmer conditions respectively.

Paired pollen and phytolith samples were examined from two stratigraphic columns at the Alkali Creek site (32DU336) (Cummings 1993). These columns exhibited sediments from the occupation at approximately 11,000 B.P. through the Leonard Paleosol (9,000–8,300 B.P.). A hiatus between the Leonard Paleosol and approximately 5,830 B.P. interrupts the pollen and phytolith records. Both the pollen and phytolith records from the Alkali Creek site exhibit similarities to the Mill Iron site data, as well as providing evidence of a vegetation community responding to increased summer insolation. An increase in Cheno-am and decrease in Poaceae pollen frequencies through the Anathermal and until the end of the Leonard Paleosol deposits indicates warming and drying conditions between 11,000 B.P. and approximately 8,300 B.P. *Artemisia* pollen frequencies are smaller at Alkali Creek than at Mill Iron, indicating that sagebrush was less dominant in the local vegetation community at Alkali Creek. It was, however, a significant contributor to the local vegetation community.

The phytolith record at Alkali Creek is less striking in terms of providing evidence of a clear increase in Chloridoid grasses as the Anathermal progressed. Festucoid grasses clearly dominate the record at Alkali Creek, possibly as a result of very close proximity to perennial water from Alkali Creek. The phytolith record from the Leonard Paleosol developed under conditions more mesic than during the previous interval between 11,000 B.P. and 9,000 B.P. This increase in moisture so well documented at the Alkali Creek site is only hinted at in the record from the Mill Iron site where samples 13 and 14 exhibit increased Festucoid phytolith frequencies, but the pollen record does not provide evidence of colder and/or more mesic conditions. Since phytoliths represent grasses, which response quickly to climatic changes and the pollen record represents a mixture of trees, shrubs, herbs and grasses, it is not unusual for the phytolith record to exhibit changes first. The phytolith record from Alkali Creek is consistent with an interpretation that by 11,000 B.P. this area of western North Dakota was already experiencing increased dryness as a result of increased summer insolation, but that the area sampled was close enough to Alkali Creek to be within a relatively wet stream margin that supported primarily Festucoid grasses. As summer solar radiation declined the area became more mesic between 9,000 and 8,300 B.P. and the Leonard Paleosol was formed.

The Tysver-Olsen Site (32DU605) in Dunn County, North Dakota, recorded xeric conditions, including decreased vegetation density and increased erosion between 9,000 and 5,000 B.P. (Scott and Lewis 1983a). This xeric interval is interrupted by a buried soil horizon at approximately 5,345 B.P., which apparently formed under relatively stable conditions. Following this, conditions ameliorate slightly, but remain primarily dry. The Marsh Hawk Site (32BI317) in Billings County also registered xeric conditions at approximately 5,000 B.P. (Scott and Lewis 1982). Mesic intervals are noted at 3,670 B.P. (site 32DU285) in Dunn County (Scott and Lewis 1983b), and at 3,570 B.P. at the Rena Wynne Site (32BI332) also in Billings County (Scott and Lewis 1983c).

Other pollen records representing pollen studies farther removed from the study area exhibit evidence of fluctuating paleoenvironmental conditions. These records extend back to approximately 12,000 B.P. At the Lost Trail Pass Bog site (Mehringer *et al.* 1977), a sagebrush steppe was identified prior to approximately 11,050 B.P. Conditions become cooler at this date, and persist until approximately 7,000 B.P., where Mazama ash is encountered. A warmer but not necessarily drier interval is recorded between the Mazama ash and approximately 5,000 B.P., when macrofossils indicate the presence of an aquatic fen. These conditions persist until approximately 4,000 B.P., when there is a return to a cooler climate, which persists until the present. Mack *et al.* (1978:504) present a summary of pollen data for sites in Washington, from which it is deduced that the period 12,500 B.P. to approximately 10,000 B.P. was cooler and/or moister than at present. This episode is followed by a transitional period to approximately 7,000 B.P., when a warmer and/or drier episode is noted on either side of the Mazama ash. The Hypsithermal follows, and lasts until 4,000 B.P., when conditions cool and become slightly more mesic. The modern climate is noted to begin approximately 2,000 B.P. Mack (1982) records warmer, drier conditions than present from 7,000–4,000 B.P. in Glacier National Park, then gradual cooling and an increase in moisture until modern conditions. Baker (1976), however, does not record a warm period until 4,000 B.P. to approximately 2,500 B.P. in samples from Yellowstone Park. The interval 7,000–4,000 B.P. was interpreted as being cooler and drier than present.

Palynological studies of a stratigraphic core near Helena, Montana yielded evidence that the Hypsithermal in that area was warmer and/or drier than present. The pines had retreated upslope, and the shrubs and grasses expanded. Climatic change was observed in the pollen record near the time of McKean occupation (4,000–5,000 B.P.), when Cyperaceae pollen enters the record, and the pine pollen increases, marking an expansion downslope during cooler and/or more mesic conditions. These conditions persisted until the present.

The pollen record from Blacktail Pond in Yellowstone National Park displays evidence of relatively low *Pinus* pollen frequencies from 14,000 B.P. until approximately 11,500 B.P. This pond is located in the extreme northwestern portion of Wyoming at an elevation of 2,018 m. This increase is mirrored at other sites in Yellowstone National Park (Baker 1976; Waddington and Wright 1974) and Lost Trail Bog (Mehringer *et al.* 1977). A dramatic increase in *Pinus* pollen is recovered from all of these locations, usually resulting in a doubling or tripling of the *Pinus* pollen frequencies near 11,500 B.P. Large quantities of *Pinus* pollen are absent from the Keller Site pollen record at the base, as is expected from its younger basal association.

A post-glacial pollen record for Grand Teton National Park and southern Yellowstone National Park indicates warming between 11,500 and 10,500 B.P. (Whitlock 1992). Continued warming is noted between 10,000 and 9,500 B.P., and indeed, until approximately 5,000 B.P. Cool, relatively moist conditions were noted late in the Holocene, affecting local vegetation. Whitlock (1992:31) also notes that changes in the seasonal cycle of solar radiation were responsible for more xerophytic vegetation during the early Holocene.

Beiswenger (1987) notes relatively cool and moist conditions in Grays Lake Basin, southern Idaho, in the glacial to late-glacial transition (13,000–12,000 B.P.). Moist conditions continue at Grays Lake until approximately 10,000 B.P. Sites farther to the east, such as Ice Slough in central Wyoming, indicate moist conditions persisted until 8,290 B.P. Beiswenger (1987) predicts that an increase in global temperatures would result in an increase in Chenopodiaceous pollen in present *Artemisia* steppe areas, while a decrease in temperatures would increase the *Artemisia* population.

The pollen record of Swan Lake in southeastern Idaho extends from 12,000 B.P. until the present. Very large quantities of *Pinus* pollen are recorded for the interval between 10,000 and 12,000 B.P., indicating that the lower limit of the conifer forest was depressed, and the environment was cooler and moister than that of today. Warming begins prior to 10,000 B.P. and continues until approximately 3,000 B.P. Conditions are interpreted to be semi-arid at Swan Lake during this interval. A short cooler and/or moister episode was recorded between 3,100 and 1,200 B.P., during which the *Pinus* and Poaceae pollen increased, and *Artemisia* pollen decreased. A return to the warm, semi-arid conditions is noted from 1,200 B.P. to the present (Bright 1966).

The pollen record at the Harrower site (48SU867) in the Overthrust Belt of southwestern Wyoming indicated a sagebrush steppe environment from 12,000 to 9,000 B.P. (Cummings 1991). The earlier portion of this interval displayed evidence of warming conditions associated with the Anathermal. Toward the middle of this interval, *Picea* frequencies increased, suggesting the onset of more mesic conditions, which may have continued until the break in deposition (ca. 9,000 B.P.). The higher *Pinus* pollen frequencies recovered indicate that the lower limit of the tree line was, indeed, at a lower elevation than present during this entire interval, suggesting cooler annual temperatures than present. The pollen record from 48SU867 displayed a hiatus in deposition from approximately 9,000 B.P. until 3,300 B.P. The lower portion of the late Neoglacial to Recent interval (3,300 B.P. to present) displayed pollen indicative

of a cooler and/or moister environment than average. The lower limit of the tree line moved upslope during the later Neoglacial to approximately its present location. The Medithermal and Recent deposits exhibited evidence of fluctuating conditions that appeared to be average or perhaps warmer and/or drier than average for most of the duration of these episodes. Slightly cooler and/or moister intervals were recorded to be of short duration.

There is considerable agreement between the paleoenvironmental record at the Mill Iron site and the combined records at several sites in the Little Missouri Badlands of western North Dakota, as well as from western Montana and Wyoming. Regional paleoenvironmental fluctuations were affecting at least this area of the Little Missouri Badlands in a consistent fashion. *Artemisia* is noted in its largest frequencies between approximately 12,000 and 9,000 B.P. on the Plains. The general vegetation trend from approximately 9,000 B.P. to at least 5,000 B.P. appears to have been decreased mesic indicators and an increase in shrubs that were drought tolerant, such as *Atriplex* (saltbush—a Cheno-am), or had deep enough roots to take advantage of moisture stored deeper in the ground, such as *Artemisia* (sagebrush). This is a similar vegetation distribution to that noted on the south-facing slope of the remnant, which experiences the lowest effective moisture rates today. As conditions became more mesic at the Mill Iron site, the Cheno-am (*Atriplex*) and *Artemisia* populations declined and the grasses increased. During the most mesic intervals the area surrounding the site probably supported a denser grass population than is noted today.

Varied vegetal resources have been present in the vicinity of the Mill Iron site for more than 11,000 years, making human occupation possible. Food plants may have been gathered, and grasses and shrubs provided food for various game animals. Among the food plants that may have been exploited is the Liliaceae family. It is interesting to note that this family of plants drops from the pollen record during the last part of Zone C, and returns towards the end of Zone B. The disappearance of this family of plants from the local vegetation may have been in response to drier paleoenvironmental conditions during the interval from late Zone C and Zone B. The extended hiatus, encompassing at least the entire Altithermal, offers no information concerning the presence or absence of this resource. Apiaceae pollen is noted primarily in Zone A. Starch granules abundant in phytolith samples near the boundary of Zones A and B represent primarily grass seeds, although some of the solid starch granules may represent members of the Apiaceae. Grass seeds are noted to produce both starch granules with hila and solid starch granules.

The phytolith record exhibits slightly elevated Festucoid phytoliths from the bonebed level, consistent with cooler and moister conditions. A transition period of warmer and/or drier conditions was noted until approximately the hiatus. This probably corresponds with the warming conditions of the Anathermal, specifically the warm, dry summers that were the result of increased solar radiation during the summer months. The interval represented by samples 11-7 exhibits elevated Chloridoid phytoliths, associated with warm/dry conditions of the Medithermal. The interval represented by samples 5-1 exhibits evidence of essentially modern vegetation in both the pollen and phytolith records.

## Climatic Modeling and The Mill Iron Site Data

The entire seasonal cycle of solar radiation was considerably different during the early Holocene than either today or at the glacial maximum (18,000 B.P.). This may be attributed to both the eccentricity of the earth's orbit and obliquity of the earth's rotational axis. Much attention recently has been focused on models of orbital eccentricity, obliquity of the rotational axis of the earth, and resulting monthly and annual insolation values (Barnosky 1987; Barnosky *et al.* 1987; Bonnischsen *et al.* 1987; COHMAP Members 1988; Davis *et al.* 1986; Kutzbach 1987; Kutzbach and Guetter 1986; Webb *et al.* 1987; and Wright 1984). While many have contributed to the formulation of a climatic model to explain paleoenvironmental changes over the past 18,000 years, a succinct statement of the model is presented by the COHMAP Members (1988).

Boundary conditions important to the formation of this model for North America include 1) the location and depth of the Laurentide ice sheet, 2) the June–August (or July) and December–February (or January) solar radiation for the Northern Hemisphere expressed as percent difference from solar radiation at present, 3) global mean annual sea-surface temperatures also expressed as percent difference from present, 4) excess glacial-age aerosol expressed on an arbitrary scale, and 5) atmospheric carbon-dioxide concentration expressed in parts per million. Particularly important factors for this model include the fact that summer solar radiation or insolation was approximately 8% greater than present at its maximum (10,000 to 11,000 B.P.) and winter solar radiation or insolation was approximately 8% less than present at its minimum, which occurred near 9,000 B.P. These factors are determined through models of obliquity of the rotational axis of the earth. As the Northern Hemisphere tilts more towards the sun, summer solar radiation or insolation will increase and winter solar radiation will decrease. This results in an intensification of seasonal climatic difference.

Also important is orbital eccentricity. Perihelion, or the time when the earth is closest to the sun, now occurs in winter for the Northern Hemisphere. Between 15,000 and 9,000 B.P., however, perihelion occurred during the summer months. At the same time, axial tilt increased, combining with perihelion during summer to increase seasonality in the Northern Hemisphere and decrease seasonality in the Southern Hemisphere. Seasonal extremes in solar radiation noted near 9,000 B.P. decrease through the Holocene toward modern values. Summer warming, which began by 12,000 B.P., reached a maximum around 9,000 B.P. due to increased summer insolation. At this time, summer temperatures in western North America are estimated to be 2–4° C warmer than at present and winters were probably correspondingly colder. By 6,000 B.P., summer temperatures were 2–4° C higher throughout the continental interior of North America, although winters should have ameliorated (COHMAP Members 1988).

Between approximately 12,000 and 6,000 B.P. the Northern Hemisphere received greater solar radiation in the summer and less in the winter than it does at present, resulting in greater seasonality. Climatic changes included changes in wind direction and velocity. Between 18,000 and 12,000 B.P., the western United States experienced easterly rather than westerly winds due to the fact that the Laurentide ice sheet had split the winter jet stream. By approximately 12,000 B.P., this was no longer the case (COHMAP Members 1988). Paleoclimatic model simulations for the early Holocene show an intensification of the northeastern Pacific Subtropical High, bringing dry, warm air to the northwestern U.S. in summer. This pattern of circulation apparently increased summer drought during the early Holocene relative to present conditions, reducing effective moisture for vegetation and resulting in warmer, drier summers. This warming pattern of the Anathermal is noted to be a summer phenomenon with winters being colder than present (Kutzbach 1987:444). Strong westerly winds are postulated near 6,000 B.P. across the Midwest, and a strong northeastern Pacific Subtropical High continues during the summer months off the west coast. Prairies are postulated to have expanded to their maximums across the American Midwest by 6,000 B.P. as a result of increased summer warmth (COHMAP Members 1988).

Davis *et al.* (1986) explain differences in vegetation response between low elevation and high elevation sites in terms of monthly insolation (Figure 9.3). They postulate that increases in insolation value during the summer months, specifically July, have a significant influence on low elevation vegetation boundaries, while high elevation vegetation boundaries appear to be more influenced by fall, specifically September, insolation. This may explain why evidence of warming is often recovered in earlier deposits at lower elevations and in later or more recent deposits at high elevations. In the Snake River Basin of Idaho, the increase in the shadscale (*Atriplex*) community reached its maximum between 10,000 and 8000 B.P., which coincides with the maximum July insolation. This model also indicates that summer temperatures increased during the Anathermal or early Holocene, while winter temperatures did not.

The period representing 11,000 B.P. for the Goshen occupation at the Mill Iron site and an indeterminate amount of time thereafter (from the base of the pollen column through sample 13), exhibits pollen and phytolith records indicating that sagebrush was a dominant element of the local vegetation, perhaps creating a sagebrush steppe. The phytolith record for this interval indicates progressive warming and/or drying until slightly before the end of this interval, when conditions abruptly become cooler and more mesic. If these sediments may be presumed to represent the period 11,000 to perhaps 8,000 B.P., the monthly insolation values for June, July, and August increase. Increased insolation during these summer months would result in a decrease of effective moisture through both increased evaporation and an intensification of the northeastern Pacific Subtropical High, a high pressure system that brings dry, warm air to the northwestern U.S. during the summer. If this high pressure system had been intensified, it would produce warmer, drier conditions than present during the summer months. Results of the warmer, drier conditions may be observed particularly in the phytolith record, in the increase in Chloridoid phytoliths, representing grasses that prefer warm, dry conditions.

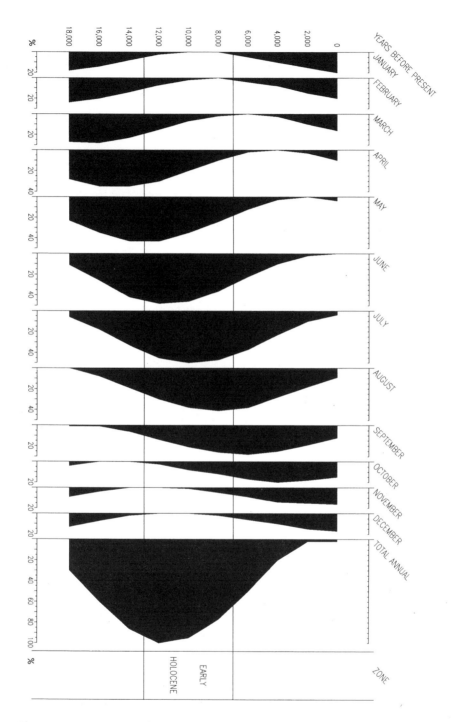

**Figure 9.3.** Monthly and annual insolation; percent change (after Davis, Sheppard, and Robertson 1986).

Expansion of the Chloridoid grass population corresponds well with increased summer insolation, producing a longer warmer growing season and drier weather. A large sagebrush population may reflect the ability of that shrub to utilize winter moisture stored in the soil to survive summer drought. This period between 11,000 and 8000 B.P. falls within the Anathermal period, which has been described as being 2 to 4° C warmer than present during the summer (COHMAP 1988). A companion effect from the increased axial tilt is an intensification of winter conditions. The Festucoid grass frequencies attest to a highly developed cool-season grass community that would manifest as green growth at the beginning and end of each growing season. As the Festucoid phytoliths decline and the Chloridoid phytoliths increase the grass population seems to be undergoing a change in response to increased summer temperatures and aridity that would prolong the hot portion of the summer. The rapid but short-lived change in phytoliths to dominance by Festucoid (cool-season) phytoliths near the end of Stratum XII may correspond with conditions that fostered the development of the Leonard paleosol elsewhere. Evidently any change toward cooler and/or more mesic conditions at the Mill Iron site were not of sufficient magnitude to create a paleosol.

The hiatus near sample 12 and the interface between strata XI and XII represents a hiatus of indeterminate time. Following the hiatus, sediments from stratum XI represent Pelican Lake deposition around 3,000 B.P. The pollen record exhibits clear evidence of a change in local vegetation. *Artemisia* (sagebrush) was becoming less dominant, while Cheno-ams increased rapidly. Following this adjustment in vegetation, both *Artemisia* and Cheno-ams declined, while Cyperaceae increases dramatically in the local vegetation. Cheno-ams were more abundant relative to the quantity of *Artemisia* present at this time than during the early Holocene (Anathermal). This vegetation pattern indicates drier conditions annually. Indeed, the phytolith record for most of Zone B indicates relatively warm, dry conditions. The only exception is in sample 12, representing the transition from stratum XII to stratum XI. The vegetation record is consistent with geomorphic evidence of accelerated erosion, probably accompanying drier conditions at this time. Lower deposits from Zone B might represent Neoglacial deposits, although the majority of samples from this zone appear to represent the warmer, drier Medithermal.

The most recent interval, Zone A, exhibits pollen and phytolith records consistent with those reported in the modern ground surface samples. The early portion of this interval exhibits evidence that *Opuntia* (prickly pear cactus) was considerably more abundant in the local vegetation than it is today. *Artemisia* (sagebrush) appears to have re-established itself as a major component of the vegetation, and sedges (Cyperaceae) are noted to be mixed with grasses. The *Pinus* (pine) population does not appear to be as large in the vicinity of the site as it is at present. The grass population moves toward a pattern observed in modern surface samples of a dominance of Festucoid phytoliths, with moderately large quantities of Chloridoid phytoliths and few Panicoid phytoliths. This represents a grass population dominated by cool-season grasses, with fewer warm-season grasses. The warm-season grasses are dominated by those preferring dry conditions. This phytolith assemblage rep-

resents a growing season with extended cool conditions and a reactively short-hot interval during the summer.

## Summary and Conclusions

The pollen record from the Mill Iron site spans the time interval from 11,000 B.P. to the present with a large hiatus between Strata XII and XI. The pollen record provides data concerning paleoenvironmental change throughout this time period. The period of occupation is marked by fluctuating *Pinus* pollen frequencies and very high *Artemisia* pollen frequencies. It should be noted that the *Pinus* pollen frequencies are higher before and at the end of the occupation than during the majority of the occupation level. This vegetation pattern appears to be part of a greater pattern that persisted for the Late Pleistocene and Anathermal episodes.

Sagebrush seems to have dominated the landscape. Grasses were included in the local vegetation, but do not appear to have been as abundant as they are today and sedges seem to have been considerably less abundant than they are today. During Zone A, the environment appears to be drying and/or warming following the Goshen occupation. Grasses present in the local vegetation were relatively evenly divided between Festucoid (cool-season) and Chloridoid (warm-season) grasses at the beginning of this zone. This changed, however, to a dominance by Chloridoid (short) grasses, which grow well under warm, dry conditions. Expansion of grasses requiring relatively warm, dry conditions at the expense of those requiring cooler and more mesic conditions is in agreement with the solar insolation models of increased solar radiation during the summer, resulting in a more pronounced warm, dry summer.

Changes in the vegetation include a decline throughout Zone B (following the hiatus) in sagebrush, and an increase in Cheno-ams during the early portion of Zone B, followed by a decrease in Cheno-ams and increase in both *Pinus* and Cyperaceae pollen near the end of Zone B. The pollen record identifying this warmer and/or drier interval after the hiatus, is not associated with accumulation of much sediment and probably represents the Medithermal. The warming and drying of the pollen record is mirrored in the phytolith record by large quantities of Chloridoid phytoliths throughout most of Zone B, with the exception of a brief interval of dominance by Festucoid phytoliths near the interface of Zones A and B. The primary impact of this brief cooler and/or more mesic interval that might represent the Neoglacial was largely on the grass and sagebrush populations in this area.

Cooler and/or more mesic conditions are recorded toward the end of Zone B and persist through Zone A until the present. A modern vegetation pattern is exhibited throughout Zone A and includes large quantities of grass and sedge in the local vegetation, accompanied by sagebrush. The pines do not appear to have been as dense, or located as close to the Mill Iron site as they are today, as the pine pollen frequencies are lower than present during most of Zone A.

The pollen record indicates that for the portion of the past 11,000 years represented, the vegetation in the vicinity of the Mill Iron site has alternated between shrubland and grassland patterns, with pine and juniper located on the nearby hills.

Sagebrush appears to have been a major shrub in this area, and has varied in frequency contributing in greater quantity to the vegetation community during the post-glacial years than at present. At no time during the time represented have paleoenvironmental changes been severe enough to cause more than a modification in the quantity of various plants that have been established in this shrubby sagebrush steppe or mixed grassland ecotone. There is no evidence of a spruce forest in this area at the end of the Pleistocene.

The stratigraphic pollen record from the Mill Iron site provides evidence that during the occupation of this site, at approximately 11,000 B.P. and for some time thereafter, the local vegetation was dominated by sagebrush (probably the result of a sagebrush steppe vegetation pattern) to a greater extent than was observed anywhere in the modern vegetation in the vicinity of the site. Immediately after the occupation, the grass population changed from including nearly equal quantities of Festucoid (cool-season) and Chloridoid (warm-season) grasses to including a larger quantity of Chloridoid grasses. This portion of the pollen and phytolith records is consistent with a model for increased insolation values during the summer months, between approximately 11,000 and 8,000 B.P., that would have functioned to increase summer drought and reduce effective moisture for vegetation. The increased solar radiation during the summer months resulting from a greater tilt to the earth's axis would have intensified the northeastern Pacific Subtropical High, bringing more warm, dry air into the area of the northwestern U.S. during the summer months.

The dramatic change in phytolith frequencies noted in the upper portion of Stratum XII might be associated with a brief event. This short-lived change in phytoliths, indicating an increase in cool-season (Festucoid) grasses, is not visible in the pollen record which records declining Artemisia (sagebrush) frequencies.

Apparent warming conditions noted in the pollen record through increased Cheno-am and Cyperaceae frequencies following this interval are supported in the phytolith record by an increase in Chloridoid (warm-season) grasses that tolerate dry conditions. This interval apparently represents the Pelican Lake period between approximately 3000 B.P. and 2000 B.P. Cooler and probably more mesic conditions are noted by Stratum V, after which the vegetation exhibits more similarity to the modern plant communities in both the pollen and phytolith records.

Comparison of the stratigraphic pollen and phytolith records from the Mill Iron site with the climatic model for the early Holocene yielded positive results. Increasing solar radiation between 12,000 and 9,000 B.P. appears to have changed the composition of grasses at the Mill Iron site from a community balanced between Festucoid (cool-season) and Chloridoid (warm-season) grasses to one dominated by Chloridoid (warm-season) grasses. This probably reflects the more intensely hot, dry summers of the Anathermal and a shortening of the cool portions of the growing season in the spring and fall, which would have been the result of increased seasonality. Sagebrush seems to have survived this warming, drying trend, which implies adequate winter precipitation to charge the soils. Vegetation communities extant at the time of occupation are not duplicated in today's vegetation communities, although many of the vegetative components are similar. Both the pollen and phytolith records for the Mill Iron site point to a vegetation community that would result from increased summer temperatures and decreased summer precipitation during the early Holocene, thus supporting the solar insolation climatic model.

Humans occupying this area had to contend with greater variation between summer and winter temperatures than today. Vegetation at the time of Goshen occupation was typical of what we consider a sagebrush steppe. Increasingly hot, dry summers are noted in the change in increasing Chloridoid phytoliths from the time of occupation at 11,000 B.P. extending over the next few thousand years. During summer months the Mill Iron area likely seemed to be dominated by sagebrush since Chloridoid grasses are short bunch grasses and cool-season grasses would have dried and turned brown. Only along riparian zones and drainages and during the spring and fall on the prairie would taller green grasses (Festucoid) be visible among the sagebrush. Trees may have formed more of a mosaic across the landscape and shrubs were more abundant. Ferns also were more numerous in the early Holocene vegetation. Changes in local vegetation would have affected not only human populations, but also animal population distribution in this area. Seasonality would have been more pronounced during the early Holocene, producing hotter, drier summers and colder winters. Human occupants of this portion of the Plains probably responded to changes in the animal population and local vegetation by changing their site settlement and/or resource procurement strategies.

## References Cited

Baker, R. G.
   1976   Late Quaternary Vegetation History of the Yellowstone Lake Basin, Wyoming. *U.S.G.S. Professional Paper 729-E.*

Baker, R. G. and Kirk Waln
   1985   Quaternary Pollen Records from the Great Plains and Central United States. In *Pollen Records of Late-Quaternary North American Sediments*, edited by Vaughn M. Bryant, Jr. and Richard G. Holloway, pp. 191–203. American Association of Stratigraphic Palynologists Foundation, Dallas.

Barnosky, Cathy W.
   1987   Late-Glacial and Postglacial Vegetation and Climate of Jackson Hole and the Pinyon Peak Highlands, Wyoming. Manuscript on file with the University of Wyoming, National Park Service Center, Laramie.

Barnosky, Cathy W., Patricia M. Anderson, and Patrick J. Bartlein
   1987   The Northwestern U. S. During Glaciation: Vegetational History and Paleoclimatic Implications. In *North America and Adjacent Oceans During the Last*

*Deglaciation*, edited by W. F. Ruddiman and H. E. Wright, Jr., pp. 189–321. Geology of North America, vol. K-3. Geological Society of America Bulletin, Boulder.

Beiswenger, Jane M.
1987 Late Quaternary Vegetational History of Grays Lake, Idaho and the Ice Slough, Wyoming. Ph.D. dissertation, Department of Botany, University of Wyoming, Laramie.

Bonnichsen, Robson, Dennis Stanford, and James L. Fastook
1987 Environmental Change and Developmental History of Human Adaptive Patterns; The Paleoindian case. In *North America and Adjacent Oceans During the Last Deglaciation*, edited by W. F. Ruddiman and H. E. Wright, Jr., pp. 403–424. Geology of North America, vol. K-3. Geological Society of America Bulletin, Boulder.

Bright, R. C.
1966 A Palynological Investigation of Postglacial Sediments at Two Locations Along the Continental Divide Near Helena, Montana. Unpublished Ph.D. dissertation, Pennsylvania State University.

Brown, D. A.
1984 Prospects and Limits of Phytolith Key for Grasses in the Central United States: *Journal of Archaeological Science* 11:345–368.

COHMAP Members
1988 Climatic Changes of the Last 18,000 Years: Observations and Model Simulations. *Science* 241:1043–1052.

Cummings, Linda Scott
1991 Pollen Analysis. Appendix E In *Archaeological Data Recovery at the Harrower Site (48SU867): LaBarge Natural Gas Project*. By Kevin W. Thompson. Cultural Resource Management Report No. 24, vol. 2: Prehistoric Mitigation. Archaeological Services of Western Wyoming College, Rock Springs.

1993 Stratigraphic Pollen and Phytolith Analysis at the Alkali Creek Site (32DU336), Dunn County, North Dakota. Manuscript on file with Metcalf Archaeological Consultants, Eagle, Colorado.

Davis, Owen K., John C. Sheppard and Susan Robertson
1986 Contrasting Climatic Histories for the Snake River Plain, Idaho, Resulting from Multiple Thermal Maxima. *Quaternary Research* 26: 321–339.

Eckerle, William
1990 Geoarchaeology of the Mill Iron Archaeological Site: Postglacial Environments on the Great Plains of Southwestern Montana. Manuscript on file with Department of Anthropology, University of Wyoming, Laramie.

Gould, F. N., and R. B. Shaw
1983 *Grass Systematics*. Texas A&M University Press, College Station.

Guthrie, R. Dale
1984 Mosiacs, Allelochemics and Nutrients: An Ecological Theory of Late Pleistocene Megafaunal Extinctions. In *Quaternary Extinctions: A Prehistoric Revolu-*

*tion*, edited by P. Martin and R. Klein, pp. 259–298. University of Arizona Press, Tucson.

Harrington, C. R., and Allan Ashworth
1986 A Mammoth (*Mammuthus primigenius*) Tooth From Late Wisconsin Deposits Near Embden, North Dakota, and Comments on the Distribution of Wooly Mammoths South of the Wisconsin Ice Sheets. In *Canadian Journal of Earth Sciences* 23:909–18.

Jones, Robert L., and A. H. Beavers
1963 Sponge Spicules in Illinois Soils. *Soil Science Proceedings* 1963: 438–440.

Kutzbach, John E.
1987 Model Simulations of the Climatic Patterns During the Deglaciation of North America. In *North America and Adjacent Oceans During the Last Deglaciation*, edited by W. F. Ruddiman and H. E. Wright, Jr., pp. 425–446. Geology of North America, vol. K-3. Geological Society of America Bulletin, Boulder.

Kutzbach, John E., and P. J. Guetter
1986 The Influence of Changing Orbital Parameters and Surface Boundary Conditions on Climatic Simulations for the Past 18,000 Years. *Journal of Atmospheric Sciences* 43:1726–1759.

Mack, Richard
1982 Pollen Analysis of Cores from Teepee Lake and McKillop Creek Pond. In *Kootenai Canyon Archeology: The 1979 LAURD Project Final Mitigation Report*, edited by T. Roll, pp. 3.1–3.9.

Mack, R N., N W. Rutter, S. Valastro, and V. M. Bryant, Jr.
1978 Late Quaternary Vegetation History at Waits Lake, Colville River Valley, Washington. *Botanical Gazette* 139(4):499–506.

Mehringer, Peter J., Jr.
1985 Late-Quaternary Pollen Records from the Interior Pacific Northwest and Northern Great Basin of the United States. In *Pollen Records of Late-Quaternary North American Sediments*, edited by Vaughn M. Bryant, Jr. and Richard G. Holloway, pp. 167–189. American Association of Stratigraphic Palynologists Foundation, Dallas.

Mehringer, Peter J., Jr., S. F. Arno, and Kenneth L. Petersen
1977 Postglacial History of Lost Trail Pass Bog, Bitterroot Mountains, Montana. *Arctic and Alpine Research* 9(4):345–368.

Rovner, Irwin
1971 Potential of Opal Phytoliths for Use in Paleoecological Reconstruction. *Quaternary Research* 1(3): 343–359.

Scott, Linda J. and Rhoda O. Lewis
1982 Stratigraphic Pollen and Phytolith Analysis of Soils from 32BI317, Billings, North Dakota. Manuscript on file with University of North Dakota Archaeological Research, Belfield.

1983a Stratigraphic Pollen and Phytolith Analysis of Soils from 32DU605, Dunn County, North Dakota.

Manuscript on file with University of North Dakota Archaeological Research, Grand Forks.

1983b    Stratigraphic Pollen and Phytolith Analysis of Soils from 32DU285, Dunn County, North Dakota. Manuscript on file with University of North Dakota Archaeological Research, Grand Forks.

1983c    Stratigraphic Pollen and Phytolith Analysis of Soils from 32BI332, Billings County, North Dakota. Manuscript on file with University of North Dakota Archaeological Research, Belfield.

Soil Conservation Service
n.d.    Unpublished soil mapping data for Natrona County, Wyoming. Soil Conservation Service, Casper.

Twiss, Page C.
1987    Grass-Opal Phytoliths as Climatic Indicators of the Great Plains Pleistocene. In *Quaternary Environments of Kansas*, edited by W. C. Johnson, pp. 179–188. Kansas Geological Survey Guidebook Series 5.

Waddington, J. C. B., and H. E. Wright, Jr.
1974    Late Quaternary Vegetational Changes on the East Side of Yellowstone Park, Wyoming. *Quaternary Research* 4:175–184.

Webb, Thompson, III, Patrick J. Bartlein, and John E. Kutzbach
1985    Climatic Change in Eastern North America During the Past 18,000 years; Comparisons of Pollen Data with Model Results. In *North America and Adjacent Oceans During the Last Deglaciation*, edited by W. F. Ruddiman and H. E. Wright, Jr., pp. 447–462. Geology of North America, vol. K-3. Geological Society of America Bulletin, Boulder.

West, Neil E.
1979    Basic Syncological Relationships of Sagebrush-Dominated Lands in the Great Basin and the Colorado Plateau. In *The Sagebrush Ecosystem: A Symposium*, pp. 33–41. Utah State University, College of Natural Resources, Logan.

Whitlock, Cathy
1992    Postglacial Vegetation and Climate of Grand Teton National Park and Southern Yellowstone National Park, Wyoming. Manuscript on file with National Park Service, Midwest Archaeological Center, Lincoln.

Wright, H. E., Jr.
1970    Vegetational History of the Central Plains. In *Pleistocene and Recent Environments of the Central Great Plains*, edited by W. Dort, Jr., and J. K. Jones, Jr., pp. 157–172. Department of Geology, University of Kansas Special Publication 3, University Press of Kansas, Lawrence.

1984    Sensitivity and Response Time of Natural Systems to Climatic Change in the Late Quaternary. *Quaternary Science Reviews* 3:91–131. Pergamon Press, Oxford, England.

# CHAPTER TEN

# Soils and Geomorphic Surfaces of the Mill Iron Site

RICHARD G. REIDER

University of Wyoming

## Introduction

Soils and geomorphic surfaces were investigated in the vicinity of the Mill Iron site in May 1985 and June 1988. Soil profiles were described (Soil Survey Staff 1975) and sampled in both natural and excavated exposures on five out of seven geomorphic surfaces of Humbolt Creek and its tributaries. Soil stratigraphy was also traced in the exposures.

The seven geomorphic surfaces are defined by Albanese (this volume). Surface 6 (S6) is the highest and oldest and Terrace 0 (T0), the modern channel of Humbolt Creek, is the lowest and youngest. Data on seven soil profiles are presented in this chapter that cover five of the seven surfaces, excluding S3 and T0. S3 was not sampled and described because it was thought to be part of T2 when field investigations were conducted. Neither was T0 so investigated because it is the active channel of the stream system and has no great bearing on the older soils and surfaces.

Soil samples were analyzed for the following: 1) particle size (Bouyoucos 1962); 2) pH (1:1 soil-water paste); 3) calcium carbonate equivalency (Piper 1950); 4) organic matter content (Walkley and Black 1934); and 5) electrical conductivity (EC) (saturated soil-water paste; Hesse 1971: 75). Soils are classified according to Soil Survey Staff (1975). Soil horizon nomenclature conforms to Guthrie and Witty (1982). Carbonate stages follow Gile et al. (1966).

This chapter summarizes the results of field work and laboratory analyses. An important aspect is that a relatively strong paleosol of the highest surface (S6), associated with Paleoindian occupation, helps to define the ages of all surfaces. Termed the Mill Iron Paleosol, it also occurs on S5 and S4. Its greater strength of development is contrasted with younger soils of the lowest two surfaces (T2 and T1) and with young soils in colluvium that frequently overlie the paleosol on the higher surfaces. The paleosol, where well preserved, has a prismatic B horizon that is secondarily enriched with carbonates and salts. It may serve as a reliable stratigraphic marker for future investigations in the area or for other Paleoindian studies in the region.

## Soils and Geomorphic Surfaces

### Character of the Mill Iron Paleosol

The Mill Iron Paleosol occurs in sediments of the upper three surfaces (S6, S5, and S4) in the site vicinity and possibly in the next lower surface (S3). It does not occur in sediments of the lowest two surfaces (T2 and T1).

At the Mill Iron site itself, the paleosol and associated soils and sediments were described at Site 1 (Figure 10.1) in a curved backhoe trench a few meters northwest of the site (Table 10.1 and Table 10.2), as well as at Site 2 (Figure 10.1) in a north-south trench located 1 m east of site datum (Table 10.3 and Table 10.4). Both sites are on S6.

The soil column at Site 1 contains three soils (Table 10.1 and Table 10.2). Soil stratigraphy with unconformities is schematically shown in Figure 10.2. Soil 1 at the ground surface has A–C horizons formed in colluvium. It is an Entisol, post-Altithermal in age, that lies unconformably on Soil 2, which in turn is marked by a truncated Bwkb horizon that also developed in colluvium. Soil 3 then lies unconformably below Soil 2. Soil 3, with Bwkzb and Ckz horizons, is formed into colluvium and underlying cross-bedded fluvial sands. Soil 3 is the Mill Iron Paleosol. The Goshen bonebed lies within the Ckz horizon of the paleosol. The paleosol is considered to be early to mid-Holocene in age, as further discussed below.

The soil column at Site 2 (Table 10.3 and Table 10.4) closely resembles that at Site 1. Three soils are present: 1) a surface Entisol, post-Altithermal in age, that developed in colluvium; 2) a calcareous soil, also in colluvium, that contains Akb and Bwkb horizons along with Late Plains Archaic artifacts (ca. 1,500–2,500 B.P.; Frison 1991); and 3) a third soil in colluvium, marked by calcareous/alkaline Bwkzb horizons, that lies unconformably below Soil 2 and which contains flaked materials described as Goshen. Soil 3 is the Mill Iron Paleosol of early to mid-Holocene age.

The Mill Iron Paleosol was also located on the S6 surface at

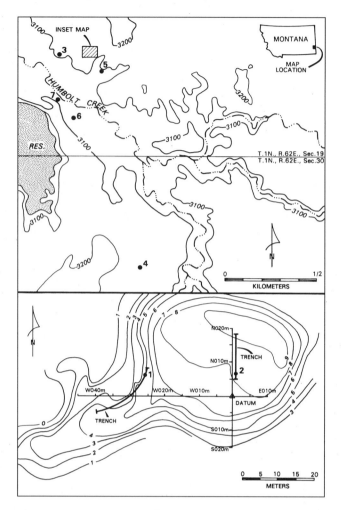

**Figure 10.1.** Locations of soil profile sites. Inset at bottom shows the locations of Sites 1 and 2.

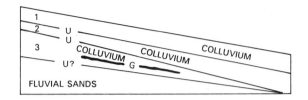

**Figure 10.2.** Schematic soil-sediment stratigraphy in trench at Site 1 showing soils 1, 2, and 3. G = Goshen cultural level; U = erosional unconformity.

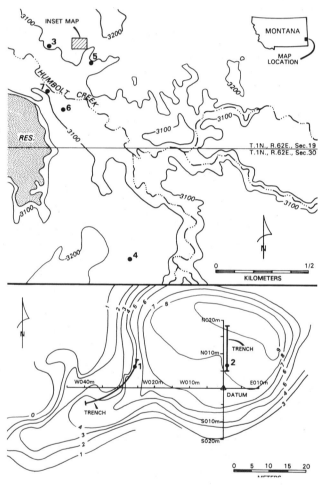

**Figure 10.3.** Soil column at Site 3. Soils 1 and 2 are post-Altithermal in age. Soil 1, developed in colluvium, is the uppermost A–C horizon sequence. Soil 2 (also in colluvium), marked by Ab and C horizons, lies below Soil 1 and contains a cultural level radiocarbon dated at 1835 ± 55 b.p. (AA-3667). Soil 3, the Mill Iron Paleosol, appears in the lower two-thirds of the photograph, consisting of Ab-Akzb-Bwkzb-Ckz horizons in colluvium and alluvium that are strongly filled with carbonates and salts as marked by the light colors. Tape extends to 170 cm. Refer to Table 10.5 and Table 10.6.

Site 3 (Figure 10.1) where the paleosol is well preserved (Table 10.5 and Table 10.6; Figure 10.3). The soil column contains three soils: 1) a surface Entisol formed in colluvium that has A–C horizons; 2) a buried Entisol in colluvium with A–C horizons that contains charcoal in its Ab horizon that was radiocarbon dated at 1835 ± 55 B.P. (AA-3667); and 3) a basal soil, Soil 3, with Ab-Akzb-Bwkzb-Ckz horizons. Soil 3, marked by prominent prismatic structure, is the Mill Iron Paleosol of early to mid-Holocene age. Soils 1 and 2 are post-Altithermal in age.

The Mill Iron Paleosol is also well preserved on S5 at Site 4 (Figure 10.1; Table 10.7 and Table 10.8), where it can be traced below a slab-lined hearth dated at 1370 ± 60 B.P. (Beta-26900). The soil column, where described, contains two soils, the surface one of post-Altithermal age formed in colluvium. The second soil, with Akzb-Bwkzb-Ckz horizons, is the Mill Iron Paleosol of early to mid-Holocene age formed in alluvium. Here, as elsewhere, the paleosol is marked by prominent prismatic structure.

**Table 10.1.**   Field Characteristics at Site 1, S6 Surface. Location: Site 24CT30, NW1/4 SW1/4, Section 19, T1N, R62E.

*Soil 1*
*Weak Soil (Entisol) in Post-Altithermal-age Colluvium*

A   0–3 cm   Dark brown to brown (10 yr 4/3, dry) sandy clay loam; very fine weak subangular blocky and single grain structure; loose to soft consistence; no effervescence; clear smooth boundary.

C   3–40 cm   Brown (10 yr 5/3, dry) sandy clay loam; fine to medium moderate subangular blockly structure; slightly hard consistence; weak effervescence; abrupt wavy boundary.

Erosional Unconformity
*Soil 2*
*Post-Altithermal-age Soil in Colluvium*

2Bkb   40–79 cm   Grayish brown (10 yr 5/2, dry) sandy clay loam; medium to coarse moderate subangular blocky structure; slightly hard consistence; strong effervescence; abrupt smooth boundary; few fine segregated carbonate filaments (Stage I).

Erosional Unconformity
*Soil 3*
*Mill Iron Paleosol of Early to Mid-Holocene Age in Colluvium Containing Goshen Cultural Level*

3Bwkzb   79–96 cm   Light gray (10 yr 7/2, dry) sandy loam; medium moderate subangular blocky (prismatic?) structure; hard consistence; violent effervescence; clear wavy boundary; disseminated carbonates (Stage II).

3Ckz   96–161 cm   Light brownish gray (10 yr 6/2, dry) sandy loam; medium moderate subangular blocky (prismatic?) structure; slightly hard consistence, abrupt irregular boundary; disseminated carbonates. Contains Goshen cultural level.

Unconformity?
*Lower Part of the Mill Iron Paleosol of Early to Mid-Holocene Age in Cross-Bedded Fluvial Sands*

4Ckz   161–212 cm   Light brownish gray (10 yr 6/2, dry) sandy loam; fine to medium weak subangular blocky structure; soft consistence; violent effervescence only along bedding planes; few segregated carbonates on seams.

**Table 10.2.**   Laboratory Data for Site 1, S6 Surface.

| Horizon/ Depth (cm) | % Gravel (> 2mm) | % Sand (2–0.05mm) | % Silt (0.05–0.002mm) | % Clay (<0.002mm) | pH 1:1 | % CaCO₃ | EC (μm mhos/cm) | % Organic Matter |
|---|---|---|---|---|---|---|---|---|
| A 0–3 | 0.0 | 53.5 | 24.3 | 22.2 | 7.6 | 0.0 | — | 2.35 |
| C 3–40 | 0.0 | 47.4 | 26.3 | 26.3 | 8.1 | 0.0 | — | 1.64 |
| 2Bkb 40–79 | 1.8 | 61.6 | 14.1 | 24.3 | 8.4 | 1.0 | — | 1.64 |
| 3Bwkzb 79–96 | 0.0 | 67.7 | 14.1 | 18.2 | 8.6 | 2.4 | — | 1.16 |
| 3Ckz 96–161 | 1.0 | 79.9 | 6.0 | 14.1 | 9.4 | 0.5 | — | 0.59 |
| 4Ckz 161–212 | 0.0 | 77.9 | 4.0 | 18.1 | 9.3 | — | — | 0.0 |

**Table 10.3.** Field Characteristics at Site 2, S6 Surface. (Location: Site 24CT30, NW1/4 SW 1/4, Section 19, T1N, R62E.)

*Soil 1*
*Weak Soil (Entisol) in Post-Altithermal-Age Colluvium*

A    0–5 cm    Brown to dark brown (10 yr 4/3, dry) sandy loam; medium moderate subangular blocky structure; soft consistence; no effervescence; clear smooth boundary; no carbonate accumulation.

C    5–38 cm    Brown to dark brown (10 yr 4/3, dry) sandy clay loam; medium moderate subangular blocky structure; hard consistence; no effervescence; clear smooth boundary; some few fine segregated carbonate filaments in the lower 4 cm.

*Soil 2*
*Post-Altithermal-Age Soil in Colluvium Containing Late Plains Archaic Artifacts*

2Akb    38–51 cm    Dark brown (10 yr 3/3, dry) sandy clay loam; medium moderate subangular blocky structure; hard consistence; weak effervescence; clear smooth boundary; few fine segregated carbonate filaments (Stage I).

2Bkb    51–78 cm    Brown to dark brown (10 yr 4/3, dry) sandy loam; medium moderate subangular blocky structure; slightly hard consistence; weak effervescence; abrupt smooth boundary; few fine segregated carbonate filaments (Stage I).

*Erosional Unconformity*
*Mill Iron Paleosol of Early to Mid-Holocene Age in Colluvium Containing Goshen Cultural Level*

3Bwkzb    78–101 cm    Grayish brown (10 yr 5/2, dry) sandy clay loam; coarse strong prismatic and subangular blocky structure; very hard consistence; violent effervescence; abrupt smooth boundary; many fine segregated carbonate filaments (Stage II). Horizon contains flakes from manufacture of Goshen artifacts.

4Bwkzb    101–195 cm    Dark grayish brown (10 yr 4/2, dry) clay; coarse strong prismatic and subangular blocky structure; very hard consistence; violent effervescence; many fine segregated carbonate filaments (Stage II). High clay content derived from bedrock.

**Table 10.4.** Laboratory Data for Site 2, S6 Surface.

| Horizon/ Depth (cm) | % Gravel (> 2mm) | % Sand (2–0.05mm) | % Silt (0.05–0.002mm) | % Clay (<0.002mm) | pH 1:1 | % CaCO$_3$ | EC (μm mhos/cm) | % Organic Matter |
|---|---|---|---|---|---|---|---|---|
| A 0–5 | 0.0 | 67.6 | 16.2 | 16.2 | 7.9 | 0.0 | — | 2.11 |
| C 5–38 | 0.0 | 61.6 | 16.2 | 22.2 | 8.0 | 0.0 | — | 1.88 |
| 2Akb 38–51 | 0.0 | 61.5 | 18.2 | 20.3 | 8.5 | 1.4 | — | 2.20 |
| 2Bkb 51–78 | 0.0 | 57.5 | 26.3 | 16.2 | 8.7 | — | — | 2.08 |
| 3Bwkzb 78–101 | 0.0 | 51.4 | 22.3 | 26.3 | 9.2 | — | — | 1.52 |
| 4Bwkzb 101–195 | 2.6 | 39.2 | 20.3 | 40.5 | 8.8 | 1.0 | — | 1.43 |

**Table 10.5.** Field Characteristics at Site 3, S6 Surface. (Location: Arroyo Cut, NW 1/4 SW 1/4, Section 19, T1N, R62E.)

*Soil 1*

*Weak soil (Entisol) in Post-Altithermal-age Colluvium*

A    0–5 cm    Grayish brown (10 yr 5/2, dry) sandy clay loam; fine weak crumb structure; soft consistence; no effervescence; clear smooth boundary.

C    5–15 cm    Brown (10 yr 5/3, dry) clay loam; fine weak subangular blocky structure; soft consistence; no effervescence; abrupt smooth boundary.

*Soil 2*

*Weak Soil (Entisol) in Post-Altithermal-age Colluvium Containing Cultural Artifacts and Charcoal Dated at 1835 ± 55 B.P. (AA-3667)*

Ab    15–29 cm    Grayish brown (10 yr 5/2, dry) clay loam; medium weak subangular blocky structure; slightly hard consistence; no effervescence; abrupt smooth boundary. Contains cultural level, 1835 ± 55 B.P.

C    29–40 cm    Brown (10 yr 5/3, dry) clay loam; medium weak subangular blocky structure; slightly hard consistence; no effervescence; abrupt smooth boundary.

*Soil 3*

*Mill Iron Paleosol of Early to Mid-Holocene Age in Colluvium*

2Ab1    40–60 cm    Grayish brown (10 yr 5/2, dry) clay loam; medium to coarse strong angular blocky structure; hard consistence; no effervescence; gradual smooth boundary.

2Akzb2    60–75 cm    Grayish brown (10 yr 5/2, dry) clay loam; medium to coarse strong angular blocky structure; hard consistence; no effervescence; gradual smooth boundary.

Unconformity?

*Lower Part of Mill Iron Paleosol of Early to Mid-Holocene Age in Alluvium*

3Bwkzb1    75–90 cm    Light brownish gray (10 yr 6/2, dry) clay loam; coarse moderate prismatic structure; hard consistence; violent effervescence; gradual smooth boundary; few fine segregated carbonate filaments and disseminated carbonates and salts (Stage II).

3Bwkzb2    90–133 cm    Light brownish gray (10 yr 6/2, dry) gravelly sandy clay loam; coarse moderate prismatic structure; hard consistence; violent efferevescence; gradual smooth boundary; few fine segregated carbonate filaments and disseminated carbonates and salts (Stage II).

3Ckz    133–170 cm    Brown (10 yr 5/3, moist) gravelly clay loam; coarse moderate prismatic and subangular blocky structure; friable consistence; violent effervescence; few fine segregated carbonate filaments and disseminated carbonates and salts.

**Table 10.6.** Laboratory Data for Site 3, S6 Surface.

| Horizon/ Depth (cm) | % Gravel (> 2mm) | % Sand (2–0.05mm) | % Silt (0.05–0.002mm) | % Clay (<0.002mm) | pH 1:1 | % CaCO$_3$ | EC (μm mhos/cm) | % Organic Matter |
|---|---|---|---|---|---|---|---|---|
| A 0–5 | 0.7 | 40.6 | 27.9 | 31.5 | 6.7 | 0.3 | 0.10 | 3.76 |
| C 5–15 | 0.0 | 36.4 | 31.0 | 32.6 | 7.8 | 0.5 | 0.10 | 1.75 |
| Ab 15–29 | 0.0 | 30.1 | 36.7 | 33.2 | 7.9 | 1.3 | 0.19 | 1.59 |
| C 29–40 | 0.0 | 30.2 | 38.1 | 31.7 | 7.9 | 0.9 | 0.16 | 1.14 |
| 2Ab1 40–60 | 0.0 | 31.9 | 35.4 | 32.7 | 8.5 | 1.0 | 0.19 | 1.04 |
| 2Akzb2 60–75 | 1.3 | 33.8 | 31.5 | 34.7 | 9.1 | 1.9 | 1.18 | 1.25 |
| 3Bwkzb1 75–90 | 17.2 | 30.2 | 34.1 | 35.7 | 9.0 | 5.6 | 2.90 | 0.69 |
| 3Bwkzb2 90–133 | 43.5 | 44.5 | 20.8 | 34.7 | 9.1 | 7.1 | 2.28 | 0.62 |
| 3Ckz 133–170 | 28.5 | 34.2 | 27.0 | 38.8 | 8.9 | 5.3 | 0.32 | 0.83 |

**Table 10.7.** Field Characteristics at Site 4, S5 Surface. (Location: Arroyo Cut, SE 1/4 NW 1/4, Section 30, T1N, R62E.)

*Soil 1*
*Weak soil (Entisol) in Post-Altithermal-age Colluvium*

A   0–10 cm   Dark brown (10 yr 3/3, moist) sandy clay loam; fine weak crumb structure; very friable consistence; no effervescence; clear smooth boundary; no carbonate segregations; no clay films.

C   10–25 cm   Dark brown (10 yr 3/3, moist) sandy clay loam; fine weak crumb structure; very friable consistence; no effervescence; abrupt smooth boundary; no carbonate segregatons; no clay films.

Disconformity?
*Soil 2*
*Mill Iron Paleosol of Early to Mid-Holocene Age in Alluvium*

2Akzb1   25–40 cm   Dark grayish brown (10 yr 4/2, dry) clay; medium to coarse strong prismatic structure; slightly hard consistence; no effervescence; clear smooth boundary; few fine segregated carbonate filaments (Stage I); no clay films.

2Akzb2   40–50 cm   Dark grayish brown (10 yr 4/2, dry) clay; medium to coarse strong prismatic structure; hard consistence; strong effervescence; clear smooth boundary; common fine segregated carbonate filaments (Stage I); no clay films.

2Bwkzb1   50–55 cm   Grayish brown (10 yr 5/2, dry) clay loam; medium to coarse strong prismatic structure; very hard consistence; violent effervescence; gradual smooth boundary; common fine segregated carbonate filaments (Stage II); very few thin clay films on ped faces.

2Bwkzb2   55–70 cm   Grayish brown (10 yr 5/2, dry) sandy clay loam; coarse strong prismatic structure; very hard consistence; violent effervescence; gradual smooth boundary; common fine segregated carbonate filaments (Stage II); very few thin clay films on ped faces.

2Bwkzb3   70–90 cm   Brown (10 yr 5/3, dry) clay loam; coarse strong prismatic structure; very hard consistence; violent effervescence; gradual smooth boundary; few fine segregated carbonate filaments (Stage II); very few thin clay films on ped faces.

2Ckz1   90–105 cm   Light brownish gray (10 yr 6/2, dry) sandy loam; coarse strong prismatic structure; hard consistence; violent effervescence; gradual smooth boundary; few fine segregated carbonate filaments.

2Ckz2   105–130 cm   Pale brown (10 yr 6/3, dry) sandy loam; coarse strong prismatic structure; hard consistence; violent effervescence; few fine segregated carbonate filaments.

**Table 10.8.** Laboratory Data for Site 4, S5 Surface.

| Horizon/ Depth (cm) | % Gravel (> 2mm) | % Sand (2–0.05mm) | % Silt (0.05–0.002mm) | % Clay (<0.002mm) | pH 1:1 | % CaCO$_3$ | EC (μm mhos/cm) | % Organic Matter |
|---|---|---|---|---|---|---|---|---|
| A 0–10 | 0.0 | 51.4 | 25.3 | 23.3 | 6.95 | 1.4 | 0.12 | 2.54 |
| C 10–25 | 0.3 | 49.3 | 28.4 | 22.3 | 7.85 | 1.5 | 0.17 | 2.05 |
| 2Akzb1 25–40 | 0.0 | 28.8 | 30.7 | 40.5 | 8.75 | 1.5 | 0.40 | 2.72 |
| 2Akzb2 40–50 | 0.0 | 31.2 | 26.9 | 41.9 | 9.20 | 3.2 | 0.41 | 1.79 |
| 2Bwkzb1 50–55 | 0.0 | 26.2 | 35.0 | 38.8 | 9.30 | 3.4 | 0.56 | 1.79 |
| 2Bwkzb2 55–70 | 0.0 | 46.8 | 20.0 | 33.2 | 9.00 | 3.5 | 0.85 | 1.39 |
| 2Bwkzb3 70–90 | 0.6 | 36.8 | 28.1 | 35.1 | 8.70 | 4.7 | 1.27 | 0.90 |
| 2Ckz1 90–105 | 0.0 | 69.8 | 12.4 | 17.8 | 8.70 | 2.3 | 0.98 | 0.63 |
| 2Ckz2 105–130 | 0.0 | 72.6 | 11.7 | 15.7 | 9.65 | 3.9 | 0.64 | 0.43 |

The Mill Iron Paleosol also occurs within the S4 surface at Site 5 (Albanese, this volume, backhoe trench 1) (Table 10.9 and Table 10.10). Where described, two soils are evident. The lowest is the Mill Iron Paleosol developed in alluvium, whereas the surface soil with A–C horizons is a post-Altithermal-age Entisol formed in colluvium. The paleosol has ABzb-Bwkzb-Ckz horizons. The B horizon has well-defined prismatic structure.

## Genesis of the Mill Iron Paleosol

The occurrence of the Mill Iron Paleosol within S6, S5, and S4 surfaces (and perhaps its potential occurrence on S3) indicates that these surfaces are early- to mid-Holocene in age. The Mill Iron Paleosol therefore ranges no older than Goshen occupation of the site area—that is, the soil overlies and is developed into sediments containing the Goshen cultural level. Conversely, the paleosol is older than the slab-lined hearth (ca. 1,400 B.P.) in S5 at Site 4, older than the charcoal-dated level (ca. 1800 BP)

is S6 at Site 3, as well as older than the Late Plains Archaic level (ca. 1,500-2,500 B.P.; Frison 1991: 24) in S6 at Site 2. Therefore, the Mill Iron Paleosol formed between the times of Goshen occupation of the Mill Iron site (ca. 11,000 B.P.) on the one hand and Late Archaic occupations on the other. Much of its formation thus spans the Altithermal period (ca. 7,000–4,000 B.P.). In part, it is the Altithermal soil (Leopold and Miller 1954; Reider 1990).

However, the paleosol has polygenetic characteristics that indicate a change in environments during its formation, resembling that described for similar-aged paleosols at Carter/Kerr-McGee and Agate Basin Paleoindian sites in northeastern Wyoming (Reider 1980, 1982, 1990). Although the prominent prismatic structures in the B horizon of the Mill Iron Paleosol suggest strong clay development, laboratory data (Tables 10.2, 10.4, 10.6, 10.8, and 10.10) in fact indicate weak clay development in B horizons relative to respective A horizons. Instead, the B horizons appear to have been Bw (cambic or color) horizons originally. Likewise, the lack of strong clay skins in

**Table 10.9.** Field Characteristics at Site 5, S4 Surface. (Location: Backhoe Trench, SE 1/4 SW 1/4, Section 19, T1N, R62E.)

*Soil 1*

*Weak soil (Entisol) in Post-Altithermal-age Colluvium*

A  0–3 cm  Brown to dark brown (10 yr 4/3, dry) sandy loam; fine weak crumb and single grain structure; loose consistence; no effervescence; clear smooth boundary; no carbonate segregations; no mottling.

C  3–44 cm  Yellowish brown (10 yr 5/4, dry) sandy loam; fine to medium weak subangular blocky structure; slightly hard consistence; no effervescence; abrupt smooth boundary; no carbonate accumulation; no mottling.

*Disconformity*

*Soil 2*

*Mill Iron Paleosol of Early to Mid-Holocene Age in Alluvium*

2ABzb  44–51 cm  Brown (10 yr 5/3, dry) sandy loam; coarse strong angular blocky structure; very hard consistence; absent to weak effervescence; clear smooth boundary; few fine segregated carbonate filaments (Stage II).

2Bwkzb1  51–68 cm  Brown (10 yr 5/3, dry) loam; fine to medium strong angular blocky to medium strong prismatic structure; hard consistence; violent effervescence; clear smooth boundary; many fine segregated carbonate filaments (Stage II).

2Bwkzb2  68–101 cm  Grayish brown (10 yr 5/2, dry) and light gray (10 yr 5/2, dry) silt loam; fine to medium strong angular blocky to medium strong prismatic structure; hard consistence; violent effervescence; clear smooth boundary; common fine segregated carbonate filaments (Stage II).

2Ckz  101–115 cm  Pale brown (10 yr 6/3, dry) clay loam; fine to medium strong angular blocky to medium strong prismatic structure; slightly hard consistence; strong effervescence; few fine segregated carbonate filaments (Stage I).

**Table 10.10.** Laboratory Data for Site 5, S4 Surface.

| Horizon/ Depth (cm) | % Gravel (> 2mm) | % Sand (2–0.05mm) | % Silt (0.05–0.002mm) | % Clay (<0.002mm) | pH 1:1 | % CaCO₃ | EC (μm mhos/cm) | % Organic Matter |
|---|---|---|---|---|---|---|---|---|
| A 0–3 | 0.0 | 55.5 | 26.3 | 18.2 | 6.9 | 0.0 | — | 3.30 |
| C 3–44 | 0.0 | 61.6 | 25.0 | 13.4 | 8.4 | 0.0 | — | 2.59 |
| 2ABzb 44–51 | 0.0 | 55.7 | 28.2 | 16.1 | 9.5 | — | — | 1.28 |
| 2Bwkzb1 51–68 | 0.0 | 49.6 | 32.3 | 18.1 | 9.6 | 2.9 | — | 1.64 |
| 2Bwkzb2 68–101 | 0.0 | 24.9 | 65.0 | 10.1 | 9.5 | — | — | 1.57 |
| 2Ckz 101–115 | 0.0 | 37.4 | 32.3 | 30.3 | 9.4 | 0.5 | — | 1.46 |

the B horizons suggests that they were Bw horizons, not Bt (argillic or clay-enriched) horizons. The few clay skins recognized in some profiles seem to be stress cutans that developed when alternate wetting and drying of the soil caused expansion and shrinkage of materials, resulting in some orientation of clays along ped faces. In fact, it appears that the prominent prismatic structures of the B horizons themselves would have formed by expansion and contraction of materials under repeated wetting and drying. The overall soil morphology resembles that of Typic Haploborolls with prismatic structure that are common to the northern Great Plains (Soil Survey Staff 1975: 289). These soils, earlier classified as Chestnut soils, have mollic over cambic horizons, usually underlain by carbonate-bearing horizons.

However, carbonates and salts secondarily fill all of the Bw horizons of the Mill Iron Paleosol and occasionally engulf its A horizons. These relationships indicate that the cambic (Bw) horizon formed first, followed by carbonate and salt impregnation, thus transforming the Bw horizon into a Bwkz horizon that is characterized by highly alkaline pH values. The soil was thus transformed into one resembling an Aridic Haploboroll or perhaps a Typic Natriboroll (Soil Survey Staff 1975: 289, 291). The latter two types were earlier considered Brown and Solonetzic soils, respectively.

In sum, relationships indicate that the Mill Iron Paleosol is polygenetic, that it evolved from a soil formed under relatively moist conditions (Typic Haploboroll), probably under tall or mixed grasses, but that it was transformed into a calcareous, highly alkaline soil under aridic conditions (Aridic Haploboroll or similar soil). The transformation likely occurred about 7,000 years ago, or near the beginning of the Altithermal. The aridic nature of the soil then became well expressed in the Altithermal, until just before Late Archaic occupations in the site area. Its calcareous, alkaline nature suggests dry conditions, perhaps marked by a short grass steppe or more desert-like vegetation.

## Younger Soils and Terraces

In contrast to the higher surfaces, weak soils (Entisols) occur in T2 and T1 terraces in alluvium as well as colluvial units that frequently mantle the surface of both terraces (Figure 10.1; Tables 10.11, 10.12, 10.13, and 10.14). Soil development of T2–T1, in relation to the restricted occurrence of the Mill Iron Paleosol to higher surfaces, indicates that T2-T1 are post-Altithermal in age.

B horizons with prominent prismatic structures, as is characteristic of the Mill Iron Paleosol, are absent on T2–T1. Only A and C horizons are present. Strongly alkaline pH values, common to the Mill Iron paleosol of the higher surfaces, are replaced in soils of T2–T1 by values that range from less than 8.0 to about 8.5, except in subsoils where strongly alkaline ground water has driven values above 9.0. On T2 (Table 10.11 and Table 10.12), strong platy structures in the 3C horizon are structures inherited from finely bedded, old alluvium. Subangular blocky structures are common in materials of the T1 terrace (Table 10.13).

The 2C horizon of the T2 terrace is formed in reworked alluvium deposited during the cut phase of this terrace, resulting in a cut terrace (strath) on relatively old, finely bedded alluvium. Young colluvium, containing weak soil development,

overlies the alluvium. However, the basal parent material of the T1 terrace is alluvial fill, deposited during the fill cycle of the T1 terrace. Weak soil development is present within young colluvium near the surface of T1.

The presence of young colluvium with weak soils (Entisols) that overlies the Mill Iron Paleosol on the higher surfaces, in addition to the presence of similar units on T2 and T1 terraces, indicates that slopes in the area were unstable during much of post-Altithermal time. Slopewash denuded upper slopes and carried colluvium, perhaps episodically, to lower slope positions wherein the Entisols formed. Soil formation in post-Altithermal time was neither long term nor intense (except for the calcareous soil containing Late Plains Archaic cultural materials at the Mill Iron site itself), but soil types suggest that short grass vegetation was dominant. Soil pH values in post-Altithermal-age colluvium are typically near neutral and lack the strong alkalinity characteristic of the Mill Iron Paleosol. The dominant weak soil development in post-Altithermal-age colluvium is common to soil-sediment units of comparable age at other archaeological sites in the region (Reider 1990).

## Summary and Conclusions

The Mill Iron Paleosol may prove to be a good stratigraphic marker in the area that can be used to identify landforms of early- to mid-Holocene age. Likewise, it may be a good indicator of sediments or landforms that contain Paleoindian cultural levels. At Mill Iron, it is easily identified by prominent prismatic structures and secondary carbonates and salts in the B horizon and sometimes in its A horizon. The paleosol may be important in identifying well-drained sites occupied by Paleoindians, unlike the paleosols identified at Carter/Kerr-McGee and Agate Basin sites in northeastern Wyoming which are useful to identify locally poorly drained sites along arroyos that once had wet meadows (Reider 1980, 1982, 1990). Testing is necessary to prove the use of the Mill Iron Paleosol as a stratigraphic marker in eastern Montana and the northern Great Plains in general.

Soil characteristics suggest that the Mill Iron Paleosol was a Typic Haploboroll when it first formed following Goshen occupation of the Mill Iron site. At that time, it probably acquired its characteristic prismatic structure in the Bw horizon that is common to many Haploborolls of the northern Great Plains. The vegetation was likely tall or mixed grasses under a relatively moist climate.

Beginning around 7,000 B.P., however, the soil was subjected to impregnation by carbonates and salts during the Altithermal when the climate became drier, lasting perhaps as late as about 3,000 B.P. The carbonates and salts, which transformed the Bw horizon to a Bwkz horizon, suggest that a short grass steppe or more desert-like vegetation replaced the tall or mixed grasses. The paleosol evolved from a Typic Haploboroll in the early Holocene to an Aridic Haploboroll or perhaps Typic Natriboroll in the Altithermal.

By contrast, weak soils, or Entisols, characterize post-Altithermal-age colluvium and alluvium of the T2–T1 terraces and two or more colluvial units that mantle the higher surfaces, except for a calcareous soil in colluvium (containing Late Plains

**Table 10.11.**  Field Characteristics at Site 6, T2 Terrace. (Location: Arroyo Cut, SW 1/4 SW 1/4, Section 19, T1N, R62E.)

*Soil 1*
*Surface and Near-Surface Horizons in Colluvium*

A   0–5 cm   Light brownish gray (10 yr 6/2, dry) clay loam; fine weak crumb structure; very friable (moist) consistence; no effervescence; clear smooth boundary.

C   5–25 cm   Light brownish gray (10yr 6/2, dry) loam; fine weak crumb structure; very friable (moist) consistence; no effervescence; abrupt smooth boundary.

*Disconformity?*
*Subsurface Horizons in Reworked and Intact Alluvium*

2C   25–37 cm   Light brownish gray (10 yr 6/2, dry) loam; fine strong platy structure (bedding planes); hard consistence; weak effervescence; abrupt smooth boundary; weak disseminated carbonates. Reworked alluvium.

*Erosional Unconformity (Strath Surface)*

3Ckz1   37–52 cm   Light brownish gray (10 yr 6/2, dry) silty clay loam; fine to medium strong platy structure (bedding planes); very hard consistence; strong effervescence; clear smooth boundary; weak disseminated carbonates. Intact alluvium.

3Ckz2   52–163 cm   Light brownish gray (10 yr 6/2, dry) sandy clay loam; fine to medium strong platy structure (bedding planes); very hard consistence; no effervescence (?); intact alluvium.

**Table 10.12.**  Laboratory Data for Site 6, T2 Terrace.

| Horizon/ Depth (cm) | % Gravel (> 2mm) | % Sand (2–0.05mm) | % Silt (0.05–0.002mm) | % Clay (<0.002mm) | pH 1:1 | % CaCO$_3$ | EC (µm mhos/cm) | % Organic Matter |
|---|---|---|---|---|---|---|---|---|
| A 0–5 | 0.0 | 29.0 | 35.3 | 35.7 | 7.7 | 1.8 | 0.30 | 2.89 |
| C 5–25 | 0.0 | 34.2 | 45.0 | 20.8 | 7.7 | 2.8 | 0.28 | 1.63 |
| 2C 25–37 | 0.0 | 28.3 | 49.2 | 22.5 | 8.2 | 5.5 | 0.43 | 1.63 |
| 3Ckz1 37–52 | 0.0 | — | — | 34.5 | 9.3 | 4.5 | 1.47 | 2.02 |
| 3Ckz2 52–163 | 0.0 | 54.9 | 22.9 | 22.2 | 8.5 | 3.8 | 1.69 | 0.87 |

**Table 10.13.**  Field Characteristics at Site 7, T1 Terrace. (Location: Hand-Dug Pit, SW 1/4 SW 1/4, Section 19, T1N, R62E.)

A   0–2 cm   Grayish brown (10 yr 5/2, dry) sandy clay loam; medium moderate subangular blocky and single grain structure; slightly hard consistence; no effervescence; clear smooth boundary. Formed in colluvium.

C   2–6 cm   Brown (10 yr 5/3, dry) sandy loam; fine weak subangular blocky and single grain structure; soft consistence; no effervescence; clear smooth boundary. Formed in colluvium.

Ab   6–10 cm   Grayish brown (10 yr 5/2, dry) sandy loam; medium moderate subangular blocky structure; slightly hard consistence; no effervescence; clear smooth boundary. Formed in colluvium.

C   10–55 cm   Brown (10 yr 5/3, dry) sandy loam; medium moderate subangular blocky and single grain structure; slightly hard consistence; no effervescence; abrupt smooth boundary. Formed in colluvium.

*Disconformity?*

2C   55–86 cm   Brown (10 yr 5/3, dry) sandy clay loam; medium weak prismatic and subangular blocky structure; slightly hard consistence; no effervescence; abrupt smooth boundary. Formed in colluvium.

*Disconformity?*

3C   86–145 cm   Pale brown (10 yr 6/3, dry) loam; medium moderate angular blocky structure; extremely hard consistence; weak effervescence on 1 mm horizontal veins in finely stratified alluvium. Formed in alluvium.

**Table 10.14.** Laboratory Data for Site 7, T1 Terrace.

| Horizon/ Depth (cm) | % Gravel (> 2mm) | % Sand (2–0.05mm) | % Silt (0.05–0.002mm) | % Clay (<0.002mm) | pH 1:1 | % CaCO₃ | EC (μm mhos/cm) | % Organic Matter |
|---|---|---|---|---|---|---|---|---|
| A 0–2 | 0.0 | 59.6 | 20.2 | 20.2 | 7.6 | 0.0 | — | 3.84 |
| C 2–6 | 0.0 | 73.8 | 14.1 | 12.1 | 7.7 | 0.0 | — | 2.53 |
| Ab 6–10 | 0.0 | 67.8 | 14.1 | 18.2 | 7.6 | 1.9 | — | 1.85 |
| C 10–55 | 0.0 | 75.7 | 6.2 | 18.1 | 8.1 | — | — | 1.28 |
| 2C 55–86 | 0.0 | 49.6 | 28.3 | 22.1 | 8.5 | 2.9 | — | 1.85 |
| 3C 86–145 | 0.0 | 43.7 | 34.2 | 22.1 | 9.7 | — | — | 1.31 |

Archaic cultural materials) that lies immediately above the Mill Iron Paleosol at the archaeological site itself. The predominance of thin Entisols in colluvium of post-Altithermal age across all surfaces signifies prevailing landscape instability. Erosion was broken only by weak, thin soils in colluvium that formed when slopes or terraces became briefly stable. The Entisols suggest that the area was dominated by short grass vegetation throughout post-Altithermal time.

The soil-geomorphic relationships near the Mill Iron site resemble the pattern recognized by Leopold and Miller (1954) for the Powder River Basin in northeastern Wyoming, especially in regard to the occurrence of the Altithermal-age paleosol, although at Mill Iron the paleosol occurs on more than one surface. The character of the paleosol reinforces the concept that the interval was relatively dry, perhaps being even desert-like in southeastern Montana.

## References Cited

Bouyoucos, C. J.
  1962  Hydrometer Method Improved for Making Particle Size Analysis of Soils. *Agronomy Journal* 54:464–465.
Frison, G. C.
  1991  *Prehistoric Hunters of the High Plains.* 2d ed. Academic Press, San Diego.
Gile, L. H., R. F. Peterson, and R. B. Grossman
  1966  Morphological and Genetic Sequences of Carbonate Accumulation in Desert Soils. *Soil Science* 101:347–360.
Guthrie, R. L., and J. E. Witty
  1982  New Designations for Soil Horizons and Layers and the New Soil Survey Manual. *Soil Science Society of America Journal* 46:443–444.
Hesse, P. R.
  1971  *A Textbook of Soil Chemical Analysis.* Chemical Publishing Co., New York.
Leopold L. B. and Miller, J. P.
  1954  *A Post-Glacial Chronology for Some Alluvial Valleys in Wyoming.* U.S.G.S. Water Supply Paper No. 1261.
Piper, C. S.
  1950  *Soil and Plant Analysis.* Interscience, New York.

Reider, R. G.
  1980  Late Pleistocene and Holocene Soils of the Carter/Kerr-McGee Archeological Site, Powder River Basin, Wyoming. *Catena* 7:301–315.
  1982  Soil Development and Paleoenvironments. In *The Agate Basin Site, A Record of the Paleoindian Occupation of the Northwestern High Plains,* edited by G. C. Frison and D. J. Stanford, pp. 331–344. Academic Press, New York.
  1990  Late Pleistocene and Holocene Pedogenic and Environmental Trends at Archaeological Sites in Plains and Mountain Areas of Colorado and Wyoming. In *Archaeological Geology of North America,* Centennial Special, vol. 4, Edited by N. P. Lasca and J. Donahue, pp. 335–360. Geological Society of America, Boulder, Colorado.
Soil Survey Staff
  1975  *Soil Taxonomy,* Agricultural Handbook 436. Soil Conservation Service, U.S. Department of Agriculture, Washington.
Walkley, A. and I. A. Black
  1934  Examination of the Degtjareff Method for Determining Soil Organic Matter and a Proposed Modification of the Chromic Acid Titration Method. *Soil Science* 37:29–38.

# CHAPTER ELEVEN

# Discussion and Conclusions

GEORGE C. FRISON
University of Wyoming

C. VANCE HAYNES, JR.
University of Arizona

MARY LOU LARSON
University of Wyoming

## Goshen, Plainview, Folsom, Clovis, and Midland

August 1966 witnessed the end of a multiyear, well-funded investigation of the Hell Gap site 48GO305 in southeast Wyoming. The site was the scene of stratified evidence of numerous Paleoindian (then referred to as "Early Man") occupations for a period of about 3,000 years. The evidence from the site established a chronology for the High Plains Paleoindian that has withstood the the test of time surprisingly well.

As the Hell Gap site excavations were drawing to a close, a productive cultural level was encountered at the bottom of the excavations in Locality 1 on August 15, 1966. At first, the investigators assumed they were in a Folsom level, but after a hurried analysis of a projectile point found in situ (Figure 1.2a) from the level on August 18, 1966, they concluded they were in a Clovis level (see Figure 11.1). After further deliberation and study of the same projectile point and two incomplete specimens (Figure 1.2d, e), they decided there were neither Folsom nor Clovis and subsequently gave them and the cultural level the name "Goshen" after the county in Wyoming in which the Hell Gap site is located. After hurried excavations in the newly designated Goshen level for a few days that resulted in the recovery of a large assemblage of tools and debitage, the Hell Gap site investigations were terminated, and the site was covered and sealed on August 26, 1966. Such was the beginning of the elusive Goshen Paleoindian cultural complex.

The Hell Gap site assemblages were only partially analyzed and only a short, summary article was published (Irwin-Williams et al. 1973). Both of the principal investigators, Henry Irwin and Cynthia Irwin-Williams no doubt intended to return to the site, but as so often happens they became over-committed to other duties and projects. Both died prematurely, and neither returned for further investigation of the Goshen complex. A Paleoindian level of apparent high integrity and as rich as the one they encountered at the Hell Gap site is an unusual occurrence, at least on the North American High Plains. This alone should have been a powerful incentive to continue

the investigations and one that few Paleoindian archaeologists could have resisted. In retrospect, however, the evidence for a Goshen cultural complex at the Hell Gap site at that time was far from straightforward. The cultural level was rich in chipped-stone tools and debitage, but diagnostics (projectile points) were few, and their technology and morphology made it difficult to convince themselves and other Paleoindian archaeologists at the time of real and quantifiable differences between these and other Paleoindian chipped-stone diagnostics such as Clovis, Folsom, Midland, and Plainview. This thinking could be reflected in their uncertainties in finally deciding to name the Goshen complex.

On the positive side, whatever the reasons why the investigators did not return to the Hell Gap site, they went to considerable effort to preserve it for future research. They cemented the floors and the ground surface, so that rain and snow runoff could not follow old trench walls and damage the profiles. An exposure of part of the site profile in Locality 1 in 1992 revealed conditions relatively unchanged from those of 1966. There is every indication that a large surface area of the Goshen level remains intact in Locality 1 and in good condition to begin further investigation when the time is right. It may have been that the investigators believed that further study of the problem at that time was not based on sufficient evidence to continue the effort, and the fact that the investigators did not pursue the Hell Gap site further might support this bit of speculation. On the other hand, the efforts spent to protect the site would suggest that they did recognize that valuable data remained there.

The identification of a Goshen culture complex on the High Plains provided Paleoindian archaeologists with a category in which to place a number of possible diagnostic projectile points from this region that heretofore were considered as Plainview, as it was known and described at the site in Texas by that name (Sellards et al. 1947). However, Irwin (1971:48; and in notes left before his untimely death) had clearly decided the Goshen projectile point as he interpreted it at the Hell Gap Site was ty-

**Figure 11.1.** The stratigraphy as it was recorded in Locality 1 at the Hell Gap site on August 18, 1966.

pologically the same as Plainview. This view is shared by one of us (Haynes 1991), who was also one of the original investigators at the Hell Gap site. The only problem this presents at present is that the radiocarbon and stratigraphic data from the Northern Plains strongly indicate a pre-Folsom age for Goshen, while Plainview on the Southern Plains is believed to be of post-Folsom age. One of us (Haynes 1991) has raised the possibility that the Plainview type site is as early as Clovis, but if Plainview in the south is younger than Goshen to the north, it would require the Goshen-Plainview continuum to have had a long life and Folsom to have come and gone within the Goshen-Plainview time frame. In addition, Goshen would have had to move southward during this time period and avoid Folsom influence in projectile point manufacture technology. If Folsom lithic technology was derived from Goshen, it would have been a one-way transmission of ideas. There remains also the possibility that Goshen and Folsom were separate and unrelated entities. Until the relationships between Goshen and Plainview are better understood, it would probably be wise to retain both Goshen and Plainview as separate, although "Goshen-Plainview" is proposed for the Northern Plains as a more suitable designation.

If any of the Goshen-Plainview relationships mentioned above should happen to materialize, somewhere along the way on both the Northern and Southern Plains, they should be confirmed by radiocarbon-dated stratigraphy. However, at this point only the stratigraphy at Hell Gap and at the Carter/Kerr-McGee sites strongly supports Goshen pre-dating Folsom. The Hell Gap stratigraphy appears to be well documented, but better radiocarbon dates with smaller standard deviations are needed. There seems little doubt that further investigation at Locality 1 at Hell Gap will yield enough charcoal from the Goshen and other components for accelerator dating purposes. Other localities at the Hell Gap site may also contain Goshen components. Both important and encouraging are the emerging results of the preliminary investigations at the Jim Pitts site 39CU1142 in the Black Hills in western South Dakota where a Goshen level with apparently high integrity is appearing underneath a Folsom level.

Goshen is in many ways a paradox in Plains Paleoindian studies; so much so that its aceptance was unlikely without a more satisfactory degree of proof than was provided at the Hell Gap site. Had it been a manifestation that could have been easily accommodated within the recognized High Plains chronology, its acceptance would have been assured. The Hell Gap stratigraphic data indicated that Goshen was present chronologically before Folsom, but it was not a projectile point type that Paleoindian archaeologists at that time or even at present would expect to see. They would expect something technologically and morphologically transitional between Clovis and Folsom, which was certainly not the case with the Goshen projectile point.

It is difficult to doubt the Hell Gap stratigraphic record, but the strong similarity between Plainview as it is known and recognized on the Southern Plains and Goshen at Hell Gap demanded caution in assigning a pre-Folsom age and, in addition, according Goshen status as a separate cultural complex. Technologically, it is difficult to conceptualize a direct Clovis derivitive going from mostly percussion biface reduction technology with fluting (Clovis) to a pressure technology with basal thinning and not fluting (Goshen) and then to Folsom with its carefully controlled fluting.

There is no doubt that better data were needed to keep the Goshen concept alive, and the Mill Iron site 24CT30 in southeast Montana appeared at an opportune moment for Northern High Plains Paleoindian studies. The Powars II Paleoindian Red Ocher Mine site 48P1330 (Sunrise Iron Mine) assemblage (Stafford 1990) found near the Hell Gap site alerted Paleoindian archaeologists once more to the presence of what could be the nebulous Goshen complex. This site produced all the commonly recognized Paleoindian projectile point types found at the Hell Gap site and, had the latter cultural materials been in the correct chronological order instead of in convoluted mine tailings, the Goshen concept would probably have been confirmed at an earlier date. This, however, was not the case, and it was not until the recovery of the Mill Iron site assemblage in a context with good integrity that included a large sample of diagnostics (projectile points) supported by accelerator radiocarbon dates that archaeologists were able to begin to consider seriously a better and more secure status for Goshen.

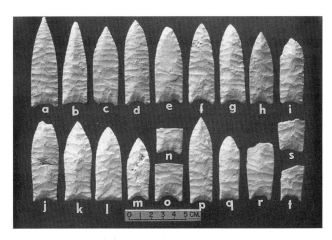

**Figure 11.2.** Projectile points from Mill Iron and Plainview sites. Mill Iron: a, c, d, f, h, j, m–o; Plainview: b, e, g, i, k, l, p; Midland: q–t. (Picture by C. V. Haynes Jr.)

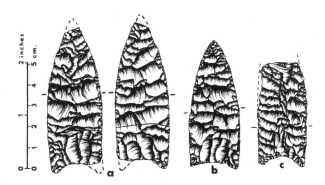

**Figure 11.3.** Projectile points from the Carter/Kerr-McGee 48CA12 (a), Kaufmann Cave 48SH301 (b), and Medicine Lodge Creek 48BH499 (c).

Unfortunately, Mill Iron was a single component Paleoindian site without stratigraphic evidence to support its place in the Paleoindian chronology. Furthermore, it has yielded two distinct populations of radiocabon dates from the same stratigraphic level.

In order to illustrate better the dilemma encountered in trying to distinguish between Goshen and Plainview diagnostics, it is of more than passing interest to take exact casts of both the Mill Iron and Plainview site projectile points, mix them together, and then attempt to separate the two assemblages on the basis of technology and morphology (Haynes 1991; Figure 11.2a-p). From this, it is easy to understand why Henry Irwin finally decided that Goshen should have been labeled Plainview, which would have avoided a good deal of contention, although the problem of the age of the two complexes would still have remained unsolved.

The Carter/Kerr-McGee site 48CA12 in the Powder River Basin in eastern Wyoming is a remnant of a large site that very nearly duplicated the Paleoindian chronology of the Hell Gap site (Frison 1984). At the time of the site investigations (1976), Goshen was still very much a question mark in High Plains Paleoindian studies, and a small assemblage of chipped-stone and bone materials that underlaid a Folsom component and was separated from it by a sterile level was identified as Clovis. After an initial analysis of the Mill Iron site materials, we realized the one complete projectile point, recovered in two pieces (Figure 11.3a), was technologically and morphologically closer to Goshen than to Clovis. Two other Goshen points were recovered in the site area but not in situ.

Another site occurrence of a Goshen projectile point should be mentioned. It was recovered in the lowest cultural level in Kaufmann Cave 48SH301, a small rock shelter in the western Powder River Basin in northern Wyoming. The projectile point (Figure 11.3b) is unmistakably Goshen, and a burned mammoth radius fragment was present at the edge of a hearth in the same level, although the latter is believed to have been par-

tially fossilized at the time it was burned. It still contained some organic material when it was burned, but there is no evidence to suggest that the mammoth was killed during the same time that the Goshen point was left at the site (Grey 1962, 1963).

Midland is another problem to resolve on both the Northern and Northwestern Plains. Irwin-Williams et al. (1973) proposed a Midland cultural complex following Folsom at the Hell Gap site within a suggested time frame of about 8,700 to 8,400 B.C. It is difficult to sort out—on the basis of careful study of the technology and morphology of projectile points from Hell Gap—which ones they labeled Midland and which Goshen. A possibility that can only be suggested at present is that at Hell Gap we might be looking at a stratigraphic sequence from early to later in Locality 1 that is Goshen-Folsom-Goshen instead of Goshen-Folsom-Midland. This, of course, would have required that Goshen and Folsom were separate but coexistent entities.

In Locality 2 at Hell Gap, a Midland level was defined on the strength of a single projectile point (Figure 1.2k), which on the basis of technology and morphology as these concepts are presently understood, could be Goshen as easily as Midland. The fact that some Folsom assemblages from the Northern and Northwestern Plains (e.g., Lindenmeier [Wilmsen and Roberts 1978], Hanson [Frison and Bradley 1980], and Agate Basin [Frison and Stanford 1982]) contain unfluted and pseudo-fluted projectile points (Folsom points in outline form made on flat-sided flakes) as well as fluted points should serve as a cautionary measure in claiming Midland as a cultural complex, at least until more reliable data are available. However, as one of us (Haynes 1991) has argued and the others are willing to accept, until that data are found, we should maintain a definition of Midland (Figure 11.2q–t) as an unfluted Folsom point.

The Middle Park area of Colorado at the headwaters of the Colorado River has potential to yield important information on Goshen-Folsom relationships, but it is still too much in the data-gathering stage to allow definitive statements. The assemblage from the Upper Twin Mountain site 5GA1513 (or Jim Chase site) is too small for meaningful comparisons, although the projectile points recovered there to date fit well both technologically and morphologically in the Mill Iron site assemblage. Neither charcoal or datable bone was recovered, but further

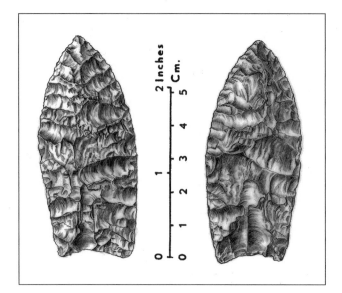

**Figure 11.4.** Projectile point from the Sheaman site 48NA211 in the Agate Basin locality in eastern Wyoming.

investigation may yield datable materials. At this time, however, nothing that can be identified as Folsom has appeared at the Upper Twin Mountain site, which is a small (15 animals) bison kill at an elevation of over 2,500 m. The site evidence does indicate that late Pleistocene bison (probably *B. antiquus*) were year-round residents of the Central Rocky Mountains high-elevation basins and were most likely not migrating out of these locations on a seasonal basis. There is a strong possibility that the Middle Park area of Colorado will eventually be one place to resolve the Goshen-Plainview chronological problem in that part of the region, but whether or not this will pertain to the more northern part of the region remains to be seen (Kornfeld et al. 1993).

Any relationships—cultural and otherwise—between Clovis and Goshen are difficult to perceive. As noted in Chapter 4, there are technological processes in biface production at the Mill Iron site that suggest a more likely relationship to Folsom than to Clovis. Part of the problem here is the extremely small assemblage of bifaces and biface reduction debitage at the Mill Iron site. The statement of Irwin-Williams et al. (1973) of a high incidence of true blades in the Goshen assemblage from the Hell Gap site needs to be better substantiated from a careful study of the assemblage. Should these claims be substantiated and if these blades prove to be the result of a systematic blade production similar to that known for Clovis, this would very likely strengthen claims of Goshen-Clovis relationships. However, there is no doubt that Clovis and Goshen projectile points are significantly different, both morphologically and technologically. Should the analysis of the extant Goshen assemblage collected earlier from the Hell Gap site not yield the needed evidence, then further data recovery from the Hell Gap site may be well justified.

The present thinking with regard to radiocarbon dates on

Clovis between 11,200 B.P. and 10,900 B.P. and Folsom beginning at very close to 10,900 B.P. (Haynes 1992:358) leaves a very small window of time Goshen could have occupied as a discrete cultural entity and at the same time have been derived from Clovis and then have evolved into Folsom. At this time, the only recourse is to almost total speculation: Goshen may have been contemporaneous with the latter part of Clovis, it may have been present between Clovis and Folsom, or it may have appeared at about the same time as Folsom. At this time also, it can be argued that the antecedents of Goshen are as poorly understood as the antecedents of Clovis.

The proposed close relationship between Goshen and Folsom projectile point lithic technology (see Chapter 4) leads to speculation as to whether or not Folsom fluting developed directly from Clovis or independently. The fact that some Folsom assemblages contain fluted, unfluted, and pseudo-fluted projectile points strengthens the possibility that Folsom could have developed directly out of the earlier Goshen complex and still retained much of the latter's lithic technology but added fluting. Further support for this idea lies in the fact that there are no indications of attempts to flute points in the Mill Iron site, the Goshen level at the Hell Gap site, the Upper Twin Mountain site, and from preliminary examinations of the Jim Pitts site assemblage. The present interpretation is that fluting as it appears in Folsom on the Northern and Northwestern plains was a post-Goshen phenomenon since there is no problem in accepting Goshen as a technological precursor of Folsom based on the Mill Iron site evidence (see Chapter 4).

Further development of the basal thinning diagnostic of Goshen projectile points into a true fluting process as seen in Folsom is not difficult to visualize. The possibility that fluting during Folsom times acquired significance beyond pure functional needs is open for speculation (see Frison and Bradley 1982:209–212), but the answer to this kind of inquiry is unlikely to be found in the archaeological record unless the future witnesses unprecedented advances in the methodology of recovery and analysis of site data that will allow retrieval of ritual and social activities.

Another area of research to be explored is that of site assemblages that datewise and technologically do not appear to fit comfortably within Clovis but still contain elements that strongly resemble Clovis. The Sheaman site in the Agate Basin site locality (Frison 1982) is an example. A recent accelerator date from the site is 10,690 ± 105 years B.P. (Beta-25836) which, if correct, seems too late for Clovis. However, the lithic technology at the site which was analyzed from a relatively large quantity of debitage is unquestionably Clovis. Some of the debitage was refitted allowing an even better biface reduction analysis, and the results appear unmistakably Clovis (Bradley 1982) but the one complete projectile point from the site (Figure 11.4), although reminiscent of Clovis, demonstrates what is difficult to identify as true fluting and appears to be more of a basal thinning. A good deal of pressure flaking is also present. The Sheaman site, on the basis of this somewhat nebulous bit of evidence, might be viewed as intermediate between Clovis and Goshen. A cylindrical ivory shaft with a single-beveled end with cross-hachuring identical to that on specimens from the Anzick Clovis Cache (Lahren and Bonnichsen 1974) was recovered at the Sheaman site (Frison and Zeimens 1980:235). Other than this, no mammoth (or possibly mastadon) remains were recovered at the site, and only bison and pronghorn were found. A mammoth rib segment modified into a tool or weapon component was recovered at the Mill Iron site (Figure 4.17). In both cases, the presence of mammoth ivory and bone is not surprising since both the mammoth and mastadon were known to be present during Clovis times, which may overlap Goshen times if the older cluster of Mill Iron site dates is correct.

Stratigraphic interpretations may be leading Paleoindian archaeologists into erroneous conclusions. When we look at a stratified site such as Hell Gap, Agate Basin, or Carter/Kerr-McGee, most of us are tempted to interpret the Paleoindian chronological record as one cultural complex evolving directly out of its stratigraphic antecedent without overlap in time, which does not necessarily have to have been the case. For example, Agate Basin complex radiocarbon dates from the Agate Basin site fall within the range of dates from known Folsom sites. Temporal overlap between Folsom and early Agate Basin has been suggested by both the Hell Gap and type Clovis sites (Haynes and Agogino 1966).

Radiocarbon dates on the Alberta-Cody materials at the Horner site are very nearly the same as Hell Gap complex dates at the Casper site and Alberta dates from the Hell Gap site. It would appear from these examples that there was coexistence of some Paleoindian cultural complexes rather than genesis of each out of an immediately preceeding one, at least on the Northern High Plains. Viewed from this perspective, there are many possible alternatives to be considered for the origins, territorial boundaries, and movements of some of the human groups operating within these cultural complexes.

To further complicate the picture, there appears to have been a dichotomy in human subsistence strategies between the foothill-mountain areas and the open plains during parts of Paleoindian time (see Frison 1992), which could be interpreted as further evidence of the presence of separate Paleoindian co-traditions. The relationship, if any, that Goshen may have had with the foothill-mountain Paleoindian groups is an area of research to pursue since the earliest known levels of some of the foothill-mountains archaeological sites and also surface-collected materials produce diagnostics (projectile points) that are very similar morphologically and technologically to those from the known Goshen site components (Figure 11.3c). Radiocarbon dates on the Goshen-like materials from the foothill-mountain area are around 10,000 years B.P. or about 1,000 years later than Goshen, although the present site sample in foothill-mountain areas is extremely limited. From this we can see that Paleoindian group relationships appear more complex than was realized even a short time ago. Different models can be proposed to demonstrate plains to foothill-mountain relationships but more data are needed even to begin to test any of these models properly.

## Paleoindian Bison Subsistence Strategies

Goshen may be the oldest of the known Paleoindian communal bison hunting groups on the Northwestern High Plains, although the bison kill at Murray Springs (Haynes 1969) in Arizona is indicative of communal bison hunting, at least in that

part of North America during Clovis times. There do not appear to have been paleoecological changes since Clovis times on the High Plains that resulted in the loss of plant species, although shifts of plants to different localities and changes in percentages of species present in different areas can be documented. Changes indicated in the pollen and phytolith record at the Mill Iron site were not of sufficient magnitude to have significantly altered bison numbers or required procurement strategies different from what would succeed at present. According to the pollen evidence, sagebrush may have been more plentiful, but grasses were also present. A close analog of Mill Iron site conditions during Goshen times would be the higher altitude (2,500 m), relatively flat-lying, sagebrush-covered areas adjacent to the mountain ranges in the upper Green River basin in northwest Wyoming, which would be good bison habitat today.

Bison bonebeds can reveal much of human activities that include seasonality through tooth eruption; population dynamics through age structure analysis; butchering, processing and utilization through osteological study; procurement through animal behavior and reconstructions of old landforms; and ecological reconstructions through pollen and phytolith analysis. As much as archaeologists like to recover data that place human behavior in neat boxes and categories, it would appear that all of these multidisciplinary bodies of data would provide the necessary information to reconstruct the cultural activities involved in subsistence strategies of the human groups involved. This, however, is not the case. The unpredictability of the length, intensity, and distribution of storms and cold periods of any given Northern Plains winter would have affected both the availability of feed for the animals and their behavioral responses and consequently determine the procurement strategy that would best apply.

Long-term changes in climate, such as glacial advances and retreats and wet and dry periods, can be detected in the paleoclimatic record. However, short-term changes in climate are not yet detectable. For example, the winter of 1886–87 on the Northern Plains was disastrous to domestic cattle and decimated most of the few remaining bison. The dust bowl days of the 1930s dramatically reduced the natural forage in the same area so that livestock either had to be moved to areas not affected or they required artificial feeding. During the winter of 1992–93, mule deer and pronghorn populations were seriously reduced in southern Wyoming because of snow and ice conditions that covered the feed supply: the winter of 1993–94 was the exact opposite with the same animals in nearly as good condition at the end as they were at its beginning. These kinds of short-term events had little effect on the major climatic episodes of the past, but to prehistoric peoples with very little in the way of protection between them and the environment, a bad winter could have been disastrous without some kind of stored surplus. The problem was that these kinds of winters were not and still are not predictable, and the human group always had to plan and prepare for the worst.

Archaeologists may have tended to place Paleoindian bison hunting groups into lifeways with subsistence strategies that are too narrowly focused toward bison procurement alone. The communal type of bison kill strategies indicated by such sites as Mill Iron, Agate Basin (Frison and Stanford 1982), Casper (Frison 1974), Hudson Meng (Agenbroad 1978), and Horner (Frison and Todd 1987) to mention a few, may represent only a small increment of the total range of subsistence activities and only those that are the most visible archaeologically. Stratified sites such as Agate Basin, Carter/Kerr-McGee, and Hell Gap indicate use of the locations throughout Paleoindian times but not occupations of a magnitude that suggest long-term, repeated annual returns to the same locations for large-scale bison hunting episodes. Bison bonebeds in the sites such as those mentioned above appear to have been the result of either discrete events or events repeated only a time or two. None contains the accumulations of bone, tools, and weaponry that would be expected if these sites were used for the same kind of communal bison procurement repeatedly, year after year, for long aggregates of years.

The bison kills at Mill Iron and other Paleoindian bison kills on the Northern Plains were cold weather kills as determined by tooth eruption schedules (Figure 11.5 and Chapter 8), but there is wide variation in the time during the cold season from late fall to early spring and also in the number of animals involved. Some are single, catastrophic events, while others suggest accumulations of smaller numbers of animals over one to several months during the cold season. This could be the results of conditions imposed by different winter weather patterns from year to year: periods of good weather favorable for coummunal bison hunting almost always occur between late October and the end of March during any given winter. However, these periods are not predictable because it is highly unlikely that any two consecutive winters will be the same. It was probably a situation of waiting until weather conditions were favorable. Such decisions would not have required scheduling ahead of time and when favorable conditions materialized could have been made early on the actual day of a kill.

There is no certain predictability either of the location of concentrations of bison from winter to winter. Bison readily and rapidly change locations in response to grass conditions and to avoid areas of deep snow, both of which can change rapidly over short distances depending on the seemingly capricious nature of annual precipitation and temperature. There can be good grass in an area one year, and it can be relatively barren of feed the next. Catastrophic events, such as hail storms, are common

**Figure 11.5.** Mandible from a calf killed in winter at the Mill Iron site. Note the deterioration of the overlying bones.

events on the plains and can destroy grass in wide strips, causing bison to move to a territory not hailed out. Careful monitoring of these conditions was necessary to be aware of bison procurement possibilities.

Topography is a limiting factor in communal bison procurement: they react differently to hunters in flat, open country from the way they do in rough and/or timbered or brushy areas. Natural traps require the proper geomorphic feature for access and containment of the animals. Corral construction depended on the availability of trees of proper size. There were limits also on the distances that bison could be successfully moved on a predictive basis by foot hunters. It may be that archaeologists are dealing with only the most visible evidence in the form of bison bonebeds, rather than the mainstream of subsistence activities. Communal Paleoindian bison kills undoubtedly produced surplusses, but whether this was necessarily done on an annual basis needs to be further investigated. Paleoindian communal bison kills may have been as important for social and ritual needs as for economic ones and could have occurred at irregular intervals as needed rather than as scheduled annual events.

The hunters had one advantage over bison in that the latter are quite predictable under given conditions—both external, such as weather, feed, and time of day or year, and internal, such as sex, age, and body condition. It was the conditions that could not be altered by the hunters but did have to be carefully monitored in order to put the proper procurement strategy in place that were the greatest concerns. Communal hunting might have been the most desirable strategy but could not always have been the most feasible because of conditions beyond the hunters' control.

Consequently, there was no such thing as a single bison procurement strategy. Success required the continual acquisition of information through monitoring not only the animals but also the elements that determined animal behavior. The bottom line is that the animals stood little chance in their life or death contests with well-trained human predators, but most of the conditions imposed were beyond the hunters' control and certainly not always what they would have preferred. Whatever the procurement strategy, it would have had to function within the restraints imposed by animal behavior and the environment, both of which could change rapidly.

There is no doubt of the adequacy for Goshen and other Paleoindian projectile points to kill bison, as experiments on modern bison have confirmed. Used with atlatl and dart, penetration of the rib cage produces internal bleeding with demise of the animal within a short period of time. Less well placed projectiles produce crippling wounds but ones that eventually assure the experienced hunter of success. The question was raised at Mill Iron if one projectile point (Figures 4.3d and 11.6) was used as a weapon or an offering for ritual purposes. An argument was made in Chapter 4 that although the quality of the technology expressed on this specimen is unexcelled in any known prehistoric flint knapping context, its morphology is not that of a functional piece of weaponry needed for killing large animals such as bison. No archaeologist can dismiss the lessons from ethnological studies which describe the ritual activities that accompany large animal procurement.

**Figure 11.6.** Projectile in situ in the Mill Iron bone bed. Could it have been a ritual offering instead of a weapon used to kill animals?

## Taphonomic Studies

Since the introduction of taphonomic principles into the study of Paleoindian archaeology more than two decades ago, no other approach has aided the interpretation of site data to the same extent. Taphonomic data are both readily observable and quantifiable and add badly needed support to archaeology, which often has difficulty defending itself as a true science. Equally important is the fact that taphonomic applications to archaeological data have expanded and show no signs of diminishing. The seasonality and bone density studies of the Mill Iron faunal materials (Chapters 7 and 8) allow an expanded base upon which to interpret past human activities. They also open the door to alternative explanations, which in turn opens the door to further research. They allow exploration of ideas that may not be at all obvious because of conditions that resulted in preservation of only selected parts of the total data base.

The use of taphonomy in certain archaeological contexts has unquestionably provided more reliable interpretations—of natural bone deterioration; carnivore, scavenger, and human alteration of bone; and butchering and processing of animal carcasses for human consumption—than were available a decade ago. Refinement of animal aging through both tooth eruption and bone ossification analysis provides a closer monitoring of Paleoindian hunting practices. The question always arises whether or or not bonebeds, such as the one at Mill Iron, represent an actual animal kill, a scavenged natural die-off, a catastrophic kill, or something else. Seasonality of kill events can rule out some events: for example, a winter kill could indicate animals that were trapped in a snowdrift-filled arroyo but not ones killed by a summer lightning storm.

The manner in which scavengers and carnivores alter faunal materials in contrast to humans is increasingly better understood. Some kinds of evidence found on bones once thought to be from human activities can now be demonstrated beyond a doubt to have been done by carnivores. Cutmarks and wear patterns can sometimes be demonstrated to occur from causes other than human butchering and processing, although some of these still cannot be separated unequivocally.

No two known Paleoindian bison bonebeds reflect the same cultural activities. The Casper site, for example, is a primary kill using a parabolic sand dune, and the butchered carcasses were left where they were killed. The same is probably true of the Alberta-Cody component at the Horner site, although use of an artificial restraining structure is postulated, but unequivocal evidence of such a feature is not present. The main Agate Basin bonebed at the Agate Basin site is believed to be a pile of surplus butchered bison carcass units that were frozen and used as needed throughout the winter. The bone remaining around the pile of carcass units appears to be what remained after carcass units were processed and utilized as food. The actual kill area location is not known but was probably a natural arroyo trap in the immediate vicinity. If, as suggested in Chapter 7, the Mill Iron bonebed is the scene of an actual kill, evidence of some kind of artificial restraining structure should be present. If, however, the bonebed is a dump for butchered bone, the kill area could have been nearby in some sort of natural trap.

Many Mill Iron bones demonstrate what appears to be postdepositional burning of the exposed surfaces, which could have been accidental. The events of the animal kill would have encouraged the growth of lush annual weeds during the summer following the kill, which would burn easily from either natural or human causes. Burning was common in later bison kills, but the causes are a matter of conjecture with a good deal of disagreement among different investigators.

Unexpected problems of bone recovery were encountered at the Mill Iron site. The normal procedure of strengthening bone with white glue before casting and removal proved unsuccessful. In this case the mixture refused to penetrate the bone and dried instead forming an undesirable surface film. Better results were obtained with a different water-mixed chemical (Acrysol) in conjunction with light plaster casts. Apparently the problem was the fact that the Mill Iron bone contained an unusual amount of unidentified salts that formed delicate, web-like crystals when the bone dried (Figure 7.16). In the final analysis, the study of the Mill Iron bonebed (Chapters 7 and 8) represents a significant advance in taphonomic method. Bone density studies will undoubtedly be incorporated into all future studies of Paleoindian and other bonebeds.

## Radiocarbon Dates

The accelerator dates on charcoal from both the bonebed and camp-processing areas at the Mill Iron site fall into two groups (see Table 1.1), but what this actually means in terms of the Paleoindian cultural chronology is open to question. It could indicate two separate site usages over 200 years apart, which is unlikely to have been the case. The oldest of the dates from the camp-processing area are about 11,250 years B.P. and are from charcoal that was derived from what is believed to have been a cultural surface hearth. If these dates are correct, it would place Goshen contemporaneous with Clovis. The younger group of dates is around 10,900 years B.P. which, if correct, would place Goshen contemporaneous with the oldest of the known Folsom dates or possibly between Clovis and Folsom. Although unproven, the older dates could represent the use of long-dead pine logs which the pollen evidence indicated would have been available. The presence of a fragment of low-grade coal in the bonebed raises the problem of contamination and the need for extreme care in collecting radiocarbon samples for dating.

## Raw Stone-Flaking Material Sources

In looking at the different raw materials used at the Mill Iron site for tool and weaponry manufacture, they appear more locally oriented than might be expected, based on evidence from other Northern Plains Paleoindian sites. The Mill Iron site is not far from the Knife River sources, but this material was not found there as it was at the Agate Basin and Horner sites located at much greater distances from the Knife River source. The only exotic material at Mill Iron is what is likely Hartville Uplift chert from eastern Wyoming about 400 km away. Absent also was the not-too-distant Phosphoria (Permian) and Amsden (Pennsylvanian) Formation cherts of exceptional quality from the Big Horn Mountains in north central Wyoming. The local Arikaree chert was utilized and is adequate but not of a quality chosen by most Paleoindian knappers. On the other hand, most of the petrified or silicified woods utilized by the Mill Iron knappers is of good quality. They were using excellent grades of porcellanite, which is common in the Fort Union Formation throughout northeast Wyoming and southeast Montana and may have negated the need for the more exotic stone-flaking materials.

In contrast, the Folsom and Agate Basin components at the Agate Basin site in eastern Wyoming contained Knife River flint, Flat Top (northern Colorado) chert, Niobrara chert and plate chalcedony from Nebraska and South Dakota respectively. Along with this were several more local materials, including Hartville Uplift cherts and quartzite and petrified woods. At the Horner site (Cody complex) in northwest Wyoming, Knife River flint, Flat Top chert, and Alibates (Texas Panhandle) silicified dolomite was recovered. Clovis caches such as Simon (Butler 1963), Anzick (Lahren and Bonnichsen 1974), and Fenn (Frison 1991a) contain exotic materials from widespread sources.

Unfortunately, many stone-flaking materials are found in so many locations over so large an area and are so similar mineralogically that pinning site samples to a given source is difficult if not impossible unless better means of separation of these sources is developed. With the amount and quality of stone flaking materials available, all Paleoindian groups shoud have been able to obtain what they needed without exploiting subsurface deposits. On the other hand, the effort expended in obtaining subsurface materials by some prehistoric groups raises the possibility that there was always the hope of acquiring something special in the way of stone-flaking materials and that these efforts were driven by more than purely economic needs. Furthermore, when the Paleoindian flintknapper did acquire a piece of superior raw stone-flaking material, it was followed by an attempt to produce something special.

## The Organization of Goshen-Plainview Technology

Consideration of raw materials, tool types, and use-wear and their spatial distribution presents some interesting information about Goshen-Plainview chipped-stone technological organization, site formation, and taphonomy at the Mill Iron site. Theoretical approaches to hunter-gatherer technological organization have been used successfully to make inferences about chipped-stone raw material procurement, production, use, discard, and loss (e.g., Bamforth 1986; Bleed 1986; Geneste 1985; Hofman 1991; Larson 1990; Nelson 1991).

The presence of numerous finished or nearly finished tools of different materials in both the camp-processing and bonebed areas suggests prior planning and use of existing tool kits for the activities pursued at the Mill Iron site. The projectile points provide the best evidence for curation. No evidence for projectile point manufacture exists, and the points tend to be manufactured out of non-local raw materials, indicating that, at least some of these points were likely carried for the longest time of any of the chipped-stone items found at Mill Iron. As well, scrapers and utilized flakes were brought into the site from other places, either as finished tools or on cores from which the tools were removed. In the case of scrapers and utilized flakes, little evidence of manufacture exists with some raw materials, but there is evidence of resharpening before discard. Since utilized flakes are the most plentiful tool type and occur in all raw material types that also have much manufacturing debris (Tables 4.2 and 4.3), some of these tools were likely manufactured on the site for immediate use. Microwear evidence of ridge rounding and multiple uses prior to a tool's final use at Mill Iron, suggests that the tools were used in a technological system that curated raw materials or particular tool shapes for multiple uses. The few bifaces at Mill Iron (n = 9) are enigmatic in their use traces, fragmentation, and raw materials. Dark brown petrified/silicified wood, of local origin, constitutes the most prevalent biface raw material type at Mill Iron, with Arikaree chert and an unidentified chert making up the remainder (Table 4.3). Either bifaces were a small part of the technology brought to Mill Iron, or bifaces were used as cores, with only a few being discarded or lost. The presence of a blade-flake technology, rather than a bifacial technology suggests the former.

As indicated by tool morphology and use-wear analysis, scraping, tool production, and tool maintenance constitute the primary activities represented in the stone assemblage from the camp-processing area at the Mill Iron site. However, the question of whether the chipped-stone remains represent activity areas or dumps remains unanswered (Chapter 2). The distribution of chipped-stone remains differs between the northern and southern parts of the camp area.

In the north, core reduction debris of primarily petrified/silicified wood and Tongue River silicified sediment predominates in the area of N19–20, W19–22, although smaller quantities of many raw materials and production debris are evident (Figures 2.8–2.11). The highest quantity of core regularization debris was found in two areas in the north: in the same area as the core reduction debris and centered on N16.5, W22 (see Figures 2.15–2.17). At the same time, tools are located slightly to the east of the production debris at N17–19, W18–20.5 (Figure 5.1a). The location of microwear IUZs (independent use zones), indicative of more highly/intensely used tools or tool edges, rather than individual tools, differs from both the production debris and tool distributions. Two peaks in IUZ distribution center on N18–W18 and N16.5–W21 (Figure 5.1b). Use-wear analysis also suggests that the tools found in the northern area were more heavily curated than those in the south (Chapter 5).

In the southern area of the camp, the highest density of production debris, tools, and IUZs cluster around one area, at N11–13, W21–23 (Figures 2.8–2.22, 5.1a, and b). Northern and southern areas are linked to one another by the refitted TRSS Core #1 (Figure 2.12). Here, the remains are of tool maintenance debris and scrapers manufactured from curated blanks (Chapters 4 and 5). The distribution of raw materials, tools, IUZs, and refitted pieces in the camp-processing area as a whole provides no easy solution to the question of whether the north and south areas in the camp represent discrete activity areas or dumps. However, the separation of high-density areas of production debris, IUZs, and tools in the north and the differences between the northern and southern tool and production types suggest that activity areas may be the most parsimonious explanation.

While the study of taphonomy using faunal and other organic remains is well developed and contributes greatly to our understanding of the formation of Mill Iron and other sites, the use of "microwear taphonomy" as defined in Chapter 5 provides further information not usually found in taphonomic or technological analyses. The presence of differential surface modification of raw materials and tool types and spatial differences in their distribution suggest the complex and not fully understood nature of the formation of the Mill Iron site in both the camp-processing and bonebed areas.

The recognition that discarded tools may carry with them important traces of their lives prior to their most recent use and that—at least at Mill Iron—these traces are complicated forms the basis for further behavioral inferences about the technological organization at the Mill Iron site. The traces of multiple use at Mill Iron make "sorting out" a particular tool's function difficult. For example, many of the Mill Iron scrapers carry with them traces of use not related to scraping, and the same is true with other tool types (see Chapter 5). This suggests that Goshen-Plainview tool kits, at least those parts discarded or lost at Mill Iron, were much more generalized and were altered to meet the immediate needs of the user. At some level, this could be used as evidence for support of Kelly and Todd's (1988) highly mobile early Paleoindian groups traveling about the landscape, as specialized hunters would require specialized tools, but the traces of multiple use on several Mill Iron tools bring questions to their argument that the high mobility was related to the search for bison. Instead, as is argued above, and elsewhere (Frison 1991a; Kornfeld 1988; Meltzer 1988), that Paleoindian subsistence and settlement may have been much less focused on bison and much more generalized for the low-density population of late Pleistocene hunter-gatherers found throughout North America. Further *in-depth* analyses of the technological systems represented by debitage, microwear, raw materials, spatial patterning, and analytical nodules at Goshen-Plainview sites including Carter/Kerr-McGee, Kaufmann Cave, Hell Gap, Upper Twin Mountain, and the Jim Pitts site will provide a means of testing some of the propositions made by Paleoindian researchers.

## Paleoecological Considerations

It is impossible to understand the parameters of archaeological site formation without a knowledge of the geological processes that were the causal agents. This is particularly true in the case of northern High Plains Paleoindian sites that have been around for longer times and survived more sequences of aggradation and degradation. Most northern High Plains Paleoindian sites barely survived: a small added amount of lateral erosion or downcutting in most cases would have eliminated all evidence. The causes of abrupt changes from arroyo filling to headcutting are not fully understood, but there is ample evidence of their occurrences.

Arroyos figured prominently in Paleoindian lifeways: arroyo bison traps were common so that extended periods of arroyo filling had to affect bison procurement. The ability to identify old landforms and the geologic activities that brought about their present configuration is a necessary tool for the archaeologist but is usually provided by special consultants. Even the partial reconstruction of old landforms from old remnants is a skill learned only from careful study and long experience. As in the case of archaeology, no two geoarchaeologists view the same data and arrive at the same conclusions. An area that has experienced as extensive an amount of erosion and filling as the Fort Union Formation soft bedrock exposures in southeast Montana can be an especially difficult area in which to attempt to reconstruct landforms as they were 11,000 or so years ago. For all of the Paleoecological expertise involved in the Mill Iron site investigation and analysis, there is still no evidence that unequivocally ties the bison bonebed and the camp-processing areas together as activities involved with the same event.

It must be admitted that the discovery of a buried Late Archaic component on the east end of the Mill Iron site butte came as a distinct surprise. The fact that it lies within a sedimentary unit that is separate and distinct from the sedimentary unit that contains the Goshen component (see Figure 1.18) is not yet satisfactorily explained to everyone's satisfaction. We know also that part of the bison bonebed was undercut postdepositionally on one side (see Figure 1.20), but the course and source of the causal agent are not yet proven.

All of these unanswered questions and many others will eventually build to the extent that someone in the future will have an adequate excuse to return to the Mill Iron site for further investigations. When the data from geological activity, soils, fauna, pollen, and phytoliths are compiled to reconstruct past environments, then the human group and the cultural data can be added with the expectation of more reliable cultural inference. Further improvement of techniques to allow better interpretation of these paleoecological factors will undoubtedly occur, and then there will be a need to reanalyze the old data along with a return to the sites for collection of new data.

## The Future of Goshen and Related Paleoindian Studies

Stratified, high-integrity Paleoindian sites have not appeared on the High Plains as frequently as hoped and expected, given the amount of earth disturbances from a wide range of activities over the past few decades. This should make all Paleoindian archaeologists cautious in using up any of the extant, relatively high-integrity Paleoindian deposits without making sure there are legitimate research questions to pursue. Further excavations at the Mill Iron site would be difficult to justify at present, but this could change within the next decade. There could be a Goshen component or components at the Agate Basin site, but this is not proven. Confirming this one way or the other would very likely entail expensive and detailed investigations, since most of the Paleoindian components known to be present there are deeply buried in alluvial and colluvial stream deposits and the context of others remains to be determined through geoarchaeological study. The Agate Basin site would probably not be a good choice if the investigators are seeking only Goshen evidence and not Paleoindian in general. The Middle Park area of Colorado still remains largely unknown, and limited investigations there may eventually provide both stratigraphic and radiocarbon data needed.

As was pointed out in the introduction (Chapter 1), the first evidence of Goshen was recognized at the Hell Gap site (Irwin-Williams et al. 1973) and this site still remains the best candidate for future research. In 1993, the stratigraphic profile (Figure 11.1) was reexposed after 27 years and a charcoal sample was collected from the Clovis (now Goshen-Plainview) level that yielded an AMS date of 10,955 ± 135 years B.P. (AA-14434). This date agrees closely with the younger series of AMS dates from the Mill Iron site and adds a strong measure of support for the Mill Iron site results and also for the age of the Goshen-Plainview Cultural Complex at about the end of Clovis times and the beginning of Folsom times on the Northern High Plains. However, the materials collected over a quarter of a century ago during the 1957–1966 Hell Gap site investigations need to be analyzed before any extensive excavation work is undertaken.

There is a good possibility that the higher altitudes will eventually yield information pertinent to the Goshen-Plainview problem. Goshen-Plainview diagnostics occur continually on the surface from the foothills to timberline. At this time there is very little stratigraphic evidence to work with, but there are high-altitude sites with good promise.

In the meantime, there is always the possibility that the ideal site will be found that will solve the chronological and other problems posed for a number of years on the Goshen Paleoindian cultural complex. Given the present geographic spread of Goshen evidence, this could occur almost anywhere on the northern High Plains. The Jim Pitts 39CU1142 site in western South Dakota mentioned above with a good sample of unmistakably Goshen-Plainview projectile points (Figure 11.7a–d) along with tools (Figure 11.7f) from a level below and separated by a sterile level from an overlying level that produced a Folsom point (Figure 11.7e) may be one of these sites.

In final conclusion, the difficulties with dropping the name Goshen as suggested by Henry Irwin in favor of Plainview are too many to consider at this time. Until the true chronological position of Goshen as pre-Folsom on the Northern Plains and as post-Folsom on the Southern Plains is resolved, the two terms are needed. The compromise at this point is to call the Northern Plains material Goshen-Plainview, so that the separation between the northern and southern materials is maintained. This can always be changed when new data demand a change.

**Figure 11.7.** Artifacts from the Jim Pitts site 39CU1142 in the western Black Hills area of South Dakota. Broken Goshen-Plainview points: a–d; Folsom point: e; a tool from the Goshen-Plainview level: f. (Specimens courtesy of James Donohue.)

## References Cited

Agenbroad, Larry D.
1978    *The Hudson-Meng site: An Alberta Bison Kill in the Nebraska High Plains.* University Press of America, Washington, D.C.

Bamforth, Douglas B.
1986    Technological Efficiency and Tool Curation. *American Antiquity* 45:1–17.

Bleed, Peter
1986    The Optimal Design of Hunting Weapons: Maintainability or Reliability? *American Antiquity* 51:737–747.

Bradley, Bruce A.
1982    Flaked Stone Technology and Typology. In *The Agate Basin Site: A Record of the Paleoindian Occupation of the Northwestern High Plains,* edited by G. C. Frison and D. J. Stanford, pp. 181–121. Academic Press, New York.

Butler, B. Robert
1963    An Early Man site at Big Camas Prairie, South-Central Idaho. *Tebiwa* 6(1):22–33.

Frison, George C.
1974    *The Casper Site: A Hell Gap Bison Kill on the High Plains.* Academic Press, New York.
1982    The Sheaman Site. In *The Agate Basin Site: A Record of the Paleoindian Occupation of the Northwestern High Plains,* edited by G. C. Frison and D. J. Stanford, pp. 143–157. Academic Press, New York.
1984    The Carter/Kerr-McGee Paleoindian Site: Cultural Resource Management and Archaeological Research. *American Antiquity* 49(2):288–314.
1991a    *Prehistoric Hunters of the High Plains.* 2d ed. Academic Press, Orlando.
1991b    The Clovis Cultural Complex: New Data from Caches of Flaked Stone and Worked Bone Artifacts. In *Raw Material Economies among Prehistoric Hunter-Gatherers,* edited by Anta Montet-White and Steven Holen, pp. 321–334. University of Kansas Publications in Anthropology 19.
1992    The Foothills-Mountains and the Open Plains: A Dichotomy in Paleoindian Subsistence Strategies between two Ecosystems. In *Ice Age Hunters of the Rockies,* edited by Dennis J. Stanford and Jane S. Day, pp. 323–342. Denver Museum of Natural History and University Press of Colorado.

Frison, George C., and Bruce A. Bradley
1980    *Folsom Tools and Technology at the Hanson Site, Wyoming.* University of New Mexico Press, Albuquerque.

Frison, George C., and Dennis J. Stanford
1982    *The Agage Basin Site: A Record of the Paleoindian Occupation of the Northwestern High Plains.* Academic Press, New York.

Frison, George C., and Lawrence C. Todd
1987    *The Horner Site: The Type Site of the Cody Cultural Complex.* Academic Press, Orlando.

Frison, George C., and George N. Zeimens
1980    Bone Projectile Points: An Addition to the Folsom Cultural Complex. *American Antiquity* 45(2):231–237.

Geneste, J. M.
1985    *Analyse Lithique d'Industries Mousteriennes du Perig-*

ord: *Une Approche Technologique du Comportement des Groups Humains au Paleolothique Moyen.* These de Docteur, Universite de Bordeaux I, France.

Grey, Donald C.
1962    The Bentzen-Kaufmann Cave Site 48SH301. *Plains Anthropologist* 7(18):237–245.
1963    Fossil Mammoth Bone from Kaufmann Cave. *Plains Anthropologist* 8(19):53–54.

Haynes, C. Vances Jr.
1969    The Earliest Americans. *Science* 166:709–715.
1991    Clovis-Folsom-Midland-Plainview Geochronology. Paper presented at the 56th Annual Meeting of the Society for American Archaeology, New Orleans.
1992    Contributions of Radiocarbon Dating to the Geochronology of the Peopling of the New World. In *Radiocarbon after four Decades,* edited by R. E. Taylor, A. Long, and R. Kra, pp. 355–374. University of Arizona Press, Tucson.

Haynes, C. Vance Jr., and George A. Agogino
1966    Prehistoric Springs and Geochronology of the Clovis Site, New Mexico. *American Antiquity* 31(6):812–821.

Hofman, Jack
1991    Folsom Land Use: Projectile Point Variability as a Key to Mobility. In *Raw Material Economies among Prehistoric Hunters and Gatherers,* edited by Anta Montet-White and Steven Holen, pp. 335–356. University of Kansas publications in Anthropology 19.

Irwin, Henry T.
1971    Developments in Early Man studies in Western North America, 1960–1970. *Arctic Anthropology* 8(2):42–67.

Irwin-Williams, Cynthia, Henry T. Irwin, George Agogino, and C. Vance Haynes, Jr.
1973    Hell Gap: Paleo-Indian Occupation on the High Plains. *Plains Anthropologist* 18(59):40–53.

Kelly, Robert L., and Larry C. Todd
1988    Coming into the Country: Early Paleoindian Hunting and Mobility. *American Antiquity* 53(2):231–244.

Kornfeld, Marcel
1988    The Rocky Folsom Site: A Small Folsom Assemblage from the Northwestern Plains. *North American Archaeologist* 9:197–222.

Kornfeld, Marcel, Jan Saysette, and James Miller
1993    Goshen-Plainview Complex at Upper Twin Mountain Sites, Colorado: One Avenue for Future Research. Unpublished manuscript on file at the Department of Anthropology, University of Wyoming.

Lahren, Larry A., and Robson Bonnichsen
1974    Bone Foreshafts from a Clovis Burial in Southwestern Montana. *Science* 186:147–150.

Larson, Mary Lou
1990    *Early Plains Archaic Technological Organization: The Laddie Creek Example.* Ph.D. dissertation, Department of Anthropology, University of California, Santa Barbara. University Microfilms, Ann Arbor.

Meltzer, David J.
1988    Late Pleistocene Human Adaptation in Eastern North America. *Journal of World Prehistory* 2:1–52.

Nelson, Margaret
1991    The Study of Technological Organization. In *Archaeological Method and Theory,* Volume 3, edited by M. B. Schiffer, pp. 57–100. University of Arizona Press, Tucson.

Sellards, E. H., Glen L. Evans, and Grayson E. Meade
1947    Fossil Bison and Associated Artifacts from Plainview, Texas, with Description of Artifacts by Alex D. Krieger. *Bulletin of the Geological Society of America* 58:927–954.

Stafford, Michael D.
1990    The Powars II Site (48PL330): A Paleoindian Red Ochre Mine in Eastern Wyoming. Unpublished Master's thesis, Department of Anthropology, University of Wyoming.

Wilmsen, Edwin N., and Frank H. H. Roberts
1978    Lindenmeier, 1934–1974. *Smithsonian Contributions to Anthropology* No. 24.

# The Mill Iron Site Local Fauna

DANNY N. WALKER
Office of Wyoming State Archaeologist
GEORGE C. FRISON
University of Wyoming

Walker (1987) and Graham, Wilson, and Graham (1987) reviewed the known status of late Pleistocene and Holocene vertebrate faunas of Wyoming and Montana. At that time, no local faunas were known from southeastern Montana, including Carter County. Excavations at the Mill Iron site during the period 1985–1988 resulted in recovery of such a fauna (Table A1.1). Ten taxa (one amphibian, one reptile, and eight mammals) were recovered from cultural deposits, primarily from the campsite or processing area (Figure A1.1), at the Mill Iron site (see also Chapter 1). *Bison antiquus* was the only taxon recovered from the bonebed area of the site. These ten taxa are included in what is here defined as the Mill Iron local fauna (Stephens 1960). The fauna is late-glacial/Pre-Boreal in age, based on radiometric dates from the occupation level. Only one taxon is extinct *(Bison antiquus),* while a second *(Microtus longicaudus)* is not reported from the extant, modern fauna.

This fauna was recovered by two processes. The first involved normal archaeological excavation techniques. This resulted in recovery of most remains of the larger forms. Some of the smaller rodents were also recovered during excavations. The second process involved a technique adapted from Hibbard (1949), using fine screen (16-mesh) and water under low pressure. The two methods were complementary and resulted in a high level of recovery.

The minimum number of individuals (Table A1.1) was determined by counting the most common element of each species. Calculation of bison minimum numbers also involved adding immature or very old animals represented by other elements (see Kreutzer, this volume, Chapter 7; Todd, this volume, Chapter 8). Kreutzer's analysis concerns only the bison bonebed. Identified bison bone recovered from the camp-processing area is presented in Table A1.2. Ribs are not included due to the extremely fragmented nature of their occurrence.

The top surfaces of bison bones from this area are badly decomposed (Figures 1.11 and A1.2), while the bottom surfaces in many cases are nearly pristine, indicating that there was little if any movement of the bone after initial deposition. How-

ever, the site is on a slope and as the exposed bone surfaces weathered, the exfoliated fragments moved downslope creating a surface cover in some areas resembling bone gravel.

Bison bone in the camp-processing area demonstrates very little in the way of modification by rodents except for the modified mammoth rib (Figure 4.17). In this case, the human use very likely resulted in the transfer of salt and other residue attractive to rodents. In this case also, the rodent activity could have occurred when the tool was used in activities prior to those at the Mill Iron site.

Bone breakage in the camp-processing area is believed to be mostly the result of human processing activities. This is further supported by the tool assemblage that is strongly oriented toward these kinds of activities. For example, the breakage of the femur in Figure 1.11 is typical of that produced by a hammerstone to gain access to the marrow cavity. Also identified in the bone assemblage were at least two bison bone "impact cones" produced by hammerstone blows at the point of impact located at right angles to long bone surfaces.

The minimum number of individual bison in the camp-processing area could very likely be increased with an intense effort at identifying more of the fragmentary bone. However, in combination with tool assemblage, it strongly supports processing activities involved with the utilization of the bison remains as human food.

## Systematic Descriptions

Abbreviations used in subsequent discussions of the faunal members are as follows: UWA = University of Wyoming Anthropology collections; M = molar; P = premolar; C = canine; I = incisor, with maxillary and mandibular specimens being upper and lower case, respectively. The abbreviation cf. is used in the sense of "showing affinities toward." MNI and NISP = "minimum number of individuals" and "number of identified specimens," respectively.

**Figure A1.1.** Excavations in progress in the camp-processing area of the Mill Iron site.

**Table A1.1.** The Mill Iron Local Fauna with MNI and NISP.

| Taxon | MNI | NISP |
|---|---|---|
| *Rana* sp. | 2 | 2 |
| *Pituophus melaneoleucus sayi* | 1 | 1 |
| *Spermophilus* cf. *tridecemlineatus* | 1 | 2 |
| *Thomomys talpoides* | 2 | 10 |
| *Reithrodontomys* cf. *megalotis* | 1 | 1 |
| *Peromyscus* sp. | 1 | 1 |
| *Microtus longicaudus* | 2 | 3 |
| *Microtus ochrogaster* | 1 | 2 |
| *M. ochrogaster* or *longicaudus* | 2 | 1 |
| *Microtus* sp. | 1 | 4 |
| Small rodent | 1 | 14 |
| *Mammuthus* sp. | 1 | 1 |
| *Bison bison* cf. *antiquus** | 1 | 1 |

*For NISP and MNI values of *Bison,* see Tables 7.13, 8.7, 8.8, and A2.2.

**Class Amphibia**
Order Anura
Family Ranidae
Genus cf. *Rana*—Frog

**Geologic range of species:** Miocene to Recent in North America (Romer 1966:364).

**Geographic distribution:** Ranid frogs are widespread across North America east of the Great Basin (Stebbins 1966:70–77). Ranid frogs occur in the vicinity of the Mill Iron site today (personal observations).

**Habitat:** As with most frogs, ranid species frequent springs, creeks, rivers, ponds, canals, and reservoirs where permanent water and abundant aquatic vegetation are found (Bernard and Brown 1978:88–91; Stebbins 1966:75–76).

**Material:** 24CT30-1626: pelvis fragment; 24CT30-1627: pelvis fragment.

**Discussion:** These two specimens are provisionally referred to this genus based on size and morphological similarity to known specimens in the UWA comparative collection. No evidence could be found that the presence of these specimens in the site deposits was due to cultural usage.

**Class Reptilia**
Order Squamata
Family Colubridae
Genus *Pituophus*
*Pituophus melanoleucus*—Gopher Snake

**Geologic range of species:** Pleistocene to Recent in North America (Romer 1966:367).

**Geographic distribution:** Several subspecies of the gopher snake occur throughout North America (Stebbins 1966:156–157). *P. m. sayi* (bullsnake) occurs in the vicinity of the Mill Iron site today (personal observation).

**Habitat:** Gopher snakes are frequently found in several habitats, including "desert, prairie, brushland, woodlands, coniferous forest" (Stebbins 1966:156). The normal habitat of the bullsnake is the "grasslands, sagebrush, and scarp woodlands" of the plains (Baxter and Stone 1980:109).

**Material:** 24CT30-1612: three vertebrae.

**Discussion:** These vertebrae are assigned to this species based on size and general morphological similarities to known bullsnakes in the UWA comparative collection. No other colubrid snake of relative size is known from this region of the plains (Stebbins 1966:156–157). No evidence for cultural usage of this snake was seen, and its presence in the site is probably due to natural causes.

**Class Mammalia**
Order Rodentia
Family Sciuridae
Genus *Spermophilus*
*Spermophilus* cf. *tridecemlineatus*—Thirteen-Lined
Ground Squirrel

**Geologic range of species:** Middle Pleistocene (Illinoian, possibly Kansan) to Recent in North America (Hibbard 1970:419–430).

**Geographic distribution:** This ground squirrel, the smallest of the genus, is found throughout the plains and prairie regions of North America (Hall 1981:391–394). It is found in Montana east of the Continental Divide (Hoffman and Pattie 1968:39). Lampe et al. (1974:12) record the species from throughout this portion of Carter County.

**Habitat:** Lampe et al. (1974:12) found this species to be "common in short grass and sagebrush throughout the area of study." It is normally found in tall grass or brushy contacts between tall grass and herbaceous vegetation (Hoffman and Pattie 1968:39) but also in short-grass prairie in Iowa (Bowles 1975).

**Material:** 24CT30-1630: humerus; 24CT30-1649: femur.

**Discussion:** This species of ground squirrel is a burrowing animal and is commonly intrusive into archaeological sites

**Figure A1.2.** Bison radius and ulna demonstrating deterioration of the upper surface from exposure before burial. Identical conditions were present on the cast metatarsal.

(Wood and Johnson 1978). Normally, bones from such intrusive animals can be distinguished, based on color and appearance. These two long bones were different in color from the rest of the rodents (except *Thomomys talpoides*, see below) and are thus considered intrusive into the cultural deposits. Their actual age is not known; they could be intrusive within a thousand years, or they could have burrowed into the site in the last hundred years.

### Family Geomyidae
### Genus *Thomomys*
#### *Thomomys talpoides*—Northern Pocket Gopher

**Geologic range of species:** Late Pleistocene (Wisconsinan) to Recent in North America (Hibbard 1958:14).

**Geographic distribution:** This species of pocket gopher is common in the western United States (Hall 1981:456–465),

and its range includes all of Montana today (Hoffman and Pattie 1968:36). Lampe et al. (1974:15–16) found it common throughout Carter County.

**Habitat:** *Thomomys talpoides* is found in many different habitats, including desert valleys, rugged desert ranges of mountains, semi-arid plains, mountain forest meadows, and above timberline (Bailey 1915:23–25).

**Material:** 24CT30-1611: lower incisor; 24CT30-1613: cranium with left and right I, P3-4, M1-2; 24CT30-1628: right mandible fragment with i, p4, m1-2; 24CT30-1631: maxilla with left I, P4, M1-3 and right I, M1-2; 24CT30-1632: right mandible with i, p4, m1-3; 24CT30-1633: left mandible with i, m1-2; 24CT30-1637: isolated m3; 24CT30-1647: lower incisor; 24CT30-1651: lower incisor; 24CT30-1653: left mandible with i, p4, m1-2.

**Discussion:** As was the thirteen-line ground squirrel, this

**Table A1.2.** Identified *Bison* Bone from the Mill Iron Site Camp-Processing Area (Ribs not Included).

| Bone | Right | Left | Side Unknown | Axial Elements |
|---|---|---|---|---|
| Scapula | 3 | 4 | | |
| Humerus | 2 | 4 | | |
| Radius | 2 | 3 | | |
| Ulna | 2 | 1 | | |
| Metacarpal | 3 | 4 | | |
| Femur | 0 | 1 | | |
| Tibia | 2 | 1 | | |
| Calcaneus | 1 | 1 | | |
| Astragalus | 0 | 2 | | |
| Metatarsal | 4 | 0 | | |
| Phalange | | | | |
| No. 1 | 3 | 2 | | |
| No. 2 | 1 | 3 | | |
| No. 3 | 1 | 3 | | |
| Lateral maleolus | 2 | 0 | | |
| Fused centrum | 3 | 1 | | |
| Intermediate carpal | 2 | 0 | | |
| Radial carpal | 1 | 1 | | |
| 4th carpal | 1 | 0 | | |
| Pubis | 1 | 0 | | |
| Mandible | 1 | 2 | | |
| Dp/4 | 1 | 0 | | |
| M/3 | 4 | 4 | | |
| M/2 | 5 | 2 | | |
| M/1 | 2 | 2 | | |
| P/2 | 0 | 1 | | |
| Sesamoid | | | 1 | |
| Thoracic vertebrae | | | | 7 |
| Cervical vertebrae (Nos. 3–7) | | | | |
| 8 | | | | |
| Atlas | | | | 2 |
| Axis | | | | 1 |
| Sacrum | | | | 1 |
| Orbit | | | | |
| Articulated Units | | | | 1 |
| Right Proximal Radius | | | | |
| Ulna* | | | | 1 |
| All (7) cervical vertebra* | | | | 1 |
| One lumbar + two thracics* | | | | 1 |
| One lumbar * one thoracic* | | | | 1 |

*Included in total counts

material is considered intrusive into the site's cultural deposits, based on coloration and preservation differences. It is also known to be a highly fossorial animal (Wood and Johnson 1978), digging burrows several feet deep. Many of these specimens appeared to be fairly "fresh" in appearance. Pocket gopher burrows were noted across the site area during the excavations.

Family Cricetidae
Genus *Reithrodontomys*
*Reithrodontomys* cf. *megalotis*

**Geologic range of species:** Late Pleistocene (Wisconsinan) to Recent in North America (Hibbard 1958:16).

**Geographic distribution:** While occurring throughout eastern Montana (Hoffmann and Pattie 1968:41), this species is apparently uncommon in Carter County (Lampe et al. 1974:18).

**Habitat:** This small, secretive, rodent is most commonly found in grassland areas, more or less brushy, but not too sparse (Hoffmann and Pattie 1968:40).

**Material:** 24CT30-1638: right mandible with i, m1.

**Discussion:** This specimen does not appear to be intrusive into the site deposits but like the *Peromyscus* specimen discussed below is probably of the same general age as the cultural occupation. No evidence for cultural usage was noted, however.

Family Cricetidae
Genus *Peromyscus*
*Peromyscus* cf. *maniculatus*—Deer Mouse

**Geologic range of species:** Late Pleistocene (Wisconsinan) to Recent in North America (Hibbard 1958:17–18).

**Geographic distribution:** This mouse is one of the most widespread species of rodent in North America (Hall 1981: 670–683). Lampe et al. (1974:19) called it "by far the most common and widely distributed mammal in Carter County."

**Habitat:** This deer mouse occurs in widely different local habitats, including swamps, watercourses, upland prairies, rocks, cliffs, and arid desert regions (Osgood 1909:26). Hoffmann and Pattie (1968:41) found it to be more common in drier rockier areas than in wet areas.

**Material:** 24CT30-1636: left mandible with m1-2.

**Discussion:** The coloration and condition of this specimen was similar to the bison bone recovered from the campsite area. Therefore, it is not considered to be intrusive into the site deposits to the extent the *Spermophilus* or *Thomomys* specimens were. It is considered to be approximately the same age as the cultural occupation. However, no evidence was present that the specimen was culturally used. It was probably a natural inhabitant of the site area.

Genus *Microtus*
*Microtus longicaudus*—Long-Tailed Vole

**Geologic range of species:** Late Pleistocene (Wisconsinan) to Recent in North America (Hibbard 1958:17).

**Geographic distribution:** *Microtus longicaudus* has been recorded from throughout the western United States and Canada (Armstrong 1972:240). A disjunct population occurs in the Black Hills (south and east of Mill Iron) (Long 1965:653–656). Lampe et al. (1974:21) did not record this taxon in Carter County.

**Habitat:** This species of vole generally occurs in montane areas (Long 1965:654), but has been known to occur in riparian habitats along streams that descend into the Transition Zone (Turner 1974:108–109).

**Material:** 24CT30-1618: left mandible with i, m1-2 (Figure A1.3a); 24CT30–1619: right mandible with i, m1 (Figure

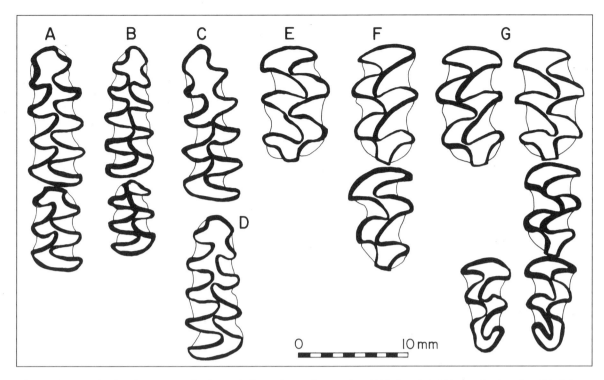

**Figure A1.3.** Occlusal patterns of vole teeth from the Mill Iron site: (A) left m1-2 *Microtus longicaudus;* (B) right m1-2 *Microtus longicaudus;* (C) left m1 *Microtus ochrogaster;* (D) right m1 *Microtus longicaudus;* (E) right M1 *Microtus* sp.; (F) left M1-2 *Microtus* sp.; (G) left M1-2, right M1-3 *Microtus ochrogaster.*

A1.3d); 24CT1620: right mandible with i, m1-2 (Figure A1.3b).

**Discussion:** This is the only taxon from the Mill Iron local fauna that has not been recorded in the modern fauna of Carter County. Hoffmann and Pattie (1968:42, 105) show southeastern Montana to be on the extreme eastern range of the species. Its presence suggests a possible expansion of the coniferous forest habitat during the Wisconsinan at the Mill Iron site. However, because no other member of the local fauna suggests a similar expansion, it is not proposed to have been widespread in the region (but see Walker 1982).

Genus *Microtus*
*Microtus ochrogaster*—Prairie Vole

**Geologic range of species:** Late Pleistocene (Illinoian) to Recent in North America (Hibbard 1958:17).

**Geographic distribution:** This species ranges from Canada to southern Texas (Hoffmann and Pattie 1968:42). Lampe et al. (1974:21) recorded the species from Carter County, Montana east and south of the Mill Iron site vicinity.

**Habitat:** Lampe et al. (1974:21) collected this species from upland meadows and semi-marshy stream banks. Normally it prefers the upland areas (Hoffmann and Pattie 1968:42) in the dry grasslands and sagebrush-grass semi-desert areas. Turner (1974:116) noted it will occupy riparian habitats when *M. pennsylvanicus* (meadow vole) is absent.

**Material:** 24CT30-1617: maxilla with right M1, M3 and

left M1-3 (Figure A1.3g); 24CT30-1621: left mandible fragment with i, m1 (Figure A1.3c).

**Discussion:** Lower first molar cusp patterns readily separate this microtine from other microtine taxa occurring in the plains. As with the *M. longicaudus* specimens, these appear to be similar in color and texture to bone known to be from the cultural occupation. Neither of these microtines burrows into the substrate; rather a complex of trails and burrows are established in the surface duff level. These microtines are thus considered definitely to be from the Wisconsinan and are not intrusive. However, no evidence for cultural usage was seen.

Genus *Microtus*
*Microtus longicaudus* or *M. ochrogaster*

**Material:** 24CT30-1615: maxilla with right M1 (Figure A1.3e); 24CT30-1616: maxilla with left M1-2 and right M1-2 (Figure A1.3f).

**Discussion:** Diagnostic teeth were not present that would enable separating these two maxilla to species. Both species show the same tooth pattern on the M1-2. M3's are diagnostic, but neither maxillae contained this tooth.

Subfamily Microtinae—Vole

**Material:** 24CT30-1614: edentulous cranium; 24CT30-1622: isolated left m3; 24CT30-1623: cranial fragments; 24CT30-1634: edentulous left mandible with i; 24CT30-1635: edentulous right mandible with i.

**Discussion:** Based on alveoli characteristics, these cranial and mandibular specimens are referred to the subfamily Microtinae. Without teeth, they cannot be identified. The isolated m3 likewise could not be identified to species. They probably all represent either *M. longicaudus* or *M. ochrogaster.*

## Order Rodentia
### Small Rodent, indet.

**Material:** 24CT30-1624: two upper incisors; 24CT30-1625: two metapodials; 24CT30-1629: long bone fragment; 24CT30-1639: femur; 24CT30-1640: vertebral fragments; 24CT30-1641: radius; 24CT30-1642: incisor fragment, caudal vertebra; 24CT30-1643: long bone fragment; 24CT30-1644: long bone fragment; 24CT30-1645: metapodial fragment; 24CT30-1646: calcaneus; 24CT30-1648: long bone fragment; 24CT30-1650: long bone fragments; 24CT30-1652: long bone fragment.

**Discussion:** These specimens were probably all from a small cricetine or microtine rodent, based on their general size. However, they could not be assigned to either genus or species, primarily because of their fragmentary nature. Also, there have been no comparative osteologies established on isolated long bones of small rodents such as these.

## Order Proboscidea
### Family Elephantidae
#### Genus cf. *Mammuthus*
##### cf. *Mammuthus* sp.—Mammoth

**Geologic range of genus:** Early (?Nebraskan) to late Pleistocene (Wisconsinan) or early Holocene in North America (Maglio 1973:61–66).

**Geographic distribution:** Widespread across North America (Maglio 1973:61–66).

**Habitat:** The mammoth was apparently primarily a grazing form, associated with Pleistocene grasslands (Tikhomirov 1958; Kurtén and Anderson 1980; Kubiak 1982).

**Material:** 24CT30-1593; rib shaft fragment.

**Discussion:** This specimen is present in the Mill Iron local fauna because of the cultural activity of the site. The rib fragment has modified into an artifact and is described elsewhere (see Frison, this volume, Chapter 4).

## Order Artiodactyla
### Family Bovidae
#### Genus *Bison*
##### *Bison* cf. *antiquus*—Bison

**Geologic range of species:** Late Pleistocene (Wisconsinan) to early Holocene in North America (Hibbard 1958:22; Wilson 1974:133).

**Geographic Distribution:** *B. antiquus* has been reported in numerous Wisconsinan and early Holocene localities in central and western North America (Wilson 1975; McDonald 1981; Walker 1986).

**Habitat:** The habitats in which this extinct subspecies occurred were probably similar to those of the extant subspecies, *B. b. bison,* that is, open grasslands or a grassland-parkland mosaic (Guthrie 1984a, 1984b, 1990).

**Material:** Over 80 fragments of identified bone (Table A1.2) were recovered from the block excavation in the camp-processing area. Additional specimens were recovered from a bonebed area that may or may not be directly associated.

**Discussion:** Kreutzer (this volume, Chapter 7) and Todd (this volume, Chapter 8) discuss the *Bison* remains from the associated bonebed area.

## Discussion

While not as extensive as other local faunas from this general time period on the Plains (see Graham, Semken, and Graham 1987), the fauna is important in that it adds to a growing database on late Wisconsinan-early Holocene faunal distributions. One amphibian, one reptile, and eight mammalian taxa are recorded for the local fauna (Table A1.1). Two of the mammals, *Thomomys talpoides* and *Spermophilus* cf. *tridecemlineatus,* were probably intrusive into the site deposits, and not directly associated with the time period of the cultural occupation. This is not to say these two burrowing animals did not occur at the Mill Iron site 11,000 years ago. They probably were present but cannot be identified as such because of their life habits.

All taxa but two from the local fauna are present in the area today. *M. longicaudus* occurs today in more of a montane habitat than that seen at the site today. Under the environmental conditions of the time (see Walker 1982, 1987), there could have been an expansion of such habitat from the Long Pine Hills and Black Hills into the area. Basing such an expansion on only one such species does make it tenuous, but it is a possibility. All other taxa from the local fauna have been known to occur in such wooded habitats.

The second taxon from the Mill Iron local fauna which no longer occurs in the area is *B. antiquus,* a bison species that went extinct during the early Holocene (see Wilson 1974, 1975; Walker 1986). While occurring throughout the plains, this species was apparently adapted to an open parkland environment (Guthrie 1990). If the montane habitat expanded over the southeastern corner of Montana during the late Pleistocene, it probably was not a solid coniferous forest. It would have been this open parkland—excellent habitat for *B. antiquus,* and its human predators.

# References Cited

Armstrong, D. D.
1972 Distribution of mammals in Colorado. *Museum of Natural History, University of Kansas, Monograph* No. 3.

Bailey, V.
1915 Revision of the Pocket Gophers of the Genus Thomomys. *U.S. Department of Agriculture, North American Fauna* No. 39.

Baxter, G. T., and M. D. Stone
1980 Amphibians and Reptiles of Wyoming. *Wyoming Game and Fish Department, Bulletin* No. 16.

Bernard, S. R., and K. F. Brown
1978 Distribution of Mammals, Reptiles, and Amphibian by BLM Physiographic Regions and A. W. Kuchler's Associations for the Eleven Western States. *U.S. Department of Interior, Bureau of Land Management Technical Note* No. 301.

Bowles, J. B.
1975 Distribution and Biogeography of Mammals of Iowa. *The Museum, Texas Tech University Special Publication* 9.

Guthrie, R. D.
1984a Alaskan Megabucks, Megabulls, and Megarams: The Issue of Pleistocene Gigantism. *Carnegie Museum of Natural History, Special Publication* 8:482–510.

1984b Mosaics, Allelochemics, and Nutrients: An Ecological Theory of Late Pleistocene Megafaunal Extinctions. In *Quaternary Extinctions: A Prehistoric Revolution*, edited by P. S. Martin and R. G. Klein, pp. 259–298. University of Arizona Press, Tucson.

1990 *Frozen Fauna of the Mammoth Steppe: The Story of Blue Babe.* The University of Chicago Press, Chicago.

Graham, M. A., M. Wilson, and R. W. Graham
1987 Paleoenvironments and Mammalian Faunas of Montana, Southern Alberta, and Southern Saskatchewan. *Illinois State Museum, Scientific Papers* 22:410–459.

Graham, R. W., H. A. Semken, Jr., and M. A. Graham (editors)
1987 Late Quaternary Mammalian Biogeography and Environments of the Great Plains and Prairies. *Illinois State Museum, Scientific Papers* No. 22.

Hall, E. R.
1981 *The Mammals of North America,* 2 vols. John Wiley and Sons, New York.

Hibbard, C. W.
1949 Techniques of Collecting Microvertebrate Fossils.

*Contributions of The Museum of Paleontology, University of Michigan* 8(2):7–19.

1958 Summary of North American Pleistocene Mammalian Local Faunas. *Michigan Academy of Science Papers* 43:3–32.

1970 Pleistocene Mammalian Local Faunas from the Great Plains and Central Lowlands Provinces of the United States. In *Pleistocene and Recent Environments of the Central Great Plains,* edited by W. Dort, Jr., and J. K. Jones, Jr., pp. 355–394. University of Kansas Press, Lawrence.

Hoffmann, R. S., and D. L. Pattie
1968 *A Guide to Montana Mammals.* University of Montana Press, Missoula.

Kubiak, H.
1982 Morphological Characters of the Mammoth: An Adaptation to the Arctic-Steppe Environment. In *Paleoecology of Beringia,* edited by D. M. Hopkins, J. V. Matthews, Jr., C. E. Schweger, and S. B. Young, pp. 281–290. Academic Press, New York.

Kurtén B., and E. Anderson
1980 *Pleistocene Mammals of North America.* Columbia University Press, New York.

Lampe, R. P., J. K. Jones, Jr., R. S. Hoffmann, and E. C. Birney
1974 The Mammals of Carter County, Southeastern Montana. *Museum of Natural History, University of Kansas, Occasional Papers* No. 25.

Long, C. A.
1965 The Mammals of Wyoming. *University of Kansas, Museum of Natural History Publications* 14(18):493–758.

McDonald, J. N.
1981 *North American Bison: Their Classification and Evolution.* University of California Press, Berkeley.

Maglio, V. J.
1973 Origin and Evolution of the Elephantidae. *American Philosophical Society, Transactions* 63(3):1–149.

Osgood, W. H.
1909 Revision of the Mice of the American Genus Peromyscus. *U.S. Department of Agriculture, North American Fauna* No. 28.

Romer, A. S.
1966 *Vertebrate Paleontology,* 3d ed. University of Chicago Press, Chicago.

Stebbins, R. C.
1966 *A Field Guide to Western Reptiles and Amphibians.* Houghton Mifflin, Boston.

Stephens, J. J.
1960    Stratigraphy and Paleoecology of a Late Pleistocene Basin, Harper County, Oklahoma. *Bulletin, Geological Society of America* 71:1675–1702.

Tikhomirov, B. A.
1958    Natural Conditions and Vegetation in the Mammoth Epoch in Northern Siberia. *Problems of the North* 1:168–188.

Turner, R. W.
1974    Mammals of the Black Hills of South Dakota and Wyoming. *University of Kansas, Museum of Natural History, Miscellaneous Publications* No. 60.

Walker, D. N.
1982    Early Holocene Vertebrate Fauna. In *The Agate Basin Site: A Record of the Paleoindian Occupation of the Northwestern High Plains,* edited by G. C. Frison and D. J. Stanford, pp. 274-308. Academic Press, New York.
1986    *Studies on the Late Pleistocene Mammalian Fauna of Wyoming.* Unpublished Ph.D. dissertation, Department of Zoology and Physiology, University of Wyoming, Laramie.
1987    Late Pleistocene/Holocene Environmental Changes in Wyoming: The Mammalian Record. *Illinois State Museum, Scientific Papers* 22:334–393.

Wilson, M.
1974    The Casper Site Local Fauna and its Fossil Bison. In *The Casper Site, a Hell Gap Bison Kill on the High Plains,* edited by G. C. Frison, pp. 125–171. Academic Press, New York.
1975    *Holocene Fossil Bison from Wyoming and Adjacent Areas.* Unpublished M.A. thesis, Department of Anthropology, University of Wyoming, Laramie.

Wood, W. R., and D. L. Johnson
1978    A Survey of Disturbance Processes in Archaeological Site Formation. In *Advances in Archaeological Method and Theory, vol. 1,* edited by M. Schiffer, pp. 315–381. Academic Press, New York.

# (A) Summary of Skeletal Parts
# (B) X-Ray Densitometry Measurements
# of Bison Bone Mineral

LEE ANN KREUTZER
National Park Service

## (A)
### Summary of Skeletal Parts

This summary of quantitative data for the Mill Iron bison bed assemblage employs element codes described in Table 7.2. Parenthetical information provided for each element describes the bone portions with which Minimum Numbers of Elements were counted.

During laboratory analysis, specimens were examined to see whether they included landmarks or portions equivalent to the scan sites used by Kreutzer (1992) in studies of bison bone mineral density. These were recorded and—for many elements—were tallied to provide MNE counts. Scan-site-based MNEs are indicated as such, below.

| Element | NISP | Portion | Freq. | L | R | N/S | Element MNE | Element MNI |
|---------|------|---------|-------|---|---|-----|-------------|-------------|
| AS | 22 | CO | 21 | 7 | 14 | 0 | — | — |
| | | US | 1 | 0 | 1 | 0 | 22 | 14 |

(MNE: 21 complete and 1 fragmentary specimens)

| Element | NISP | Portion | Freq. | L | R | N/S | Element MNE | Element MNI |
|---------|------|---------|-------|---|---|-----|-------------|-------------|
| AT | 25 | CO | 6 | — | — | — | — | — |
| | | CN | 2 | — | — | — | — | — |
| | | CNN | 3 | — | — | — | — | — |
| | | CNW | 3 | — | — | — | — | — |
| | | NA | 2 | — | — | — | — | — |
| | | US | 9 | — | — | — | 12 | 12 |

(MNE: vertebral wing, scan site AT3)

| Element | NISP | Portion | Freq. | L | R | N/S | Element MNE | Element MNI |
|---------|------|---------|-------|---|---|-----|-------------|-------------|
| AX | 25 | CO | 3 | — | — | — | — | — |
| | | CN | 16 | — | — | — | — | — |
| | | CNN | 2 | — | — | — | — | — |
| | | CNS | 1 | — | — | — | — | — |
| | | US | 3 | — | — | — | 21 | 21 |

(MNE: dens, scan site AX1)

| Element | NISP | Portion | Freq. | L | R | N/S | Element MNE | Element MNI |
|---------|------|---------|-------|---|---|-----|-------------|-------------|
| CA | 3 | CO | 3 | — | — | — | 3 | — |

(MNE: 3 complete elements)

| Element | NISP | Portion | Freq. | L | R | N/S | Element MNE | Element MNI |
|---------|------|---------|-------|---|---|-----|-------------|-------------|
| CB | 35 | — | — | — | — | — | — | — |
| CE | 87 | CO | 19 | — | — | — | — | — |
| | | AP | 21 | — | — | — | — | — |
| | | CN | 17 | — | — | — | — | — |
| | | CNN | 19 | — | — | — | — | — |
| | | CNS | 3 | — | — | — | — | — |
| | | NAS | 6 | — | — | — | — | — |
| | | PEP | 1 | — | — | — | — | — |
| | | US | 1 | — | — | — | 46 | 9.2 |

(MNE: anterior centrum with scan site CE1)

| Element | NISP | Portion | Freq. | L | R | N/S | Element MNE | Element MNI |
|---------|------|---------|-------|---|---|-----|-------------|-------------|
| CL | 18 | CO | 11 | 5 | 6 | 0 | — | — |
| | | DS | 2 | 0 | 1 | 1 | — | — |
| | | DSE | 1 | 0 | 1 | 0 | — | — |
| | | PR | 2 | 0 | 2 | 0 | — | — |
| | | US | 2 | 0 | 1 | 1 | 14 | 10 |

(MNE: scan site CA2)

| Element | NISP | Portion | Freq. | L | R | N/S | Element MNE | Element MNI |
|---------|------|---------|-------|---|---|-----|-------------|-------------|
| CPF | 13 | CO | 11 | 5 | 4 | 2 | — | — |
| | | US | 2 | 0 | 1 | 0 | 12 | 5 |

(MNE: 11 complete and 1 fragmentary specimens)

| Element | NISP | Portion | Freq. | L | R | N/S | Element MNE | Element MNI |
|---------|------|---------|-------|---|---|-----|-------------|-------------|
| CPI | 10 | CO | 10 | 5 | 5 | 0 | 10 | 5 |

(MNE: 10 complete elements)

| Element | NISP | Portion | Freq. | L | R | N/S | Element MNE | Element MNI |
|---------|------|---------|-------|---|---|-----|-------------|-------------|
| CPR | 11 | CO | 9 | 3 | 5 | 1 | — | — |
| | | US | 2 | 0 | 1 | 0 | 10 | 6 |

(MNE: 9 complete and 1 fragmentary elements)

| Element | NISP | Portion | Freq. | L | R | N/S | Element MNE | Element MNI |
|---------|------|---------|-------|---|---|-----|-------------|-------------|
| CPS | 19 | CO | 18 | 6 | 12 | 0 | — | — |
| | | US | 1 | 1 | 0 | 0 | 19 | 12 |

(MNE: 18 complete and 1 fragmentary specimens)

| Element | NISP | Portion | Freq. | L | R | N/S | Element MNE | Element MNI |
|---------|------|---------|-------|---|---|-----|-------------|-------------|
| CPU | 12 | CO | 12 | 6 | 6 | 0 | 12 | 6 |
| CRN | 62 | MX TW | 12 | 0 | 4 | 8 | — | — |
| | | OCC | 11 | — | — | — | 2 | — |
| | | PET | 23 | — | — | — | 16 | — |
| | | SKO | 9 | — | — | — | — | — |

| Element | NISP | Portion | Freq. | L | R | N/S | Element MNE | Element MNI |
|---|---|---|---|---|---|---|---|---|
| | | MX | 3 | — | — | — | — | — |
| | | US | 4 | — | — | — | — | — |
| FB | 102 | US | — | — | — | — | — | — |
| FM | 26 | CO | 0 | 0 | 0 | 0 | — | — |
| | | CDL | 1 | 0 | 0 | 1 | — | — |
| | | DS | 3 | 1 | 0 | 2 | — | — |
| | | DSE | 1 | 1 | 0 | 0 | — | — |
| | | DSH | 1 | 0 | 1 | 0 | — | — |
| | | HE | 6 | 1 | 2 | 3 | — | — |
| | | PRS | 2 | 0 | 2 | 0 | — | — |
| | | PSH | 3 | 2 | 1 | 0 | — | — |
| | | SH | 9 | 6 | 2 | 1 | 11 | 4 |

(MNE: heads and proximal ends with heads, scan site FE1)

| Element | NISP | Portion | Freq. | L | R | N/S | Element MNE | Element MNI |
|---|---|---|---|---|---|---|---|---|
| HM | 28 | CO | 0 | 0 | 0 | 0 | — | — |
| | | DDS | 1 | 0 | 1 | 0 | — | — |
| | | DPR | 3 | 0 | 1 | 2 | — | — |
| | | DS | 4 | 2 | 1 | 1 | — | — |
| | | DSE | 1 | 0 | 1 | 0 | — | — |
| | | DSH | 8 | 4 | 4 | 0 | — | — |
| | | DSS | 7 | 4 | 3 | 0 | — | — |
| | | HE | 1 | 0 | 0 | 1 | — | — |
| | | SH | 3 | 0 | 3 | 0 | 18 | 10 |

(MNE: trochlea, scan site HU5)

| Element | NISP | Portion | Freq. | L | R | N/S | Element MNE | Element MNI |
|---|---|---|---|---|---|---|---|---|
| HY | 4 | ANG | 2 | — | — | — | — | — |
| | | US | 2 | — | — | — | — | 1 |
| IC | 23 | US | — | — | — | — | — | — |
| IM | 61 | CO | 7 | 6 | 1 | 0 | — | — |
| | | AC | 9 | 1 | 1 | 7 | — | — |
| | | ACL | 12 | 6 | 5 | 1 | — | — |
| | | ACP | 5 | 3 | 1 | 1 | — | — |
| | | ACS | 4 | 3 | 1 | 0 | — | — |
| | | IL | 6 | 3 | 1 | 2 | — | — |
| | | ILC | 3 | 2 | 0 | 1 | — | — |
| | | IS | 3 | 0 | 1 | 2 | — | — |
| | | ISC | 3 | 2 | 1 | 0 | — | — |
| | | PB | 6 | 1 | 2 | 3 | — | — |
| | | PBS | 1 | 0 | 0 | 1 | — | — |
| | | US | 2 | 0 | 0 | 2 | 38 | 13 |

(MNE: ilium with acetabulum, scan site IL2)

| Element | NISP | Portion | Freq. | L | R | N/S | Element MNE | Element MNI |
|---|---|---|---|---|---|---|---|---|
| LB | 102 | US | — | — | — | — | — | — |
| LM | 37 | CO | 5 | — | — | — | — | — |
| | | AEP | 1 | — | — | — | — | — |
| | | CN | 15 | — | — | — | — | — |
| | | CNN | 8 | — | — | — | — | — |
| | | CNS | 2 | — | — | — | — | — |
| | | NAS | 2 | — | — | — | — | — |
| | | PZG | 1 | — | — | — | — | — |
| | | US | 3 | — | — | — | 24 | 5 |

(MNE: anterior centrum, scan site LU1)

| Element | NISP | Portion | Freq. | L | R | N/S | Element MNE | Element MNI |
|---|---|---|---|---|---|---|---|---|
| LTM | 6 | CO | 6 | 0 | 4 | 2 | 6 | 4 |

(MNE: 6 complete elements)

| Element | NISP | Portion | Freq. | L | R | N/S | Element MNE | Element MNI |
|---|---|---|---|---|---|---|---|---|
| MC | 8 | CO | 5 | 2 | 3 | 0 | — | — |
| | | DSH | 1 | 0 | 1 | 0 | — | 5 |
| | | PSH | 2 | 0 | 2 | 0 | 7 | — |

(MNE: 5 complete and 2 proximal, scan site MC1)

| Element | NISP | Portion | Freq. | L | R | N/S | Element MNE | Element MNI |
|---|---|---|---|---|---|---|---|---|
| MCF | 3 | CO | 0 | 0 | 0 | 3 | — | — |
| MMX | 30 | — | — | — | — | — | — | — |
| MMR | 10 | — | — | — | — | — | — | — |
| MP | 14 | CDL | 7 | 0 | 0 | 6 | — | — |
| | | DDS | 2 | 0 | 0 | 2 | — | — |
| | | DS | 3 | 0 | 0 | 3 | — | — |
| | | PR | 2 | 0 | 0 | 2 | 1 | 1 |

(MNE: 1 fragmentary proximal, scan site MC1)

| Element | NISP | Portion | Freq. | L | R | N/S | Element MNE | Element MNI |
|---|---|---|---|---|---|---|---|---|
| MR | 106 | CO | 15 | 7 | 8 | 0 | — | — |
| | | ANG | 2 | 0 | 0 | 2 | — | — |
| | | BDR | 9 | 0 | 0 | 9 | — | — |
| | | DRM | 24 | 8 | 11 | 5 | — | — |
| | | HRM | 2 | 1 | 1 | 0 | — | — |
| | | RAM | 15 | 4 | 7 | 4 | — | — |
| | | SYM | 9 | 4 | 2 | 3 | — | — |
| | | TW | 21 | 8 | 8 | 5 | — | — |
| | | US | 9 | 0 | 0 | 9 | — | — |
| MT | 13 | CO | 2 | 2 | 0 | 0 | — | — |
| | | DDS | 1 | 0 | 0 | 1 | — | — |
| | | DSE | 1 | 0 | 0 | 1 | — | — |
| | | DSS | 2 | 0 | 2 | 0 | — | — |
| | | PSH | 4 | 1 | 3 | 0 | — | — |
| | | PRS | 2 | 0 | 1 | 1 | — | — |
| | | SH | 1 | 0 | 1 | 0 | 8 | 5 |

(MNE: proximal, scan site MR1)

| Element | NISP | Portion | Freq. | L | R | N/S | Element MNE | Element MNI |
|---|---|---|---|---|---|---|---|---|
| MUN | 7 | — | — | — | — | — | — | — |
| PH | 4 | HE | 3 | — | — | — | — | — |
| | | US | 1 | — | — | — | — | — |
| PHF | 67 | CO | 57 | — | — | — | — | — |
| | | US | 2 | — | — | — | — | — |
| | | PR | 5 | — | — | — | 64 | 8 |

(MNE: body, scan site P12)

| Element | NISP | Portion | Freq. | L | R | N/S | Element MNE | Element MNI |
|---|---|---|---|---|---|---|---|---|
| PHS | 51 | CO | 46 | — | — | — | — | — |
| | | SH | 1 | — | — | — | — | — |
| | | US | 2 | — | — | — | — | — |
| | | HE | 2 | — | — | — | 50 | 6.25 |

(MNE: complete and distal articular ends, scan site P23)

| Element | NISP | Portion | Freq. | L | R | N/S | Element MNE | Element MNI |
|---|---|---|---|---|---|---|---|---|
| PHT | 31 | CO | 23 | — | — | — | — | — |
| | | PR | 6 | — | — | — | — | — |
| | | US | 2 | — | — | — | 30 | 3.75 |

(MNE: all articular ends and 1 fragment, scan site P31)

| Element | NISP | Portion | Freq. | L | R | N/S | Element MNE | Element MNI |
|---|---|---|---|---|---|---|---|---|
| PMR | 6 | — | — | — | — | — | — | — |
| PMX | 15 | — | — | — | — | — | — | — |
| PT | 7 | CO | 7 | — | — | — | 7 | — |
| PUN | 2 | CO | — | — | — | — | — | — |
| RB | 657 | BL | 570 | 23 | 19 | 1 | — | — |
| | | CO | 6 | 2 | 3 | 1 | — | — |
| | | HE | 7 | 1 | 0 | 6 | — | — |
| | | PR | 24 | 8 | 8 | 7 | — | — |
| | | PRS | 36 | 12 | 7 | 17 | — | — |

| Element | NISP | Portion | Freq. | L | R | N/S | Element MNE | Element MNI |
|---|---|---|---|---|---|---|---|---|
| | | PSH | 6 | 0 | 4 | 2 | 65 | 3 |

(MNE: proximal ribs, scan site RI2)

| Element | NISP | Portion | Freq. | L | R | N/S | Element MNE | Element MNI |
|---|---|---|---|---|---|---|---|---|
| RD | 31 | CO | 8 | 2 | 6 | 0 | — | — |
| | | DS | 1 | 1 | 0 | 0 | — | — |
| | | DPR | 1 | 0 | 0 | 1 | — | — |
| | | DSE | 3 | 3 | 0 | 0 | — | — |
| | | DSH | 2 | 0 | 2 | 0 | — | — |
| | | DSS | 2 | 2 | 0 | 0 | — | — |
| | | FK | 2 | 1 | 0 | 1 | — | — |
| | | PR | 1 | 0 | 0 | 1 | — | — |
| | | PRS | 6 | 6 | 1 | 0 | — | — |
| | | PSH | 3 | 2 | 1 | 0 | — | — |
| | | SH | 1 | 1 | 0 | 0 | 17 | 8 |

(MNE: complete and proximal elements)

| Element | NISP | Portion | Freq. | L | R | N/S | Element MNE | Element MNI |
|---|---|---|---|---|---|---|---|---|
| SA | 11 | CO | 1 | — | — | — | — | — |
| | | CN | 4 | — | — | — | — | — |
| | | CNW | 3 | — | — | — | — | — |
| | | US | 3 | — | — | — | — | — |
| SC | 67 | CO | 7 | 5 | 2 | 0 | — | — |
| | | BL | 14 | 3 | 1 | 10 | — | — |
| | | GN | 13 | 1 | 3 | 0 | — | — |
| | | GNB | 25 | 8 | 13 | 4 | — | — |
| | | GS | 3 | 3 | 0 | 0 | — | — |
| | | SP | 4 | 1 | 0 | 3 | — | — |
| | | US | 1 | 0 | 0 | 1 | 37 | 17 |

(MNE: specimens with more than half the glenoid fossa)

| Element | NISP | Portion | Freq. | L | R | N/S | Element MNE | Element MNI |
|---|---|---|---|---|---|---|---|---|
| SE | 22 | CO | — | — | — | — | 22 | — |
| TA | 17 | CO | 0 | 0 | 0 | 0 | — | — |
| | | DS | 2 | 0 | 2 | 0 | — | — |
| | | DSE | 3 | 1 | 1 | 1 | — | — |
| | | DSH | 6 | 4 | 2 | 0 | — | — |
| | | FK | 1 | 1 | 0 | 0 | — | — |
| | | PRE | 1 | 0 | 0 | 1 | — | — |
| | | SH | 2 | 0 | 1 | 1 | — | — |
| | | US | 2 | 0 | 0 | 2 | 9 | 4 |

(MNE: distal epiphyses, scan site TI5)

| Element | NISP | Portion | Freq. | L | R | N/S | Element MNE | Element MNI |
|---|---|---|---|---|---|---|---|---|
| TFR | 94 | — | — | — | — | — | — | — |
| TH | 64 | CO | 11 | — | — | — | — | — |
| | | CNN | 12 | — | — | — | — | — |
| | | CNS | 11 | — | — | — | — | — |
| | | CN | 9 | — | — | — | — | — |
| | | NAS | 8 | — | — | — | — | — |
| | | SP | 13 | — | — | — | 33 | 2.4 |

(MNE: anterior end, scan site TH1)

| Element | NISP | Portion | Freq. | L | R | N/S | Element MNE | Element MNI |
|---|---|---|---|---|---|---|---|---|
| TRC | 14 | CO | 10 | 5 | 5 | 0 | — | — |
| | | US | 4 | 3 | 1 | 0 | 12 | 6 |

(MNE: 10 complete and 2 fragmentary specimens)

| Element | NISP | Portion | Freq. | L | R | N/S | Element MNE | Element MNI |
|---|---|---|---|---|---|---|---|---|
| TRS | 7 | CO | 7 | 3 | 4 | 0 | 7 | 4 |
| TTH | 62 | — | — | — | — | — | — | — |
| UL | 26 | ANC | 4 | 3 | 1 | 0 | — | — |
| | | PR | 1 | 0 | 1 | 0 | — | — |
| | | PRS | 7 | 5 | 1 | 1 | — | — |
| | | PSH | 2 | 0 | 2 | 0 | — | — |

| Element | NISP | Portion | Freq. | L | R | N/S | Element MNE | Element MNI |
|---|---|---|---|---|---|---|---|---|
| | | SH | 7 | 2 | 1 | 0 | — | — |
| | | US | 5 | 0 | 0 | 5 | 14 | 8 |

(MNE: trochlear notch, scan site UL2)

| Element | NISP | Portion | Freq. | L | R | N/S | Element MNE | Element MNI |
|---|---|---|---|---|---|---|---|---|
| US | 702 | — | — | — | — | — | — | — |
| VT | 194 | — | — | — | — | — | — | — |

## (B)
### X-Ray Densitometry Measurements of Bison Bone Mineral

In collecting densitometry data for bison skeletons, Kreutzer (1992a, 1992b) followed the scan site illustrations provided by Lyman (1982, 1984). Here are presented the criteria used in placing scan sites consistently within element classes and how the bones were positioned under the scanner. These descriptions are most effectively used in conjunction with the illustrations presented in Figure 7.12. All bones scanned with the Hologic QDR 1000 (dual X-ray machine) were placed on a block of 5 cm thick Lucite, to compensate for the lack of soft tissue, for which the device is calibrated. Smaller sheets of Lucite or foam rubber were sometimes positioned to hold bones in place or to keep long bone shafts parallel to the table and transverse to the X-ray beam alignment.

### Mandible

The mandible is positioned lateral side up, with the angle propped with Lucite sheets to keep its surface level. Because the X-ray densitometer operates in English units, scan site measurements are reported in inches. All other measurements are presented in metric units, the scientific standard.

**DN1:** The scan line is oriented transversely across the specimen, mid-way between the incisors and the mental foramen.

**DN2:** The scan line is transversely oriented, mid-way between mental foramen and $P_2$.

**DN3:** The scan line is transversely oriented, immediately anterior to $P_2$. The scan proceeds in an anterior direction, so that tooth mineral is not measured with the bone.

**DN4:** The scan line is transversely oriented between $P_4$ and $M_1$. It is measurable only when one of these teeth is missing; otherwise, tooth mineral would be included in the bone scan.

**DN5:** The mandible is rotated and the scan line begins on the posterior side of $M_3$. It continues diagonally across the element to the muscle scar on the inferior border of the mandible.

**DN6:** The scan line is positioned as a 45-degree diagonal, proceeding from the mid-point of the angle.

**DN7:** The scan line is positioned across the width of the ascending ramus, directly below the mandibular condyle.

**DN8:** The scan line lies transversely across the base of coronoid process, immediately above the superior notch.

## Hyoid

**HY1:** The scan is aligned across the greatest breadth of the angle.

## Vertebrae

Vertebrae are placed dorsal side up, unless otherwise noted. Where necessary, they are propped with Lucite to keep them from tipping to one side. Some bison vertebrae are too wide for the Hologic's 6 in maximum scan field, and must be measured half at a time. Vertebrae exhibited a high degree of morphological variation among skeletons, making it difficult to place scan lines in precisely the same place on all specimens.

**AT1:** The atlas is placed ventral side up. The scan line runs lengthwise (cranio-caudally) through the middle of the centrum.

**AT2:** Still ventral side up, the atlas is rotated 90 degrees. The scan site is aligned across the width of the vertebra and through its center.

**AT3:** Still ventral side up, the atlas is rotated 90 degrees to its original position. The scan line runs lengthwise (cranio-caudally) through the wing, centered on the anterior articular process for the skull.

**AX1:** The axis is propped at its caudal end, so that the body of the vertebrae is parallel to the table. The scan line is transverse to the body. It begins at the base of the dens and moves cranially.

**AX2:** The axis is propped at its caudal end. The scan line runs across the width of the vertebra, caudal to the intervertebral foramenae, and does not include the post-zygopophyses.

**AX3:** The axis is propped at its caudal end. The scan line is transverse to the body, begins caudal to the spine, and measures the post-zygopophyses.

**CE1:** The scan is lined up at the posterior base of the spine, and moves toward the anterior end. It includes the spine and pre-zygopophyses.

**CE2:** The scan line runs across the width of the vertebrae, from the base of the post-zygopophyses. Scan direction is toward the caudal end.

**TH1:** The vertebra is propped in anatomical position. The scan line runs across the width of the element, beginning at the base of the spine. Scan direction is toward the cranial end.

**TH2:** The vertebrae is positioned horizontally, on one side, with the tip of the spine propped to keep it parallel to the table. The scan line is at the center of the length of the spine.

**LU1:** The specimen is propped with sheets of Lucite under one transverse process to hold it in anatomical position. The scan is aligned across the width of the bone, beginning at the posterior base of the pre-zygopophyses. Scan direction is toward the anterior end.

**LU2:** Still propped, the scanner is aligned at the anterior base of the post-zygopophyses, and the scan proceeds toward the posterior end.

**LU3:** The vertebrae is turned 90 degrees and one transverse process is propped to hold it in position. The scan begins at the base of one transverse process, and moves laterally across it.

**SC1:** The caudal end of the sacrum is raised with sheets of Lucite so that the dorsal surface is level. The scan is aligned across the width of the sacrum, at the center of the auricular surfaces. When the vertebrae is more than 6 in wide, halves are scanned separately.

**SC2:** The caudal end is still propped. The scan line is positioned immediately behind the dorsal sacral foramena, and the scan proceeds toward the caudal end.

Caudal vertebrae and sternebrae were not available for densitometry measurement.

## Ribs

**RI1:** The scan encompasses the rib head.

**RI2:** The scan encompasses the tubercle.

**RI3:** The scan line is positioned transversely across the proximal portion of the blade, starting at its narrowest point. Scanning proceeds toward the blade end.

**RI4:** The length of the blade is measured, and the scan line is positioned transversely at two-thirds of the distance down the blade.

**RI5:** The scan line lies across the distal rib blade at its point of maximum width.

## Scapula

The scapula is placed with the subscapular fossa facing upward, and with the vertebral border propped up by Lucite sheets. Although the illustration depicts the element from a lateral view, it was found that the high projection of the spine "confused" the scanner and caused it to malfunction. Turning the spine away from the scanner appeared to solve the problem.

**SP1:** The scan is aligned across the neck at the point of its smallest depth.

**SP2:** The scan line is positioned transversely across the scapula, and begins 4 cm dorsally from the acromion.

**SP3:** The scan is aligned across and transverse to the cranial border. The distance between scan site SP4 and the vertebral border is measured, and SP3 is positioned mid-way between the two. The scan line begins at the cranial border and extends to the posterior base of the spine.

**SP4:** The distance between the caudal lip of the glenoid fossa and the vertebral border is measured along the caudal border. The scan line is positioned at two-thirds of this length. The line is transverse to the caudal border, extends 10 cm from that border toward the spine.

**SP5:** The scan line extends transversely from the caudal border, for 10 cm. It is positioned at the vertebral border.

## Humerus

The humerus is positioned on its posterior side. The head may be propped to keep the shaft parallel to the table.

**HU1:** The line is transverse across the center of the head, at the point of greatest breadth of the proximal end.

**HU2:** The scan line is transverse across the proximal shaft, under the lip of the head and at the deltoid crest.

**HU3:** The scan line is positioned at the point of the least breadth of the diaphysis.

HU4: The scan line is positioned immediately above the olecranon fossa at the distal end of the shaft, at the greatest breadth of the distal shaft.

HU5: The scan is aligned transversely across the greatest breadth of the distal end of the element, between the medial and lateral epicondyles.

## Radius-Ulna

The radius-ulna was positioned with its anterior face on the table. Radius measurements include the ulnae, where the two elements are fused. In measuring the proximal ulna, the fused bones were arranged with their lateral sides facing upward.

UL1: The element is aligned diagonally so that the scan line will be positioned across the greatest depth of the olecranon process. This generally follows the line of epiphyseal fusion across the process.

UL2: The scan is oriented transversely across the trochlear notch at the point of its least depth.

RA1: The scan line follows the greatest breadth of the proximal end.

RA2: The scan line is aligned across the point of greatest breadth of the proximal shaft.

RA3: The scan line follows the line of least breadth of the mid-shaft.

RA4: The scan follows the line of greatest breadth across the distal end of the radius.

RA5: The scan is aligned transversely across the distal epiphysis, at the styloid process; the scan proceeds toward the proximal end.

## Carpals

Each carpal was scanned across its entire length and breadth.

## Metapodials

The positioning of metacarpal and metatarsal scan sites are herein described collectively.

MC–MT1: The scan is aligned across the greatest breadth of the proximal end.

MC–MT2: The scan is aligned across the greatest breadth of the proximal shaft.

MC–MT3: The scan is positioned at the point of least breadth of the diaphysis.

MC–MT4: The scan lies across the distal shaft, proximal to the nutrient foramen in the vascular groove.

MC–MT5: The scan is aligned across the greatest breadth of the distal shaft.

MC–MT6: The scan is positioned transversely across the medial condyle.

## Phalanges

Phalanges are placed with their lateral sides upward. Second phalanges are generally too small to make three ½ in scans (Lyman's were ⅛ inch scans), so I make only two measurements on those elements.

P11 and P21: The scan line follows the greatest depth of the proximal end.

P12: The scan follows the least depth of the diaphysis.

P13 and P23: The scan is positioned across the greatest depth of the distal end.

P31: The scan is aligned across the greatest depth of the phalanx.

## Innominate

Most of the specimens were complete pelves, which were difficult to position because of their size and irregular shape. I found it helpful to brace the element with large blocks of foam rubber.

IL1: Because the breadth of the bison ilium always exceeds the 6 in width limit of the scanning device, the pelvis must be rotated until the ilium lies within that limit. At the same time, care must be taken to avoid positioning the other ilium between the scanner and the target. As a result, the scan line will not actually lie across the relatively flat, lateral surface of the ilium, as it appears in the illustration. Once the pelvis is oriented correctly, it must be positioned so that the scan line crosses the greatest breadth of the ilium.

IL2: The pelvis is rotated to expose the greatest surface of the ilium, and the scan site is aligned transversely, across the least breadth of the ilium.

AC1: Keeping the pelvis braced in this position, the scanner is then trained across the center of the acetabulum.

PU1: The pelvis is positioned so that it rests on its pubic symphysis. The element is then rotated so that the scan will lie transversely across the portion of the pubis that is anterior to the symphysis. The scan site follows the least breadth of that portion of the pubis.

PU2: The scan line follows the least breadth of the pubis at the symphysis.

IS1: With the pelvis still resting on its pubic symphysis, the element is rotated so that the scan line follows the least breadth of the ischial body.

IS2: The scan line follows the least breadth of the ischial ramus.

## Femur

The femur is placed anterior face up with the proximal end raised with sheets of Lucite to make the shaft parallel to the table. These small sheets are repositioned under the shaft as necessary, so that they do not directly underlie any scan site during scanning.

FE1: The scan line is positioned diagonally, following the line of epiphyseal fusion of the head. The scan proceeds cranially—toward the fovea—and does not include any portion of the shaft.

FE2: The scan is aligned across the greatest breadth of the proximal shaft.

FE3: The scan is positioned transversely across the proximal shaft, distal to the trochanteric fossa and through the lesser trochanter.

**FE4:** The scan follows the line of least breadth of the diaphysis.

**FE5:** The scan line follows the greatest breadth of the distal shaft, proximal to the patellar groove.

**FE6:** The scan lies across the greatest breadth of the distal end.

## Patella

**PA1:** The element is positioned with its cranial side upward. The scan is aligned across its greatest breadth.

## Tibia

The tibia is positioned with its anterior side upward and its distal end propped with Lucite to hold the shaft parallel to the table.

**TI1:** This scan follows the line of greatest breadth of the proximal end of the element.

**TI2:** The scan line is positioned at the point of the element's greatest depth on the proximal shaft.

**TI3:** The scan lies at the least depth of the diaphysis.

**TI4:** The scan is aligned along the greatest breadth of the distal shaft.

**TI5:** The scan is positioned at the greatest breadth of the distal epiphysis.

## Astragalus

The astragalus is placed with its dorsal side upward.

**AS1:** This scan site is aligned along the element's least length.

**AS2:** The specimen is rotated 90 degrees, and the scan is positioned transversely, across the point of its greatest depth.

**AS3:** The scan is positioned across the greatest breadth of the distal trochlea.

## Calcaneus

The calcaneus is placed on its lateral side.

**CA1:** The distal end is scanned across the line of its greatest depth.

**CA2:** The body is scanned dorsal to the sustentaculum and along the line of its greatest depth.

**CA3:** The scan is aligned across the sustentaculum at its greatest depth.

**CA4:** The scan site lies across the medial articular surface of the proximal calcaneus, at its greatest depth.

## Small Tarsals

Small tarsals are scanned along their entire length and breadth.

## Naviculo-Cuboid

The element is placed with its distal articular surfaces upward and is propped with Lucite blocks.

**NC1:** The scan is aligned across the articular surfaces for the metatarsals.

**NC2:** The element is rotated 90 degrees, and the scan is aligned in the groove between the articular surfaces for the metatarsal. This coincides with the element's greatest breadth.

**NC3:** The scan is positioned across the articular surfaces for the metatarsal and that for the fused second and third tarsals.

## References Cited

Kreutzer, L. A.
  1992A  Bison and Deer Bone Mineral Densities: Comparisons and Implications for the Interpretation of Archaeological Faunas. *Journal of Archaeological Science* 19: 271–294.
  1992b  Taphonomy of the Mill Iron, Montana (24CT30) Bison Bonebed. Ph.D. dissertation, University of Washington, Seattle. University Microfilms, Ann Arbor.

Lyman, R. L.
  1982  The Taphonomy of Vertebrate Archaeofaunas: Bone Density and Differential Survival of Fossil Classes. Ph.D. dissertation, University of Washington, Seattle. University Microfilms, Ann Arbor.
  1984  Bone Density and Differential Survivorship of Fossil Classes. *Journal of Anthropological Archaeology* 3: 259–299.

# Size Comparison of the Mill Iron Site Bison Calcanea

MATTHEW GLENN HILL
University of Wisconsin

Diminution in size of bison during the late Pleistocene/early Holocene transition has been noted by several researchers (e.g., Guthrie 1980, 1984a, 1984b, 1990; Hillerud 1980; Reher 1974; Todd 1986, 1987; Wilson 1974a, 1974b, 1975, 1978). Although the reasons for the decrease in stature are beyond the scope of this short appendix, it has been proposed that a longer somatic growth season resulting from an extended period of dietary protein availability may have been an important factor in accounting for the larger size of bison during the late Pleistocene (Guthrie 1980, 1984a, 1984b, 1990).

Most size comparisons among the various subspecies of bison undertaken to date have relied on craniometrics (e.g., McDonald 1981; Skinner and Kaisen 1947; Wilson 1974a, 1974b, 1975, 1978). Other researchers have used limb bones (e.g., Bedord 1974; McDonald 1981; Peterson 1977; Peterson and Hughes 1980; Todd 1983, 1986, 1987; Zeimens 1982), phalanges (e.g., Zeimens 1982), or astragali (e.g., Hoffecker et al. 1991; Zeimens 1982; Zeimens and Zeimens 1974). More recently, Morlan (1991) demonstrated, despite a small sample size, that bison carpals and tarsals are untapped sources of information for aging and sexing post-cranial bison bones. Taking Morlan's research a step further, several additional osteometric observations have been developed for bison calcanea (Figure A3.1, Table A3.1, Hill 1994:174–176). These metric observations were then applied to mature bison calcanea in the University of Wyoming, Department of Anthropology, zooarchaeological comparative collections (UWAC). Only calcanea with complete fusion of the calcaneal tuber were measured. The results indicate the measurements on modern bison are significantly smaller than the bison of the late Pleistocene/early Holocene (see Table A3.2).

Calcanea are ideally suited to this type of metric analysis for a number of reasons. First, they are relatively high in bone mineral density (Kreutzer 1992a, 1992b). As a result, their ability to withstand destructive processes is high. Second, calcanea have relatively low food utility (Emerson 1990). Thus, they may be less subject to transport by people or carnivores unless articulated to larger anatomical units (Binford 1981; Burgett 1990). Additionally, the process of epiphyseal union of the calcaneal tuber permits analysis to be restricted to only those specimens displaying comparable degrees of proximal union (e.g., Todd 1987:122). For bison, complete union of the calcaneal tuber occurs during the fifth year of life in bulls and during the sixth year for cows (Empel and Roskosz 1963:282). Such considerations make calcanea well suited for synchronic and diachronic studies of herd composition and size diminution. The extremely poor preservation of bison bone from the Mill Iron site 24CT30 excluded most of the carcass elements from use as size determiners, but fortunately a small number of intact calcanea was recovered.

Measurements of calcanea from several bison bonebed assemblages are presented in Table A3.2. Shaft length (CL9 in mm) of calcanea plotted against greatest breadth (CL4 in mm) of calcanea for these bonebed assemblages and the UWAC assemblage is presented in Figure A3.2. Although the Mill Iron site sample is small (Table A3.3), the results indicate that based on the calcaneal measurements the size of the bison from the site is well within the size range of bison from other North American Paleoindian bonebed assemblages (Figure A3.2). This is as expected, given the radiocarbon dates of around 11,000 years ago for the Goshen cultural component at the Mill Iron site.

**Table A3.1.** Description of Measurements Recorded for Bison Calcanea.

CL1     (greatest length; osteometric board):    The lateral surface of the calcaneus is positioned over the slide groove with the distal end fixed against the end of the board. The slider contacts the calcaneal tuber (Figure A3.1, a–b).

CL2     (greatest breadth proximal end; osteometric board):    The caudal surface of the proximal calcaneus rests on the board in a transverse orientation. The lateral surface of the proximal end and the cranial portion of the shaft at the point where is extends off the board are fixed against the end of the board. The slider contacts the medial border of the calcaneal tuber (Figure A3.1, c–d).

CL3     (greatest depth of proximal end; osteometric board):    The medial surface of the proximal calcaneus rests on the board in a transverse orientation. The lateral surface of the proximal end and the cranial portion of the shaft are fixed against the end of the board. The slider contacts the caudal surface of the calcaneal tuber (Figure A3.1, e–f).

CL4     (greatest breadth; osteometric board):    The lateral surface of the calcaneus and the caudal surface of the element are fixed against the end and base of the board, respectively. The slider contacts the medial-most point of the sustentaculum (Figure A3.1, g–h).

CL5     (greatest depth; osteometric board):    The caudal surface of the calcaneus is fixed against the end of the board. The medial surface of the sustentaculum rests on the base of the board. The slider contacts the most medial point of the lateral malleolus facet (Figure A3.1, i–j).

CL6     (distal width; sliding calipers):    The calcaneus is held in a vertical position with the caudal surface toward you and distal end up. One jaw of the calipers is placed in a slight sulcus adjacent to muscle attachments on the lateral surface. The rack of the calipers passes along the cranial surface of the element, and the other jaw contacts the medial slope of the talus facet (Figure A3.1, k–l).

CL7     (greatest length of the naviculocuboid facet; sliding calipers):    The calcaneus is held in a vertical position with the lateral surface toward you and distal end up. One jaw of the calipers is fixed against the proximal edge of the naviculocuboid facet. The rack of the calipers passes along the medial surface of the element, and the other jaw contacts the distal edge of the naviculocuboid facet (Figure A3.1, o–b).

CL8     (greatest length of talus facet; sliding calipers):    The calcaneus is held in a vertical position with the lateral surface toward you and distal end up. One jaw of the calipers is fixed against the cranial edge of the articular surface of the talus facet. The rack of the calipers passes along the medial surface of the talus facet and the other jaw contacts the distal edge of the articular surface (Figure A3.1, m–n).

CL9     (greatest length of shaft; sliding calipers):    The calcaneus is held in a horizontal position with the cranial surface up and lateral surface toward you. One jaw of the calipers is fixed against the cranial surface of the talus facet. The rack of the calipers passes along the medial surface of the shaft, and the other jaw contacts the most proximal point of the calcaneal tuber (Figure A3.1, n–a).

CL10     (greatest length [only on elements with unfused proximal epiphysis]; osteometric board):    This measurement is taken on calcanea with unfused proximal epiphyses. The lateral surface of the calcaneus is positioned over the slider groove with the distal end fixed against the end of the board. The slider contacts the most proximal point of the epiphyseal surface (Figure A3.1, a–b).

CL11     (greatest length of shaft [only on elements with unfused proximal epiphysis]; sliding calipers):    This measurement is taken only on calcanea with unfused proximal epiphyses. The calcaneus is held in a horizontal position with the cranial surface up and lateral surface toward you. One jaw of the calipers is fixed against the cranial surface of the talus facet. The rack of the calipers passes along the medial surface of the shaft, and the other jaw contacts the most proximal point of the epiphyseal surface (Figure A3.1, n–a).

Table A3.2. Summary of Selected Measurements of Bison Calcanea from Several Bison Bone Bed Assemblages.

| Measurement* | Cows | | | | | Bulls | | | | |
|---|---|---|---|---|---|---|---|---|---|---|
| | N | Mean | Min | Max | SD | N | Mean | Min | Max | SD |
| *CL1 (Greatest Length of Calcaneus)* | | | | | | | | | | |
| AB Agate Basin level[b] | 24 | 159.9 | 148.0 | 170.0 | 5.6 | 2 | 182.5 | 179.0 | 186.0 | 4.9 |
| AB Folsom level[b] | 2 | 156.0 | 155.0 | 157.0 | 1.4 | 2 | 176.0 | 172.0 | 180.0 | 5.7 |
| Casper | 36 | 157.5 | 150.0 | 166.0 | 4.6 | 7 | 174.6 | 170.0 | 180.0 | 3.9 |
| Frasca | 15 | 157.0 | 150.0 | 165.0 | 4.7 | 15 | 173.7 | 165.0 | 183.0 | 5.8 |
| Lindenmeier | 5 | 164.0 | 160.0 | 167.0 | 2.9 | 10 | 184.4 | 179.0 | 192.0 | 4.0 |
| Lipscomb | 17 | 160.3 | 151.0 | 170.0 | 5.4 | 4 | 178.5 | 172.0 | 188.0 | 7.2 |
| Mill Iron | 4 | 159.5 | 156.0 | 163.0 | 3.5 | 0 | — | — | — | — |
| UWAC[c] | 19 | 145.5 | 135.0 | 155.0 | 5.5 | 8 | 155.9 | 152.0 | 160.0 | 3.6 |
| *CL4 (Greatest Breadth of Calcaneus)* | | | | | | | | | | |
| AB Agate Basin level | 15 | 54.5 | 49.0 | 62.0 | 3.4 | 1 | 65.0 | 65.0 | 65.0 | — |
| AB Folsom level | 2 | 55.5 | 55.0 | 56.0 | 0.7 | 2 | 64.5 | 64.0 | 65.0 | 0.7 |
| Casper | 37 | 53.6 | 50.0 | 58.0 | 2.0 | 7 | 60.9 | 59.0 | 64.0 | 2.0 |
| Frasca | 19 | 53.3 | 48.0 | 57.0 | 2.3 | 18 | 60.7 | 56.0 | 65.0 | 2.6 |
| Lindenmeier | 2 | 55.0 | 55.0 | 55.0 | 0.0 | 5 | 66.0 | 63.0 | 68.0 | 2.1 |
| Lipscomb | 18 | 54.1 | 48.0 | 58.0 | 2.5 | 6 | 61.7 | 47.0 | 69.0 | 8.0 |
| Mill Iron | 3 | 55.0 | 54.0 | 56.0 | 1.0 | 2 | 62.0 | 62.0 | 62.0 | 0.0 |
| UWAC | 19 | 48.2 | 42.0 | 52.0 | 2.9 | 8 | 54.3 | 52.0 | 57.0 | 1.7 |
| *CL5 (Greatest Depth of Calcaneus)* | | | | | | | | | | |
| AB Agate Basin level | 17 | 64.1 | 58.0 | 69.0 | 3.0 | 2 | 73.5 | 72.0 | 75.0 | 2.1 |
| AB Folsom level | 2 | 64.0 | 64.0 | 64.0 | 0.0 | 2 | 72.5 | 72.0 | 73.0 | 0.7 |
| Casper | 36 | 61.9 | 56.0 | 69.0 | 2.5 | 7 | 67.4 | 64.0 | 70.0 | 2.1 |
| Frasca | 18 | 61.6 | 58.0 | 65.0 | 2.1 | 13 | 68.6 | 64.0 | 73.0 | 2.7 |
| Lindenmeier | 4 | 62.5 | 61.0 | 66.0 | 2.4 | 10 | 69.8 | 65.0 | 75.0 | 3.3 |
| Lipscomb | 19 | 63.3 | 58.0 | 69.0 | 2.7 | 8 | 69.4 | 67.0 | 73.0 | 2.5 |
| Mill Iron | 4 | 63.8 | 62.0 | 65.0 | 1.3 | 1 | 75.0 | 75.0 | 75.0 | — |
| UWAC | 19 | 54.9 | 47.0 | 61.0 | 3.6 | 8 | 60.8 | 56.0 | 68.0 | 4.5 |
| *CL9 (Greatest Shaft Length of Calcaneus)* | | | | | | | | | | |
| AB Agate Basin Level | 31 | 105.1 | 96.7 | 110.7 | 3.8 | 3. | 121.1 | 117.1 | 123.3 | 3.5 |
| AB Folsom level | 2 | 102.8 | 102.6 | 103.0 | 0.2 | 2 | 117.7 | 115.4 | 119.9 | 3.1 |
| Casper | 36 | 103.0 | 95.9 | 109.4 | 3.0 | 7 | 114.3 | 110.2 | 116.0 | 2.2 |
| Frasca | 23 | 102.6 | 97.3 | 110.9 | 3.3 | 26 | 115.4 | 108.2 | 122.5 | 4.2 |
| Lindenmeier | 6 | 106.0 | 100.9 | 110.3 | 3.3 | 11 | 119.5 | 113.7 | 123.6 | 3.1 |
| Lipscomb | 33 | 106.2 | 98.5 | 114.6 | 3.9 | 8 | 120.0 | 116.1 | 126.5 | 3.9 |
| Mill Iron | 5 | 105.0 | 103.2 | 106.7 | 1.4 | 1 | 116.4 | 116.4 | 116.4 | — |
| UWAC | 18 | 95.5 | 88.8 | 99.5 | 2.9 | 8 | 102.8 | 99.4 | 106.1 | 2.6 |

[a]Only calcanea with complete union (PF = 3) of the calcaneal tuber are included here; all measurements in millimeters; N, number of measurable calcanea; MIN, minimum; MAX, maximum and SD, standard deviation; see Table A3.1 for description of measurement.
[b]Agate Basin site, Wyoming.
[c]University of Wyoming, Department of Anthropology, modern comparative specimens.

**Table A3.3.** Measurements of Bison Calcanea from the Mill Iron Site.

| No. | ELE | POR | SEG | Side | PF[b] | Sex | CL1 | CL2 | CL3 | CL4 | CL5 | CL6 | CL7 | CL8 | CL9 | Comments |
|---|---|---|---|---|---|---|---|---|---|---|---|---|---|---|---|---|
| 3037 | CL | PSH | CO | R | 3 | F | 0.0 | 40.0 | 42.0 | 0.0 | 0.0 | 0.0 | 0.0 | 37.2 | 103.2 | |
| 3042 | CL | CO | CO | L | 4 | ? | 0.0 | 0.0 | 0.0 | 0.0 | 0.0 | 0.0 | 0.0 | 0.0 | 0.0 | Complete but unmeasurable |
| L13-16-122 | CL | CO | CO | L | 4 | ? | 0.0 | 0.0 | 0.0 | 52.0 | 64.0 | 0.0 | 39.9 | 0.0 | 0.0 | |
| L13-16-130 | CL | CO | CO | R | 3 | F | 157.0 | 0.0 | 0.0 | 54.0 | 65.0 | 45.5 | 0.0 | 0.0 | 104.0 | |
| L13-19-100 | CL | CO | CO | L | 4 | ? | 0.0 | 0.0 | 0.0 | 0.0 | 0.0 | 0.0 | 0.0 | 0.0 | 0.0 | Complete but unmeasurable |
| L13-25-158 | CL | CO | CO | R | 3 | F | 163.0 | 0.0 | 45.0 | 55.0 | 64.0 | 45.0 | 43.9 | 34.8 | 105.9 | |
| L13-23-81 | CL | CO | CO | R | 4 | ? | 0.0 | 0.0 | 0.0 | 0.0 | 0.0 | 0.0 | 0.0 | 0.0 | 0.0 | Complete but unmeasurable |
| L13-24-111 | CL | CO | CO | R | 4 | ? | 0.0 | 0.0 | 0.0 | 50.0 | 64.0 | 45.9 | 39.3 | 34.7 | 0.0 | |
| L13-24-93 | CL | CO | CO | R | 4 | ? | 0.0 | 0.0 | 0.0 | 50.0 | 61.0 | 44.4 | 40.9 | 35.3 | 0.0 | |
| L13-25-49 | CL | CO | CO | R | 3 | F | 162.0 | 42.0 | 44.0 | 46.0 | 64. | 47.6 | 0.0 | 36.4 | 106.7 | |
| M13-17-11 | CL | CO | CO | R | 4 | M | 0.0 | 0.0 | 0.0 | 62.0 | 75.0 | 56.4 | 0.0 | 41.1 | 0.0 | |
| M13-3-90 | CL | CO | CO | L | 4 | ? | 0.0 | 0.0 | 0.0 | 0.0 | 0.0 | 0.0 | 0.0 | 0.0 | 0.0 | Complete but unmeasurable |
| M14-10-110 | CL | CO | CO | L | 3 | F | 156.0 | 0.0 | 0.0 | 0.0 | 62.0 | 0.0 | 40.6 | 0.0 | 105.4 | |
| M14-11-53 | CL | DS | LT | R | 4 | M | 0.0 | 0.0 | 0.0 | 0.0 | 0.0 | 0.0 | 50.9 | 0.0 | 0.0 | Conjoin with M14-11-54 |
| M14-11-54 | CL | PSH | CO | R | 3 | M | 0.0 | 0.0 | 0.0 | 62.0 | 0.0 | 0.0 | 0.0 | 0.0 | 116.4 | |

[a]All measurements in millimeters; see Table A3.1 for description of measurement.
[b]Stage of proximal union of the calcaneal tuber: 3 = complete; 4 = indeterminate.

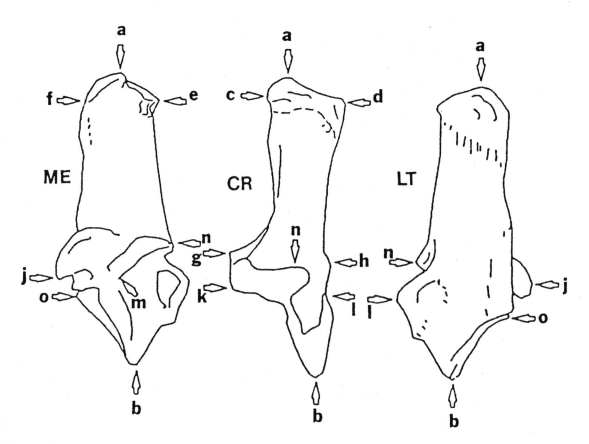

**Figure A3.1.** Measurements for bison calcanea. CL1:a–b; CL2:c–d; CL3: e–f; CL4:g–h; CL5:i–j; CL6:k–l; CL7:o–b; CL8:m–n; CL9:n–a.

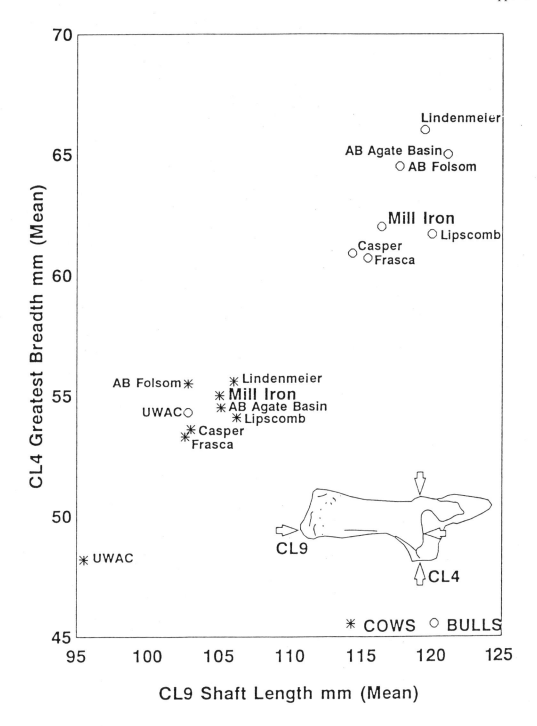

**Figure A3.2.** Calcaneal shaft lengths plotted against greatest breadth for several Paleoindian bison bonebeds and the bison from the University of Wyoming comparative collection (UWAC).

## References Cited

Bedord, J. N.
   1974    Morphological Variation in *Bison* Metacarpals and Metatarsals. In *The Casper Site: A Hell Gap Bison Kill on the High Plains,* edited by G. Frison, pp. 199–240. Academic Press, New York.

Binford, L. R.
   1981    *Bones: Ancient Men and Modern Myths.* Academic Press, New York.

Burgett, G. R.
   1990    *The Bones of the Beast: Resolving Questions of Faunal Assemblage Formation Processes through Actualistic Research.* Unpublished Ph. D. dissertation, Department of Anthropology, University of New Mexico, Albuquerque.

Emerson, A. M.
   1990    *Archaeological Implications of Variability in the Economic Anatomy of* Bison bison. Unpublished Ph. D. dissertation, Department of Anthropology, Washington State University, Pullman.

Empel, W., and T. Roskosz
   1963    Das Skellet der Gliedmassen des Wisents, *Bison bonasus* (Linnaeus, 1758). *Acta Theriologica* 37:259–279.

Guthrie, R. D.
   1980    Bison and Man in North America. *Canadian Journal of Anthropology* 1:55–73.

   1984a   Mosaics, Allelochemics and Nutrients: An Ecological Theory of Late Pleistocene Megafaunal Extinctions. In *Quaternary Extinctions: A Prehistoric Revolution,* edited by P. S. Martin and R. G. Klein, pp. 259-298. University of Arizona Press, Tucson.

   1984b   Alaskan Megabucks, Megabulls, and Megarams: The Issue of Pleistocene Gigantism. In *Contributions in Quaternary Vertebrate Paleontology: A Volume in Memorial to John E. Guilday,* edited by H. H. Genoways and M. R. Dawson, pp. 482–510. Carnegie Museum of Natural History Special Publication No. 8.

   1990    *Frozen Fauna of the Mammoth Steppe: The Story of Blue Babe.* University of Chicago Press, Chicago.

Hill, M. G.
   1994    *Subsistence Strategies by Folsom Hunters at Agate Basin, Wyoming: A Taphonomic Analysis of the Bison and Pronghorn Assemblages.* Unpublished Master's thesis, Department of Anthropology, University of Wyoming, Laramie, Wyoming.

Hillerud, J. M.
   1980    Bison as Indicators of Geologic Age. *Canadian Journal of Anthropology* 1:77–80.

Hoffecker, J. D., G. Baryshnikov, and O. Potapova
   1991    Vertebrate Remains from the Mousterian Site of Il'skaya I (northern Caucasus, U.S.S.R.): New Analysis and Interpretation. *Journal of Archaeological Science* 18:113–147.

Kreutzer, L. A.
   1992a   Bison and Deer Bone Mineral Densities: Comparisons and Implications for the Interpretation of Archaeological Faunas. *Journal of Archaeological Science* 19:271–294.

   1992b   *Taphonomy of the Mill Iron, Montana (24CT30) Bison Bonebed.* Unpublished Ph. D. dissertation, Department of Anthropology, University of Washington, Seattle.

McDonald, J. N.
   1981    *North American Bison: Their Classification and Evolution.* University of California Press, Berkeley.

Morlan, R. E.
   1991    Bison Carpal and Tarsal Measurements: Bull Versus Cows and Calves. *Plains Anthropologist* 36: 215–227.

Peterson, R. R., Jr.
   1977    *Sexual and Morphological Characteristics of Bison Populations from Communal Kill Sites in and Near Wyoming: Radiographic Analysis of the Metacarpals.* Unpublished Master's thesis, Department of Anthropology, University of Wyoming, Laramie, Wyoming.

Peterson, R. R., Jr., and S. S. Hughes
   1980    Appendix 2: Continued Research in Bison Morphology and Herd Composition using Chronological Variation in Metapodials. In *The Vore site, 48CK302, a Stratified Buffalo Jump in the Wyoming Black Hills,* edited by C. Reher and G. Frison, pp. 170-190. Plains Anthropologist Memoir, No. 16.

Reher, C. A.
   1974    Population Study of the Casper Site Bison. In *The Casper Site: A Hell Gap Bison Kill on the High Plains,* edited by G. Frison, pp. 113–124. Academic Press, New York.

Skinner, M. F., and O. C. Kaisen
   1947    *The Fossil Bison of Alaska and Preliminary Revision of the Genus.* American Museum of Natural History Bulletin No. 89: 127–256.

Todd, L. C.
   1983    *The Horner Site: Taphonomy of an Early Holocene Bison Bonebed.* Unpublished Ph. D. dissertation, Department of Anthropology, University of New Mexico, Albuquerque.

   1986    Determination of Sex of *Bison* Upper Forelimb Bones: The Humerus and Radius. In *Papers for George C. Frison, Wyoming State Archaeologist, (1967-1984),* edited by D. Walker. *Wyoming Archaeologist* 29(1-2):109–123.

   1987    Taphonomy of the Horner II Bonebed. In *The Horner Site: The Type Site of the Cody Cultural Complex,* edited by G. Frison and L. Todd, pp. 107–198. Academic Press, Orlando.

Wilson, M.
   1974a   The Casper Local Fauna and its Fossil Bison. In *The Casper Site: A Hell Gap Bison Kill on the High Plains,*

edited by G. Frison, pp. 125–171. Academic Press, New York.

1974b    History of Bison in Wyoming, with Particular Reference to Early Holocene Forms. In *Applied Geology and Archaeology: The Holocene History of Wyoming,* edited by M. Wilson, pp. 91–99. Geological Survey of Wyoming, Reports of Investigations No. 10.

1975    *Holocene Fossil Bison from Wyoming and Adjacent Areas.* Unpublished Master's thesis, Department of Anthropology, University of Wyoming, Laramie, Wyoming.

1978    Archaeological Kill Site Populations and the Holocene Evolution of the Genus *Bison.* In *Bison*

*Procurement and Utilization: A Symposium,* edited by L. Davis and M. Wilson, pp. 9–22. Plains Anthropologist Memoir, No. 14.

Zeimens, G. M.
1982    Analysis of Postcranial Bison Remains. In *The Agate Basin Site: A Record of the Paleoindian Occupation of the Northwestern High Plains,* edited by G. Frison and D. Stanford, pp. 213–240. Academic Press, New York.

Zeimens, G. M., and S. Zeimens
1974    Volumes of Bison Astragali. In *The Casper Site: A Hell Gap Bison Kill on the High Plains,* edited by G. Frison, pp. 245–246. Academic Press, New York.

# Index